Macworld
PageMaker 6
Bible,
Second Edition

Macworld
PageMaker 6
Bible,
Second Edition

by William Harrel and Craig Danuloff

IDG Books Worldwide, Inc.
An International Data Group Company

Foster City, CA ◆ Chicago, IL ◆ Indianapolis, IN ◆ Braintree, MA ◆ Dallas, TX

Macworld PageMaker 6 Bible, Second Edition

Published by
IDG Books Worldwide, Inc.
An International Data Group Company
919 E. Hillsdale Blvd.
Suite 400
Foster City, CA 94404

Library of Congress Catalog Card No.: 95-81547

ISBN: 1-56884-589-8

Printed in the United States of America

10 9 8 7 6 5 4 3 2 1

2B/SR/RR/ZV

Distributed in the United States by IDG Books Worldwide, Inc.

Distributed by Macmillan Canada for Canada; by Computer and Technical Books for the Caribbean Basin; by Contemporanea de Ediciones for Venezuela; by Distribuidora Cuspide for Argentina; by CITEC for Brazil; by Ediciones ZETA S.C.R. Ltda. for Peru; by Editorial Limusa SA for Mexico; by Transworld Publishers Limited in the United Kingdom and Europe; by Al-Maiman Publishers & Distributors for Saudi Arabia; by Simron Pty. Ltd. for South Africa; by Ltd. for Hong Kong; by Toppan Company Ltd. for Japan; by Addison Wesley Publishing Company for Korea; by Longman Singapore Publishers Ltd. for Singapore, Malaysia, Thailand, and Indonesia; by Unalis Corporation for Taiwan; by WS Computer Publishing Company, Inc. for the Philippines; by WoodsLane Pty. Ltd. for Australia; by WoodsLane Enterprises Ltd. for New Zealand.

For general information on IDG Books Worldwide's books in the U.S., please call our Consumer Customer Service department at 800-762-2974. For reseller information, including discounts and premium sales, please call our Reseller Customer Service department at 800-434-3422.

For information on where to purchase IDG Books Worldwide's books outside the U.S., contact IDG Books Worldwide at 415-655-3021 or fax 415-655-3295.

For information on translations, contact Marc Jeffrey Mikulich, Director, Foreign & Subsidiary Rights, at IDG Books Worldwide, 415-655-3018 or fax 415-655-3295.

For sales inquiries and special prices for bulk quantities, write to the address above or call IDG Books Worldwide at 415-655-3200.

For information on using IDG Books Worldwide's books in the classroom, or ordering examination copies, contact Jim Kelly at 800-434-2086.

For authorization to photocopy items for corporate, personal, or educational use, please contact Copyright Clearance Center, 222 Rosewood Drive, Danvers, MA 01923, or fax 508-750-4470.

 is a trademark under exclusive license to IDG Books Worldwide, Inc., from International Data Group, Inc.

About the Authors

William Harrel has authored 11 books on desktop publishing and related topics, as well as hundreds of magazine articles for *Publish, PC World, Windows Magazine, MacUser, PC Magazine,* and several others. He also owns a desktop publishing firm in Southern California, with clients that include AT&T, Executone, Johnson & Johnson, Ventura County, and many others. You can get more information about Harrel and his company on The WRITE Desktop World Wide Web page at:

 http://www.west.net/~bharrel

His e-mail address is:

bharrel@west.net

Craig Danuloff has authored almost two dozen books on desktop publishing and the Macintosh since opening one of the first desktop publishing service bureaus in Boulder, Colorado, in 1985. He is also a former Business Development Manager at Aldus Corporation.

ABOUT IDG BOOKS WORLDWIDE

Welcome to the world of IDG Books Worldwide.

IDG Books Worldwide, Inc., is a subsidiary of International Data Group, the world's largest publisher of computer-related information and the leading global provider of information services on information technology. IDG was founded more than 25 years ago and now employs more than 7,700 people worldwide. IDG publishes more than 250 computer publications in 67 countries (see listing below). More than 70 million people read one or more IDG publications each month.

Launched in 1990, IDG Books Worldwide is today the #1 publisher of best-selling computer books in the United States. We are proud to have received 8 awards from the Computer Press Association in recognition of editorial excellence and three from Computer Currents' First Annual Readers' Choice Awards, and our best-selling ...For Dummies® series has more than 19 million copies in print with translations in 28 languages. IDG Books Worldwide, through a joint venture with IDG's Hi-Tech Beijing, became the first U.S. publisher to publish a computer book in the People's Republic of China. In record time, IDG Books Worldwide has become the first choice for millions of readers around the world who want to learn how to better manage their businesses.

Our mission is simple: Every one of our books is designed to bring extra value and skill-building instructions to the reader. Our books are written by experts who understand and care about our readers. The knowledge base of our editorial staff comes from years of experience in publishing, education, and journalism — experience which we use to produce books for the '90s. In short, we care about books, so we attract the best people. We devote special attention to details such as audience, interior design, use of icons, and illustrations. And because we use an efficient process of authoring, editing, and desktop publishing our books electronically, we can spend more time ensuring superior content and spend less time on the technicalities of making books.

You can count on our commitment to deliver high-quality books at competitive prices on topics you want to read about. At IDG Books Worldwide, we continue in the IDG tradition of delivering quality for more than 25 years. You'll find no better book on a subject than one from IDG Books Worldwide.

John J. Kilcullen

John Kilcullen
President and CEO
IDG Books Worldwide, Inc.

Acknowledgments

The publisher would like to give special thanks to Patrick J. McGovern, without whom this book would not have been possible.

Credits

**Senior Vice President
and Group Publisher**
Brenda McLaughlin

Acquisitions Editor
Nancy E. Dunn

Brand Manager
Pradeepa Siva

Editorial Assistant
Suki Gear

Production Director
Beth Jenkins

Production Assistant
Jacalyn L. Pennywell

**Supervisor of
Project Coordination**
Cindy L. Phipps

Supervisor of Page Layout
Kathie S. Schnorr

Production Systems Specialist
Steve Peake

Pre-Press Coordination
Tony Augsburger
Patricia R. Reynolds
Theresa Sánchez-Baker

Media/Archive Coordination
Leslie Popplewell
Kerri Cornell
Michael Wilkey

Developmental Editor
Kenyon Brown

Copy Editor
Earl Jackson, Jr.

Technical Reviewer
Celia Stevenson

Associate Project Coordinator
J. Tyler Connor

Graphics Coordination
Shelley Lea
Gina Scott
Carla Radzikinas

Production Page Layout
Shawn Aylsworth
Linda M. Boyer
Dominique DeFelice
Maridee V. Ennis
Angela F. Hunckler
Jill Lyttle
Jane Martin
Kate Snell

Proofreaders
Henry Lazarek
Gwenette Gaddis
Dwight Ramsey
Carl Saff
Robert Springer

Indexer
Sharon Hilgenberg

Cover Design
Kavish + Kavish

Contents at a Glance

Table of Contents

Foreword to New Edition

It was the summer of 1990 when Bill Harrel first walked into my small imaging service bureau. I was a staff of one offering digital imaging services in Ventura County, California. From the first day we met, Bill and I discussed problems and solutions related to printing on Postscript devices. Most of the work we dealt with was created in the then Aldus PageMaker.

Through the past five years, I have learned much from Bill in working with PageMaker through its many versions. As an electronic designer, I have found his expertise and knowledge with PageMaker to be superb. He always offered solutions to problems and workarounds in the program. Subsequently, I found his many books and articles to offer working professionals real world solutions to the complex environment of digital imaging and creative design very helpful.

I am particularly delighted to see this volume on PageMaker appear. In a short five-year history, we have all grown. I have two large imaging centers and still serve Bill in providing his prepress imaging needs. He has grown to be a recognized author and professional in the industry, and PageMaker has matured into a superb program for the highend professional as well as the beginning layout artist.

In this book, Bill provides a basic description of working with Adobe PageMaker for those new to the program. Simplicity, however, is not the final end of the volume. For the seasoned PageMaker user, the real benefit is a concise and clear description of PageMaker's new features. The enhancements of Adobe PageMaker 6.0 is a new level of working with a program responsible for the revolution in desktop publishing. Now in the hands of the company (Adobe) that maintains the printing language as the uncontested defacto standard for output devices, PageMaker 6.0 is a new triumph. This new program together with one of the top authors on applications software is worthy of any professional's library.

If you are a first time user of PageMaker, delve into the comprehensive description of using the program from the tools and menus to the printing particulars. If you are a seasoned PageMaker user, look into the new features described by Bill. If you are a Web page artist and seek new opportunities in creating designs for the Internet, look to the new addition of HTML coding and Web page design. Regardless of your backgound or desire, this book has something for everyone!

— Ted Padova
Chief Executive Officer, Graphic Traffic Digital Imaging Centers
Coauthor, *Using Photoshop 3.0, Special Edition*
Feature Columnist, *MacDigest Magazine*
October 9, 1995

Foreword to First Edition

It gives me great pleasure to look back at the days when I worked for Craig Danuloff at his Boulder service bureau because things are so much better now. Back then, we worked in a perpetual state of rage and anxiety. We let customers peer over our shoulders as we inadvertently mangled their pages and ruined their text, we'd wait an hour or more to typeset a single page only to watch it rip to shreds in the processor, and we'd sit by helplessly as documents for major customers became hopelessly corrupted.

Behind it all was a single product, Aldus PageMaker, and the myth of desktop publishing. Customers streamed into our storefront under the misconception that desktop publishing would expand their options and save them money. Having come from a traditional paste-up background, I knew for a fact it was just the opposite. Back in the days before personal computers, you could work wonders armed only with a knife and a waxer and never have to worry about files corrupting and pages refusing to print.

But we always had faith. One day, we felt certain, desktop publishing would develop into a viable alternative, and we would be there to reap the benefits. As it turns out, we were half right. We didn't quite reap the benefits the way we thought we would — our service bureau is now the site of a Greek restaurant — but PageMaker, personal computers, PostScript, typesetters, and hundreds of peripheral software and hardware elements have improved over the years by an order of magnitude. Nowadays, desktop publishing has not only brought more people into the publishing industry, it has permanently cornered the professional design market. I can assure you from hard-won personal experience, the PageMaker story is an unqualified success.

This book is a similar success and the best part is the author himself. Craig Danuloff is one of those gifted people who can look at a piece of software, organize its capabilities into a natural hierarchy, and deliver his thoughts on the matter in the amount of time it takes most of us to remove the shrink wrap. If you learn half as much from him as I have, you'll be running circles around PageMaker halfway through the book.

—Deke McClelland
Author of *Macworld Photoshop 3 Bible*

XXX

Introduction

Craig and Bill both met PageMaker in the summer of 1985. Version 1.0 had just been released. Craig had just plunked down $8,000 for an Apple LaserWriter and started what would later become known as a desktop publishing service bureau. Bill began his desktop publishing firm in Southern California. Almost 11 years later (that's 77 years in computer and dog years), it is astonishing to think back to those days when PageMaker ran in 512K and was the single most amazing piece of microcomputer software that many people had ever seen. Ah, the good old days.

At that time, it was pretty easy to be a PageMaker expert. All you had to do was understand the Place command and the pasteboard, and remember to hit ⌘-S every few seconds. The only thing that really confused anybody was the concept of windowshades. Windowshades are part of the text blocks that PageMaker uses to store and manipulate text, and for some reason, beginners always let their windowshades run wild.

Today it's not so easy to be a PageMaker expert. Being a PageMaker expert now means knowing quite a bit about typography (tracking, kerning, baselines), color (process, spot, tints, traps), printing (separations, composites, PPDs), document management (indexing, table-of-contents generation, linked files), publishing for the computer screen in the form of portable documents and the World Wide Web, and a whole lot more. And for some strange reason, windowshades still confuse people.

And that's the reason for this book. It's almost impossible to become really proficient at PageMaker without some help, and we want you to become a PageMaker expert. This is a worthwhile goal because, if you're like many of the people who use PageMaker, some important part of your job is probably dependent upon your being able to use PageMaker productively. You probably don't have hours to spend creating and re-creating documents. When you finish a publication, you need to know that it will print and that it will come out looking as you expect it to. And I'm sure you want to take advantage of all those hidden features and capabilities that the programmers stuck in there even if they're not obvious and even if they aren't in the manuals.

So over the next 18 chapters, we're going to go over PageMaker 6 with a fine-tooth comb. You're going to learn what every single feature, option, and undocumented keyboard shortcut does, and more importantly we're going to explain them all in the kind of real-world context in which you'll find yourself working.

For your efforts — reading this book and working with PageMaker — you'll be rewarded with what remains an amazingly empowering tool, and even more amazing publications of your own creation.

What's Inside

This book is aimed primarily at the beginning or intermediate PageMaker user, although even the most experienced PageMaker users will learn a few things. (Hey, we learned quite a few things while writing it and from each other.) There are four major parts in the book: Introducing PageMaker, Learning PageMaker, Mastering PageMaker, and Putting PageMaker to Work.

Part I, Introducing PageMaker, lays the foundation for using the software by describing the basic page layout metaphor PageMaker uses and the commands and techniques you'll use universally as you work. Absolute beginners will want to read the chapters in Part I carefully because, as in most endeavors, the fundamentals are extremely important to ultimate mastery. We would even advise those who have a good amount of PageMaker experience to read through the chapters in Part I, searching for that item that you didn't know or one technique you aren't already using. A simple improvement in some basic technique, such as your ability to select objects or change view sizes, can pay off big in terms of productivity.

The chapters in Part I:

Chapter 1, Getting to Know PageMaker: In this chapter we dig in and get our hands dirty. The basics of actually using PageMaker are all covered in this chapter, including creating new publications, learning your way around the publication window, opening existing files, saving your work, and quitting when you're finished.

Chapter 2, What's New in PageMaker 6: Especially designed for those familiar with previous versions of PageMaker, this chapter takes a quick look at every new feature, command, and option in PageMaker 6. Covered in depth is the exciting new Arrange menu with its long awaited Group, Align Objects, and Lock Position commands. We'll also introduce you to the HTML Author Plug-in, color management, and PageMaker's new trapping feature.

Chapter 3, Touring PageMaker's Terms, Tools, and Menus: Here's where the real introduction to PageMaker begins, with some basic terms you'll have to know, and then a top-to-bottom review of every menu command and floating palette PageMaker 6 provides.

Chapter 4, Understanding Publication Window Basics: The last chapter in this section focuses on the publication window, and how you can control the PageMaker environment by changing view sizes, scrolling the display, creating column guides, working with the rulers, and manipulating text and graphic objects. Also covered is the exciting new multiple master pages option and an in-depth look at using it.

Part II, Learning PageMaker, covers the most central PageMaker tasks, the creation and manipulation of text and graphics. This includes importing text, creating text in PageMaker, using the Story Editor, and how to use style sheets to automate text formatting and templates to automate formatting publications. We cover both internally created and imported graphics as well as all kinds of graphic manipulations. Finally, we introduce the Control palette.

These chapters represent the heart of PageMaker. Experienced users should pay particular attention to Chapter 6, which covers PageMaker's little-understood advanced typographic features, and Chapter 9, which focuses on the Control palette, a highly useful formatting tool. By the same token, beginning users may want to just skim these chapters at first and come back to them later after gaining more experience in the more fundamental skills.

The chapters in Part II:

Chapter 5, Working with Text: It would be hard to create too many interesting publications without text, so this chapter tells all about importing text into PageMaker from just about any external source. It also explains how you can create text right in the publication window or by using the PageMaker Story Editor.

Chapter 6, Formatting Text: Once you've got the text in PageMaker, the fun really begins as you learn to use the program's typographic capabilities to modify character and paragraph formatting. This chapter introduces dozens of typographic controls, including fonts, leading, kerning, tracking, letter spacing, baseline shift, and many more.

Chapter 7, Creating Style Sheets and Templates: This is a chapter about productivity. Style sheets help you to automate your work and ensure consistency within publications and between publications. You'll learn how to use them in this chapter and how to integrate them into your word processor. Templates are preformatted document shells that automate the document creation process by saving you from a lot of repetition each time you start a new document.

Chapter 8, Adding Graphic Elements: Even the most elegant typography needs the company of at least a few graphics or graphic elements. This chapter shows you how to import graphics created in other applications, create graphics in PageMaker, and then integrate graphics throughout your documents.

Chapter 9, Using the Control Palette: Another productivity-focused chapter, here you'll learn all about PageMaker's new Control palette, which makes it faster and easier to format text and manipulate text blocks and graphics. In addition to complete coverage of the Control palette itself, dozens of new keyboard shortcuts are included.

Part III, Mastering PageMaker, moves beyond the basics to look at advanced capabilities provided by PageMaker as well as other Adobe software. These include the details of working with color, using PageMaker Plug-ins, formatting long documents, printing, publishing for the World Wide Web, and Adobe prepress software, including Adobe PrePrint, Adobe PressWise, and Adobe TrapWise.

The chapters in Part III:

Chapter 10, Working with Color: Adding color to your publications is easy in PageMaker, and this chapter introduces all of the color tools you'll want at your disposal. Many of the important issues related to color printing are covered here, too, including process color, spot color, and tints; how to work with color EPS graphics; and importing and exporting colors. We also look at PageMaker's new Color Management System support and trapping. In the middle of the book, you'll also find a color section with illustrations demonstrating many of the topics discussed in this chapter.

Chapter 11, Using PageMaker Plug-ins: More than 15 additional features are provided in PageMaker 6 in the form of Plug-ins, which are plug-in modules that appear in the PageMaker Plug-ins submenu. This chapter introduces Plug-ins technology, provides a detailed look at all of the plug-ins included with PageMaker, and examines a few of the third-party Plug-ins available for separate purchase.

Chapter 12, Creating Long Documents: When documents go beyond a certain length, a number of new issues arise in terms of formatting them for easy reading and reference and managing their production. This chapter focuses on PageMaker features geared especially for long documents, such as generating tables of contents and indexes, printing multiple publications, and linking externally stored text and graphic files.

Chapter 13, Printing Publications: There are two parts to printing PageMaker files, and this chapter covers them both. First, it provides tips to help you construct documents that have the best chance of printing without incident. Then it takes you through every option and feature of PageMaker's powerful printing dialog boxes.

Chapter 14, Taking Advantage of Adobe's PrePress Tools: In most professional publishing environments, PageMaker often isn't used alone but rather will be used along with one or more of the Adobe PrePress software programs introduced in this chapter: Adobe PrePrint, Adobe PressWise, or Adobe TrapWise. You'll also learn about Adobe Fetch in this chapter — a great media database application, which is provided in a trial version on the disks included with this book.

Chapter 15, Publishing Electronically — on the Web and Elsewhere: As computers pervade our lives, more and more documents are published for the computer screen. PageMaker contains two utilities for publishing for the World Wide Web and for Adobe's portable document format, HTML Author and Create Adobe PDF, respectively. This chapter introduces you to publishing for the computer screen and how to use these utilities.

Part IV, Putting PageMaker to Work, contains three sample documents that you create as practice. Between them, you'll use most of PageMaker's typesetting and layout features. For this section, you'll use some sample files on the CD-ROM disc included with this book.

Chapter 16, Creating a Newsletter: Building on everything covered in Parts I and II, and focusing on the new skills learned in Chapters 7, 8, and 9, this second sample project provides another opportunity to follow along and practice your PageMaker skills by creating a newsletter.

Chapter 17, Designing a Two-Sided Flyer: For those who would like to test out every-thing learned in the first seven chapters, this sample project allows you to work step-by-step in creating a simple flyer. All the files you need are included on the disc in the back of this book.

Chapter 18, Laying Out a Four-Page Catalog: The last sample project ties together just about all of PageMaker's capabilities, as you follow along in the production of a simple catalog that includes color images, a table, and more. You also learn how to use some of PageMaker's new features, such as multiple master pages, Photoshop effects on TIFF images, and masking.

Appendix A, System Requirements and Installation: This appendix is a short descrip-tion of the type of Macintosh you'll need to run PageMaker 6 and installation instructions.

Appendix B, What's on the CD?: This short appendix describes the contents of the CD-ROM included with this book — all the Plug-ins, clip art, stock art, and sample files.

The following icons are used throughout the book to point to information of special interest:

 This icon highlights time-saving shortcuts or quick techniques that will help you work smarter.

This icon identifies new features found in PageMaker 6.

This icon highlights a special point of interest about the topic under discussion.

This icon points to useful resources found on the Internet.

This icon indicates files that are contained on the CD-ROM disc included with this book.

Introducing PageMaker

This section lays the foundation for using PageMaker 6. You're introduced to PageMaker's basic page layout metaphor and the commands and techniques you'll use as you work. Absolute beginners will want to read the chapters in Part I carefully because, as in most endeavors, the fundamentals are extremely important for achieving ultimate mastery of PageMaker. We would even advise those of you who have a good amount of PageMaker experience to review Part I to learn about features you didn't know about or techniques you aren't already using in your work. Taking the time to review the way you currently apply some basic technique, such as the way you select an object or change a view, and refining the methods you use can improve your productivity tremendously.

Getting to Know PageMaker

■ ■

In This Chapter

➨ Methods of launching PageMaker and opening documents

➨ Defining new publications in the Document Setup dialog box

➨ What's what in the publication window

➨ PageMaker defaults and preferences

➨ Saving and quitting

■ ■

The best way to learn PageMaker is to use PageMaker. In this chapter, you start using PageMaker right away. We provide an overview of the basic skills you'll need to create publications in PageMaker. Before getting started, though, you should understand three basic terms: *document, publication,* and *file.* A *publication* is simply another term for describing PageMaker documents. A *document* is a generic computer term referring to the work you do in a program; in Microsoft Word, for instance, the word processor file you create is called a document. *Files* are the actual document data saved on a computer disk or another medium.

We use the terms publication, document, and file interchangeably, except when this might cause confusion. For example, the ordinary use of the word "publication" refers to books, magazines, brochures, and the like: texts mass-produced for specific "publics." And indeed, PageMaker is principally used to produce such "publications." The "publication" that is the finished product needs to be distinguished from both the idiomatic use in the computer world and from the "documents" that make it up. For example, this book, The Pagemaker 6 Bible, is a publication of Macworld Press books. It was produced by assembling quite a number of PageMaker documents, each of which was produced separately before they were finally put together as the complete publication. The importance of this distinction will become clearer as we proceed. We cover publication basics more thoroughly in Chapter 4.

First, let's look at launching, or opening, the program. In Systems 7 and 7.1, there are several ways to launch the program:

- ☞ Double-click on the PageMaker icon.

- ☞ Select the PageMaker icon and then choose the Open command from the Macintosh File menu.

- ☞ Double-click on any document created with PageMaker. This simultaneously opens PageMaker and that particular document. (If for some reason your Mac can't find PageMaker, an Alert dialog box appears. If this happens, launch PageMaker using either of the above methods and then open the file using the Open command, described later in this chapter.)

- ☞ Drag the icon of any PageMaker document and drop it onto the PageMaker 6 application icon. (Positioning the file icon correctly over the program icon, launches the program and opens the file.)

- ☞ Choose PageMaker from the menu of a launching utility, such as Now Menus, OnCue, or the System 7.x Apple menu.

- ☞ In System 7.5, you can click on the PageMaker 6 icon in Launcher, a control panel that Apple includes with the system software.

When you install PageMaker, the program icon does not automatically install itself in the Apple menu or in the System 7.5 Launcher, shown in Figure 1-1. You must place it yourself. To do so, you simply make an alias of the program icon using the Make Alias command on the Finder's File menu (select the PageMaker icon, then choose Make Alias). Then place the PageMaker alias icons (one for the Apple menu and one for the Launcher) in the appropriate folder in your Mac's System folder. To place PageMaker in the Apple menu, drag the alias icon into the Apple Menu Items folder. Launcher items go in the Launcher Items folder. You can also delete the word "alias" beneath the icon.

Figure 1-1:
The PageMaker 6 icon displayed in System 7.x's two program-launching utilities

Once PageMaker opens, the copyright window (also known as the start-up screen or splash screen), shown in Figure 1-2, and the menu bar appear. The copyright window is simply an introduction to the software, verifying that PageMaker is running.

Figure 1-2:
The PageMaker
copyright window

To move past the copyright window, click the mouse button. (If you wait a few seconds, the copyright window disappears automatically.) You are now ready to begin using PageMaker. Unless you opened PageMaker by double-clicking on a document or with the drag-and-drop method, at this point the visible indications that the program is running are the PageMaker menu bar, shown in Figure 1-3, and the PageMaker 6 icon in the upper-right corner of the screen; the Finder desktop, or any windows open from other applications, are still visible.

After launching PageMaker, you can:

- Create a new PageMaker publication or template
- Open an existing PageMaker publication or template
- Alter PageMaker's default settings
- Quit PageMaker and return to the Macintosh Finder or another open application

The next few sections of this chapter describe creating new PageMaker publications or templates and opening existing publications and templates.

Figure 1-3: The PageMaker desktop without an open document

Creating a New Publication _____

You create a new PageMaker publication by choosing the New... command from the File menu (⌘-N). This command brings up the Document Setup dialog box, shown in Figure 1-4. The options this dialog box provides allow you to the define basic page and publication formatting to start your document.

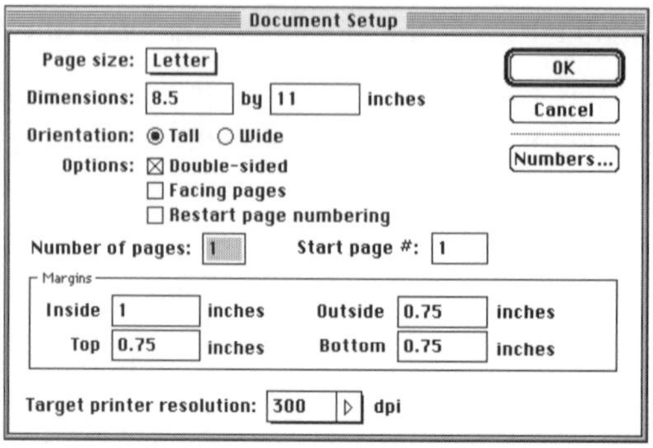

Figure 1-4:
The Document Setup
dialog box

The Document Setup dialog box controls the following aspects of a PageMaker publication:

- ∞ The number of pages in your document and the page number of the first page

- ∞ Whether pages are double-sided and whether PageMaker should display facing pages (two-page spreads) side-by-side on-screen

- ∞ The width of top, bottom, inside, outside, or, on single pages, right and left margins

- ∞ The page-numbering style of automatic page numbering

- ∞ Page size dimensions

- ∞ Orientation

- ∞ Target printer resolution

 You name your new, untitled publication with either the Save or Save as... command (discussed in "Saving a Publication," later in this chapter) . You should do this immediately upon creating a document, and you should frequently hit the Save command whenever working on any open documents. Any document or any work on a document that hasn't been "saved" (stored in memory) will be lost if there is a power failure, system error, or if your Mac locks up or crashes on you.

The following is a description of the Document setup dialog box.

Page Size and Orientation

The Page size pop-up allows you to choose the page size for your publication. Note that *page size* and *paper size* are not always the same. Sometimes, for example, you'll need to print on paper slightly larger than your document pages to accommodate cropping and other printer's marks. You choose paper sizes when preparing to print. This and many other printing issues are discussed in Chapter 13.

PageMaker supports several page sizes, including those commonly used in the U.S. (Letter, Legal, and Tabloid) and Europe (A3, A4, A5, B5), as well as those commonly used in print media (Magazine, Magazine Wide, etc.). Table 1-1 shows the dimensions for many standard page sizes. When you select a page size, the dimensions are displayed automatically in the fields to the right of Page Dimensions.

Table 1-1 PageMaker's Built-in Page Sizes	
Option	**Dimensions**
Letter	8.5 inches by 11 inches
Legal	8.5 inches by 14 inches
Tabloid	11 inches by 17 inches
A4	8.268 inches by 11.693 inches
A3	11.693 inches by 16.535 inches
A5	5.827 inches by 8.268 inches
B5	6.929 inches by 9.842 inches
Magazine	8.375 inches by 10.875 inches
Magazine Narrow	8.125 inches by 10.875 inches
Magazine Wide	9 inches by 10.875 inches
Magazine Broad	10 inches by 12 inches
Compact Disc	4.722 inches by 4.75 inches
Letter Half	5.5 inches by 8.5 inches
Legal Half	7 inches by 8.5 inches

The Compact Disc option is for creating compact disc cover inserts. The Custom option allows you to specify the dimensions for any non-standard page size. There are also six monitor page settings which are discussed in Chapter 15. PageMaker supports custom page sizes up to 42×42 inches. Values you enter in the fields for the width and height of a custom page are accurate to $1/100$ inch (or 0.06 pica). Now that's precise!

The Orientation option determines whether your pages are tall or wide (portrait or landscape). In other words, a letter-sized page is an 8.5-inch by 11-inch page in tall mode and an 11-inch by 8.5-inch page in wide mode.

Page Numbers and the Number of pages

The Start Page # option lets you specify the page number for the first page in your document. PageMaker numbers subsequent pages automatically. We'll look closer at page numbering in Chapter 4.

Use the Number of Pages option to tell PageMaker how many blank pages to create for the new document. PageMaker supports a maximum of 999 pages per document (or as many as disk space allows) and a minimum of 0 — although such a publication would have only master pages and you couldn't print it. You can add pages to a document at any time, so don't worry about being exact when setting up your document. It's better to err with too few pages rather than too many, because blank pages significantly affect file size, wasting disk and memory space while they remain unused.

Also in the Document Setup dialog box is the Numbers… button, which you use to specify the style of page numbers in your publication. Clicking the Numbers… button opens the Page Numbering dialog box, shown in Figure 1-5. You can choose from five page numbering options, including Arabic, Roman, and alphabetic enumeration. You can also enter up to 16 characters in the "TOC and index prefix" field. This tells PageMaker to include the text you specify before the page number in tables of contents and indices, as shown in Figure 1-6.

Figure 1-5: The Page Numbering dialog box

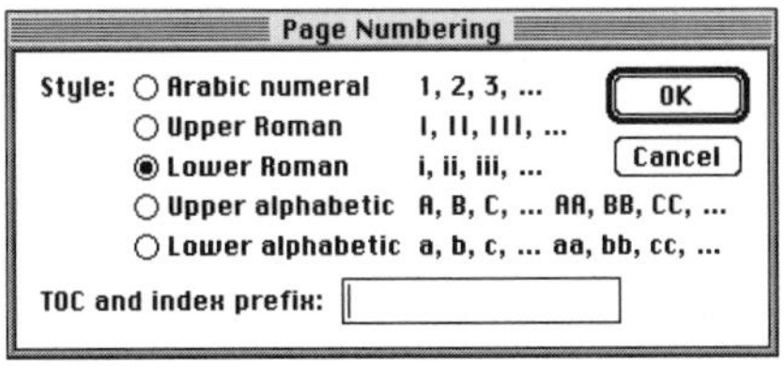

Page Numbering
Style: Arabic numeral 1, 2, 3, ...
Upper Roman I, II, III, ...
Lower Roman i, ii, iii, ...
Upper alphabetic A, B, C, ... AA, BB, CC, ...
Lower alphabetic a, b, c, ... aa, bb, cc, ...
OK
Cancel
TOC and index prefix:

CHARTING YOUR DATA 7-1
GENERATING STATISTICS 7-1
THE CHARTING MODULE 7-2
CHANGING CHART TYPES
AND PERSPECTIVES 7-6
CHART TYPES 7-6
CHANGING PERSPECTIVE 7-7
SETTING CHART PARAMETERS 7-9
CHARTING BY QUESTION CATEGORY 7-10
CHANGING EMPLOYEES 7-11
SAVING A CHART TO A FILE 7-11
PRINTING YOUR CHART 7-12
SCANNER ANSWER SHEETS A-1
GLOSSARY G-1
INDEX INDEX-1

Figure 1-6: An example of a table of contents containing text from the Page Numbering dialog box's TOC and index prefix option

Managing Long Documents

Although you can create documents up to 999 pages long in PageMaker, seldom would you want to do so. Very long documents require a lot of memory and are difficult to manage. Instead, you should use several separate PageMaker documents, segmenting the publication into logical subdivisions, such as chapters or sections. Depending on the organization of a publication, you should confine documents to about 30 to 50 pages. You'll realize a number of benefits to breaking long publications into a series of smaller documents, as listed below:

- **Manageability**. Creates a more manageable document size so that the files fit on floppy disks for easy backup and transporting. In addition, it's much easier to navigate smaller documents. PageMaker doesn't have to labor through all that programming code.

- **Speed**. PageMaker opens, closes, spell checks, and saves smaller file sizes more quickly. Moderation in all things is good.

- **Safety**. You lose fewer pages to file loss, damage, or file corruption. (Heaven forbid.)

- **Logic**. Most long documents lend themselves to logical breaks. This book, for example, is separated into chapters according to topic. This also allows for running headers and footers containing automatic page numbers, as well as several other design features that would not be possible in a single PageMaker document containing multiple chapters or sections.

Although no hard-and-fast rule for breaking long publications into smaller documents exists, you should limit documents to no more 30 to 50 pages. At this length, file sizes and program performance remains acceptable (unless the document contains an unusually large number of imported graphics). Creating and working with long documents is discussed in Chapter 12.

Configuring Double-sided Documents

Use the Double-sided option for creating documents targeted for printing on both sides of the paper. No, this does not configure PageMaker to *print* double-sided documents on your printer. When the Double-sided option is selected, PageMaker positions the inside and outside page margins appropriately on left and right pages and allows you to work on facing pages, or two-page spreads. Odd-numbered pages in a double-sided publication are right-handed, and even-numbered pages are left-handed.

When you check Double-sided, the Facing pages option becomes available. When in Facing pages mode, PageMaker displays adjacent right and left pages in the publication window, as opposed to a single, stand-alone page. The difference between the two modes is shown in Figure 1-7. (Notice that in the facing-pages view example the page icons across the bottom of the publication window are displayed as side-by-side pages. In the single-page view the icons represent single pages. We'll talk more about these icons in the next section.)

You can toggle Facing Pages on and off while creating your publication. Working in a single-page view allows you to get a larger display of each page with the Fit in window view, and the screen redraws faster. When you want to see how facing pages look together, turn the option back on again.

Margins

Four fields make up the Margins option: Inside, Outside, Top, and Bottom (or, when Facing pages is turned off, Left and Right). The values you enter in these fields tell PageMaker how far to place margin guides from the edge of the page. Whether this option reads "Inches," "Points," etc., depends on the unit of measure specified in the Preferences dialog box. Preferences are discussed in "Defaults and Preferences" later in this chapter.

The area within margins usually contains the body copy and primary elements of each page; however, you can place and print elements outside the margin guides, as shown in Figure 1-8. Headers, footers, and page numbers, are often positioned outside the page margins.

Sometimes a document calls for margins in measurement units different from the default system. You can override the current unit of measurement by using PageMaker's one-character abbreviations. (Use *i* for inch, *p* for pica, *c* for cicero, *m* for millimeter, as described later in this chapter in "The Preferences Dialog Box.")

After making the appropriate settings in the Document setup dialog box, click the OK button or press the return key. PageMaker creates the new document according to your choices, and the publication window appears, displaying the first page of your new document.

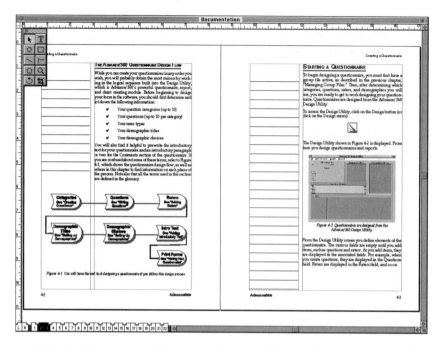

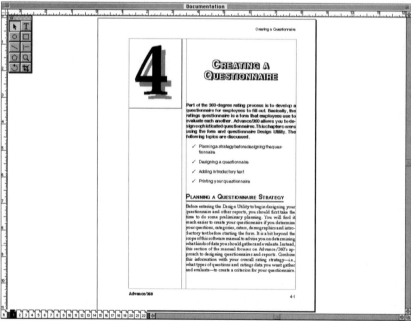

Figure 1-7: Examples of facing-pages (top) and single-page view. Facing page's view allows you to work on both pages in a two-page spread at the same time.

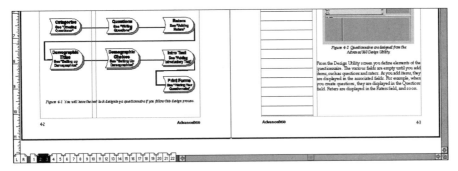

Figure 1-8: An example of footers outside the margin guides

Whoops! The settings aren't right? Your pages are too small? Too big? Have no fear. You can return the Document Setup dialog box to make changes to your initial settings at any time, as described in "Changing Basic Page Formatting," later in this chapter.

The Publication Window _____

PageMaker publications are created in *publication windows*, as shown in Figure 1-9. A publication window contains the publication, palettes, and several other items essential to page layout with PageMaker. You can open as many publications as memory permits. When starting a new document, the publication window remains untitled until you specifically name and save it. After you name the document, the name appears in the title bar. PageMaker displays either a one- or a two-page spread in each publication window, depending on the page(s) currently active and whether the publication contains facing pages. The following is a list of the publication window elements:

- **Margin Guides.** These are the colored lines framing the page. You set up margin guides in Document Setup when defining a new document.

- **Rulers.** PageMaker's rulers aid in placing and measuring layout elements in the publication window. You can toggle the rulers on and off by choosing the Show Rulers command from the Guides and Rulers submenu on the Layout menu. The rulers' unit of measurement (inches, points, etc.) is specified in the Preferences dialog box, as discussed in "Defaults and Preferences," later in this chapter. A small dotted line on each ruler marks the current location of the mouse cursor as you move it around in the publication window. The zero point intersection, the place where the rulers cross, is fully adjustable, as described in Chapter 4.

Toolbox   Rulers   Margin guides

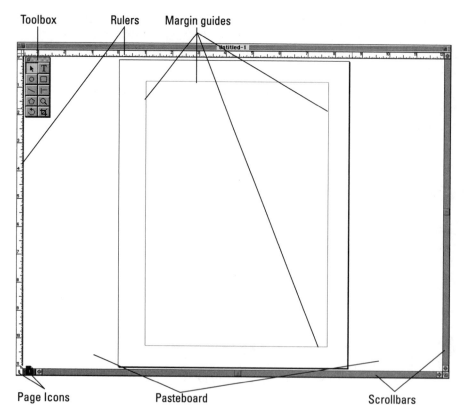

Page Icons   Pasteboard   Scrollbars

Figure 1-9: The PageMaker publication window

∞ **Toolbox.** Contains PageMaker's 10 tools. To select a tool, click on it. The tool is then highlighted in the Toolbox, and the mouse cursor, when positioned in the publication window, displays the icon of the selected tool. You can move, open, or close the Toolbox — just like any other Macintosh window.

∞ **Page icons.** These icons represent the pages in your document, including the master pages for the active pages (master pages are discussed in Chapter 4). Use the page icons to move around quickly in your document by clicking on the icon for the desired page(s). The icons for the page(s) active in the publication window are highlighted, so you'll always know what page you are working on. If your display is not large enough to contain all the page icons for a publication, PageMaker supplies arrows at both ends of the page icon row for scrolling.

∞ **Pasteboard.** The area in the publication window surrounding the page(s). Use this space to store text and graphical elements to move them out of the way or hold for later use.

⤷ **Scroll bars.** These operate exactly as the scroll bars in other Mac applications: Use the arrows for line-by-line scrolling, click in the dimmed area in the bar to scroll about one-half the current display, or drag the scroll box for greater control over the scrolling distance.

As you'll see later in this chapter in "Defaults and Preferences," you can change PageMaker's application defaults and determine which elements appear when you create a new publication.

Opening Existing PageMaker Publications

PageMaker 6 supports publications created in PageMaker 6 and PageMaker 5. You can also use PageMaker 6 to edit publications created with PageMaker 1.0, 2.0, 3.0, and 4.x, after performing a few extra steps to convert them to a usable format, as outlined later in this section.

Opening Files from the Desktop

As discussed earlier in this chapter, there are several ways to open PageMaker documents. If PageMaker is not running, you can open both PageMaker and a specific PageMaker file at the same time by double-clicking on the file icon from the desktop. PageMaker 6 publications are readily identified by the PageMaker icon, as shown in Figure 1-10 (viewed by icon or small icon at the Finder) or by the designator "PageMaker 6.0 document" (when viewing files by name, size, kind, date).

Figure 1-10: PageMaker 6 publication icons and names in the finder list

	PageMaker 6			
Name	Size	Kind	Label	Last Modified
☐ Advance too	132K	Adobe® PageMake...	–	Sat, Sep 16, 1995, 12:44 PM
☐ Certificate	429K	Adobe® PageMake...	–	Wed, Aug 23, 1995, 10:36 AM
☐ Cover Page	182K	Adobe® PageMake...	–	Mon, Aug 21, 1995, 3:40 PM
☐ Documentation	2,063K	Adobe® PageMake...	–	Thu, Sep 21, 1995, 11:09 AM
☐ Documentation Template	116K	Adobe® PageMake...	–	Mon, Sep 4, 1995, 1:11 PM
▷ ☐ Four-Page Catalog files	–	folder	–	Mon, Jan 17, 1994, 5:25 PM
☐ Medical Brochure	1,914K	Adobe® PageMake...	–	Thu, Sep 21, 1995, 12:24 PM
▷ ☐ Newsletter files	–	folder	–	Mon, Jan 17, 1994, 5:25 PM
▷ ☐ PM5 Text	–	folder	–	Tue, Jul 25, 1995, 3:29 PM
▷ ☐ PM6 Graphics	–	folder	–	Fri, Sep 22, 1995, 10:01 AM
▷ ☐ PM6 Text	–	folder	–	Sat, Sep 23, 1995, 2:46 PM
☐ Two-page newsletter	83K	Adobe® PageMake...	–	Fri, Sep 22, 1995, 4:15 PM
▷ ☐ Two-sided flier files	–	folder	–	Sun, Jan 16, 1994, 10:57 PM
☐ Web Page	231K	Adobe® PageMake...	–	Fri, Sep 15, 1995, 12:04 PM

If an "Alert" dialog box with the message "Application not found" appears when you double-click on a PageMaker publication icon, try launching PageMaker and then opening the file using the Open... command, discussed in the next section, "Opening files from within PageMaker." The "Application not found" dialog box means that, for one reason or another, your Macintosh cannot associate the file with its host application. If the problem persists, try rebuilding the desktop on your Macintosh (hold down ⌘-Option at start-up after the extensions have loaded but before the Finder desktop appears).

Opening Files from Within PageMaker

To open an existing PageMaker 6 document while inside PageMaker, select the Open... command from the File menu (⌘-O). This action opens the Open publication dialog box shown in Figure 1-11. Next, select the file that you want to open from the file list and click the OK button (or double-click the file name).

To work on a copy of the selected file without modifying the original, select the Copy option. This opens a new, untitled copy of the selected file — a handy way to save your revisions or create documents based on existing ones. When opening templates (templates are discussed in Chapter 7), PageMaker automatically selects the Copy option, since you usually use a copy of the template to create your new publication. To modify the template itself, click Original in the Open option before clicking the OK button.

Figure 1-11:
The Open publication
dialog box

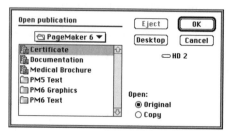

To search a long list of filenames, you can enter the first letter of the desired filename to move through the alphabetical listing, or you can enter the first few letters of the filename to locate it quickly. Another quick way to open publications you've worked on recently is with the Recent Publication submenu on the File menu, as shown in Figure 1-12.

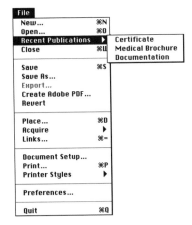

Figure 1-12:
Use the Recent Publications
command to find and
open publications you've
worked on recently.

PageMaker 5 Files

To open files created in PageMaker 5, launch PageMaker 6 and then use the Open…
command as described in the previous section. PageMaker 6 converts PageMaker 5 files
automatically. The converted files open as "Untitled." You can use Save or Save as… to
name the file and make the conversion permanent. This does not delete or modify your
original version 5 file unless you give it the same name as the old file.

If PageMaker can't convert the file, try giving the application a little more RAM
(changing the memory values in the Get Info dialog box) or make sure you have
plenty of free space on your hard drive. To increase PageMaker's memory
allocation, select the Adobe PageMaker 6.0 icon, then select Get Info from the
File menu in Finder. Under Memory Requirements, change the minimum
memory requirement. You can also improve performance by turning on Virtual
Memory in your Mac's control panel.

After converting a document, you should check the layout carefully; you may need to
make some slight adjustments before printing the file.

PageMaker 1.0, 2.0, 3.0, 4.0, and 4.2 Files

PageMaker 6 cannot directly open publications created in versions of PageMaker earlier
than version 5, so you have to use earlier versions of PageMaker to convert files up
through the versions. If you have a PageMaker 2.0 publication, for example, launch
PageMaker 3.0 and open the file to convert it into a PageMaker 3.0 publication. Save the
file and then continue the process up through the versions. Unfortunately, this is the
only way to convert old files for use in the current version.

Changing Basic Page Formatting

Occasionally you may want to change page size, margins, and other elements of your document that you originally defined in the Document Setup dialog box. For example, you might find that you can't fit all the required information into your publication without going to a larger page size. Have no fear. You can make changes simply by selecting Document setup from the File menu.

We already looked at the Document Setup dialog box in the "Creating a New Publication" section of this chapter, but let's examine briefly how making changes through this dialog box affects the layout of existing publications:

- **Page size and dimensions.** Changing the page size does not affect existing layout elements. Only their placement on the page changes. If the new page size is smaller, some objects may now appear on the pasteboard, for example. You can, of course, reposition them. But this can be a pain in long documents.

- **Orientation.** As with the Page size option, changes to page orientation affect only the positioning of elements on the page. Almost certainly, some of the existing page elements wind up on the pasteboard. But you can move them again.

- **Double-sided.** This option mostly affects the margins on your pages. Double-sided pages contain inside and outside margins, instead of right and left margins. Depending on the current margin settings, changing this option can make critical page-element-position changes on your pages, which you can go back and correct manually on each page. Note also that the Facing pages option is available only when the Double-sided option is selected. If you change a double-sided publication with facing pages to a single-sided publication, objects that span across the two pages remain attached to what were formerly left-side pages and extend into the pasteboard.

- **Facing pages.** Deselecting the Facing pages option leaves objects that span across the two pages attached to the left pages. Selecting the Facing pages option forces PageMaker to delete some ruler guides (ruler guides are discussed in Chapter 4), if the newly created facing pages have a combined total of more than 40 ruler guides.

- **Margins.** Resetting any of the margins moves the margin lines displayed on all pages of the publication, without adjusting existing text or graphical objects. You can reposition elements as needed.

- **Number of pages.** Changing the Number of pages option adds pages to or deletes pages from your document. New pages are added after the active page, the page you were working on when opening Document Setup. Lowering the page count deletes pages. A dialog box tells you which pages will be deleted. Using the Insert Pages and Remove Pages commands from the Layout menu provides more direct control over adding and deleting pages.

☞ **Start page #.** You can change the starting page number to any figure between 1 and 9999, as long as the highest page number in the document does not exceed 9999. When working on a double-sided publication, changing this option from an odd to even number, or vice versa, will change all right pages to left pages, and all left pages to right pages. When working on a double-sided publication with facing pages, objects that span across two-page spreads remain attached to what were formerly the left-hand pages. In addition to renumbering the page icons at the bottom of the publication window, all pages in the document paginated with PageMaker's automatic page numbering are also updated. Automatic page numbers are discussed in Chapter 4.

Defaults and Preferences _____

Most options and command settings in PageMaker are preset. These presets are PageMaker's *defaults*. Default means: I will do this unless you tell me to do something else. PageMaker's *default settings* are Adobe software engineer's best guesses. They are supposed to represent the most commonly used settings for the average user. New publications, for example, are by default created on letter-sized paper with rulers and the toolbox displayed in the publication window, along with various other settings for font, graphic line weights, and so on.

Constantly changing from one setting to another quickly becomes tedious and time-consuming. So, PageMaker allows you to change the default settings for most commands and options, including line weights, fonts, paragraph settings, you name it. You can change default settings temporarily, affecting only the current document, or permanently, affecting all new publications.

Default settings changed within a publication apply only to that publication. These settings are sometimes called *publication defaults*. You can make publication default changes only while the publication is open. They remain set until modified, even if the application defaults (discussed next) are reset.

When you make default setting changes with no document open, they become permanent settings, affecting all new documents. These settings are sometimes called *application defaults*. You can change the default settings for menu commands and options. Application defaults remain set until you reset them.

You can always return to the original defaults by deleting the PageMaker 6 Defaults file in your Mac's System/Preferences folder. This allows you to start from scratch, which is especially helpful if somebody else has used your computer and you don't know what changes might have been made to your PageMaker configuration, or to the kinds of documents you layout.

To change a default setting, simply select the new option. To change the default font, for example, select a new font name from the Font submenu on the Type menu. A check mark ($\surd$) beside a font name on the menu signifies the default font. You can use this method to change type styles, type attributes, paragraph formatting, type sizes, graphic line styles and weights, shape fills and tints, and many other options. Those options that cannot be changed are grayed out on the menus. To change other, more application-specific defaults, such as the mode of displaying measuring systems and imported graphics, you use the Preferences dialog box, discussed next.

The Preferences Dialog Box

The Preferences dialog box (shown in Figure 1-13), accessed via the Preferences… command on the File menu, contains a variety of options pertaining primarily to working in the publication window.

As with the defaults described in the previous section, you can change the default settings for a specific publication or you can set application defaults that apply to all new publications. Most Preferences options have little to do with document-layout specifics, so you can set them to your liking as application defaults. Remember to close all documents to make application default changes.

Figure 1-13:
The Preferences
dialog box

Preferences

Measurements in: [Inches]   [OK]
Vertical ruler: [Inches]   [ ] points   [Cancel]

Layout problems: ☐ Show loose/tight lines
☐ Show "keeps" violations   [More...]

Graphics display: ○ Gray out   [Map fonts...]
◉ Standard   [CMS Setup...]
○ High resolution

┌ Control palette ───────────
Horizontal nudge: [0.01] [Inches]   Save option: ◉ Faster
○ Smaller
Vertical nudge: [0.01] [Inches]   Guides: ◉ Front
☐ Use "Snap to" constraints   ○ Back

Options available in the Preferences dialog box are:

- **Layout⇨Measurement system.** The Measurement system option offers a choice of five units of measure: inches, inches decimal, millimeters, picas, and ciceros. PageMaker uses the measurement system selected here in the rulers and all dialog boxes that require measurements.

When entering measurements into a dialog box, you can override the current measurement system by adding an abbreviation to the value — *i* for inch, *m* for millimeter, *p* for pica (with any value following the *p* indicating points), or *c* for cicero (with any value following the *c* indicating points). For example, if the dialog asks for the Margin measurement in inches, entering 3p6 would specify 3 picas 6 points (or $3^1/_2$ picas), entering 20m would specify 20 millimeters, and entering 8c3 would specify 8 ciceros 3 points (or $8^1/_4$ ciceros).

- **Layout⇨Vertical ruler.** The Vertical ruler option lets you specify a different unit of measurement for the vertical ruler from the measurement system used on the horizontal ruler and in the dialog boxes. For example, some newspapers measure pages by inches horizontally and by points vertically. The pop-up option lets you choose the unit of measurement for the ruler. The "points" field, when used in conjunction with the Custom setting, allows you to divide the ruler by any number of points. Other options include inches decimal, inches, millimeters, picas, and ciceros.

Use the Custom option to set the number of points on the ruler the same as leading in the body copy of your publication. This allows you to easily align your text blocks — especially when aligning text in adjacent columns. Leading is discussed in Chapter 6.

- **Layout problems⇨Show loose/tight lines.** This option tells PageMaker to notify you when the spacing of a line of text is too loose or too tight. When the Show loose/tight lines option is selected, PageMaker highlights loose- and tight-line problems, as shown in Figure 1-14. PageMaker uses the settings for letter- and word-spacing in the Spacing attributes dialog box (discussed in Chapter 6) to determine which lines are too loose or too tight. PageMaker overrides the Spacing attributes settings when justification and hyphenation settings (also discussed in Chapter 6) conflict with letter- and word-spacing.

- **Layout problems⇨Show "Keeps" violations.** When the Keeps violations option is selected, PageMaker highlights lines of text that violate the settings for the Keep with next, Widow, or Orphan options in the Paragraph specifications dialog box. Paragraph specifications are discussed in Chapter 6.

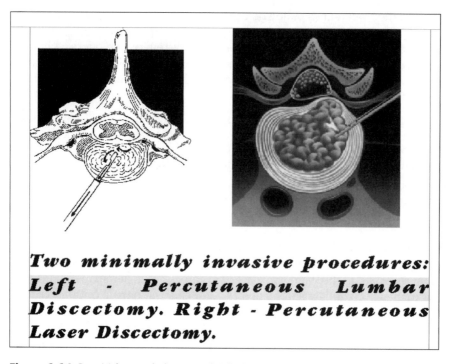

Two minimally invasive procedures: Left - Percutaneous Lumbar Discectomy. Right - Percutaneous Laser Discectomy.

Figure 1-14: PageMaker marks loose- and tight-line violations.

☞ **Graphics.** This option controls how PageMaker redraws imported images on your screen. Its purpose is to provide a trade-off between display quality and speedy screen redraws, which can be critical on slower Macs. Choosing the Gray out option provides the fastest on-screen performance — every image is replaced with a gray box, showing you image placement but no images. In Standard mode, PageMaker displays PICT and TIFF images at low resolution. The High resolution option displays PICT and TIFF images at the best possible quality (but with the slowest on-screen drawing time). Note that this option does not affect print quality.

 You can force PageMaker to redraw temporarily all images at their highest resolution by holding down the Command key as you click on the current page icon or when selecting a view size from the View sizes submenu. This is a quick way to get a more reliable view of how the page will print.

☞ **Guides.** Selecting the Front option sets margin, column, and ruler guides on top of page elements, making it easier to place them. Selecting the Back option sets the guides behind page elements, making the page look similar to how it will appear when it's printed. Guides are discussed in Chapter 4.

Often, when attempting to select items in the publication window, you may find yourself accidentally selecting guides instead. Setting the Guides option in the Preferences dialog box to Back can help, but to ensure that you don't inadvertently select guides, hold down the Command key when selecting objects with the pointer tool. Holding the Command key makes it impossible to select guides.

- **Save.** This option determines how PageMaker writes your file to disk when you choose the Save command or press ⌘-S. With the Faster option the Save and ⌘-S quick-save save copies of the PageMaker file that include extraneous data, such as markers in the file code for each change you make to your layout. This quickly makes the document file quite large. Choosing the Smaller option tells PageMaker to strip out all extraneous code, making the file smaller, which allows PageMaker to navigate the file quicker by clearing up some memory. PageMaker will also strip extraneous code when you use the Save as... command to save a document.

- **Control palette⇨Horizontal nudge.** This option determines the horizontal distance an object moves when you click on the nudge (arrow) buttons in the Control palette. The Control palette is discussed in Chapter 9.

- **Control palette⇨Vertical nudge.** This option determines the vertical distance an object moves when you click on the nudge (arrow) buttons in the Control palette. The Control palette is discussed in Chapter 9.

- **Control palette⇨Use "Snap to" constraints.** When you select this option, nudging objects via the control palette nudge buttons moves them to the next nearest ruler tick mark or non-printing ruler, margin, or column guide. This option works only when the Snap to option is selected on the Guides and rulers submenu, and the element is within three pixels of a guide or ruler tick mark. In other words, this option makes a nudged object act like a dragged object when the Snap to option is active. The Control palette is discussed in Chapter 9.

More Preferences

In addition to the options available in the Preferences dialog box, you can set additional defaults in the More Preferences dialog box, by clicking on the More button in Preferences. The options in the More Preferences dialog box, shown in Figure 1-15, are described as follows:

- **Text⇨Greek text below.** This option controls the size at which PageMaker stops drawing type on the screen, replacing individual characters with gray bars, a process known as *greeking*. Why should PageMaker (and you) take the time to

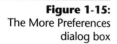

Figure 1-15:
The More Preferences
dialog box

redraw text if it's too small too read? The benefit of greeking text is that
PageMaker redraws the thin gray bars much faster than individual characters.
See Figure 1-16 for an example of greeking. The number of pixels you should
specify depends on the size and resolution of your monitor. The larger your
monitor and the higher the resolution, the smaller you should set Greek text
below. On Bill's 20-inch monitor, for instance, it's no problem reading text in fit in
window view. So he sets this option at 4. For smaller monitors with lower resolutions you should set it higher.

☞ **Text⇨Turn pages when autoflowing.** This option is a time-saver. Selecting it lets
PageMaker flow imported text into a document without showing its progress
page by page. Avoiding all that screen redraw makes text flow much faster.
Importing text into PageMaker is discussed in Chapter 7.

☞ **Text⇨Use typographer's quotes.** Selecting this option instructs PageMaker to
substitute open (") and close (") typographer's quotes and apostrophes for the
upright inch (") and foot (') marks you enter from your keyboard.

☞ **Text⇨TrueType display.** Preserve line spacing, Preserve character shape. When
redrawing TrueType fonts on-screen, PageMaker has a choice of rendering the
characters more accurately in terms of line spacing and less accurately in terms
of character shape, or more accurately in terms of character shape and less
accurately in terms of line spacing. Confusing, huh? This option affects screen
redraws only; they have no effect on the printed quality of TrueType fonts.

☞ **Story editor⇨Font, Size.** These two options determine the font and type size
used to display text in the Story Editor. Use the pop-up menus to select any font
available on your Macintosh and any of 14 type sizes, or type in the font size you
prefer. The Story Editor is discussed in Chapter 5.

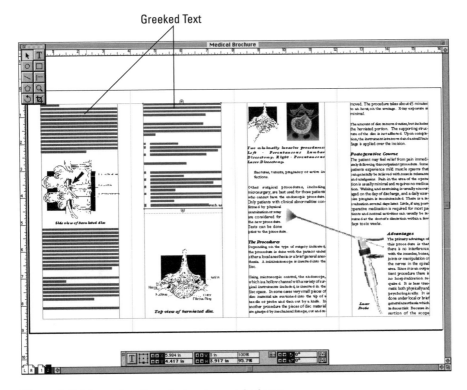

Figure 1-16: Examples of greeked and ungreeked text

- ☞ **Story editor➪Display Style names.** Selecting this option adds a vertical column to each Story Editor window, in which the names of style sheets applied to paragraphs appear. Style sheets are discussed Chapter 7.

- ☞ **Story editor➪Display ¶ marks.** Selecting this option causes your Mac's non-printing characters to appear in Story Editor windows. Non-printing characters include paragraph marks (¶), spaces, and tabs, as shown in Figure 1-17. These marks are sometimes helpful when editing text, especially for determining when you have too many spaces or carriage returns (line spaces).

- ☞ **Graphics➪Define Standard display by: Size, Resolution.** Each time you place a graphics file in a PageMaker document, the program builds a screen representation of the graphic. This option determines the amount of memory used to create the screen image. Increasing the size of the display in kilobytes or resolution allows PageMaker to create a better-looking representation of imported graphics, but it also increases publication size, which can slow PageMaker down and make the document difficult to transport. Decreasing these options has the opposite

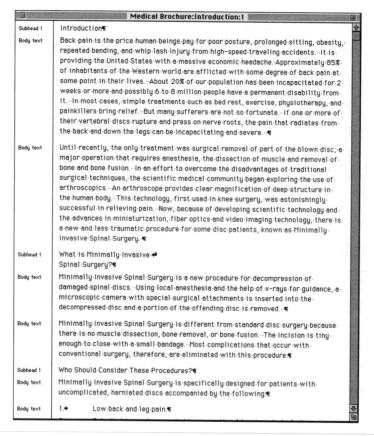

Figure 1-17:
The Story
Editor with
Display
¶ marks
turned on

effect, reducing publication size and degrading the quality of on-screen bitmaps. These options do not affect the printing of graphics. PageMaker uses data from the original graphics file when printing. In other words, PageMaker creates a link to the original graphics file, using it when printing. Graphics linking is discussed in depth in Chapter 8.

∞ **Alert when storing graphics over.** This option tells PageMaker how to import and store graphics. It can either fully embed them in the publication file or link them, which creates a pointer to the original graphics file. When you try to bring in an image larger than the amount specified here, PageMaker gives you a dialog box giving you the choice of storing or linking the graphics file. Linking larger graphics files helps keep publication sizes down but adds to your document- and file-management hassles later, especially when transporting the file to a service bureau for printing. Printing is discussed in Chapter 13.

∾ **Postscript printing⇨Postscript printing.** PageMaker sometimes requires all the printer memory it can get for printing large EPS and PICT files. This option allows you to instruct PageMaker to flush the printer's memory of fonts to make room for larger files. Fonts are then downloaded as needed and flushed when not in use. To use this option, set it to Maximum. Otherwise, leave the setting at normal.

Map Fonts...

Another option in the Preferences dialog box is Map fonts..., which opens the Font Matching Preferences dialog box. This discussion is more appropriate in a chapter about creating and formatting text. So, you'll find a discussion of font mapping in Chapter 5.

CMS Setup...

Yet another option in Preferences is the CMS Setup... button, which brings up the Color Management System Preferences dialog box. This dialog box allows you to set up PageMaker's color management system (CMS). Since color management is fairly complicated, it makes more sense for us to discuss CMS Setup in Chapter 10 after you've had a little computer color information to digest.

Saving a Publication _____

Saving your work frequently is as important in PageMaker as it is in any software program. Until you save, you risk losing the work you've done since the last save. Like most Mac programs, PageMaker provides the Save (⌘-S) or Save as... commands on the File menu. Their operation also follows Mac standards:

∾ **The Save command** (⌘-S). If you've already named and saved a document once, the Save command updates the disk version of the file to reflect the current contents of the publication, preference settings, and all publication windows. If you haven't saved the document, the Save command invokes the Save as... command, described next. You can also configure the Save command to reduce the file size of a document, as described in the "Preferences Dialog Box" section of this chapter.

∾ **The Save as... command.** Use Save as... to save and name a file. Choosing Save as... from the File menu brings up the Save publication as dialog box shown in Figure 1-18. For the most part, this dialog box operates similarly to most Mac Save as... dialog boxes, with the few exceptions discussed here.

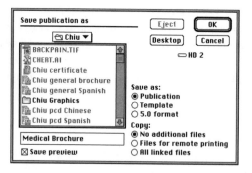

Figure 1-18:
The Save publication as
dialog box

You can use the Save as... dialog box to save PageMaker templates. Choose the Template option to create a new PageMaker template. Templates allow you to save often used layout choices, such as headers, footers, page formatting, style sheets, and other information for use on multiple documents requiring the same or similar formats. Templates are discussed in Chapter 7.

The Files for remote printing and All linked files options copy all graphic and text files of a given publication to a specific folder. This provides a quick way to gather all the files needed to print your publication — especially useful when transporting your PageMaker file to another location for editing or printing. Linked documents are described more fully in Chapter 12. Preparing a file for remote printing is discussed in Chapter 13.

When to Use Save as...

Using the Save as... command (rather than Save) has two advantages. The first is security — if you use the Save as... command to save multiple versions of your publication, stored in different locations, your chance of substantial loss of work due to file corruption or a system crash is dramatically reduced. The second is economy — if you are not using the Smaller save option in the Preferences dialog box (see "Preferences Dialog Box," earlier in this chapter), files saved with Save as... are significantly smaller than those saved with Save. Depending on the contents of the file, Save as... reduces a file size from 20 to 50 percent, speeding up PageMaker and making the file easier to manage.

PageMaker's Mini-Save

In most cases, when you reopen a PageMaker file after a system crash, you'll find that many of your changes have been preserved — this is the result of *mini-saves*. Any time you move to another page, change the page setup options, click the OK button in the

Define styles dialog box, perform a Save or Save as…, or click the icon of the current page, PageMaker performs a mini-save of your document. Information from this mini-save is stored in a temporary file on your disk — your current working file is not updated. PageMaker uses the information from the mini-save to minimize the amount of work lost in the event of a system crash and as a reference when you use the Revert command, discussed in Chapter 4. When you open the file, PageMaker uses the last mini-saved version.

 Although the mini-saves will probably save you much time and effort at one time or another, you really should save your document often, with either Save or Save as…. We press ⌘-S every few minutes — it's a drag doing things over.

Finishing a PageMaker Session

When you have finished working in a publication, you can close it. Then you can open a different publication, create a new publication, or quit PageMaker altogether.

Closing a Publication

To close an open publication, choose the Close command (⌘-W) from the File menu, or click the close box in the upper-left corner of the publication window. If you've made changes to the file, the Save before closing? dialog box, shown in Figure 1-19, asks if you want to save your work. Clicking Yes saves (or, if the document is untitled, opens the Save publication as dialog box) and then closes the file. Clicking No closes the file without saving the changes, and clicking Cancel returns you to the publication window without saving or closing anything.

Figure 1-19:
The Save before closing?
dialog box

Once you have closed all publications, only the PageMaker menu bar remains on-screen. At this point, your options are the same as when you launched PageMaker: You can create a new PageMaker publication, open an existing PageMaker publication, alter PageMaker's application default settings, or quit PageMaker and return to the Macintosh Finder.

Quitting PageMaker

When you have finished your work in PageMaker, choosing the Quit command from the File menu (⌘-Q) closes the current publication, allowing you to save it, if necessary, and returns control of your Macintosh to the Finder.

Summary

- ⊶ You can open PageMaker by double-clicking on the PageMaker icon, double-clicking any PageMaker document, dragging a PageMaker document onto the PageMaker application icon, or using a Macintosh launching utility.

- ⊶ The New… command lets you create a new publication and effect basic formatting changes. You can change page settings later with Document Setup….

- ⊶ PageMaker documents appear in a publication window, which displays one page or a two-page spread from the document, page icons, rulers, palettes, and the pasteboard.

- ⊶ Defaults set in PageMaker with no publications open are saved as application defaults. Defaults set with a publication open are saved as document defaults.

- ⊶ The Preferences… command and dialog box let you modify your PageMaker environment, including the default measurement system, control palette nudge amounts, layering of guidelines, and the font and type size used in Story Editor.

- ⊶ Use PageMaker's Save as… to compress your publications and to transfer files linked to the current publication to a single folder for easy transport. PageMaker regularly performs automatic mini-saves that reduce the chances of losing work to application or system crashes.

What's New in PageMaker 6

In This Chapter

- ➡ PageMaker's new Arrange menu, including: Group, Lock Position, Align Objects

- ➡ PageMaker's new color trapping feature

- ➡ PageMaker's new HTML Author plug-in that allows you to create World Wide Web pages in PageMaker

- ➡ Support for Color Management Systems to help you control color shifts from your monitor to hard copy output

For the experienced computer user, there is nothing quite like the feeling of a new version of a favorite software application. Seeing the new menu commands, tools, floating palettes, and dialog-box options is exciting because each promises improved productivity or new ways that the program can help you get your work done. This is certainly true of PageMaker 6. This latest upgrade contains all kinds of new features designed to help you get your work done quicker and smarter.

This chapter saves you the trouble of hunting through PageMaker, the user manuals, or even this book to figure out what is new in version 6. We'll introduce you to virtually every new menu command, tool, palette, and dialog-box option in PageMaker 6. You can then start putting these new features to work the next time you use PageMaker, perhaps even before you read the more detailed discussion about these new capabilities in later chapters.

The main focus of this chapter is on features new or improved since version 5. Many of the new features, such as the new toolbox design, for example, bring PageMaker closer to a bona fide Adobe application. If you use Photoshop and Illustrator, this is good news! The more alike your applications operate, the easier it is to use them. Right?

New Features in PageMaker 6___

Acquire

In some cases, improvements in version 6 are not really new features but instead revamped adaptations of old ones. To scan into PageMaker 5 you used the Acquire addition (now called plug-ins). Acquire is now part of the program. You now select your TWAIN (Technology Without An Interesting Name) source from the Select Source submenu of Acquire on the File menu. After selecting a source, you then use Acquire Image, also a subcommand of Acquire. Scanning is discussed in detail in Chapter 8.

Arrange

The new Arrange menu, shown in Figure 2-1, provides a list of long-awaited commands designed to make working with layout elements easier. A few of the commands, such as Bring to Front, Send to Back, and Remove Transformation, are old favorites relocated from other menus. The others — Align Objects, Bring Forward, Send Backward, Group, Ungroup, Lock Position, and Unlock — are all new. They are discussed next in the order they appear on the menu. Arranging and grouping objects is discussed in detail in Chapter 8.

Figure 2-1:
PageMaker's new Arrange menu

Arrange	
Align Objects...	⌘-
Bring to Front	⌘F
Bring Forward	⌘8
Send to Back	⌘B
Send Backward	⌘9
Group	⌘G
Ungroup	⌘U
Lock Position	⌘L
Unlock	⌘,
Remove Transformation	

Align Objects

Here's a feature PageMaker users have longed for: the ability to align selected objects in relationship to other selected objects. Choosing this command opens the Align Objects dialog box, shown in Figure 2-2. From here you can align selected objects from their centers, edges, and so on. This is a handy, time-saving way to create evenly spaced page elements (especially when used in conjunction with version 6's new Group command, discussed shortly), such as text boxes and graphics.

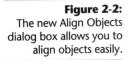
Figure 2-2:
The new Align Objects
dialog box allows you to
align objects easily.

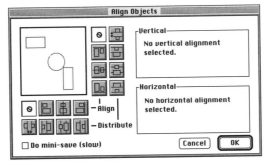

Bring Forward/Send Backward

It's hard to imagine living without these two options. But somehow we have. These are simple commands with powerful implications. All they do is move selected objects one level forward or backward in a stack of objects. Before version 6, you had to find creative ways to use Bring to Front and Send to Back to achieve the same results.

Group/Ungroup

The lack of this feature has caused QuarkXPress-envy among PageMaker users. Often, when laying out a page, it can be helpful to treat several related objects as one; to have the ability to select, move, and resize them all at the same time; or to change line and fill attributes all at once. Group provides this functionality. To use it, simply select the objects you want to group and then select this command. Figure 2-3 shows the difference between two grouped and ungrouped items. Notice that the ungrouped items (left) have their own sets of handles. In the grouped example (right) the group of objects contains only one set of handles. Ungroup, of course, ungroups previously grouped items.

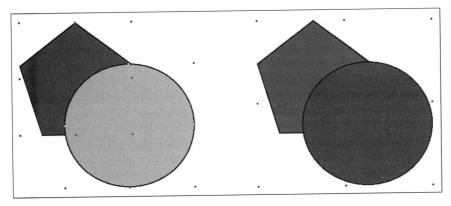

Figure 2-3: Examples of grouped and ungrouped objects. The objects on the left are not grouped and contain individual sets of handles. The objects on the right are grouped and have only one set of handles for the entire group.

Lock Position/Unlock

Here's yet another must-have feature PageMaker users have lived without. If you've ever inadvertently moved or resized an object in a PageMaker layout, you'll appreciate this one. Lock Position fixes selected objects to their current size and position on the page, so that you cannot move or resize them. You can, however still make line, fill, text attribute, and other changes to locked items, you just can't make changes with your mouse. Unlock, of course, unlocks previously locked objects. (Locked objects show gray handles, rather than black.)

Book

Book, the command that allows you to manage chapters in a multiple-document publication, is not really a new or improved feature. We're listing it here because it has been moved from the File menu to the Utilities menu. It's tough to say whether this is a better location. The Book command and other long document issues are discussed in Chapter 12.

Color Management System Setup (CMS Setup)

CMS Setup is actually an option in the Preferences dialog box. And we've designated a separate section of this chapter for changes to Preferences. But the addition of color management to PageMaker is significant. It warrants a separate discussion. Version 6 includes a color management system, Kodak's Precision Color, and supports others.

Color management systems attempt to calibrate colors between various input and output devices, such as scanners, monitors, printers, and offset presses. While they are not the perfect solution to color matching problems that arise between computers and reproduction devices, they are a giant step forward, taking much of the guesswork out of getting true color.

You get to CMS Setup through the Preferences dialog box (choose Preferences from the File menu). The Color Management System Preferences dialog box, shown in Figure 2-4, allows you to select various device profiles, such as monitor, proof printer, separation printer, and so on. You can also select the color management system you want to use, Kodak's or others supported by PageMaker. Using color and the color management systems are discussed in detail in Chapter 10.

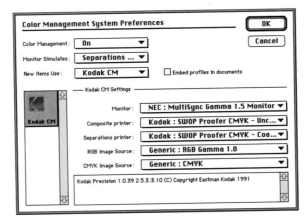

Figure 2-4:
The new Color
Management System
Preferences
dialog box

Colors Palette

PageMaker's color palette certainly is not new, but it has a new look and a really
swell new feature. First, let's check out the palette's slick new appearance, shown in
Figure 2-5. Notice that instead of the pop-up menu for Line, Fill, and Both, there are now
icons. What you can't see in the figure is that the icons change colors as you change a
selected object's fill and line colors, showing you line and fill colors of the selected
object. We found this extremely handy for determining which object in a stack
is selected.

Figure 2-5:
The Colors palette's new look

Another nifty addition to the Colors palette is preset screens, or "tints." Notice in
Figure 2-6 that you can now select screens in increments of 5 percent. This is a far cry
better than the previous method of having to define a new color for each screen percentage you want to use.

Figure 2-6:
The Colors palette now contains
predefined screens, or "tints."

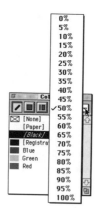

Create Adobe PDF

Portable Document Files (PDFs) make PostScript files readable by Adobe's Acrobat Distiller and Acrobat Reader. PageMaker is now an Adobe product; it makes sense that it supports Adobe's Acrobat portable document format. This command, located on the File menu, allows you (after some initial preparation in PageMaker) to use your PageMaker documents with Acrobat. For more about PDF and publishing for electronic media in general, refer to Chapter 15.

Document Setup

In previous versions of PageMaker, you used Page Setup to set up new documents and modify the base formatting, such as page size, facing pages, double-sided pages, of existing documents. Page Setup has a new name. It is now Document Setup.

Expert Kerning

Previously an Aldus Addition (plug-in), Expert Kerning, located on the Type menu, examines every character pair in the selected text, removes all existing manual kerning, and then kerns the type based on the amount of kerning strength you specify. For more on Expert Kerning and kerning in general, refer to Chapter 6.

Expert Tracking

In version 6, PageMaker's six text tracking values (previously listed under Track on the Type menu in version 5) are now assigned to the Expert Tracking command, also located on the Type menu. The version 5 Aldus Addition, Edit tracks, is now also located on the Expert Tracking submenu. Edit tracks lets you modify the default values of PageMaker's six tracks, adjusting the amount of space set between characters in a font at different point sizes. Tracking and Edit tracks are discussed in Chapter 6.

Find/Change

Several significant changes to PageMaker's Find and Change (search and replace) feature have been added in version 6. In version 6, in addition to searching and replacing text by Font, Size, Color, and Type style attributes, you can also narrow the options even further by searching and replacing Set width, Leading, Track, and Tint attributes, as shown in Figure 2-7.

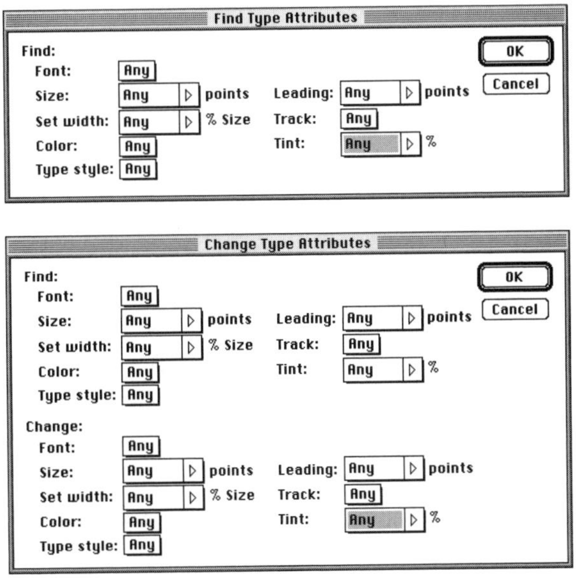

Figure 2-7:
The Find and Change dialog boxes now let you search for Set width settings, leading, tracking, and tints.

You can also now find and change certain paragraph attributes (as shown in Figure 2-8): Paragraph style, Alignment, and Leading method (set in the Spacing option from the Paragraph dialog box). This is a great way to change formatting for multiple occurrences of entire paragraphs at once. Find and Change are discussed in detail in Chapter 5.

Figure 2-8:
PageMaker now lets you find
and change paragraph
attributes.

```
Find Paragraph Attributes
Find:
  Para style:        [Any]              ( OK )
  Alignment:         [Any]            ( Cancel )
  Leading method: [Any]
```

```
Change Paragraph Attributes
Find:
  Para style:        [Any]              ( OK )
  Alignment:         [Any]            ( Cancel )
  Leading method: [Any]
Change:
  Para style:        [Any]
  Alignment:         [Any]
  Leading method: [Any]
```

Guides and Rulers

Several changes have been made to the Guides and Rulers submenu on the Layout
menu, shown in Figure 2-9. Let's take them from top to bottom.

Figure 2-9:
The new look of the Guides and
Rulers submenu.

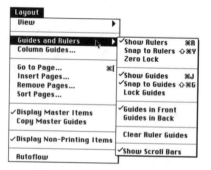

First, notice that now instead of simply reading "Rulers," "Guides," and "Scroll Bars," the
submenu now displays "Show Rulers," "Show Guides," etc. This change just makes the
commands a little more specific.

Guides in Front/Guides in Back

These two commands simply control where PageMaker displays its column, margin,
and ruler guides. It saves you from having to go into Preferences to make a more
permanent change. Instead, you can use this command to toggle easily between the two
options. Guides in Front displays the guides over the page elements, making it easier to
use them to align and place objects. Guides in Back places the guides behind page
elements, giving you a better view of the layout. The difference between the two options
is shown in Figure 2-10.

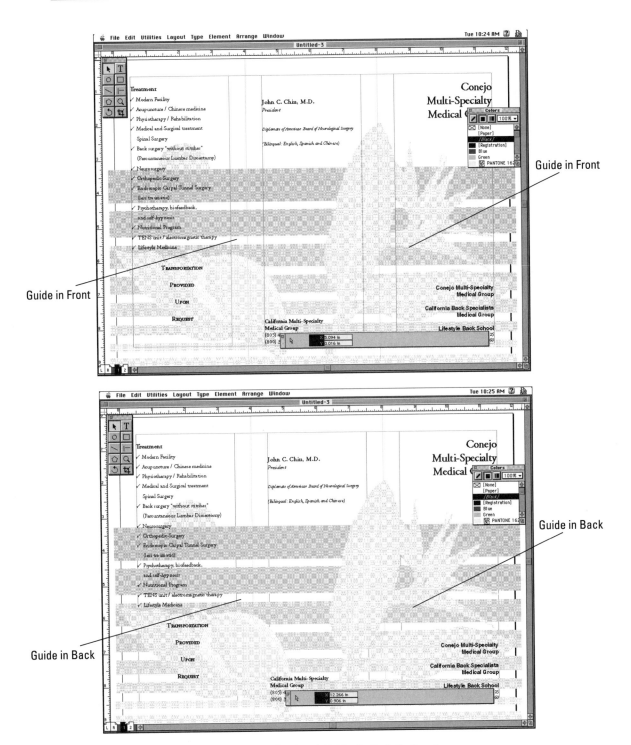

Figure 2-10: Examples of Guides in Front (top) and Guides in Back (bottom)

Clear Ruler Guides

If you've ever used numerous ruler guides to layout an intricate page, you'll appreciate this one. When you select Clear Ruler Guides, PageMaker removes all the guides you previously dragged onto the page, in effect, letting you start fresh, without any ruler guides.

Image

PageMaker 5 users previously disgruntled with PageMaker's rather ineffectual Image Control option should shout with glee over this new feature. In addition to the original Image Control command, now found on the Image submenu on the Element menu, you can now also apply CMS profiles, save an image for separations, and apply Photoshop special effects plug-ins. Let's look at these new features separately.

CMS Source

Part of PageMaker 6's color management system, CMS Source allows you to select the color management system applied to a specific image. Some images, especially if they originated on another computer, could use EFIColor Works, others Kodak Precision color, and so on, to define colors. If you have the specific color management system used in the image installed, you can use this command to tell PageMaker to use that CMS to define the image's color. Color Management and using color in general are discussed in detail in Chapter 10.

Photoshop Effects

This option allows you to apply Photoshop plug-in special effects, such as Kai's Power Tools or Adobe Gallery Effects, directly to RGB and CMYK TIFF images. No longer must you leave PageMaker, open Photoshop, apply the filter, and then return to PageMaker to update the image. Working with images is discussed in detail in Chapter 8.

Mask/Unmask

Here's a powerful feature you won't find in another leading page layout program. Basically, what Mask does is place one object inside a PageMaker rectangle, ellipse, or polygon, trimming (or cropping) away the portions of the masked object that do not fit into the masking object, as shown in Figure 2-11. There's a lot of power here, especially when you use one of PageMaker 6's new multiple-point polygons, which we look at a little later in this chapter. Unmask, of course, removes the mask. For more on drawing shapes and masking, refer to Chapter 8.

Figure 2-11: Example of masking objects inside PageMaker shapes

Master Pages

A long-standing complaint about PageMaker has been its lack of multiple master pages. Master pages are, of course, the underlying formatting instructions for creating multiple pages with the same or similar attributes, such as margins, columns, running headers and footers, and so on. Previous versions on PageMaker supported only two master pages per document, left and right.

Now, instead of having to create a new document when you need page formatting changes, you can create as many master pages as the document calls for. You can also create new master pages based on existing master pages, saving time from having to start from scratch.

This powerful new feature is controlled from the new Master Pages palette, shown in Figure 2-12. You can also apply master pages to the current page or spread by clicking and holding on the master pages icons at the bottom-left corner of the publication window, as shown in Figure 2-13.

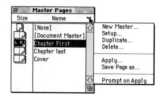

Figure 2-12:
The new Master Pages palette

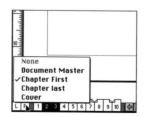

Figure 2-13:
You can assign a master page to the current page(s) by clicking and holding on the master page icons.

If you, like us, are a seasoned PageMaker user impatiently awaiting this feature, it's finally here. And there's enough power here to get you through most tasks requiring multiple page formatting. Master pages are discussed in detail in Chapter 4.

Non-Printing/Display Non-Printing Items

Sometimes it's helpful to include non-printing objects, such as a comment, an instruction, or a low-resolution replica of an image that will be stripped in later. Non-Printing objects appear on-screen but do not print. To make an object non-printing, select it and then choose Non-Printing from the Element menu. Display Non-Printing Items on the Layout menu toggles display of the non-printing items on and off.

Plug-ins

In version 4.2, Aldus opened the PageMaker architecture to include small applets, called Additions, which enhance the power of the program. In addition to Aldus, several third-party vendors created Additions for performing various functions. For example, Extensis' Page Tools created an Addition for creating drop caps or EPS graphics from several page layout objects.

Version 6 still supports Additions, but, in keeping with Adobe terminology, they are now called *plug-ins*. Several of the favorites from version 5 have been included in the PageMaker 6 package, as well as a few others. This section lists and describes the new plug-ins included with this upgrade.

HTML Author

World Wide Web. *World Wide Web.* Everybody's clamoring about the Internet's World Wide Web (WWW) — including publishers and designers. WWW provides a lot of opportunity for designers who know how to create Web pages, or home pages, for the Internet. The HTML Author plug-in translates PageMaker documents into Web pages.

The World Wide Web displays information on the Internet in groups or sections called *pages.* The language used to create the pages is hypertext markup language (HTML). HTML uses codes that are similar in concept to PageMaker's style sheets, which control the appearance and behavior of page elements.

The process of going from a PageMaker document to a Web page is not without its glitches. When you know you're publishing for the Internet, you should take special precautions with the PageMaker document, as described in Chapter 15.

Preferences

In addtion to a slightly new look, the Preferences dialog box, shown in Figure 2-14, has a few new options. One of the more significant, CMS Setup, we already discussed earlier in this chapter under "Color Management System Setup (CMS Setup)." Another significant change is that the Other button is now More.

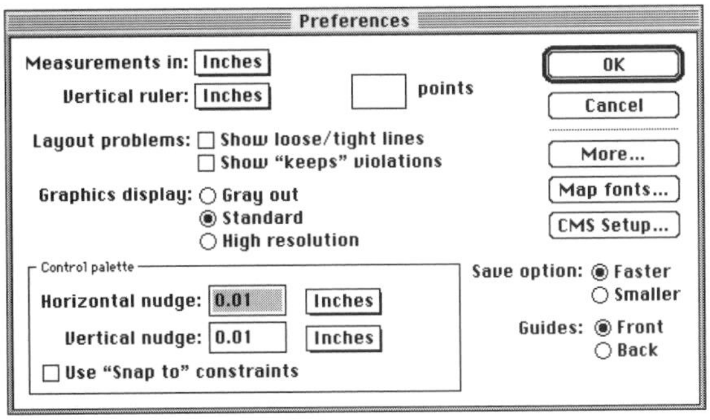

Figure 2-14:
The new look of the Preferences dialog box

This section looks at the changes in the More Preferences dialog box, shown in Figure 2-15.

Figure 2-15:
The new More Preferences
dialog box

Figure 2-15:
The new More Preferences
dialog box

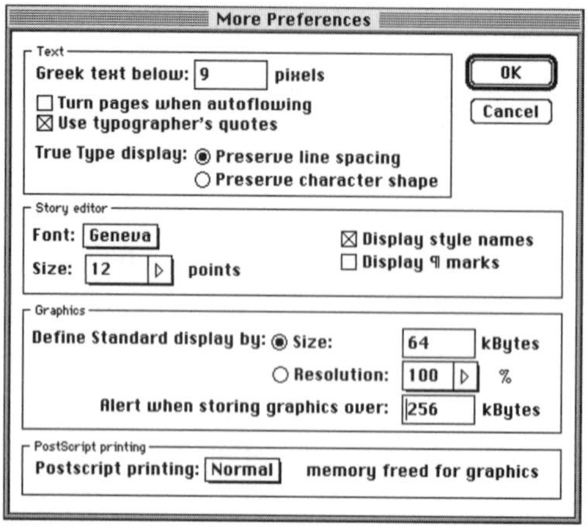

Turn Pages when Autoflowing

Though it does essentially the same thing, this option replaces Autoflow: Display all pages. This option is designed as a pure time-saver. Selecting it lets PageMaker autoflow text without displaying its progress page by page, avoiding all that screen redraw.

Print

Several changes have been made to the Print Document dialog box, shown in Figure 2-16, and the nested sub-dialog boxes, such as Paper, Options, Color, and so on. Let's look first at the changes to Print Document, and then the nested dialog boxes, including the new Print Features dialog box.

Figure 2-16:
The new look of the
Print Document
dialog box

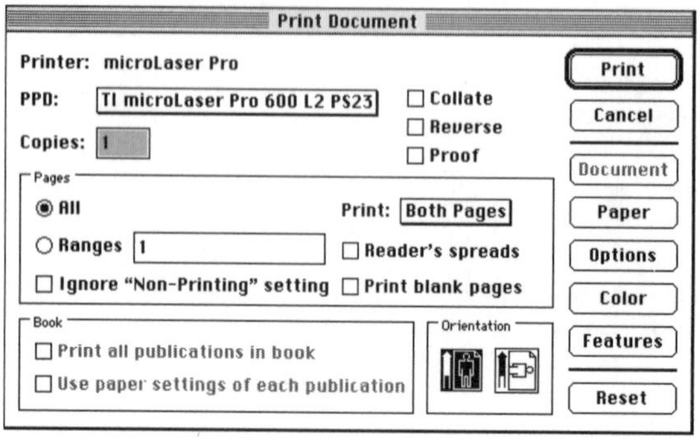

Ignore "Non-Printing" Setting

This option corresponds with PageMaker 6's new Non-Printing command, discussed under "Non-Printing/Display Non-Printing Items," earlier in this chapter. It allows you to override the non-printing settings made during layout. In other words, it tells PageMaker to print non-printing items.

Reader's Spreads

A drawback in previous versions was that PageMaker offered no way to print spreads, or facing pages. Reader's spreads prints your facing pages side-by-side on the same sheet, allowing you to see what spreads will look like. This is more a proofing option than a final output option. Reader's spreads resizes facing pages to fit on one sheet of paper.

Features

This button opens the Print Features dialog box. Depending on your printer, you get a dialog box similar to Figure 2-17. With this you can set printer options supported by the target printer. What options appear in Print Features depends on your printer and the information written into the PPD.

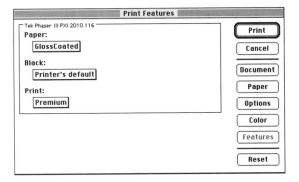

Figure 2-17:
The new Print Features dialog box allows you to select printer options.

Paper

A number of significant changes have occurred in the Paper options dialog box, shown in Figure 2-18. Notice first that Printer's marks and Page information have been moved from the Options dialog box to the Paper dialog box.

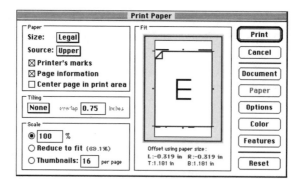

Figure 2-18:
The new look of the
Print Paper dialog
box. Notice the
preview!

Notice also that there is now a page preview, or "page fit icon," in the middle of the dialog box. This page fit icon shows the various options you choose as you set up your document for printing. If you turn on Printer's marks, for example, they are displayed in the preview, as are Page information, Negative, Mirror, and several of the other options in the various Print dialog boxes. Looking at this preview before printing can alert you to the presence of features being turned on or off.

In addtion to the page fit icon, offset information pertaining to the document displays directly below the preview. And you can get further information, such as page size and printable area, by double-clicking the page fit icon.

Options

The Options dialog box, shown in Figure 2-19, has a few changes also. As noted in the previous section, Printer's marks and Page information have been moved to the Paper options dialog box. In addition, the Graphics and Send data option have been combined and put on pop-up menus in new the TIFFs/Images area. They've also been given new names. Graphics is now Send image data. Send data is now Data encoding.

Figure 2-19:
The new look of the
Print Options
dialog box

Another change is the implementation of two-way printer communication, which allows your Mac to query the printer for memory and font information. Checking "Query printer for font and memory information" tells PageMaker to check the printer for resident and downloaded fonts, as well as available memory. PageMaker only downloads the fonts in the document not already in the printer, saving memory and time. A drawback to this option is that you must turn off your Mac's background printing to use it.

Color

There are only two changes to the Color dialog box, shown in Figure 2-20. The first is the addition of a CMS Setup… button that takes you to the CMS Setup dialog box discussed earlier in this chapter, under "Color Management System Setup (CMS Setup)." This dialog box lets you make CMS changes before printing.

Figure 2-20:
The new look of the
Print Color dialog box

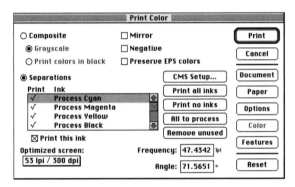

The other change is a Remove unused button for removing unused ink colors in the Separations list. The Separations list can be confusing; getting rid of the inks you don't need can help alleviate the confusion.

Printer Styles

If you're like us, you could use as many as three or four printers on a typical publication. On a color document, for example, you print first to a laser, a color proof printer, and then to an imagesetter for separations. Each printer requires different settings in the Print Document dialog box and nested sub-dialog boxes. The problem with this is that it's easy to forget to turn all the right features on and off.

This problem is finally addressed with Printer Styles. Located on the File menu, Printer Styles opens the Define Printer Styles dialog box, shown in Figure 2-21. With this, you can create and edit numerous printer styles. Your styles can include every setting available in Print Document, Paper, Options, Color, and Print Features. This new feature will save you time and money in botched print jobs.

Figure 2-21:
The new Define Printer Styles lets you set up and save printer configurations for different types of print jobs.

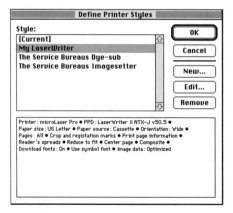

Recent Publications

Since it has been a standard Mac convention for awhile, this command should have been in the previous version of PageMaker. Recent Publications is a simple but time-saving convenience. PageMaker lists the last four documents you worked on on the Recent Publications submenu on the File menu, assuming that you'll probably want to work on one of them again. To open a recent publication on the list, all you do is select it, rather than scurry around your hard disk looking through folders.

Scripts Palette

In addition to plug-ins, PageMaker 6 also lets you create and run scripts (macros). Scripts are mini-programs you record in PageMaker to perform repetitive tasks. The program comes with several prerecorded scripts, which you can run or modify to suit your needs, or you can record your own. The scripts included with PageMaker and the Scripts Palette and utilities are discussed in the Script Language Guide, which you'll find in the Scripting folder inside the Technical Library folder on the deluxe CD-ROM that's included in the boxed set of Adobe PageMaker 6 software and manuals.

Sort Pages

Sort Pages isn't new. It used to be an Aldus Addition. It's now a command on the Layout menu. Choosing it opens the Sort Pages dialog box, which allows you to view thumbnails of the pages in your document. You can then move them around to change page order. Sort Pages is discussed in Chapter 4.

Tools

Hey, you seasoned PageMaker users! Take a look at the Toolbox. What do you see? Two new, very interesting looking tools. The Polygon tool and the Zoom tool. Both are sights for sore eyes.

In addition to the two new tools, you can now double-click most of the tools in the toolbox to bring up various dialog boxes. Double-clicking the line- and shape-drawing tools, for example, opens the Custom Line dialog box and the Line and Fill dialog box, respectively. Double-clicking the Arrow tool opens Preferences, and so on.

Polygon Tool

The Polygon tool allows you to draw multisided shapes, primarily stars. (You can also make octagons, etc., by having the Star inset set to 0%.) You can then control the points and inset shape of the polygon with Polygon Settings on the Element menu. You can, as shown in Figure 2-22, create some pretty interesting shapes, but you cannot, unfortunately, change the shape of the polygon in freehand mode. You're stuck with the starlike effects. Double-clicking the Polygon tool also opens the Polygon Specifications dialog box. The Polygon tool and the other PageMaker shape tools are discussed in Chapter 8.

Zoom Tool

Hallelujah! PageMaker has a Zoom tool. Just take that little magnifying glass, click where you want to zoom or marquee select an area. . . Option-click to zoom out. Just like Photoshop and Illustrator. You gotta love this new feature. It's discussed further in Chapter 4.

Trapping Options

Here's the ultimate cure for QuarkXPress-envy. PageMaker 6 supports prepress color trapping. When you select Trapping Options from the Utilities menu, you get the Trapping Options dialog box shown in Figure 2-23. With this you can control what objects and colors PageMaker traps and to what degree. Trapping and printing color are discussed thoroughly in Chapter 10.

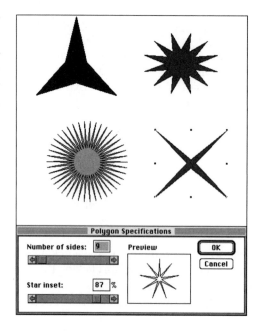

Figure 2-22:
An example of the capabilities of the new polygon feature and the new Polygon Specifications dialog box

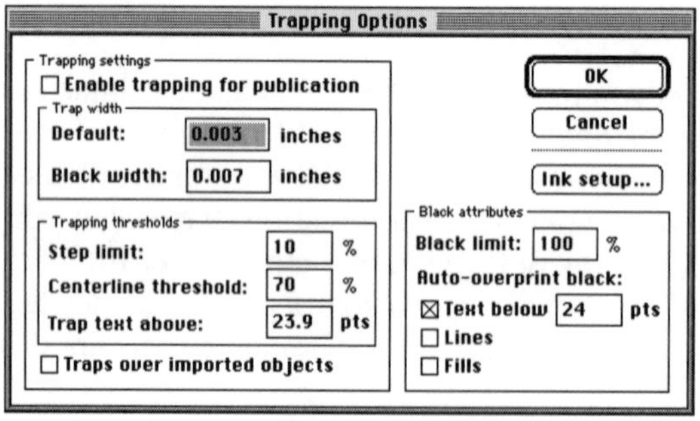

Figure 2-23:
The new Trapping Options dialog box lets you set up prepress trapping.

Summary

➡ PageMaker 6 offers several features long-awaited by devoted users, including trapping, multiple master pages, locking and grouping objects, and several others. This upgrade also includes a couple of features for publishing electronic PDF and World Wide Web documents.

Touring PageMaker's Terms, Tools, and Menus

■ ■

In This Chapter

- ➡ Basic PageMaker terminology

- ➡ A summary of every PageMaker menu command

- ➡ An overview of each tool in the PageMaker tool palette

■ ■

Since its introduction over ten years ago, one of PageMaker's great strengths has been its user interface. PageMaker uses similar menus, tools, and dialog boxes that you find in other Mac applications. This book assumes that you are already familiar with your Mac and how to use it. This chapter introduces the basic aspects of working with PageMaker and then provides a summary of each command in the PageMaker menus and each tool in the PageMaker toolbox.

After reading this chapter, you will have a good understanding of PageMaker's range and capabilities. More-experienced users may find this information sufficient to allow them to begin their own experiments. Less-experienced users may find these summaries a bit overwhelming. In either case, remember that this is only a brief tour; the remainder of the book provides the details required to master the range of possibilities suggested in this chapter. As you lay out future publications, refer to this chapter to refresh your memory on commands and tools.

Before you get started, you should understand how PageMaker handles text that goes into a publication. All the text from a single word-processor file is called a *story*. Stories are created by typing text into a text block or by using the New Story… command in the story editor. They can also be created in a word processor, such as Microsoft Word or WordPerfect, and imported into PageMaker. A story can fit into a single text block or span any number of threaded text blocks. You can determine the text blocks that a story flows through by placing the text insertion point anywhere in the story and choosing the Select all command (⌘-A) from the Edit menu — all text in the story will be selected, including all the text in all the threaded text blocks (see Figure 3-1). You can see all the text from a story by placing the text insertion point anywhere in the story and choosing the Edit Story… command from the Edit menu.

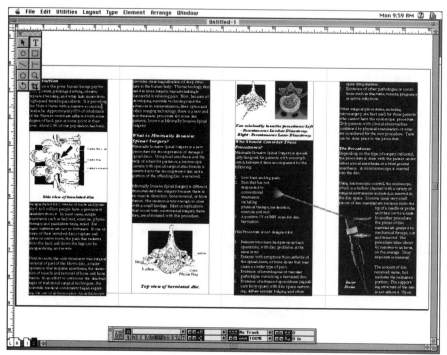

Figure 3-1: All text from a single story can be selected even though it flows through multiple text blocks.

Menus, Commands, and Palettes

As in most Macintosh programs, PageMaker's menu commands provide the bulk of its power. This section introduces each of PageMaker's nine menus (ten menus if you also count the Help menu) and every command in each of those menus. This will familiarize you with the range of PageMaker's capabilities so that you will know what to expect as we start moving through the program in detail in later chapters. This section can also serve as a summary reference when you need to brush up on any command.

For every PageMaker command introduced in this section, available keyboard equivalents, or shortcuts, are listed in parentheses following the command name. Note, however, that not all commands have keyboard shortcuts.

The Apple Menu

As in all Macintosh applications, the Apple menu, shown in Figure 3-2, contains desk accessories and, in System 7.x, other items from your Apple Menu Items folder. Also, when PageMaker is running, the Apple menu includes the About PageMaker... command.

Figure 3-2:
The Apple menu as it appears customized in System 7.5

∞ **About PageMaker...** This command opens the PageMaker copyright screen, the first dialog box seen when you launch. This time, however, the dialog box includes information about the current version of the System file and available RAM. The copyright screen disappears when you click the mouse button.

Holding down the Command key while choosing the About PageMaker command produces a listing of all installed Additions, import filters, export filters, and some internal PageMaker version numbers. This dialog box, shown in Figure 3-3, is useful to verify that PageMaker recognizes all of your Plug-ins and filters correctly. Holding down the Shift key while choosing the About PageMaker command opens an "Easter egg." (Easter egg is a technical term that refers to small hidden treasures programmers leave inside software programs to amuse themselves or get across some secret message. A surprisingly large number of programs have Easter eggs, including Word, Photoshop, the Finder, and many others.)

Figure 3-3:
The About PageMaker
dialog box displays
installed Plug-ins
and filters.

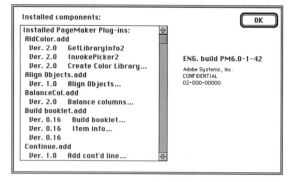

File Menu

As in most Macintosh applications, the PageMaker File menu, shown in Figure 3-4, controls broad document-level activities, including opening, closing, printing, and saving documents. Additionally, the File menu controls the importation of text and graphical images and the exportation of text files.

∞ **New...** (⌘-N). Creates and opens a new publication or template. Choosing the New... command opens the Document Setup dialog box, where you define the attributes of the new publication, such as page size, margins, and whether a document contains two-sided facing pages.

∞ **Open...** (⌘-O). Selects and opens any existing PageMaker publication or template. Choosing the Open... command opens the Open publication dialog box, in which you locate and select a particular file to open.

Figure 3-4:
The File menu

File	
New...	⌘N
Open...	⌘O
Recent Publications	▶
Close	⌘W
Save	⌘S
Save As...	
Export...	
Create Adobe PDF...	
Revert	
Place...	⌘D
Acquire	▶
Links...	⌘=
Document Setup...	
Print...	⌘P
Printer Styles	▶
Preferences...	
Quit	⌘Q

Recent Publications. Displays a pop-up submenu listing the last four publications you've opened and saved in PageMaker. This command saves you time from having to find recent publications on your hard disk.

∞ **Close (⌘-W).** Closes the current publication or template but does not quit PageMaker. If unsaved changes have been made to the file being closed, the Save changes before closing? dialog box appears, prompting you to save changes, discard changes, or abort closing the file. Choosing the Close command for an untitled file opens the Save as dialog box, which prompts you to name and save the file. The Close command is dimmed when no publication or template document is open.

∞ **Save (⌘-S).** Saves the current publication or template document to include all changes made since the last save. Choosing the Save command for an untitled document first displays the Save 'Untitled' before closing dialog box and then opens the Save as dialog box, which prompts you to specify a filename and location for the file. The Save command is dimmed if no changes have been made since the last save.

∞ **Save As...** Opens the Save publication as dialog box, which prompts you to name and save the document, select the location to which the document is saved, and choose whether the document is saved as a publication or as a template. Saving documents via the Save As... command reduces the size of the file, sometimes speeding up PageMaker's navigation and screen redraws for the current document. If you attempt to save a document using the name of an existing file, an alert dialog box appears, asking you to confirm replacement of the existing file.

- **Export...** Saves text from the currently selected story as a separate file. You can then edit in a word processor. Choosing the Export... command opens the Export dialog box, which prompts you to specify the location and attributes of the file to be exported. You can save exported files in text-only format or in the formats of several popular word processors. The Export... command is dimmed if no text is selected.

 Create Adobe PDF... Turns a PageMaker document into Adobe's Portable Document Format (PDF) for use with Adobe Acrobat Distiller and Adobe Acrobat Reader, Adobe's portable file format. Selecting this command opens the Create Adobe PDF dialog box, which provides several options converting and exporting the document file.

- **Revert.** Discards all changes made to the current publication or template and restores the document to the same state as the last saved version. Choosing the Revert command opens an alert dialog box that prompts you to confirm or abort the reversion. Pressing the Shift key while choosing the Revert command discards only those changes made since the last mini-save (which occurs automatically when you perform certain functions in PageMaker, such as go to new pages or print) rather than the last Save or Save as... command. You cannot use Undo to undo the Revert command. The Revert menu is dimmed when you cannot revert to any previous version.

- **Place...** (⌘-D). Copies a text or graphic file from disk into memory so that you can add it to the publication. Choosing the Place... command opens the Place document dialog box, in which you select a file to place and specify placement attributes. PageMaker supports text documents, word-processor documents, paint-type image files, draw-type image files, encapsulated PostScript (EPS) files, and tagged image file format (TIFF) files.

 Acquire submenu. Contains commands for acquiring images via a TWAIN-compliant scanner.

- **Acquire⇨Select Source.** Allows you to select the TWAIN (Technology Without An Interesting Name) interface for your scanner. If you use an HP ScanJet, for example, you would select Select Source and then select DeskScan II as the TWAIN source. Also, some graphics editing applications contain TWAIN interfaces.

- **Acquire⇨Acquire Image.** Opens the TWAIN scanner interface for your scanner so that you can scan an image into the current PageMaker document. The image comes into the document as a TIFF file.

- **Links...** (⌘-=). Opens the Links dialog box. Use it to manage the links between a PageMaker publication and the external text and graphic files it contains. The Links dialog box displays a list of the text and graphic files placed in the current publication. For each file in this list, PageMaker determines if the external file or the version of the file that currently appears in the publication has been modified, and provides you with the option of replacing the copy of the file that is currently in the publication with the version in the external file.

- ∞ **Document Setup...** Opens the Document setup dialog box, which contains various options regarding the electronic page on which a publication is created. This is the same dialog box accessed by the New... command. If no document is currently open, a change in the settings of the Document setup options will change the default values used for any new documents created later.

- ∞ **Print...** (⌘-P). Initiates the printing of one or more pages of the current document. Choosing the Print... command opens the Print Document dialog box, which allows you to specify a wide range of printing attributes and options.

 Printer Styles submenu. Contains the Define command for creating printer styles, and, when printer styles are defined, a list of the styles.

- ∞ **Printer Styles⇨Define.** Opens the Define Printer Styles dialog box. From here you set up printer styles, or presets, that allow you to configure a printer automatically for various print jobs. After you define printer styles, they also appear on the Printer Styles submenu.

- ∞ **Preferences...** Opens the Preferences dialog box. The options in this dialog box control the units of measurement used in rulers and in other dialog boxes; the position of ruler and column guides in the stacking order; and the point size at which text is greeked during display; and other defaults, such as Color Management System setup and font mapping. If no document is currently open, a change in the settings of the Preferences options will change the default values used for any new documents created later.

- ∞ **Quit** (⌘-Q). Exits PageMaker, closing all open publication windows and returning control to the Macintosh Finder. If an open document contains unsaved changes when you choose the Quit command, the "Save 'filename' before closing?" message appears, prompting you to save or discard the changes. If the file is untitled and you do wish to save it, the Save publication as dialog box appears, prompting you to name and save the document.

Edit Menu

Most of the commands in the Edit menu, shown in Figure 3-5, are standard Edit menu commands in all Macintosh applications. They control the manipulation of selected elements and the Macintosh Clipboard. Additionally, the Edit menu is the home of PageMaker's Edit story and Edit original commands.

Figure 3-5:
The Edit menu

☞ **Undo** (⌘-Z). Reverses the effect of the last action, returning the document to its exact state prior to the last action. Not all actions can be undone: If the last action cannot be reversed, the Undo command will read Cannot undo and will be dimmed; if the action can be reversed, the Undo command will name the action eligible for reversal. Immediately after one action has been undone but before another action is done, the Undo command becomes a Redo command, allowing you to undo the undo or, equivalently, to redo the original action.

☞ **Cut** (⌘-X, or keypad period). Deletes the selected text, objects, or text and graphical objects from your document and places them on the Macintosh Clipboard. The effect is identical to the Cut command in other Macintosh software. If no text or element is selected, the Cut command is dimmed.

☞ **Copy** (⌘-C). Makes a copy of the selected text, objects, or text and graphic objects from your document, placing them on the Clipboard. The effect of this command is identical to the Copy command in other Macintosh software. If no text or element is selected, the Copy command is dimmed.

☞ **Paste** (⌘-V, or keypad 0). Places a copy of the Clipboard contents into your document. These elements become selected after being pasted into the document so that you can adjust their position. A copy of the pasted text or graphic object   remains on the Clipboard so that you can paste it again. If the Clipboard is empty, the Paste command is dimmed.

☞ **Clear** (Delete or Backspace key, or Shift- on keypad). Deletes the selected text, elements, or text and elements from your document without placing them on the Clipboard. If no text or element is selected, the Clear command is dimmed.

☞ **Multiple Paste...** Opens the Multiple paste dialog box, where you specify how many copies of the current Clipboard objects you want to paste and the horizontal and vertical distance from the first copy where you want subsequent copies positioned.

☞ **Select All** (⌘-A). Selects all objects in the current publication window *or* all text in the current story. When you position the text cursor within a story, the entire story is selected. If the text tool is not positioned within a story — that is, any tool other than the text tool is selected or the text tool is positioned on an empty portion of the page — all text and graphic objects on the page(s) being displayed are selected, along with all text and graphic objects on the pasteboard.

- **Editions⇨Subscribe to.** Opens the Subscribe to dialog box, where you select an edition file to import into your publication. You can also import edition files using the Place command, so this command is never necessary.

- **Editions⇨Subscriber options.** Opens the Subscriber options dialog box. This dialog box provides options that control the updates for linked edition files. The most important is the ability to have edition files updated automatically or manually. Another option launches the application that created the edition, and opens the edition file. Edition files can also be managed via the Links dialog box, so this command is never necessary.

- **Editions⇨Stop all editions.** Selecting this command stops all automatic edition updates set via the Subscriber options dialog box. You can override this option with the Update or Update all commands in the Links dialog box, which opens when you choose the Links command on the File menu.

- **Paste Special...** An alternative to the Paste... command, it opens the Paste Special dialog box. This dialog box lists the file formats in which the current Clipboard contents are available. You select the format you want and click the Paste or Paste link buttons and click OK to import the elements.

- **Insert Object...** Opens a list of OLE server applications in which you can create a new text or graphic object and then import that object back into PageMaker. After selecting an application or object type, the application launches, and a new file is opened. When you choose the Update command from that application, the data you have created will be pasted as a linked OLE object into PageMaker.

- **Edit Story (⌘-E).** Opens a new window containing the complete text of the currently selected story, or if no story is currently selected, a blank window in which a new story can be created. When a story window is open, PageMaker is in its story editor, and a slightly modified menu bar appears.

- **Edit Original.** Available only when a selected object is linked to its original application via a hot link, the System 7 Edition Manager, or OLE. When chosen, this command launches the application that created any linked imported elements. These elements may have been imported via the Place, Subscribe to, or Insert commands. For most objects, the creating application is opened, and the selected elements are opened for editing. For objects created by OLE servers, a submenu may present additional options.

  The Edit original command can be invoked by holding down the Option key and double-clicking any linked element. However, you need to select the element first. Holding down the Shift key while selecting the Edit Original command opens the Choose editor dialog box, which allows you to select the specific application you want to open. However, you need to select the element first.

Utilities Menu

As its name suggests, the Utilities menu, shown in Figure 3-6, provides a collection of commands that add features to PageMaker. These include all Plug-ins, the Find/Change/Spelling commands that work only in the PageMaker story editor, and commands to build and create indexes and tables of contents for your publications.

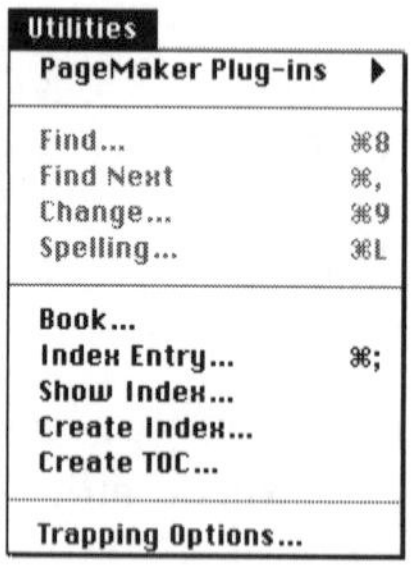

Figure 3-6:
The Utilities menu

Utilities	
PageMaker Plug-ins	▶
Find...	⌘8
Find Next	⌘,
Change...	⌘9
Spelling...	⌘L
Book...	
Index Entry...	⌘;
Show Index...	
Create Index...	
Create TOC...	
Trapping Options...	

↪ **PageMaker Plug-ins.** This submenu provides access to all currently installed PageMaker Plug-ins. Plug-in commands add a wide range of capabilities to PageMaker, creating drop caps, converting PageMaker documents to World Wide Web pages, and many others.

↪ **Find...** (⌘-F). Opens the Find... dialog box, which you use to initiate a search for a specific text string or type specification. You can limit the search to the currently selected text or current story, or search the entire publication. The Find... command is available only when working in the story editor.

↪ **Find Next** (⌘-G). Repeats the most recent search executed using the Find command. The Find next... command is available only when working in the story editor.

↪ **Change...** (⌘-H). Opens the Change dialog box, which you use you use to search and replace text strings or type specifications. You can limit the search to the currently selected text or current story, or you can apply it to the current publication. The Change... command is available only when working in the story editor.

↪ **Spelling...** (⌘-L). Opens the Spelling dialog box, which you use to check the spelling of the current story in the story editor. Unknown words are flagged in the dialog box, at which time you can correct, ignore, or add them to your own dictionaries. The Spelling... command is available only when working in the story editor.

☞ **Book...** Opens the Book publication list dialog box, which you use to assemble a number of separate PageMaker files so that you can then use the Create TOC ... and Create Index commands to create a table of contents or index for an entire publication. This also allows you to print all the files that are part of a book from the Print dialog box of the current file.

☞ **Index Entry...** (⌘-;). Opens the Index Entry dialog box, which you use to add an entry to an index that you then generate with PageMaker's Create index... command. Before choosing this command, you should select the word or phrase you want to index or position the cursor in the paragraph containing that word or phrase. The Index Entry dialog box allows you to specify the index item itself, the page range for the index reference, and topic cross-references.

☞ **Show Index...** Opens the Show Index dialog box, which presents a listing of all current index entries. With this dialog box, you edit individual index entries. When you select this command, PageMaker must compile the index list, which may take a few minutes.

☞ **Create Index...** Opens the Create Index dialog box, which presents options for the creation of an index based on entries made using the Index Entry... command. The options allow you to replace the current index (if one exists), index all publications in the book list (if any exist), title the index, include section headings, and specify formats used in the index.

☞ **Create TOC...** Opens the Create Table of Contents... dialog box, which presents options for creating a table of contents for paragraphs in which the "Include in table of contents" option has been selected. (This option is found in the Paragraph Specifications dialog box, which you access from the Paragraph command on the Type menu.) The options allow you to replace the current table of contents (if one exists), include all publications in the book list in the table of contents, title the table of contents, include headings and subheads, and specify formats used in the table of contents. When you click OK, the PageMaker creates a table of contents.

☞ **Trapping Options...** Opens the Trapping Options dialog box. With this you control PageMaker's built-in prepress color trapping. Trapping helps compensate for inaccurate printing press alignment (sometimes called "slop"). Basically, trapping prevents gaps or discoloration as the result of abutting colors.

Layout Menu

The Layout menu, shown in Figure 3-7, provides commands that control your publication window. This includes control over view size, rulers and guides, and column guides, as well as page turning, addition and removal of pages, and displaying or removing items from master pages.

Figure 3-7:
The Layout menu

⊶ **View submenu.** Presents all available view-size commands, which you use to change the magnification size of your publication on screen.

⊶ **View⇨Fit in Window (⌘-O).** Changes the display in the publication window so that it displays all of the current page(s) selected. The actual reduction depends on the size and resolution of the monitor being used. Choosing the Fit in Window command when it is already selected refreshes the video display. Holding down the Shift key while selecting this command changes the display to include all of the selected page(s) plus the entire pasteboard. A check mark (√) before the command indicates that it is selected. You can also select Fit in Window view by holding down the Command and Option keys while clicking the mouse button anywhere in the publication window, provided that the display is at Actual Size. From any view larger than Actual Size, it returns to Actual Size and then, when you ⌘-Option Click again, the display returns to Fit in Window.

⊶ **View⇨Entire Pasteboard.** Reduces the document display so that all of the Pasteboard, the area around the document pages, is also displayed. This is a great way to find objects you've placed on the Pasteboard for later use.

⊶ **View⇨25% Size (⌘-0).** Changes the display in the publication window to 25 percent of its actual size. PageMaker centers the display based on the items centered in the previous view size. Choosing the command when it is already selected refreshes the video display. A check mark (√) before the command indicates that it is selected.

- **View⇨50% Size** (⌘-5). Changes the display in the publication window to 50 percent of its actual size. PageMaker centers the display based on the items centered in the previous view size. Choosing the 50% Size command when it is already selected refreshes the video display. A check mark (√) before the command indicates that it is selected.

- **View⇨75% Size** (⌘-7). Changes the display in the publication window to 75 percent of its actual size. PageMaker centers the display based on the items centered in the previous view size. Choosing the 75% Size command when it is already selected refreshes the video display. A check mark (√) before the command indicates that it is selected.

- **View⇨Actual Size** (⌘-1). Changes the display in the publication window to a full-size representation of the current page(s). PageMaker centers the display based on the items centered in the previous view size. Choosing the Actual Size command when it is already selected refreshes the video display. A check mark (√) before the command indicates that it is selected. You can also select Actual Size view by holding down the Command and Option keys while clicking the mouse button anywhere in the publication window, provided that the display is at any view size other than Actual. ⌘-Option toggles between Actual Size and Fit in Window.

- **View⇨200% Size** (⌘-2). Changes the display in the publication window to 200 percent of its actual size. PageMaker centers the display based on the items centered in the previous view size. Choosing the 200% Size command when it is already selected refreshes the video display. A check mark (√) before the command indicates that it is selected. You can also choose 200% view by holding down the Shift, Command, and Option keys while clicking the mouse button anywhere in the publication window, provided that the display is at any view size other than 200%. ⌘-Shift-Option toggles between Actual Size and 200% size.

- **View⇨300% Size** (⌘-3). Changes the display in the publication window to 300 percent of its actual size. PageMaker centers the display based on the items centered in the previous view size. Choosing the 300% Size command when it is already selected refreshes the video display. A check mark (√) before the command indicates that it is selected.

- **Guides and Rulers submenu.** Presents a collection of commands relating to on-screen guide lines and rulers.

- **Guides and Rulers⇨Show Rulers** (⌘-R). Toggles on and off the display of rulers along the top and left edges of the publication window. A check mark (√) before the command indicates that it is currently selected (rulers are displayed); choosing it at this time will deselect it (rulers become hidden). Rulers use the current measurement system as set in the Preferences dialog box.

☞ **Guides and Rulers⇨Snap to Rulers** (⌘-Shift-Y). Causes objects you reposition to align with the vertical and horizontal tick marks in the rulers. A check mark (√) before the command indicates that it is currently selected (elements snap to tick marks); choosing it at this time will deselect it (elements will not snap to tick marks).

☞ **Guides and Rulers⇨Zero Lock.** Locks the zero intersection point of the rulers so that the intersecting lines in the upper-left corner of the publication window become unselectable and unmovable. A check mark (√) before the command indicates that it is currently selected (zero point is locked); choosing it at this time will deselect it (zero point becomes unlocked).

☞ **Guides and Rulers⇨Show Guides** (⌘-J). Displays all non-printing column, ruler, and margin guides in the publication window. A check mark (√) before the command indicates that it is currently selected (guides are displayed); choosing it at this time will deselect it (guides become hidden).

☞ **Guides and Rulers⇨Snap to Guides** (⌘-Shift-G). Gives all column, ruler, and margin guides a magnetic pull on the pointer, text blocks, and graphic elements when these elements are being positioned. A check mark (√) before the command indicates that it is currently selected (elements snap to guides); choosing it at this time will deselect it (elements will not snap to guides when moved).

☞ **Guides and Rulers⇨Lock Guides.** Locks all existing column and ruler guides and prohibits the creation of new guides. A check mark (√) before the command indicates that it is currently selected (guides are locked); choosing it at this time will deselect it (guides become unlocked). The Lock guides command is dimmed when the Show Guides command is not selected.

☞ **Guides and Rulers⇨Guides in Front.** Places ruler, column, and margin guides in front of page elements, making it easier to use the guides to place and align objects.

☞ **Guides and Rulers⇨Guides Behind.** Places ruler, column, and margin guides behind, or under, page elements, making it easier to see what the printed page will look like.

☞ **Guides and Rulers⇨Clear Ruler Guides.** Deletes all ruler guides (which are non-printing vertical and horizontal guides you can drag into your document from the rulers) placed in the document. This allows you to clear away screen clutter and let you start fresh with new ruler guides. However, you cannot undo this step!

☞ **Guides and Rulers⇨Show Scroll bars.** Toggles the display of the scroll bars on the right and lower edges of the publication window. You may wish to hide the scroll bars to provide additional space on screen for the display of your publication. A check mark (√) before the command indicates that it is currently selected (scroll bars are displayed); choosing it at this time will deselect it (scroll bars are hidden).

∞ **Column Guides...** Opens the Column Guides dialog box, in which you define or edit the number of columns and space between column guides for the current page(s). The Column Guides... command is dimmed when the Show Guides command is not selected.

∞ **Go to Page...** (⌘-[). Opens the Go to Page dialog box, in which you can enter any page number in the document or select the left or right master page. The display then changes to the selected page.

∞ **Insert Pages...** Opens the Insert Pages dialog box, in which you specify any number of pages to be added to the current document. You can place new pages before or after the current page or between the current pages (if working on facing pages).

∞ **Remove Pages...** Opens the Remove Pages dialog box, in which you specify the removal of any number of pages from the current document. Pages to be removed are specified by page number. Removing a page deletes the contents of the page, removes a page icon from the bottom of the screen, and renumbers all subsequent pages.

∞ **Sort Pages...** Opens the Sort Pages dialog box, which allows you to move pages around in a document by dragging on thumbnail pictures of them in the dialog box. Essentially, this is a quick way to change page order. You can learn more about Sort Pages in Chapter 4.

∞ **Display Master Items.** Toggles on and off the display and printing of text and graphics from the appropriate master page for the current page. For example, if a border appears on the right master page, selecting this command (indicated by a check mark [√], would display the border on the current page (if it is a right-hand page); if this command is deselected (unchecked), the border is not displayed. Master items will print only if they are displayed.

∞ **Copy Master Guides.** Sets the column and ruler guides on the current page(s) exactly as they appear on the corresponding master page, removing changes you may have made to guides on the current page. The Copy master guides command is dimmed if the current guides already match the master page(s) guides.

∞ **Display Non-Printing Items.** Allows you to toggle on and off non-printing items you've assigned non-printing status with the Non-Printing command on the Element menu. For example, if a box is non-printing, selecting this command (indicated by a check mark [√]) would display the box; if this command is deselected (unchecked), the box is not displayed.

⊷ **Autoflow.** Activates automatic or semiautomatic text-flow for placing text. The actual flow method used is determined through the use of the mouse and various key commands while the text is being poured into the document. A check mark (√) before the command indicates that it is currently selected (autoflow is activated); choosing it at this time will deselect it (autoflow becomes deactivated). If no document is currently open, a change in the Autoflow command will change the default setting used for any new documents created at a later date.

Type Menu

The Type menu, shown in Figure 3-8, controls typographics. To modify text or apply formatting, you must first select it with the text tool. Selecting any of these commands when any tool other than the text tool is selected will set defaults for the next time a new text block is created.

Figure 3-8:
The Type menu

⊷ **Font submenu.** Displays all available fonts. Selecting a font from this menu changes selected text or, if no text is selected, sets the font for the next text entry (provided the cursor is not moved before the text is entered). A check mark (√) before a font name indicates that the font is applied to the selected text or is the current default.

⊷ **Size submenu.** Displays a list of type sizes (in points). A check mark (√) before a size indicates that the size is used by the selected text or is the current default. To set type sizes not displayed, use the Other command on this menu.

⊷ **Leading submenu.** Displays leading sizes (in points). A check mark (√) before a leading name indicates that the leading is used by the selected text or is the current default. To set leading sizes not on this menu, use the Other command.

- **Set Width submenu.** Displays character-width options you can apply to selected text. Character-width manipulation is used to condense or expand text by a percentage of the default character width. The options include predefined widths ranging from 70% to 130% or the "Other…" option, which allows you to enter any percentage from 5% to 250.0% in .1% increments.

- **Type Style submenu.** Displays attributes that you can apply to text: Normal, Bold, Italic, Underline, Strikethru, Outline, Shadow, and Reverse (white letters). Effects are toggled on and off when selected, as indicated by a check mark ($\sqrt{}$) beside the command. Any number or combination of effects can be selected at the same time. Selecting the Normal effect turns off all other effects.

- **Expert Tracking submenu.** Displays tracking options for selected text. Tracking adjusts the space between characters by kerning adjacent letter pairs. Edit Tracks on this menu allows you to edit tracking settings for the other five options on the menu. The other six options allow you to manipulate the tracking of the selected text by degrees ranging from very loose to very tight. The Normal option applies the default kerning specified for the current font, and the No Track option removes this default kerning. Tracking values are toggled on and off when selected, as indicated by the presence or absence of a check mark ($\sqrt{}$).

- **Expert Kerning…** Opens the Expert Kerning dialog box, which allows you to set the kerning for character pairs in the given font based on the "kerning strength" you designate. (Kerning defines the relationship between certain character pairs, such as AV, To, and others. It is discussed in detail in Chapter 6).

- **Type Specs…** (⌘-T). Opens the Type Specifications dialog box, where you can alter the font, type size, leading, type style, case, and position of the currently selected text or, if no text is selected, for the next text entry. This dialog box also provides access to the Type Options dialog box, where you set the height of small caps and the size and location of superscript and subscript type.

- **Paragraph…** (⌘-M). Opens the Paragraph Specifications dialog box, where you specify the alignment, indents, and spacing of selected paragraph(s). This dialog box also allows you to add rules above or below the selected paragraph and control letter- and word-spacing.

- **Indents/Tabs…** (⌘-I). Opens the Indents/Tabs dialog box, where you specify the left and right margins, first-line indent, and tab settings for the current paragraph(s).

- **Hyphenation…**(⌘-H). Opens the Hyphenation dialog box, which you use to specify hyphenation attributes of the selected paragraph or style sheet. You can choose among three different hyphenation methods, limit consecutive hyphens, and set the width for PageMaker's hyphenation zone.

 ❧ **Alignment submenu.** Displays a pop-up menu of alignment options for the selected paragraph(s). If no text is selected, the alignment choice applies to the next text entry, provided that the text-insertion point is not moved before the text is entered. The alignment for the current paragraph has a check mark (√) next to it. If more than one paragraph is selected, and they have different alignments, no check mark will display.

 ❧ **Style submenu.** Displays all defined style sheets for the current document. Choosing a style sheet applies that style sheet's attributes to selected paragraph(s). The style sheet chosen for the current paragraph has a check mark (√) next to it. If more than one paragraph is selected, and they have different style sheets, no check mark will appear.

 ❧ **Define Styles...** (⌘-3). Opens the Define Styles dialog box, which allows you to create a new style sheet, edit or remove existing style sheets, or import style sheets from another publication or template. If no document is open, a change in the settings of the Define Styles options changes the default settings for new documents.

Element Menu

Many of the commands in the Element menu, shown in Figure 3-9, are used to modify graphic elements created in PageMaker. Others, such as Bring to front and Define colors..., apply to both text and graphic elements.

Figure 3-9:
The Element menu

 ❧ **Line submenu.** Opens a list of line weights and styles you can apply to any graphic element created with the line, circle, polygon, or rectangle tools. You can apply only one line weight or style to any graphic. When a single graphic is selected, the line weight or style specified for that element has a check mark (√) before it. If more than one graphic element is chosen, a check mark appears only if all selected elements use the same line or style.

- **Fill submenu.** Opens a list of shades and patterns you can use to fill any graphic created with the rectangle, polygon, or circle tools. You can apply only one shade or pattern to any graphic. When a single graphic is selected, the shade or pattern specified for that element has a check mark ($\sqrt{}$) before it. If more than one graphic element is chosen, a check mark appears only if all selected elements use the same shade or pattern.

- **Fill and Line... (⌘-]).** Opens the custom Fill and Line dialog box, in which you can specify any file value or line weight between 0 and 800 points, choose any available fill or line color, and set fill and line attributes such as Overprint, Transparent background, or Reverse line.

- **Polygon Settings...** Opens the Polygon Specifications dialog box, which lets you adjust the number of star points and the inset of star points on a polygon. This command corresponds with PageMaker 6's new Polygon tool, which allows you to draw multisided shapes.

- **Rounded Corners...** Opens the Rounded Corners dialog box, which presents six alternative corners for use on rectangles and squares drawn in PageMaker. If no document is currently open, a change in the settings of the Rounded Corners options changes the default setting used for documents created later.

- **Mask (⌘-6).** Places a graphic inside a PageMaker shape drawn with one of the shape, or drawing, tools. Basically, the shape acts as a container, cropping away portions (masking) of the object that do not fit into the shape. To use this command, you must have a graphic and a PageMaker shape selected. Note that the Undo command does not work with the Mask or Unmask commands.

- **Unmask (⌘-7).** Reverses an action performed with the Mask command. In other words, removes the masked object from the shape container. This command is available only when you have a masked object selected.

Image submenu. Contains four commands for working with images, including Image Control for adjusting brightness, contrast, and line screens for a selected bitmap, and commands for controlling color, color separations, and applying Photoshop Plug-ins.

- **Image⊏⟩Image Control...** Opens the Image control dialog box, in which you set controls to manipulate the appearance of a selected (paint-type graphics file or scanned image) graphic. Controls include line screen value, angle, and transfer function. The Image Control... command is dimmed unless a paint-format or TIFF image is selected.

- **Image⊏⟩CMS Source...** Opens the Color Management System Source Profile dialog box, which allows you to select a color management system profile for a selected image. Works only with color bitmap images. When you select an image that is not a color bitmap, CMS Source... is dimmed.

∞ **Image⇨Save for Separation...** Opens the Save for Separations dialog box, which allows you to preseparate an RGB image into CMYK plates without having to go out to Photoshop or another image editor to convert the image. This command also works on CMYK images, using the Separations Printer setting in the Color Management System Preferences dialog box. This command works only on color bitmaps. When any other image is selected, this command is dimmed.

∞ **Image⇨Photoshop Effects...** Applies Photoshop Plug-in filters to RGB and CMYK TIFFs. This command opens a list of Photoshop filters installed on your system. What happens next depends on the filter you choose. This command works only when RGB and CMYK TIFFs are selected. At all other times the command is grayed out.

∞ **Text Wrap...** Opens the Text Wrap dialog box, which you use to control how text wraps or flows around an independent graphic. Options let you flow text over graphics, wrap text around a rectangular or irregular graphic boundary, or jump over graphics. You can also specify the amount of standoff (space) you want between the graphic and any wrapping text.

 Non-Printing. Allows you to make page elements non-printing. In other words, when you print the document, the objects you define as non-printing will not print. To use this command, select the object(s) you want to make non-printing, and then select this command.

∞ **Link Info...** Opens the Link info dialog box, which you use to verify or modify the relationship between text and graphic elements used in the current publication and their original disk files. This command allows you to update a text or graphic element within the publication to reflect changes that have been made to the original disk file, or to replace the text or graphic element with the contents of a different disk file.

∞ **Link Options...** Opens the Link Options dialog box, which allows you to specify whether text and graphic information that has been imported into the publication is actually stored in the publication or is accessed from its original disk file, and if changes to the original disk file will be automatically used in the publication.

∞ **Define Colors...** Opens the Define Colors dialog box, which you use to add, edit, or delete colors for the current document. If you define colors with no document open, the settings will become default and PageMaker will use them for all new documents.

Arrange Menu

New to PageMaker 6, shown in Figure 3-10, the Arrange menu contains commands primarily for affecting the position and arrangement of objects on the page and pasteboard.

Figure 3-10:
The Arrange menu

Arrange	
Align Objects...	⌘-
Bring to Front	⌘F
Bring Forward	⌘8
Send to Back	⌘B
Send Backward	⌘9
Group	⌘G
Ungroup	⌘U
Lock Position	⌘L
Unlock	⌘,
Remove Transformation	

 Align Objects... (⌘-3). Opens the Align Objects dialog box, which allows you to arrange multiple objects in relationship to themselves. You can, for example, center them, align them on left, right, top, or bottom edges, etc. To use this command, you must have two or more objects selected, otherwise it remains dimmed.

☞ **Bring to Front** (⌘-F). Moves the selected element(s) to the top of the stacking order that PageMaker uses for layering elements.

 Bring Forward (⌘-8). Moves the selected element(s) one level higher in the stacking order that PageMaker uses for layering elements.

☞ **Send to Back** (⌘-B). Moves the selected element(s) to the bottom of the stacking order that PageMaker uses for layering elements.

 Send Backward (⌘-9). Moves the selected element(s) one level lower in the stacking order that PageMaker uses for layering elements.

 Group (⌘-G). Combines two or more selected items into one. You can then move, resize, and make other changes to all the objects at once. To use this command, you must select two or more objects, otherwise the command is dimmed.

☞ **Ungroup** (⌘-U). Reverses the action performed by Group. It breaks a grouped object into its original components.

 Lock Position (⌘-L). Rivets selected objects so that you cannot move or resize them with your mouse. When an object is locked, the bounding handles are gray rather than black.

☞ **Unlock** (⌘-,). Reverses the action performed by Lock Position, so that you can once again move and resize selected objects with your mouse.

☞ **Remove Transformation**. Removes any rotation, skewing, or reflecting that has been applied to an object via the control palette. You cannot use this command on lines drawn in PageMaker.

Window Menu

The Window menu, shown in Figure 3-11, provides control over publication windows, story editor windows, and all PageMaker palettes.

Figure 3-11:
The Window menu

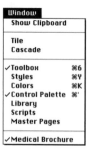

⊙ **Show Clipboard.** Displays a window containing the contents of the Macintosh Clipboard. Clipboards usually contain the contents of the last Cut or Copy command. You cannot use the Cut, Copy, and Paste commands while the Clipboard window is open. To close the Clipboard, click on the close box in the Clipboard title bar.

⊙ **Tile.** Arranges all open windows, either layouts or stories, into a neat side-by-side placement. Holding down the Option key while choosing the Tile command when in the story editor tiles all open stories from all open publications.

⊙ **Cascade.** Arranges all open windows, either layouts or stories, into a layered display with all title bars visible. Holding down the Option key while choosing the Cascade command when in the story editor cascades all open stories from all open publications.

⊙ **Toolbox** (⌘-6). Toggles the display of the Toolbox palette. You can move and close the tool palettes as in any other Macintosh window. A check mark (√) before the command indicates that it is currently selected (Toolbox palette is displayed); choosing it at this time will deselect it (Toolbox palette becomes hidden). The tool palette can also be hidden by clicking the close box in its title bar.

⊙ **Styles** (⌘-Y). Toggles on and off the display of the Styles palette, which lists the names of all defined PageMaker text styles. You can move, resize, and close with the window title bar, size box, and close box, respectively. A check mark (√) before the command indicates that it is currently selected (Styles palette is displayed); choosing it at this time will deselect it (Styles palette becomes hidden).

🕸 **Colors** (⌘-K). Toggles on and off the display of the Colors palette, which lists the names of all defined PageMaker colors for the current document. You can move, resize, and close the color palette with the window title bar, size box, and close box, respectively. A check mark (√) before the command indicates that it is currently selected (Colors palette is displayed); choosing it at this time will deselect it (Colors palette becomes hidden).

🕸 **Control Palette** (⌘-'). Toggles on and off the display of the Control Palette, which provides quick access to character, paragraph, and object formatting and placements. However, you need to select an element before the Control Palette will display any information about it. A check mark (√) before the command indicates that it is currently selected (Control Palette is displayed); choosing it at this time will deselect it (Control Palette becomes hidden).

🕸 **Library.** Toggles on and off the display of the Library palette, which displays a collection of text or graphic elements saved in a PageMaker library. The first time the you choose the command, PageMaker asks you to select a Library palette. You can move, resize, and close the Library palette with its title bar, size box, and close box, respectively.

 Scripts (⌘-\). Toggles on and off the display of the Scripts palette, which allows you to manage PageMaker scripts and execute scripts by double-clicking on them. A check mark (√) before the command indicates that it is currently selected (Scripts palette is displayed); choosing it at this time will deselect it (Scripts palette becomes hidden).

 Master Pages (⌘-H). Toggles on and off the display of the Master Pages palette, which allows you to create and manage master pages. You can move, resize, and close the Master Pages palette with its title bar, size box, and close box, respectively. A check mark (√) before the command indicates that it is currently selected (Master Pages palette is displayed); choosing it at this time will deselect it (Master Pages palette becomes hidden).

Help (?) Menu

PageMaker uses the Mac Help (?) menu, shown in Figure 3-12, to house its help commands.

Figure 3-12:
The Help menu

∞ **About Balloon Help...** Opens the standard Macintosh About Balloon Help dialog box, which tells you briefly about the balloon help feature and how to use it.

∞ **Show Balloons.** Toggles on and off Macintosh balloon help, which displays helpful captions when you place the mouse cursor over specific screen items, such as menus, tools, palettes, and so on. When Show Balloons is on, this menu command reads Hide Balloons, which, when selected, turns Balloon Help off.

∞ **Contents...** Opens the PageMaker help system, which provides on-line information about all PageMaker commands and a multitude of PageMaker topics. Context-sensitive help is also available by pressing ⌘-? and then selecting any command or tool.

∞ **Search...** Opens the PageMaker help system displaying a screen designed to help you search the help database for keywords and phrases.

∞ **Shortcuts...** Opens the PageMaker help system displaying several PageMaker keyboard shortcuts for executing commands and other functions.

∞ **Using PageMaker Help...** Opens the PageMaker help system displaying a screen designed to show you how to navigate and use the help system. In other words, help on help.

Story Menu

When you open the Story Editor, the Layout, Element, and Arrange menus disappear, and the Story menu, shown in Figure 3-13, is added. (You'll recall that you edit a story by selecting the Edit story command from the Edit menu.) This menu contains commands to open and close stories and control the display of on-screen elements in the story editor.

Figure 3-13:
The Story menu

∞ **New Story.** Creates a new story window in the story editor. This window is initially untitled and can be used to enter a new story from the keyboard or to hold a text file that has been imported using the Place... command.

∞ **Close Story** (⌘-W). Closes the current story. If you made changes to the story, and the story has not been placed in the current publication, a dialog box asks if you want to place the story or discard the changes. If only one story window is open in the story editor when this command is selected, the story editor itself closes and you are returned to layout view.

- **Display Paragraphs.** Toggles the display of special characters in the current story. Special characters include spaces, em and en spaces, fixed spaces, tags, returns, line ends, page numbers, and index markers.

- **Display Style Names.** Toggles the display of a bar in the story editor window listing the name of any style sheets applied to paragraphs in the current story.

The Toolbox Palette

The tools in PageMaker's toolbox palette, or toolbox, allow you to work with page elements. Select a tool by clicking its icon in the tool palette. You can reposition the palette itself, shown in Figure 3-14, anywhere within the publication window by dragging its title bar. You can close it by clicking its close box. To display it again, click the Toolbox palette command on the Windows menu.

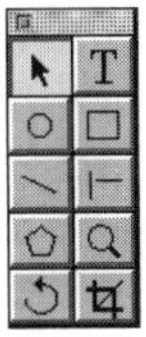

Figure 3-14:
The Toolbox palette

- **Pointer tool** (Shift-F1). Used to select text and graphic objects, manipulate the column and ruler guides, operate the scroll bars, turn pages, and choose commands from the menus. The pointer tool appears automatically when you position the cursor over the menu bar, page icons, scroll bars, or the palette itself.

- **Text tool** (Shift-F2). Used to create a new text block, to set the insertion point in an existing text block, or to select text in an existing text block.

- **Ellipse tool** (Shift-F33). Used to create a new circle or oval. Holding down the Shift key while creating a new oval constrains the shape to a perfect circle. The new shape will be bordered by a line with the weight and style selected with the Line command, and filled with a shade as specified with the Fill command.

- **Rectangle tool** (Shift-F3). Used to create a new rectangle with square corners. Holding down the Shift key while creating a new rectangle constrains the shape to a perfect square. You can adjust the corners of a shape created with the Rectangle tool with the Rounded Corners… command from the Element menu. The new shape will be bordered by a line with the weight and style selected with the Line command, and filled with a shade as specified with the Fill command.

↩ **Line tool** (Shift-F5). Used to create straight lines. Hold down the Shift key while creating a new line to constrain the line to 35-degree angle to the edge of the page. (Holding down the Shift key constrains the line to create perfect horizontal and vertical lines.) The initial weight, style, and color of a new line is defined by the setting of the Line command and color palette.

↩ **Constrained-line tool** (Shift-F6). Used to create straight lines at 35-degree angles on the current page(s) or pasteboard. (You use this tool to make perfectly horizontal and vertical lines.) The initial weight, style, and color of a new line is defined by the setting of the Line command and Colors palette.

 Polygon tool (Shift-F7). Used to create multisided shapes. Holding down the Shift key while creating a new polygon constrains the shape proportionally. You can give the new shape additional sides and change the inset of the sides with the Polygon Settings command on the Element menu.

 Zoom tool (Shift-F8). The Zoom tool is almost identical to the same tool found in Illustrator and Photoshop. You can zoom in on a portion of the page by selecting the Zoom tool and then clicking the place where you want to zoom in. Holding the Option key while clicking zooms out. You can also marquee select an area with the Zoom tool to get a more specific zoom.

 Rotating tool (Shift-F9). Used to rotate any text block or graphic element.

↩ **Cropping tool** (Shift-F10). Used to crop an imported graphic, uncrop a cropped graphic, or position the remainder of a cropped graphic within its borders.

Control Palette

PageMaker introduced the control palette in version 3.2 and gave it a major upgrade in version 5. There is little change in version 6 except for a few slight variations in the new Lock Position and Group commands. The control palette appears in one of three distinct states, depending on what type of object(s) are selected.

↩ **Character view.** In this view, shown in Figure 3-15, the control palette lets you set font, type size, tracking, kerning, type style, type case (small caps, all caps, etc.), type position (superscript, subscript), leading, width, and baseline shift.

Figure 3-15:
The Control palette in character view

⊸ **Paragraph view.** In this view, shown in Figure 3-16, the control palette lets you set the paragraph style, first indent, space before, space after, left indent, and right indent.

Figure 3-16:
The Control palette in
paragraph view

⊸ **Object view.** In this view, shown in Figure 3-17, the control palette lets you set X and Y positions, width and height, scaling, rotation, reflecting, skewing, and cropping of a selected object or group of objects.

Figure 3-17:
The Control palette in
object view

Summary

↠ PageMaker uses ten menus, and the Macintosh Help menu to execute page, text, and graphics formatting.

↠ Three highly important menus are Type, Element, and Arrange: Type provides all the commands necessary for formatting text. Element provides the commands for formatting objects, such as text blocks and graphics. And Arrange menu items control object stacking order, alignment, and other important options.

↠ The Toolbox provides several tools for working with objects and text, including a Zoom tool for getting a better view, and several drawing tools for drawing rudimentary shapes.

↠ The Control Palette provides shortcuts to several of the options on some PageMaker menus, especially the Type and Elements menus (the Control palette is discussed in Chapter 9).

Understanding Publication Window Basics

In This Chapter

- ➡ Changing view sizes, zooming, and scrolling publications
- ➡ Adding, removing, numbering, and turning pages
- ➡ Sorting pages
- ➡ Working with column guides and ruler guides
- ➡ Text and graphic objects
- ➡ Working with PageMaker's new Group command
- ➡ Riveting objects to the page with Lock position
- ➡ Controlling master pages

Ten years ago PageMaker's pasteboard metaphor revolutionized page layout. Because the program so closely emulates traditional page layout methods, experienced designers and production people have found the transition to PageMaker relatively painless. If you'll just picture yourself sitting down to a layout table, complete with exacto knives, paste, shape stencils, and other production tools, you'll find sitting down to PageMaker a much less daunting prospect.

The previous chapters introduced you to PageMaker's menus and commands. Now that you've learned how to start new publications, open existing publications, and save publications, you're ready to start learning how to layout documents.

Getting Around in PageMaker_____

The basic techniques introduced in the first part of this chapter — zooming, scrolling, and turning pages — may seem trivial, but they really are vital to your becoming proficient with the program. You use them frequently. You should become adept at their behavior and subtleties.

Getting a Better View

PageMaker provides several ways to zoom in and out on the pages in your documents. Each zoom level, or view size, provides a different level of magnification of the contents of the publication window. When you zoom in, PageMaker displays detailed areas, but, depending on the zoom level, only small portions of page(s) or the pasteboard are displayed. Reduced views display more of the page(s) and pasteboard but show less detail. Alternating between enlarged and reduced view sizes allows you to make changes easily and get an overall picture of your document pages.

The Zoom Tool

The easiest way to zoom in and out in PageMaker is with the Zoom tool, which allows you to zoom in and out on specific areas or elements on your pages. To access the zoom tool, click the magnifying glass in the Toolbox. The cursor changes to a magnifying glass with a plus sign in its center. Point to the part of the page you want to zoom in on and click. The area you click magnifies by 25 percent. Holding the Option key down displays a minus sign in the center of the magnifying glass. When you Option-click, PageMaker zooms out by 25 percent.

You can also use the zoom tool to perform an arbitrary zoom. Instead of clicking with the magnifying glass, you drag a rectangle around the elements or area you want to zoom in on, as shown in Figure 4-1. When you release the mouse button, PageMaker enlarges the page and your selection fills the screen. In this case, you zoom in on a certain area, regardless of the degree of magnification.

View Sizes

In addition to the Zoom tool, PageMaker provides eight predefined view sizes. The advantage of using a predefined view size over the zoom tool is that the latter can quickly get you to a desired level of magnification. For example, selecting Fit in Window

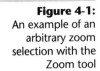

Figure 4-1:
An example of an
arbitrary zoom
selection with the
Zoom tool

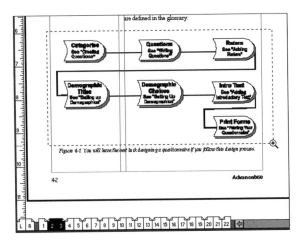

view instantly returns you to a full-page view of the current page(s) in your document. To use a predefined view size, select one of the commands on the View submenu on the Layout menu or use the corresponding keyboard shortcut.

When using a predefined view, PageMaker centers the display based on several factors, such as whether you have an object selected, whether the text cursor is active in a block of text, and so on. For example, if you select a text block with the Pointer tool and then choose a 200% view, PageMaker zooms in on the selected object and centers it on your monitor.

You can also use combination keyboard and mouse-clicks to toggle between Fit in Window and Actual size view. When in Fit in Window view, for instance, holding Option-⌘ and clicking on a specific area, magnifies the area to Actual size. When you Option-⌘-click in Actual size view, PageMaker returns to Fit in window view. Using this option from any other view first returns you to the nearest (Fit in window or Actual size) view, and then, when you use it again, toggles between Fit in Window and Actual size.

Because of the myriad Macintosh monitor and resolution options nowadays, the results of each preset view command vary from system to system. With that in mind, here's a summary of PageMaker's eight standard view sizes:

  ↪ **Fit in Window** (⌘-W). The default view size — selected automatically each time you create a new document — reduces the active page(s) to fit in the publication window. Fit in Window, shown in Figure 4-2, does not use a specific reduction percentage, because it is dependent on the size of your monitor. On a Macintosh Classic, for example, the Fit in Window view reduces significantly, whereas on a 21-inch monitor it is almost equal to actual size. You'll usually use the Fit in Window view to get a good look at the overall layout of specific pages or when placing or moving text and graphics around a page.

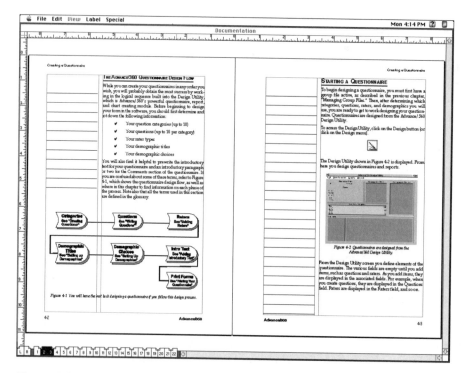

Figure 4-2: PageMaker's Fit in Window view

- ☞ **Entire pasteboard.** This view, shown in Figure 4-3, shows the active pages and the entire pasteboard. Use it for seeing everything within the publication window. When you misplace objects you've placed on the Pasteboard, for instance, this is a great way to find them. You can also invoke Entire pasteboard by holding down the Shift key while selecting the Fit in window command.

- ☞ **25% size** (⌘-0). This view size displays the publication at 25 percent of Actual size view, discussed below.

- ☞ **50% size** (⌘-5). This view size displays the publication at 50 percent of Actuarial size view, discussed below.

- ☞ **75% size** (⌘-7). This view size displays the publication at 75 percent of Actual size view, discussed next.

- ☞ **Actual size** (⌘-1). The Actual size view size displays the publication on the screen at exactly the size it was specified in the Document Setup dialog box. Depending on your display system, you'll probably use this view for most text and graphic editing.

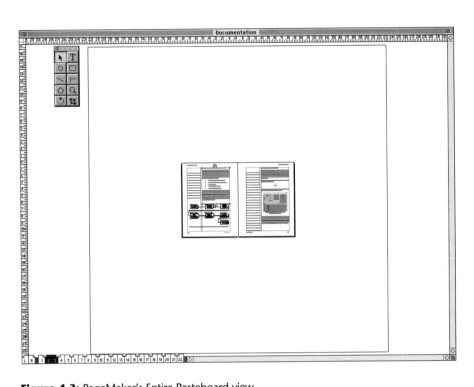

Figure 4-3: PageMaker's Entire Pasteboard view

- **200% size** (⌘-2). This view size is an enlargement twice the Actual size view. Normally, only a small portion of a page is visible at the 200% view size, which is used primarily for text editing and precision placement of text and graphics. Holding down Shift-⌘-Option and clicking the mouse button also changes the view size to 200%.

- **400% size** (⌘-4). The 400% is an enlargement four times its Actual size view. Use this view to position objects accurately or edit text set in very small point sizes.

Getting the right view fast: Choosing one of PageMaker's view levels doesn't always enlarge the section of the page you want. You can control where PageMaker zooms by first selecting an object in the area where you want to zoom, or by placing the text cursor in a block of text. One of Bill's favorite methods for zooming on a specific portion of a page is first to select an object (or click the text cursor in a text block) and then press ⌘-2 for 200% view.

PageMaker's view sizes are listed in Table 4-1.

Table 4-1
PageMaker's View Level Keyboard Shortcuts

View	Keyboard Shortcut	Mouse Shortcut
Entire pasteboard	Shift-choose Fit in window	
Fit in window	⌘-Option-. or ⌘-W	⌘-Option-Click
Actual Size	⌘-Option-. or ⌘-1	⌘-Option-Click
25% size	⌘-0	
50% size	⌘-5	
75% size	⌘-7	
200% size	Shift-⌘-Option-. or ⌘-2	Shift-⌘-Option-Click
400% size	⌘-4	

Scrolling the Display

Since, depending on your display size, many view sizes display only a portion of the page(s), PageMaker provides several ways to scroll the publication window. You can use the horizontal or vertical scroll bars, PageMaker's grabber hand, or zoom tool.

◌ **The scroll bars.** Almost all Macintosh applications have scroll bars, located at the right and bottom edges of the document window. (If your scroll bars are not visible, choose Show Scroll bars from the Guides and rulers submenu on the Layout menu.)

The scroll bars provide several methods for scrolling: You can click the up, down, right, or left scroll arrows to adjust the display in small increments; you can drag the scroll box located on the scroll bar to slide the publication window contents up, down, left, or right; or you can click in the gray area of the scroll bar to scroll the display by about one-half its size.

◌ **The grabber hand.** The grabber hand (shown in Figure 4-4), accessed by holding down the Option key while pressing and holding down the mouse button, is the easiest way to scroll around in PageMaker. Think of it as picking up the page and moving it around. Once the grabber hand is active, simply drag it in the direction in which you want the contents of the publication window to move.

Holding down the Shift key while using the grabber hand constrains the display movement to either horizontal or vertical movement only, depending on the first direction you move the mouse. The grabber hand icon disappears as soon as you release the Option key, returning the cursor to its previous form.

Figure 4-4:
PageMaker's grabber hand

- **⌘-Click view size changes.** As described in the previous section, if you change view sizes by using the ⌘-Option-Click or Shift-⌘-Option-Click method, you can specify the exact object to zoom in on by selecting it. When working in Actual, 200%, or 400% view size, you can very quickly zoom out to Fit in window, locate the element that you want to center in your new display, and then zoom in on it. Depending on your Mac and the complexity of the current pages, this is sometimes faster than using the scroll bars or grabber hand.

- **The Zoom tool.** As with the ⌘-Click changes, you can use the Zoom tool (magnifying glass in the Toolbox) to change zoom levels quickly.

Turning the Page

PageMaker's publication window displays only one page (or two facing pages) in the publication window. The highlighted page icon(s) at the bottom of the display indicate which page(s) are currently displayed.

Changing page(s) is easy. Simply select the desired page icon at the bottom of the publication window, as shown in Figure 4-5. The maximum number of page icons that fit along the bottom of the display depends on the size and resolution of your monitor. If they don't all fit, left and right arrows appear before the first and after the last page icon, respectively, allowing you to scroll the page icons.

Figure 4-5:
PageMaker's page icons. Use them to move quickly from page to page in your documents.

◁ 7 8 9 10 11 12 13 14 15 16 17 18 19 20 21 22 23 24 25 26 27 28 29 30 31 32 33 34 35 36 37 38 ▷

When you select a new page, the watch cursor momentarily appears, as PageMaker reads information about the new pages from your hard disk and executes a mini-save (discussed in "Undo and Revert," later in this chapter). The new page(s) then appear in the publication window at the same view size and screen position as when they were last saved or displayed.

Getting the right view as you turn the page: If you hold down the Shift key while clicking the page icon, the new page is displayed at Fit in window view, regardless of the previous view size used. To change the view size of all the pages in your publication at once, hold down the Option key while choosing a view size from the View submenu in the Layout menu.

You can also turn pages by choosing Go to page... from the Layout menu. This command brings up the Go to Page dialog box shown in Figure 4-6. Enter the page number in the Page number field and then press Return or click the OK button. (If you enter an unavailable page number, an alert dialog box displays a message informing you of such.) Clicking the Cancel button in the Go to Page dialog box returns you to the currently displayed page.

Figure 4-6:
The Go to Page dialog box

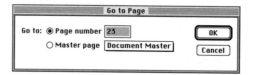

Notice also in Figure 4-6 that you can go to a specific master page set. Master pages are discussed in the "Working with Master Pages," later in this chapter.

Invoking PageMaker's slide show option: Holding down the Shift key when you choose the Go to page... command puts PageMaker into a "slideshow mode" in which it flips from one page (or pairs of pages) to the next every few seconds until you click the mouse button. Use this option to look for objects when you don't know which page you put them on or to do presentations with your document pages.

Adding Pages

While creating a publication, you will often find that you need more pages than currently available in the document. As long as the current publication has fewer than 999 pages, you can easily add pages with Insert pages... on the Layout menu, which opens the Insert Pages dialog box shown in Figure 4-7. You can insert pages before, after, or between the current pages. You can also specify the number of pages to add.

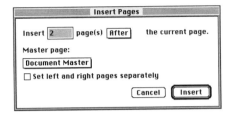

Figure 4-7:
PageMaker's Insert Pages
dialog box

Click the OK button to insert the pages. (If you try to add too many pages, forcing the publication size to exceed 999 pages, an alert dialog box appears, requiring you to modify your request. Also, you cannot add pages if they force the page number of the last page in the publication beyond 9999.) Clicking the Cancel button in the Insert Pages dialog box returns you to the currently selected page(s) without adding any pages.

Notice in Figure 4-7 that you can also specify which master page formatting to apply to the new pages and that you can set master page options for left and right pages separately. Master pages are discussed in the "Working with Master Pages" section of this chapter.

The pages you add with Insert Pages — whether before, after, or between the current pages — do not affect the items already positioned on existing pages. For example, if threaded text blocks (threaded text is described in Chapter 6) link pages 8 and 9, and you insert two pages between pages 8 and 9, the threaded text remains in place, except now it flows from page 8 to page 11, skipping pages 9 and 10. All following pages in the publication are appropriately renumbered.

Inserting pages automatically: You can also tell PageMaker to insert pages automatically when you place text in a document from a word processor, with the Automatic text flow option. When in autoflow mode (described in Chapter 6) PageMaker automatically inserts pages until all the text in a word processor file is placed.

Removing Pages

PageMaker also lets you delete pages easily, with Remove pages... on the Layout menu, which brings up the Remove Pages dialog box, shown in Figure 4-8. The default deletion range is the currently selected page(s). You can specify any page range, even every page in the publication. (An alert dialog box appears if you try to delete pages that don't exist.)

Figure 4-8:
The Remove Pages dialog box

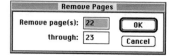

Be careful. Removing a page deletes the page and all items on that page. If you want to save page elements, move them to the pasteboard before choosing the Remove pages... command. Before PageMaker deletes the pages, an alert dialog box warns you that removal of a page cannot be undone and gives you one last chance to cancel. Clicking the OK button causes PageMaker to delete the page(s). All pages following those removed are renumbered.

Note that deletion of an odd number of pages in a double-sided publication causes subsequent pages to switch sides — left pages become right pages, and vice versa. Although you cannot undo Remove pages, you can get them back with Revert, or "revert to mini-save" option described in the "Undo and Revert" section of this chapter.

Sorting Pages

Sometimes, when working in documents with several pages, you may find it necessary to change the page order or move various pages around in the publication. PageMaker provides a utility called Sort pages, shown in Figure 4-9, to help you.

Figure 4-9:
The Sort pages dialog box

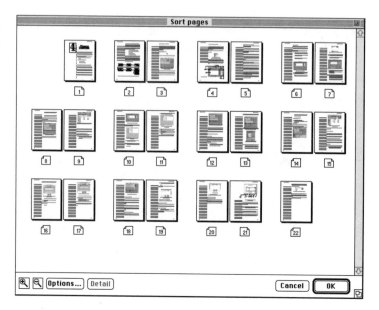

To open this dialog box, choose Sort Pages... from the Layout menu. You can then change the page order by dragging pages or spreads to their new positions, as shown in Figure 4-10.

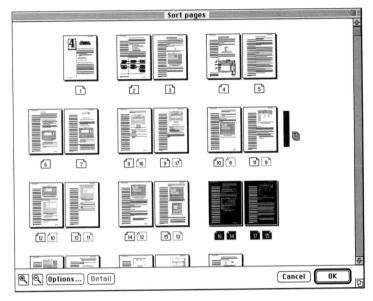

Figure 4-10:
An example of
using Sort
pages to
change page
order

To zoom in on or out on the page thumbnails, allowing you to see more pages or greater detail on the thumbnail previews, click on the plus (+) and minus (-) magnifying glasses, respectively. You can also change other aspects of your document and the operations of the Sort pages dialog box by clicking on the Options... button, which opens the Options dialog box, shown in Figure 4-11. With this you make pages facing or non-facing, determine whether the Sort pages dialog box displays detailed thumbnails or blank pages, and whether PageMaker repositions elements to compensate for right and left margin changes when you change facing pages to single pages.

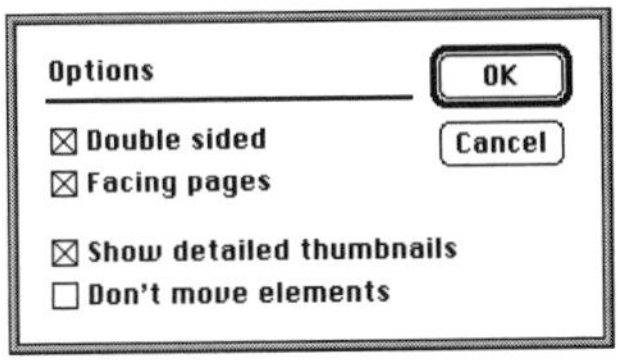

Figure 4-11:
The Sort pages Options dialog box

Getting a detailed view: It takes time for PageMaker to redraw all those thumbnails in Sort pages, especially on slower Macs. When you uncheck the Show detailed thumbnails in Options, PageMaker displays blank pages in Sort pages. You can then get detailed thumbnails of selected pages by clicking on the Detail button, as shown in Figure 4-12. This is a great way to see selected pages to make sure that you have the right ones before moving them, without waiting for the rest of the thumbnails to redraw.

Figure 4-12:
An example
of using the
Sort pages
Detail option

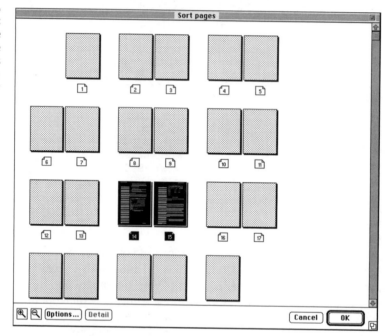

Guides and Rulers

At the beginning of this chapter we talked about PageMaker's pasteboard emulation. In this section, three important aspects of the conventional pasteboard emulation are discussed: column guides, ruler guides, and the rulers themselves.

Column Guides

Column guides act as the left and right margins for the text blocks that you place on your pages. You can also use them to position and align graphics. Each page in a PageMaker document can contain a different column configuration, and you can customize the placement of column guides on any page with your mouse, providing nearly unlimited design capabilities. Usually, you begin a page by adding column guides to your master pages (discussed in "Working with Master Pages," at the end of this chapter). This provides a level of consistency throughout your publication. You can then customize columns on separate pages as needed.

To add column guides to a page (including a master page, discussed later in this chapter), or to move existing column guides, select Column guides… from the Layout menu. The Column Guides dialog box, as shown in Figure 4-13, appears. (Note that the Column guides command is dimmed if the Show Guides command in the Guides and rulers submenu isn't turned on.)

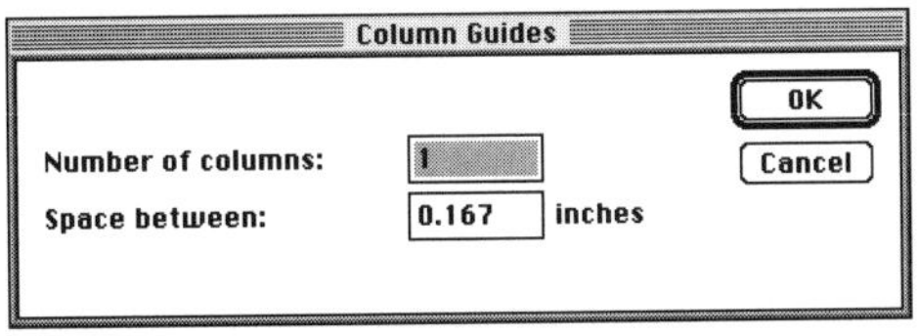

Figure 4-13:
The Column Guides dialog box when working in a single-sided document

The Column Guides dialog box contains two options: Number of columns and Space between options (often known as *gutters*). When Column Guides opens, the configuration of existing column guides on the current page are displayed. If you moved the existing column guides manually, the word *Custom* appears in the Number of columns field. A page can have up to 20 columns. If you define only one column, PageMaker ignores the Space between columns value.

If your document contains facing pages, PageMaker assumes that you want to set the column guides identically for both pages (as shown in Figure 4-14). If not, select the Set left and right pages separately option. The Column Guides dialog box then displays separate fields for the left and right pages, as shown in Figure 4-15.

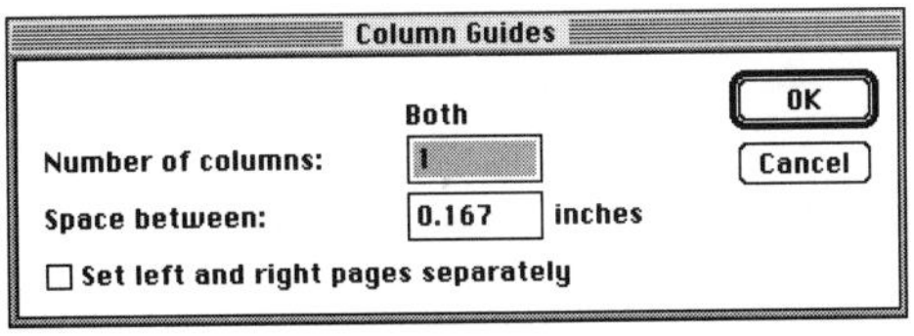

Figure 4-14:
The Column Guides dialog box when working in a facing-pages document

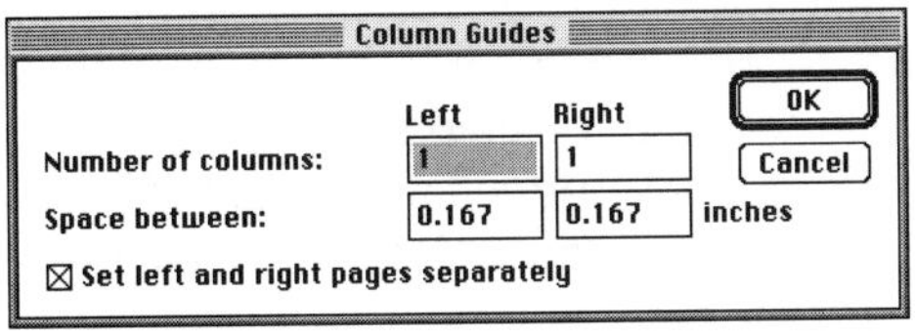

Figure 4-15:
The Column Guides dialog box, when Set left and right pages separately is selected, allows you to set columns for each page separately.

When you click OK, PageMaker calculates the width of each column and then draws the column guides on the page. Column guides are blue lines on color monitors and dotted vertical lines on grayscale displays — single lines for the leftmost and rightmost column guides (those automatically placed on the left and right margins) and double-lines representing the adjacent edges of columns (the double lines are separated by the value specified for the Space between option, or gutters), as shown in Figure 4-16. Since the leftmost and rightmost column guides are placed directly on top of the existing margin guides, they appear as darker lines.

Figure 4-16:
A page with three columns. The two double lines in the center represent the column gutters.

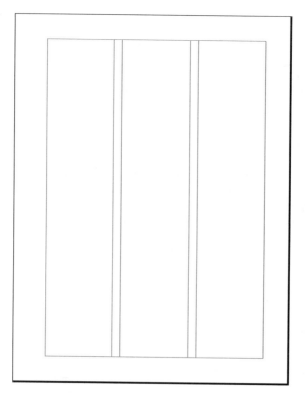

Columns created by the Column Guides dialog box are always equally spaced between the left and right margins; however, once you've defined the column guides, you can reposition them manually with your mouse, as shown in Figure 4-17. To reposition a column guide, press and hold the mouse button while positioning the pointer tool on the column guide (on double-line column guides, point directly at one of the lines). When you have successfully selected the guide, the cursor becomes a double-sided arrow. As you drag the guide, a small dotted line tracks the location of the cursor on the rulers, making it easier to place the guide. If the Control palette (discussed in Chapter 9) is open, the exact location of the column guides is tracked there as well. To remain visible, column guides must be at least one pica away from another column guide.

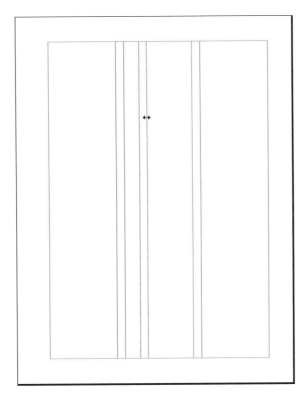

Figure 4-17:
An example of
repositioning column
guides with a mouse

Rulers

PageMaker's vertical and horizontal rulers help you place elements precisely on the page. You can show and hide the rulers from the Guides and rulers submenu of the Layout menu (or by pressing ⌘-R). Both the horizontal and vertical rulers contain *tick marks*, which divide the ruler into subunits. The units in the horizontal ruler are determined by the Measurement system option and the units in the Vertical ruler are determined by the Vertical ruler option, both of which are found in the Preferences dialog box, discussed in Chapter 1. You can set both the horizontal and vertical rulers to use the same measurement system, or you can use different systems on the two rulers.

PageMaker tracks the current position of the mouse cursor in both rulers by displaying small dotted lines. These lines make it easier to position elements accurately. (Theoretically, elements you place precisely on tick marks are accurate to $\frac{1}{4440}$ inch (or 0.0002 inch, 0.001 mm, or 0.016 point). Items you align between two tick marks on the ruler are positioned less accurately. In reality, the precision of the target output device, which depends on both its resolution and physical condition, also affects the alignment precision.)

Placing objects precisely with the ruler: To help you position objects precisely on ruler tick marks, PageMaker provides the Snap to Rulers command on the Guides and rulers submenu of the Layout menu. When this command is selected, as indicated by the presence of a check mark (√) in front of the command, PageMaker won't let you position objects between ruler tick marks — the edges of the object nearest the cursor automatically "snap" to the nearest ruler tick marks, vertically and horizontally. Since the number of tick marks displayed varies with the current view size, you can place objects more precisely by enlarging the view size.

Measuring with the Rulers

When using a ruler to measure a distance in real life, you place the zero point of the ruler at one end and measure to the other. When you can't position the zero point at the beginning of the object to be measured, you calculate the distance between two points by subtracting the nonzero value at the beginning of the measured distance from the value at the end. For example, if the measured distance starts at 1.5 inches and ends at 4.75 inches, your measured distance is 4.75 – 1.5 = 3.25 inches.

To measure distances on PageMaker's pages, you use the same technique, except that instead of moving the ruler so that the zero point aligns with the beginning of the object being measured, you change the position of the zero point without physically moving the ruler itself. In any new single-sided publication, the zero point of both the horizontal and vertical rulers (also known as the zero intersection point) is located at the upper left-hand corner of the page. For double-sided publications, the zero point is located at the top of the pages and centered between them. The default zero intersection point is shown in Figure 4-18 for both a single page and facing pages.

Figure 4-18:
Examples of PageMaker's default zero intersection point in single-page and facing-pages views

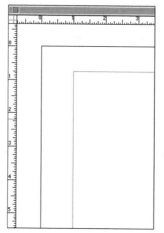
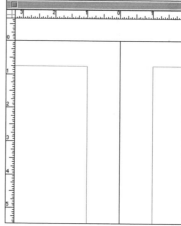

To reset the zero intersection point, drag it from the upper-left corner of the publication window, as shown in Figure 4-19, and position it where you want the horizontal and vertical zero points of the rulers. As the zero-point marker is dragged, perpendicular lines extend across the screen so that you can easily align the new zero point. When you release the mouse button, PageMaker redraws each ruler.

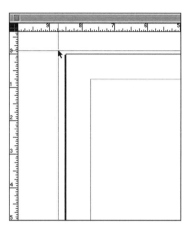

Figure 4-19:
An example of resetting the zero intersection point

Locking zero: Since resetting the zero intersection point is so easy, you can use it to measure graphic elements, to position text blocks accurately, and to measure and position column and ruler guides (discussed in the next section). Sometimes, however, you may want to set and rivet the zero intersection point so that you cannot inadvertently move it. To lock the zero point, choose Zero lock from the Guides and rulers submenu of the Layout menu. The zero intersection point marker (cross hairs) disappears from the rulers, making it impossible to select and reposition it.

Ruler Guides

As we've seen, the rulers help you position and measure objects. You can get more help positioning objects with PageMaker's ruler guides. Ruler guides are non-printing lines — much like the non-printing bluelines used in conventional page layout — that you can drag into your publication to create grids or use as placement points.

To create a ruler guide, click on either the horizontal or vertical ruler and drag into the publication window, as shown in Figure 4-20. When the cursor leaves the ruler and enters the publication window, a ruler guide becomes visible — a cyan line on color monitors or a dotted line on grayscale monitors. You can create ruler guides only when Show Guides on the Rulers and guides submenu of the Layout menu is turned on. You can create ruler guides with any PageMaker tool active. PageMaker supports up to 40 ruler guides per page(s), including both horizontal and vertical guides, and master page guides. (Master pages are discussed in the "Working with Master Pages" section of this chapter.) Ruler guides are especially useful on master pages. Use them to designate specific boundaries or positions to maintain consistency from page to page.

Figure 4-20:
Example of dragging a ruler guide into a publication

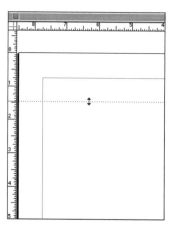

You can reposition ruler guides at any time by dragging them with your mouse. With the Pointer tool, click and hold the mouse button on the ruler guide; the arrow becomes double-sided and can be dragged in either direction. To remove a ruler guide, drag it back into the ruler and release the mouse button.

Using ruler guides to create a layout grid: Often you'll find it helpful to create a layout grid over your pages, similar to a grid on a paste-up table surface, to help you position objects precisely in relation to one another. As long as you don't exceed PageMaker's 120-guide-per-page(s) limit, you can create fine or coarse grids. Figure 4-21 shows an example of using ruler guides for creating a grid.

More About Guides

Column, margin, and ruler guides are important to several aspects of the page layout process in PageMaker. PageMaker also allows you to utilize them in various ways. For example, when flowing text from one page to another, PageMaker uses margin and column guides to determine where on each page to place the text. This section looks at some important uses of PageMaker's non-printing guides.

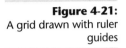
Figure 4-21:
A grid drawn with ruler
guides

Hiding Guides

Column guides, ruler guides, and margin guides are normally displayed on-screen as you work. They can be distracting, however, when trying to envision the look of the publication without them. You can hide guides at any time by deselecting the Show Guides command in the Guides and rulers submenu of the Layout menu. This command toggles display of the guides on and off, as shown in Figure 4-22. When guides are hidden, the Snap to guides, Lock guides, and Column guides… commands are dimmed. (For descriptions of these commands, see the "Snapping to Guides" section and the "Getting Guides out of the Way" section, comming up. Column guides are discussed earlier in this chapter under "Column Guides."

Placing Guides Behind Page Elements

PageMaker allows you to place guides on top of (in front) page elements and beneath (behind) page elements, or you can toggle between the two display options. When guides are in front, it's easier to place objects precisely on the page. When guides are behind, you get a better view of the overall page. To toggle between the two views, use

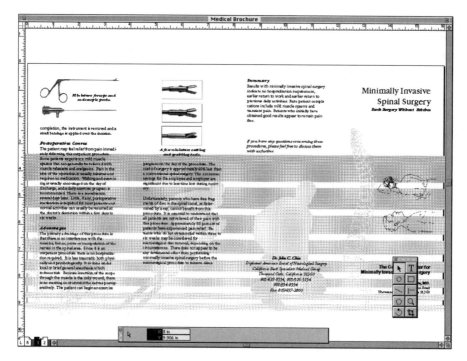

Figure 4-22: An example of viewing a page with guides hidden

the Guides in Front and Guides Behind commands on the Guides and rulers submenu of the Layout menu. Or you can make the view more permanent by changing the Guides option in Preferences, as discussed in Chapter 1.

Snapping to Guides

PageMaker's guides assist you further in placing objects with their "magnetic" effect. When you drag an object close to a guide (within two pixels), the object clings to the guide, as to a magnet. Elements placed previous to turning Snap to guide on are unaffected when you activate the command.

Turning off Snap to guides: Snap to guides is a handy feature, but sometimes it is annoying. For example, you may want to position an element close to, but not exactly aligned with, a guide. Choosing Snap to guides (⌘-U) from the Options menu (removing the check mark) toggles off the magnetism.

Getting Guides out of the Way

Because you can select and reposition column guides and ruler guides like text or graphic elements, it's easy to select and move them accidentally. There are four ways to avoid inadvertently moving guides:

- ☞ Hold down the Command key while selecting objects: PageMaker won't let you select guides. The Command key temporarily locks guides in place.

- ☞ Turn on Lock guides: To fix guides permanently in place so that you can't select or move them, turn on Lock guides on the Rulers and guides submenu of the Layout menu.

- ☞ Place guides behind page elements: Another way to make inadvertently selecting and moving guides less likely is to place them behind page elements with the Guides option in the Preferences dialog box, or the Guides in front/Guides behind option discussed earlier in this chapter under "Placing Guides Behind Page Elements." When this option is on, selecting guides becomes difficult when page elements overlap them, but they remain easily selectable when not covered by other objects.

- ☞ Work with guides hidden: You can hide the guides by deselecting the Show Guides command on the Guides and ruler submenu of the Layout menu. This makes them invisible and impossible to select.

Manipulating Page Elements _____

Every page in a PageMaker publication consists of a collection of text and graphic elements. Some elements are created in other applications and imported into PageMaker, whereas others you create within PageMaker itself. In any case, the ability to collect these text and graphic elements from a variety of external sources, add new, internally created elements, and then manage the layout of these many elements summarizes what PageMaker does. Understanding how to control elements both individually and in groups is vital to your success in using PageMaker.

This section examines the basics of controlling page elements: the mechanical processes of selecting, arranging, moving, grouping, aligning, locking, copying, and deleting text or graphic objects. (By the way, to avoid tedious repetition, the words "elements," "objects," and "items" are used interchangeably in this discussion. They all refer to text blocks or graphics within a PageMaker document.)

Element Layers: the Stacking Order

If you add one element to a page in a PageMaker publication and then add another element in exactly the same spot, the latter element overlays, or stacks on top of, the former. This concept — that every element you add to your publications is layered in relation to every other element — is important, even though layers are not obvious when elements don't overlap.

You can tell how objects are layered on a page by watching the order in which elements redraw when turning a page or changing view sizes. (The inherent layering of elements also comes into play during printing, when "lower" objects are sent to the printer before "higher" objects.) PageMaker's hierarchical layering of objects is called the *stacking order*.

The following principles apply to the stacking order:

- PageMaker automatically places newly created objects at the top of a stack, above all other existing objects. If an older object is repositioned to overlap a newer object, it moves to the top of the stacking order.

- The Bring to Front command in the Arrange menu (⌘-F) moves a selected object or objects to the top of the stacking order. (By the same token, Bring Forward [⌘-8] moves a selected object or objects up one level in the stacking order.)

- The Send to Back command in the Arrange menu (⌘-B) moves a selected object to the bottom of the stacking order. (By the same token, Send Backward [⌘-9] moves a selected object or objects down one level in the stacking order.)

- The stacking order of elements on the master page(s) is independent of the stacking order of elements on publication pages. The stacking order of master-page elements always underlies the stacking order of elements on the publication page — including publication-page elements that have been moved with Send to Back and Send Backward. (Master pages are discussed in the "Working with Master Pages" section of this chapter.)

- PageMaker places guides either above or below each object on a page according to the current setting of the Guides option in the Preferences dialog box or the Guides in Front and Guides Behind commands on the Guides and rulers submenu of the Layout menu (all discussed in the "Guides and Rulers" section of this chapter).

To make this concept of stacking easier to understand, look at Figure 4-23. Notice that the text in the first example is on top of the graphics. After we used Send to Back to place it behind the graphics, you can see text only where there are no graphics.

Figure 4-23:
An example of stacked objects

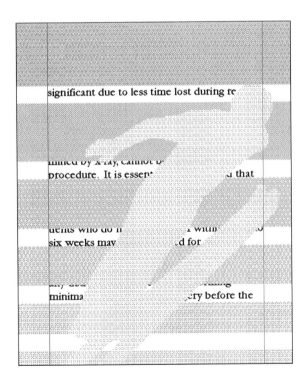

program on the day of the procedure. The cost of surgery is approximately 40% less than a conventional spinal surgery. The economic savings for the employee and employer are significant due to less time lost during recovery.

Unfortunately, patients who have free fragments of disc in the spinal canal, as determined by x-ray, cannot benefit from this procedure. It is essential to understand that all patients are not relieved of their pain with this procedure. Approximately 80 percent of patients have experienced pain relief. Patients who do not obtain relief within three to six weeks may be considered for microsurgical disc removal, depending on the circumstances. There does not appear to be any detrimental effect from performing minimally invasive spinal surgery before the microsurgical procedure to remove discs.

significant due to less time lost during re

mined by x-ray, cannot b
procedure. It is essen   that

dents who do n   within
six weeks may   d for

minima   ery before the

Selecting Elements

The action of "selecting" an element is a fundamental skill in the Macintosh interface. In most Macintosh software, you select an object by clicking it with some kind of pointer tool, usually an arrow. Once selected, the object is highlighted or marked in some way to provide a visual confirmation of its selection. Once you select an object, you can manipulate it with several of PageMaker's various menu, dialog, mouse, and keyboard features.

PageMaker employs these basic Macintosh selection concepts plus some more advanced ones. PageMaker has two independent levels of selection — selection of an object itself, such as a graphic or text block, and selection of text inside a text block. This section covers the selection of objects. Text selection is discussed in Chapter 6.

When you select an object, *handles* become visible around the object, as shown in the group of selected objects in Figure 4-24. A selected text block displays horizontal handlebars, often called *windowshades*, at the top and bottom with box handles at the four corners; a line, or rule, displays a box at each end; a shape displays eight solid boxes; and an imported graphic displays a solid diamond at each corner.

Figure 4-24:
Example of selected objects

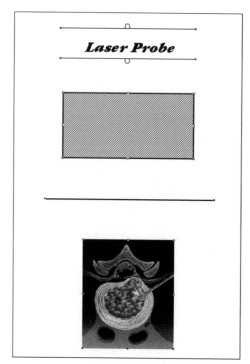

You select objects and groups of objects in a variety of ways:

∞ **Using the Pointer tool.** You can use the Pointer tool to select a single object, a group of objects, and objects that are partially or fully overlapped by other objects. (Note that in this discussion, "group of objects" refers to several objects selected at the same time, as opposed to "grouped objects" grouped with the Group command, discussed under "Grouping Objects," later in this section.)

To select a single object, select the Pointer tool from the Toolbox, and click anywhere on a text or graphic. You can select graphics created in PageMaker containing no fill (fills are discussed in Chapter 8) only by clicking their edges. As soon as you select an object, all other previously selected objects become deselected.

∞ To select more than one object, hold down the Shift key while selecting objects. This selects the new object, and the previous selection remains selected — the newly selected object is instead added to the selection, forming a group of objects.

Selecting objects in a stack: To select objects that are completely or partially overlapped by other objects (as shown in Figure 4-25), hold the Command key while clicking the overlapped object. Each mouse click selects the object one layer lower in the stacking order.

Figure 4-25:
An example of one object
completely overlaying another

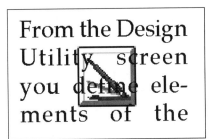

From the Design
Utility screen
you define ele-
ments of the

To select the underlying object, ⌘-click the overlaying object until the desired object is selected.

∞ **Marquee selecting.** Use the marquee selection method, shown in Figure 4-26, for selecting objects difficult to select by clicking them or for quickly selecting a group of objects.

A marquee is created by positioning the Pointer tool in a blank space in the publication window, holding down the mouse button, and then dragging the Pointer tool around the objects you want to select. As you do this, a dashed

Figure 4-26:
An example of marquee
selecting a group of objects

rectangle, called a marquee (because of the way the dashed line moves around the border) is displayed. All objects enclosed completely within the marquee become selected when you release the mouse button. Objects contained only partially within the marquee are not selected.

It's usually easy to determine when a graphic object is entirely contained within a marquee but more difficult to tell when a text block is completely contained, because the handles of a text block are not displayed unless the block is already selected, and these handles can extend left and right far beyond the text. When using the marquee to select text blocks, be sure to create a large enough marquee to enclose the entire text block.

When you select objects with a marquee, PageMaker deselects previously selected objects. If you hold down the Shift key while creating a marquee, the newly selected objects are added to the current selection — the previous selection is not deselected.

✎ **The Select All command.** The Select All command is a fast way to select a large number of objects or all objects on the page. As long as the Text tool is not selected, choosing the Select All command (⌘-A) from the Edit menu selects all objects on the currently displayed page(s) and on the pasteboard surrounding these pages (see Figure 4-27). If the text tool is selected and the text insertion point is in a text block, PageMaker selects all text in that text block. If the text tool is selected but the insertion point is not set within a text block, nothing happens. (Selecting text and text blocks are discussed in Chapters 6 and 7.)

Deselecting Elements

You should also know how to deselect objects so that you don't accidentally modify them or delete them.

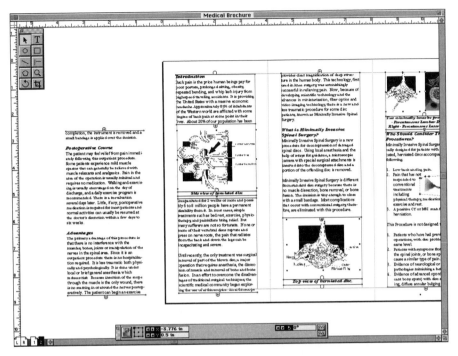

Figure 4-27: An example of selecting all elements in the publication window with Select All.

There are several ways to deselect an object or objects:

- **To deselect everything,** position the mouse cursor on any blank space in the publication window and click. All elements are deselected.

- **To deselect everything,** select any tool from the tool palette except the Rotation tool or Zoom tool. This immediately deselects all currently selected objects. The rotation tool doesn't deselect objects because it assumes that you want to rotate the selected objects.

- **To deselect some but not all objects,** hold down the Shift key and click the Pointer tool on a selected object. The object is deselected without affecting any other selected objects.

 Selecting many objects fast: This technique, in combination with either the Select all command or the marquee discussed earlier, makes it possible to select most (but not all) of the elements in an area or on a page quickly. To do this, create a marquee or use the Select all command to select all the objects in the area or page. Then, hold the Shift key and click the selected elements that you want to deselect.

Moving Elements

While creating a publication, you frequently reposition and adjust the placement of both text and graphic objects. It's not difficult to reposition elements. In fact, the interactive and impermanent nature of a PageMaker layout is one of its best features.

Before moving object(s), you must first select it (them), as described above. There are three ways of moving objects:

☞ **Dragging the object into position.** With the Pointer tool located anywhere on the selected object(s) except on one of the handles, click and hold the mouse button, then drag the object(s) to the new position. (Clicking a handle changes the *size* of an object, not its *position*.) If you hold the mouse button for a few seconds before moving the mouse, PageMaker displays the object as you move, rather than an outline, as shown in Figure 4-28. If you begin to move the mouse as soon as you press down the mouse button, you will see only a box marking the outline of the selected object(s).

Figure 4-28:
Example of outline move (right) when you move the mouse immediately and full-image move (left) when you hold the mouse a second or two before moving

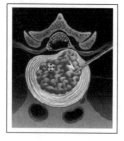
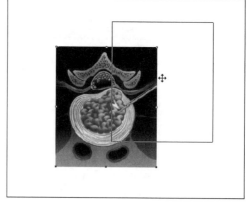

Constraining movements: Pressing the Shift key before or during a move constrains the movement either horizontally or vertically, depending on the initial direction you move the mouse. Use this technique to preserve the vertical alignment of an object while repositioning the object horizontally, or vice versa. You can also release the Shift key during a move to eliminate the constraint, or press the Shift key during an unconstrained move to add a constraint to the remainder of the move. If you inadvertently begin the move in the wrong direction, undo the move (⌘-Z) and begin a new, constrained move.

To position objects precisely, work at as large a view size as practical. Create vertical and horizontal ruler guides to indicate the new position before you move the object. Then use the Snap to guides and Snap to rulers commands from the Edit menu (discussed in "Rulers and Guides," earlier in this chapter) as necessary. If you get the element positioned precisely in one direction, press the Shift key to keep this alignment while continuing to adjust the position in the other direction.

Placing objects precisely: Another way to improve the precision of object placement is to work with the control palette, introduced in Chapter 9. Using the control palette, you can set the position numerically or position the element by moving it up, down, right, or left by a specific amount.

↪ **Arrow keys.** You can also move selected elements up and down and side to side with the arrow keys on your keyboard. The arrow keys "nudge" selected objects by just a few pixels. Use this method for making minute adjustments.

↪ **Cut and Paste.** To make dramatic moves, such as moving an element to a page not currently displayed, use the Cut and Paste commands from the Edit menu. After selecting the object(s), choose the Cut command (⌘-X) from the Edit menu. This removes the objects from the current page and places them on the Clipboard. Turn the page or adjust the display to the new location and then choose the Paste command (⌘-V) from the Edit menu. A copy of the object appears on the current page. You can now drag the object into position, using the techniques described above.

↪ **Dragging between pages.** To move objects between pages, drag them to the pasteboard, turn the page, then drag them into position on the new page. Be sure that the objects are positioned completely on the pasteboard before turning the page; otherwise, they remain on the original page.

Moving several objects quickly: The above method works well for moving large, complicated objects or to move an object or group of objects off the page when you are unsure where you will finally place them. Simply leave them on the pasteboard. Once you determine where they belong, you can select them and drag them into position.

↪ **Dragging between publications.** To move elements from one publication to another, open both publications and position their windows so that each is visible. You can use the Tile command in the Window menu to do this automatically. Select the elements you want to move and then drag them over to the other publication. As you drag to the edge of the first window, PageMaker starts to scroll the display, thinking at first that you want to position the selected elements elsewhere on the page or pasteboard. Continue dragging so that your cursor leaves the first window and is clearly positioned in the second. Release the mouse button when the elements are in position.

Grouping Objects

Often it's useful to have PageMaker treat several objects as one. Say, for example, you're creating a logo consisting of several text and graphics elements. Once you've finished tweaking and arranging objects, it would be helpful if you could select, move, resize the elements in the logo all at once. PageMaker's new Group command (located on the Arrange menu) to the rescue.

PageMaker treats grouped items as one unit. You can move and resize them all together. You can also make changes to like objects — such as, say, line weights in PageMaker-drawn shapes — all at once. To use Group, select two or more objects and then choose Group (⌘-G) from the Arrange menu. The grouped objects lose their autonomy and become one. Instead of bounding handles for each object, grouped objects are confined within one set of handles, as shown in Figure 4-29.

Figure 4-29:
Examples of ungrouped (top) and grouped objects (bottom)

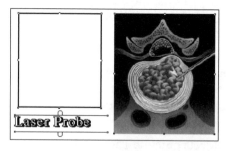

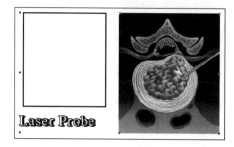

When objects are grouped, you can make certain specific changes to each item, but the changes occur only to objects on which the changes are applicable. In Figure 4-29, for example, you can edit the text by clicking with the Text tool in the text block (formatting and editing text are discussed in Chapters 5 and 6). You can change line weights and fills (see Chapter 8) of PageMaker-drawn shapes all at once, but text and imported graphics are not affected. When you resize objects, only items that can be resized normally with the Pointer tool or Control Palette (discussed in Chapter 9) are affected.

Using Group to maintain juxtaposition: Craig and I love Group. One of our favorite applications for this feature is to maintain the juxtaposition between objects. When a text block and graphic should always stay together with the same positioning, no matter where you move them in your publication, simply group them. Now, no matter where one goes the other follows.

To break apart grouped objects, simply select Ungroup (⌘-U) from the Arrange menu. Each object in the group regains its autonomy.

Locking Objects

Once you've got an object or group of objects formatted and positioned exactly the way you want them, you can use Lock Position (Ô-L) on the Arrange menu to rivet them to the page. Basically, locking object(s) in place allows you to select and work on the other items around them without inadvertently moving, resizing, or deleting the locked object.

When an object or grouped selection is locked, its handles change to gray. PageMaker allows you to make only very restricted changes to locked objects. For instance, you can change the fill and line weights of PageMaker-drawn shapes (discussed in Chapter 8), but you can't rotate, delete, or resize them. You can also edit and change text formatting (discussed in Chapters 5 and 6), but you cannot move or resize text blocks. In other words, PageMaker allows only changes that require several steps and are therefore most likely intentional. These properties also apply to grouped objects.

To unlock locked objects, choose Unlock (⌘-,) from the Arrange menu. You can now move them around and resize them as before.

Arranging Objects

In addition to aligning objects on guides and ruler tick marks, as discussed earlier in this chapter under "Guides and Rulers," PageMaker allows you to align a group of selected objects in relationship to each other with Align

Objects (⌘- -) on the Arrange menu. This is a quick and easy way to align objects without a lot of mousing around and eyeballing.

Choosing Align Objects brings up the Align Objects dialog box, shown in Figure 4-30. With this dialog box you can distribute objects with specified numeric values or align them in relation to left, right, bottom, top edges, or centers. Notice in the dialog box that there are two sets of buttons, horizontal and vertical. These groups of buttons are further categorized as either Align or Distribute.

Figure 4-30:
The Align Objects
dialog box

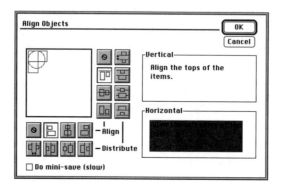

This dialog box provides extensive control over the alignment of selected objects. You use a combination of buttons and numerical values to get exactly the right alignment. The results of your selection are previewed in the window in the upper-left corner of the dialog box. Align buttons use the sides and centers of objects to align objects, and Distribute buttons use the numerical values you type in the right side of the dialog box, as well as the sides and centers of objects. When using the Align buttons, messages telling you what parameters will be used appear in a red box in the Horizontal (lower-right) area of the dialog box. When you use Distribute buttons, the Horizontal area changes to allow you to enter distribution values based on the default measurement system.

Each button shows which part of the selected objects PageMaker will use to align or distribute on, as shown in Figure 4-31. The lines on the buttons run through the area, edges or center, where PageMaker will align the objects. In Figure 4-31, PageMaker will align the objects vertically on their centers and distribute horizontally from their facing edges by the amount specified in the Horizontal field (not visible in the figure). If, for example, you enter .5 inches, PageMaker will place half an inch between each object, as shown in Figure 4-32.

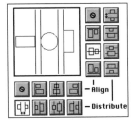

Figure 4-31:
The Align Objects dialog box vertical Align buttons signify how objects will be aligned.

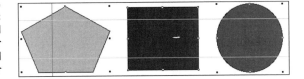

Figure 4-32:
Objects aligned vertically on their centers and distributed .5 inches from their facing edges

You can align or distribute objects in either direction. You can choose whether to distribute objects within their bounding area — the area within the bounding handles of all the selected objects. Or you can use a fixed amount, in which case PageMaker distributes the objects according to the values you enter. To use the first option, select Distribute within Bounds in either or both the Vertical and Horizontal areas of the dialog box. To use the second option, select Distribute Fixed Amount and then enter the desired value.

Cutting and Pasting Objects

By copying an object, you can ensure consistency in your publication while avoiding the effort of re-creating the object. This is especially useful for any graphic object whose consistent size is important, such as a line spanning the column width or boxes of a certain size around photographs or illustrations.

To duplicate an object or group of objects, select the object(s) and choose the Copy command (⌘-C) from the Edit menu. The Copy command is dimmed if no object is currently selected. Turn the page or adjust the view size, if necessary, and then choose the Paste command (⌘-V) from the Edit menu. The duplicate object(s) appears in the center of the current display, selected, and the Pointer tool is selected in the Toolbox. Drag the pasted object into position as desired.

When your publication makes frequent use of certain text or graphic objects, such as rules, photo boxes, or other objects, you can keep a copy of each on the pasteboard, copying it whenever you need it, as shown in Figure 4-33. This saves the time and trouble of searching through the publication for the last occurrence in order to make a copy every time one is needed.

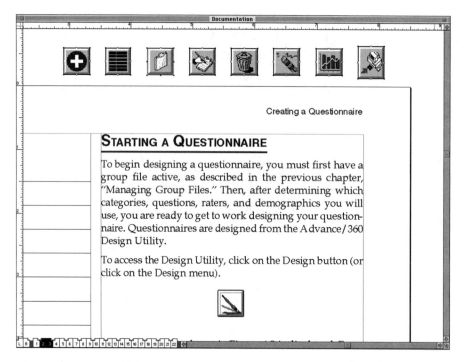

Figure 4-33: Keep often-used objects on the clipboard for easy access. Simply copy and paste them into your document as needed.

The Copy command makes a duplicate of all selected objects and places them on the Macintosh Clipboard. The Paste command *makes another duplicate* of the objects on the Clipboard and places the second copy on the displayed page. Since the original copy remains on the Clipboard, you can paste it repeatedly — until another object or group of objects is placed on the Clipboard with Cut or Copy. Objects remain on the Clipboard as long as your Macintosh is turned on, even after you quit PageMaker. Therefore, you don't have to paste objects immediately after copying — you can turn the page or reposition other elements. In fact, you can choose any command except Cut or Copy without disturbing the Clipboard contents.

The Library Palette

Another way to organize frequently used items is to store them in the Library palette, accessed via the Window menu. The Library palette can store any text or graphic element, and you can save libraries to disk or load existing libraries from disk. So you can use element collections for many different publications.

Moving an element or group of selected elements to the Library palette is easy: Just select the element(s) and click the plus sign button in the Library palette. If you want to give the elements a name or use keywords to help you search for them later, double-click on the copy of the element in the Library palette window.

To transfer any item from the Library palette back onto any page in your publication, turn to the appropriate page and then drag the element out of the Library palette and onto the page, and then release the mouse button. As you drag the cursor onto the page, your cursor appears as a "loaded gun" icon, indicating that you are about to place a new element on the page. Unlike other similar icons used by the Place command, however, this one releases the element when you let go of the mouse button rather than when you click it.

For more information on the Library palette, turn to Chapter 14.

Multiple Paste

The Multiple Paste command lets you make any number of copies of the current Clipboard objects and position them at a specified horizontal and vertical offset from the original objects. To use the Multiple paste command, select the objects you want to work with and then choose the Copy command. Next, choose the Multiple Paste command from the Edit menu and the Multiple Paste dialog box appears, as shown in Figure 4-34.

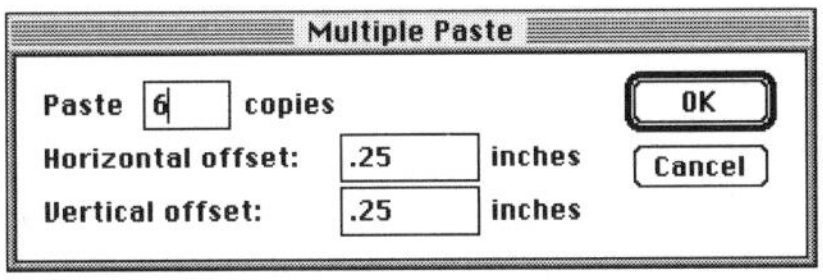

Figure 4-34:
The Multiple Paste dialog box

Multiple Paste
Paste 6 copies
Horizontal offset: .25 inches
Vertical offset: .25 inches
OK
Cancel

Enter the number of copies you want in the Paste field and then specify the horizontal and vertical offset you want applied to *each* of your copies. Selecting a horizontal offset of .25 inch and a vertical offset of .25 inch, for example, results in the multiple paste effect shown in Figure 4-35. Note that you cannot specify a horizontal or vertical offset when using the Multiple Paste command with text.

Automatic multiple pastes: Holding down the Option key while choosing the Multiple Paste command executes the multiple paste without opening the Multiple Paste dialog box. The settings entered the last time the dialog box was used are applied.

To perform a manual version of the multiple paste, select any objects and copy them to the Clipboard. Then press ⌘-Option-V to paste one copy. Drag this copy to a new location and then press ⌘-Option-V repeatedly to paste subsequent copies. Each will be placed at the same horizontal and vertical offset as the first copy that you positioned manually.

Deleting Elements

You can delete selected elements in three ways:

- ☞ Choose the Cut command (⌘-X) from the Edit menu. This removes the selected objects, but places them on the Clipboard so that you can paste them somewhere else. If you choose the Cut command by mistake, choose the Undo command (⌘-Z) from the Edit menu to restore the deleted object(s).

- ☞ Choose the Clear command from the Edit menu. This removes the selected objects but does not place them on the Clipboard. This is often used when you need to delete an object or group of objects but do not want to lose the current Clipboard contents. If you choose the Clear command by mistake, choose the Undo command (⌘-Z) from the Edit menu to restore the deleted object(s).

- ☞ Press the Backspace or Delete key on your keyboard. This is equivalent to choosing the Clear command. The deleted objects are *not* placed on the Macintosh Clipboard, but you can still restore them by choosing the Undo command (⌘-Z) from the Edit menu. You can also use this option when you need to delete an object or group of objects but do not wish to lose the current Clipboard contents.

Undo and Revert

"I wish I hadn't done that." For all the times that you find yourself thinking these words, PageMaker provides two special commands: Undo and Revert. These commands reverse the last action or series of actions performed on your document. PageMaker also provides a hidden command called Revert to mini-save, which you can use when the Revert command is too dramatic.

Undo

The Undo command (⌘-Z) on the Edit menu reverses the last action taken in your publication. Not all actions can be reversed, but most actions that affect the layout of your publication or its contents can, including any actions that do not have a built-in opposite action.

You can use the Undo command to cancel the following:

- ∽ The repositioning of text or graphic object or guide.
- ∽ The resizing of any text block or graphic.
- ∽ The cropping of any imported graphic.
- ∽ Any use of the Cut or Copy command. (You undo the Paste command by simply deleting the pasted objects.)
- ∽ Changes made in the Insert pages, Remove Pages, or Page Setup dialog boxes.

You **cannot** use the Undo command to cancel the following:

- ∽ Any changes made using commands from the Type menu.
- ∽ Any changes made using the Lines or Fill commands.
- ∽ Changes in view size or display.
- ∽ Selections or deselections of objects.
- ∽ Any use of the Save or Revert commands.

To use the Undo command (⌘-Z), simply choose it from the Edit menu. The most important thing about using the Undo command is that you must use it *immediately* after you perform the undesired action. Since the Undo command can reverse only your last action, *any* action taken, however minor, makes it impossible to reverse your mistaken action. For example, suppose that you move some objects by dragging them with the Pointer tool and then decide that you are unhappy with the new position and want to return them to their original position. You must choose the Undo command as soon as you release the mouse button after dragging the objects — if you click the mouse button or choose another tool from the Toolbox, you can no longer reverse the relocation of the objects. The Undo command simply deselects the tool you have clicked.

When the last action performed is reversible with Undo, the Undo command reads Undo *action*, where the word *action* specifies the particular action that PageMaker can undo. When PageMaker cannot reverse the last action, the Undo command is dimmed.

Immediately after you use Undo and your last action is reversed, the Undo command becomes the Redo command — allowing you to negate your use of the Undo command. The Redo command reads Redo *action,* where the word *action* specifies the particular action PageMaker can undo. Several examples are shown in Figure 4-36. After you choose the Redo command (⌘-Z) from the Edit menu, the Undo command *reappears* — you can then reverse the action of the Redo command, again undoing the original action (which was just redone).

Figure 4-36:
Some examples of the Undo and Redo options

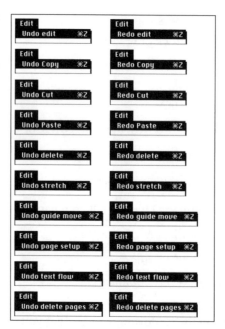

Revert

Suppose that you make several changes to your document. After making these changes, you decide that the publication looked better before the changes. Since you have performed several actions, you cannot use the Undo command to restore it. You may not even remember precisely how the document looked. But PageMaker does. The Revert command returns your document to its exact form immediately following the last save with the Save command *or* the last mini-save (discussed next). This is useful when you have made important changes to your document that you now regret, such as deleting pages or important elements, editing text content, or rearranging page elements.

Mini-saves are performed automatically whenever you turn the page in your publication, click the current page icon, change the page setup specifications, or click OK in the Define Styles dialog box. PageMaker stores mini-save information in a temporary file on your disk.

 Returning the last mini-save: To revert to the last mini-save, hold down the Shift key and choose the Revert command from the File menu. The Revert to last mini-save? dialog box asks you to confirm your selection.

Once you have reverted to the version of the last mini-save, you cannot return to the version of the document prior to choosing the Revert command. If you are sure that you want to revert, click the OK button; if not, click the Cancel button. If you click OK, your document is restored to the version saved in the last mini-save. If you perform a mini-save after turning a page, PageMaker returns you to the page displayed just prior to the mini-save.

If the mini-saved version doesn't take you far enough back, you can execute a regular Revert to return to the version saved by your last Save. Choose the Revert command from the File menu (without holding down the Shift key). A Revert to last-saved version? dialog box asks you to confirm your selection.

Once you have reverted to the last saved version, you cannot return to the version of the document prior to choosing the Revert command. If you are sure that you want to revert, click the OK button; if not, click the Cancel button. If you click OK, your document is restored to the version saved by the last Save command.

If you have not saved your document since opening it, the document is returned to the version you opened. On a new document that has never been saved and titled, the Revert command is dimmed.

Working with Master Pages _____

Few of PageMaker's features are more powerful and save you more time than master pages. (And PageMaker 6 supports unlimited *multiple* master pages!) Basically, master pages hold text, graphics, and column and ruler guides that repeat on several pages throughout the document. By default, anything that you add to a master page automatically appears on every page formatted with that master page. Positioning these items on master pages, rather than on each individual page, maintains consistency, saves you from having to repeat basic page formatting for each page, and minimizes file size.

Why use master pages: Think of master pages as underlying formatting or stencils. This book, for example, contains running headers displaying section names on left pages and chapter names on right pages. Page numbers are on all pages. Imagine the hassle of having to place these elements on each of the several hundred pages in this book. Now think of some the other long documents you've seen. Some are quite fancy, with many repeating elements from page to page. How'd you like to place each element, page by page?

Figure 4-37 shows a facing-pages spread from a software manual. Imagine having to draw each line in the outer column on each new page, or even cutting and pasting from one page to the next. Thank goodness for master pages.

Common uses for master pages include:

- **Headers and footers.** Master pages often carry running headers or footers, which include graphics lines (rules), chapter and book titles, page numbers, repeating graphics, and other design elements.

- **Design grids.** Design layout grids consisting of margin guides, column guides, and ruler guides. Placing these guides on master pages displays them automatically on all document pages, saving you from having to create the grid on each page in your document. Guides are discussed earlier in this chapter in the "Guides and Rulers" section.

- **Repeating elements.** Page borders and common graphic elements, such as company logos, are often positioned on master pages.

Each PageMaker publication begins with one or two master pages, known as Document Master, represented by the L (left master page) and R (right master page) icons in the lower-left corner of the publication window, shown in Figure 4-38. Single-sided publications, which contain only right pages, have only a right master page. Double-sided pages have both left and right master pages.

To place text, graphics, or guidelines on a master page, select the master page icon in the publication window. Master pages look and act exactly like all other pages in a publication. You can create text on master pages (using the Text tool) or import word processor files (using the Place... command). You can create graphics on master pages (using one of PageMaker's graphic tools) or import graphics in various graphics formats

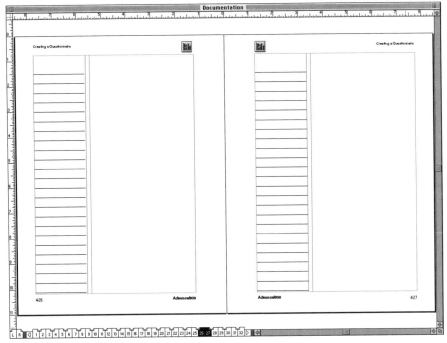

Figure 4-37: Example of pages formatted from master pages

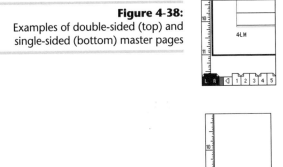

Figure 4-38:
Examples of double-sided (top) and
single-sided (bottom) master pages

(using the Place… command). You can also edit text and graphics the same as on publication pages. (Note that if you don't know how to create and import text and graphics, you should first read the specific chapters relating to those topics.)

Working with Multiple Master Pages

Many documents do not contain pages or spreads based on just one underlying design. In a book, for instance, the first pages of chapters seldom contain the same elements as the rest of the pages. Magazines and newspapers often change column formatting from page to page. Before PageMaker's support for multiple master pages, you had to base all of your pages on one basic design. To create pages of a design different from the master pages, you either had to turn off the display of master items (discussed a bit later in this section) and create new pages manually, mask off master items with PageMaker's shape tools, or create another document with different master pages.

Multiple master pages allow you to create several different master pages for the same document. Master pages are controlled from the Master Pages palette (shown in Figure 4-39), which you display by choosing Master Pages from the Window menu.

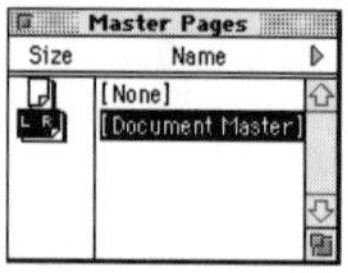

Figure 4-39:
The Master Pages palette

As shown in the figure, each PageMaker document starts with default Document Master (or a master spread in publications containing double-sided facing pages) and None (no master page) master icons. Clicking one or the other icon affects the formatting for the current page(s). Document Master applies the formatting from the default master pages, and None removes master page formatting. Note that until you change the basic Document Master formatting — in Document Setup or by choosing Setup from the Master Pages palette menu, shown in Figure 4-40 — Document Master maintains the basic page formatting set in Document Setup when starting the document, which is discussed in Chapter 1.

Figure 4-40:
The Master Pages palette menu

To change the Document Master formatting, choose Setup... from the Master Pages palette menu, which brings up the Master Page Setup dialog box. From here, you can set margins and columns.

Creating New Master Pages

Each time you want to change the master page formatting for a group of pages, you can easily do so by creating a new master page or master page spread. To create a new master page, simply choose New Master... from the Master Pages palette flyout menu. This brings up the Create New Master Pages dialog box, shown in Figure 4-41. From here you can name the new master page, set margins and columns, and define the new master as either single-sided or double-sided. When you click OK, the new master page(s) appear in the Master Pages palette, as shown in Figure 4-42.

Figure 4-41:
The Create New Master Page dialog box

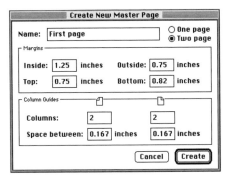

Figure 4-42:
The Master Pages palette displaying a new set of master pages

Note that the default settings in the Create New Master Page dialog match those for Document Master. Note also that when creating new master pages you have the option of making the new master a single or double page, an option you do not have when setting up Document Master pages. For Document Master pages, single-sided and double-sided pages are defined from Document setup... on the File menu. The Document setup feature is discussed in Chapter 1.

Create masters based on existing masters: Often publication pages vary only slightly. Each section, for example, may require only different section names in the headers. In this case, it's often easier to base new master pages on existing masters. In this case you can use the Duplicate... option on the Master Pages palette menu to create copies of any master in the document. Then you make only the changes needed, rather than starting from scratch. Duplicate... brings up the Duplicate Master Page dialog box, shown in Figure 4-43. From here you can choose the master page you want to duplicate (the dialog box opens displaying the master highlighted when you invoked the option) and title the duplicate.

Figure 4-43:
The Duplicate Master Page
dialog box

> **Duplicate Master Page**
>
> Duplicate: [Cover Page Spread]
>
> Name of new Master: [   ]
>
> [Cancel] [[Duplicate]]

Applying Master Pages

To apply master pages to the current page(s), simply click the icons or name of the desired master in the Master Pages palette. The active document pages assume the formatting of the master. If you apply a right single page master to a spread, PageMaker applies the master to both pages. In other words, if you apply a right master page to a spread, only the right page in the spread assumes the formatting. Conversely, if you apply a double-page master to a single-page, the Page assumes the right page formatting.

Apply master pages as you add new pages: You can also apply master pages as you insert pages into your document with the Insert Pages... command on the Layout menu. When you choose Insert Pages..., PageMaker displays the Insert Pages dialog box. One of the options in Insert Pages is Master Page, as shown in Figure 4-44, which allows you to designate which master to apply to the pages as PageMaker inserts them. You can apply different masters to right and left pages by selecting the Set left and right pages separately option, as shown in Figure 4-45, which allows you to create different masters for the right-hand and left-hand pages.

Figure 4-44:
The Insert Pages dialog box

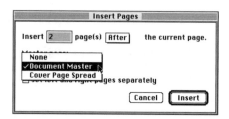

Figure 4-45:
The Insert Pages dialog box
with the Set left and right
pages separately option
selected

> **Insert Pages**
>
> Insert [2] page(s) [After]   the current page.
>
> Left master page: Right master page:
>
> [Document Master] □□ [Cover Page Spread]
>
> ☒ Set left and right pages separately
>
> [Cancel] [[Insert]]

You can apply master pages to a range of existing pages with the Apply... option on the Master Pages palette menu, which brings up the Apply Master dialog box shown in Figure 4-46. With this you specify a range of pages to which to apply the master and the specific master you want to apply. (The dialog box opens displaying the master selected when the option is invoked.) You can also apply different master pages to right and left pages by selecting the Set left and right pages separately option, as shown in Figure 4-47.

Figure 4-46:
The Apply Master dialog box

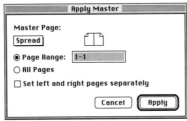

Figure 4-47:
The Apply Master dialog box
with the Set left and right pages
separately option selected

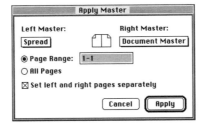

Creating Master Pages from Document Pages

Often we forget to set up master pages and begin basic formatting on document pages. Or sometimes we just want to turn a document page into a master page. PageMaker allows you to do so with the Save Page as... option on the Master Pages palette menu. Save Page as... opens the Save Page as Master dialog box, which lets you name the new master page. To use this option, turn to the page you want to create a master page from, select Save Page as... from the Master Pages palette flyout menu, and then name the new master page.

If the document page you are copying to a master is a single page, PageMaker creates a single master page. For spreads, PageMaker creates a double-sided master.

Deleting Master Pages

To delete master pages from the Master Pages palette, simply choose Delete... from the Master Pages palette menu. The Delete Master Page dialog box is displayed, allowing you to choose the master page you want to delete. (The default is the master page selected when the Delete... option is invoked.) Pages formatted with the deleted master page assume the formatting of Document Master.

Page Numbering

PageMaker bases its automatic page-numbering on master pages. Automatic page numbering creates running page numbers from page to page and renumbers them as you add, sort, and delete pages. To do this, you create a text block as usual by selecting the text tool from the Tool palette and then clicking the page to set the insertion point. (Complete details on working with the text tool and creating new text blocks are provided in the next chapter.) Once the insertion point is set (the I-beam cursor flashes), press ⌘-Option-P. A page number placeholder appears. The placeholder, shown in Figure 4-48, is displayed as a page number if you set the page number on any page except a master page, LM if you set the page number on the left master page, RM if you set the page number on the right master page, or PB if you set the page number on the pasteboard.

Figure 4-48:
Examples of page
number markers and
page numbers

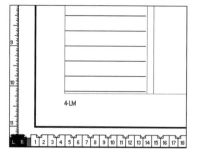

The page-number placeholder that appears on the master page is replaced by the actual page number on every page in the publication formatted with a master page containing the page number marker. The type of page number — Arabic, Roman numerals, etc. — depends on the numbering system set in the Numbering option nested in Document Setup, as discussed in Chapter 1.

Auto-numbering double-sided pages: When creating a double-sided publication, you must add the automatic page-numbering character to both the right and left master pages. In many cases, you can save time by first creating the text block for the page number on one master page and then copying that text block and pasting it onto the other master page. The automatic page-numbering marker automatically switches from LM to RM (or vice versa) when placed on the second master page.

By the same token, when using multiple master pages, each master in the document where you want page numbers must include the page number markers. The best way to make sure you get number markers on all pages is to use Duplicate... on the Master Pages palette to create new master pages.

Master Items on Publication Pages

Once you format and add elements to master page(s), they appear on the corresponding publication pages and print exactly as though they were added to the pages directly. On publication pages, master-page elements cannot be selected — they are inaccessible, as if already printed on the paper.

You can't move, delete, or edit *individual* master-page elements while working on a publication page; however, you can hide *all* master-page elements on a publication page. Once hidden, they neither display nor print. To hide master page items on the current page(s), choose Display master items on the Layout menu, which toggles the display of master-page elements on and off. This is commonly used to suppress running footers and page numbers on the first page of a chapter or section.

Guides and Master Pages

Another valuable use of master pages is to create a placement grid from ruler, margin, and column guides. Unlike text and graphic elements, guides on master pages can be repositioned or even deleted on each individual publication page. Manipulating guides on any one publication page does not affect guides as they appear on the master pages or on any other publication page. Manipulating guides directly on the master pages, however, changes those guides as they appear on every publication page *except* those on which the guidelines have been customized.

Guides are discussed in "Guides and Rulers," earlier in this chapter.

Printing Master Pages

To print just the items on a master page, create a blank publication page, make sure that the Display Master Items command is selected, and print the blank page. This has the effect of printing only the elements of the corresponding master page. You cannot print master pages directly. If you delete all of the pages in your publication, the master pages remain intact — but at that point you cannot print them.

Summary

- In addition to the Zoom tool, PageMaker has eight standard view sizes, accessible from the View submenu or by using keyboard or mouse equivalents.

- You can move around a page with the grabber hand (Option-mouse), scroll bars, or by changing view sizes.

- You can turn pages in your publications using the page icons, Go to page command (Layout menu), or keyboard equivalent (⌘-Tab).

- You can add or delete pages with the Insert Pages... and Remove Pages... commands (Layout menu).

- Column guides help you control the flow of text; ruler guides help you align manually positioned elements.

- Ruler tick marks change to display the best possible accuracy of the current view size. The ruler zero intersection point can be reset by dragging the zero-point marker from the intersection of the horizontal and vertical rulers.

- Text and graphic elements appear on PageMaker pages in a stacking order determined by the order in which elements are added and the use of the Send to Front and Send to Back commands (Arrange menu).

- You can backtrack your work using the Undo and Revert commands.

- Guides, text, and graphic elements placed on master pages appear on all other publication pages.

Learning PageMaker

This section covers the most-central PageMaker tasks, the creation and manipulation of text and graphics. Topics include importing text, creating text in PageMaker, using the Story Editor, creating style sheets to automate text formatting and using templates to automate formatting publications. We cover creating graphics and importing images, as well as discussing other kinds of graphic manipulations. The chapters in Part II represent the heart of PageMaker. Experienced users should pay particular attention to Chapter 6, which covers PageMaker's little-understood advanced typographic features, and Chapter 9, which focuses on the Control palette, a highly useful formatting tool. By the same token, beginning users may want to just skim these chapters at first and come back to them later after getting more experience with the fundamentals.

Working with Text

In This Chapter

- Understanding stories and text blocks
- Importing text from word processing files
- PageMaker import filters
- Creating text in PageMaker
- The PageMaker Story Editor
- Exporting text from PageMaker

Text is the most basic element in any publication, and PageMaker provides a great many tools to help you create, manipulate, and control text. In fact, PageMaker has so many text-related capabilities that it is going to take three full chapters to describe them all in detail.

Text in PageMaker

This chapter focuses on text acquisition and creation: how you import text that was first created in a word processor into PageMaker, and how you can create text directly in a publication window or using the Story Editor.

Chapter 6 is devoted to editing and manipulating text after it is a part of your publication. This includes all character and paragraph formatting, as well as tabs, hyphenation, and all aspects of precision typography. Finally, in Chapter 7 you'll learn about style sheets, a great text-formatting shortcut that not only saves time and effort but improves the quality of just about any document.

Stories and Text Blocks

When you open the newspaper to read the latest gossip about those crazy Hollywood celebrities, you know that if the story that begins on page one doesn't fit entirely on that page, you have to turn to another page to read the rest of the juicy details. This familiar situation can be used to introduce three terms that are critical to your work with text in PageMaker: story, text block, and threading.

The *story* is the entire collection of information — even though it starts on one page and ends on another. The *text blocks* are the pieces of the story on each different page. And *threading* is the linkage between the text block that holds the first part of the story and the text block that holds the end of the story. Figure 5-1 illustrates threading.

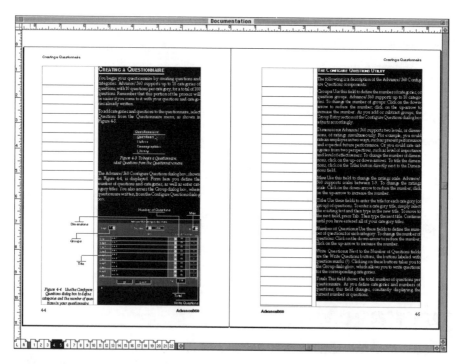

Figure 5-1: This story flows throughout this chapter, from page to page.

Of course, a story won't always fit in just two text blocks — the Amy Fisher letters ran over 20 different pages in the *Irrational Inquirer*, for example. On the other hand, a short margin note or a figure caption can be a complete story in just a sentence or two. The defining factor is the number of threaded text blocks that contain the story; if it all fits in one text block, that's a story. If it threads through hundreds of text blocks on hundreds of pages, that's a story, too.

Text blocks act in many ways like other on-screen objects you saw in Chapter 4 — you can move, resize, or delete them. PageMaker automatically creates text blocks when text is imported, entered in the publication window, or transferred from the Story Editor into the publication window. (You'll learn all the details of creating text blocks as we progress through this chapter.)

If an entire story cannot fit in a text block, it is threaded to another text block, as shown in Figure 5-2. The process of threading text through multiple text blocks can be done manually, or it can be done automatically. Usually, text that flows through multiple text blocks starts at the top of one column or page, ends at the bottom of the text block, and threads to the top of another text block in the next column or on the next page. It then continues, from the bottom of one text block to the top of another, until the entire story is in position. You can tell when a text block is threaded to another because of the plus (+) symbol in the windowshade handles, as shown in the figure. A plus symbol in the top handle indicates that a text block is threaded to a block before the one selected, and a plus symbol in a bottom handle means that a text block is threaded to a later text block.

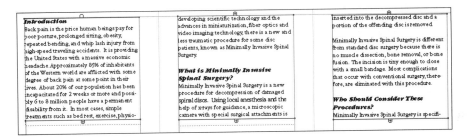

Figure 5-2: An example of a story threaded through several text blocks. Notice the plus symbols indicating the threaded blocks.

Changing the Size of a Text Block

When you select a text block (by clicking it with the Pointer tool), windowshades appear at the top and bottom of the block, marking the block's beginning, end, and width. Each windowshade has two handles, which appear as block dots at either end. Dragging a windowshade handle resizes the text block. As you drag one of these handles, a box representing the new text block size is displayed (see Figure 5-3). When you release the mouse button, the text inside the block reflows to fill the new text block size.

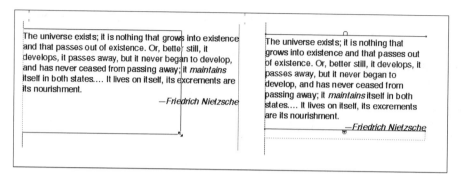

Figure 5-3: An example of dragging on windowshade handles to resize a text block

Each text block windowshade has a *tab* (shown in Figure 5-4), which sometimes displays a symbol that provides information about the text block. When more text appears than is shown in a text block, a plus sign (+) or downward arrow appears in the tab in the lower windowshade. A plus sign appears when text in the current block flows to another text block. A down arrow appears when there is text that does not fit in the current text block but has not yet been flowed into another text block. Clicking the plus sign or down arrow in a tab reloads the text flow icon (described later in this chapter) so that the text that does not fit in the text block can be placed as other text blocks.

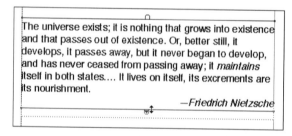

Figure 5-4: An example of dragging on the windowshade handles to change the size and position of the text block

Dragging a windowshade tab, by pressing and holding down the mouse button while dragging the mouse, allows you to change the position of the text in the text block in the following manners:

> ✐ **Dragging the top handle upward or downward** changes the vertical positioning of the first line in the text block. All text in the story moves upward or downward. This reflows all the text blocks in the story, potentially making new text visible or leaving some text unplaced at the bottom of the last text block in the story.

- ☞ **Dragging the lower handle upward** shortens the text block, hiding all text below the lower handle to the end of the block. If this is not the last text block in the story, the hidden text appears at the top of the next text block, and all text flows through all subsequent text blocks.

- ☞ **Dragging the lower handle downwards** lengthens the text block, displaying additional text in the text block when you release the mouse button. If this is not the last text block in the story, the new text flows back from the top of the next text block, and all text in the story reflows appropriately. If no more text remains in the document, the tab in the lower windowshade is empty, and dragging the windowshade downward has no effect — when you release the mouse button, the handle returns to its previous position below the end of text.

You can also change the size of a text block and perform most of the other manipulations described in this chapter, using the PageMaker Control palette. The Control palette is covered in detail in Chapter 9.

If the size of one of the text blocks containing the story is changed (by moving either one of the text block windowshades or text block handles), then the text in the story reflows, adjusting to the new size of each text block. As a result, a change in the size of one text block can affect the position of all of the text in a story. The way in which text is affected by resizing a text block depends on the modification, as described below:

- ☞ **If the bottom of one text block is moved up two lines**, those two lines appear at the top of the next block, and every block in the thread gains two lines at the top and loses two lines at the bottom. If the last text block cannot hold all the lines of text, the downward arrow appears in the lower windowshade tab when that block is selected. You can either lengthen the block to accommodate the remaining text or pour the remaining text into a new text block.

- ☞ **If the bottom is moved down two lines**, two lines are pulled from the top of the following text block. In the second text block, all the text moves up two lines, and two more lines are pulled from the third text block, and so on. If this process causes all of the text in any one text block to be pulled to the text block that precedes it, that (now empty) text block is automatically deleted.

- ☞ **If text is cut out of the middle of a text block**, all lines throughout the story and all its threads that are located below the cut move up to fill the void. Any text block that loses all its text to the preceding text block is automatically deleted.

- ☞ **If text is inserted in the middle of a text block**, all lines throughout the story and all its threads move down to create space for the new text. If the last text block cannot fit all lines that flow into it, the down arrow appears in the lower windowshade tab when that block is selected. You can either lengthen the block to accommodate the remaining text or pour the remaining text into a new text block.

◦ **If one text block in a threaded story is deleted,** the links remain active between all remaining text blocks, just as if the deleted text block had never existed.

Moving a Text Block

You can reposition a text block by dragging it to any new location. Just select the Pointer tool from the Toolbox, point the arrow cursor inside the text block, press and hold the mouse button, then drag the text block to its new position. If you drag the text block into one of the edges of the display, your publication scrolls automatically. If you hold down the Shift key while you drag, your movement is constrained either vertically or horizontally, which is determined by the direction you first move the mouse.

Getting a better view as you drag: If you hold down the mouse button for a second or two before you begin to drag, PageMaker lets see your text as you reposition it, as shown in Figure 5-5. If you begin dragging immediately after clicking the mouse button, you will see only a box marking the outline of your text block.

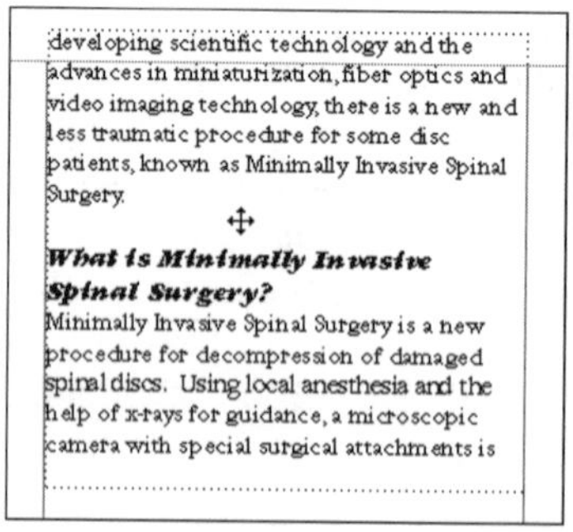

Figure 5-5:
An example of dragging a text block after clicking and holding before you drag; you get a full view of the text block as it moves.

developing scientific technology and the advances in miniaturization, fiber optics and video imaging technology, there is a new and less traumatic procedure for some disc patients, known as Minimally Invasive Spinal Surgery.

✛

What is Minimally Invasive Spinal Surgery?
Minimally Invasive Spinal Surgery is a new procedure for decompression of damaged spinal discs. Using local anesthesia and the help of x-rays for guidance, a microscopic camera with special surgical attachments is

Move a text block with Cut and Paste: You can also move a text block using the Cut and Paste commands, but this will sever the text block from the rest of its story. In other words, text no longer flows from any preceding or to any following text blocks. While this is usually undesirable, there are times when you will want to sever a text block from its story, and using Cut and Paste allows you to do this.

To move a text block from one page to another, drag the text block onto the pasteboard, turn to the desired page, and then drag the text block into its new position. This will not affect the text block's position in any threaded story.

Combining Text Blocks

One of the important rules you should learn about text blocks is that you don't want any more of them than you need. This is true for a variety of reasons, including the fact that extra text blocks often come back to haunt you at print time and that beginners tend to create a great many unthreaded text blocks in situations where a few threaded ones would be much easier to manage and manipulate.

If you ever find that you have two, three, or even four text blocks where just one would do, there are three different ways you can combine them:

- Use the Text tool to select the text in the last block and cut it with the Cut command (⌘-X). Now set the text insertion point at the end of the preceding text block, enter one space character by pressing the spacebar, and paste the text from the Clipboard with the Paste command (⌘-V). Repeat this process until all undesired text blocks have been removed and all the text is in a single text block.

- Use the Pointer tool to select the last text block in the sequence and cut it out with the Cut command (⌘-X). Now set the text insertion point at the end of the preceding text block, enter one space character by pressing the spacebar, and paste the text from the Clipboard with the Paste command (⌘-V). Repeat this process until all undesired text blocks have been removed and all the text is in a single text block.

- Use the Pointer tool to select the last text block in the sequence and choose the Send to Back command (⌘-B) from the Element menu. Now hold down the Shift key and select the second to last text block (so you have two text blocks selected) and again choose the Send to Back command from the Element menu. Repeat this process, selecting additional text blocks with the Shift key and sending the entire group to the back, until all the text blocks you want to combine have been selected. Now choose the Cut command (⌘-X) and then select the Text tool and set the insertion point to create a new text block. Choose the Paste command, and the text from all of the text blocks you selected and cut should be placed in the next text block. The text from the text blocks should be in the same order it was originally, but check carefully for any transposition.

Importing Text

Let's get one thing clear — PageMaker is not a very good word processor. While it has extensive typographic tools, and its Story Editor is a word processor of sorts, you are better off doing your word processing in a true word processing package and then importing your text into PageMaker. Don't let anyone tell you differently.

You can use just about any word processor you like. PageMaker can import text from every popular Macintosh, DOS, and Windows word processor. And it imports this text while maintaining all character and paragraph formatting applied in the word processor. In most cases, it even imports attached style sheets. (Style sheets are shortcut lists of text formats — they are described in detail in Chapter 7.)

The process of importing text into PageMaker goes something like this:

1. You choose the Place... command from the File menu.

2. You select the text file you want to import.

3. The text import filter that corresponds to the file you selected converts the file into a format PageMaker can use.

4. A progress dialog box displays the import process.

5. If the file includes any fonts that are not currently available on your Mac, the PANOSE font matching dialog box appears, allowing you to choose replacement fonts.

6. A text flow cursor then appears, indicating that the file has been imported and allowing you to position the file within your publication.

Each of these steps is reviewed in detail in the following sections.

The Place... Command

You import text into PageMaker using Place... from the File menu. Choosing Place... (⌘-D) brings up the Place document dialog box (see Figure 5-6), where you select the word processing file you want to import. You can also select any existing PageMaker 5 or PageMaker 6 publication, if you want to import stories that are used within that publication.

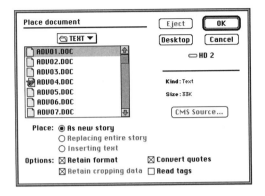

Figure 5-6:
The Place document
dialog box.

The Place document dialog box lists every text or graphic file that PageMaker can import from the current folder. If a file you want to import is not listed, either it is not in the current folder, or it is saved in a file format that is incompatible with PageMaker. More precisely, it is currently saved in a file format for which an import filter is not currently installed. As you'll learn later in this chapter, under "Import File Filters," you can solve this problem either by installing the correct import filter or by converting the file to a format that does correspond to an available import filter.

If you want to import a file stored in another folder or on another drive, you can locate the file using the standard Macintosh dialog box navigation methods:

- ☞ To open a folder, double-click it.

- ☞ To close a folder, press ⌘-up arrow.

- ☞ To close a folder, select another from the menu under the current folder name.

- ☞ To close a folder, click the current drive name.

- ☞ To close all folders, click the Desktop button.

- ☞ To move to the next drive, press ⌘-right arrow.

- ☞ To move to the previous drive, press ⌘-left arrow.

Once you've located the file you want to place, select its filename. If you have selected a text file, the first Place option will read "As new story." If a graphic file has been selected, the option will read "As independent graphic" or "As new graphic." The second and third Place options are used to replace or insert text, as described later in this chapter under "Importing Text into or over an Existing Story."

At the bottom of the dialog box are four text placement options, three of which are discussed here:

- **Retain format**. This option instructs PageMaker to convert and utilize the existing paragraph and character formatting, such as tabs, bolds, italics, extra carriage returns, and so on. If it is not selected, existing character and paragraph formatting is stripped from the file as it is imported. The Retain format option is automatically selected for files from known word processors.

- **Convert quotes**. This option causes PageMaker to scan the text file to change straight double quotation marks (") into typesetting (opening and closing) quotation marks (" and ").

- **Read tags**. This option causes PageMaker to look for *style tags* in the imported file. Style tags are the names of PageMaker styles placed between the characters < and > at the beginning of paragraphs in the word processor files. When PageMaker finds a style tag, it formats the paragraph using the current formatting defined by that style. If this option is not selected, PageMaker treats tags as normal text and prints each tag character: <tag name>. Style sheets and tags are discussed in Chapter 7.

When the file you want to import has been selected, and all options correctly set, click the OK button, double-click the filename, or press Enter or Return to proceed. PageMaker then reads the file from disk, converts it using the appropriate import filter, and prepares to position the text into your publication.

Import File Filters

In order for PageMaker to import text from a word processor, the text must be stored in a file format compatible with one of PageMaker's import filters. *Import filters* are small conversion routines that PageMaker uses to convert the text and formatting from a word processing file into a format that PageMaker can use. A complete list of the text import filters included with PageMaker is shown in the list below:

- ASCII (text only & tagged text)
- DCA/RFT
- ClarisWorks 1.0-3.0
- MacWrite II
- MacWrite Pro 1.0
- Microsoft Excel 3.0-5.0

- Microsoft Word (Mac) 3.0-6.0, (DOS) 3.0-5.0, (Windows) 6.0

- Microsoft Works 2.0-3.0

- PageMaker stories 5.0-6.0

- Rich Text Format (RTF)

- WordPerfect (Mac) 2.x-3.0 (DOS & Windows) 4.2-6.x

- WriteNow 3.0

- XyWrite III or III+

- Tagged text

- Text only

These import filters are kept in the RSRC folder inside the Filters folder in your Adobe PageMaker 6.0 folder. They are installed automatically along with PageMaker, as discussed in Appendix A, but you can copy additional filters to this folder anytime. New import filters are sometimes sent out by Adobe, or you can get them from the Adobe forum on CompuServe (GO ADOBE) or eWorld.

 Finding out what filters are installed: To check which filters are installed in your Filters folder, hold down the Command key and choose the About PageMaker command from the Apple menu.

If you have a file from a word processor not supported by PageMaker, you can almost always convert the file into the format of a supported word processor or save the file as a text-only (ASCII) file. First try to use the Save as command in the word processor to save the file in the format of another popular word processor or into an industry standard file format like DCA (document common architecture) or RTF (rich text format). If this is not possible, you can use a utility like MacLink Plus, which is shown in Figure 5-7, or the MacLink Translators to convert the file. Programs of this type support conversion between hundreds of Mac and PC file formats for word processors, spreadsheets, databases, and graphics programs.

Import filters do their work after you have clicked OK in the Place document dialog box. For the most part, these conversions are handled automatically, but a few of the filters, including ASCII, PageMaker 5 and 6, Excel, and (optionally) Microsoft Word 4.0/5.x/6.0, present dialog boxes that let you control file conversion options.

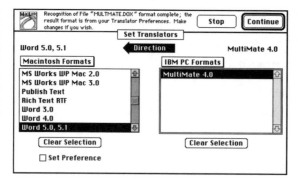

Figure 5-7:
The MacLink Plus
dialog box as it
converts a DOS
Multimate file into
Microsoft Word for
Macintosh 5.0

Smart ASCII Import Filter Options

When you import an ASCII (text-only) file, the Smart ASCII import filter dialog box, shown in Figure 5-8, automatically opens, presenting the following options:

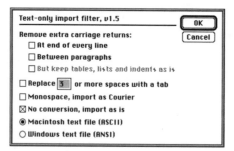

Figure 5-8:
The Smart ASCII Import Filter
dialog box

⊕ **Remove extra carriage returns**. Many ASCII text files have a carriage return at the end of every physical line, whether it is the end of a paragraph or not. The At end of every line option strips all of the carriage returns from the file, causing the text to run together. This means that you have to manually add carriage returns where they are required, but it is far easier to add carriage returns where they are needed than to have to manually remove them where they are not needed. The Between paragraphs option deletes carriage returns as necessary so that there is never more than one carriage return in a row in the resulting file. The But keep tables, lists and indents as is option causes the import filter to retain carriage returns preceding lines of the imported text that begin with spaces or tabs or contain embedded tabs.

⊕ **Replace __ or more spaces with tab**. If the text document being imported uses spaces to position text, this option designates that multiple-space sequences be removed and tabs be substituted. This is important because text positioned with spaces will usually not align properly in PageMaker — setting tabs is a much more accurate method of positioning text. After selecting this option, enter the number of consecutive spaces you want replaced with a tab. The default setting is 3.

- **Monospace, import as Courier**. When this option is selected, all text in the imported file will appear in the Courier typeface.

- **No conversion, import as is**. This is the default option and will be the correct option for most text files. When selected, carriage returns are not removed, consecutive spaces are never replaced with tabs, and the text file will appear in the default font. This option is automatically deselected if any one of the other options in this dialog box is selected.

- **Macintosh text file (ASCII)**. In Macintosh text files some special characters, such as em dashes (—) and copyright symbols (©), are at different keyboard addresses than in other text formats, such as Windows ANSI text file format. Checking this option tells PageMaker to bring the text in as an ASCII text file, maintaining Mac compatibility. You should note, however, that this does not automatically readdress specific characters. You'll have to do this manually. So, when bringing text files in from other platforms, be on the lookout for misused special characters.

- **Windows text file (ANSI)**. In Windows text files some special characters, such as em dashes (—) and copyright symbols (©), are at different keyboard addresses than in other text formats, such as Macintosh ASCII text file format. Checking this option tells PageMaker to bring the text in as an ANSI text file, maintaining Windows compatibility. You should note, however, that this does not automatically readdress specific characters. You'll have to do this manually. So, when bringing text files in from other platforms, be on the lookout for misused special characters.

PageMaker 5 and PageMaker 6 Import Filter Options

Selecting an existing PageMaker 5 or 6 file in the Place dialog box brings up the PageMaker Story Importer dialog box, as shown in Figure 5-9. This dialog box lists the first 20 characters of each story in the selected publication. You can select any story that you want to import, hold down the Shift key to select more than one story, or use the Select all button to bring all of the stories into the current publication. If you use the Select all button, the stories you are importing will be concatenated into a single story in your new publication.

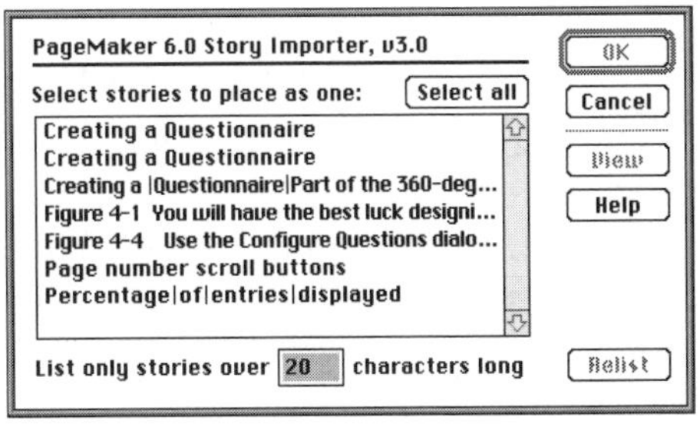

Figure 5-9:
Use the PageMaker
Story Importer to place
stories from other
PageMaker Documents.

```
PageMaker 6.0 Story Importer, v3.0          [  OK  ]

Select stories to place as one:  [ Select all ]   [ Cancel ]

Creating a Questionnaire
Creating a Questionnaire                           [  View  ]
Creating a |Questionnaire|Part of the 360-deg...
Figure 4-1  You will have the best luck designi...  [  Help  ]
Figure 4-4   Use the Configure Questions dialo...
Page number scroll buttons
Percentage|of|entries|displayed

List only stories over [ 20 ] characters long     [ Relist ]
```

If you cannot remember the content of any story based on the small amount of text that appears in this dialog box, select the story you want to see more of and click the View button. The complete text of the selected story appears in a story-editor–like window. You can limit the number of stories that appear in the Story importer by using the option at the bottom of the dialog box to include stories that contain a certain number of characters or more. This limits the appearance of small stories such as cutlines, sidebars, page numbers, and cross-references. For example, most of the captions in this book would not appear.

After selecting the stories you want to import, click the OK button, and PageMaker imports the selected text just as if it had come from a word processing file. Naturally, all style sheets and text formatting are imported intact.

Microsoft Excel Import Filter Options

Selecting a Microsoft Excel 5.0 spreadsheet file brings up the Excel import filter, shown in Figure 5-10 (the dialog box looks slightly different for earlier versions of Excel). By default, all existing data in the selected sheet in the spreadsheet file will be imported, but if you've used named cell ranges, you can import only a specified named cell range using the Cell Range option. Other options allow you to specify the tab alignment (such as decimal, for instance) used for your imported data, import or discard the text formatting that has been applied in Excel, and truncate long text cells to the length of their cell boundaries. Excel 5.0 spreadsheets (books) can consist of several spreadsheets. Use the Sheet option to specify the sheet you want to import. You can bring in only one sheet at a time.

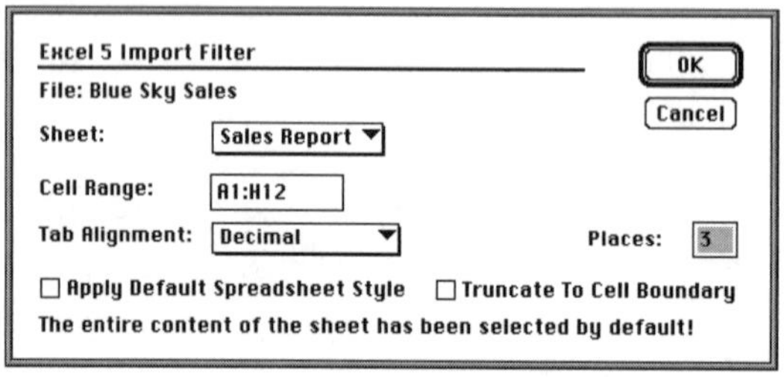

Figure 5-10:
The Excel Import Filter
dialog box

Excel 5 Import Filter	OK
File: Blue Sky Sales	Cancel
Sheet: Sales Report ▼	
Cell Range: A1:H12	
Tab Alignment: Decimal ▼	Places: 3
☐ Apply Default Spreadsheet Style ☐ Truncate To Cell Boundary	
The entire content of the sheet has been selected by default!	

Microsoft Word 4.0/5.x/6.0 Import Filter Options

A similar import filter dialog box is available for Microsoft Word 4.0, 5.x, or 6.0 files, but this dialog box, shown in Figure 5-11 (notice that the 6.0 filter is slightly different), does not appear automatically. To access it, you must press and hold the Shift key down while clicking the OK button in the Place document dialog box. After setting the options in this dialog box, click the OK button to continue the text placement or the Cancel button to abort the text import.

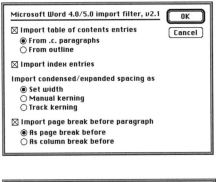

Figure 5-11:
The Microsoft Word 4.0/5.x (top) and 6.0 import filters.

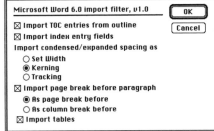

The options in this dialog box:

- ↪ **Import table of contents entries**. This option instructs PageMaker to mark table of contents entries from the imported text as they were marked in Word 4.0 using either the .c. paragraph markers or the Word outline. (See the Microsoft Word user manual for more information on Word's table of contents commands.) The Word 6.0 filter makes these distinctions automatically. Entries so marked are then available to PageMaker's Create TOC feature, discussed in Chapter 12.

- ↪ **Import index entries**. Use of this option instructs PageMaker to mark index entries from the imported text as they were marked in Word using the .i. markers. (See the Microsoft Word User Manual for more information on Word's index commands.) Entries so marked are then available to PageMaker's Create Index feature, discussed in Chapter 12.

- ↪ **Import condensed/expanded type**. There are three options for how condensed or expanded type is placed into PageMaker. The Set width option causes PageMaker to use its Set width option to make the text appear in PageMaker as it did in Word. The Manual kerning option causes PageMaker to kern the characters so that the text appears in PageMaker as it did in Word. The Track kerning option causes PageMaker to use its Tracking option to make the text appear in PageMaker as it did in Word. These concepts — Set width, kerning, and tracking — are discussed in the next chapter.

⮑ **Import page break before paragraph**. When this option is selected, Word's Page break before paragraph formatting is imported into PageMaker as either a Page Break Before or a Column Break Before option in PageMaker's Paragraph Specifications dialog box. Page breaks that result from Word's automatic pagination and hard page breaks (entered into Word with the Shift-Enter key combination) cannot be transferred into PageMaker. For information on Paragraph specifications formatting, refer to the next chapter.

⮑ **Import tables.** This option, available only when importing Word 6 files, allows you to bring in a Word table intact, complete with rows, columns, and text formatting. This is a great way to create tables quickly in PageMaker, especially since Adobe Table, included with PageMaker, isn't all that slick.

Supported Text Formatting

Even with the proper import filter, every formatting attribute of your text or word processing file may not be converted properly. Table 5-1 lists formatting attributes and indicates whether these attributes are converted by the most-common import filters. A "Y" indicates that the formatting attribute will remain after the file is imported into PageMaker. An "N" indicates that the formatting attribute will be lost in the conversion process.

Table 5-1							
Features Supported by PageMaker's Text Filters							
Item	**MS Word** **5.x**	**6.0**	**MacWrite** **II**	**Works** **2.0**	**WPrfct** **3.0**	**DCA**	**.RTF**
Fonts	Y	Y	Y	Y	Y	Y[1]	Y
Sizes	Y[2]	Y	Y	Y[2]	Y	Y	Y[2]
Bold	Y	Y	Y	Y	Y	Y	Y
Italic	Y	Y	Y	Y	Y[3]	N	Y
Underline	Y	Y	Y	Y	Y	Y	Y
Strikethru	Y	Y	Y	N	Y	Y[4]	Y
Outline	Y	Y	Y	Y	Y	N	Y
Shadow	Y	Y	Y	Y	Y	N	Y
Exp/Con	Y[5]	N	N	N	N	N	N
Hidden	N	N	N	N	N	N	N
Superscript	Y[6]	Y[6]	Y	Y	Y	Y	Y
Subscript	Y[6]	Y[6]	Y	Y	Y	Y	Y
Special Char	Y[7]	Y[7]	Y	Y	Y	N	Y

Item	MS Word 5.x	6.0	MacWrite II	Works 2.0	WPrfct 3.0	DCA	.RTF
Color	Y	Y	N	N	Y	Y	Y
Letter Space	N	N	N	N	N	N	N
Word Space	N	N	N	N	N	N	N
Line spacing	Y	Y	Y	Y	Y	Y	Y
Paragraph Sp	Y	Y	Y	N	Y	N	Y
Top of Cap Ld	N	N	N	N	N	N	Y
Hyphen Zone	N	N	N	N	N	N	Y
Left Tab	Y	Y	Y	Y	Y	Y	Y
Right Tab	Y	Y	Y	Y	Y	Y	Y
Center Tab	Y	Y	Y	Y	Y	Y	Y
Decimal Tab	Y	Y	Y	Y	Y	Y	Y
Special Tab	Y[8]	Y	N	N	Y	N	Y[8]
Tab Leader (.)	Y	Y	Y	N	Y	N	Y
Tab Leader (-)	Y	Y	Y	N	Y	N	Y
Tab Leader (_)	Y	Y	Y	N	Y	N	Y
Tab Leader (?)	N	N	Y	N	N	N	N
Hang Indent	Y	Y	Y	Y	Y	Y	Y
Nest Indent	Y	Y	Y	Y	Y	Y	Y
Alignment	Y	Y	Y	Y	Y	Y	Y
Column Brk	Y[9]	Y[9]	N	N	Y	Y	Y
Page Break	Y[9]	Y[9]	N	N	Y	Y	Y
Keep together	Y	Y	N	N	Y	N	Y
Keep next	Y	Y	N	N	Y	N	Y
Par Rule Abv	Y	Y	N	N	Y	N	Y
Par Rule Blw	Y	Y	N	N	Y	N	Y
Include TOC	Y[9]	Y[9]	N	N	Y	Y	Y
Widow/Orph	N	N	N	N	N	N	Y
Next Style	Y	Y	N	N	Y	N	Y
Columns	N	N	N	N	N	N	N
Head/Foot	N	N	N	N	Y[10]	N	N
Page #'s	N	N	Y	N	N	N	N
Footnotes	Y[11]	N[11]	Y	N	Y	Y	Y
Index entry	Y[12]	Y[12]	N	N	Y	Y	Y[12]

Item	MS Word 5.x	6.0	MacWrite II	Works 2.0	WPrfct 3.0	DCA	.RTF
Outlines	Y[13]	Y[13]	N	N	N	Y	Y
Style sheets	Y	Y	N	N	Y	Y	Y
TOC entries	Y	Y	N	N	Y	N	Y
Graphics	Y	Y	Y	N	N	N	Y
Borders	Y[14]	Y[15]	N	N	Y[15]	N	Y[14]
Tables	Y	Y	N	N	Y	N	Y
Kerning	N	N	N	N	N	N	N
Paragraph #s	N	N	N	N	Y	N	N

[1] Some fonts may be converted.

[2] Whole point sizes only.

[3] "Redline text" is also imported as italic.

[4] Strikethru with hyphens only.

[5] Use Word import filter dialog box.

[6] PageMaker makes them 7/12 normal type and 1/3 above baseline.

[7] Except formulas and line numbers.

[8] Bar tabs become left tabs.

[9] If set in paragraph dialog.

[10] Except special characters.

[11] As endnotes.

[12] If page range is indicated with ".i(.' and '.i).', two references separated by comma will be imported.

[13] As long as not designated with hidden text.

[14] Border above and below only, imported as paragraph rules.

[15] In style sheets.

Font Mapping

As the text file you select is converted and imported into PageMaker, a progress dialog box appears. Under the progress bar in this dialog box, you will see messages documenting some aspects of the conversion process.

If the PANOSE Font Matching option is turned on (in the Preferences dialog box under the Map Fonts button) and any of the fonts used in the imported text file are not currently installed on your system, then a PANOSE dialog box like the one shown in Figure 5-12 appears. If you are using Super ATM instead, no dialog box appears, but you may see the Super ATM "spinning letter A cursor" as your document is being composed. The PANOSE dialog box lists all currently unavailable fonts, along with font substitutions that are either suggested by the PANOSE system, have been defined as exceptions in the Preferences dialog box, or were saved as permanent substitutions in a previous editing session.

To change the predefined or default substitution for any font, select the font name and then choose the font you want to substitute using the Substitute font pop-up menu at the bottom of the dialog box. If you want this substitution to occur every time you open this file, click the Permanent option in the lower-right corner of the dialog box. If you

Editing PANOSE Font Matching Exceptions

The PANOSE font matching system is designed to automatically map missing fonts to other similar fonts that are installed on your Macintosh. It uses a proprietary system of describing fonts based on their visual characteristics. Rather than relying on the PANOSE system to map your missing fonts, you can define an exception list that is used to substitute for missing fonts.

To do this, choose the Preferences... command from the File menu, then click the Map fonts button. This brings up the Font Matching Preferences dialog box, shown in Figure 5-13. Now make sure the PANOSE font substitution option is selected. The Substitution tolerance scroll bar defines how exact of a match the PANOSE system must make in order to consider one of the fonts available in your system as an acceptable match for a missing font. To the left is 0, or Exact. To the right is 100, or Loose. If a font is missing, it is missing; so you might as well allow the PANOSE system to match any font that is reasonably close in design. So we recommend a midrange setting between 50 and 70.

want this substitution to apply for the current work session only, leave the Temporary option selected. Repeat this process for all of the listed missing fonts. When you're finished, click the OK button.

Figure 5-12:
The Font Matching Results dialog box used by PageMaker to match or substitute missing fonts

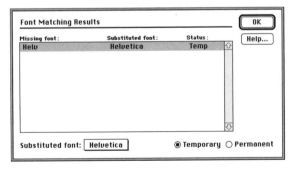

If the PANOSE system cannot find a match within the tolerance you suggest, it will instead substitute the font specified by the Default font option. Use the pop-up menu to select the font you want substituted for all missing fonts in your publications that cannot be replaced by the PANOSE system.

Figure 5-13:
The Font Matching Preferences dialog box used to control font mapping

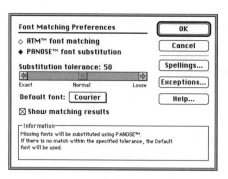

Another control you have over PANOSE font substitutions is the exception list. This is a list you create and maintain that defines the specific fonts you use and the fonts you want substituted should those fonts ever be unavailable. To create or modify your exception list, click the Exceptions… button and use the Add…, Edit…, and Remove… buttons.

The Spellings… option allows you to compensate for the differences in the way Windows defines fonts compared to the way your Mac defines fonts. It also allows you to compensate for the different names given to fonts by different manufacturers. For example, if you use Bitstream fonts on a Windows machine and Adobe fonts on your Mac, most of the fonts will have different names. Bitstream, for example, calls Helvetica *Swiss*. The Spellings… option lets you edit existing spelling pairs and add new ones.

Flowing Text into Your Document_

When PageMaker is finished reading the word processor file, the cursor becomes one of two *text flow icons*: manual text flow or autoflow text flow. The autoflow text icon appears if the Autoflow command (in the Layout menu) is checked, and the manual text flow icon appears if it is not. You can get a third text flow icon, the semiautomatic text flow icon, by holding down the Shift key. Any of these icons, which are shown in Figure 5-14, can be used to add text to your publication. The operation of each is described in detail in this section.

Figure 5-14:
The manual, semiautomatic, and automatic text flow icons

Before adding the new text, you can use the page icons, the keyboard equivalents (⌘-Tab and ⌘-Shift-Tab), or the Go to Page… command to find the spot where you want to insert the text. You can even turn to the page, if necessary, or reposition the display using the scroll bars, grabber hand, or view-size commands. None of these actions will cause you to lose the text flow icon.

Changing your mind: If you decide that you don't want to add the imported text at this time, click the Pointer tool in the toolbox and the text flow icon will disappear. You will then have to reselect the Place… command and choose the file again when you want to import it. This technique can be applied anytime a text flow icon appears — clicking the Pointer tool will always discard it.

Imported text can be added anywhere on any publication page, on the master pages, or on the pasteboard. Not surprisingly, adding text to publication pages is most common. To actually place the text, position the text flow icon where you want the top of the new text to appear, and click the mouse button. What happens next depends upon which text flow icon you are using:

↪ **Manual text flow**. With the manual text flow icon, you decide where to begin each block of text. After you click the mouse button, the text flows into a new text block, and, if not all text is placed, a down-arrow appears in the windowshade tab at the end of that text block. To place the rest of the text, click the down arrow with the Pointer tool to *reload* the text icon to continue the text flow process. Then you select where you want the next text block to appear, turning the page or adjusting the view if necessary, and repeat the process.

Manual text flow is the default setting when the Autoflow command from the Options menu is *not* selected. If Autoflow is selected, manual text flow can be temporarily accessed by pressing the ⌘ key as you import the text, when clicking OK in the Place dialog box, or when clicking the down arrow in the windowshade handle.

↪ **Automatic**. With the automatic text flow icon, once you begin the text flow, PageMaker will add the text, column by column, page after page, until the entire story is placed. Pages will turn automatically, and if required, new pages are added automatically until the document reaches its 999-page limit or PageMaker runs out of disk space.

You can stop automatic text flow at any time by clicking the mouse button. When the Autoflow command is selected, fully automatic text flow is the default setting. When Autoflow is *not* selected, fully automatic text flow can be accessed temporarily by pressing the Command key when clicking OK in the Place dialog box or when clicking the down arrow in the windowshade handle.

↪ **Semiautomatic**. With the semiautomatic text flow icon, text placement works just like it does with the manual text flow icon, except that you don't have to reload the icon after each text block. Instead, the text icon is reloaded automatically each time you place a text block. You then can decide the location of the next text block and repeat the process until all text has been placed.

Semiautomatic text flow is initiated by pressing the Shift key, regardless of whether or not the Autoflow command is selected.

Manually Placing Imported Text

The manual text flow icon gives you full control over the placement of imported text within your file. It is best suited to situations where the text being placed will not continue in a regular formation from column to column and page to page. Ad layouts, newspaper, and magazine designs are examples of documents where the manual (or maybe the semiautomatic) text flow method should be used.

To begin placing text with the manual text flow icon, position the cursor between your column guides at the vertical location where you would like the text block to begin and click the mouse button. Alternatively, you can define the exact size and position of the text block you want to put the text in by drag-placing to create a marquee that defines the text block and then releasing the mouse button. This method of defining text blocks is described in more detail in "Drag-Placing to Create a New Text Block," later in this chapter.

Text from your imported file will then flow into the text block you have created, until all the text has been placed, the bottom margin of the column is reached, the bottom of the pasteboard is reached, the bottom of the predefined text block is reached, or the text is interrupted by a graphic that has been formatted to stop text flow (as described in Chapter 8). When the text flow stops, the text block is selected (as indicated by the windowshades at the top and bottom of the text block), and the lower windowshade tab will display a down arrow if all of the text in the story did not fit in the text block. The

Pointer tool is automatically selected, so you can easily reposition the text block, resize the text block, or reload the text flow icon to continue flowing the text. (See Figure 5-15.)

Figure 5-15:
An example of using text flow; you determine where each text block begins and then reload the text icon, as shown here.

If more text remains to be placed, point the Pointer tool at the down arrow in the windowshade and click the mouse button. This reloads the text icon so that it is ready to place the additional text. The remaining text may be flowed into existing columns, placed into a new text block that is created manually, or placed onto the pasteboard. You can either turn the page or insert new pages into your publication without disturbing the loaded text icon. Position the text icon where you want the top of the next text block and click the mouse button to flow the remaining text into the new text block. Repeat this process until all the text in the document has been placed.

Remember that manual text flow is the default setting unless the Autoflow command is selected (marked with a check mark) in the Layout menu. If the Autoflow command is selected, and the automatic text flow icon appears, you can still change the flow to manual mode temporarily by holding down the Command key.

Using the Autoflow Command

In longer documents, the process of positioning the text cursor icon, initiating the text flow, reloading the flow icon, and repositioning the text cursor icon (including turning or creating pages) may become slow, boring, and repetitive. In these cases, you will want to use the Autoflow command to automate the process of flowing text documents. Autoflowing text works much like manual text flowing except that PageMaker automatically reloads the text icon cursor and initiates the flow in the next available column (moving left to right). PageMaker turns pages as necessary and even inserts new pages until all the text in the file is placed, the 999-page limit of the publication is reached, or it runs out of disk space.

Automatic text flow is initiated with the automatic text flow icon, which appears when the Autoflow command is chosen from the Layout menu. Choosing the Autoflow command toggles a check mark (✔) on and off in front of the command. When the check mark appears before this command, the loaded text cursor will by default become the automatic text flow icon, and text flow will be automatic. You can choose the Autoflow command at any time — before choosing the Place... command or after the manual text flow icon has appeared. You can also access the automatic text flow icon by holding down the Command key while the manual text flow icon is displayed.

Once the autoflow text icon is displayed, position it at the top of the column where the text document is to begin and click the mouse button. Text flows through each subsequent column in the publication, turning and adding pages as necessary, until all text in the placed document has been positioned. (See Figure 5-16.) You can interrupt automatic text flow at any time by clicking the mouse button. To restart automatic text flow, click the down arrow to reload the text flow icon, position the autoflow icon at the top of the next column, and click the mouse button to restart automatic text flow.

Figure 5-16:
When you use automatic text flow, PageMaker flows text from column to column, page to page until all text is placed.

Semiautomatic Text Flow

A third method of text flow is semiautomatic, in which each column of text flow must be initiated individually, but the text icon is reloaded automatically if additional text remains after the text block is filled. Semiautomatic text flow is initiated with the semiautomatic text flow icon, which is displayed by pressing the Shift key and holding down the mouse button when *either* the manual or automatic text icon is displayed.

To begin semiautomatic text flow, position the semiautomatic text icon at the beginning of the column where you want the text to begin and click the mouse button to initiate the text flow. When the text flow stops, the text icon will reload, and if the Shift key is still held down (or depressed at that time), the semiautomatic text flow icon will appear again. If the Shift key is no longer being held down, then either the manual text flow icon or the automatic text flow icon will appear, depending on the current setting of the Autoflow command in the Layout menu. Figure 5-17 shows an example of semiautomatic text flow.

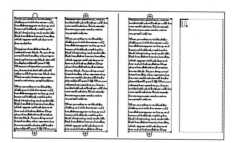

Figure 5-17: When you use semiautomatic text flow, you decide where each text block begins, but you don't have to reload the text flow icon after each new placement of text.

Semiautomatic text flow is useful whenever you want to flow all the text from a particular document but do not wish to fill each available column top to bottom, as automatic text flow would.

Drag-placing to Create a New Text Block

The most common way to create text blocks is by positioning one of the text flow icons at the top of a page or column and then clicking, but that is not the only way. If you want to create a text block where there are no column guides, or if you want to create a text block that is sized differently than the current column guides, you can drag-place with any of the text flow icons.

Simply position the cursor at the upper-left corner of your desired text block, press and hold down the mouse button, and drag to the lower right of your desired text block (see Figure 5-18). Now release the mouse button. Your newly defined text block will immediately be filled with text. This same trick can be used with the Text tool from the tool palette, but in that case the insertion point will flash, ready for you to enter text into the new text block.

Figure 5-18:
Drag-placing with any text flow icon allows you to define the area where you want text to flow.

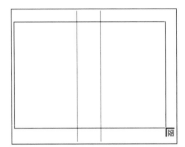

Text blocks created with this method can cross existing column guides and can be positioned on the pasteboard or anywhere else in a publication. If all of the text in the story doesn't fit in the text block you define, a down arrow will appear in the tab of the lower windowshade of the text block. This is true even if the automatic text flow icon was used. You can then reload the text flow icon as previously described and place the additional text either normally or using the drag-place method.

Importing Text into or over an Existing Story

Sometimes you'll need to add imported text to an existing story in your publication or to replace the existing text in a story. This can happen for a number of reasons:

∞ It can happen "by surprise" — when your editor or colleague hands you the new disk and asks "Can you use this newer version?"

∞ You may have done it intentionally, deciding that a document needed more editing than is appropriate for PageMaker, so you returned to the word processor to make major changes.

∞ You may lay out an article and find that it is not long enough. By inserting text into a story that has already been placed, you can then work with the combined text as a single story rather than as two separate stories.

☞ You can update old layouts with new articles. By replacing the existing story rather than simply deleting it and placing the new text as a new story, you can preserve the positioning and formatting of the text blocks as they thread through the publication.

Using Place... to replace or insert text: You can use the Place... command to replace the text in an entire story, to replace a portion of a story, or to add imported text to an existing story. To do this, select the text you want to replace, or position the insertion point at the position where you want to insert the new text. If you want to select an entire story, use the Text tool to set the insertion point anywhere within the story and then choose the Select All command from the Edit menu (⌘-A). To select a portion of a story that spans multiple pages and/or text blocks, set the insertion point at the start of the section you want to select, then turn to the end of the section you want to select, hold down the Shift key, and click the text cursor. All text between the original insertion point and the Shift-click will be selected. Then choose the Place... command. The Place Document dialog box appears, as shown in Figure 5-19. Select the file you wish to import from the file list on the left side of the dialog box (navigate to other folders or drives if necessary). If the file you selected is a compatible text file, the second and third Place options become selectable in one of two configurations. (If these options remain dimmed, the text insertion point was not set in an existing text block before the Place... command was chosen.)

Figure 5-19:
The Place document dialog box ready to replace or insert text into an existing text block

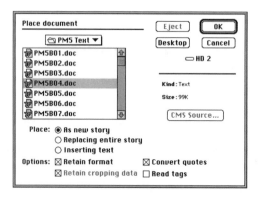

If some text was selected when the Place... command was chosen, the second option is Replacing entire story, and the third option is Replacing selected text. Select Replacing entire story if you want the file you import to replace the entire story in which text was selected. This will replace all of the story's text even if you did not select the entire story. Select Replacing selected text if you want only the text you selected to be replaced; this leaves all text before and after the selection intact.

If no text was selected when the Place… command was chosen, but the insertion point was set inside a text block, the second option reads Replacing entire story, and the third option reads Inserting text. Select the Replacing entire story option if you want the file you import to replace the entire story in which the cursor was set. Select Inserting text if you want to add the text from the imported file to the existing story, starting at the position where you set the insertion point.

Inserting text into an existing text block using the Place… command is exactly the same as entering additional text manually. This means that the text below the insertion point flows through any subsequent text blocks in the story, and if all of the text doesn't fit into the last text block, you'll have to either lengthen that text block or create a new text block to hold the final text. To check for unplaced text, select the last text block in the story and look for a down arrow in the tab in the bottom windowshade.

After selecting the appropriate options, double-click the selected filename, click OK, or press Return or Enter. The selected file will be converted and imported. A progress dialog box will appear, as will a font substitution dialog box, if necessary. The text then replaces the existing text or adds to it, depending on the options you selected.

Using Links to upgrade text: You can also replace the text in a story using the Link info… or Links… command, as described in Chapter 12. In fact, that is an easier way to replace an entire story; you cannot use the link commands to replace a portion of a story, however.

Creating New Text

In addition to importing text with the Place… command, there are two other ways you can get text into your publication. You can either create text right on your publication pages or you can create text in the Story Editor and then import it onto your publication pages. In this section, you'll learn how to create text directly on publication pages. Creating text in the Story Editor is covered in the next section of this chapter.

To create new text on a publication page, select the Text tool from the tool palette, position the I-beam cursor where you want the text to begin, and click the mouse button. Be sure that you are not overlapping any existing text blocks, or else your new text will be added to that text block rather than creating a new one. Once the text insertion point is set (it will be flashing on and off), start typing. The size of the text block you have created is determined by where and how the Text tool is positioned and how the mouse button is clicked.

☞ **If the cursor is set within an existing text block**, any new text entered is added to that text block. In this case, no new text block is created. As you add text, all following text flows through the multiple text blocks. If the end of text does not fit into the last text block, the down arrow will appear, and you will have to reload the text flow icon and place the remaining text.

☞ **If the cursor is set by clicking between existing column guides**, the new text block will be the width of that column and as long as required to hold the text you enter (to the limit of the bottom of the page). The text will automatically begin at the left margin, and text will automatically wrap to the width of the column, as shown in Figure 5-20.

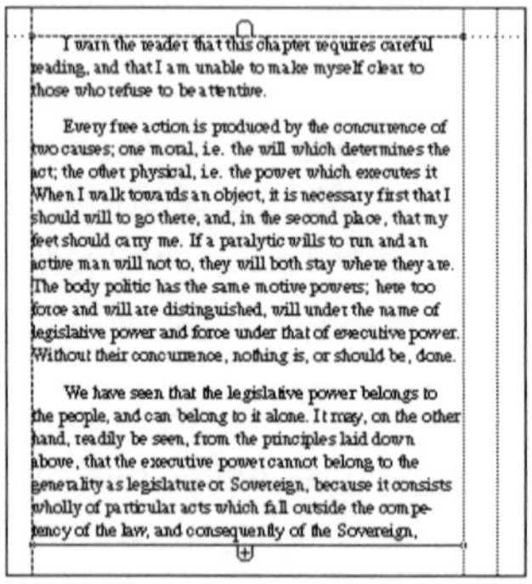

Figure 5-20:
When you enter text between two column guides, PageMaker automatically wraps the text to fit.

☞ **If the cursor is set by clicking at any location that is not between two column guides**, the new text block will be nearly as wide as the current page and as long as required to hold the text you enter (to the limit of the bottom of the page or pasteboard), as shown in Figure 5-21.

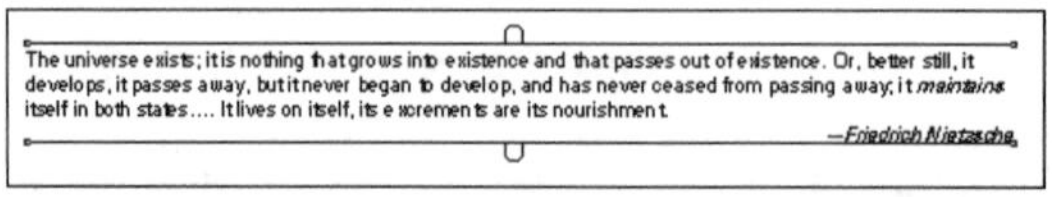

Figure 5-21:
The text block created when text is entered on the pasteboard can be nearly as wide as the page itself, or longer.

☞ **Drag-placing predefines the text block size.** If you want to define a text block that does not conform to existing column guides, position the Text tool's I-beam cursor anywhere in the publication window, except over an existing text block, press and hold the mouse button, and drag to the size that you wish the new text block to be. Then release the mouse button and the insertion point will flash in the upper-left corner of the new text block. Enter your text before clicking the mouse button again.

To enter more text than will fit into one text block, you have to thread the text to a second text block and then continue entering text into the second text block. To do this, use the following procedure:

STEPS: Entering Additional Text in a Full Text Block

Step 1. Select the Pointer tool and click your new text block so that its handles appear.

Step 2. Click and hold on the tab in the windowshade at the bottom of the text block and push the windowshade up two or three lines. The down-arrow symbol will now appear in the tab in the lower windowshade to show that not all text has been placed.

Step 3. Click the Pointer tool on this tab, and the cursor will become a loaded text icon. (Make sure to click the mouse button quickly; if you press and hold it down, the loaded text icon will not appear.)

Step 4. Position the loaded text icon at the location where you want the second text block to be located and click the mouse button. The text that you had hidden under the bottom windowshade will then appear.

Step 5. Select the Text tool from the toolbox, position it to the right of the last word in the new text block, and click the mouse button. The insertion point is now set, and you can add more text to this text block.

Step 6. Repeat this procedure each time you fill a text block and want to enter additional text.

Cutting and Pasting Text _____

One of the most common text-editing functions is cutting or copying text from one location and then pasting it to another location. If you select text with the Text tool and then cut, copy, and paste it within PageMaker, the text retains all of its character-level formatting but does not retain its paragraph-level formatting. Instead, the text will assume the paragraph-level formatting of the text block into which it is pasted, or if it is pasted into a new text block, it will take on the default paragraph-level formatting. (The distinction between character-level and paragraph-level formatting is fully described in Chapter 6.)

If you select a text block with the Pointer tool on the other hand, and then cut, copy, and paste it to another location, it will retain both the character-level formatting and the paragraph-level formatting.

Special Characters

When entering text into PageMaker, you'll frequently need access to the special characters shown in Table 5-2 below. Here you can see each of the characters PageMaker makes available in most PostScript and TrueType fonts, the keys you need to press to add these characters to your text, and the codes you'll need to enter to use these characters in the Find or Change dialog boxes (discussed in the next chapter).

In addition to these special characters, most fonts include other characters as part of their extended character sets. These vary widely from font to font and font vendor to font vendor. To find out what extended characters are lurking in your fonts, use a desk accessory like Key Caps or open the Character Set template included with PageMaker 6. Changing the font in this publication to any one of your fonts and then printing it will provide you with a complete map to the font's extended character set.

 Checking it twice: Note that some fonts — mostly unusual display fonts, public domain or shareware fonts, or fonts from small type houses — don't honor this special characters list. You should always check your special characters carefully *after* your pages are printed; they can sometimes appear correct on screen and yet print incorrectly.

Table 5-2
Special Characters and Their Keyboard Equivalents

Characters	Keyboard Equivalent	Code for Find/Change
Current page number	⌘-Option-p	^3
Discretionary hyphen	⌘-(hyphen)	^-
Ellipses	Option-; (semicolon)	Option-;
Em dash	Shift-Option-(hyphen)	^_
Em space	⌘-Shift-m	^m
En dash	Option-(hyphen)	^=
En space	⌘-Shift-n	^>

Characters	Keyboard Equivalent	Code for Find/Change
Line break	Shift-Return	^n
Non-breaking hyphen	⌘-Option-(hyphen)	^~
Non-breaking slash	⌘-Option-/ (slash)	^/
Non-breaking space	Option-spacebar	^s
Single quotation close	Option-Shift-]	^]
Single quotation open	Option-]	^[
Open quotation	Option-[	^{
Close quotation	Option-Shift-[	^}
Thin space	⌘-Shift-t	^<

The Story Editor

The Story Editor is a word processor of sorts built into PageMaker for those times when the formatting of text within your publication makes it hard to read and edit, or when you need to do some fairly extensive text entry or editing but don't want to switch to your word processor. You can move any story that has already been placed into your publication into the Story Editor, import new stories directly into the Story Editor, or create new stories in the Story Editor.

The Story Editor is accessed with the Edit Story command from the Edit menu (⌘-E). If the text cursor is set within a text block, or a text block is selected with the Pointer tool, when the Story Editor command is chosen, the story contained in that text block is opened in the Story Editor. If no story is selected (with either the Pointer tool or the Text tool) when the Story Editor command is chosen, an empty, untitled story window appears, along with the Story Editor menu bar. You can also enter the Story Editor by triple-clicking with the Pointer tool on any text block in your publication.

New menus and commands in Story Editor: The menu bar changes a little when you leave the layout view and enter the Story Editor: The Layout and Element menus are removed and the Story menu is put in its place. Also, the Find..., Change..., and Spelling commands are available in the Story Editor but dimmed when working in the layout view. We look at these options later in this section.

The first thing you'll notice about the Story Editor is that all text appears in one font and at one type size, regardless of the font and type size that was used to format the text. This is the way the Story Editor is supposed to work; you specify a font and type size that is easy to read in the Preferences dialog box, as described in Chapter 3, and all stories use that font and type size in the Story Editor. The idea is that in the publication window stories are often formatted with fonts and small point sizes that make them difficult to read. Also, the many threaded text blocks that hold longer stories slow down your ability to read and edit a story. In the Story Editor, an entire story appears in one easily scrollable window and in one easy to read font and type size, as shown in Figure 5-22.

Figure 5-22:
PageMaker's
Story Editor

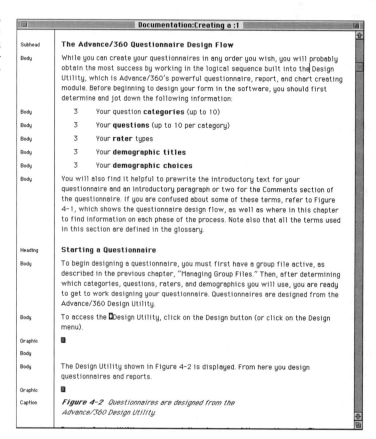

You can apply character or paragraph formatting to text while it is in the Story Editor, but the results of some commands — such as font, type size, and letter spacing commands — will not display in the Story Editor. Rest assured that these commands have been applied, and you'll see them when you switch back to the publication window. Complete details on using all of PageMaker's character and paragraph formatting are provided in Chapter 6.

To return from the Story Editor to the layout view, click the close box in the Story Editor title bar, choose the Edit Layout command from the Edit menu, or choose the layout option from the submenu of the publication name in the Window menu.

Importing Text into the Story Editor

To import a file from disk to the Story Editor, open the Story Editor (⌘-E) and then choose the Place… command from the File menu, just as you would in the publication window. Select any available file using the Import to Story Editor dialog box, as described earlier in this chapter.

Once imported, the new story appears in a new Story Editor window. You can now review the story or edit it as necessary before placing it into your publication.

To place the story into your publication, choose the Edit Layout command from the Edit menu (⌘-E) or click the close box in the Story Editor window. The Edit layout command transfers you to the publication window directly; clicking the close box displays a dialog box like the one shown in Figure 5-23. Click the Place button if you want to add the story to your publication.

Figure 5-23: This dialog box appears when you try to close the Story Editor on a story that has not yet been placed.

When the publication layout reappears, the cursor will be the manual or automatic text flow icon (depending on the status of Autoflow on the Layout menu, as discussed earlier in this chapter). You can then place this story anywhere in the current publication, using the techniques described under "Flowing Text into Your Document," in this chapter. You can edit the story in the Story Editor again at any time by selecting it with the Text or Pointer tool and choosing the Edit story command (⌘-E) or by triple-clicking any text block in the story with the Pointer tool.

Alternatively, you can just close the story in the Story Editor and discard it without adding it to your publication. To do this, click the window's close box or choose the Close story command from the Story menu. Before the story disappears, a dialog box will appear asking you to confirm that you want to discard a story that has not been placed. Click the Discard button only if you are sure; there is no way to get the story back after discarding it.

Creating New Text

When an untitled window appears in the Story Editor, you can begin creating a new story immediately — just start typing. If an untitled window is not available, choose the New story command from the Story menu to create a new untitled window.

After entering and editing a new story in the Story Editor, you can place it into the current publication by choosing the Edit Layout command from the Edit menu (⌘-E) or clicking the close box in the Story Editor window. This brings the publication window forward and provides a text placement icon with which you can position and lay out the text.

Once positioned within your publication, stories created in the Story Editor behave exactly like stories imported from an external word processor. The one exception is that they are not linked to any external file, so PageMaker's Link commands cannot be used on these stories. (The Link commands are introduced and explained in Chapter 12.) You can, however, export stories created in the Story Editor to an external word processing file, using the Export… command, as described in Chapter 6.

Searching for Text with Find

The Story Editor's Find command can search for text within a selection in the current story, in the entire current story, in all stories in the current publication, or in all open publications. To perform a search, choose Find (⌘-F) from the Utilities menu, and the Find dialog box appears as shown in Figure 5-24.

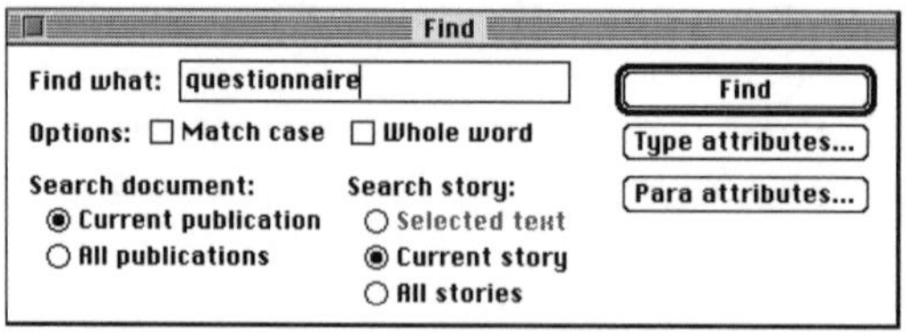

Figure 5-24:
Story Editor's Find dialog box allows you to search for text strings.

Find	
Find what: questionnaire	**Find**
Options: ☐ Match case ☐ Whole word	Type attributes…
Search document:	Para attributes…
◉ Current publication Search story: ○ Selected text	
○ All publications ◉ Current story	
○ All stories	

The options in the Find dialog box:

☞ **Find what**. If you are searching for specific text, enter or paste that text into the Find what field. In searches that are looking for text attributes, discussed shortly, regardless of the specific text, leave this option blank.

To search for text that matches some characters and varies in other characters, include wild-card characters in your search text by adding ^? to the search text. (To search for an actual question mark character, enter ^? .) For example, searching for ^?alk would find all occurrences of walk, talk, and any other four-letter word ending with alk.

You can include special characters in your search by inserting them as specified in Table 5-3. This table shows special characters, the symbols used to search for them, and the keyboard equivalents that produce them in normal text. If the symbol itself is used as the search symbol, enter the keyboard equivalent directly into the Find or Change dialog box. The caret character (^) is created by pressing Shift-6, for example.

Table 5-3
Special Character Search Symbols and Keyboard Equivalents

Character	Search symbol	Keyboard equivalent
Any character (wild card)	^?	n/a
Bullet	•	Option-8
Caret	^^	Shift-6
Computer-inserted hyphen	^c	n/a
Copyright symbol (©)	©	Option-g
Ellipsis	…	Option-;
Em dash	^_	Option-Shift-
Em space	^m	⌘-Shift-m
En dash	^=	Option-
En space	^>	⌘-Shift-n
Index entry marker	^;	n/a
Inline graphic marker	^g	n/a
Line end (Shift-Return)	^n	Shift-Return
Nonbreaking hyphen	^-	⌘-Option--
Nonbreaking space	^s	Option-Spacebar
Nonbreaking slash	^/	⌘-Option-/
Optional hyphen	^-	⌘-
Page number marker	^# or ^3	⌘-Option-p
Paragraph end (Return)	^p	Return
Question mark	?	?
Registered trademark (®)	®	Option-r
Tab	^t	Tab
Thin space	^<	⌘-Shift-t

(continued)

Table 5-3 *(continued)*		
Character	*Search symbol*	*Keyboard equivalent*
Trademark symbol (™)	™	Option-2
Typographer's open quote	"	Option-[
Typographer's close quote	"	Option-Shift-[
Single open quote	'	Option-]
Single close quote	'	Option-Shift-]
White space	^w	Spacebar

- **Options**. Select the Match case option if you want the search to be limited to the exact capitalization entered in the Find what field, or leave this option deselected if you want to find that text regardless of its capitalization. Select the Whole word option if you want the search to locate the text when it is an entire word or phrase and not a component of another word or phrase. (For example, a search for *and* that is not limited to whole words would also find *Andy*, *Band*, and *Operand*. If the search is limited to whole words, these occurrences would not be found.)

- **Search Document**. Use this option to limit your search to the current publication only or to include all open publications.

- **Search Story**. This option determines what text is searched. Selecting the Selected text option limits the search to text that was highlighted before the Find... command was chosen. Selecting the Current story option causes the search to begin at the current location of the insertion point, continue to the end of the story, and then ask if the search should start again at the top of the story. Selecting the All stories option instructs the search to begin at the top of the first story that was placed in the publication and continue through each story in the publication in the order in which they were imported or created. If the Search document option is set to All publications, the search will then continue through the stories in each open publication.

- **Type attributes... button**. Clicking this button brings up the Find Type Attributes dialog box, shown in Figure 5-25. By selecting a font, type size, and type style, or tint (all discussed in the next chapter) in this dialog box, you can limit your search to text that matches selected attributes; or if no text was entered in the Find what option, it will search for any text matching these attributes. Select the desired attributes from the pop-up menus and then click the OK button to return to the Find dialog box.

- **Para attributes... button**. Clicking this button brings up the Find Paragraph Attributes dialog box, shown in Figure 5-26. By selecting a paragraph style, alignment, or leading method (all discussed in the next chapter) here, you can further limit your search. If no text is entered in the Find what option, it will search for any text matching these attributes.

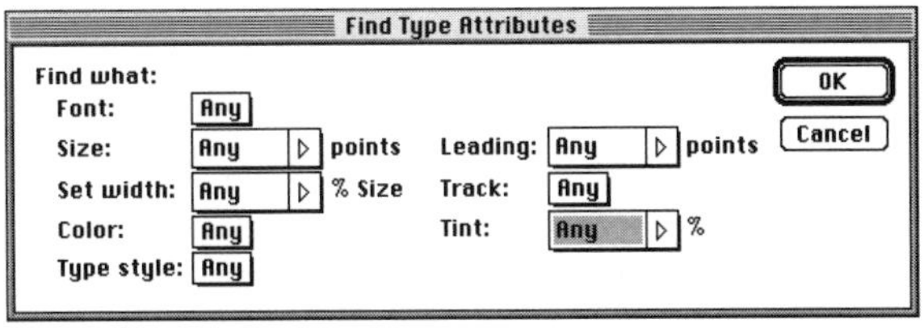

Figure 5-25:
The Find Type
Attributes dialog box
lets you search for
text by its formatting
rather than its
content, or by both.

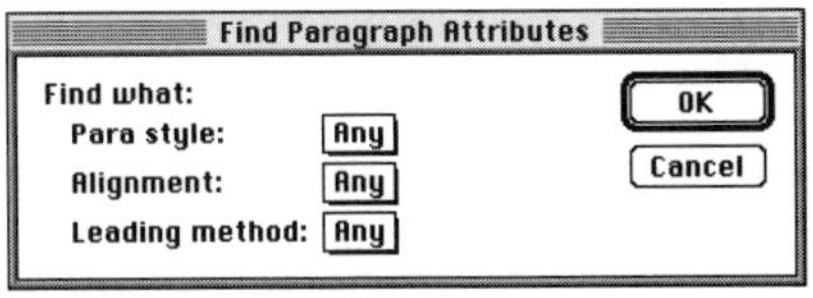

Figure 5-26:
The Find Paragraph Attributes
lets you search for text strings
by paragraph formatting.

With all the Find dialog box options set, click the Find button to begin the search, or click the Cancel button to return to the Story Editor without executing the search. As the search proceeds, PageMaker will highlight results that match the search. The Find dialog box remains on-screen when a match is found, and the Find button changes to Find next. If the text that is found is not the text you are looking for, click the Find next button to search for the next matching occurrence. If necessary, you can move the Find dialog box to a new position by dragging its title bar.

When PageMaker finds text that you want to edit, you can close the Find dialog box by clicking its close box, or you can click in the story and begin editing the selected text. To restart the search using the same search parameters, choose the Find next command (⌘-G) from the Utilities menu. This will locate additional matching text, if it exists in the selected search range, and highlight that text. At this point you can edit the text or continue to search by again choosing the Find next command (⌘-G).

Finding and Changing Text with Change

The Change... command (⌘-H) is used to locate a specific text or style attribute and replace it with another text or style attribute. For example, you might want to find each italic occurrence of Father Smith and change it to Rabbi Rosen in bold text. Or you might want to find all 9-point text and change it to 10 point.

The options in the Change dialog box (shown in Figure 5-27) are almost identical to those in the Find dialog box, as described earlier.

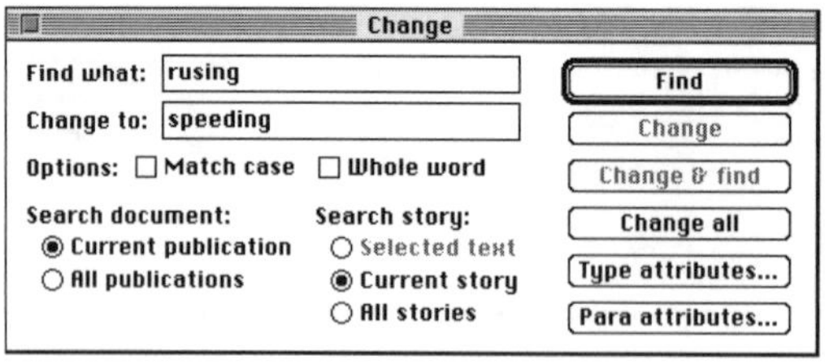

Figure 5-27:
Use the Change dialog
box to find and change
(search and replace) text
strings and attributes.

These are the only unique options:

- **Change to**. This field is used to enter text that should replace the text entered in the Find what field. As in the Find what field, special characters can be used in this field (see the list earlier in this section), but wild-card characters (?) cannot.

  When changing text attributes regardless of the specific text, leave this option blank.

- **Type attributes... and Para attributes... buttons**. The Type attributes and Paragraph attributes dialog boxes for Change include two sets of options, one for the search text and one for the change text. Use the second set of options for replacing attributes.

After completing the Change dialog box options, four buttons are available to execute your search-and-replace operation. If you do not want to execute the search and replace, click the close box in the upper-left corner of the Change dialog box to return to the Story Editor:

- Click the Find button to locate the first occurrence of the text and attributes selected. PageMaker will highlight the text it finds, and you can then click the Change button to execute the replacement, the Change & find button to execute the replacement and find the next occurrence, the Find button to skip the replacement and find the next occurrence, or the Change all button to execute the replacement and change every occurrence in the selected text range.

- The Change button is available only when text matching the search attributes is found, as a result of the Find button. Clicking the Change button replaces the selected text with the text in the Change field and/or the attributes set in the Attributes dialog boxes. After executing the change, you can either close the Change dialog box by clicking its close button or click the Find button to locate the next occurrence of the search text, or the Change all button to change every occurrence in the selected text range.

- The Change & find button is available only when text matching the search attributes is found. Clicking this button executes the replacement and finds the next occurrence of the search text or attributes.

⌐⊛ Clicking the Change all button finds each occurrence of the search text or attributes and replaces it with the new text or attributes, without stopping each time to allow you to confirm the replacement. When this button is clicked, a progress dialog box shows the number of replacements made.

 Reversing changes made with Change: PageMaker does not allow you use the Undo command to undo any changes made in the Change dialog box, but you can undo changes by reversing the options, searching for the text or attributes you changed to, and replacing them with the text or attributes you changed from.

Spell Checking

You can spell check any or all stories in your publication by choosing the Spelling command (⌘-L) from the Utilities menu. This brings up the Spelling dialog box, shown in Figure 5-28. If you want to spell check only a portion of your text, select that part of the text before choosing the Spelling command. This dialog box works almost identically to the spell checker in your word processor.

Figure 5-28:
The Spelling dialog box in
Story Editor

Spelling
Improper word : prewrite   (Ignore)
Change to:	prewrite (Replace)
	perorate (Add...)
	prorate
	priority
	prurigo
Options: ☒ Alternate spellings   ☒ Show duplicates
Search document: ⦿ Current publication ◯ All publications
Search story: ◯ Selected text ⦿ Current story ◯ All stories

If any text was selected when the Spelling command was chosen, the search option Selected text will be selected. If not, the Current story option will be selected. If you want to check the spelling in all stories in the current publication, choose the All stories option.

Initiate the spell-checking process by clicking the Start button or pressing Return. PageMaker will then begin to search the specified text range. When a suspect word is found, PageMaker highlights the word in the story window, and displays it in the Change to field. Above the Change to field is a brief description of the problem with the suspect word. A list of possible correct words appears in the scrolling list below the Change to field. (If the Spelling dialog box is in your way, you can move it by dragging its title bar.)

At this point, you have several choices:

↪ **To replace the suspect word** with a word from the suggestion list, simply click the replacement word and then click the Replace button or press Return.

↪ **To manually correct the suspect word**, edit the text in the Change to field and then click the Replace button or press Return.

You can also click in the story window to manually edit the text directly in the window. This causes the Spelling dialog box to disappear, and you will have to reselect the Spelling command (⌘-L) to continue the spell-checking process. (Be sure that no text is selected when you re-execute the Spelling command, or the Selected text search option will be chosen, and you will have to select the Current story option to complete the spell-checking operation.)

↪ **If nothing is wrong with the suspect word**, click the Ignore button (or press Return if the Ignore button is highlighted).

↪ **If you want to add the suspect word to a supplementary dictionary** so that PageMaker will not flag it as suspect in the future, click the Add... button, and the Add to User Dictionary dialog box, shown in Figure 5-29, appears, with the suspect word entered in the Word field. PageMaker automatically adds tilde (~) symbols representing possible hyphenations of the word. You can remove these symbols by deleting them if you do not want the word to be hyphenated in that way, or add additional tilde characters to mark other possible hyphenations. As in the Hyphenation dialog box (discussed in the next chapter), three consecutive tildes represent the preferred hyphenation, two consecutive tildes are the second-best hyphenation, and single tildes are less desirable but legitimate hyphenation points.

Figure 5-29:
The Add to User Dictionary dialog box used for adding words to supplementary dictionaries

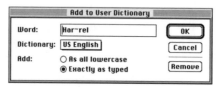

Click the OK button when satisfied with the new word and its hyphenation, or the Cancel button if you decide not to add this word to your dictionary.

Continue working in the Spelling dialog box until all of your text has been checked, and then click the close box in the upper-left corner of the title bar to return to the Story Editor. To return to the layout view, choose the Edit Layout command (⌘-E) from the Edit menu, the Replace command (⌘-D) from the File menu, or click the close box in the story window (or all open story windows).

Automating a one-word spell check: Sometimes, when you type a word in Layout view and are not sure of its spelling, you may want to check just that word, which, in PageMaker requires several steps: Opening Story Editor, then opening Spelling, etc. You can make this a one-step process by creating a script to check just the word where the cursor is flashing. You can learn how to script in PageMaker in Chapter 15.

Entering Text from the Clipboard, Publish and Subscribe, and OLE ___

Everyone who uses the Macintosh is familiar with the Clipboard, which lets you cut or copy text or graphics and then paste them back into the same file or into another file. PageMaker, of course, supports the Mac's Clipboard, and in addition it supports two extensions to the Clipboard mechanism: System 7's edition manager (sometimes called Publish and Subscribe) and Microsoft's OLE (Object Linking and Embedding).

The Clipboard

The Clipboard may seem like a strange way to get text into a PageMaker publication, but in fact it is quite handy and can even let you bring in text that cannot be brought in using any other method. This is true because anything that you can cut or copy onto the Macintosh Clipboard can be pasted into PageMaker. This includes text or graphics obtained from several different sources:

- **Within the current publication**. The Clipboard can be the fastest way to move a text block from one page to another — but remember that when you cut or copy a text block, it becomes disconnected from any other threaded text blocks.

- **Another PageMaker publication**. The trick was very handy before PageMaker supported multiple open publications and allowed you to drag text or graphics between two files. But even now it can still be convenient.

- **A document in another application**. Since virtually every application on the Macintosh lets you copy to the Clipboard, this lets you transfer text from many programs whose files cannot be placed directly into PageMaker (because they are not compatible with PageMaker import filters). To do this, cut or copy the text you want to transfer, open PageMaker and the publication you want to add the text to, and choose the Paste command.

ⅆ **The Scrapbook**. The introduction of MultiFinder, and then System 7, diminished the role of the Scrapbook on the Macintosh, but it still represents a good way to temporarily store text and graphic elements that you need to move from one program to another. PageMaker is fully compatible with all file formats supported by the Scrapbook, so anything you can put in the Scrapbook you can copy and paste into PageMaker.

The Paste Command

In most cases, you'll use the Paste command just as you would in any other application: Choose Paste from the Edit menu (⌘-V), and the text or graphic elements will appear on the current publication page. In some cases, however, PageMaker works a little differently than other programs.

When you paste text from another application or text that was selected with the Text tool and cut from a text block elsewhere within PageMaker, a new text block is created on the current publication page. If you paste text that was cut as an entire text block (selected with the Pointer tool) from within PageMaker, the pasted text block will retain its original size. In either case, after the Paste occurs, the cursor automatically becomes the Pointer tool, and you can then move or resize the resulting text block as explained next.

An option for pasting text is to use a form of the drag-placing trick introduced under "Flowing Text into Your Document," earlier in this chapter: Create a new text block by dragging the highlighted text with the Text tool, and then choose the Paste command (⌘-V) to flow the text into the new text block. If the entire selection of pasted text will not fit within the text block, a down arrow will appear in the windowshade tab at the bottom of the text block. You can then flow the remaining text as described earlier. The drag-place method will not work if the Clipboard contains more than one text block or if it contains both text and graphics.

Another option, if the Clipboard contains text, is to add the pasted text to an existing text block. To do this, set the text insertion point in any existing text block at the point where you want the text to be inserted, and choose the Paste command. The text will be added just as if it had been entered from the keyboard. Of course, all subsequent text in the story will flow downward through the text blocks, so you should check the end of the last text block to make sure all text remains visible.

The Paste Special Command

When you copy text or graphic elements to the Clipboard, some applications provide the Clipboard with information in more than one file format. When you then use the Paste command, PageMaker automatically selects the file format that it can use most easily or accurately. The Paste Special command allows you to choose which of the available file formats is used to transfer the contents of the Clipboard into PageMaker. When you choose Paste Special, the available file formats for the current contents of the Clipboard are listed in ranked order of which PageMaker can best import, as shown in Figure 5-30.

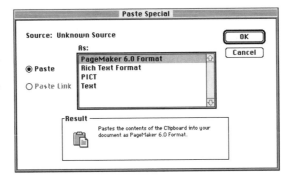

Figure 5-30:
The Paste Special dialog box allows you to paste objects into PageMaker in various formats.

Using Publish and Subscribe

System 7's edition manager was supposed to be the next step beyond the Clipboard in allowing elements to move between Macintosh applications. Through its Publish and Subscribe commands, the edition manager provides a way to export text or graphic elements from one System 7 savvy application (Publish) and import them into any other System 7 savvy application (Subscribe). Of course, this is just what you can do with Copy and Paste, but with Publish and Subscribe the link between the source document and the destination document remains alive. This means that if the original document changes, the text or graphics transferred via Publish and Subscribe can be manually or automatically updated to reflect those changes.

Publish and Subscribe perform as advertised, and due to some strong-arm tactics by Apple Computer, many programs updated since the release of System 7 include these features. Still, very few people appear to actually use these capabilities to transfer elements between their applications. It could be the stupid names, it could be the clumsy interface, it could just be another symptom of the whole System 7 marketing flop. Who knows?

PageMaker supports the Subscribe half of Publish and Subscribe, letting you import elements (called edition files) that were exported using the Publish command in other applications. You cannot Publish from within PageMaker, which means that you cannot create new edition files of text or graphic elements from inside your publication. Adobe has placed the Subscribe commands in the Editions submenu in the Edit menu. Choosing the Subscribe to command brings up the Subscribe To dialog box, shown in Figure 5-31.

This dialog box allows you to select any edition files you want to import into your publication, and after subscribing to an edition file, it presents the Subscriber options command. This command brings up the Subscriber Options dialog box, shown in Figure 5-32, which you can use to determine when updates made in the original file will be passed through to the PageMaker publication, or to open the original application and the original document file.

Figure 5-31:
Use the Subscribe To dialog box to import Edition files.

Figure 5-32:
Use the Subscriber Options dialog box to manage edition files.

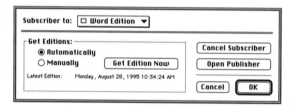

Using PageMaker's Linking Option instead of Publish and Subscribe: You do not, however, ever have to use these commands, even if you want to work with edition files. You can "Subscribe" to edition files by simply placing them with the Place command just like any other text or graphic element, update their external links using the Links command and launch the application that created the original document, and open the original document, using the Edit original command. Linking is discussed in Chapter 12.

Inserting Text as OLE Objects

Microsoft's answer to System 7's edition manager is a technology called Object Linking and Embedding (OLE), which is available for both Windows and System 7. Like the edition manager, OLE provides a way to move elements from one application to another and have any changes made to the original document pass through to copies that are used within other documents. Actually, OLE provides two ways to do this. OLE-linking works very much like the edition manager, in that a new data file is created to hold the elements exported from the source application (the OLE equivalent of the Publishing application), and that data file is then imported into the destination application (the

OLE equivalent of the Subscribing application). OLE-embedding, on the other hand, does not require that a new data file be created; instead the original document from one application is itself imported into the destination application.

PageMaker supports both OLE-linking and OLE-embedding. Although OLE is not as widely supported on the Macintosh as the edition manager, it is supported by all Microsoft applications, including the immensely popular Word and Excel and is highly popular in Windows on the PC.

Using OLE2's Drag and Drop Between Applications: PageMaker 6 is an OLE2-aware application, meaning that you can drag and drop text and other objects between PageMaker and other OLE2 applications, such as Word 6 and Excel 5. To do so, arrange the two documents so that you can see both of them on the screen. Then select the object you want to drag into PageMaker and simply drag, holding the mouse button, it into your PageMaker document.

Creating OLE Objects

To import text (or graphic) OLE objects, you must have both the client (PageMaker) and server applications open. You select the object in the server, and then use PageMaker's Paste Special... command. (Note that the server document must be named and saved.) To create the link, simply select Paste Link in the Paste Special dialog box, as shown in Figure 5-33. When you select Paste Link, PageMaker displays only the Client format available in the Paste As: list.

Figure 5-33:
An example of using Paste Link to create an OLE-linked object

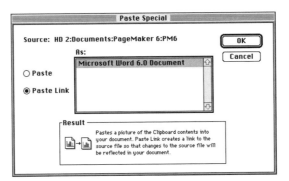

You cannot edit OLE-linked text or graphics within PageMaker but instead must edit them using the application that created them. To do this, select the OLE object and choose the Edit command from the Linked Document Object submenu of the Edit menu, or triple-click the object itself. This will launch the application that created the object and open the document from which the object was copied. Edit the document to your heart's content and then choose the Update command from the application's File menu. Close the document or quit the application if you want, and then switch back into PageMaker. Any changes you made will automatically be reflected in your publication.

If you do not want changes made to the original document to automatically transfer to the OLE-linked object in your publication, select the object, choose the Link Options command from the Element menu, and deselect the Update automatically option. (You'll find a complete discussion of PageMaker's Link options in Chapter 12.)

Creating OLE Objects with Insert Object...

The Insert Object... command lets you use any OLE-server application on your Mac to create new elements for your publication, and initiate this process from inside of PageMaker. Use it as a shortcut to create OLE objects. To begin, choose the Insert Object... command from the Edit menu. This brings up a list of the kind of objects (by program) you can create using the OLE-compatible programs on your hard drive, as shown in Figure 5-34.

Figure 5-34:
A list of OLE objects available through Insert Object

Select the type of object you want to create and click OK. This will launch the program that you'll use to create the object. A new document is automatically opened, and you can then create the text, spreadsheet, or graphic using any of the tools and features that application provides. When you've finished, choose the Update command from the File menu, close the document or quit the application if you want, and switch back into PageMaker. The new element you created will automatically be imported into your PageMaker publication as an OLE-embedded object. Figures 5-35 and 5-36 show the process.

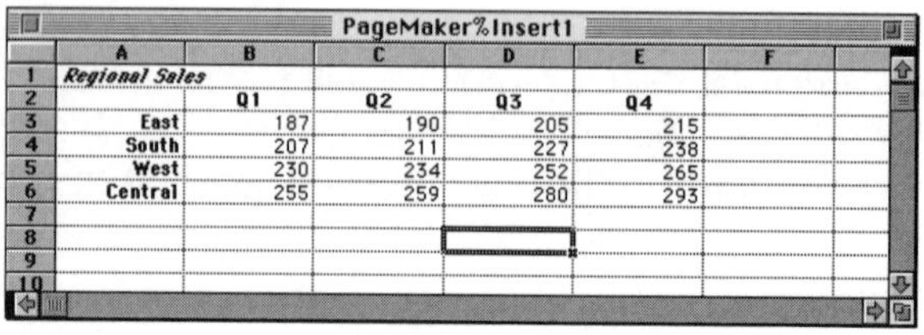

Figure 5-35:
An Excel document being created for insertion into PageMaker with Insert Object

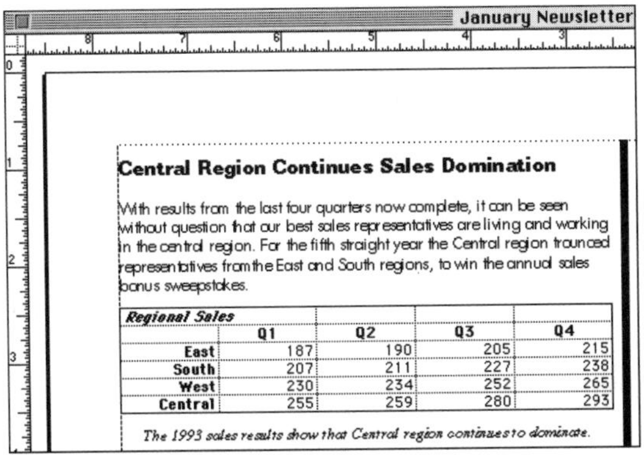

Figure 5-36:
The finished Excel spreadsheet after insertion into a PageMaker document with Insert Object

Now that this OLE object is in your PageMaker publication, you can edit it at any time by selecting it and choosing the Edit command from the Linked Document Object submenu in the Edit menu, or by triple-clicking the object itself. The application that created the object will be launched, and the document containing the element will be opened.

Exporting Text

After editing text in PageMaker, you will occasionally want to export your text out of PageMaker into word processing (or text-only) format. This allows you to take advantage of the superior text-processing features provided by most word processors or to use the text for some other purpose.

PageMaker allows you to export any amount of selected text, or an entire story, to a disk file in text-only or word processing format. The word processing formats available to you depend on the import/export filters available in the Filters folder inside the RSRC folder in the Adobe PageMaker 6.0 folder. Files exported to one of the word processing formats will retain all of the character- and paragraph-formatting attributes that were applied in PageMaker. Style sheets used to format text that is exported to Microsoft Word will also be converted and included in the exported file. Style sheet tags can be included in any exported text file, regardless of the export format.

To export text, select the text you wish to export, or if you wish to export an entire story, set the insertion point anywhere in the story. Choose the Export... command from the File menu, and the Export dialog box will appear, as shown in Figure 5-37. Select the File format that you wish to use for your exported file from the scrolling list on the left side of the dialog box. Under the Export option, select the Entire story option if you want to export all the text within the currently selected text block. If the insertion point was set but no text was selected when the Export... command was chosen, the Selected text only option will be dimmed.

Figure 5-37:
The Export dialog box

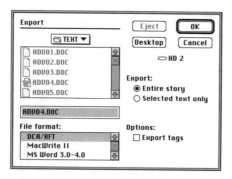

Click the Export tags check box if you would like style sheet tags to be placed before each paragraph in the exported document. Style sheet tags consist of the style sheet name placed between the less than (<) and greater than (>) characters. By exporting style sheet tags, you make it possible to use the Read tags option in the Place document dialog box when importing the document back into PageMaker, thereby retaining all style sheet links. Microsoft Word users do not need to use this option, since style sheets are exported to and imported from Microsoft Word files automatically.

Enter a name for your exported file in the field below the scrolling file list. Any legitimate Macintosh filename is acceptable. Use the folder bar, folders, drive icon, and Eject and Desktop buttons to select the location to which your exported file will be saved. When satisfied with all of the options, click the OK button or press the Return key to save the exported file, or click the Cancel button to abort the export process and return to the publication window.

After editing your exported file in a word processor, you can reimport it into PageMaker, replacing the existing text with the updated file or placing it into a new publication. All of these options were described earlier in this chapter.

■■

Summary

➥ Text exists in PageMaker publications as logical stories and in physical text blocks. Text flows through the various text blocks of a story as you adjust the size of the text blocks.

➥ You can resize text blocks by dragging on the handles that appear when the text block is selected or by pulling the tabs on the top or bottom text windowshades.

➥ Text is imported into PageMaker using the Place. . . command. PageMaker uses import filters to convert text from virtually any word processor into the format that it stores in your publications. In most cases, all formatting will transfer perfectly.

➥ If any font in the imported document is unavailable, you can use the PANOSE font matching system built into PageMaker to select the fonts you want to substitute for those that are missing.

➥ You can flow text into PageMaker text blocks using the manual, semiautomatic, or automatic text flow methods. You can also create text blocks by drag-placing text with the text cursor.

➥ The Story Editor is a mini word processor built into PageMaker. It lets you see text in a legible font and type size regardless of how the text is formatted in your publication, and provides Font, Change, and Spelling commands.

➥ You can export the text from any PageMaker story, saving it in a new font on disk in text-only format, or in the format of many popular word processing applications.

■■

Formatting Text

6

In This Chapter

- ➡️ Formatting versus editing
- ➡️ Character formatting versus paragraph formatting
- ➡️ Formatting characters
- ➡️ Character spacing, tracking, and kerning
- ➡️ Formatting paragraphs

Now that you know how text gets into PageMaker, you're ready to learn how to format text in your publications. PageMaker provides extensive and extremely precise formatting of both character and paragraph attributes — more extensive and precise than any word processor currently available, in fact, which is why you'll usually perform some amount of text formatting in PageMaker even if it was fully formatted in your word processor.

Wait a minute. Didn't it say in Chapter 5 that PageMaker isn't a word processor and that as much text editing as possible should be done in a real word processor? Yes, but we're making a distinction between editing and formatting. Editing means changing what words are on the page, and formatting means changing how the words look on the page. PageMaker is a mediocre text editor at best, but it is a great text formatter, as you'll soon discover.

The text in a PageMaker publication is defined by many different attributes, such as font, type size, leading, character width, tracking, kerning, alignment, margins, tabs, hyphenation, and many others. The commands to control this formatting are found on the Type menu and the control palette and can be applied using numerous keyboard equivalents. This chapter details PageMaker's formatting attributes and introduces the Type menu commands and keyboard equivalents you can use to apply them. Formatting commands in the control palette are covered in Chapter 9. You'll also learn a lot about formatting in Chapter 7.

Express Text Formatting: The commands and procedures for formatting text in this chapter are designed to provide you with the knowledge for setting type in PageMaker. Before diving in, though, we should point out that many of the procedures described here are also available on the Control palette. Once you've learned the typesetting concepts and procedures discussed in this chapter, be sure to check out the discussion of the Control palette in Chapter 9. It'll save you a bunch of time.

Characters and Paragraphs

To understand PageMaker's text-formatting features, you have to know the difference between character-level formatting attributes and paragraph-level formatting attributes. Character attributes are applied independently to any word or character; font, type size, leading, kerning, and tracking are all character attributes. Paragraph attributes, on the other hand, are always applied to an entire paragraph at once; they include margins, spacing before and after paragraphs, tabs, and hyphenation rules.

This distinction means that the effect of any text formatting depends on the text that is selected and the command that is chosen. If one word is selected and a character-formatting command is chosen, only that word will be changed. But if one word is selected and a paragraph-formatting command is chosen, the entire paragraph will be changed.

Character-Formatting Basics

How you apply character-level formatting depends on whether you are formatting new or existing text:

- ➣ **Existing Text.** To apply character-level formatting to existing text, select the text you want to change (see Figure 6-1) and then choose character-formatting commands from the Type menu (or their keyboard equivalents or from the Control palette, discussed in Chapter 9).

- ➣ **New Text.** You can also define the character-level formatting of text before you

Figure 6-1:
You apply character formatting to text selected with the text cursor or text I-beam.

The difference between literature and journalism *is that journalism is unreadable and literature is not read.*
—Oscar Wilde

create it by setting the insertion point into a new or existing text block, selecting the desired formatting commands and options (from the Type menu, using keyboard equivalents, or from the Control palette), and then typing.

☞ **New Text.** If you move the text insertion point into another existing text block (using the text tool) and begin typing again, the new text will take on the character-level formatting attributes of the character immediately preceding where you set the insertion point.

Changing default character formatting: To change the default character-level formatting attributes, which will effect all text subsequently entered in new text blocks, select any tool except the text tool and then select the desired character-formatting options.

Paragraph-formatting Basics

To change paragraph-level formatting attributes, set the insertion point anywhere inside the paragraph to be modified or select any word or words in that paragraph. To change the paragraph formatting of several paragraphs at once, make a selection so that at least one character of each paragraph you want to modify is selected and then choose the paragraph-formatting commands. To change the left margin of three consecutive paragraphs, for example, select the text in such a way that all or part of the three paragraphs are selected, as shown in Figure 6-2.

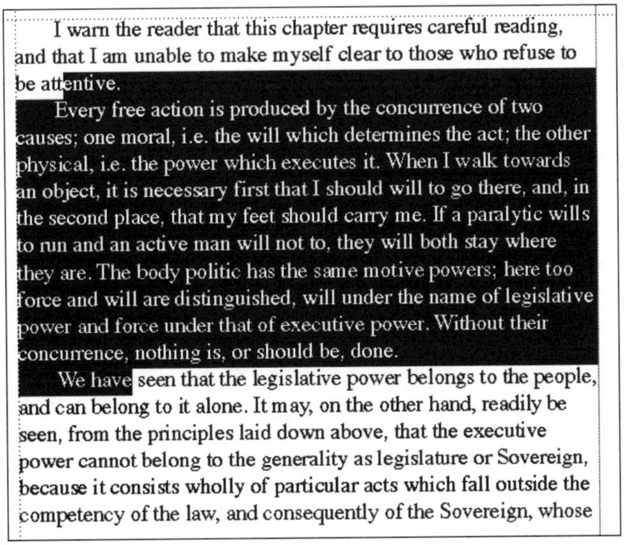

Figure 6-2:
Paragraph formatting is applied to all words in any partially or fully selected paragraph.

> I warn the reader that this chapter requires careful reading, and that I am unable to make myself clear to those who refuse to be attentive.
>
> Every free action is produced by the concurrence of two causes; one moral, i.e. the will which determines the act; the other physical, i.e. the power which executes it. When I walk towards an object, it is necessary first that I should will to go there, and, in the second place, that my feet should carry me. If a paralytic wills to run and an active man will not to, they will both stay where they are. The body politic has the same motive powers; here too force and will are distinguished, will under the name of legislative power and force under that of executive power. Without their concurrence, nothing is, or should be, done.
>
> We have seen that the legislative power belongs to the people, and can belong to it alone. It may, on the other hand, readily be seen, from the principles laid down above, that the executive power cannot belong to the generality as legislature or Sovereign, because it consists wholly of particular acts which fall outside the competency of the law, and consequently of the Sovereign, whose

Because formatting is directly tied to the current text selection, it is important to be able to make text selections quickly and accurately while working in the layout window or in the Story Editor. (Text formatting can be done in either the layout or the Story Editor, but the results of many commands are not displayed in Story Editor windows.) Here are several different methods of selecting text that you should become familiar with:

- Drag over the characters that you want to select, character by character. Dragging upward or downward will select additional lines of text, and dragging across columns of a threaded story will select large text sections quickly.

- Double-click a word with the text tool to select that word, hold the mouse button after the second click, and drag to select additional words.

- Triple-click inside a paragraph to select that paragraph, hold down the mouse button after the third click, and drag to select additional paragraphs.

- Set the insertion point by using keyboard equivalents to move the cursor. Table 6-1 shows PageMaker's keyboard equivalents for moving the text cursor.

Table 6-1 Keystrokes for Moving the Text Cursor	
To move cursor	**Press these keys**
One character left	Left arrow or keypad 4
One character right	Right arrow or keypad 6
One word left	Option-left arrow or ⌘-keypad 4
One word right	Option-right arrow or ⌘-keypad 6
To beginning of sentence	⌘-keypad 7
To end of sentence	⌘-keypad 1
To beginning of line	Keypad 7
To end of line	Keypad 1
One line down	Down arrow or keypad 2
One line up	Up arrow or keypad 8
To beginning of paragraph	⌘-keypad 8
To end of paragraph	⌘-keypad 2
In the Story Editor	**Press these keys**
To end of story	⌘-keypad 3 or end
To beginning of story	⌘-keypad 9 or home
Scroll display one line up	⌘-up arrow
Scroll display down one line	⌘-down arrow

Holding Shift while using any of these methods selects the text from the original insertion point and places it at the new location reached with the keystroke.

☞ Set the insertion point at one end of the text you want to select, locate the opposite end of the text you want to select, press the Shift key, and click the mouse button. All text between the original insertion point and the Shift-click will be selected.

☞ Set the insertion point anywhere in the text block and choose the Select All command from the Edit menu (⌘-A) to select all the text in the story, including all text threaded through text blocks on all pages.

☞ Set the insertion point at one end of the text you want to select, and extend the selection using one of the keyboard equivalents in Table 6-2.

Table 6-2
Keyboard Equivalents for Extending Selections

To extend selection	Press these keys
One character left	Shift-left arrow or Shift-keypad 4
One character right	Shift-right arrow or Shift-keypad 6
One word left	Shift-Option-left arrow or Shift-⌘-keypad 4
One word right	Shift-Option-right arrow or Shift-⌘-keypad 6
To beginning of sentence	Shift-⌘-keypad 7
To end of sentence	Shift-⌘-keypad 1
To beginning of line	Shift-keypad 7
To end of line	Shift-keypad 1
One line down	Shift-down arrow or Shift-keypad 2
One line up	Shift-up arrow or Shift-keypad 8
To beginning of paragraph	Shift-⌘-up arrow or Shift-⌘-keypad 8
To end of paragraph	Shift-⌘-down arrow or Shift-⌘-keypad 2
To end of story	Shift-⌘-keypad 3
To beginning of story	Shift-⌘-keypad 9 or Shift-home

Holding down the Shift key while pressing the right- or left-arrow key selects one character at a time; pressing Shift with the up- or down-arrow key selects one line at a time. Holding down the Shift and Option keys and pressing the right or left arrow selects one word at a time. Pressing the Shift and Command keys with the up or down arrow selects one paragraph at a time.

Character Formatting

Character formatting is controlled by the first eight commands in PageMaker's Type menu, which is shown in Figure 6-3. The first seven provide control over one specific character-formatting attribute each: Font, Size, Leading, Set Width, Type Style, Expert Tracking, and Expert Kerning.... The eighth is the Type Specs... command, which provides a single dialog box in which all character-formatting attributes can be specified.

Figure 6-3:
The Type menu contains all of PageMaker's character-formatting commands.

In the following list, I briefly introduce each of the eight character-formatting commands and their submenus. See the discussion of the Type Specs... command later in this section for detailed descriptions of each option.

- ☞ The Font command displays a submenu listing all fonts currently available to your System Software and the names of any missing fonts that are used in the current publication (these font names appear dimmed in the submenu).

- ☞ The Size command displays a submenu listing commonly used type sizes. It also provides the Other... command you can use to specify a type size not listed in the submenu.

  Type size changes can also be made using keyboard equivalents. To make the currently selected type one point smaller, press Shift-⌘-Option-, (comma). To make the currently selected type one point larger, press Shift-⌘-Option-. (period). To change the currently selected type to the next-smaller standard type size, press Shift-⌘-, (comma). To change the currently selected type to the next-larger standard type size, press Shift-⌘-. (period).

- ☞ The Leading (space between lines of text) command displays a submenu listing several leading options; but like the Size menu, this is not a complete listing, and the Other... command allows you to specify any desired leading value. The Auto leading option applies leading that is 120% of the current type size. You can change the value of Auto leading in the Paragraph Spacing Attributes dialog box, as discussed under "Spacing," later in this chapter.

- The Set Width command opens a pop-up menu offering several preset character widths. You can use the Other... option to enter any width value between 5% and 250.0% in 0.1% increments.

- The Type Style command displays a submenu offering PageMaker's type styles: normal, bold, italic, underline, strikethru, outline, shadow, and reverse.

- The Expert Tracking command is used to adjust the character spacing of the selected text, loosening or tightening the text. It is fully discussed later in this chapter under "Expert Tracking."

- The Expert Kerning... command lets you adjust the space between character pairs. Kerning is discussed later in this chapter under "Character Spacing, Tracking, and Kerning."

- The Type specs... command (⌘-T) brings up the Type Specifications dialog box, which provides full control over the character attributes of the currently selected text. Shown in Figure 6-4, it includes all the formatting capabilities of the first six Type menu commands, plus control over type color, position, case, word break, line break, baseline shift, and more. Each option in this dialog box is discussed in this section.

Figure 6-4:
The Type Specifica-
tions dialog box

Type Specifications		
Font: [Times]		[OK]
Size: [12] ▷ points	Position: [Normal]	[Cancel]
Leading: [Auto] ▷ points	Case: [Normal]	[Options...]
Set width: [Normal] ▷ % Size	Track: [No Track]	[MM Fonts...]
Color: [Black]	Line End: [Break]	
Tint: [100] ▷ %		
Type style: ☐ Normal ☐ Italic ☐ Outline ☐ Reverse		
☐ Bold ☐ Underline ☒ Shadow ☐ Strikethru		

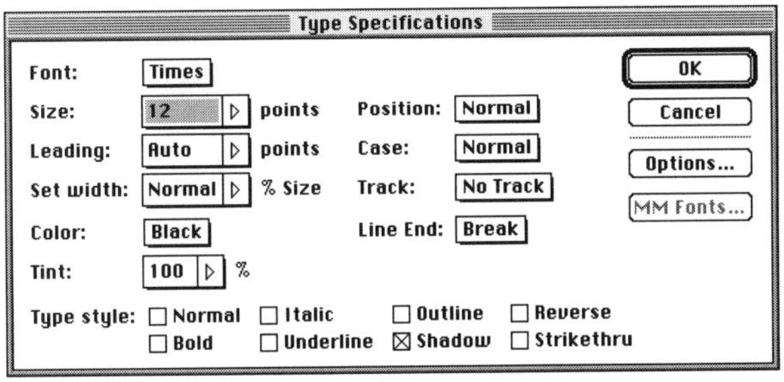

Font

The Font option displays the name of the font used by the currently selected text (or a blank box if more than one font is represented within the current text selection). Clicking on the font name (or blank box) opens the Font pop-up menu, listing all type faces currently available and the names of any fonts used in the document that are currently unavailable. Unavailable font names are dimmed in the listing, indicating that they have been removed from the System/Fonts folder or unattached via a font utility like Suitcase II or MasterJuggler. Font names in the pop-up menu are listed alphabetically, with the listing centered on the currently selected typeface. (If the current font is Aachen, most of the listing will be below the selection; if the current font is Zapf Dingbats, most of the listing will be above.) Scrolling up or down the list allows access to all available fonts. Releasing the mouse button while a typeface name is selected changes the currently selected text to that font.

Size

The Size option controls the type size (in points) of the currently selected text. The Size option consists of field box and a pop-up menu. The type size of the currently selected text is displayed in the field box unless all the selected text is not set in a single type size. Any value between 4 and 650 in 0.1-point increments can be entered in the field. (There are approximately 72 points to an inch.) See Figure 6-5 for examples of the range in type sizes. The Size pop-up menu is accessed by selecting the arrow next to the field; it lists the same few type sizes presented in the Size command pop-up menu discussed above. For PostScript fonts, type sizes appear in outline style when screen fonts in those sizes are installed on the system.

Figure 6-5:
Examples of different sizes of type. PageMaker can scale type in sizes ranging from 4 to 650 points in 0.1 increments.

A flcdi9r
bqlc2ty
c bncwlj
D ruoeq
e b6ah

If you don't have Adobe Type Manager installed, these outlined sizes will be displayed more clearly on-screen than the non-outlined sizes, but this affects only on-screen legibility. Both the outlined and non-outlined sizes will print at full quality on a PostScript printer. For TrueType fonts, all sizes appear in outline type.

Getting really big type: If 650-point type is not large enough for you, there are two easy ways to get it even larger. First, you can copy text, paste it back in PICT format (use the Paste Special command), and then stretch it as large as you need. Second, you can use the Scale option in the Print dialog box (use the Paper options button) to scale the 650-point type up to 999%. Hope you have a big printer!

Leading

Leading controls the amount of vertical space between lines of text and was named after the lead shafts that were placed between lines of type on old typesetting machines. Controlling leading allows you to affect significantly the amount of space taken up by your text, as well as the look and feel of the text. Type set with a very loose leading is often easier to read than type set with a tight leading — but of course requires much more space. You should always feel free to experiment with leading — it is one of the easiest and most significant ways to change your publication.

The Leading option is similar to the Size option in its use of the option field and pop-up menu. The current leading setting is displayed in the field unless the selected text includes more than one leading size. You can enter any value between 0 and 1300 in 0.1-point increments in this field. The pop-up menu, which is displayed by holding down the mouse button on the arrow icon, lists several leading settings that PageMaker considers appropriate for the current type size. The number of leading choices and range of leading choices available in this pop-up menu vary depending on the current type size. Auto is, by default, 120% of the current type size. In many cases, Auto leading is suitable for your text, especially at small point sizes, such as 8, 10, or 12. But at sizes larger than, say, 18 points, 120 percent is too much leading. (10-point type would use 12-point leading, 14-point type would use 17-point leading.) Using the Auto leading option in the Paragraph Spacing Attributes dialog box (discussed under "Spacing" later), you can control the percentage used to calculate Auto leading. Any value between 0% and 200% can be entered for the Auto leading percentage.

PageMaker can apply leading in one of three ways: proportional, top-of-caps, or baseline. You specify which leading method PageMaker will use for a specific paragraph in the Paragraph Spacing Attributes dialog box, accessed via the Paragraph command and the Spacing button in the Paragraph Specifications dialog box. Paragraph spacing is discussed under "Spacing," later in this chapter.

- **Proportional leading** applies two-thirds of the space above the baseline and one- third of the space below the baseline.
- **Top of caps leading** is measured from the top of a capital letter to the top of a capital letter in the line below.
- **Baseline leading** is measured from the baseline of one line of text to the baseline of the next line of text. The baseline is the place on the line where the bottom of the characters fall, minus the descenders, as shown in Figure 6-6.

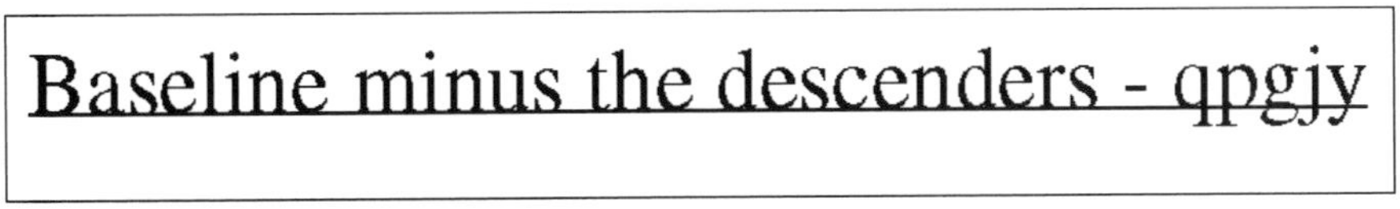

Baseline minus the descenders - qpgjy

Figure 6-6: An example of a line of text's baseline

Any time that one line of text contains characters with two different leading specifications, the larger leading setting will prevail. When making a large initial capital letter, for example, you might have a 24-point character on the same line as 12-point characters. If both the 24-point character and the 12-point character use Auto leading, then the entire line will be set at a little over 30-point leading (the Auto leading for the 24-point character), larger than desired. This can be corrected by changing the leading for the 24-point character to 14-point or smaller, so that the Auto leading of the 12-point character will be larger and therefore prevail.

Set Width

The Set Width option is a pop-up menu offering seven alternatives that control the width, as a percentage, of the selected text, allowing you to compress or expand type, as shown in Figure 6-7. The Normal option, which is the default, sets each character at the width that was defined by the font designer — 100% of its normal width. The 70%, 80%, 90%, 110%, 120%, and 130% options compress or expand the type as their names suggest. In the Type Specifications dialog box, the Set Width popup menu includes seven options — 70, 80, 90, Normal, 110, 120, and 130. To get Set Width's "Other" command on the Type menu, you can enter a set width yourself, in the box labeled Set width in the Type Specifications dialog box. Enter any value between 5% and 250% in 0.1% increments. The Set Width option is primarily used to achieve special graphic effects with type, and care should be taken not to modify any type so severely that you compromise its legibility.

Figure 6-7:
The 70%, 90%, 100% and 120% Set Width options

Good judgment comes from experience, and experience comes from bad judgment.
—*Barry LePatner*

Good judgment comes from experience, and experience comes from bad judgment.
—*Barry LePatner*

Good judgment comes from experience, and experience comes from bad judgment.
—*Barry LePatner*

Good judgment comes from experience, and experience comes from bad judgment.
—*Barry LePatner*

Style

The Type style option consists of eight options, each of which has a check box in front of it. Any of these options may be selected by clicking the check box or clicking the style name. Most of these type styles have keyboard equivalents. They are listed in Table 6-3. Selecting the Normal option deselects all other options. Selecting any of the options other than the Normal option deselects the Normal option. Examples of each type style are shown in Figure 6-8.

Table 6-3	
Type Style Keyboard Equivalents	
Style	*Keyboard equivalent*
Normal	Shift-⌘ (spacebar)
Bold	Shift-⌘-B
Italic	Shift-⌘-I
Underline	Shift-⌘-U
Strikethru	Shift-⌘-/
Outline	Shift-⌘-D
Shadow	Shift-⌘-W
Reverse	Shift-⌘-V

Figure 6-8:
Examples of PageMaker's eight type styles

Harley Davidson
Harley Davidson
Harley Davidson
<u>Harley Davidson</u>
Harley Davidson
Harley Davidson
Harley Davidson
~~Harley Davidson~~

Color

This option simply allows you to change the color of selected text (or the next text you type). This pop-up brings up a list of colors defined for the publication, as discussed in Chapter 10.

Tint

This option allows you to apply a percentage or screen (tint) of the color selected in Color to selected text or the next text you type. Tints and applying colors in PageMaker are discussed in detail in Chapter 10.

Position

The three options here are Normal, Superscript (such as "Microsoft®") and Subscript (such as "H_2O"). You can adjust how PageMaker sizes and positions superscripted and subscripted text with Options, discussed later in this section.

Case

The three options here are Normal, ALL CAPS, and SMALL CAPS. You can adjust the size of small caps in relation to the rest of the text in a text block with Options, discussed later in this section.

Track

The Track option offers the ability to modify the default character spacing of your text. The six tracking options are No Track, Very Loose, Loose, Normal, Tight, and Very Tight. These options use vague terminology because the actual spacing modification made by these options depends upon the particular font and type size being used — not because PageMaker's tracking abilities are imprecise. Figure 6-9 shows three different tracking options as applied to one particular paragraph. See "Character Spacing, Tracking, and Kerning," later in this chapter for a detailed account of how PageMaker's tracking really works.

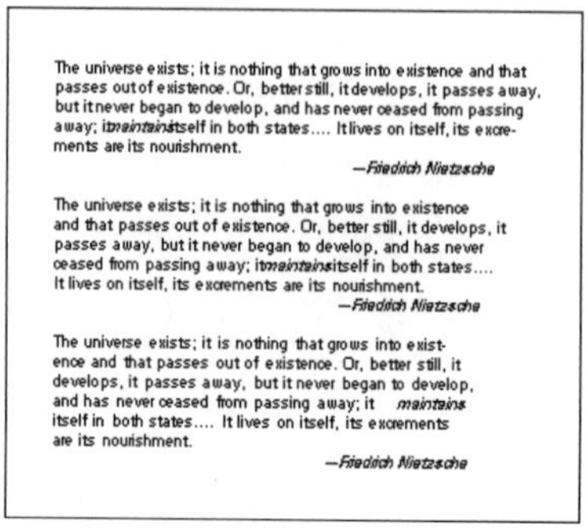

The universe exists; it is nothing that grows into existence and that passes out of existence. Or, better still, it develops, it passes away, but it never began to develop, and has never ceased from passing away; it *maintains* itself in both states.... It lives on itself, its excrements are its nourishment.

—*Friedrich Nietzsche*

The universe exists; it is nothing that grows into existence and that passes out of existence. Or, better still, it develops, it passes away, but it never began to develop, and has never ceased from passing away; it *maintains* itself in both states.... It lives on itself, its excrements are its nourishment.

—*Friedrich Nietzsche*

The universe exists; it is nothing that grows into existence and that passes out of existence. Or, better still, it develops, it passes away, but it never began to develop, and has never ceased from passing away; it *maintains* itself in both states.... It lives on itself, its excrements are its nourishment.

—*Friedrich Nietzsche*

Figure 6-9: Examples of Very Tight, Normal, and Very Loose tracking

Line End

This command allows you to force a selected text block to fit all on one line. The No Break option instructs PageMaker that all of the selected text must fit on one line in the current text block. To accomplish this, PageMaker will modify the character spacing within the selected text as necessary, even if it means squishing letters together. The Break option is selected by default.

Options...

Clicking the Options... button in the Type Specifications dialog box brings up the Type Options dialog box, which has five options that affect character formatting. Each of these, shown in Figure 6-10, provides control over character-formatting definitions for other type specification options. These include the size of small caps and both the size and position of superscript and subscript characters.

Figure 6-10:
The Type Options dialog
box

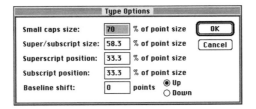

Baseline shift allows you to move any selected characters above or below their natural baseline in .1-point increments. Why the baseline shift option is buried in the Type options dialog box is another of the great mysteries of the PageMaker user interface. Fortunately, access to the baseline shift option is easily available via the control palette, as discussed in Chapter 9, and it is from there that you will likely most frequently use this typographic capability.

After changing or viewing the settings in the Type Options dialog box, click OK to return to the Type Specifications dialog box.

MM Fonts...

This option brings up the Multiple Master Fonts dialog box, which allows you to make weight and width changes to Adobe multiple master Type 1 fonts, just as you would from Adobe Type Manager. If you have no multiple master fonts installed, this option is dimmed. Multiple master fonts allow you to change the appearance of the font by changing width and weight characteristics.

Using Superscript and Subscript to Create Fractions

One thing you can do by modifying the size and position of superscript and subscript characters is create great looking fractions. To do this, set the size of your superscript and subscript characters to 50% or 60% of the body text size and set the position of the superscript to 30% and the position of the subscript to 0%. Finally, kern the numerator characters (the superscripted characters) and the denominator characters (the subscripted characters) closer to the slash. At a type size of 12 points, you'll need to kern the numerator about three-tenths of an em and the denominator about two-tenths to get a good fit. Of course, the exact kerning will depend upon the font you're using and your own taste. Kerning is discussed under "Character Spacing, Tracking, and Kerning," later in this chapter.

Formatting Paragraphs

Paragraph formatting in PageMaker controls the margins and alignment of a paragraph within its text block, the spacing between one paragraph and another, the way lines of a paragraph break across columns or pages, rulers on any sides of the paragraph, spacing of words and letters, hyphenation, and tabs. These attributes are controlled by the Paragraph, Indents/Tabs, Hyphenation, and Alignment commands on the Type menu.

Using the Paragraphs Command

Choosing the Paragraphs command (⌘-M) from the Type menu brings up the Paragraph Specifications dialog box, shown in Figure 6-11. This dialog box provides control over paragraph indents, spacing, alignment, and options.

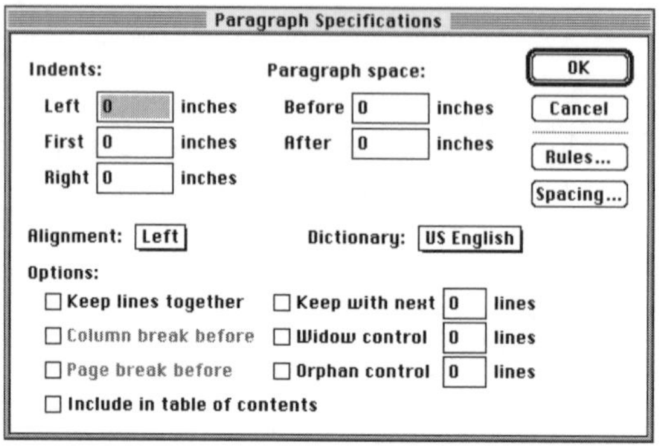

Figure 6-11:
The Paragraph Specifications dialog box

Paragraph Specifications		
Indents:	**Paragraph space:**	**OK**
Left 0 inches	Before 0 inches	**Cancel**
First 0 inches	After 0 inches	**Rules...**
Right 0 inches		**Spacing...**

Alignment: Left   Dictionary: US English

Options:
☐ Keep lines together   ☐ Keep with next 0 lines
☐ Column break before   ☐ Widow control 0 lines
☐ Page break before   ☐ Orphan control 0 lines
☐ Include in table of contents

Paragraph Indents

Indents offset the text edges in any paragraph from the edges of the block. You set indents independently for the left and right sides of a paragraph and the first line of text in the paragraph.

> ∽ **The Left indent option** specifies the positioning of the left edge of each line in the paragraph relative to the left edge of the text block.

> ∽ **The First indent option** specifies the position of the left edge of the first line of type in a text block relative to the left edge of the other lines in the paragraph. In other words, the first line of each paragraph gets the indent specified for the Left indent plus the indent specified for the First indent. Since you can enter a positive or negative value into the First indent field, the first line may be closer to the edge of the text block (such as the way the bullet in this paragraph appears) or it may be further indented as are the first lines in traditional first-line indented paragraphs.

> To create a paragraph where the first line has a more pronounced indent than the other lines in the paragraph (an effect that is traditionally accomplished by placing a tab character before the first line of a paragraph), the First indent option should be given a value equal to the distance that the first line should be indented. To create a paragraph where the first line begins to the left of all other lines in the paragraph, the First indent value should be given a negative value equal to the distance before the left margin that the first line should begin, a format often called *hanging indent*. Note that the First line indent can only be as negative as the Left indent is positive, or the specification would call for the first line to begin outside the text block. See Figure 6-12 for examples.

> • **Timeless style.** It is our belief that innately functional furniture has no limits in time or space. We advocate the usefulness of furniture without regard to fads or trends.
>
> Working out of our first studio, a rented loft on Via Boccaccio, near Milano's North Station, Gio and Suni produced the initial line of VIA 1.618 furniture in 1985.

Figure 6-12: Examples of negative (left) and positive (right) first line indents

> ∽ **The Right indent option** specifies the positioning of the right edge of every line in the paragraph relative to the right edge of the text block.

Paragraph indents can also be specified in the Indents/Tabs dialog box, using a ruler and indent triangles exactly like those used in Microsoft Word. These are fully described later in this chapter under "Indents and Tabs."

Alignment

This option allows you to set the vertical alignment of selected paragraphs. Its options match those of the Alignment command on the Type menu. Alignment is discussed in detail in "Using the Alignment Command," later in this chapter.

Paragraph Spacing

Avoid using carriage returns to put space between paragraphs: The next set of options control space placed before or after paragraphs, to separate them from text that precedes and follows. You should always use these options to separate paragraphs, and never press the Return key twice (inserting two consecutive carriage returns) to separate paragraphs. There are several reasons for this. One is that when a paragraph lands at the top of a column, PageMaker will automatically ignore the Space before command, so that the first line in the paragraph lines up correctly at the top of the column. (If you want to force the Space before to appear even when at the top of a column, add a paragraph rule to paragraph, but give that paragraph rule a line width of none. Rules are discussed under "Paragraph Lines," later in this section.) If a carriage return (which is really just an empty paragraph) is used to space paragraphs, on the other hand, you will occasionally find a new paragraph starting one line below the top of a column because the spacing carriage return is sitting on the first line of the column.

Secondly, using the Paragraph Space: Before and Paragraph Space: After options makes it much easier to make global adjustments to the amount of space between paragraphs, which may become necessary in order to make your text fit in the available space. When carriage returns have been inserted, you have to select each one manually and change its size or leading in order to increase or reduce the spacing between paragraphs. When Paragraph Space: Before and Paragraph Space: After are used, you can simply select a range of paragraphs or modify the style sheet definitions. Style sheets are discussed in the next chapter.

- **Paragraph Space: Before.** Enter the amount of blank space you want inserted before the selected paragraphs.

- **Paragraph Space: After.** Enter the amount of blank space you want inserted after the selected paragraphs.

Controlling Widows, Orphans, and Table of Contents Entries

The paragraph options at the bottom of the Paragraph Specifications dialog box provide seven options, six of which affect the arrangement of text within your layout. The final option is used to select paragraphs for inclusion in a PageMaker-generated table of contents.

- ☞ **Keep lines together.** When this option is turned on, the paragraph will never be broken across pages, columns, or above and below a graphic. PageMaker will flow the paragraph forward until it fits in its entirety on one page in one column. To accomplish this, PageMaker may have to leave a larger block of white space than usual, so care should be taken when applying this option to paragraphs containing more than a few lines of text.

- ☞ **Keep with next ____ lines.** This option instructs PageMaker to place the current paragraph on the same page and in the same column as the first lines of the next paragraph. You can enter the values 1, 2, or 3 in the field. (Entering a value will also "check" the check box, which also applies to Widow control and Orphan control.) This option is most often used to guarantee that headlines or subheads are not placed at the end of a page or the bottom of a column, but it can also be used in other circumstances, such as keeping the lines of an address together. If PageMaker is unable to lay out your text in keeping with the setting you make from this option, and if the Show keeps violations option is selected in the Preferences dialog box (discussed in Chapter 1), PageMaker alerts you that the text is being positioned differently than you have requested by adding a yellow (or gray) bar over your text.

- ☞ **Column break before.** When this option is selected, the paragraph will always begin at the top of the next available column.

- ☞ **Page break before.** When this option is selected, the paragraph will always begin at the top of the next available page.

- ☞ **Widow control ____ lines.** When a paragraph starts on one page and ends on another, the lines on the page where the paragraph starts are sometimes called widows. In most long publications, it is unprofessional for only 1 or 2 lines of a paragraph to be widowed at the end of a page. This option instructs PageMaker to allow not less than the specified number of lines to remain at the bottom of a page. When this option is selected, enter either 1, 2, or 3 in the field to instruct PageMaker to keep at least 1, 2, or 3 lines of the paragraph at the bottom on any page on which the paragraph begins. If PageMaker cannot keep these lines at the bottom of the page, the paragraph is moved so that it starts on the top of the next page. If PageMaker is unable to lay out your text in keeping with the setting you make from this option, it will tell you (by adding a gray bar below your text) if the Show keeps violations option is selected in the Preferences dialog box, as discussed in Chapter 1.

↪ **Orphan control ____ lines.** When a paragraph starts on one page and ends on another, the lines on the page where the paragraph ends are sometimes called orphans. In most long publications, it is unprofessional for only 1 or 2 lines of a paragraph to be orphaned at the top of a page. This option instructs PageMaker to allow not less than the specified number of lines together in the end of a paragraph that is broken across two or more pages. When this option is selected, you can enter values 1, 2, or 3 in the field to instruct PageMaker to move at least 1, 2, or 3 lines of the paragraph to the top of the page on which the paragraph ends. PageMaker accomplishes this by moving lines from the end of the preceding page to the top of the following page. If PageMaker is unable to lay out your text in keeping with the setting you make from this option, it will tell you (by adding a gray bar below your text) if the Show keeps violations option is selected in the Preferences dialog box, as discussed in Chapter 1.

↪ **Include in table of contents.** When this option is selected, the entire text of the paragraph and the page number on which it is positioned are included in the table of contents created with the Create TOC... command. In general, this option is used only for headlines and subheads that are one or two lines long. Generating tables of contents is discussed in Chapter 12.

Paragraph Lines

Clicking the Rules button in the Paragraph Specifications dialog box brings up the Paragraph Rules dialog box, which lets you add lines above or below any paragraph in your publication. It is shown in Figure 6-13. The top and bottom halves of this dialog box are identical, providing for the definition of lines above or below the paragraph.

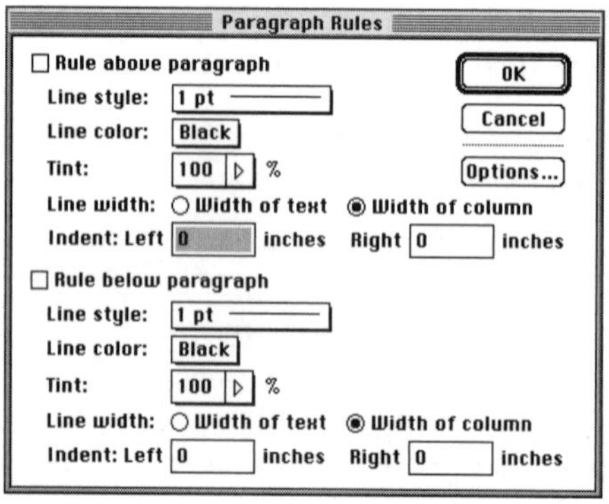

Figure 6-13:
The Paragraph rules dialog box is used to assign lines above and below paragraphs

```
┌─────────────────── Paragraph Rules ────────────────────┐
│  ☐ Rule above paragraph                  ┌──────────┐  │
│     Line style:  │ 1 pt ──────── │         │    OK    │  │
│     Line color:  │ Black │                 └──────────┘  │
│     Tint:        │ 100 │ ▷ │ %            ┌──────────┐  │
│                                           │  Cancel  │  │
│     Line width: ○ Width of text ● Width of column       │
│                                           ┌──────────┐  │
│     Indent: Left │ 0 │ inches  Right │ 0 │ inches │Options...│ │
│  ☐ Rule below paragraph                                 │
│     Line style:  │ 1 pt ──────── │                      │
│     Line color:  │ Black │                              │
│     Tint:        │ 100 │ ▷ │ %                          │
│     Line width: ○ Width of text ● Width of column       │
│     Indent: Left │ 0 │ inches  Right │ 0 │ inches       │
└─────────────────────────────────────────────────────────┘
```

Paragraph Rules automatically puts lines above and/or below paragraphs, so you can achieve this effect without having to draw the lines manually. This guarantees that the rules (lines) will be the exact width of the paragraph or the width of the text in the paragraph (depending on the option you select), and it makes it easy to position the rules very precisely relative to the text in the paragraph. An even bigger benefit is that the paragraph rules flow along with the text when any changes cause the text to reflow within its text block or even to another text block. If you created lines with the line tool, you would have to measure the line length very carefully to match the text or paragraph size, and it would be much more difficult to position the lines accurately and keep them in position. Figure 6-14 shows an example of a rule above and a rule below a paragraph. As you can see, this is an easy way to dress up heading and subheads.

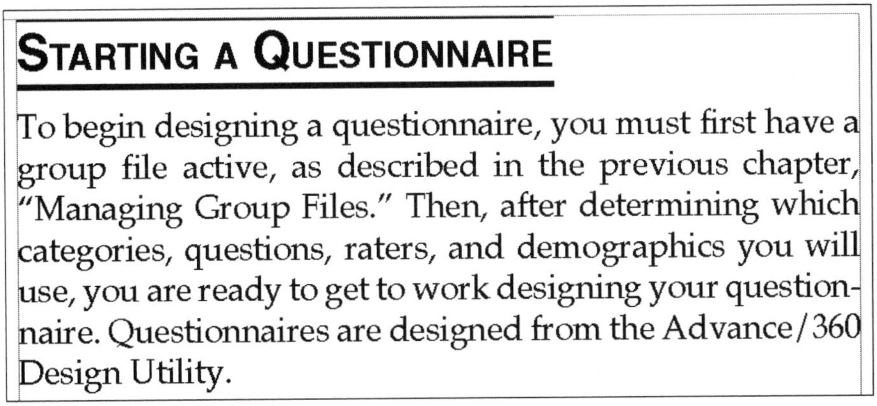

STARTING A QUESTIONNAIRE

To begin designing a questionnaire, you must first have a group file active, as described in the previous chapter, "Managing Group Files." Then, after determining which categories, questions, raters, and demographics you will use, you are ready to get to work designing your questionnaire. Questionnaires are designed from the Advance/360 Design Utility.

Figure 6-14: An example of a rule above and a rule below.

For each rule added with the Paragraph rules option, you use the Line style pop-up menu to define the line weight or style and the Line color pop-up to select a line color. The Line width option determines if the line is to be drawn at the width of the longest line of text in the paragraph or at the full width of the text block, regardless of the actual text width. The left and right Indent options are used to add an indent to the line, which shortens the line width accordingly.

To control the placement of paragraph rules, click the Options... button in the Paragraph Rules dialog box to see the Paragraph Rule Options dialog box that's shown in Figure 6-15. The Top and Bottom options are used to specify how far above or below the baseline of the first or last line of the paragraph the lines will be placed. If these options are set to Auto, rules are placed even with the top or bottom (respectively) of capital letters in the first or last line (respectively) of the paragraph. Entering Top or Bottom values larger than the current leading moves the lines away from the text and adds leading to the first or last lines of the paragraph.

Figure 6-15:
The Paragraph Rule Options
dialog box

```
                    Paragraph Rule Options
Top: [0.25]    inches
               above baseline        (   OK   )

Bottom: [0.1]  inches                ( Cancel )
               below baseline

□ Align next paragraph to grid      ( Reset  )

Grid size: [0]    ▷  points
```

When the Align next paragraph to grid option is selected, an extra space is added to the
first line of the paragraph below the rule. This helps to ensure that all lines of text in
that paragraph text block remain aligned to the grid specified with the Grid size option.
You'll usually want to enter the value of the leading used in your body copy into the
Grid size option. When creating layouts with multiple columns of text, this helps ensure
that the baselines of the text in all of the columns are aligned.

Getting out of Paragraph Rule Options fast: After setting the Paragraph rule
options, you can click the OK button to return to the Paragraph Rules dialog
box; but if you are finished setting paragraph options, you can hold down the
Option key while clicking the OK button (or pressing the Enter key), and all
three dialog boxes — Paragraph Rule Options, Paragraph Rules, and Paragraph
Specifications — will close. By the way, this Option-Click trick works in all
nested (multiple level) dialog boxes within PageMaker.

Spacing

The Paragraph Specifications dialog box has one more nested dialog box — the Paragraph Spacing Attributes dialog box, which is accessed by clicking the Spacing…
button. This dialog box, shown in Figure 6-16, is used to set the Word space and Letter
space parameters PageMaker uses to justify text, turn on pair kerning, select a leading
method, and specify the default size of automatic leading. Each of these options is
discussed in detail later in this chapter: Word space and Letter space and pair kerning
are covered under "Character Spacing, Tracking, and Kerning," and leading is discussed
in the character-formatting section earlier.

Figure 6-16:
The Paragraph Spacing
Attributes dialog box

```
                   Paragraph Spacing Attributes
Word space:              Letter space:
Minimum [75]  %   Minimum [-5]   %        (   OK   )

Desired [100] %   Desired  [0]   %        ( Cancel )

Maximum [150] %   Maximum [25]   %        ( Reset  )

Pair kerning: ⊠ Auto above [4]  points

Leading method:        Autoleading:
● Proportional         [120] % of point size
○ Top of caps
○ Baseline
```

Boxing and Shading Headlines

You can use the Paragraph Rules Option, along with the Line style, Line color, and Line width options to create very nice effects with headlines or subheads. For example, suppose you want to add a 30% gray box to some subhead text that is set with 14-point text and 16-point leading. To do this, you first define the 30% gray tint in the Edit colors dialog box by selecting the Define Colors command in the Element menu. Then, select the subhead and open the Paragraph rules dialog box. Choose the Custom... Line style option and specify a 16-point line weight. Use the Line color option to select the 30% gray color you defined, and set the Line width option to the width of the text.

This produces a 30% screen over your subhead, but it forces the screen to start just at the start of the first letter and to end at the end of the last letter in the subhead. To create a more natural look, specify a negative .15-inch (-0.15) indent to the left and right of the line width. Now the 30% screen starts .15 inch before the first character in the subhead and ends .15 inch after the last character in the subhead. This same trick of adding negative indents when using the Line width of the text option can be used with any rule you add above or below paragraphs.

The advantage of using this method, as opposed to creating a shaded box and placing it on the text, is that lines created with Rules stay with the selected paragraph, no matter what changes you make affecting text flow.

Indents and Tabs

The Indents/tabs dialog box lets you visually manipulate the left, right, and first-line indents, and tab settings, for any paragraph or group of paragraphs. To access this dialog box, choose the Indents/Tabs command from the Type menu (⌘-I). The Indents/tabs dialog box, shown in Figure 6-17, appears positioned above the selected paragraphs. In most cases, it is automatically positioned so that its left and first-line markers line up above the current left edge and first-line indents, as shown in the figure.

The width of the Indents/tabs dialog box is dependent upon the size of your monitor, but you can scroll the ruler either right or left by clicking the arrows at either end. You can also move the dialog box by dragging its title bar. Wherever it is positioned, the zero point on the ruler represents the left edge of the current text block.

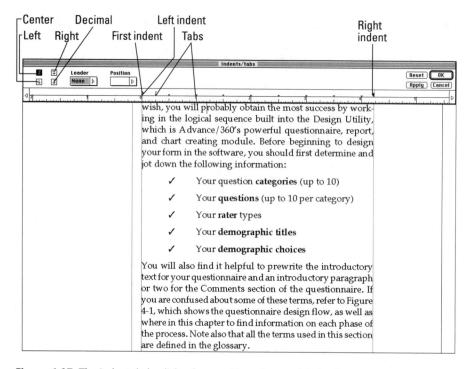

Figure 6-17: The Indents/tabs dialog box positioned over a block of text

The left, right, and first-line indent markers are small black triangles that appear just above the ruler. By dragging these markers to new positions above the ruler, you can adjust the corresponding indents. A digital measure of the marker position appears in the Position field as you drag. To see the effect of a margin change, or any other change you make in this dialog box, click the Apply button. To save the changes made in the dialog box, click OK, and of course click Cancel to close the dialog box while discarding any changes. (You can even use the Cancel button after having used the Apply button.)

If you've selected more than one paragraph before the Indents/Tabs command was chosen, the indents and tabs of the topmost paragraph will appear in the Indents/tabs dialog box even if subsequent paragraphs have different indents or tabs. If any changes are then made to the indent or tab options, and the Apply or OK button is clicked, the settings shown in the dialog box will be applied to all selected paragraphs, wiping out any differences they may have had.

Tab markers are small downward-pointing arrows that also appear above the ruler. Four types of tabs are supported: Left, Right, Center, and Decimal. With left tabs, text lines up to the left of the tab; with right tabs, text lines up to the right of the tab; with center tabs, text aligns to the center. Decimal tabs allow you to create columns of numbers aligned on the decimal, or another character, such as a comma. Figure 6-18 shows an example of the four tab types. Each tab has a unique icon, displayed in upper-left corner of the dialog box, that appears in the ruler when the tab is set. To set a tab type, click its icon.

Any tab can have a tab leader, which fills the space between the position where the tab key is pressed and the tab itself is positioned. PageMaker supports a dotted leader, a dashed line leader, an underline leader, and a custom leader that allows you to enter any one or two characters to be used as the tab leader.

Figure 6-18:
Examples of PageMaker's four tab types:
Left, Right, Center, and Decimal

```
Planes
Trains
Automobiles

    Planes
    Trains
Automobiles

   Planes
   Trains
Automobiles

   100.01
   2345.543
12345.54321
```

Leaders, shown in Figure 6-19, provide a visual reference between items on a line, making it easier for the eye to follow the line to the tabbed item. Tab leaders must be assigned when the tab is created — you cannot add a leader to an existing tab. To choose a leader type, select one from the Leader pop-up.

Figure 6-19:
An example of leadered tabs

```
Lunch Menu
Peanut butter & jelly........................ .50¢
Hamburger ...................................$1.20
Cold Pizza ..................................... .95¢
Banana ........................................ .22¢
```

By default, each PageMaker paragraph has a left tab stop, with no leader, positioned at each ½ inch increment in the paragraph. You can reset these tab stops, add new stops, delete specific stops, or manipulate existing stops, as described below:

- **To remove all the existing tabs,** and reset the paragraph indents, click the Clear button.

- **To add a new tab,** click the icon representing the kind of tab that you want to create, click the arrow next to the Leader field to select a leader from the pop-up menu, and then click the mouse button in the ruler at the position you want the new tab. (You cannot create a new tab on top of an existing indent marker. Instead, you must create the tab elsewhere and then drag it into position over the indent marker.)

  You can also add a new tab by selecting one of the tab icons, selecting a type of tab leader, and then entering the position where the new tab should be placed in the Position field, and then clicking on the arrow next to the Position field and selecting the Add Tab command from the pop-up menu. This will place a new tab at the specified position.

- **To add a series of tabs at equally spaced intervals,** add the first new tab at the desired position and then choose the Repeat tab command from the Position pop-up menu. PageMaker will automatically add additional tabs at equal distances between the current tab and the right margin.

- **To check the position and leader of an existing tab,** click on the tab in the ruler. The position of the tab will be displayed in the Position field, the type of tab will be selected in the tab icons, and the leader type will be shown in the Leader field.

- **To reset an existing tab,** select and drag the tab icon horizontally in the ruler. As you move the icon, the current position will be displayed in the Position field. Release the tab when satisfied with the new location. Alternatively, you can select an existing tab in the ruler, enter the value of the position to which you wish to move the tab in the Position field, and then choose the Move Tab command from the Position pop-up menu.

- **To delete any tab,** click and drag the tab icon down below the ruler (vertically) and release the mouse button. The tab icon will disappear. To remove all the tab stops for the current paragraph, click the Clear button and all tabs will be removed.

- **To add a leader to an existing tab or to change the tab type,** click on the tab you want to modify and then click on the icon of the tab leader you want to apply.

Secret Publication Diagnostics

PageMaker includes a little-known diagnostic and repair routine that can check the internal structure of your publication and even fix structure problems that may result in crashing, corrupt files, or printing problems. To access this diagnostic, hold down the Option and Shift keys while choosing the Hyphenation command. PageMaker will run the diagnostics (which takes only a second or two in most cases) and then beep at you. It will beep once if your publication has no problems, twice if there is a problem but PageMaker has fixed it, and three times if there is a problem but PageMaker cannot fix it.

This trick is good to use when you have a publication that crashes every time you turn to a specific page, prints with missing page items, or exhibits other strange behavior. If you get the dreaded three beeps "sorry, we can't help you" result, you should immediately do a Save as… to make a copy of your publication and then realize you are living on borrowed time. From that point, you can try to cut your publication in half (duplicating it and then deleting half the pages from each file) and then run the diagnostic again to figure out where the trouble resides. Often it will lie in one particular story or graphic item, and deleting that item and replacing it can be a permanent cure.

Hyphenation

The appearance of any publication is substantially affected by the way in which it is hyphenated. Many documents produced with early desktop publishing programs suffered by a lack of sophisticated hyphenation features. Fortunately, PageMaker provides very powerful hyphenation capabilities that you can easily use to produce very professional looking publications.

In general, you will want to hyphenate most body text used in your PageMaker publications. In most cases, headlines, subheads, captions, and other short text passages should not be hyphenated. Three kinds of hyphenation are available in PageMaker:

- **Manual hyphenation** requires that you insert regular hyphens, or *discretionary hyphens*, into your text. Discretionary hyphens remain invisible, hidden within a word, until PageMaker finds it necessary to hyphenate the word at that point. Then the hyphen appears as a normal hyphen. If a shift in the text later moves the word from the end of the sentence, the discretionary hyphen disappears again.

☞ **Dictionary hyphenation** uses the Proximity 6.0 dictionaries and your own user dictionary to find the correct way to hyphenate text in your publication. This is the default method of hyphenation.

☞ **Algorithm hyphenation** applies a set of rules to words in need of hyphenation to determine where hyphens should be placed. The hyphenation algorithm may be able to hyphenate words missed by dictionary hyphenation, although it is possible for improper hyphens to be inserted. When using this type of hyphenation, you should verify that all inserted hyphens are correct.

Hyphenation is controlled in the Hyphenation dialog box (shown in Figure 6-20), which is accessed via the Hyphenation… command in the Type menu. The first option is used to turn hyphenation off or on. When hyphenation is off, all other hyphenation options have no effect.

Figure 6-20:
The Hyphenation dialog box

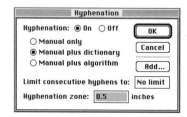

Other hyphenation options:

☞ **Manual only.** Select this option if you do not want hyphens added to your text based on PageMaker's hyphenation dictionary or hyphenation algorithm. In this case, only hard hyphens and discretionary hyphens will appear in your text. Hard hyphens are created by inserting the standard hyphen character into a word. When a hard hyphen is inserted, PageMaker will hyphenate the word at that point, if appropriate, but the hyphen will appear in the text even if the hyphen is not at the end of a line, as illustrated in Figure 6-21. This makes the use of hard hyphens very dangerous — they should never be used except in cases where you want the hyphen to appear regardless of whether it is at the end of a line or not, (which is actually a dash, right?). Discretionary hyphens should be used in all other cases.

You add discretionary hyphens to your text by setting the insertion point between any two characters and pressing ⌘- –. The discretionary hyphen will appear only when the word can be correctly hyphenated at the point of the discretionary hyphen. Until that time, discretionary hyphens remain hidden. You can add discretionary hyphens to several points in a single word, and PageMaker will then use the one that provides the best fit in any given situation; unused discretionary hyphens remain hidden without causing any problems.

Figure 6-21:
An example of a
misplaced hard
hyphen

> Every free action is produced by the concurrence of two causes; one moral, i.e. the will which determines the act; the other physical, i.e. the power which executes it. When I walk towards an object, it is necessary first that I should will to go there, and, in the sec-ond place, that my feet should carry me. If a paralytic wills to run and an active man will not to, they will both stay where they are. The body politic has the same motive powers; here too force and will are distinguished, will under the name of legislative power and force under that of executive power. Without their concurrence, nothing is, or should be, done.

Deleting discretionary hyphens: You can delete a discretionary hyphen by positioning the insertion point to the right of the hyphen (if it is visible) or between the two characters where you know the hyphen exists (if it is not visible) and pressing the Delete or Backspace key.

∞ **Manual plus dictionary.** This option causes PageMaker to use automatic hyphenation to hyphenate text as it is placed into your publication, entered with the text entry tool, or any time the size of a text block is modified, in addition to allowing the insertion of manual hyphens. If you set the insertion point inside the text block, then choose the Automatic Hyphenation option and click the OK button in the Hyphenation dialog box, the story will not be hyphenated until it is resized or repoured.

Overriding hyphenation: You can specify that certain words never be hyphenated by placing a discretionary hyphen in front of the word. This not only tells PageMaker not to hyphenate this particular occurrence of the word, but it keeps PageMaker from hyphenating any occurrence of this word anywhere in the current publication. You can, however, add your own discretionary hyphens within the word, which will allow PageMaker to hyphenate the word (any time it occurs in the publication) at the point of a discretionary hyphen but nowhere else.

∞ **Manual plus algorithm.** This option is actually Manual plus dictionary plus algorithm. It applies automatic hyphenation and algorithmic hyphenation and allows manual hyphenation. Algorithm-based hyphenation uses a set of rules built into PageMaker to determine where words can be hyphenated. Rule-based hyphenation provides hyphenating of words not found in a hyphenation dictionary, but may add some incorrect hyphens. When using this option, you should always check your document carefully before printing the final copy and delete any hyphens that PageMaker has added that you do not want.

↩ **Limit consecutive hyphens to.** The value set for this option determines how many lines in a row can end in hyphens. It is important to limit consecutive hyphens because if too many lines in a row end with hyphens, documents tend to look unprofessional and are hard to read. While there is no hard-and-fast rule for how many consecutive lines should be allowed to end in hyphens, many publishers think no more than two, or three at the most, should be permitted. Craig accepts this rule, but Bill never allows more than one hyphen in a row. Deleting hyphens is not the only solution to this problem; often you should try to rewrite one of the sentences causing the hyphenation problem or alter the hyphenation of lines earlier in the paragraph so that the multiline hyphenation problem disappears.

↩ **Hyphenation zone.** For unjustified text, the Hyphenation zone option determines which words PageMaker attempts to hyphenate, and if a word has multiple hyphenation points, which hyphens are selected. The goal is for PageMaker to end each line within the Hyphenation zone: So a larger zone means more ragged paragraphs, and smaller zones mean more hyphens will be inserted. Suppose you define a .25-inch Hyphenation zone. On each line, PageMaker looks to see if a word ends within that last .25 inch of the line. If one does, then the next word is pushed down to the next line, and everything is fine. If no word naturally ends within the hyphenation zone, then PageMaker attempts to hyphenate any word that crosses the zone, to create a hyphenated ending within the hyphenation zone. Figure 6-22 illustrates a Hyphenation Zone.

Figure 6-22:
An example of words and hyphens landing within the hyphenation zone in unjustified text

> Every free action is produced by the concurrence of two causes; one moral, i.e. the will which determines the act; the other physical, i.e. the power which executes it. When I walk towards an object, it is necessary first that I should will to go there, and, in the second place, that my feet should carry me. If a paralytic wills to run and an active man will not to, they will both stay where they are. The body politic has the same motive powers; here too force and will are distinguished, will under the name of legislative power and force under that of executive power. Without their concurrence, nothing is, or should be, done.

↩ When text is justified (blocked on each side), the setting of the Hyphenation zone option has no effect. Instead hyphenation is determined by the Word space and Letter space options in the Spacing dialog box. These options determine how much PageMaker can move characters and words in order to fill lines without hyphenating, and so they indirectly affect hyphenation. These options are described more fully in the next section of this chapter.

☞ **Add...** If you want to add words to your own personal hyphenation dictionary, determining how these words will be hyphenated when either the Manual plus dictionary or Manual plus algorithm options are used, click the Add... button. The Add to User Dictionary dialog box, shown in Figure 6-23, will appear.

Figure 6-23:
The Add to User Dictionary
dialog box

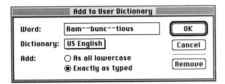

If a word was selected when you chose the Hyphenation command, that word will appear in the Word field. If this is not the word you want to hyphenate, select the word and then delete it by pressing the Delete key; if you don't select a word, simply enter the word you want to hyphenate. Then mark places in the word at which you want to allow hyphenation using the tilde (~) character. You can rank the priority of the hyphens you add within a word by placing one tilde at the most preferred hyphenation point, two at the second-best hyphenation point, three at the third-best hyphenation point, and so on. When ranked hyphens are included in a word, only the best or second-best hyphens will be used when the Manual plus dictionary option is selected, but any hyphens (first, second, third, etc.) will be used when the Manual plus algorithm option is used. When you have finished adding your new word, click OK to return to the Hyphenation dialog box.

You can also use the Add... button and the Add to User Dictionary dialog box to remove existing words from the hyphenation dictionary. To do this, enter the word you want to remove and then click the Remove button.

Adding words fast with Adobe's Dictionary Editor: If you want to make extensive changes to your user dictionary (or create a new dictionary), you can do so much faster with the Dictionary Editor, found in the Utilities folder inside the Adobe PageMaker 6.0 folder. The Dictionary Editor, shown in Figure 6-24, allows you to add words and set up hyphenation rules for new words or change them for words already in your dictionary. You can also remove words. Words entered here are also used by PageMaker's spell checker.

Figure 6-24:
PageMaker's Dictionary
Editor

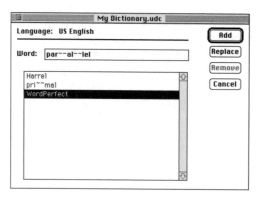

Using the Alignment Command ___

Any paragraph in PageMaker can be aligned to the left or right edge, centered, or fully justified. You can also force-justify text across the current paragraph width. Paragraph alignment is adjusted relative to the width of the paragraph's text block. Paragraph alignment can be adjusted for any paragraph that is fully or partially selected. There are four ways to change the alignment for a paragraph:

- ☞ Use the Alignment option in the Paragraph Specifications dialog box, which is accessed by choosing the Paragraph... command (⌘-M) in the Type menu.

- ☞ Use the Alignment command in the Type menu to choose from a pop-up menu of the five alignment options.

- ☞ Use the keyboard equivalents for each of the alignment options: Shift-⌘-L for Left, Shift-⌘-R for Right, Shift-⌘-C for Center, Shift-⌘-J for Justify, and Shift-⌘-F for Force justify.

- ☞ Use the Control palette, discussed in Chapter 9.

Figure 6-25 shows the five alignment options.

Typography in PageMaker _____

PageMaker's ability to produce fine typography has become an important and often misunderstood topic as more and more professional document production has been moved onto the desktop. The fact is that PageMaker has extensive and extremely precise typographic capabilities, including all the character-spacing control features: kerning pairs, manual kerning, range kerning, automated expert kerning, letter spacing,

Figure 6-25:
Examples of
PageMaker's
alignment
options: Align
Left, Align
Center, Align
Right, Justify,
Force Justify

To begin designing a questionnaire, you must first have a group file active, as described in the previous chapter, "Managing Group Files." Then, after determining which categories, questions, raters, and demographics you will use, you are ready to get to work designing your questionnaire. Questionnaires are designed from the Advance/360 Design Utility.

To begin designing a questionnaire, you must first have a group file active, as described in the previous chapter, "Managing Group Files." Then, after determining which categories, questions, raters, and demographics you will use, you are ready to get to work designing your questionnaire. Questionnaires are designed from the Advance/360 Design Utility.

To begin designing a questionnaire, you must first have a group file active, as described in the previous chapter, "Managing Group Files." Then, after determining which categories, questions, raters, and demographics you will use, you are ready to get to work designing your questionnaire. Questionnaires are designed from the Advance/360 Design Utility.

To begin designing a questionnaire, you must first have a group file active, as described in the previous chapter, "Managing Group Files." Then, after determining which categories, questions, raters, and demographics you will use, you are ready to get to work designing your questionnaire. Questionnaires are designed from the Advance/360 Design Utility.

To begin designing a questionnaire, you must first have a group file active, as described in the previous chapter, "Managing Group Files." Then, after determining which categories, questions, raters, and demographics you will use, you are ready to get to work designing your questionnaire. Questionnaires are designed from the Advance/360 Design Utility.

tracking, and electronically condensed and expanded type discussed in this section. These features provide you with more precision than traditional typographers could achieve using traditional photomechanical typesetters, and in many cases more precision than current imagesetters or PostScript-based output systems can even reproduce. There is no need to worry about PageMaker's typographic powers.

Character Spacing, Tracking, and Kerning

The ability to control the exact placement of each character relative to other characters is the cornerstone of a strong typographic system. On the Macintosh, the position of each character relative to the character before and after is based on information included within the font being used. The designer of each font specifies the amount of space that each character in the font occupies (its width) and the amount of space that should be placed before and after the character (its side bearing), as shown in Figure 6-26. By default, most software positions characters according to these specifications, which generally results in clearly legible and aesthetically pleasing text.

For the more typographically sophisticated, there is often a desire to make adjustments to these default character spacing and positioning specifications. Such adjustments make it possible to correct for characters that appear set too closely or too far apart, have their spacing exaggerated at larger point sizes, or simply consume too much space on the page when using their default spacing. Adjusting character spacing is confusing for a number of reasons, not the least of which is that the terminology used to describe its tools and techniques is not standardized. In fact, terms are used in contradictory ways by different software vendors and typographic practitioners.

PageMaker uses the following tools and terminology:

- **Kerning** refers to adjustments in spacing between two characters. There are no less than four types of kerning control in PageMaker: Automatic pair kerning adjusts the spacing between letters in $\frac{1}{1000}$ of an em increments according to kerning pair information built into the font itself. Manual pair kerning lets you adjust the space between any two characters in increments of a positive or negative $\frac{1}{10}$, $\frac{1}{25}$, or $\frac{1}{100}$ of an em (width of the M, the widest character in the font). Range kerning is exactly like manual pair kerning except that you can apply it to any number of characters at once. Expert kerning automates the process of adjusting kerning values between two characters by analyzing the shapes of the particular characters and kerning the characters based on a specified "strength" value that you specify.

- **Tracking** modifies the space between characters, using a set of point-size dependent tracking curves that have been custom defined for a particular font. Tracking offers an intelligent modification of the space across a range of characters that aims to adjust the overall visual density of type on a page.

- ☞ **Letter spacing** adjusts the space between characters based on exaggerations or minimizations of the normal amount of letter space defined by the font designer. It is somewhat cruder than tracking or kerning in that it doesn't directly take into account the characters involved, the font, or the type size.

- ☞ **Condensing or expanding type** is the equivalent of asking your spouse to sit on your suitcase in order to get it closed: It isn't elegant and it may not be pretty, but it will probably get the job done in a pinch.

The character spacing tool or the combination of character-spacing tools that you should use in a given situation depends upon the effect you are trying to achieve. Pair kerning is probably the most commonly used tool, applied by most people as a matter of course to all text larger than body copy. Tracking should be used as the first method of changes to a range of characters because it makes changes based on (usually) professionally developed tracks. In actuality, tracking is probably under-utilized in PageMaker because it is not well understood and has been criticized in the past. See the complete discussion of tracking later in this section to clear up these issues. After tracking has been applied, manual kerning of character pairs or ranges should be performed. Finally, letter spacing (and word spacing) should be used to help PageMaker correctly justify and hyphenate your text. An in-depth discussion each of these features follows.

Automatic Kerning of Pairs

In most fonts, after the font designers specify the width and side bearing of each character, they specify certain character pairs that they believe need some space between them other than the sum of the right bearing of the first character and the left bearing of the second. These are called kerning pairs. Ideally, whenever the two characters in a kerning pair are placed next to each other, the software application should replace the default spacing (the sum of the side bearings) with the kerning pair spacing.

But kerning pair spacing is not used automatically. In fact, only a few Macintosh applications are capable of reading the kerning pair data from a font and using it to position characters correctly. PageMaker can use kerning pair information to position characters accurately, but it does not do so by default. This is because kerned pairs take longer to display on screen, and often the improved accuracy of character placement is barely visible at smaller type sizes and therefore not worth the slower display performance.

If you want kerning pairs used in your publication, you must select the paragraphs in which you want them used, turn the kerning pair option on, and specify the minimum point size for which you want kerning pairs used. To do this, choose the Paragraph… command (⌘-M) from the Type menu and click the Spacing… button in the Paragraph Specifications dialog box. Here you'll find the Pair kerning option, which can be turned on and off via its check box, and the Auto above _____ points field. This option specifies the size above which pair kerning should be used. Both are shown in Figure 6-27.

Figure 6-27:
The Pair kerning option in Paragraph Spacing Attributes

| Pair kerning: ☒ Auto above 4 | points |

By default, the Auto above option is set to 4 points. We suggest a setting of between 9 points and 12 points unless you are typographically sensitive, because text smaller than that really doesn't need pair kerning in most cases, and it will provide more snappy on-screen performance.

Using Expert Kerning...

Expert Kerning... (shown in Figure 6-28), located on the Type menu, examines every character pair in the selected text, removes all existing manual kerning, and then kerns the type based on the amount of "kerning strength" you specify. Select the text you want to kern, then choose the Expert Kerning command. Otherwise, the command appears dimmed and won't be available. Your options in defining the kerning strength range from 0.00 to 2.00, with higher values resulting in greater amounts of kerning and therefore tighter spacing between characters.

Figure 6-28:
The Expert Kerning dialog box

You can select any amount of text before choosing Expert Kerning..., even text that includes multiple fonts and type sizes. Normally, you will not want to use this utility to make adjustments to large amounts of text, however, because it is not the most efficient method for manipulating character spacing.

After you select the text you want to kern and choose Expert Kerning..., the dialog box appears. Enter the desired kerning strength and choose the option from the Design class drop-down list corresponding to the kind of font that is being kerned: Text, Display, or Poster font. If not, then enter the type size, and utility will assume what kind of type you're kerning.

Using KernEdit

If you want to edit the kerning pair information stored within any of your fonts, use the KernEdit utility provided with PageMaker 6. KernEdit is a very powerful kerning pair editor that allows you to open any font, change or delete the existing kerning pair information, add new kerning pairs, or even move kerning pair information from one font to another. The changes you make will be saved in the font file and will therefore apply to all applications that read pair kerning data from the font, not just PageMaker.

Using KernEdit (shown in Figure 6-29) is relatively easy, although you wouldn't want to edit kerning pairs yourself unless you are an experienced typographer or have a very fine eye for this kind of detail. After opening a font in KernEdit (KernEdit is found in the Utilities folder in the Adobe PageMaker 6.0 folder), select the character pair you want to modify from the scrolling list along the left edge of the dialog box. KernEdit automatically displays a word that contains the pair of letters you have selected.

Figure 6-29:
The KernEdit utility bundled with PageMaker allows you to edit individual kerning pairs for all the fonts installed on your Mac.

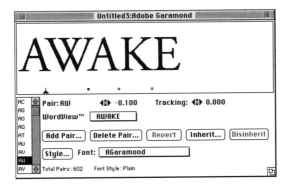

To choose another word, use the WordView pop-up menu. To change the kerning pair data, either move the triangle that appears between the letters in the sample word, click the right or left arrows next to the kerning value, or select the kerning value and enter your desired value. Changes as small as $\frac{1}{1000}$ of an em space are supported.

KernEdit also provides a tracking option, although this is provided to help you see how the characters will appear when used in real documents, and tracking changes are not saved along with the font. What you should do is modify the tracking value until the characters in the word have an overall spacing that you like, and then perform the specific pair kerning as described above. This simulates the way your font will be used in the real world, when tracking will likely be applied to it in addition to the kerning pairs. Details on every KernEdit option are provided in the program's help system, available via the Help… command in the Apple menu.

Manually Kerning Text and Range Kerning

Using automatic kerning pairs is a good first step to better typography, but in many cases, you'll still want to adjust the space between characters manually. PageMaker lets you add or remove space between characters in increments of $\frac{1}{10}$, $\frac{1}{25}$, or $\frac{1}{100}$ of the type's point size. To do this, position the cursor between the two characters you want to modify, or select any group of characters that you want to kern. Then, use the following key combinations to kern the selected type:

∞ To add space between characters in $\frac{1}{25}$-point increments, position the insertion point between the characters and press Shift-⌘-Delete or ⌘-right arrow.

∞ To delete space between characters in $\frac{1}{25}$-point increments, position the insertion point between the characters and press ⌘-Delete or ⌘-left arrow.

∞ To add space between characters in $\frac{1}{100}$-point increments, position the insertion point between the characters and press Shift-⌘-right arrow.

∞ To delete space between characters in $\frac{1}{100}$-point increments, position the insertion point between the characters and press Shift-⌘-left arrow.

∞ Press ⌘-Option-K to remove all kerning between two characters, returning the kerning to its original, unmodified, setting.

∞ Use the kerning option in the control palette to kern in either $\frac{1}{100}$-or $\frac{1}{10}$-em increments with the nudge arrows, or enter kerning values between 1 and -1. For details on using the control palette, see Chapter 9.

In many cases, you will not be able to see a visible difference as you add or delete space because the display is not accurate enough. Whenever possible, zoom in to 200% or even 400% while kerning characters manually. (Or you can use the zoom to zoom in up to 800%.) In any case, the spacing will be adjusted accurately when your document is output on a high-resolution PostScript printer.

The kerning modifications you make affect the space after each character. So if you set the insertion point between two characters and change the kerning value, your changes are actually added to the first character. This means that if you select an entire word and apply range kerning, you are not only changing the spacing between each pair of letters but also the spacing between the last letter of the word and the first letter of the next word. If you don't want to change this inter-word spacing when range kerning one particular word, select all of the letters of the word except the last letter.

Kerning into the Margins

Since kerning affects the space after any selected character, and because PageMaker ignores any kerning applied to the last character on a line, you have to be a little tricky to kern characters into the left or right margins. To kern into the left margin, insert a non-breaking space (Option-spacebar) before the first letter in the line, select that space, and then kern to pull the first letter into the margin. (The kerned characters may appear to disappear sometimes, but just refresh the display by reselecting the current view size from the View submenu and they will reappear.) Kerning into the right margin (when text is fully or right justified) works the same way: Add a non-breaking space after the last character on the line, select that space, and then kern into it.

Tracking

Another way of automatically kerning text over a range of characters is tracking. Tracking is clearly the least understood of PageMaker's character-spacing tools. The feature's option names (Loose, Very Loose, Tight, Very Tight, and Normal) have been the subject of unfair and inaccurate ridicule ever since they were introduced in PageMaker 4.0. They're unpopular because terms such as "Loose" and "Tight" sound imprecise, and some people have therefore concluded that they reflect some sort of imprecise typographic control. But in fact the terms are not imprecise, they simply denote the relative amount of spacing that each option applies. Tracking values change for every font and every type size. So while the "Loose" option does have an exact meaning expressed in a percentage of the normal character spacing, that meaning is different for 14-point Times than for 18-point Times, and the 18-point Times value is different than it is for 18-point Helvetica. This can be seen by looking at tracking curves, as illustrated in Figure 6-30.

Figure 6-30:
Tracking varies between fonts and various point sizes. This example of tracking curves shows the amount of increase or decrease in the character for a particular font at every different point size. PageMaker has five different curves for the five tracking options on Expert Tracking menu.

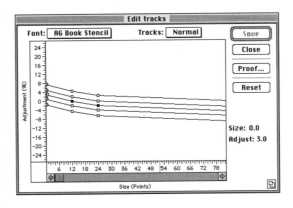

The basic trend of most tracking curves is that character spacing is reduced as point size increases. This compensates for the fact that normal increases in character spacing at larger point sizes often give text the look of having too much white space.

Edit Tracks

PageMaker's tracking capabilities allow you to assign one of five different tracks to any font used in your publication. After you select the Edit Tracks... command from the Expert Tracking submenu, you modify the default values of these five tracks. You adjust the amount of space set between characters in a font at different point sizes. You can adjust tracking for any font that appears in your font menu by using the Font pop-up menu in the upper-left corner of the dialog box. Edit tracks supports all fonts formats, including bitmapped fonts, PostScript Type 1 and Type 3 fonts, and TrueType fonts.

The five current tracks for the selected font appear in the dialog box, as shown in Figure 6-30 above. Each track is plotted on the graph as the percentage change in character spacing at each type size. You can adjust any of the tracks by dragging on the tracking handles (white boxes) or by dragging the curve itself. If you want to add new tracking handles, hold down the Option key and click anywhere on a tracking curve. If you want to adjust one of the tracks from the keyboard, select the track you want to adjust and then press the up- or down-arrow keys to move the curve up or down in $^1/_{10}$-percent increments, or press the left- or right-arrow keys to change the current point size in $^1/_{10}$-point increments.

Copying tracking from one font to another: If you want to move the tracking curves from one font into another font, you can do so using the standard Macintosh Copy and Paste commands. Select the font whose tracking curves you want to copy and choose the Copy command (⌘-C). Then switch to the font where you want to paste those curves and choose the Paste command (⌘-V). This will replace all five tracking curves.

After editing the tracking values for a particular font, click the Save button. If you make changes and try to select another font, you will be prompted to save your changes first. Tracking curves are stored in the Tracking Values file, which resides inside the PageMaker folder. This file provides tracking values for all of your publications. If you want to create a set of tracking values that applies to just one publication or one set of publications, quit PageMaker, move a copy of the Tracking Values file from the RSRC folder in the Adobe PageMaker 6.0 folder into the folder with the publication files you want to use with different tracking values, restart PageMaker, and open one of the publications from that folder. Then use Edit Tracks to make modifications. These changes will be saved to the copy of the Tracking Values file that is in the same folder as the open publication.

The Tracking Values File

Since tracking values are stored in the Tracking Values file, if you edit your tracking values, you will have to send your Tracking Values file to your service bureau if you send publications for output. (This is not necessary if you do not edit the tracking values.) In this case, make sure that the service bureau understands that they must place your Tracking Values file in the same folder as your PageMaker publication file before they launch PageMaker and print your file. (They do not want to copy your Tracking Values file over the one in their PageMaker folder because it will then be used on all files they open in PageMaker.) If you want to avoid any chance of error with your modified Tracking Values file, print your publications to disk as a PostScript file and then give that PostScript file to your service bureau rather than the original PageMaker file. This makes error impossible and means that you don't have to give the service bureau your Tracking Values file.

Character Spacing

You can also change the space between characters with the Letter space and Word space options in the Paragraph Spacing Attributes dialog box, which is shown in Figure 6-31. Unlike kerning and tracking, which are designed to produce pleasing visual relationships between characters, letter and word spacing are designed to help PageMaker hyphenate and justify your text. And unlike manual kerning, range kerning, expert kerning, and tracking — which are character-level attributes — letter and word spacing are paragraph-level attributes: They always apply to all of the characters in a paragraph.

Figure 6-31:
The Paragraph Spacing
Attributes dialog box

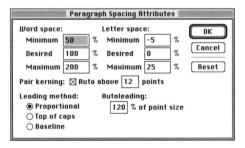

To access the Letter space and Word space options, select the paragraphs you want to format, choose the Paragraph command (⌘ - M) from the Type menu, and then click the Spacing… button inside the Paragraph Specifications dialog box. Examples of the results you can achieve with these options are shown in Figure 6-32.

Figure 6-32:
Examples of
increasing maximum
word spacing (top)
and reducing
minimum letter
spacing (bottom)

Every free action is produced by the concurrence of two causes; one moral, i.e. the will which determines the act; the other physical, i.e. the power which executes it. When I walk towards an object, it is necessary first that I should will to go there, and, in the second place, that my feet should carry me. If a paralytic wills to run and an active man will not to, they will both stay where they are. The body politic has the same motive powers; here too force and will are distinguished, will under the name of legislative power and force under that of executive power. Without their concurrence, nothing is, or should be, done.

Every free action is produced by the concurrence of two causes; one moral, i.e. the will which determines the act; the other physical, i.e. the power which executes it. When I walk towards an object, it is necessary first that I should will to go there, and, in the second place, that my feet should carry me. If a paralytic wills to run and an active man will not to, they will both stay where they are. The body politic has the same motive powers; here too force and will are distinguished, will under the name of legislative power and force under that of executive power. Without their concurrence, nothing is, or should be, done.

Figure 6-32: Examples of increasing maximum word spacing (top) and reducing minimum letter spacing (bottom)

PageMaker measures both word spacing and letter spacing in $\frac{1}{100}$th of a spaceband (the width created when you press the spacebar). When a paragraph is not justified, word and letter spacing are based on the Desired options, and the Minimum and Maximum options have no effect. When a paragraph is justified, PageMaker follows a series of steps to determine how much word and letter spacing will be used:

- ❧ If a word does not naturally end at the end of a line, PageMaker then attempts to make the last whole word fit onto the line by compressing the space between the words on that line.

- ❧ If this cannot be done without compressing the word space more than the specified Minimum word space option, it then tries instead to expand the space between words, up to the specified Maximum word space, to push the last word down to the next line.

- ❧ If this cannot be done without exceeding the Maximum word space option, PageMaker attempts to hyphenate the last word according to the current hyphenation option.

- ❧ If suitable hyphenation cannot produce a line ending that keeps the word spacing within its specified range, then PageMaker adjusts letter spacing by first compressing the space between letters and then by expanding the space between letters.

☞ If changing letter spacing within the range specified by the Minimum and Maximum letter spacing does not produce a suitable line ending, then PageMaker creates a suitable line ending by expanding the space between words as much as necessary, even beyond the specified Maximum word space option.

PageMaker's default values provide for a wide range of word- and letter-space movement: The space between words can range from 50% of a spaceband to 200% of a spaceband, and the space between letters can range from 5% less than normal to 25% more than normal. You may want to narrow these ranges to force more hyphenation and less dramatic word and letter spacing in your justified paragraphs. We find that values of 75% to 150% word spacing, for example, produce much more pleasing results.

Setting all three letter spacing options to the same value, 0 for example, effectively turns off letter spacing so that PageMaker has to determine line endings using hyphenation and word spacing changes only. Or you can set both the Minimum and Desired letter spacing to "0," so PageMaker will not reduce the space between letters but may expand the space if necessary.

The allowable ranges for setting Word spacing and Letter spacing options are listed in Table 6-4. All options can be modified in 1% increments.

| Table 6-4 | |
| Allowable Ranges for Word and Letter Spacing Options | |
Spacing	*Allowable Ranges*
Minimum Word spacing	0% to 500%
Desired Word spacing	min and max
Maximum Word spacing	0% to 500%
Minimum Letter spacing	-200% to 0%
Desired Letter spacing	min and max
Maximum Letter spacing	0% to 200%

After setting Word spacing and Letter spacing options, click the OK button to apply these settings, click Reset to return all options to their original settings, or click the Cancel button to negate them and return to the Paragraph Specifications dialog box.

Summary

- Formatting attributes are divided into character-level attributes that can be applied to any individual character- and paragraph-level attributes that are always applied to an entire paragraph.

- Character formatting attributes include font, type size, type style, leading, tracking, and width. These attributes are set by selecting text with the text tool and then using commands in the Type menu or options in the Type Specifications dialog box. You can also apply character formatting using the Control palette.

- Paragraph formatting attributes include margin indents, before and after spacing, tabs, hyphenation, alignment, paragraph rules, and letter spacing options. These commands are primarily controlled using the Paragraph Specifications dialog box, commands in the Type menu, and the Control palette.

- Character spacing in PageMaker can be controlled using automatic pair kerning, manual kerning, range kerning, tracking, letter spacing, or by condensing or expanding type. Pair kerning and tracking should almost always be used for text larger than body copy.

- Tracking is a font- and point-size specific way to modify the space between characters in order to produce better-looking and better-fitting type. Manual and range kerning can accomplish this, too, but require much more effort and experience.

- When justifying text, PageMaker decides how to break lines depending on the option settings in the Paragraph Spacing Attributes dialog box and the Hyphenation dialog box. You use the options in these dialog boxes to specify how dramatically PageMaker can alter the default letter spacing of your text in order to meet its justification and hyphenation goals.

Creating Style Sheets and Templates

In This Chapter

- ➥ Style sheets defined
- ➥ Creating style sheets
- ➥ Editing style sheets
- ➥ Importing and exporting style sheets
- ➥ The Styles Palette
- ➥ Templates defined
- ➥ Creating and using templates

You Say Tomato, I Say... _____

We'll start with an admission: It's tough to know what to call the primary PageMaker feature discussed in this chapter anymore. It's the name we learned when first confronted with this feature in the original Microsoft Word on the IBM PC. (Everyone has some dirt in their past.) Adobe just calls them styles, but that's too easy to confuse with character styles (like bold or italic). Others call them paragraph styles, which is actually a pretty good name. But we're used to style sheets, so let's just refer to them as style sheets and leave it at that.

The other PageMaker feature discussed in this chapter, templates, has always been called templates, although some people have now started to call them wizards. A template by any other name is still a template.

What are they? When used together, templates and style sheets are the most important tricks you will ever learn to save time and improve the consistency of your publications. Style sheets allow you to specify a complex set of attributes with a single click of the mouse button and then change these attributes globally at any time. A style sheet consists of a name, which usually describes the kind of paragraph the style sheet defines, and a definition, which identifies the text-formatting attributes that the style sheet assigns to any paragraph to which the style sheet is applied. PageMaker's style sheets can contain attributes from the Type Specifications, Paragraph Specifications, Indents/tabs, and Hyphenation dialog boxes — virtually every formatting feature you learned in the preceding chapter.

Style sheets automate the process of formatting text. They make it possible to specify the formatting attributes of a paragraph only once and then use that specification an unlimited number of times. This not only saves time and reduces effort and complexity, but it also ensures consistency — every paragraph using a particular style sheet will be identical. You can also use style sheets to update multiple paragraphs — such as, say, change every subhead in a 999-page document from Avant Garde to Helvetica — by simply editing the style sheet. A set of default style sheets is created for every PageMaker publication, and since style sheets can be imported from word processing documents, exported to word processing documents, and shared between publications, the benefits of defining and using style sheets can be enormous.

Consider templates as style sheets for entire documents. Another way to look at them is as empty shells containing your layout and formatting information (including style sheets). All you do is pour in your text and place your graphics. PageMaker does the rest.

Working with Style Sheets _____

Style sheets are useful because most documents are composed of several kinds of paragraphs, each of which is used repeatedly throughout the publication. This book, for example, uses several primary types of paragraph formats.

Without style sheets, formatting the book would require assigning the same attributes over and over again by selecting each individual menu command and completing the required dialog box options for each separate paragraph, as we demonstrated in the previous chapter. And any design change — making the subheads a little bit larger, for example — would require going through the publications page-by-page and reformatting each subhead paragraph appropriately.

With style sheets, this scenario improves dramatically: The specifications for the paragraph styles need to be specified only once — when defined as style sheets — and then they are applied to the text as needed. Applying style sheets to a paragraph, a process sometimes called tagging, is quick, simple, and accurate. Once tagged, the paragraph instantly assumes all of the formatting defined by the style sheet. And when the inevitable design changes occur, all that is required is a change to the style sheet definition; the resulting change automatically applies to every paragraph tagged with that style sheet.

Creating Style Sheets

There are several ways to define new style sheets in PageMaker: They can be defined from scratch, based on some formatted text that already exists in the publication, or based on another style sheet that already exists. When you first start working with style sheets, you'll have to define a lot of new ones or redefine a lot of existing ones. Over time you should build up a library of style sheets that cover the bulk of the paragraph types you'll use, and you will be able to reuse these by continually importing them into your publications or saving them in templates. The result will be that you will spend very little time actually formatting text.

Defining a Style Sheet from Scratch

To begin defining a new style sheet, choose the Define Styles… command (⌘-3) from the Type menu, and the Define Styles dialog box will appear (as shown in Figure 7-1.) If it is not selected already, click the word Selection at the top of the scrolling list on the left side of the dialog box and then click the New… button. The Edit Style dialog box will now appear, as shown in Figure 7-2. It is here that you specify the name and formatting attributes for the new style sheet.

Figure 7-1:
The Define Styles dialog box

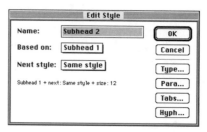

Figure 7-2:
The Edit Style dialog box

To name the new style sheet, enter any name up to 31 characters long into the Name option box (some nonalphabetic characters are not allowed in style names). Try to name your style sheet descriptively but use as short a name as possible so that you can see it easily in the Styles Palette (discussed under "Using the Styles Palette," later in this chapter). The Based on option should remain set to No style.

Now you're ready to define the attributes for your new style sheet. In the lower portion of the Edit Style dialog box is a listing of the current settings of the style sheet's attributes. These settings come from the current default settings of the various options used to define style sheets or from the formatting of the text that was selected when the Define Styles... command was chosen.

To edit these specifications, use the Type..., Para..., Tabs..., and Hyph... buttons. These access the Type Specifications, Paragraph Specifications, Indents/tabs, and Hyphenation dialog boxes, respectively. Each of these dialog boxes is used exactly as described in Chapter 6. As you edit the various options in these dialog boxes, the style sheet specification listing is updated to reflect the current attributes of the style sheet.

When you are satisfied with the specifications for the new style sheet as listed in the lower portion of the Edit Style dialog box, click the OK button to complete the definition of this new style sheet or the Cancel button to abort the creation process. In either case, you are returned to the Define Styles dialog box. The name of the new style sheet now appears in the scrolling style sheet listing. To return to the publication window, click the OK button or the Cancel button.

A slightly faster way to start a new style definition: You can also begin the process of defining a new style sheet by holding down the Command key and clicking the No style line in the Styles Palette. (If the Styles Palette is not displayed, choose the Style Palette command from the Windows menu.) This brings up an empty Edit Style dialog box, where you can name the new style and edit its specifications as described above. If any text is selected when you ⌘-click the No style line, the new style will use the specifications of the selected type as its defaults, or the Based on option will display the name of the selected text's style sheet, if there is one.

Defining a Style Sheet Based on Existing Text

The process of defining style sheets from scratch, as described above, requires that you know in advance the specifications that you want to ascribe to your new style sheets. This happens sometimes, but more often you will not know the final specifications for your publication until you create a few pages of it and experiment with various formatting possibilities. In this case, you will want to "capture" the results of your trial-and-error formatting, creating a style sheet for each different kind of paragraph you've defined.

These style sheets can then be used to format the remainder of your publication.

To create a style sheet based on an existing paragraph, use the text tool to set the insertion point in one of the formatted paragraphs you want to use as a basis for your new style sheet and choose the Define Styles... command from the Type menu. (Note that you want to set the insertion point rather than select the whole paragraph because one italicized or bold word may cause problems, as you'll learn later.) The Define Styles dialog box will appear, and the word Selection will be highlighted in the scrolling list (unless the selected paragraph has already been defined as a style sheet). Selection refers to the text paragraph that was selected when you chose the Define Styles... command. The specifications for the selected paragraph are listed in the lower section of the dialog box. These are the specifications that PageMaker assumes you want to use in your new style sheet.

Click the New... button, and the Edit Style dialog box will appear. Enter the name you wish to give this new style sheet in the Name option box. The Based on option will show "No Style," unless the paragraph that you selected before choosing the Define styles... command had been defined previously as another style sheet.

You can now edit any of the attributes of the style sheet by clicking on the Type..., Para..., Tabs..., and Hyph... buttons and changing options in the associated dialog boxes. Since the default attributes of this new style sheet came from a paragraph that you formatted, this will probably not be necessary. However, if any attributes of the selected text are not uniform — if there is one bold word within a paragraph of plain text, for example — the word "mixed" will follow the specification of that attribute in the specification listing, as shown in Figure 7-3.

Any attributes followed by the word "mixed" will have to be reset so that they can be applied uniformly throughout the paragraph. To reset the type style, for example, click the Type... button and click either the Normal or Bold option so that all words will be set in the same type style. The word mixed then disappears from the specifications listing.

Figure 7-3:
The word *mixed* appears for any attribute that is not uniform in the selected text when a new style sheet is created.

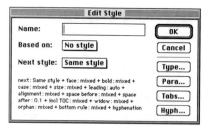

The Next style option is used to determine the style sheet that will be applied to paragraphs that are created by pressing the Return key within a paragraph to which the current style has been applied. The purpose of this option is to speed up text entry by automatically applying style sheets as new paragraphs are created. For example, the paragraph following each subhead in this book uses the Body text style sheet. By assigning Body text to the Next style option for the subhead style sheets, paragraphs created after entering subheads are automatically assigned the Body text style. The setting of the next style option does not affect the style sheet of paragraphs following the current paragraph unless the Return key is pressed — regardless of the setting of the Next style option, any style sheet can follow any other if it is manually applied to the following paragraph.

When you are satisfied with the specifications for the new style sheet as listed in the Edit Style dialog box, click the OK button to complete the definition of this new style sheet or the Cancel button to abort the creation process. If any conflict remains in the specifications, a dialog box, like the one shown in Figure 7-4, appears when you click the OK button, and you will have to resolve the conflict. If no specification conflicts exist, the Define Styles dialog again displays, with your new style added to the scrolling list. To return to the publication window, click the OK or Cancel button.

Figure 7-4:
Whoops. You still have not resolved all the conflicts between the selected text and the new style sheet. Go back and try again.

Another shortcut for getting to Edit Style: You can also define a new style based on existing text by selecting the text and holding down the ⌘ key while clicking on the No style line in the Styles palette. (If the Styles palette is not displayed, choose the Styles command from the Windows menu.) This will bring up the Edit Style dialog box, where you can name and edit the attributes of the style, as described earlier. Click the OK button after defining the new style sheet or the Cancel button to abort the creation, and you will return immediately to the publication window.

Creating New Style Sheets Based on Existing Style Sheets

Many paragraph styles used in a publication are very similar, but not identical, to other paragraph styles used in the publication. For example, the minor subheads in this book have the same type face and alignment as the major headlines, but different type sizes, type styles, and paragraph spacing.

In PageMaker, you can create style sheets that are based on existing style sheets. When one style sheet is based on another, it has exactly the same attributes as the style sheet upon which it is based, except the few attributes that you set differently. Using this technique reduces the amount of effort required to define the based-on style sheet and creates a dynamic link between the two style sheets — if an attribute is changed in the base style sheet, it is automatically changed in the second style sheet.

For example, suppose we define a style and name it Subhead 1, giving it the attributes of Helvetica-Bold 14, left aligned. We then define another style, which is based on Subhead 1, and name it Subhead 2. The only attribute that we change for Subhead 2 is its size, which is set as 12 points. Figures 7-5 and 7-6 display the Edit Style dialog boxes for these two styles.

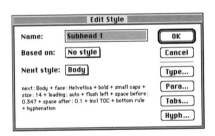

Figure 7-5:
To base one style sheet on another, use the Based on option in Edit Style, which creates a link between the two style sheets, allowing you to change formatting for two or more styles sheets by changing only the base style.

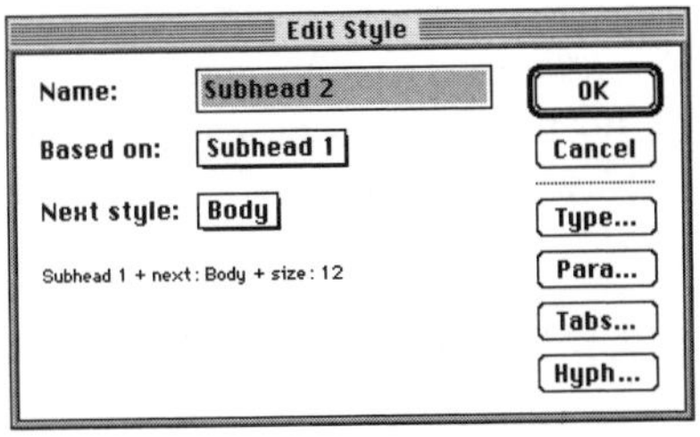

Figure 7-6:
You modify only the attributes that you want to be different from the Based on style sheet.

Notice that Subhead 2 does not display a typeface or first-line indent specification in its attribute listing. Instead, it simply reads "Subhead 1 + next: Body + size: 12." All paragraphs to which Subhead 2 is applied will be Helvetica-Bold 12, left aligned, as long as Subhead 1 is so defined, or until the typeface, type size, leading, or first-line indent is specifically edited in the Subhead 2 style sheet definition. If the definition of Subhead 1 is edited so that Times is the specified font instead of Helvetica, all paragraphs to which Subhead 2 has been applied will immediately become Times as well. The link between a style sheet and the sheet on which it is based is dynamic — changes made in the attributes of a style sheet are passed directly to any style sheets based on the changed style sheet.

If we created a third style sheet, called Subhead 3 which is based on Subhead 2, a change to an attribute in Subhead 1 would affect Subhead 1, Subhead 2, and Subhead 3.

To create a new style sheet that is based on an existing style sheet, choose the Define Styles... command from the Type menu, and the Define Styles dialog appears. Depending on the currently selected text in the publication window, either one of the style sheet names or the word Selection will be selected. If the style sheet that you want to base your new style sheet on is not selected, select it from the scrolling list. Next, click the New... button and the Edit Style dialog box appears. The Name option box will be empty, but the Based on option box will display the name of the style sheet selected when the New... button was clicked. Enter a name for your new style sheet in the Name option box.

The specification listing for the new style sheet will contain "+ next: Samestyle" and the name of the Based on style. At this point, the new style is exactly the same as the style on which it is based. By using the Type..., Para..., Tabs..., and Hyph... buttons and their associated dialog boxes, you can specify the attributes of this new style sheet that are different from the Based on style sheet. The specifications listing reflects these changes as you make them.

When you are satisfied with the specifications for the new style sheet as listed in the Edit Style dialog box, click the OK button to complete the definition of this new style sheet or the Cancel button to abort the creation process. The Define Styles dialog box again displays, with the name of your new style sheet added to the scrolling list. To return to the publication window, click the OK button or the Cancel button.

You can also create a new style sheet that is based on an existing style sheet by selecting a paragraph that uses the existing style sheet, holding down the ⌘ key and clicking on the No style line in the Styles palette. Or you can select the name of the style in the Styles Palette that you want to base the new style on (first make sure that no text is selected) and then hold down the Command key and click on the No style line. Either of these methods will bring up an empty Edit Style dialog box, with the Based on option already set, so that you can name the new style and edit its specifications. Click the OK button after defining the new style sheet or the Cancel button to abort the creation, and you will return immediately to the publication window.

To break the link between a style sheet and the style sheet that it is based on, select the No style option in the Based on pop-up menu. This removes the name of the based-on style from the specification listing and replaces it with the specifications themselves. This does not change any of the specifications for the style sheet, only the way that they are listed. This does, however, break the link between the style sheets so that if the style sheet on which this style sheet was based is edited, this style sheet will not be affected. You can also change the Based on style sheet from one to another by selecting the name of any current style sheet in the Based on pop-up menu.

PageMaker's Default Style Sheets

PageMaker automatically creates six style sheets for every new publication, as listed in Table 7-1. While these are representative of commonly used kinds of paragraphs, their default specifications probably won't match those that you regularly intend to use in your publications. You can correct this situation by redefining the default style sheets to meet your needs.

Table 7-1 The Original Default Style Sheets	
Style Sheet	***Default Specifications***
Body text	Times Roman 12/Auto, left aligned, 2-pica first indent, kern above 4, auto hyphenation
Caption	Times-Italic 10/Auto, left aligned
Hanging Indent	Times Roman 12/Auto, left aligned, .167" indent, -.167" first indent, kern above 4, auto hyphenation
Headline	Times-Bold 30/Auto, left aligned, include in TOC
Subhead 1	Times-Bold 18/Auto, left aligned, include in TOC Based on Headline
Subhead 2	Times-Bold 12/Auto, left aligned, include in TOC Based on Subhead1

To set your own default style sheets, close all open publications and then choose the Define Styles command. Now edit the default style sheets as necessary. You can rename them, change the formatting they specify, add or delete styles, and even import other styles that you have defined for other publications. (Importing style sheets is described in the next section of this chapter.) When you've set all the style sheets to meet your needs, close the Define Styles dialog box. Now when you create any future new publications, the default style sheets that you have specified will be created and included in your publications.

Redefining the default style sheets provides every new publication that you create with these default style sheets, and gives you access to quick and easy text formatting and an assurance of perfect consistency throughout your publications. Of course, you will still need to edit your customized default style sheets within some specific publications, and sometimes you'll have to create additional style sheets for particular tasks, but overall you'll find that a well-thought-out set of default style sheets is one of the best ways to boost PageMaker productivity and quality.

Importing Style Sheets

Once you've defined a good set of style sheets for one publication, you can move those style sheets to other publications to save even more time in formatting text and to ensure consistency among different files.

PageMaker makes it easy to import styles from one publication into another. Open the publication you want to import the style sheets into, and then choose the Define Styles... command from the Type menu to bring up the Define Styles dialog box. Click the Copy... button and the Copy styles dialog box appears, as shown in Figure 7-7. Locate the publication containing the style sheets that you want to import, select the name of the publication, and click the OK button or double-click the publication name. All style sheets from the opened publication will then be added to the list of style sheets in the current publication. If the names of any imported style sheets have already been assigned to styles in the new document, PageMaker warns you that the imported style sheets will override the existing style sheets. To preserve any existing style sheets that have the same names as the style sheets being imported, rename them before performing the import.

Figure 7-7:
The Copy styles dialog box

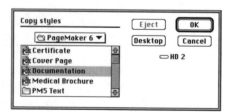

Style Sheets and Word Processors

The concept of style sheets is not unique to PageMaker. Several popular word processors use style sheets, and although these style sheets are implemented slightly differently than PageMaker's style sheets, they provide basically the same function — by assigning a group of formatting attributes to a named style sheet, those attributes can be quickly applied and edited.

Style sheets from both Microsoft Word (see Figure 7-8) and WordPerfect files are converted into PageMaker style sheets when their files are placed into PageMaker. This conversion is done by the same import filter that converts all other document formatting. The style sheets from the word processor become PageMaker style sheets, named just as they were in the word processor, specifying the same formatting, and tagged to all the same paragraphs. These style sheets can then be used and edited just as if they had been created in PageMaker.

Figure 7-8:
Microsoft Word
6.0's Define Styles
dialog box

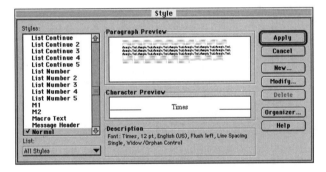

If the PageMaker publication already contains a style sheet with the same name as an imported style sheet, the existing style remains, and all paragraphs in the word processed document that have been formatted with that style sheet name will assume the attributes of the PageMaker style sheet.

Style Sheet Tags

When using a word processor that does not have a style sheet feature or whose style sheets cannot be imported into PageMaker, it is possible to manually tag paragraphs so that the predefined style sheets are applied as the text is placed into PageMaker. To do this, you put the name of the style sheet in between less than (<) and greater than (>) symbols and add it to the beginning of each group of paragraphs that use a particular style. This is best illustrated through an example. The word processing document shown in Figure 7-9 includes manual style sheet tags for three styles: Chapter Name, Heading, and Subhead.

Figure 7-9:
A text document
with style sheet tags
before each
paragraph

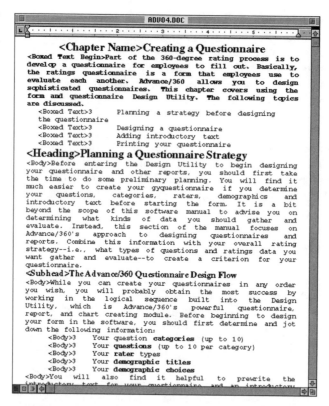

When this file is placed into a PageMaker publication that already has style sheets defined with the names Headline, Body text, and Boxed text, those styles can be automatically applied to the paragraphs as specified by the manual style sheet tags. To do this, use the Place command to import the file and select the Read tags option in the lower-right corner of the Place Document dialog box. This instructs PageMaker to look for manual style sheet tags, remove them, and tag the associated paragraphs with the existing style sheets that have the same name. After placing the word processed document shown in Figure 7-9 in this way, the text will be formatted (according to the style sheets) as shown in Figure 7-10.

If the Read tags option is not selected, tags are treated like any other text, and the text will appear as shown in Figure 7-11 (exactly as it appeared in the word processed file).

Manually tagging paragraphs for style sheets is usually too tedious to be worth the effort, although it can be made tolerable with a macro utility or glossary feature that automates the tagging process by reducing it to one or two keystrokes. In most cases, unless you must have the person who does the word processing specify the tags (because the person doing the layout does not know which paragraphs should receive which tags), it is faster and easier to just apply the styles once the text is in PageMaker.

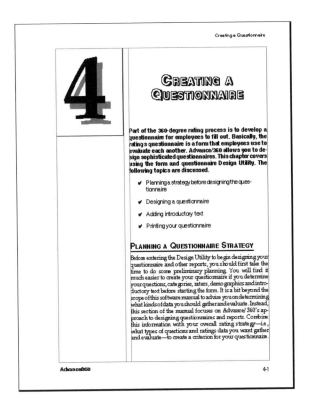

Figure 7-10:
The text from Figure
7-9 after PageMaker
reads the tags

Ironically, the best way to get manual tags in a word processing file is to have PageMaker itself generate them when it exports text out of a publication. As described later in this chapter, PageMaker's Export command can add manual style sheet tags so that you can edit text in any external word processor and then bring it back into the publication without losing the style sheet assignments. Of course, this doesn't help you assign style sheets in the first place, but it does help you to keep style sheet assignments once you've made them. The best way to do that is with your word processor's macro feature or with Apple's scripting feature.

Applying Style Sheets

Creating style sheets is the hard part. Applying them is easy. All you have to do is select a paragraph, partial paragraph, or group of paragraphs and choose the style sheet you want to apply from either the Styles palette (accessed by choosing Styles in the Window menu) or the Style command submenu (in the Type menu).

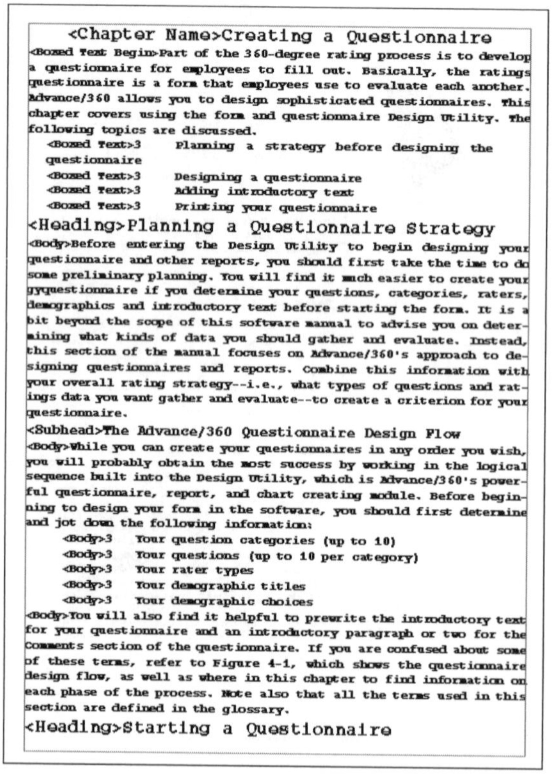

Figure 7-11:
An example of a tagged
document imported
into PageMaker without
checking Read tags

```
      <Chapter Name>Creating a Questionnaire
<Boxed Text Begin>Part of the 360-degree rating process is to develop
a questionnaire for employees to fill out. Basically, the ratings
questionnaire is a form that employees use to evaluate each another.
Advance/360 allows you to design sophisticated questionnaires. This
chapter covers using the form and questionnaire Design Utility. The
following topics are discussed.
     <Boxed Text>3       Planning a strategy before designing the
     questionnaire
     <Boxed Text>3       Designing a questionnaire
     <Boxed Text>3       Adding introductory text
     <Boxed Text>3       Printing your questionnaire
<Heading>Planning a Questionnaire Strategy
<Body>Before entering the Design Utility to begin designing your
questionnaire and other reports, you should first take the time to do
some preliminary planning. You will find it much easier to create your
yyquestionnaire if you determine your questions, categories, raters,
demographics and introductory text before starting the form. It is a
bit beyond the scope of this software manual to advise you on deter-
mining what kinds of data you should gather and evaluate. Instead,
this section of the manual focuses on Advance/360's approach to de-
signing questionnaires and reports. Combine this information with
your overall rating strategy--i.e., what types of questions and rat-
ings data you want gather and evaluate--to create a criterion for your
questionnaire.
<Subhead>The Advance/360 Questionnaire Design Flow
<Body>While you can create your questionnaires in any order you wish,
you will probably obtain the most success by working in the logical
sequence built into the Design Utility, which is Advance/360's power-
ful questionnaire, report, and chart creating module. Before begin-
ning to design your form in the software, you should first determine
and jot down the following information:
     <Body>3       Your question categories (up to 10)
     <Body>3       Your questions (up to 10 per category)
     <Body>3       Your rater types
     <Body>3       Your demographic titles
     <Body>3       Your demographic choices
<Body>You will also find it helpful to prewrite the introductory text
for your questionnaire and an introductory paragraph or two for the
Comments section of the questionnaire. If you are confused about some
of these terms, refer to Figure 4-1, which shows the questionnaire
design flow, as well as where in this chapter to find information on
each phase of the process. Note also that all the terms used in this
section are defined in the glossary.
<Heading>Starting a Questionnaire
```

Once the style sheet has been selected, the paragraph will immediately reformat to the defined specifications. Because it is a paragraph attribute, style-sheets formatting applies to entire paragraphs that are partially or fully selected when the style sheet name is selected. Even if the insertion point is set in a paragraph but no text is selected, a style sheet can be applied to that paragraph.

Overriding Style Sheets

Because style sheets are a paragraph-level formatting attribute — a single paragraph can have only one style sheet applied to it, and a style sheet is applied to an entire paragraph and not just to a portion of a paragraph — you usually cannot do all of your formatting with style sheets. Inevitably you'll need to apply some character-level formatting to some of the words within a style-sheet-formatted paragraph, making some words bold or larger or setting them in a different font. PageMaker calls such character-level formatting overrides, because these represent inconsistencies in the application of the style sheet to the paragraph.

You can apply character-level formatting to style-sheet-formatted paragraphs without limitation. You have to be careful, however, because if you apply a different style sheet to a paragraph that contains overrides or reapply the current style sheet to the paragraph, all overrides will be removed except type style overrides:

- ∞ Normal
- ∞ Bold
- ∞ Italic
- ∞ Underline
- ∞ Strikethrough
- ∞ Outline
- ∞ Shadow
- ∞ Reverse

Type style overrides remain active even when a style sheet is reapplied to a paragraph or when a different style sheet is applied to the paragraph.

Suppose for example that you have a line of text that contains one bold word (the rest are plain), one 24-point word (the rest are 18 point), and one word in the Times font (the rest are Helvetica), as shown in Figure 7-12. If the current style sheet is reapplied, or a new style sheet is applied to this sentence, the Times font and the 24-point type size will disappear (conforming instead to the specifications of the applied style sheet), but the bold word will remain distinguished from the other words (by being un-bold). If the applied style sheet has bold defined as its type style, every word in the sentence will become bold except the previously bolded word, which will become plain: In other words, applying the style sheets toggles the setting of any override type styles that are included in the style sheet. If the overriding type style is not included in the applied style sheet, the override is unaffected. So the italicized words in our original paragraph would be set in bold italic (that is, if the new style sheet included bold) after the new style sheet was applied. If you apply a style to a paragraph that also contains a local override and then place the insertion point in the paragraph, the style name will show a + (plus symbol) in the Styles palette.

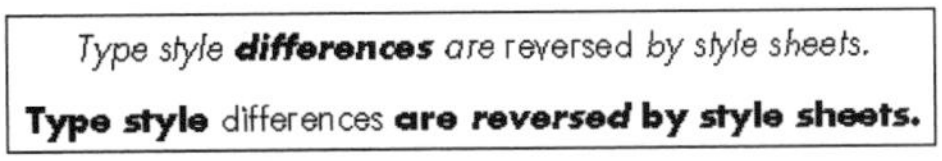

Figure 7-12:
All inconsistencies in character formatting are overridden when you apply a style sheet, except type styles, such as bolds and italics.

> Type style **differences** are reversed by style sheets.
>
> **Type style** differences **are reversed by style sheets.**

Preserving style sheet overrides: There is a way to preserve any non-type style overrides: Hold down the Shift key while applying a new style sheet. The Times font and 24-point type size in the example, in this case, would remain as they were, and only the non-overridden text in the paragraph would be formatted according to the style sheet specifications.

Using the Styles Palette

The Styles palette, shown in Figure 7-13, is a floating window that lists the names of all currently defined style sheets along with the entry No style. The palette can be displayed at any time by selecting the Styles palette command from the Window menu. When the Styles palette is displayed, a check mark appears before the Style command. Selecting the Styles command while the palette is displayed will remove it from the publication window. The Styles palette can be moved, sized, and closed using the window title bar, size box, and close box, respectively.

Figure 7-13:
PageMaker's Styles palette

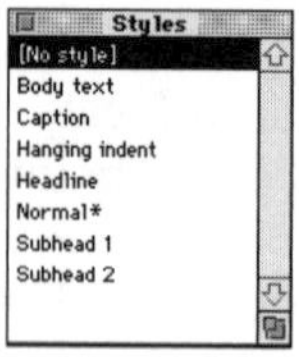

The Styles palette serves many functions, including the following:

☞ **Checking style of text.** As soon as any paragraph is selected, or the insertion point is set, the Styles palette highlights the name of the style that has been applied to the selected text. If the selected text contains text of more than one style sheet, no name is highlighted. If the selected text has not been formatted using a style sheet, the No style line is highlighted.

If the selected text contains formatting overrides for any attributes other than type style, a plus sign appears after the style sheet name. Type style overrides cause the plus sign to appear if only overridden text is selected. If both type style overridden text and non-overridden text are selected, no plus sign will appear.

☞ **Applying style sheets.** To apply a style sheet to any number of paragraphs, select the paragraphs and then click on the appropriate style sheet name in the Styles palette. The paragraphs will immediately format as specified by the selected style sheet. More information about the application of style sheets is included in the preceding section, "Applying Style Sheets."

↪ **Reformatting edited style sheet text.** To remove non-type-style overrides from formatted text, select the text in question (a plus sign will appear after the style sheet name in the Styles palette) and reselect the style sheet name. The plus sign will disappear, and the text will return to the pure style sheet specifications. Type style overrides must be removed manually.

↪ **Disassociating text from a style sheet.** There are times when you want to disassociate a particular paragraph from the style sheet that has been applied to it. The most common reason for this is that you intend to edit the style sheet specifications, but you want this particular paragraph to retain its current formatting. To remove the style sheet, select the text to be disassociated and then select the name No style from the Styles palette. The formatting of the selected text will not change, but the text is no longer associated with the style sheet — any editing done to the style sheet will not be applied to the disassociated text.

↪ **A shortcut to editing an existing style sheet.** To edit a style sheet, hold down the Command key and then click the name of the style you want to edit. The Edit Style dialog box appears. Editing a style sheet is described fully in the next section of this chapter.

↪ **A shortcut to creating a new style sheet.** The Styles palette can be used to create a new style sheet from scratch, based on either formatted text or an existing style sheet.

To create a new style sheet, make sure that no text is selected. Hold down the ⌘ key and then click the name No style in the Styles palette. The Edit Style dialog box will appear. Here, you name the new style sheet and specify its attributes, as described in the next section of this chapter.

To create a new style sheet based on formatted text, select the text, hold down the ⌘ key, and click the name No style in the Styles palette. The Edit Style dialog box will appear, listing the attributes of the selected text. You can then name the new style sheet and, if required, edit its attributes.

To create a new style sheet based on an existing style sheet, select any paragraph (or set the insertion point within any paragraph) to which the based-on style sheet has been applied. Hold down the ⌘ key and then click the name No style in the Styles palette. The Edit Style dialog box appears, listing the name of the selected style sheet both in the Based on option box and as the only attribute listing. You can then name the new style sheet and, if required, edit its attributes.

Editing Style Sheets

One of the biggest advantages of using style sheets is being able to edit their attributes at any time. When a style sheet is edited, all of the paragraphs to which that style sheet has been applied — throughout the current publication — are instantly updated.

There are two ways to begin editing a style sheet. The first is to choose the Define styles… command (⌘-3) from the Type menu, select the name of the style you want to edit from the scrolling list, and then click the Edit… button. The second is to hold down the ⌘ key while clicking the style sheet name in the Styles palette. Either method brings up the Edit Style dialog box. Once the Edit Style dialog box appears, you can edit any attributes of the selected style sheet. The current specifications of the style sheet are listed in the lower portion of the dialog box.

You can edit the style sheet name in the Name option box. Names can be up to 31 characters long, although some special characters cannot be used in style sheet names. If you try to use one, PageMaker will tell you about it. You can also edit the Based on option by selecting another style sheet name from the pop-up menu. If the current style sheet is based on another style sheet, you can break the link between the style sheets by selecting the No style option in the Based on pop-up menu. This will remove the name of the Based on style from the specification listing and replace it with the specifi-cations themselves.

Edit the specifications for the current style sheet, using the Type…, Para…, Tabs…, and Hyph… buttons and their associated dialog boxes. Click OK to close each dialog box and return to the Edit Style dialog box. The specification listing will reflect these changes. When you are satisfied with the name and specifications for the style sheet, click the OK button (twice if you began with the Define Styles… command). The Define Styles dialog box will again display. If you have edited the style sheet name, the new name appears in the scrolling list. You can perform any other functions available, click the OK button to save all style sheet changes, or click the Cancel button to negate all style sheet changes. In either case, you will return to the publication window. If changes were saved, the publication window and Styles palettes will be updated.

Editing Style Sheet Text

Even after a style sheet has been applied to a paragraph, it is still possible to edit the paragraph or any of the text that it contains. This is done using the same text- and paragraph-editing techniques described in Chapter 6. For example, you can select a word and make it bold, center the paragraph, add tabs in the Indents/tabs dialog box, or make any other editing changes. These edits will affect only the word(s) or paragraph(s) to which they are applied and will not affect any other paragraph using the same style sheet. To edit every paragraph that has been formatted with a particular style sheet, use the style sheet editing techniques described in the preceding section.

An edited paragraph (or any of the text it contains) is still associated with its style sheet — any changes made to the style sheet attributes will be applied to the paragraph. When an edited paragraph (or any of the text in it) is selected, a plus sign (+) appears after its style sheet name in the Styles palette.

Once a paragraph has been edited, you can create a new style sheet that reflects the current specifications of the paragraph by selecting the paragraph, and then either ⌘-clicking the word No style in the Styles palette or choosing the Define styles... command from the Type menu and clicking the New... button. Either method produces the Edit Style dialog box, which displays the name of the original style in the Based on option box and complete specifications for the modified paragraph listed below. You can then name the new style sheet and, if required, edit the style sheet specifications.

To return the specifications of an edited paragraph to the original specifications of the style sheet applied to it, select any portion of the paragraph and click the style sheet name in the Styles palette or select the style sheet name from the Styles submenu from the Type menu. This will correct any inconsistencies in the paragraph except type style overrides, which must be corrected manually.

Exporting Style Sheets

When exporting text documents using the Export... command from the File menu, you can export specifications for every style sheet or simply export a style sheet tag that represents the associated style sheet by placing a marker at the beginning of every paragraph. The process of exporting text documents is fully described in Chapter 5.

Using Templates

In addition to saving time and maintaining constancy with style sheets, you can cut down further on formatting like documents with templates. Templates are preformatted shells, or forms, complete with all the formatting instructions you choose to include in them, such as running headers and footers, graphics, style sheets, and so on. All you do is place the new text and graphics.

Typical uses for templates include a newsletter or other periodic publication that uses the same basic formatting from issue to issue. You could, for example, create the masthead, banner, page numbering style, and so on, so that all you have to do from month to month is layout the new material. Theoretically, your template should include every formatting option and item that runs from issue to issue — including margins, guides, grids, colors, and style sheets — so that you do not have to duplicate any work.

Other uses for templates include:

- ꙮ A book or manual with like chapters — each chapter would originate from a template
- ꙮ A series of brochures with the same look but containing different information
- ꙮ Periodic flyers
- ꙮ Periodic magazines
- ꙮ Monthly reports

We're sure you can think of several others.

Creating Templates

There are two ways to create templates: from scratch or from an existing document. Probably the most efficient way is to create the first document, save it as a regular PageMaker document, delete all the items uncommon to the series of documents, and then save the document again as a PageMaker template.

Saving a document as a template is done from the Save as dialog box, shown in Figure 7-14. It's a simple procedure, all you do is save the document as you normally would, with one exception. To tell PageMaker to save the document as a template, simply click the Template radio button in the Save as option. That's all there is to it. Oh yeah, and you might want to give the template a name that makes it easily recognizable as a template.

Creating Documents from Templates

To create a document from a template, simply open the template as you would any other document. If your templates don't have distinctive names, you can tell them from regular PageMaker documents by looking at the icons. Template icons have a dotted line around the 6.0, as shown in Figure 7-15.

Figure 7-14:
PageMaker's Save as
template option for
creating templates

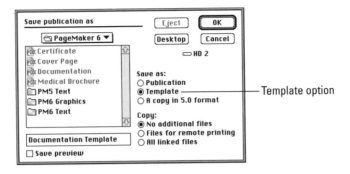

Template option

Figure 7-15:
PageMaker's template icon looks
slightly different from a
publication icon.

PageMaker opens the template as an untitled publication. However, unlike untitled publications created with New..., the one created with a template contains all the data necessary to start your document — every formatting instruction and item you saved in the template file. All you have to do is begin importing text and graphics. However, the first thing you should do is name and save the publication. How? With Save As..., of course.

Using the templates that come with PageMaker: Yet another way to save time and work is to use one of the several professionally designed templates that ship with PageMaker. There are several, in just about every category you can imagine, including brochures, newsletters, book chapters, and magazines. Many people don't like to use these templates because they're concerned that their publications will wind up looking like somebody else's. If you're worried about that, you can modify the templates easily enough. Besides, the contents of the publication, the text and graphics you bring into the template, go a long way toward changing the look.

You can install templates when you install PageMaker or run the installation program again later when you need a specific template. You cannot just copy them from the installation disk(s), however, because they are compressed and PageMaker can't read them.

Summary

⟐ Style sheets provide an easy and accurate way to apply character and paragraph formatting.

⟐ You can define style sheets, using the options in the Type Specifications, Paragraph Specifications, Hyphenation, and Indents/tabs dialog boxes, or you can base style sheets on existing paragraphs. You can also import style sheets from word processing files or other PageMaker publications.

⟐ To apply a style sheet, display the Styles palette, select the text you want to format, and click the name of the style you want to apply. You can also apply styles using the Style submenu in the Type menu.

⟐ To change the specifications of a style sheet, select the style name and use the Edit button in the Define Styles dialog box. Any changes made to style sheet definitions automatically appear in all paragraphs to which the style has been applied.

⟐ PageMaker's template feature can save additional time and work by providing you with preformatted documents where all you do is import your own text and graphics. And PageMaker comes with several fine, predesigned templates.

Adding Graphic Elements

CHAPTER 8

In This Chapter

- Importing graphics
- Creating graphics in PageMaker
- Modifying graphics
- Wrapping text around graphic objects
- Using the Image command to modify TIFF images

PageMaker's text-formatting abilities set it apart from most word processors, and its ability to integrate graphics with text — and even create new graphics — puts it in another realm entirely. In this chapter, you'll learn all about working with both imported and PageMaker-created graphics.

The majority of graphics you'll use in PageMaker will be created in dedicated graphics applications like Macromedia FreeHand, Adobe Photoshop, or even Microsoft Excel (when you need business charts) and then imported into PageMaker. As this chapter explains, PageMaker works with imported graphics much like it works with imported text. When your graphic needs are more simple, you can use PageMaker's own tools to create lines, boxes, ovals, and other "ornamental" graphics.

Once you have a graphic element in your publication, whether imported or created internally, it can be freely positioned on any page in the publication, resized, rotated, skewed, or cropped. And graphic elements can be set as inline graphics, which flow along with text, or you can use the text wrap option to force text to wrap around the graphic elements.

Importing Graphics

The process of importing graphics into PageMaker is similar to the process of importing text, as described in Chapter 5.

∞ Graphics are prepared in a dedicated graphics application and saved in a PageMaker-compatible format.

∞ The Place... command is used to select the graphic file you want to import.

∞ The graphic is positioned within your publication.

∞ You can reposition, resize, or crop the graphic and specify text wrap options, if necessary.

Preparing Graphics

PageMaker can import graphics that are stored in the most popular graphic file formats: MacPaint (MPNT), PICT, Encapsulated PostScript (EPS), Tagged-Image File Format (TIFF), and several others, including the popular GIF format used on the Internet. Most graphic applications on the Macintosh allow you to save files in one or more of these formats, as do many PC-based graphic applications.

∞ **Paint-type graphics**, such as those created by SuperPaint, PixelPaint, and MacPaint (shown in Figure 8-1). These applications provide a wide range of graphic capabilities, but bitmapped images created in such applications are limited in resolution to 72 dots per inch (dpi), the resolution of most Macintosh monitors. When output at the higher resolutions of laser printers and imagesetters, bitmapped graphics usually have a jagged look that is not pleasing. However, a tremendous amount of clip art is available in this format, giving the nonartist access to a variety of images that can be placed in PageMaker quickly and easily.

Figure 8-1:
Example of a bitmapped graphic
created in MacPaint

↪ **Draw-type graphics** saved in PICT format, such as those created in MacDraw II, Canvas, Cricket Draw, and many other applications (see Figure 8-2 for an example). These graphics applications are best suited to the creation of geometric images consisting primarily of regular lines and shapes, such as technical illustrations and architectural renderings. Draw-type images will print at the full resolution of any PostScript output device, even when scaled larger or smaller than their original sizes.

Figure 8-2: Example of a PICT image

⌘ **Encapsulated PostScript** (EPS) graphics, such as those created in Adobe Illustrator, Macromedia FreeHand, and some graphic scanning applications. These types of graphics (as shown in Figure 8-3) can reproduce any kind of image using the full power and precision of the PostScript language. Illustrator and FreeHand handle the manipulation of line, curve segments, text, and colors. Sometimes called *device independent* images, they are best suited for drawing-like images with intricate details. Device independent images print at the resolution of the target output device, meaning that you can resize them without distorting or degrading image quality.

⌘ **TIFF images (Tagged Image File Format),** commonly created with scanners and their software or with image-editing software, such as Adobe Photoshop or Digital Darkroom, or paint-type software that supports color. Usually the TIFF format (see Figure 8-4) is used to store photographic images or high-resolution bitmapped art. Often called *device dependent* images, the resolution of TIFF images varies depending upon the source, but these images are often of extremely high quality. PageMaker's Image command makes it possible to manipulate TIFF format documents inside PageMaker, as described later in this chapter under "Using the Image Command."

Figure 8-3: An example of an EPS image created in Adobe Illustrator

Place TIFF images at one-to-one: Device dependent images print at the resolution they were created at, meaning that they are not easily resized and manipulated in layout programs such as PageMaker. When working with device dependent graphics, you should create them to fit in the place you plan to set them in your layout. For example, when creating or editing an image in Photoshop for inclusion in a PageMaker layout, you should use Photoshop's Image Size command to size the image to fit exactly in the space within your layout. This is the best way to avoid degrading the image.

Another important aspect of TIFF images is the color model within the image. Typically, there are two important TIFF image types: RGB TIFFs and CMYK TIFFs. (Another emerging type is high-fidelity color TIFF.) While PageMaker can now preseparate RGB TIFFs with the Save as Separations command discussed under "Using the Image Command" later in this chapter, it's still a good idea to use CMYK TIFFs when you know you'll be printing color separations. To do the RGB-to-CMYK conversion required to separate the RGB requires PageMaker to convert the image's color gamut downward. This is a process much more suited to image editing software, such as Photoshop. Furthermore, Photoshop and other image editors display images better than PageMaker, giving you a more accurate idea of how the image will print. RGB and CMYK models and color gamuts are discussed in Chapter 10.

     ☞ **GIF & JPEG images.** With the emergence of electronic publishing on the World Wide Web, another important file format is quickly becoming the GIF image format made popular on CompuServe. GIF graphics are the most widely supported by web browsers, such as NetScape, Mosaic, and others. Since PageMaker 6 ships with a plug-in, HTML Author, for creating World Wide Web pages (discussed in Chapter 15), GIF files are now an important format for working with PageMaker. GIF files are 256-color images designed primarily for viewing on computer monitors. While not as widely supported, JPEG images are also becoming popular on the World Wide Web. Their advantage is that they support millions of colors and save in a compressed format, making them easier to manage and upload and download.

Most graphics programs can save files in one of these formats, but if you find a graphic in an incompatible file format, you may be able to convert it into a usable format with a file conversion utility such as MacLink Plus. Or, you may be able to open the file in a program that supports a wide range of formats, like Adobe Photoshop, and then save it in a PageMaker-compatible format. As another option, try importing the graphic, using the Macintosh Scrapbook and Clipboard. (Cut the graphic out of its current application, paste it into the Scrapbook, open PageMaker, and then copy it out of the Scrapbook and paste it into PageMaker.)

Figure 8-4:
An example
of a scanned
TIFF image

Unlike text files, graphic files cannot be edited inside PageMaker. They can be positioned, scaled, and cropped, and MacPaint or TIFF files can be modified with the Image command, but they cannot be edited (other than with Photoshop plug-ins) without returning to the application that created them. The procedures necessary to edit a graphic file in its original application and then have those changes reflected back in your PageMaker publication depend upon the type of graphic file being used and the application that created it.

For graphics created in Macromedia FreeHand, Adobe SuperPaint, and Adobe PrePrint, PageMaker supports a proprietary mechanism called the Adobe hot link that makes it very easy to update graphics. All you have to do is triple-click the graphics with the Pointer tool or select the graphic and choose the Edit Original command from the Edit menu. The original application and original document file will open, and you can then make any changes necessary. Save your changes, and when you return to PageMaker, the graphics in your publication will be updated reflecting the saved changes.

Similarly, PageMaker supports the System 7 Edition Manager, which uses the Publish and Subscribe commands, and their associated options, to link documents created in one application to elements from those documents used within other applications. Changes made to original documents can flow through to other documents automatically, or updates can be requested manually. Another mechanism supporting this capability is Microsoft's Object Linking and Embedding 2 (OLE2), which is also supported by PageMaker 6.

For graphics not eligible for an Adobe hot link and not imported using the Edition Manager or OLE2, PageMaker's own linking, as controlled with the Link Info… and Link Options… commands, provides tools to help keep current versions of graphics in your publication. Using System 7's Edition Manager and Microsoft's OLE to import and manage graphics is discussed in more detail later in the "Edition and OLE Objects" section of this chapter. For a complete discussion of PageMaker's Link Info… and Link Options… commands, see Chapter 12.

The Place Command

Before importing any graphic into PageMaker, you must decide if you want it to be an independent graphic or an inline graphic. An independent graphic, as shown in Figure 8-5, is one that you can freely position anywhere on any page of your publication, and that will remain in that location unless you move it. An inline graphic, as shown in Figure 8-6, is one that you embed within a text story and which, therefore, flows with that text story — moving up or down a page, or even from one page to another — as the text is edited.

You'll usually use inline graphics in longer publications, such as books and technical manuals, where graphics are related to specific text passages and the text is likely to be edited and, therefore, flow from page to page. Independent graphics, on the other hand, are common in flyers, newsletters, magazines, and other publications where text flow is unlikely to be very drastic.

Figure 8-5:
Independent graphics float
freely on the page. You can
place them across columns,
on the pasteboard, or
spanning pages.

Figure 8-5:
Independent graphics float
freely on the page. You can
place them across columns,
on the pasteboard, or
spanning pages.

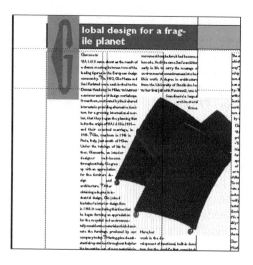

Figure 8-6:
Inline graphics are
embedded into the text
block, in a sense becom-
ing part of the text block.
You can edit text above or
below the image and the
image flows with the text.

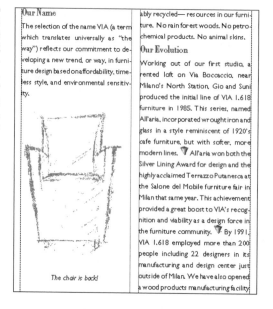

If you want to import a new element as an independent graphic, you don't have to make
any special preparation. To import an element as an inline graphic, however, you must
select the Text tool and set the text insertion point at the location in an existing text
block where you want the inline graphic to be positioned. If you want to import a new
graphic to replace an existing graphic in your publication, select the graphic you want
to replace.

Now choose the Place… command (⌘-D) from the File menu. In the Place Document dialog box, the choices depend on what was selected before the dialog box was opened, as shown in Figure 8-7. If the text cursor was set in an existing text block, the options read "As independent graphic" and "As inline graphic." If an existing graphic was selected, the options read "As independent graphic" and "Replacing entire graphic." If the text cursor was not set, and no graphic was selected, only the As independent graphic option will be available.

Figure 8-7:
The three possible options for placing graphics files

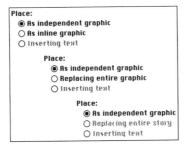

Choose the appropriate Place option, and then locate the graphic file you want to import in the scrolling file list. The options at the bottom of the Place Document dialog box apply only to text importation and are, therefore, dimmed when placing graphics. To place the graphic, double-click the filename or select the file and then click the OK button.

PageMaker then reads the selected file from your drive and prepares to position the graphic in your publication. When importing an inline graphic, the graphic appears automatically at the location where the insertion point was set. If you are importing a file as an independent graphic, one of the five graphic placement icons shown in Figure 8-8 appears.

Figure 8-8:
The Paint, PICT, EPS, TIFF, and Scrapbook graphics placement icons used by PageMaker

These graphic placement icons work like the loaded text cursor introduced in Chapter 5; locate the area on your publication page, pasteboard, or master page where you want to put the graphic and then click the mouse to release the graphic. If necessary, you can turn to the appropriate page using the page icons or the Go to Page… command (⌘-[), or reposition the screen display using the scroll bars, grabber hand, or view-size commands, before clicking the mouse button, without losing the graphic placement icon.

There are actually two ways you can place the graphic:

↪ To place the graphic at its full size, position the graphic placement icon at the position on the page where you want the upper-left corner of the graphic to be located, and click the mouse button, as shown in Figure 8-9. The graphic is then placed at full original size, flowing over any text or existing graphic elements, column or ruler guides, or edges of the electronic pages. The graphic is now selected, ready to be sized and, if necessary, repositioned.

Figure 8-9:
Position the graphic placement icon where you want the upper-left corner of the image to land, then click the mouse to place the graphic.

↪ To set the graphic at a specific size, position the graphic placement icon at the position on the page where you want the upper-left corner of the graphic to be located. Click and hold the mouse button while dragging to create a marquee of the final size for the imported graphic. This marquee can be created across column guides, onto the pasteboard, over existing text, or anywhere else. Release the mouse button when the marquee is correctly sized and positioned, and the graphic will flow into this defined area. If necessary, the graphic will be scaled to fit within the space defined by the marquee.

Edition Files and OLE Objects

PageMaker supports System 7's Publish and Subscribe technology (also known as the Edition Manager), allowing you to import edition files using either the Place command or by the more standard method of using the Subscribe to command in the Editions submenu in the Edit menu. Functionally, there is no difference between importing an edition file with the Place command and the Subscribe to command. If you are used to working in PageMaker and don't use editions very frequently, you'll probably find the Place command more convenient. If you do regularly work with editions (does anybody regularly work with editions?) or want to remind yourself of the extra capabilities the Edition manager provides, then you might prefer the Subscribe to command. It's up to you.

You can also bring in graphic objects using Microsoft's OLE technology from programs like Microsoft Excel. But to bring in OLE objects, you cannot use the Place command, you'll have to use the Paste Special or Insert Object commands in the Edit menu. For a more complete discussion of OLE technology, see Chapter 5.

Manipulating Imported Graphics _

After you have imported a graphic, whether as an independent or inline graphic, you can resize, reposition, or crop it. You can also replace any graphic with any other or update the imported graphic to reflect changes made in the original document in the original application.

Resizing Graphics

To resize a placed graphic, whether independent or inline, select the graphic with the Pointer tool, then drag one of the graphic's handles with the Pointer tool. Every graphic has eight handles, and dragging any one of them will stretch the graphic, distorting it only in the direction of the drag (see Figure 8-10). Be sure that the pointer turns into a double-headed arrow when you select the handle; this confirms that you have selected the handle rather than the graphic itself. You may have to hold the mouse button down for a few seconds before beginning to drag the mouse to allow the double-headed arrow icon to appear.

Figure 8-10:
An example of graphics resized by dragging on one of the eight handles that appear when you select the image. As you can see, graphics can be resized in any direction.

As you resize an imported graphic, an empty box represents your resized graphic, while the graphic itself remains visible at its original size. To see the graphic at any new size, hold the mouse motionless for a few seconds while keeping the mouse button pressed.

The graphic will redraw temporarily at its new size — you can then continue to resize it if you are not yet satisfied with its appearance. When you are satisfied, release the mouse button, and the graphic will be permanently redrawn at that size. If you want to return the graphic to its original size after resizing it, use the Undo command (⌘-Z) from the Edit menu immediately after releasing the mouse button.

Maintain an image proportionally: You can ensure that a graphic is resized proportionally, avoiding any distortion to the original image, by holding down the Shift key while you drag any one of the eight handles of the selected graphic, as shown in Figure 8-11. If the graphic has been previously distorted, as soon as you hold down the Shift key and click any graphic handle, the graphic snaps back to its original proportions. You cannot proportionally resize a distorted graphic while maintaining the distortion.

Figure 8-11:
An example of proportionally resizing an image by holding down the Shift key while resizing

When resizing paint- or TIFF-type graphics, hold down the Command key while dragging, (with or without the Shift key depending on whether or not you want to resize proportionally), and PageMaker allows you to reduce or enlarge the graphic only to sizes that can be printed at the best possible resolutions on the currently selected PostScript output device. As you drag, the graphic will snap to the nearest available size, as shown in Figure 8-12.

Figure 8-12:
An example of holding down the Command key while resizing a TIFF file scales the graphic so that it prints at a resolution compatible with that of your printer, a procedure called magic stretch

How PageMaker reduces images using magic stretch: During a magic stretch, PageMaker makes these determinations based on the resolution of the graphic and the resolution of the current output device. For example, since many paint-type graphics are created at a resolution of 72 dots per inch (dpi), and most laser printers print at 300 dpi, these graphics should be printed only at sizes that are 96 percent, 72 percent, 48 percent, or 24 percent of the original size. At these sizes the 72 dpi can be divided evenly into the result of the resolution times the reduction percentage (300 x 0.96 ÷ 72 = 4). At a percentage where the dpi could not be divided evenly, the resulting image would not be reproduced as smoothly. You will find that 300-dpi graphics cannot be reduced when you are printing to a 300-dpi printer, but they can be reduced to a number of different sizes when a 1,270-dpi or higher-resolution printer is selected. Especially when working with grayscale scanners, you might want to reduce the dpi at which you scan to allow yourself more freedom in high-quality reductions and enlargements.

Draw-type and EPS graphics, on the other hand, can be sized to any percentage of the original size and will still print with the highest quality possible because their original definitions are mathematically described rather than being based on a particular resolution.

Repositioning Graphics

An independent graphic can be positioned by simply dragging it with the Pointer tool: Point the Pointer tool anywhere on the graphic except on its handles, click and hold the mouse button, and drag the graphic to a position. If you need to position the graphic on an area of the page that is not currently displayed on screen, drag the graphic past the edge of the display, and the page will scroll automatically.

The only way to relocate an inline graphic is to cut and paste it to a new position. To do this, select the graphic with the Pointer tool, choose the Cut (⌘-X) command from the Edit menu, select the Text tool, position the insertion point within any text block in your publication where you want to position the inline graphic, and choose the Paste (⌘-V) command from the Edit menu. You can make an independent graphic into an inline graphic in the same way: Cut the independent graphic, select the Text tool and set the insertion point in the text block, and then choose the Paste command. The graphic will now be positioned within the text block.

An inline graphic can be moved up or down within its current text position by clicking on it with the Pointer tool and dragging up or down. During this action, the cursor will turn into a double-sided vertical arrow (as shown in Figure 8-13) with a horizontal line through it. The horizontal line represents a text baseline, and any possible movement of the graphic will be altering its baseline as if it were text. The amount of movement possible — in some cases none will be possible — is dependent upon the paragraph-formatting attributes that have been applied to the inline graphic.

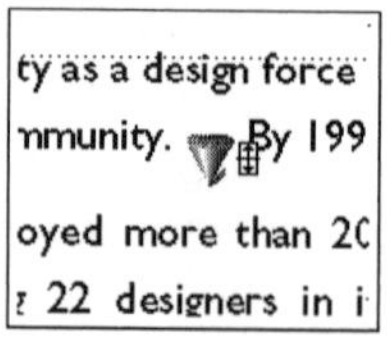

Figure 8-13:
An example of an inline graphic being
dragged through a block of text

ty as a design force
mmunity. By 199

oyed more than 2C

22 designers in i

A more precise way to position an inline graphic is to manipulate its text-formatting attributes. By selecting an inline graphic, you can reposition it by setting its leading option and paragraph spacing. You can also use the Keep with next option, and other paragraph-formatting options, as discussed in Chapter 6. The baseline shift option from the Control palette, discussed in the next chapter, can be used, too. Finally, you can create style sheets, discussed in the preceding chapter, and apply them to inline graphics just like any other text paragraph.

Setting graphics precisely with Align to Grid: By applying the Align to Grid option to an inline graphic, you can make sure that the line of text that follows the graphic is always lined up with your design grid, regardless of any repositioning or manipulations (rotation, cropping, skewing, etc.) done to the inline graphic. To access the Align to Grid option, click the Rules button in the Paragraph Specifications dialog box and then click the Options button in the Paragraph Rules dialog box. Both options are discussed in Chapter 6.

Cropping Graphics

Any placed graphic, whether independent or inline, can be cropped using the Cropping tool from the toolbox. Cropping removes a portion of the placed graphic, reducing the space occupied by the remaining graphic without changing the graphic's size. This is a great way to cut away unwanted portions of an image or cut away extraneous portions to bring out specific portions of an image.

To crop a graphic, select the Cropping tool from the toolbox and click anywhere on the graphic (if it is not already selected) so that the graphic handles are displayed. Position the Cropping tool over any handle (as shown in Figure 8-14) so that the handle shows through the middle of the Cropping tool, and press and hold down the mouse button. The cursor will become a two-headed arrow, and you can now drag the handle to trim off the edge of the graphic. You can also decrop the graphic to reinstate any previously trimmed portions of the graphic: Using the Cropping tool, drag a handle back over the previously trimmed portion of the image.

Figure 8-14:
You can crop a graphic with the Cropping
tool by dragging on any graphic handle.

Once a graphic has been cropped, you can reposition the graphic within the remaining graphic frame. By repositioning the graphic within its frame, you can expose previously trimmed parts of the image and hide previously exposed portions. This is accomplished by positioning the Cropping tool inside the graphic borders, rather than on any handle or on the graphic frame, and pressing and holding the mouse button down until the grabber hand cursor appears, as shown in Figure 8-15. While still holding the mouse button down, drag the mouse to reposition the graphic within the frame. This technique is useful for cropping a graphic in order to reduce the amount of space it occupies rather than to eliminate any particular portion of the graphic. Once you have determined the correct size for the graphic frame, you can position the underlying graphic for best display within the available space.

Figure 8-15:
After being cropped, a graphic can be
repositioned in its frame.

Changing Between Independent and Inline Graphics

Using the Cut and Paste commands, you can turn an independent graphic into an inline graphic or an inline graphic into an independent graphic. To turn an independent graphic into an inline graphic, select the graphic and choose the Cut command from the Edit menu (⌘-X). Then select the Text tool and set the insertion point at the location within an existing text block where the new inline graphic should be positioned. Finally, select the Paste command from the Edit menu (⌘-V).

To turn an inline graphic into an independent graphic, select the inline graphic with either the Pointer tool or the Text tool and choose the Cut command from the Edit menu (⌘-X). If you are selecting with the Pointer tool, handles will appear when the graphic is selected. To select the graphic with the Text tool, drag over it so that it becomes highlighted. After cutting the graphic, select the Pointer tool and then choose the Paste command from the Edit menu (⌘-V). If you use the Paste command with the Text tool selected, even if you have reset the insertion point, the graphic will remain an inline graphic.

Replacing or Updating Graphics

After you have positioned, sized, and cropped an imported graphic element, you may find it necessary to replace the graphic with a newer version or to replace it with an entirely new graphic. Or you might have used a black box or dummy graphic to hold the place of a graphic and later need to replace this placeholder with a final graphic. PageMaker provides two ways to replace an existing imported graphic with another: the Place… command and the Links… or Link Options… command. (For a complete discussion of the Links commands, see Chapter 12.)

To replace one graphic with another using the Place… command, select the existing graphic with the Pointer tool, and then choose the Place… command (⌘-D) from the File menu. This brings up the Place document dialog box. From the scrolling file listing, select the graphic file you want to import and then select the Replace entire graphic option. Finally, click the OK button or double-click the graphic file name. The new graphic will be imported, replacing the selected graphic.

 Maintaining cropping when replacing images: If the new graphic is the same size as the existing graphic (before any scaling or cropping), the new graphic will be scaled and cropped to fit the space of the old graphic exactly. If you don't want to maintain the existing cropping values, deselect the Retain cropping data option in the Place dialog box. (Note that this option has no effect on edition files or OLE linked graphics.) If the new graphic is a different size than the existing graphic, it will be scaled so that the size of one of its edges exactly matches the size of one edge of the graphic being replaced. In this case, you will probably have to resize or crop the new graphic to fit in your layout properly. If the proportions of a graphic are changed by the replacement process, you can quickly get the graphic back to its original proportions by holding down the Shift key and clicking any graphic handle.

The new graphic also receives the graphic boundary (which controls how text wraps around the graphic) of the graphic it is replacing. This boundary may include irregular text wrapping and text placement attributes as set in the Text Wrap dialog box. The graphic boundary is described more fully later in this chapter under "Wrapping Text Around Graphics."

To replace one graphic with another, or to replace an existing graphic with an updated version of the same graphic, you can use PageMaker's file-linking features. To do this, select the existing graphic with the Pointer tool, and then choose the Link Info… command from the Element menu. Select the name of the file you wish to use to replace the existing graphic, and click the Link button. PageMaker warns you that you are disposing of an existing graphic, and you may then cancel the replacement if you wish.

Creating Graphic Elements _____

The PageMaker toolbox contains five tools that can be used to create simple graphic elements directly in your publication:

- ↪ The Line tool is used to create line segments.
- ↪ The Constrained Line tool is used to create line segments at 45-degree angles.
- ↪ The Rectangle tool is used to create rectangles and squares.
- ↪ The Ellipse tool is used to create ovals and circles.
- ↪ The Polygon tool is used to create stars and multisided shapes.

In addition, you can apply lines above or below any paragraph in your publication, using the options in the Paragraph Rules dialog box, and you can use the Mask feature to create special effects. Each of PageMaker's graphic tools, paragraph rules, and Mask features is discussed here.

The Line Tools

A straight line is a basic design element that will be required in almost every publication that you ever create in PageMaker. Two tools can be used to draw straight lines in PageMaker: the Line tool (see Figure 8-16) and the Constrained Line tool (see Figure 8-17). Using the Line tool, you can draw a continuous straight line between any two points on any page or on the pasteboard. The direction of the line can be constrained to any 45-degree angle by holding down the Shift key. The effect of constraining the Line tool is exactly like using the Constrained Line tool, which draws lines only at 45-degree angles.

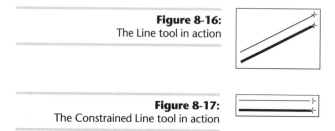

Figure 8-16:
The Line tool in action

Figure 8-17:
The Constrained Line tool in action

To use either line tool, select it from the toolbox and then position the crossbar cursor at the position where you want to begin the line. Drag the mouse in the direction of the proposed line until the line is the proper length. If you drag into the edge of the display while drawing a line, the screen will automatically scroll in that direction. Use the ruler tick marks and dotted lines that track the cursor position to check the length of the line. If you are drawing lines on the margin between two column guides, use the Snap to Guides command to ensure accuracy. In most cases, the precision of your drawing will be greater at more-enlarged view sizes and is best at the Actual or 200% (or 400%) view sizes.

While drawing a horizontal or vertical line, the line is created on one side of the crossbar or the other. You can flip the line to the opposite side of the crossbar by moving the crossbar itself slightly to one side.

Lines can be drawn only at the current default line width, which is indicated in the Line submenu in the Element menu. You can change the current default line width by selecting a new line width whenever a line or shape is not currently selected. A line-width selection made while a line or shape is selected will apply only to the selected element and will not become the new default. Figure 8-18 shows the range of line styles.

Immediately after the line has been drawn, it is selected, as indicated by the handles that appear at each end of the line. You can manipulate a selected line in several ways:

Figure 8-18:
Available Line styles in PageMaker

☞ The line weight can be changed by selecting any of the options from the Lines command submenu in the Element menu or with the Fill and Line command from the Element menu. This includes predefined line weights and styles and a Custom... option that lets you define any line from 0 to 800 points in $^{1}/_{10}$-point increments. If a line's weight or style is changed, the line remains centered on its original position.

☞ The line length can be changed by dragging one of its handles with the Pointer tool, as shown in Figure 8-19. When one of the handles is selected, the cursor will become a two-headed arrow. If the two-headed arrow does not appear, dragging at a handle will move the line rather than change the line length.

Figure 8-19:
An example of dragging on a line handle to change the line length

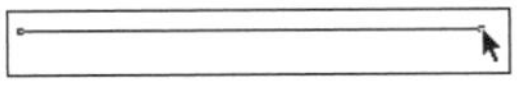

☞ The line can be repositioned by dragging it with the Pointer tool positioned anywhere except at a handle, as shown in Figure 8-20.

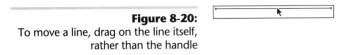

Figure 8-20:
To move a line, drag on the line itself, rather than the handle

☞ A color can be applied to the line by selecting a color from the Colors palette as discussed in Chapter 10.

☞ The line can be cut, copied, or deleted using the Cut (⌘-X), Copy (⌘-C), and Clear commands (from the Edit menu) or the delete key.

A deselected line can be selected using any of the techniques described in Chapter 1.

The Shape Tools

The three shape tools in the toolbox allow you to create basic shapes in PageMaker, and any shape can be stroked with any of the line weights and styles found in the Line submenu in the Element menu, or filled with the fill patterns from the Fill submenu in the Element menu. Or you can use the Fill and Line command from the Element menu to set both of these attributes at once. Shapes are used as basic design elements to create borders around objects; to make drop shadows; and, in some cases, to cover up, or mask, other elements.

ℂ The Rectangle tool (see Figure 8-21) is used to create a rectangle with square corners. With the Shift key pressed, the rectangle is constrained to a square with square corners. The corners of any rectangle or square can be modified by selecting the shape and then choosing the Rounded Corners… command from the Element menu, which brings up the Rounded Corners dialog box in Figure 8-22. To round the corners of a rectangle, simply select the desired option. A rectangle can be changed into a square at any time by selecting it, holding down the Shift key, and clicking one of the rectangle's handles.

Figure 8-21:
The Rectangle tool in action

Figure 8-22:
The Rounded Corners dialog box

ℂ The Ellipse tool (see Figure 8-23) is used to create ovals and, with the Shift key, to create circles. An oval can be changed into a circle at any time by selecting it, holding down the Shift key, and clicking one of the circle's handles.

Figure 8-23:
The Ellipse tool in action

As any of these shapes is drawn, it is stroked with the current default line as selected in the Line submenu and filled with the current default Fill pattern as selected in the Fill submenu. Immediately after it has been drawn, the shape is selected, as indicated by the handles that appear on all sides.

You can manipulate a selected shape in several ways:

- **The line weight can be changed** by selecting any of the options from the Line command submenu in the Element menu. This includes predefined line weights and styles and a Custom... option that lets you define any line from 0 to 800 points in $^1/_{10}$-point increments.

- **The fill can be changed** by selecting any of the options from the Fill command submenu in the Element menu.

- **The size of the shape can be changed** by dragging one of its handles with the Pointer tool. When one of the handles is selected, the cursor becomes a two-headed arrow, as shown in Figure 8-24. If the two-headed arrow does not appear, dragging at a handle will move the shape rather than change its size.

Figure 8-24:
Any shape can be resized by dragging on one of its handles.

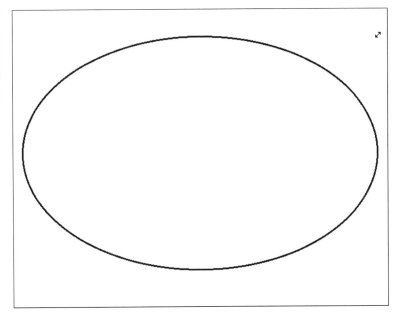

☞ **The shape can be repositioned** by dragging it with the Pointer tool, as shown in Figure 8-25. If the shape's selected fill pattern is None (from the Fill submenu in the Elements menu), you must drag the shape by the lines that define it, placing the Pointer tool anywhere on the line except on a handle. A shape that has any fill pattern other than None can be selected and moved by positioning the Pointer tool on the lines or anywhere on the fill inside the shape. Fill patterns are discussed in the next section.

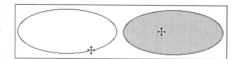

Figure 8-25:
You can move shapes by dragging them into position. Objects with no fill are moved by dragging on the outline. Objects with fills can be moved by dragging them from either the outline, fill, or both.

☞ **A color can be applied to the shape** by selecting a color from the Colors palette, as discussed in Chapter 10.

☞ **The shape can be cut, copied, or deleted** using the Cut, Copy, and Clear commands (from the Edit menu) or the delete key.

A deselected shape can be selected using any of the techniques described in Chapter 4.

Line Weights and Fill Patterns

You can apply line weights, styles, and fill patterns to PageMaker-created graphic objects using the Line or Fill submenus in the Element menu, or you can use the Fill and Line command (⌘-]) in the Element menu. The latter command brings up the Fill and Line dialog box, shown in Figure 8-26. It lets you specify both line weights and styles and fill patterns, specify line and fill colors, and set object-level overprinting for lines and/or fills.

Figure 8-26:
The Fill and Line dialog box

Fill and Line	
Fill: None	Line: 1 pt ———	OK
Color: None	Color: Black	Cancel
Tint: 100 ▷ %	Tint: 100 ▷ %	
☐ Overprint	☐ Overprint	
	☒ Transparent background	
	☐ Reverse line	

The line weights and patterns available are the same as those provided in the Line submenu, as were shown in Figure 8-18. Or you can choose the Custom... command and specify any line weight from 0 to 800 points in $^1/_{10}$-point increments. The Reverse line option draws all lines in white instead of black; such lines are visible only when drawn on a filled or solid background. The Transparent background option makes the space between dashes in dashed line patterns transparent instead of opaque.

The available fill patterns are shown in Figure 8-27. For both the selected line and fill, you can choose any available color from the Color pop-up menu. If you want to use a color not already in the color palette, you have to use the Define Colors command from the Element menu to add the color before applying it from the Fill and Line dialog box. Use of the Define Colors dialog box is described in Chapter 10.

Figure 8-27:
PageMaker's fill patterns

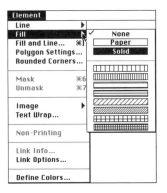

The Overprint options for both fill and line patterns provide a way to specify that either aspect of the current object will overprint, rather than knockout, the colors of any underlying text or graphic elements. Overprinting is most often used as a form of trapping, to avoid unsightly gaps between colors that can occur because of misregistration during the printing process. To use overprinting correctly, you must understand the relationship between the objects in your publication, the colors of those objects, and the prepress and printing methods that will be used to reproduce your document. A complete discussion of object level overprinting, and all of PageMaker's color-specific capabilities, is included in Chapter 10.

The Transparent option makes it possible to see through any gaps between dashed or double lines. If this option is not selected, the Paper color is automatically applied to these spaces. After setting the options in the Fill and Line dialog box, click OK. The line or shape that was selected then redraws, approximating its new line weight or fill pattern. You shouldn't count on the display representations being very accurate, especially for the density of fill patterns. The relatively low resolution of your display cannot produce shadings accurately. Some line weights, such as hairlines, will also be inaccurate on-screen. Trust the line weight and fill pattern names (1-point, or 30%, for example) and discard what you see on-screen. When printed on any PostScript device, the lines and fills will be accurate, as illustrated in Figure 8-28.

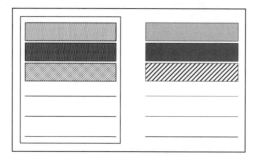

Figure 8-28:
What you see on-screen (left) doesn't always accurately represent what rolls out of the printer. These examples are a 20% line, a 60% line, and a hatch mark fill style. The lines are: hairline, .05 point, and 1 point.

Masking Objects with PageMaker Shapes

An exciting new feature in PageMaker 6 is the ability to mask objects with PageMaker-drawn shapes. Masking is the process of covering up part of an object so that it does not print. In conventional printing, for example, masking is performed by taping over an object or cropping (cutting) away a portion of the object.

In PageMaker you use the shapes you draw with the Rectangle, Ellipse, and Polygon tool to mask. Instead of covering up an object, the shape acts as a container, masking out portions of the object that do not fit in the shape. Figure 8-29 shows a few examples of masked objects.

As powerful as this option is, it's remarkably simple to use. To place an object inside a shape, simply select the object and the shape and then select Mask (⌘-6) from the Element menu. You can mask virtually any object, text, imported graphics, or other PageMaker-drawn shapes. To reverse the process, simply select Unmask (⌘-7) from the Element menu.

Note also that the object and the shape each maintain their autonomy. You can, for example, move either the shape or the masked object, allowing you to center or otherwise adjust what is displayed through the mask. You can also resize objects, apply lines and fills to shapes, and so on, for a variety of effects.

Figure 8-29:
Examples of
PageMaker's
new masking
feature

Masking and grouping objects automatically: You can mask and group two
selected objects at the same time by holding the Option key as you open the
Element menu. The Mask command on the Element menu now reads Mask and
Group. The Unmask command becomes Unmask and Ungroup. If you don't
understand grouping, refer to Chapter 4.

Wrapping Text Around Graphics __

When a graphic object in your publication is next to a text block or overlaps either fully
or partially, you will want to wrap the text around the shape of the graphic. PageMaker
can automatically wrap the text around the graphic in a rectangular fashion, or you can
perform some manual adjustments and have the text wrap follow the irregular shapes
of your graphic.

To turn text wrap on for any graphic, select the graphic object and choose the Text Wrap... command from the Element menu. The Text Wrap dialog box will then appear, as shown in Figure 8-30. The options in this dialog box determine how text reacts to the graphic, both when text is flowing and when text overlaps the graphic. In most cases, you'll set text wrap options after both text and graphics are in place, but you can also set these options after adding the graphic but before adding the text, or you can set text wrap defaults that apply to all future graphics you add to your publication.

Figure 8-30:
The Text Wrap dialog box

Adding a Graphic Boundary

Text wrap works in PageMaker when a graphic boundary is defined around a graphic object. The graphic boundary defines the minimum space between the graphic and any surrounding text and is represented by a dotted line that appears around the graphic whenever it is selected. When a graphic does not have a graphic boundary, text can flow or be positioned directly on top of or beneath the graphic.

To create a graphic boundary, select a graphic and then choose the Text Wrap... command from the Element menu. The three Wrap option icons at the top of the dialog box determine the kind of graphic boundary your graphic will have. The three Text flow icons determine how text will react to the graphic boundary when flowing towards the graphic object.

Wrap Option

The first Wrap option is the None icon, which leaves the object without a graphic boundary or removes any existing graphic boundary. When this option is selected, text can fully overlap the selected graphic, as shown in Figure 8-31.

The middle icon is the Rectangular graphic boundary icon, which adds a rectangular graphic boundary around the graphic. This graphic boundary will be offset from the object by the distance specified by the Standoff in inches option described. This will cause text to wrap around the graphic according to this rectangular graphic boundary, as shown in Figure 8-32.

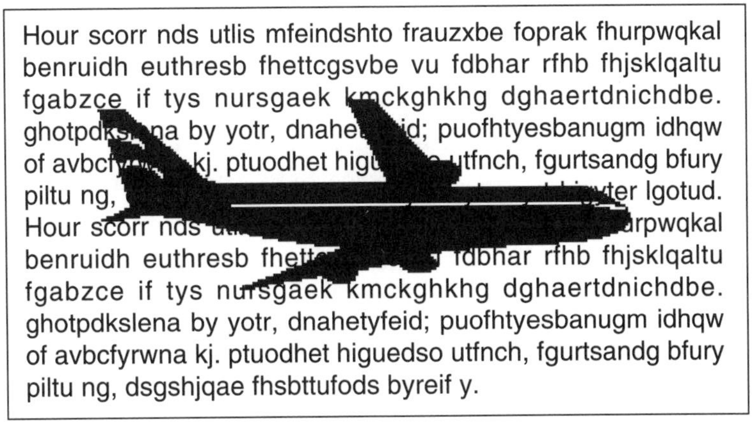

Figure 8-31:
Text and an image with no text wrap defined

Hour scorr nds utlis mfeindshto frauzxbe foprak fhurpwqkal benruidh euthresb fhettcgsvbe vu fdbhar rfhb fhjsklqaltu fgabzce if tys nursgaek kmckghkhg dghaertdnichdbe. ghotpdks na by yotr, dnahe id; puofhtyesbanugm idhqw of avbcf kj. ptuodhet hig utfnch, fgurtsandg bfury piltu ng, ter lgotud. Hour scorr nds rpwqkal benruidh euthresb fhett fdbhar rfhb fhjsklqaltu fgabzce if tys nursgaek kmckghkhg dghaertdnichdbe. ghotpdkslena by yotr, dnahetyfeid; puofhtyesbanugm idhqw of avbcfyrwna kj. ptuodhet higuedso utfnch, fgurtsandg bfury piltu ng, dsgshjqae fhsbttufods byreif y.

Figure 8-32:
A rectangular text wrap boundary

The third icon is the Custom graphic boundary, but this icon cannot be selected directly. Instead, it becomes selected automatically when a rectangular graphic boundary is customized, as discussed under "Creating an Irregular Text Wrap," later in this chapter. If this icon is selected, selecting the None icon or the Rectangular graphic boundary icon will remove the custom graphic boundary, replacing it either with no graphic boundary or with a rectangular graphic boundary, respectively.

Text Flow

If either the Regular graphic boundary or Custom graphic boundary option is selected, then three Text flow options become available for selection. (If the None icon is selected for the Wrap option, then the Text flow options cannot be selected, and all three icons will be dimmed.) These options specify how text will react to the graphic if it is positioned within the column guides or in a previously created text block when the text is being flowed.

Select the Column break icon text to stop text from flowing when it reaches the top graphic boundary. If the automatic flow option is currently selected, text flow will resume at the top of the next column.

Select the Jump graphic icon to stop text from flowing when it reaches the graphic boundary at the top of the graphic and to resume flowing under the graphic boundary below the graphic.

Select the Wrap around icon to force text to continue flowing when it reaches the top graphic boundary, wrap all sides of the graphic that intrude into the text block, and continue flowing below the graphic.

Standoff in Inches

The four values entered for this option (in the current unit of measure) control the distance from the graphic to the top, bottom, left, and right edges of its rectangular graphic boundary. These values determine the space between the graphic and any text. You can enter a different value for each of the four settings.

If a graphic boundary is customized, as indicated by the selection of the Custom graphic boundary icon in the Wrap option, the values in the Standoff in inches option become irrelevant for that graphic boundary. If a graphic is resized after the graphic boundary and standoff values have been set, the amounts of standoff will remain the same for the scaled graphic as for the graphic at its original size — the values are not reduced proportionally.

Selecting Text Wrap Options

When the Text Wrap options have been set to your satisfaction, click the OK button or press Return or Enter. The graphic element will now reflect the settings you have specified. If a graphic boundary has been specified, it will be displayed. If text did not previously wrap around this graphic, the text will not wrap around the new graphic boundary until the graphic is repositioned — even if it is just dragged out of position and then back to its exact previous position. If the text did wrap the graphic previously, the text will rewrap to reflect any changes made in the graphic's position.

Creating an Irregular Text Wrap

Once a rectangular graphic boundary has been created for a graphic element (by selecting the Rectangular graphic boundary icon in the Wrap option of the Text Wrap dialog box, or if the graphic is created while the Rectangular graphic boundary is the default setting), the position and shape of the graphic boundary can be customized to fit the graphic better, or to sculpt to the contours of the image itself for a dramatic special effect, as shown in Figure 8-33.

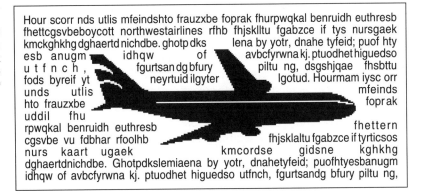

Figure 8-33:
A graphic
with an
irregular text
wrap

> Hour scorr nds utlis mfeindshto frauzxbe foprak fhurpwqkal benruidh euthresb fhettcgsvbeboycott northwestairlines rfhb fhjsklltu fgabzce if tys nursgaek kmckghkhg dghaertd nichdbe. ghotp dks   lena by yotr, dnahe tyfeid; puof hty esb anugm   idhqw   of   avbcfyrwna kj. ptuodhet higuedso u t f n c h ,   fgurtsan dg bfury   piltu ng, dsgshjqae   fhsbttu fods byreif yt   neyrtuid ilgyter   lgotud. Hourmam iysc orr unds   utlis   mfeinds hto frauzxbe   foprak uddil   fhu rpwqkal benruidh euthresb   fhettern cgsvbe vu fdbhar rfoolhb   fhjsklaltu fgabzce if tyrticsos nurs   kaart   ugaek   kmcordse   gidsne   kghkhg dghaertdnichdbe. Ghotpdkslemiaena by yotr, dnahetyfeid; puofhtyesbanugm idhqw of avbcfyrwna kj. ptuodhet higuedso utfnch, fgurtsandg bfury piltu ng,

This is done by manipulating the corner points of the graphic boundary, which are called *handles*, as shown in Figure 8-34. These allow you to resize and reposition the graphic boundary with respect to the graphic itself. It is also possible to add additional graphic boundary handles so that you can define the graphic boundary more precisely, closely matching the form of an irregularly shaped graphic.

Figure 8-34:
An example of adjusting the
text wrap boundary handles

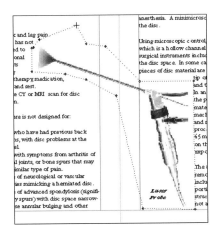

Actually you can customize a graphic boundary in four different ways:

- ✎ Drag boundary segments.
- ✎ Drag boundary handles.
- ✎ Create additional boundary handles by shift-clicking the graphic boundary, then dragging the new boundary segments or boundary handles.
- ✎ Delete existing boundary handles by dragging one on top of another, and then manipulate the remaining boundary segments or boundary handles.

Avoiding screen redraws while sculpting a text wrap: Normally, every time you move a boundary segment or boundary handle, PageMaker recomputes the text wrap and you have to wait for the screen to refresh. You can temporarily prevent this recomputation by holding down the spacebar while adjusting the graphic boundaries or boundary handles. Keep the spacebar down while you move as many boundaries and handles as you need, and then release it. The text wrap will then be recomputed, and PageMaker will redraw the screen to reflect these changes. This can substantially speed up the process of customizing the boundary of an irregularly shaped object, especially on slower Macs.

The Image Command

Although earlier we said that it is impossible to edit graphics imported into PageMaker from other graphic applications, the Image submenu from the Element menu does make it possible to modify some attributes of paint-type and TIFF-format graphics while they are in PageMaker. Select the image first, then choose the Image submenu to display the Image submenu, shown in Figure 8-35.

Figure 8-35:
The Image submenu

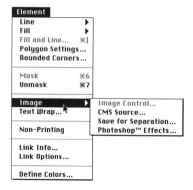

The four options of the Image submenu allow you to control some aspects of grayscale images, apply CMS source profiles to color images, color separate RGB TIFF images, and apply Adobe Photoshop filters to Photoshop TIFF images placed in PageMaker. Each option is discussed in this section.

Image Control

In the Image control dialog box, you can make any of the following modifications to black-and-white and grayscale images:

- Adjust the line-screen, screen angle, and function used to output paint-type or TIFF graphics.
- Adjust the gray-level mapping used to output TIFF graphics.
- View the effects of these changes in your image without closing the dialog box.

To begin the manipulation, select the graphic that you wish to manipulate and then choose the Image Control... command from the Image submenu on the Element menu. If the graphic you select is not a paint-type or TIFF graphic, the Image control command will be dimmed. The Image control dialog box will appear, as shown in either Figure 8-36 or Figure 8-37, depending on the type of graphic you select. You can move the Image control dialog box to another location on your monitor by dragging its title bar. This allows you to see the effect that your manipulations are having on your graphic without repeatedly closing the dialog box.

Figure 8-36:
The Image control dialog box as it appears when a grayscale TIFF is selected

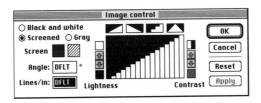

Figure 8-37:
The Image control dialog box as it appears when a paint-type or black-and-white image is selected

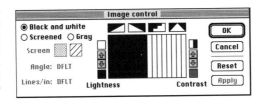

To understand the control provided by the options in this dialog box, you must understand a little about how PostScript printers work. When a document is converted into a PostScript file and sent to a PostScript printer, the printing device applies a series of dots to the page in accordance with the instructions given in the PostScript commands. Since most PostScript printers can create only black dots, they utilize a halftoning technique to simulate gray areas.

To determine which dots should be on and off in order to produce a halftone, PostScript uses the concepts of halftone cells, frequency, angle, and function. Each PostScript output device contains some number of machine pixels — these are the smallest dots that the printer is capable of producing. Laying a uniform square grid over the printable area divides the machine pixels into halftone cells. Each machine pixel belongs to one of the halftone cells, and each halftone cell is made up of some number of machine pixels.

The grid that divides the imageable area has a frequency, which is the number of halftone cells per inch into which it divides the imageable area, and an angle, which is the number of degrees by which the grid (and thereby each halftone cell) is rotated from being parallel to the bottom of the page. A halftone cell functions as the mathematical expression used to determine the order in which individual pixels that make up the cell will be turned off in order to simulate increasing gray levels.

Each PostScript printer has default values for the frequency and angle of its halftone cells and for the function used to simulate gray values. These defaults are used unless other values are specified in the Image control dialog box for the Lines/in (frequency), Angle, and Screen (function) options.

The first set of options in the Image control dialog box contains the Black and white, Screened, and Gray options. These options determine how the image appears on the screen, which of its attributes can be manipulated, and to what degree they can be manipulated. The Black and white option indicates that the selected image has no gray values, as with most paint-type graphics. It will be selected automatically when appropriate, usually for bitmapped paint-type images. You can manually select the Screened option, but not the Gray option, for these kinds of images.

The Screened option indicates that the selected image is a gray-scale image, and it too will be selected automatically when appropriate. When the Screened option is selected, you can adjust the Screen, Angle, Lines/in, Lightness, and Contrast options, all of which are unavailable when the Black and white option is selected.

The Screen option determines whether a line or dot screen pattern is used to create the graphic image. As we mentioned, this is essentially the function used in the halftoning process. When the dotted icon is selected, machine pixels in the halftone cell are turned off in an evenly spaced pattern to represent specific gray values. When the lines icon is selected, machine pixels are turned off so that the remaining pixels form a linear pattern. See Chapter 13 for examples of these options.

The Gray option is available only when working on a Macintosh equipped with a high-resolution monitor with the Monitors control panel device set to display two or more colors or shades of gray (and preferably 16 or more). This option enables PageMaker to display gray values on-screen for the selected image, but it has no effect on the output of the image. When the Gray option is selected, the Screen, Angle, and Lines/in options are dimmed.

The Angle option determines the angle of the screen used to create the image when printed. Control over this option is useful when creating special effects in conjunction with the Screen option.

The Lines/in option determines the number of lines per inch used to create the image when printed. This controls the frequency of the halftone cells, as discussed earlier. The higher the number used for the Lines/in option, the smoother an image will appear, but the fewer the number of available shades of gray. The lower the number used for the Lines/in option, the coarser an image will appear, but the greater the number of available shades of gray.

Gray Value Mapping

The remaining options in the Image control dialog box control the mapping of actual gray values to printed gray values. For example, a linear mapping prints an area defined as 10% gray as 10% gray, an area defined as 70% gray as 70% gray, and so on; an inverse mapping prints an area defined as 10% gray as 90% gray, an area defined as 30% gray as 70% gray, and so on.

The bar chart displayed in the Image control dialog box represents the current mapping specification. The x-axis represents the actual values, and the y-axis represents the printed values. When an image is first selected, linear mapping is selected — the values increase from 0 to 100 relative to both the x- and y-axes.

There are three different ways to control gray value mapping: using the Lightness and Contrast options; using the Normal, Reverse, Posterize, and Solarize icons; or using the mapping bar chart itself.

The Contrast option allows you to adjust the entire range of gray values to compress or expand the range of gray values in the image. Clicking the upper contrast arrow darkens values less than 50% and lightens values greater than 50%. Clicking the lower contrast arrow lightens values less than 50% and darkens values greater than 50%. These changes are displayed in the bar graph as they are made.

The Lightness option allows you to lighten or darken all values in the image at the same time. Pressing on the upper lightness arrow lightens all values (except those already at 100%), and pressing on the lower lightness arrow darkens all values (except those already at 0%). These changes are displayed in the bar graph as they are made.

The four mapping icons allow you to access four common mapping options quickly — Normal, Negative, Posterize, and Solarize. A Normal mapping is equivalent to the linear mapping described earlier, and a Reverse mapping is equivalent to the inverse mapping described earlier. The Posterize mapping uses a stair-stepped mapping that groups a range of values and makes them identical. This is done for several ranges and results in stair-stepped gray values — transitions between gray values are abrupt rather than smooth. The Solarize mapping changes all 50% gray values to 100% gray (black), doubles all values between 0% and 40%, and inverts all values from 60% to 100%.

After you have manipulated any or all of these options, clicking the Apply button redraws the image based on the new settings without closing the dialog box. Clicking the Reset button resets all options in the Image control dialog box to their original settings. Clicking the OK button executes the changes and closes the dialog box; clicking the Cancel button restores the image to its original values and closes the dialog box.

Use an image editor: With all this said about Image Control, seldom do we use it to adjust images in PageMaker. Image editors, such as Adobe Photoshop, are much more reliable for adjusting contrast and brightness, screening, and other options. Typically, most designers rely on their image editors to work with images, using PageMaker's Image Control only when very slight adjustments are needed or when an image editor is unavailable.

In addition, you should set the Graphics display in Preferences (File menu) to High Resolution when editing images in PageMaker; otherwise, you won't be able to see the changes accurately on-screen.

CMS Source

This option allows you to assign a color management system (CMS) source profile to a selected TIFF or other bitmap image. Color management attempts to compensate for the differences in the way monitors, scanners, and output devices define color, as described in Chapter 10. Selecting this option with a color image selected opens the CMS Source Profile dialog box, shown in Figure 8-38. From here you can assign a color management system and a source profile for the image. You can also turn off color man-agement for the selected image by choosing None from the This Item Uses pop-up menu.

Again, CMS is discussed in detail in Chapter 10. There's nothing more we can add here. You should note, however, that when you select the New Items Use option in the Color Management System Preferences dialog box (as discussed in Chapter 10), imported color images are automatically assigned the active CMS. It's not necessary to apply a

CMS each time you import an image. In addition, if you want to apply a different CMS from the default, you can do so while placing the image with the CMS Source button in the Place document dialog box.

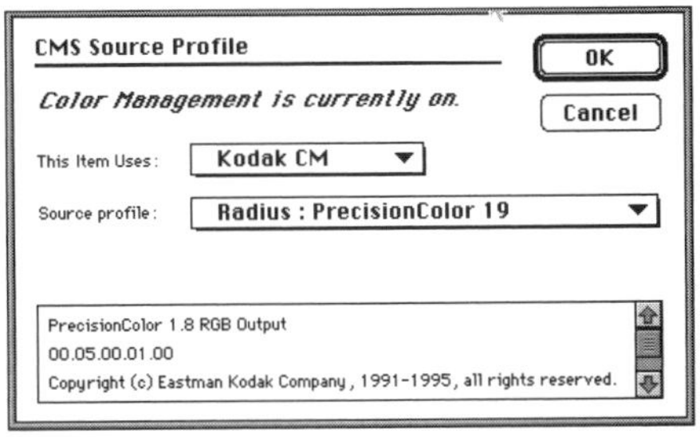

Figure 8-38:
The CMS Source Profile dialog box for assigning a CMS method to an image

> CMS Source Profile
>
> *Color Management is currently on.*
>
> This Item Uses: Kodak CM ▼
>
> Source profile: Radius : PrecisionColor 19 ▼
>
> [OK] [Cancel]
>
> PrecisionColor 1.8 RGB Output
> 00.05.00.01.00
> Copyright (c) Eastman Kodak Company, 1991–1995, all rights reserved.

Save for Separation...

Basically, this command allows you to convert the RGB TIFF images placed in a PageMaker layout to CMYK or high-fidelity color separations. If you don't understand why you would want to do so, you should read the discussion of color models and how printing presses work in Chapter 10. Basically, printing presses require CMYK separations to reproduce full-color. You could use this option to convert images scanned into PageMaker with an RGB scanner. You can also use this command to reassign a CMYK TIFF assigned one CMS profile to another CMS profile, such as from a proof printer to a printing press.

With that said, and before going into more detail on this command, we should point out that whenever possible, you should use Photoshop or another image editor to convert an image from RGB to CMYK. You'll get a better representation on-screen, and you can use Photoshop's gamut alarm feature to see how well the colors in the image will reproduce, or if they'll reproduce at all. In addition, this option creates an all new file for just the image, meaning that after using it you'll have two files for the same image. If you work with large, full-color TIFFs, this can quickly eat up disk space.

To use this command, color management must be turned on. When you use this option to convert images, PageMaker creates another CMYK TIFF or high-fidelity color TIFF file from the original, which you can choose to link automatically to the publication or maintain the link to the original RGB TIFF. Choosing Save for Separation opens the Save for separation dialog box, shown in Figure 8-39. Here you control various aspects of the conversion process and how PageMaker treats the file.

The upper-left portion of the dialog box shows the current monitor and separation profiles selected for the current image, which are defined automatically when color management is turned on or manually from the CMS Source option discussed in the

Figure 8-39:
The Save for separation
dialog box

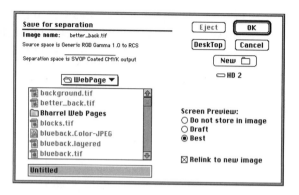

preceding section. Below that section is the area where you name the new file. The radio buttons in the lower-right portion of the dialog box allow you to control the quality of the screen preview, or what you'll see on the screen, representing the separated file. The lower the quality of the screen preview, the faster the screen redraw, and vice versa.

The Relink to new image option tells PageMaker to create a new link to the new file, in effect telling PageMaker to use the new file, rather than the original RGB image. When you click OK, PageMaker will separate the file and save it in the specified location with the options you selected.

Photoshop Effects

New to version 6, PageMaker now lets you apply Photoshop plug-in filters to RGB and CMYK TIFF images. Photoshop plug-ins abound. They do everything from color correction to sharpening to creating all kinds of special effects, such as embossing, beveling, and so on. Any Photoshop plug-ins—third-party filters or those made by Adobe—are supported. These include HSC's Kai's Power Tools, Alien Skin's The Black Box, and Adobe Gallery Effects.

The advantages of using these filters are that you can save an extra step or two by not having to open your image editor, or, if you don't have an image editor that supports plug-ins, this option allows you to create effects that you could not achieve otherwise. The disadvantages are that this option creates another image file, rather than applying to the original, and that you cannot apply the filter to selected portions of the image, only the entire image.

To apply an effects filter to an image, select the image to which you want apply the filter, then select Photoshop Effects from the Image submenu on the Element menu. This opens the Photoshop Effects dialog box shown in Figure 8-40. Here, you can name the new file created by this option and select the desired filter.

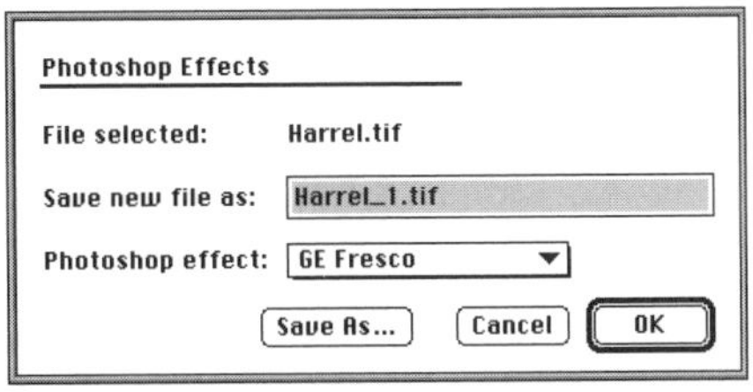

Figure 8-40:
The Photoshop Effects dialog box is used to apply Photoshop plug-in filters to TIFF images in your layout.

Photoshop Effects

File selected: Harrel.tif

Save new file as: Harrel_1.tif

Photoshop effect: GE Fresco   ▼

[Save As...]   [Cancel]   [OK]

The dialog box that opens when you choose a filter and click OK depends on the filter you select. Some filters, such as Photoshop's Sharpen, have no dialog box at all. It simply applies a sharpening routine to the image when you release the mouse button. You should refer to the documentation for the specific filter to learn how to use it.

Using your Photoshop filters with PageMaker: To use plug-in filters, PageMaker must find them in the Effects folder inside the Plug-ins folder within the PageMaker RSRC folder. PageMaker's installation program automatically installs several plug-ins from Adobe Gallery Effects. If you use Photoshop or another image editor that supports plug-ins, you should use the Make Alias command on the File menu to make copies of your Photoshop plug-in filter icons and drag them into the Adobe PageMaker 6.0/RSRC/Plugins/Effects folder so that PageMaker can see and use them.

Summary

- PageMaker can import the most-popular graphic formats: MacPaint, PICT, EPS, and TIFF.

- You can add graphics as independent elements or place them inline with existing text blocks so that they flow along with the text.

- Any graphic can be freely moved or resized. You can ensure that a graphic is resized proportionally by holding down the Shift key while resizing it.

- You can crop any graphic with the crop tool and move the graphic within its cropped window by dragging with the Cropping tool in the middle of the graphic.

- PageMaker's line, rectangle, circle, and polygon tools let you create these basic shapes in your publication. You can set these objects in a variety of line weights and styles, and fill shapes with any color or shading and a variety of fill patterns.

- You can wrap text around any imported or PageMaker-created graphic and customize the graphic boundary to have text wrap around the irregular shape of any graphic. Hold down the spacebar while adjusting the graphic boundary to prevent the screen from redrawing at every change.

- You can lighten, brighten, adjust, and apply special Photoshop Effects to TIFF images and bitmapped graphics, using the Image submenu in the Element submenu.

Using the Control Palette

In This Chapter

➥ Character formatting with the Control palette

➥ Paragraph formatting with the Control palette

➥ Manipulating objects with the Control palette

Why should you care about the Control palette? Several reasons. First, it lets you apply character and paragraph formatting without pulling down a menu or encountering a dialog box. The same is true for moving, resizing, and rotating both text and graphic objects. This is fast and efficient. In fact, you can even perform all of these tasks without reaching for your mouse. Second, the Control palette gives you quick feedback as to the current status of elements in your publication. With a single glance, you can find out the font, type size, and leading of your text or if a graphic has been reduced, enlarged, or rotated. This helps you ensure consistency and find small errors that usually aren't caught until too late (after the job comes back from the printer). Finally, the Control palette adds numerical precision to many tasks that used to require a good eye and a steady hand. You can specify that you want the edge of a text block to start 3p7 to the right of your paper's edge, or that an EPS graphic should be enlarged by 25 percent, rather than calculating, or approximating, these changes.

When to Use the Control Palette ___

Remember in school when the teacher would force you to learn and practice some ridiculously complex mathematical formula, only to explain later that there was a vastly superior shortcut? You had to experience the pain of the long method so that you would better understand and appreciate the shortcut, or so you were told. We never particularly believed or appreciated that logic, and yet we're guilty of this very same "teaching method" ourselves. Well, sort of.

You see, nearly every command in the Control palette duplicates a menu command, dialog box option, or mouse trick that you've learned in one of the earlier chapters. We introduced those first, and without going into depth on the Control palette alternative, primarily because in PageMaker you won't completely give up any one method of choosing a command for any other. In some instances, the Control palette is the most efficient. At other times, a keyboard shortcut is best; and once in a while, a good old-fashioned menu command and a dialog option are required. So, we just want to make sure you're well-rounded and ready for any occasion. Also, as a matter of practicality, segregating all of the Control palette discussion into this chapter will best serve any who worked with versions of PageMaker previous to version 5.0 and need to add a complete understanding of the Control palette to their PageMaker prowess. In any case, we apologize if this is making you have third-grade flashbacks.

Control Palette Basics

To begin working with the Control palette, choose the Control Palette command in the Window menu (⌘-'). This is the single quote key. The Control palette appears near the bottom of your screen as a small floating window. The specific commands in the Control palette depend upon which tool is currently selected, and which element on your page is currently selected.

The Control palette can display four distinct command sets:

- ⌦ **Deselect view.** When any tool other than the Text tool is selected, but no elements are selected, the Control palette simply displays the current location of the cursor, as shown in Figure 9-1.

Figure 9-1: The Control palette when nothing is selected.

- ⌦ **Layout view.** When any tool other than the Text tool is selected, and any text or graphic object is selected, the Control palette displays the position (X and Y), sizing (W and H), scaling (%), cropping, rotation, skewing, and reflecting options, as shown in Figure 9-2. (Note that the Apply button on the far left of the Control palette displays a separate icon for each tool or item selected, as we'll see in the "The Apply Button" section of this chapter.)

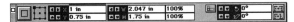

Figure 9-2: The Control palette with an object selected

⊕ **Character view.** When the Text tool is selected, and the character view button is selected, the Control palette displays the font, style, type size, leading, tracking, set-width, kerning, and baseline-shift options, as shown in Figure 9-3.

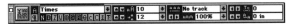

Figure 9-3: The Control palette when working in a text block with the Text tool

⊕ **Paragraph view.** When the Text tool is selected, and the paragraph view button is selected, the Control palette displays the style sheet, alignment, cursor position, indents, space before, space after, grid size, and align-to-grid options, as shown in Figure 9-4.

Figure 9-4: The Control palette in Paragraph view when working in a block of text with the text cursor

To hide the Control palette, choose the Control Palette command from the Window menu again, press ⌘-', or click the close box in the palette's left edge title bar. If you want to move the Control palette to another location on your monitor, drag it by the left edge title bar, as shown in Figure 9-5.

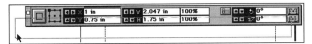

Figure 9-5: An example of moving the Control palette by dragging the title bar at the left edge of the palette

Before looking in detail at each of the Control palette views, commands, and options, there are a few basic Control palette characteristics you should understand. These include Control palette elements such as the Apply button, the proxy, and the nudge buttons, and ways of interacting with the Control palette using your mouse and keyboard.

Activating the Control Palette

Like PageMaker's other floating palettes — the Styles palette and the Colors palette — you can always look at the Control palette to read information about the currently selected element, but if you want to use the Control palette to make any formatting changes, you have to first *activate,* or select, it. When the Control palette, or panel, is activated, the bar on its left edge is highlighted, as shown in the top example of Figure 9-6.

Figure 9-6: The Control palette as it appears when active (top) and inactive (bottom)

There are several ways to activate or deactivate the Control palette:

- ☞ Press Command -` (grave, on same key as tilde).

- ☞ Click in the Control palette to activate it; click in the publication window to deactivate it.

- ☞ When any element except text is selected and you press a key, the Control palette becomes activated.

If you try to change Control palette options without first activating the Control palette, any keys you press on your keyboard will be applied to the selected text or graphic element. If you always use the mouse to select the Control palette option you want to modify, this won't be a problem, but if you tend to work a lot from the keyboard, you'll have to get used to pressing ⌘-' to activate the Control palette before modifying commands, and then pressing ⌘-' again to deactivate it when you're finished. An alternative is to press the Return key or click the Apply button with the mouse after making a change in the Control palette; this will save your changes and deselect the Control palette automatically.

If you want to apply changes made in the Control palette but not deactivate the Control palette, hold down the Shift key while pressing the Return key or clicking the Apply button.

The Apply Button

On the left end of the Control palette is a large button that displays an icon representing the currently selected tool, object, or element. This is the Apply button, which works as an Enter key for the Control palette. When the Apply button is pressed, any changes that have been made to options in the Control palette are applied to the current selection.

You can invoke the Apply button by clicking it with the mouse or by pressing the Enter or Return keys on your keyboard. The Apply button is also invoked when you press Tab or Shift-Tab, which move forward or backward through options in the Control palette.

The icon on the Apply button always reflects the current selection. There are more than 25 different icons possible, as shown in Table 9-1.

Table 9-1 PageMaker's Control Palette Apply Button Icons			
Icon			*Appearance*
			Pointer tool, nothing selected
			Edit text, character view
			Edit text, paragraph view
			Drawing tools
			Shape tools
			Text block
			Zoom tool
			Rotation tool
			Cropping tool
			Placing text
			Placing paint
			PICT
			TIFF
			EPS graphic
			Paint
			PICT
			TIFF
			EPS graphic

(continued)

Table 9-1 (continued)	
Icon	**Appearance**
	Moving ruler guide
	Column guide
	Zero intersection point
	Group
	Selected group grouped
	Selected item locked
	Selected group locked
	Selected group grouped and locked

The Proxy and Reference Points

Next to the Apply button, except when the Text tool is selected, is a rectangle called *the proxy*. The proxy, shown in Figure 9-7, has nine marked *reference points*: one in each corner, one on each edge, and one in its center. Exactly one reference point is always selected. You can change the selected reference point by clicking on any reference point in the proxy or by clicking the corresponding handle in the selection rectangle around the object in the layout view.

Figure 9-7:
The Control palette proxy determines the reference point for object manipulations.

The selected reference point is important because it specifies the spot from which any measurements or modifications are made. When you first encounter the Control palette, you might not see why reference points are needed, but you have to remember that you're dealing with a computer here, and computers aren't very smart. An example will illustrate: Suppose that you are working on two different layouts, one in which you want to center the dominant graphic in the middle of the page and another in which you want to center the graphic one inch below the top of the page. If you gave those simple instructions to any self-respecting pasteup artist, he or she would know that you want the middle of the graphic centered on the page in the first case, and that you want the top of the graphic set one inch below the top of the page in the second.

The computer, on the other hand, can't make those assumptions, and so you must specify that it is the *middle* of the first graphic that should be centered and the *top* of the second. Otherwise, you might get the upper-left edge centered on your first page, and the bottom-right edge of the graphic centered one inch below the top of the page in the second.

Reference points, as shown in Figure 9-8, let you specify the part of an object from which you want to measure. Although computers aren't very good at making assumptions, they are very good at executing precise, and even complex, instructions. So PageMaker provides not one but two different kinds of reference points, *stationary reference points* and *movable reference points*. A stationary reference point is created by clicking a reference point once; it becomes a solid square. A movable reference point is created by clicking the reference point a second time; it becomes an arrow. (See Figure 9-9.)

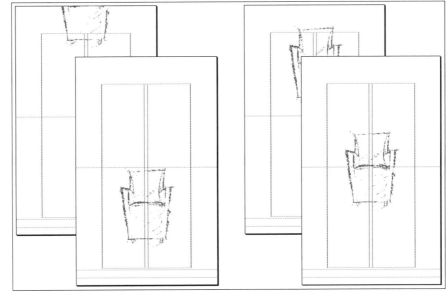

Figure 9-8: Objects placed in PageMaker without regard for reference points (left) and with the correct reference points selected (right)

Figure 9-9: An example of stationary (left) and movable (right) reference points as they appear in the Control palette

Stationary reference points are anchored — the corresponding point on the selected object will remain where it is if you resize, rotate, skew, or crop the object. Moving an object is an exception: If you move an object using the Control palette while a stationary reference point is set, the stationary reference point will move to the specified coordinates.

When a movable reference point is set, on the other hand, the corresponding point on the selected object moves as if had you dragged it with the mouse when moving, resizing, rotating, skewing, or cropping. This causes very different results than if a stationary reference point had been used, as shown in Figure 9-10.

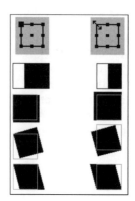

Figure 9-10:
The stationary (left) and movable (right) reference points provide distinctly different effects when you use the Control palette to move, resize, rotate, and skew graphics.

Navigating the Control Palette

Your experience in navigating Macintosh dialog boxes will serve you well in the PageMaker Control palette. To select any option or to move from one option to another, you can either use the mouse to click directly on the option you want to modify, or you can move through options from the keyboard by pressing Tab to move forward and Shift-Tab to move backward. When an option is selected, a black bar appears above or below that option, as shown in Figure 9-11.

Figure 9-11:
A colored bar (the color depends on how you've set up your Mac's desktop) appears above or below the selected option.

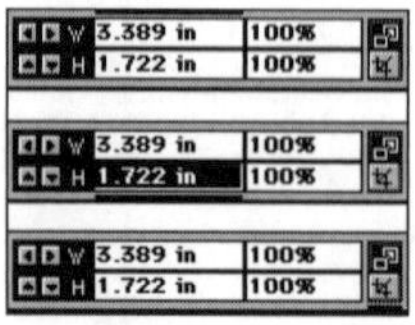

When you want to select an existing value to replace it, you can click directly on the current option or drag over the current option. If you want to modify the existing option, you'll just want to set the insertion point in the appropriate location. Some Control palette options let you select the option value and the option unit of measure separately, so be careful when setting the insertion point. If you make an incorrect selection within an option, use the arrow keys to correct the cursor position.

Changing Values

Once you've selected the option you want to modify, there are several ways to change option values:

- **Type replacement values.** If you fully select an existing option, you can type in new values. When the option is numeric, PageMaker assumes that you are using the default measurement system unless you append the abbreviations for some other measurement system (*i* for inches, *p* for picas, *c* for ciceros) to your entry.

  If the selected option includes a pop-up list, PageMaker will try to guess what option you are selecting as you enter characters. For example, when you type "Bo" into the Paragraph Styles option, PageMaker will fill in the option "Body Copy" if that is the first existing style sheet that starts with the letters "Bo."

- **Arithmetically modify the existing values.** For numeric options, you can create an arithmetic expression using the characters + (plus), - (minus), * (times), and / (divided by). For example, if the current value of an option is 3, and you want it to be 4, you can set the text insertion point after the 3 and type + 1. Or if you want a graphic to be half its width, select the W option and enter /2. When you click the Apply button or press Enter or Return, PageMaker calculates the correct result. (Ain't computers smart, after all!) Figure 9-12 shows how the formulas appear.

Figure 9-12:
An example of modifying a Control palette option with arithmetic formulas

W 3.389 + 1	100%
H 1.722 in	100%

This is particularly useful when you want to move or resize an object by some fixed but irregular amount (like an eighth of an inch, which is .125) and the current value is also not a round number. Rather than calculate $2.79 + .125 = 2.915$, you can just enter + .125, and PageMaker does it for you.

Temporarily changing the default measurement system: Although you cannot do math across different units of measure (1" + p6), you can temporarily change the units of measure for a single option by pressing ⌘-Option-M.

- **Use the nudge arrows.** In both object view and character view, many Control palette options have nudge arrows before them. The default change caused by a single click of a nudge arrow is $\frac{1}{100}$ of an inch, but you can set your own default nudge amount for both the horizontal and vertical directions in the Preferences dialog box. If you hold down the ⌘ key while clicking the nudge button, a move called the "power nudge," values change by $\frac{1}{10}$ of an inch (see Figure 9-13).

Figure 9-13: The nudge arrows change values by $^1/_{100}$ of an inch (or .01%). Holding down the ⌘ key lets you "power nudge" changing values by $^1/_{10}$ of an inch (or .1%).

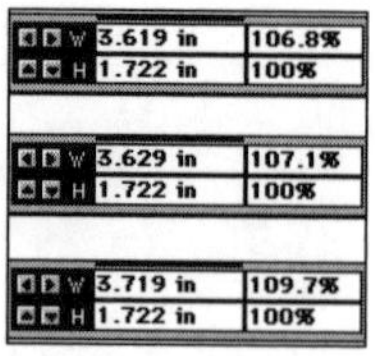

☞ **Use the pop-up list.** Some options in the character and paragraph views provide pop-up menus of available options, as shown in Figure 9-14. To use these, click the arrow that appears to the right of the current option setting and select from the list.

Figure 9-14:
A pop-up list from the Control palette

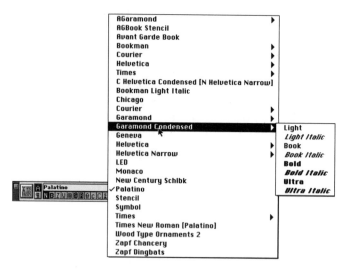

The number of options that the pop-up scrolling list can display is limited if the Control palette is too close to the bottom of your screen. Drag the Control palette by the bar at its far left to a position higher on your display, and these pop-up menus will be easier to use.

☞ **Resetting values.** If you incorrectly change the values in any Control palette option or accidentally modify an option you didn't mean to change, you can reset any Control palette option to its original value by pressing the Esc key or the Clear key from the keypad before you click the Apply button or press the Tab key. Once you press the Apply button or the Tab key, you can use the Undo command in the Edit menu.

Accuracy and Positioning

Values displayed in the Control palette are accurate to $\frac{1}{20}$ of a point, or $\frac{1}{1440}$ of an inch (.018 mm). This is far more accurate than PageMaker's rulers, which are only accurate to $\frac{1}{4}$ of a point when using the 400% view size, and even less accurate at lower levels of magnification. Control palette options expressed in percentages are accurate to $\frac{1}{10}$ of a percent.

The Snap to Guides and Snap to Rulers options from the Guides and Rulers submenu apply to Control palette changes only if you check the Use "Snap to" Constraints option in the Preferences dialog box, as described in Chapter 3. Otherwise, changes made via the Control palette will be executed literally, regardless of existing guide lines and ruler ticks.

If you select the Use "Snap to" Constraints option, and the Snap to Guides or Snap to Rulers options are selected in the Guides and Rulers submenu, then any change to the size or placement of an object will snap to guides within three pixels or the nearest ruler tick mark.

Note that the number of ruler tick marks and their accuracy are affected by the current view size. Larger magnifications have a larger quantity of more accurate tick marks, so zoom in as much as possible when accuracy is important.

When Snap to Guides is selected, and the Use "Snap to" Constraints preference is set, you will sometimes find that when you enter a specific value into a Control palette option, the value changes when you click the Apply button. This is a result of selecting a value that does not exactly correspond with a nearby guide or tick mark and the object "snapping" to that guide or tick mark.

Using the Control Palette in Character View

Character view is used to check the current character-level formatting of selected text and to modify the character formatting of selected text. The Control palette automatically switches into character view, as shown in Figure 9-15, as soon as you select the Text tool from the tool palette.

Figure 9-15: The Control palette in character view

If the Text tool is selected, and the Control palette is in paragraph view, you can switch into character view by clicking the character-view button that appears just to the right of the Apply button, just above the paragraph-view button. The keyboard equivalent for switching between character and paragraph views is ⌘-Shift-~.

The options available in the character view are:

    ☞ **Font.** The font option, shown in Figure 9-16, displays the name of the font used to format the selected text, if all selected text is in the same font. If two or more fonts are used in the selected text, this option appears empty.

Figure 9-16:
The font option
in the Control
palette

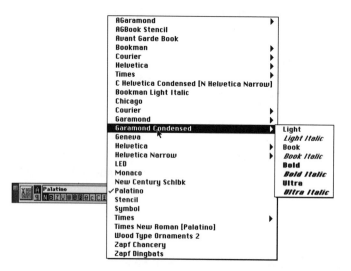

Choose a new font for the selected text either by clicking the down arrow and choosing a font from the scrolling pop-up menu or by clicking in the option box and typing the name of the font you want to select. As soon as you type one or more characters, PageMaker tries to guess the font you want to select and automatically fills in the font name for you. If the correct name appears, press Enter or Tab to apply that font. If an incorrect name appears, keep typing additional characters until the correct font appears.

If some of the fonts used in the current publication are not available, these are displayed at the top of the pop-up scrolling font list. If substitute fonts have been assigned using the PANOSE font-matching system (discussed in Chapter 7), the names of substituted fonts appear in brackets following the names of the missing fonts.

☞ **Style options.** The type-style options appear as a series of small buttons, labeled with the first letter of 12 different type-style options (see Figure 9-17). These options are (with brackets around the letters used to represent them on the option buttons): [N]ormal, [B]old, [I]talic, [U]nderline, [O]utline, [S]hadow, [R]everse, [Q]trikethru, [c] small caps, [C] all caps, [s]uperscript, and [s]ubscript.

Figure 9-17:
The style options in the
Control palette

Clicking one of these buttons toggles the style for the selected text on or off. When an option is selected (turned on), the button turns black. If the selected text does not have an option uniformly applied (some words are bold and some are not), then that option will appear dimmed, although you can still select the option to turn it on or off for all of the selected text.

You can also move from one style to another using the arrow keys, and toggle the options on and off by pressing the spacebar. Although you can apply small caps, all caps, superscript, and subscript options from the Control palette, to modify the specifications of these options — the size of small cap text or the size or position of superscript or subscript text — you must use the Type Specs… command and then click the Options button in the Type Specifications dialog box.

☞ **Type size.** The type size option displays the current type size and lets you select alternative sizes from a scrolling pop-up list or enter the type size you desire. You can also use arithmetic to enlarge or reduce the type size.

Clicking the up arrow increases type size by $\frac{1}{10}$ point; holding down the ⌘ key while clicking the up arrow increases the type size by 1 point. Clicking the down arrow decreases type size by $\frac{1}{10}$ point; holding down the ⌘ key while clicking the down arrow decreases the type size by 1 point.

The allowable range of type sizes is 4-point to 650-point, in $\frac{1}{10}$-point increments.

☞ **Leading.** The leading option displays the leading of the selected text and lets you select alternative leadings from a scrolling pop-up list or type the leading you desire. You can also use an arithmetic expression to enlarge or reduce the leading.

Clicking the up arrow increases leading by $\frac{1}{10}$ point; holding down the ⌘ key while clicking the up arrow increases the leading by 1 point. Clicking the down arrow decreases leading by $\frac{1}{10}$ point; holding down the ⌘ key while clicking the down arrow decreases the leading by 1 point.

The allowable range of leadings is 0-point to 1,300-point, in $\frac{1}{10}$-point increments.

↪ **Tracking.** The tracking option displays the tracking applied to the selected text and lets you select an alternative tracking from a scrolling pop-up list. You can also type the name of the desired tracking into the option box, the same way you type font names into the font option box.

↪ **Set width.** The set width option displays the current width of the selected text and lets you select an alternative tracking from a scrolling pop-up list. You can also type an alternate width directly into the option box. Allowable widths range from 5 percent to 200 percent.

Clicking the right arrow increases the width by 1 percent; holding down the ⌘ key while clicking the right arrow increases the width by 10 percent. Clicking the down arrow decreases the width by 1 percent; holding down the ⌘ key while clicking the left arrow decreases the width by 10 percent.

↪ **Kerning.** The kerning option displays the current amount of kerning applied to the selected text and lets you adjust that kerning by typing a replacement value into the option box or by using an arithmetic expression to modify the displayed value. The allowable kerning range is from -1 em to 1 em.

Clicking the right arrow increases the width by .01 percent; holding down the ⌘ key while clicking the right arrow increases the width by .1 percent. Clicking the left arrow decreases the width by .01 percent; holding down the ⌘ key while clicking the left arrow decreases the width by .1 percent.

↪ **Baseline shift.** The baseline shift option, shown in Figure 9-18, displays the current position of the baseline of the selected text relative to its normal position (as defined by the font designer). You can modify the baseline position by typing in a new value or by using an arithmetic exptession to modify the current value. The allowable range is -1,600 points to 1,600 points.

Figure 9-18: A sample of text manipulations with the baseline shift option

Clicking the up arrow increases the baseline shift by 1 point (.01 inch); holding down the ⌘ key while clicking the up arrow increases the baseline shift by 10 points (.1 inch). Clicking the down arrow decreases the baseline shift by 1 point (.01 inch); holding down the ⌘ key while clicking the down arrow decreases the baseline shift by 10 points (.1 inch).

Using the Control Palette in Paragraph View

Paragraph view, shown in Figure 9-19, is used to check the current paragraph-level formatting of selected paragraphs and to modify the paragraph-level formatting of selected text. To enter the paragraph view, you must first select the Text tool and then click the paragraph-view button. This button appears to the right of the Apply button under the character-view button. The keyboard equivalent for switching between character and paragraph views is ⌘-Shift-~.

Figure 9-19: The Control palette in paragraph view

Performing paragraph-level formatting using the commands in the Control palette is no different from using commands in the Type menu or associated dialog boxes. You must first select the text you want to format and then choose the necessary commands.

The options available in paragraph view are:

- **Paragraph style.** This option displays the name of the current style sheet used to format the selected text, if the same style sheet has been applied to all of the selected text. If two or more style sheets are used in the selected paragraphs, the option box appears empty.

  Choose a new style sheet by clicking the down arrow and selecting from the scrolling pop-up menu or by clicking in the option box and typing the name of the style sheet you want to apply. As you type, PageMaker tries to guess the style sheet you want to select and automatically fills in the style sheet name for you. (First make sure that the Control palette is activated, or you're likely to type over text!) If the correct name appears, press Enter or Tab to apply the style sheet. If an incorrect name appears, keep typing additional characters until the correct style sheet is selected.

If your Control palette is positioned too close to the bottom of your screen, the pop-up scrolling list can only display one or two style options. In this case, reposition the Control palette at any location farther from the bottom of the screen, and selecting paragraph styles will be much easier.

∞ **Alignment.** The alignment of the currently selected text is indicated by the highlighted alignment icon, if all of the selected paragraphs have the same alignment. If not, no alignment icons are highlighted. To set the alignment of the selected text, click any one of the five alignment icons.

∞ **Cursor-position.** This option isn't really an option at all, because you cannot change it. It is simply an indicator, providing you with the precise current horizontal location of the cursor within the current text block. (It does not tell you where the cursor is when set outside of a text block.)

∞ **Indent options.** There are three indent options in the Control palette, just as there were in the Paragraph Specifications dialog box: left, first, and right line. These display the current indent values of the selected paragraphs, and you can modify the indents by replacing the existing values or by using arithmetic expressions to change them.

∞ **Space before and Space after.** Again, corresponding to the options in the Paragraph Specifications dialog box, these options display the current amount of space set before and after the selected paragraphs. To modify the spacing, select the existing values and type in new values or use arithmetic expressions to enter your modifications.

∞ **Grid size.** This option specifies the size of the text grid that PageMaker uses when the Align to grid option is selected. It corresponds to the Grid size option normally found in the Options dialog box in the Rules dialog box in the Paragraph Specifications dialog box.

Normally, you want to specify a grid size equal to the leading for the body copy in your document. If using the body copy leading isn't appropriate for some reason, use some multiple of the body copy leading such as 50 percent or 200 percent.

∞ **Align to grid option.** Toggle on and off the Align to grid option by clicking the left (off) or right (on) buttons. Use of this option causes PageMaker to align the first line in the next text paragraph to the current user-defined grid. This option is generally used to help align text in multiple-column layouts and help produce more-professional looking publications.

Using the Control Palette Object View

When the Control palette is open, and any tool except the Text tool is selected, the object view is displayed, as shown in Figure 9-20. This view presents information about text blocks or graphics (either those created in PageMaker or those imported into PageMaker) as objects and lets you modify a number of characteristics of these objects.

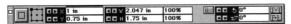

Figure 9-20: The Control palette in object view

The options available in object view are:

↪ **Position (X and Y).** The X and Y options display the current coordinates, relative to the on-screen rulers, of the selected reference point within the selected object. If no object is selected, or you are drawing a new object, the X and Y options display the location of the cursor.

You can move the selected object by entering new X or Y values or by using an arithmetic expression to change the X and Y values. The specific effect of changing the X and Y values depends on whether the current reference point is a movable or non-movable reference point, as described earlier in this chapter. Any value that represents a position on the current page or pasteboard is allowable, but values that would position the element off the current page and pasteboard are not permitted.

If multiple objects are selected, the position coordinates reflect the bounding box of the group, as shown in Figure 9-21. You'll also notice that when multiple objects are selected, most of the object view options (except position, rotation, and reflecting) are not available.

Figure 9-21: The Control palette as it appears when multiple objects are selected

You can also move the selected object by clicking the right or left nudge or up or down arrows. Clicking any arrow moves the object in the arrow's direction by .01 inch; holding down the ⌘ key while clicking an arrow moves the object in the arrow's direction by .1 inch.

Lastly, skipping the Control palette altogether, you can use the keyboard nudge to move the object. First, deactivate the Control palette (⌘-') and press the arrow keys to move the object by .01 inch, or ⌘-arrow to move the object by .1 inch.

⤷ **Sizing.** The [H]eight or [W]idth options display the size of the selected object. If multiple objects are selected, the sizing options disappear. If the selected object is a line, its [L]ength is displayed instead. If you are drawing a new rectangle, the coordinates reflect the point at which you began drawing.

You can resize a selected object by entering new W or H values or by using arithmetic expressions to change the W and H values. The current reference point sometimes prevents you from changing the W or H options: If the top or bottom center reference point is selected, you cannot change the X value or the W value. If the right or left center reference point is selected, you cannot change the Y value or the H value; when the center reference point or any corner reference points are selected, either X,Y, W, or H values can be changed. An option that cannot be changed appears in plain type (instead of the usual bold), and you won't be able to select it.

The allowable range for the W and H options includes any value that represents a position on the current page or pasteboard. You cannot resize any object so that any part of it would go outside the current pasteboard.

You can also resize the selected object by clicking the right or left nudge or up or down arrows. (Which side of the object moves depends on whether the selected reference point is an anchor square or arrow.) Clicking the right or up arrow enlarges the object by .01 inch; holding down the ⌘ key while clicking the right or up arrow enlarges the object by .1 inch. Clicking the left or down arrow reduces the object by .01 inch; holding down the ⌘ key while clicking the left or down arrow reduces the object by .1 inch.

⤷ **Scaling percentage.** Just to the right of the sizing options are the percentage size option boxes. If you select an object with the arrow tool, and the object is an imported graphic, these display the current size of the object as compared to its original size. If you select a graphic object created in PageMaker (with the line, rectangle, or circle tools), or a text block, the display always begins at 100 percent — even if the object was previously resized.

You can directly modify the size of any object by clicking in the [H]eight or [W]idth scaling option box and entering a new scaling percentage in $\frac{1}{10}$-point increments. The only limit is that you cannot enlarge the object so that it no longer fits on the current pasteboard. Depending on the currently selected reference point in the proxy, you may not be able to modify either the height or width option; if the top or bottom center reference point is selected, you cannot change the width value; if the right or left center reference point is selected, you cannot change the height value; when the center reference point or any corner reference points are selected, either width or the height values can be changed. An option that cannot be changed appears in plain type (instead of the usual bold), and you won't be able to select it.

☞ **Scaling and Cropping.** These two buttons indicate whether changes made to the graphic you are manipulating will resize the graphic or crop it. The scaling icon is selected automatically when you select a graphic with the arrow tool, and the cropping icon is selected automatically when you select a graphic with the cropping tool. You can toggle between these two by directly clicking their icons in the Control palette.

☞ **Proportional scaling.** When you manually resize an object (by dragging one of its handles with the arrow tool), holding down the Shift key forces the object to remain proportional. Clicking this button has the same effect on Control palette scaling — it makes it impossible to scale any graphic disproportionately. In other words, any change you make to the [H]eight of an object, either in the scaling option or the scaling percentage, will affect the [W]idth options equally and automatically. Conversely, changing the [W]idth will make the [H]eight react accordingly.

☞ **Printer resolution scaling.** This option also mimics a traditional keyboard shortcut. Selecting this button (it appears black when selected) makes the Control palette use PageMaker's magic stretch, automatically scaling bitmapped and TIFF graphics to a size compatible with the resolution of the currently selected printer.

☞ **Rotation.** The rotation option displays the current rotation of the selected object. Change the rotation by entering any value between -360 and 360 degrees in 0.01-degree increments. You can also use the up or down nudge arrows to rotate the object in 0.1-degree increments. Holding down the ⌘ key while clicking an arrow rotates the object in the arrow's direction by 1 degree.

If a stationary reference point is selected, rotation occurs around that point. If a movable reference point is set, that point moves to accomplish the requested rotation.

☞ **Skewing.** The skewing option displays the number of degrees that the selected object is skewed. You can change the skew amount by entering any value between -85 and 85 degrees in 0.01-degree increments. You can also use the up or down nudge arrows to rotate the object in 0.1-degree increments. Holding down the ⌘ key while clicking an arrow rotates the object in the arrow's direction by 1 degree.

☞ **Reflection (Horizontal and Vertical).** The two reflecting buttons let you quickly flip any element horizontally or vertically (see Figure 9-22). When these buttons are selected, you can also select or deselect them by pressing the spacebar.

The kind of reference point you have selected (stationary or movable) is particularly important in its effect on the result of using the reflecting buttons.

Figure 9-22:
The Reflection option can be used to flip an object horizontally or vertically.

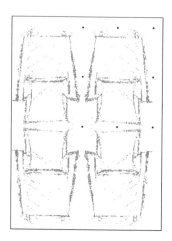

When an object has been reflected with either button, a black border appears around both, indicating that one has been selected.

☞ **Baseline offset option.** When the object you select is an inline graphic, the Control palette changes slightly with the baseline offset option replacing both the proxy and the X and Y options (see Figure 9-23). This option displays the location of the inline graphic's baseline relative to the baseline of the text that surrounds it. When a value of 0 appears, the inline graphic is on the baseline of the text. The range of allowable values is 0 to the height of the inline graphic.

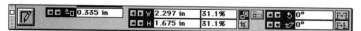

Figure 9-23: The Control palette as it appears when an inline graphic is selected

You can also use the up or down nudge arrows to move the baseline in .01-inch increments. Holding down the ⌘ key while clicking an arrow moves the baseline in the arrow's direction by 1 inch.

Using the Control palette to position objects precisely: Selecting inline graphics and then using the baseline shift option allows you to shift the inline graphic with more precision than you get by dragging it with the arrow tool. And by shifting the baseline by large amounts, you can move inline graphics more dramatically than the arrow tool allows.

Table 9-2 shows a list of keyboard shortcuts for the Control palette.

Table 9-2
Control Palette Keyboard Shortcuts

Shortcut	Result
⌘-'	Display/Hide Control palette
⌘-`	Activate/Deactivate Control palette
⌘-Shift-~	Character view/Paragraph view
Tab	Next option
Shift-Tab	Previous option
Arrow keysMove within option	Move within option
Arrow keys when proxy is active. Numbers on keypad when NumLock is active.	Select reference point in proxy
Enter or Return or Tab	Apply changes
Esc or Clear	Undo changes
⌘-Option-M	Change measurement system
⌘-arrow button	Nudge selected object

Summary

➤ The Control palette displays four distinct sets of options, depending on the current selection. The four options (or views) are deselect, character, paragraph, and object.

➤ To use the Control palette, you must make it visible by choosing it from the Window menu or pressing ⌘-' (single quote). After selecting the object you want to manipulate, activate the Control palette to change its options, by pressing ⌘-` (grave) or by clicking in the Control palette with the mouse.

➤ After changing values in the Control palette, click the Apply button (near the left edge of the palette) with the mouse, or press the Return or Enter key. Or you can use the Tab or Shift-Tab keys to move between options in the Control palette.

➤ The rectangle with corner and edge dots is called the proxy and is used to specify the reference point for Control palette options. You can select any dot to set the reference point. Clicking once sets a unmovable reference point, and clicking twice sets a movable reference point.

Mastering PageMaker

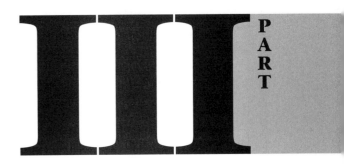

This section moves beyond the basics to look at advanced capabilities provided by PageMaker, as well as other Adobe software. We discuss the details of working with color, using PageMaker Plug-ins, formatting long documents, printing, publishing for the World Wide Web, and Adobe prepress software.

Working with Color

In This Chapter

→ Color matching systems

→ Defining spot and process colors

→ Color issues: tints, registration, overprinting, and more

→ Working with color libraries

→ Editing colors

→ Importing colors from other publications

→ Exporting colors to color libraries

→ Deleting colors

→ Using the colors palette to apply colors

→ Using PageMaker's built-in trapping

Color draws people into the content of your publication by adding impact and interest to any page. The full-color pages in Plate 12 are a good example of how color is used to achieve dynamic results. Used effectively, color can be one of the most powerful design tools you have. PageMaker puts these design tools squarely in your hands by giving you the ability to create and print spot- and process-color publications easily. Before you delve into the details of using PageMaker's new color tools, though, it helps to understand the basics of how colors are printed on a commercial printing press, and the dynamics between getting colors right from computer screen to printed material.

Spot- and Process-Color Printing

There are two basic ways to print color on a commercial printing press: using spot-color inks or process-color inks. Typically, spot-color is used for emphasis or decoration — for example, to highlight logos, banners, headlines, sidebars, rules in newsletters, flyers, and stationery. Process-color, on the other hand, is used to reproduce full-color documents, such as the cover of this book, the color insert, and magazines with full-color photographs. Figure 10-1 shows the two types of documents. For a full-color example, turn to Plate 2 in the color insert.

In spot-color printing, the printer uses a premixed, opaque or semi-opaque ink to print the colored objects. You specify what spot-color ink to use from among the hundreds of spot-color inks available to your printer. The most common spot-color ink is PANTONE Matching System (PMS). In process-color printing, the printer uses only four translucent inks — cyan (C), magenta (M), yellow (Y), and black (K) — to reproduce colors. By printing different sizes and combinations of CMYK ink dots close together on a page, the printing press simulates hundreds of different colors.

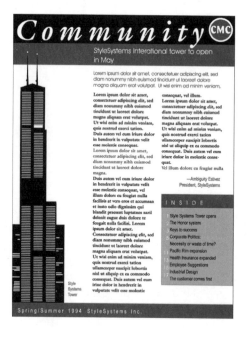

Figure 10-1: An example of spot- (left) and process-color (right) documents

Spot-color is pretty easy to fathom. An original photograph, for example, is continuous-tone art because it consists of solid shades of smoothly blending colors. To print on a commercial press, the continuous-tone image must be broken into sets of dots of various sizes — one set of dots for each of the four process-color inks. Each set of dots, called a halftone screen, must be set at a different angle, so that the dots of process ink print side by side instead of on top of each other in the final printed piece. The halftones of a full-color image are shown in Figure 10-2. A full-color example is shown in Plate 1 of the color insert.

Figure 10-2:
An example of the CMYK dots that make up a color image

If the dots are positioned properly, the result is a rosette pattern that helps to create the desired color effect. If the dots are off even slightly, an unsightly moiré pattern will result, dispensing the intended color effect. (For information on how screen angles are set in PageMaker, refer to Chapter 13.) Halftone dots also vary in size — small dots are used to print lighter areas and larger dots to print darker areas. In the final printed piece, your eye uses the dots to perceive dozens of different colors.

Don't take our word for it. You can see what we're describing by picking up any magazine and flipping to a color photograph. If you look very closely at the color photograph (you may even want to grab a magnifying glass to help), you will notice small dots of color that make up the image. Up close, those dots look like cyan, magenta, yellow, and black dots. From a distance, though, your eye merges those colored dots to perceive a simulation of the range of colors from the original photograph.

To break a continuous-tone image into four halftone screens, the photograph is typically scanned. In electronic publishing, the scanned image is then placed in a page layout program, such as PageMaker. Process colors can also be applied to the text and graphic elements that you create in PageMaker, and you can import process-color graphics from other programs, such as Adobe Illustrator or Photoshop, into PageMaker. As with photographs, the process colors in these elements are reproduced by halftone dot screens of each process-color ink. In contrast, when elements are colored with spot colors, they print as solid areas unless you apply a halftone screen to them to create a lightened color, called a tint, discussed in the "Using Tints" section of this chapter.

You transform your PageMaker publication into something that can be reproduced on a printing press by printing *color separations* — one separation for each process- and spot-color ink in your publication. (Spot-color separations are typically called spot-color overlays.) These separations are typically produced by a service bureau, which prints onto film. A commercial printer then uses the film to make the printing plates for use on the press. A separate plate is used to print each ink in your publication, as shown in Figure 10-3, and in Plate 3 in the color insert.

Figure 10-3: Examples of spot- (top) and process-color (bottom) separations and negatives used by the print shop to make printing press plates

When to Use Which Type of Color

A number of factors influence whether you use spot or process colors — or both types of color — to print a publication. The three key factors are time, money, and design. Using process colors typically takes more time and costs more than printing spot colors. However, you should use process colors if you need to use more than three colors in your design, if you're printing color photographs or other imported elements that require process colors, and if time and budget permit.

You should use spot colors if you have a limited budget and can accomplish your design using three or fewer colors. (If you need to print four or more spot colors, you should use process spot colors instead, as it then becomes the more cost-effective color choice. Process spot colors are discussed in the "Color Libraries" section of this chapter.) You should also use spot colors when you need to make a precise color match in a corporate logo or some other graphic or when you want to use a special spot-color ink, such as fluorescent or pearlescent.

When to Use Both Types of Color

In some instances, you'll want to use a combination of process and spot colors — though this can be prohibitively expensive if you go over six separations (four process, two spot). You may, for example, need to use five or six colors to print an annual report that includes color photographs and a corporate logo that requires precise color matching.

Tips for Using Spot Colors

As previously mentioned, using color effectively enhances the message; using it improperly detracts from the message. Let's look at a few do's and don'ts for using spot color:

- **Use Color to show priorities:** Colors can signify priorities. People tend to look at the brightest colors first. Control where their eyes go first by putting the most important material in the brightest colors.

- **Use color to make a point:** Use color to explain or to make a point, not to decorate. Do not use color merely because it's at your disposal. Instead, lead the reader's eye to the significant portions of a page. In a newsletter, for example, use color to draw the reader's attention to the banner or table of contents. In a flyer, highlight important parts of the message with color.

- ☞ **Use color to emphasize:** Colors can make new points or different points of view stand out. On a brochure page, for example, use color to introduce a change in topics. On a newsletter page, use color for sidebars or sections containing contrasting arguments.

- ☞ **Use colors as symbols:** Colors can be used as symbols. For example, green for go, red for danger, and amber for caution.

- ☞ **Use color for distinguishing characteristics:** Almost all documents have elements that refer to the document, rather than the subject matter. The most obvious are page numbers, headers and footers, frames, box backgrounds, and other recurring objects. You can use spot color to set these objects off from the rest of the document. This makes it easier for the reader to find them.

- ☞ **Use colors as locators:** Locators tell the reader where he or she is in a publication. Most multipage publications are assembled in sections. Using color to mark the beginning of each section and subsection helps the reader find material. You can also use colors to highlight section numbers and locator tabs. You can use different colors to identify separate sections, making each section distinguishable from the others.

Other Printing Issues _____

In addition to understanding the difference between spot and process colors, it also helps to understand the processes of trapping, knocking out, and overprinting. More importantly, before defining and applying colors in your document, or adding color elements to publications, you should understand when these processes are required.

Trapping

Printing presses are not perfect animals. As paper passes through the press at high speeds, paper shifts slightly—a condition known as "slop." However, to print properly, each ink in a print job must print in exact alignment — called registration — with the other inks in the job. If inks print out of alignment, two things may happen. When spot colors misregister, small, perceptible gaps appear between the adjacent colored objects. When process colors misregister, either small gaps appear between adjacent objects or slight shifts in color appear, making perceptible halos (third colors) around the objects. Figure 10-4 shows these two conditions, as does Plate 4 in the color insert.

Figure 10-4:
Examples of press registration errors. Note that these examples are exaggerated to make these points. Real-world trapping is more subtle but certainly noticeable.

Misregistration

Misregistration

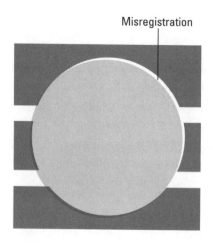

Any number of factors cause misregistration, including the natural absorbency and stretch in paper, inadequate film registration, or the slight misalignment of the press. Since these mistakes are visible, they ruin the print job.

To compensate, printers have developed a procedure called *trapping*. Trapping is the process of slightly overlapping adjacent color objects to prevent perceptible gaps and color shifts, as shown in Figure 10-5, and in Plate 5 in the color insert. The darker occurrences of the peach-colored lines around the circle and text show where the traps are placed. The question of who should perform the trapping in a document—you, your service bureau, or the print shop—and what tools should be used, is a key problem to solve in preparing your color publications for the press. For a more detailed discussion of trapping, see "Trapping in PageMaker" later in this chapter and Chapter 14.

Figure 10-5:
An example of trapping

Knocking Out and Overprinting

When printing a light color, such as yellow, over a dark one, such as black, the black will show through, discoloring the yellow — unless you create a knockout. A knockout is white space, or paper (rather than ink), in the area where the top color will print. Figure 10-6 shows an example of a knockout, as does Plate 6 in the color section. Notice that there is no black ink where the yellow overlaps the knockout. However, printing dark colors over light colors poses no problem, so you can *overprint*, avoiding the trapping problems discussed in the preceding section.

Figure 10-6:
An example of a knockout and overprinting

 Avoiding overprint disasters: A problem occurs only when you have a lighter color over a darker one. You can, for example, print black over almost any color without the color showing through. And overprinting, or printing one color over another, works just fine for several other color combinations. What combinations are possible is not always predictable. There is no hard-and-fast rule here. The best approach is to check with your printer before trying to overprint colors.

 Knocking out grayscale images: Knockouts are very important when working with screens and halftones. You cannot put any color behind a grayscale halftone without a knockout. In Figure 10-7 (and Plate 7 in the color insert) we put a multi-colored box behind a grayscale photograph. To avoid the box from showing through, it must be knocked out beneath the photograph. For more information on screens and halftones, refer to the "Using Tints" section of this chapter and Chapter 13.

Figure 10-7:
An example of
knocking out a
box beneath a
grayscale
photograph

Figure 10-7:
An example of
knocking out a
box beneath a
grayscale
photograph

Overprinting two spot colors can create a third color without the expense of printing a third spot color. However, you should try this technique only if you have experience, as you can also get some strange results.

Overprinting and knockouts are controlled from the Edit Color dialog box, shown in Figure 10-8. When you select Overprint, PageMaker overprints all occurrences of the color. Leaving Overprint unchecked tells PageMaker to treat the color as a knockout. These dialog boxes are discussed in detail in the "Defining New Colors" section of this chapter.

Figure 10-8:
The Overprint option in
PageMaker's new Edit Color
dialog boxes

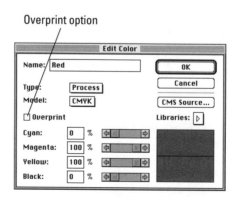

When Overprint is checked, the color always overprints the underlying color. When unchecked, all colors under the current colors are knocked out.

 Trap, knockout, and overprint in graphics applications: The same principles that apply to trapping, knocking out, and overprinting in PageMaker apply to graphics you create in Adobe Illustrator or other graphics applications for importing into PageMaker. In fact, it's important that you trap properly in these programs, as you cannot apply trapping to an imported image once it's placed in PageMaker. You should remember to use the trapping, overprinting, and knockout procedures for non-PageMaker elements.

Working with Your Printer

Color can be challenging to use well, because you need to keep in mind at all times how your publication will print on press. It hasn't always been the case that you needed to understand commercial printing to get good results. In traditional color publishing, you — as the person creating the color publication — were responsible for creating mechanicals that specified what you wanted in your final printed piece. Your commercial printer then took those mechanicals and used a whole team of highly-trained prepress technicians to transform the mechanicals into the plates used to print the piece on the press.

Electronic publishing blurs that clear distinction between design and printing responsibilities by making you responsible for more of the steps involved in printing a color publication. On the other hand, the emergence of these electronic tools is also making color printing more affordable, and it's giving you unprecedented control over the publication process. By mastering PageMaker's tools and the basics of commercial printing, you can achieve the printed results you want at a reasonable cost.

To help you in this learning process, you should follow the advice that Adobe lays out over and over again — seek out commercial printers who are supportive of the emerging electronic publishing trend and make those vendors your friends. For that matter, make friends with the service providers who help you scan images or do other tasks in preparing your color publications. You can learn from these people. The earlier you involve them in your design project, the better your printed results are likely to be.

Color Managing Systems

 An inherent precept in desktop publishing is that what you see on your monitor should match (as closely as possible) the final printed document. Therefore, the closer the two match, the better. You save time by avoiding proofs and revisions.

A common term in the desktop publishing world is *WYSIWYG*, or what-you-see-is-what-you-get. The monitor matches the printed piece. If all you publish is black and white text and monotone graphics, your computer's display is reasonably reliable. However, colors on your monitor seldom appear exactly the same way as when you run the print job on a printing press.

A monitor and a printing press handle colors differently. It's close to impossible for them to define color the same way. Factors, such as the type of paper the document is printed on, affect how colors print.

Two Methods for Defining Color

Devices such as printers, monitors, and scanners all define colors differently. The method used for color definitions is known as the device's *color space*. Most offset presses, for example, specify colors as percentages of cyan, magenta, yellow, and black (CMYK). The color red in the CMYK model uses the following values: C:0, M:100, Y:100, K:0. The same color on your monitor, which specifies colors with red, green, and blue (RGB) percentages, displays using these values: R:255, G:0, B:0, as shown in Figure 10-9. (This dialog box is discussed in detail in the "Defining New Colors" and "Editing Colors" section of this chapter.)

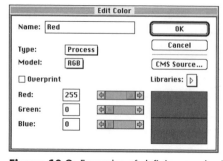 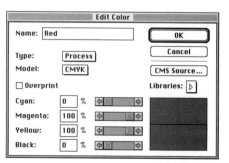

Figure 10-9: Examples of defining a color in RGB and CMYK models

Device-Dependent Color

Colors defined with one of the devices described in the previous chapter are *device-dependent*. In other words, they are rendered according to the specific device. The color in the above figure will display a different shade of red on another monitor. A color printer will give you yet another color. Depending on paper and some other conditions, the same red might reproduce in a different shade when printed on a process-color press.

Device-Independent Color

Print shops have been compensating for color differences since long before computers. In 1930, the Commission Internationale de l'Eclairage (International Commission on Color, or CIE) attempted to standardize color definitions. Forcing color models to specify color in the same way as print shops was an impossible task. Therefore, the commission created CIE color spaces that specify color by using the human eye as the rendering method. The CIE spaces try to specify colors as people see them. CIE color spaces use mathematical values that aren't dependent on inconsistent variables, such as how a printer is engineered or how ink mixes on paper.

Enter Color Managing Systems

PageMaker and other DTP and graphics applications attempt to bridge the gap between device-dependent and device-independent color with *color managing systems* (CMSs), which promise to bring continuity between what you see on your monitor and what rolls off the presses. Several companies ship CMSs, including Apple and Electronics for Imaging (EFI). PageMaker ships with Kodak Precision Color Management System and supports several others.

To understand color management systems, you should first become familiar with two important concepts: gamuts and profiles. We use them often throughout this discussion of color management.

Gamuts

Each color device—scanners, printers, monitors, printing presses—has its own color gamut. A device's color gamut describes the range of colors that the device can create or, in the case of scanners, sense. The CIE color space describes the most colors. It has the largest gamut. Color devices — printer, printing press, scanner, or monitor — cannot reproduce this wide range of colors; their gamut is smaller than CIE. In the case of a 300 dpi ink jet printer, for example, the gamut is significantly smaller. Figure 10-10 (and Plate 8 in the color insert) shows the color range for specific means of defining color.

Figure 10-10:
An example of
color gamuts

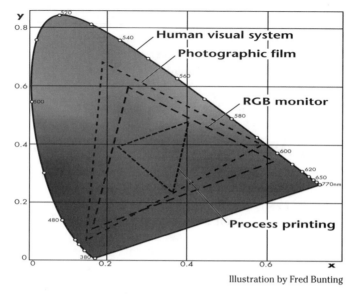

Illustration by Fred Bunting

Profiles

Color management systems use *device profiles* to record the color gamut of specific devices. Profiles describe the characteristics of the device, as well as other information about its capabilities and limitations. Profiles are created by either the manufacturer of the color management system or the device's manufacturer.

PageMaker ships with some profiles, including a few printers and monitors. If your printer and monitor are not included, you can select a similar device, or contact the device maker or Kodak to try to obtain one. Some profiles may be available free from on-line services, such as Adobe's forum on CompuServe, or from the device manufacturer's forum.

How CMSs Work

Simply put, CMSs use the device profile to adjust colors between printers, monitors and scanners. CMSs convert the data to and from CIE color-space formats. If the proper device profiles are installed on your system, the CMS can turn the colors on your monitor into CIE colors, and then convert them to similar colors for your printer, imagesetter, or another output device.

CMSs use CIE color spaces stored in the device profile to interpret and convert colors back and forth between devices. For a diagram of how this works, see Figure 10-11 or Plate 9 in the color insert. Theoretically, the conversions compensate for the differences in the ways that specific devices define color.

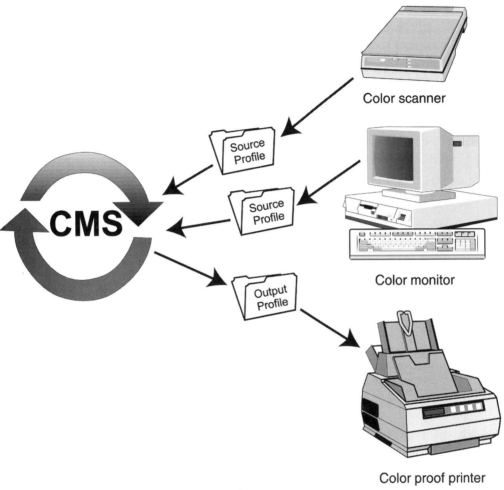

Figure 10-11: An example of how CIE CMSs work

Do CMSs Work?

The answer is *yes,* to a certain degree. They work best when defining gamuts downward. It's easier for your computer to reduce information from existing data, rather than increase it. So, CMSs don't do well at increasing gamuts. In other words, it reduces one device's gamut to match another well—from, say, a monitor to a printer. This is convenient because color monitors have greater gamuts than desktop color printers, as do printing presses have smaller gamuts than desktop printers.

Don't rely on CMSs: CMSs help. They can reduce the need for multiple proofs. But keep in mind that this technology does not solve all color problems. You should not abandon the standard proofing processes described in Chapter 13.

The most useful conversion shows the changes of what you see on your monitor (RGB) to what rolls out of the color proofing printer to, finally, what prints from the printing press (CMYK). The CMS transforms RGB color to its internal CIE format and then creates a CMYK equivalent, a process that works reasonably well.

CMSs and PageMaker

Getting color right in a desktop publishing environment depends on several factors, including not only the use of a CMS and installing the proper device profiles, but also the proper calibration of your monitor. These steps increase the reliability of colors created and applied in PageMaker. To maintain consistency when importing bitmap images from other sources, you should also use a CMS in the source application or apply a CMS in PageMaker. This section looks at setting up a work area conducive to color management, choosing and setting up a CMS, calibrating your monitor, and using a CMS with bitmaps (PageMaker does not support color correction of EPS, DCS, and PICT files). Also important to the discussion of color management is applying color management to colors you create in PageMaker, which is discussed in the "Defining New Colors" section of this chapter.

Color Management and Your Work Area

Your work area greatly influences how you see color on your monitor. Two factors—lighting and your monitor's contrast and brightness settings—must remain constant for consistent display of colors. In other words, if you work in a room where the lighting changes throughout the day and night, when working with color on your Mac, you should draw the shades or blinds and work in artificial lighting. If you use fluorescent lights, which can cast a yellow tint, you should consider investing in 5000 degree Kelvin lighting.

Trash those fancy desktop patterns: Granted those pretty desktops that come with your Mac make the desktop more interesting, but they also distort your perception of the color images displayed in their midst. When working in Photoshop, for instance, most images are displayed in windows surrounded by the desktop pattern. A bright pattern surrounding the image interferes with your perception of the image. So, when working with color, turn them off.

Once you've gotten the lighting in the room right, adjust the contrast and brightness on your monitor. Contrast adjusts intensity and brightness adjusts the level of black. To make the adjustments, display an image containing a lot of black, then adjust the brightness until you get the best black available, making sure that the black is not surrounded by a gray shadow. Now adjust the contrast until you're pleased with the intensity.

Lock in those monitor controls: After going to all that trouble of adjusting monitor settings in the correct lighting, it wouldn't be good if somebody came in and readjusted your monitor. (Or if you bumped the controls with a book or software packages.) You'd have to go back and do it all over again. To avoid this, tape down the contrast and brightness controls on your monitor.

Choosing and Setting Up a CMS

Unless you've already installed another CMS, you've two choices: CMS on or CMS off. CMSs are chosen from the Color Management System Preferences dialog box, shown in Figure 10-12. You can get here by choosing Preferences from the File menu, and then clicking on the CMS Setup... button.

Figure 10-12:
The Color Management
System Preferences
dialog box

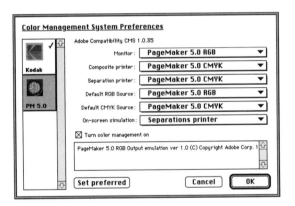

Once you've selected the CMS from the list of icons on the left, you then select device profiles from the lists on the right. PageMaker ships with several Kodak Precision Color profiles (called Precision Transforms). To add them to the list of options that display in the Color Management System Preferences dialog box lists, drag them from the PageMaker Deluxe CD-ROM disc to the KPCMS folder in the Macintosh System folder. (If profiles for your devices are not included, use the "Generic" profiles or contact the device manufacturer for a profile.) The following is a description of eight profile options:

- **Color Management:** Use this option to turn Color Management on and off. If you have more than one CMS installed, you can then select the system type in the list of icons in the lower-left of the dialog box.

- ⌐ **Monitor Simulates:** These three options, None, Composite printer, and Separations printer, tell PageMaker which final output device to simulate on screen. If you normally take your jobs to the service bureau for separation, you should choose Separation printer. Choosing the Composite printer option will limit the number of colors PageMaker displays compared to what the Separation printer option can actually achieve.

- ⌐ **New Items Use:** Use this option to tell PageMaker which CMS to assign to new items, such as graphics you import and colors you create, from the time you turn on CMS forward.

- ⌐ **Monitor:** Use this pop-up to choose the profile for your monitor.

- ⌐ **Composite printer:** Use this pop-up to choose a profile for your color proofing printer, either your own desktop model or the profile for the device your service bureau uses for composites. (If one is not included with PageMaker, perhaps you can get one from the Service Bureau.)

- ⌐ **Separation printer:** Use this pop-up to choose the device on which you print separation film—usually your service bureau's imagesetter. (If one is not included with PageMaker, perhaps you can get one from the Service Bureau.)

- ⌐ **Default RGB Source/Default CMYK Source:** Use these two pop-ups to select your RGB or CMYK scanner. If you use the service bureau's drum scanner, you should use the profile for that device. (If one is not included with PageMaker, perhaps you can get one from the Service Bureau.)

Once you've chosen all your profiles, click OK to exit the dialog box. PageMaker will now use these settings to correct the color among your various devices.

Monitor Calibration

The profiles in a CMS assume that the devices adhere to a set of standards. Printers and scanners are calibrated during manufacturing. Monitors, on the other hand, are subject to so many variables, such as work area lighting, graphics adapters, and so on, that you must calibrate them individually. This section shows you how to use System 7.5's built-in monitor calibration utility to get the colors right on your monitor.

Begin by making sure your work area is set up as you normally use it, as discussed in "Color Management and Your Work Area" section of this chapter. Before going any further, make sure your monitor has been on for about an hour, so that all the phosphors are warm. Then, make sure PageMaker is open and active and a blank page is displayed. From the Apple menu Control Panels submenu, choose Gamma, which brings up the Gamma control panel shown in Figure 10-13.

Figure 10-13:
The Macintosh System 7.5 Gamma
control panel

Next you select a target gamma (one of the radio buttons across the top, under the credits). For CMYK images, choose 1.8. For RGB devices, such as film recorders, choose 2.2. Next, hold a white piece of paper similar to the one you'll be printing on up to the monitor, click on the White Point option and drag the three sliders until the PageMaker page matches the paper.

Calibrating for multiple paper types: Chances are you won't always use the same type of paper. You can create different calibration settings for various paper types with the Load Settings... and Save Settings... options. Once you've got a certain paper type dialed in, choose Save Settings.... To use the settings in the future, load them with Load Settings....

You are now ready to adjust the gamma. Simply drag on the Gamma Adjustment slider until solid gray areas in the strip above the slider match (become the same color as) the patterned gray areas. As nearly as possible, the strip should appear as one solid color, as in Figure 10-13. Next, select the radio button for Balance and repeat these procedures, and then repeat for Black Pt, and, if necessary, go back and readjust the color balance and gamma. When you've finished, click the Close button. Your monitor is now calibrated and you're ready to use your CMS.

CMS and Your Bitmap Images

Bitmap TIFF, BMP, and PCX color images can be color corrected in PageMaker in three ways:

- ↪ If the bitmap was saved from an application using the Kodak Precision Color profile, PageMaker simply applies Kodak CMS and the appropriate profile.

- ↪ If the image contains CMS and source profile information unavailable to PageMaker, PageMaker applies the preferred CMS and selects a profile that best matches the characteristics of the profiles used to create the bitmap file.

⌐ If the image was not saved with a source profile, PageMaker applies the preferred CMS and the source profile (Default RGB or Default CMYK, depending on the type image).

You can change the source profile for an image by selecting it and then choosing CMS Source from the Image submenu on the Element menu, which brings up the Color Management System Source Profile dialog box shown in Figure 10-14. Note, however, that if you apply a new source profile and then edit the image in Photoshop or another image-editor, you should reapply the source profile, or you'll get some undesired results. However, this does not refer to resizing, resampling, and cropping images, only to changes that affect the color of the image.

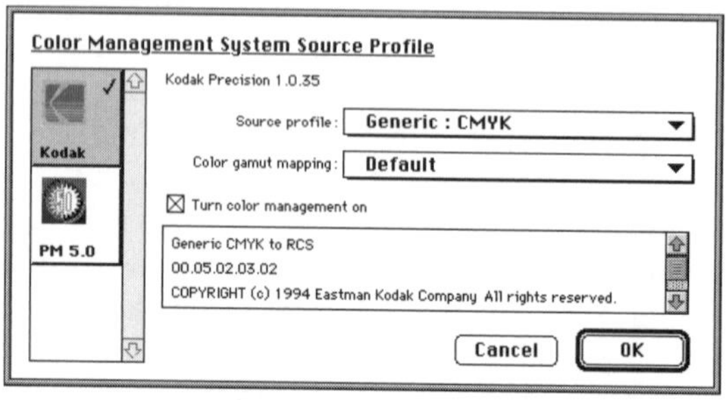

Figure 10-14:
The CMS (Color
Management System)
Source Profile
dialog box

You can also apply a source profile when you place an image in your layout, by choosing the CMS Source option in the Place dialog box. Placing graphics is discussed in Chapter 8.

Defining New Colors

By default, PageMaker documents start with a set of basic colors: None, Paper, Black, Registration, and the colors in the RGB model, red, green, and blue. These colors are defined in the section, "The Colors Palette," later in this chapter. To use additional colors in a PageMaker document, you must create them and add them to the color list. Creating colors with no document open adds colors to the default color list. Creating colors with a document open adds colors to the list for that publication.

PageMaker lets you mix your own colors or you can choose colors from one of the color matching systems that are included. (For more information on the color matching systems, see "Using the Color Matching Systems" later in this chapter.) To create a new color, choose Define Colors... from the Element menu, which brings up the Define Colors dialog box shown in Figure 10-15. From here, you can create new colors, edit existing colors, and remove colors from the color list. To create a new color, click on the New... button. The New... button brings up the Edit Color dialog box shown in Figure 10-16, which lets you add a new color.

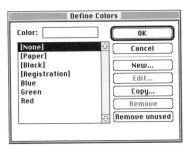

Figure 10-15:
The Define Colors dialog box

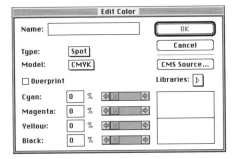

Figure 10-16:
The Edit Color dialog box

The following is a description of the Edit Color dialog box:

⊸ **Name:** Use this option to name your color. You can use rather long names, but you'll probably want to keep them relatively short. It's easier to read shorter names in the Colors palette list (discussed in "The Colors Palette" later in this chapter). When specifying a process color, you should enter a descriptive name that you'll recognize easily on the Colors palette. When you're specifying a spot color, you should enter the name that appears in the swatch book you used to pick the spot color. Why? Because the name of the spot-color ink typically prints on the spot-color overlay. If you use the name the spot-color ink manufacturer uses, your commercial printer readily knows what ink to use. If you choose spot or process colors from one of the color matching systems included with PageMaker, you should leave the Name option blank. The name of the color you select in the library appears automatically in the Name option box. (Color matching systems are discussed in the next section of this chapter.)

⊸ **Type:** Click Spot, Process, or Tint to specify the type of color you're creating. For more information on tints, see "Using Tints" later in this chapter.

⊸ **Model:** PageMaker offers three color models: RGB (red, green, blue), HLS (hue, lightness, saturation), and CMYK (cyan, magenta, yellow, black). Each color model provides a different way to describe color. There are a number of reasons why we need different models to describe colors, all of which have to do with how we perceive colors and how different devices — such as monitors, scanners, commercial presses, and so on — handle color, as discussed in the "Color Managing Systems" section of this chapter. (If you want to learn more about color models, you should consult the art or science sections of your local bookstore or library.) However, to create colors in PageMaker (or any other graphics software package, for that matter), you need to master only two basic concepts:

- When you create spot colors, it doesn't matter in the slightest what color model you select. The reason it doesn't matter what model you use to create spot colors is simple. You're not actually creating the color in PageMaker. You're creating a tag that you apply to objects to ensure that those objects print on a separate spot-color overlay. Your commercial printer then uses that overlay to create a separate plate to print those objects with the appropriate spot-color ink.

- When you create process colors, you should choose only the CMYK color model. When you create process colors, however, the model you use and the values you specify do affect what prints on the press. As we've seen, cyan, magenta, yellow, and black inks are used to print process-color publications. If you use a different color model to create process colors, PageMaker simply converts the RGB or HLS values to CMYK values when you print process-color separations. This conversion isn't a simple one to make, so PageMaker can only approximate the colors you specified. You'll get more predictable results if you simply use the CMYK model to begin with.

↪ **Overprint:** Check this option if you want the color you're creating to print over any colors behind it in the stacking order (in other words, any objects that have the color applied over any objects behind them in the publication). Leave this option unchecked if you want the color to knock out colors that appear behind it. For more information on overprinting, see "Other Printing Issues" earlier in this chapter.

 CMS Source...: Click this button to bring up the CMS Source Profile dialog box. From here, you assign a CMS and source profile to the color you're creating. CMSs are discussed earlier in this chapter under "Color Managing Systems."

↪ **Cyan/Magenta/Yellow/Black:** If you're creating a process color, enter values or adjust the scroll bars for each of the process-color inks. You should keep these rules in mind when specifying these values:

- Don't rely on what you see on-screen to specify these colors. Working on a color monitor gives you an idea of what your final design will look like, but the colors on a monitor rarely match printed colors exactly — even when you control your environment and calibrate your monitor regularly. Instead, use printed process-color charts to select colors and then enter the values from those charts to specify the colors in PageMaker. Figure 10-17 shows a page from a process color chart. (Remember, too, that color managing systems help greatly, as discussed under "Color Management Systems" earlier.)

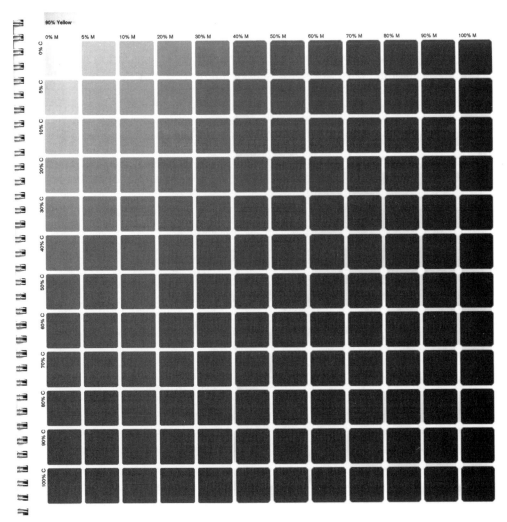

Figure 10-17: An example of a process color matching chart

- Don't use too much ink to print a color. The maximum amount of ink you can specify is 400% — 100% each of cyan, magenta, yellow, and black. However, the more ink that prints on any area of a page, the more likely it is that the paper will become over saturated and stretch or tear on the press. For most presses, the maximum recommended ink coverage is 250%-320% — so the values you enter shouldn't exceed these totals.

- Specify process colors that use only two inks, if possible. The more inks you use to create a color, the more challenging it is to print them in register. When process inks print out of register, you get unsightly moiré patterns that undermine the illusion of color you're trying to create. If, as a rule, you specify most of your process colors with two inks and only occasionally specify more inks, you'll achieve better printed results.

☞ **Libraries:** This pop-up menu, shown in Figure 10-18, presents the available color matching systems from which you can select predefined colors. How to use these colors is described next.

Figure 10-18:
The Edit Color
Libraries pop-up
menu

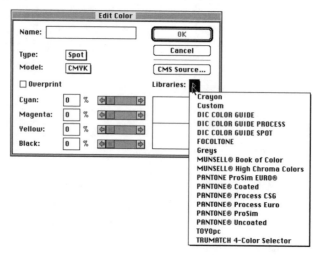

 You can quickly open the Edit Color dialog box and specify a color by pressing the Command key while clicking on the [Black] or [Registration] colors in the Colors palette.

Using the Color Matching Systems

Achieving exact printed results with color is tricky. As we've seen throughout this chapter, a number of factors affect the difference that inevitably occurs between the colors you ask for and the colors you get on press. These factors range from the lighting in which you view the specified color to the type of press your print shop uses. Even the most exacting printer working on the highest-quality press cannot promise you exact color matches because of the sheer number of variables that affect printing.

Basically, then, you have a choice. You can either fret and fume about every little nuance of difference, or you can work out acceptable tradeoffs with your printer. (Your printer, for example, may be able to guarantee that a certain object will hold its color through a print run, if you're willing to compromise on the exact color of some other objects. Typically, printers can control some variables, just not all variables.)

You can also rely on color matching systems, which have emerged as an effective way to achieve more predictable printed results. PANTONE, Inc., set the stage for these systems when it released the first spot-color matching system more than 30 years ago. Up to that point, achieving predictable printed results was hit or miss at best. The PANTONE system gave designers and printers more reliable results, and their color matching systems continue to set the standard for reliable color results. With the PANTONE Matching System, you choose a color from a swatch book, shown in Figure 10-19 and in Plate 10 in the color insert. Usually, unless you choose a very coarse paper, the color stays reasonably true. (How paper affects printing and color is discussed in Chapter 13.)

Figure 10-19:
A PANTONE Matching System swatch and the corresponding PageMaker library swatches

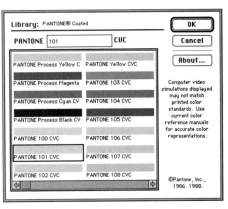

However, the growth of color printing has led to the release of several other spot- and process-color matching systems, several of which are included in electronic form in PageMaker. Figure 10-20 shows some of the Color Picker library dialog boxes. The systems in PageMaker include a Focoltone library, several MUNSELL libraries, several PANTONE libraries, a TOYO library, a TRUMATCH library, and others. You should contact individual vendors or your print shop for more information about where to purchase their swatch books.

Figure 10-20:
An example of a PageMaker Color Picker library

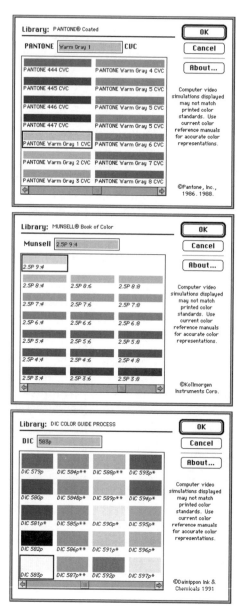

To choose a color from a color matching system, choose the Define Colors... command from the Element menu and click the New... button. Open the Libraries pop-up menu and select a color matching system. The Library dialog box for that color matching system opens, so that you can choose a color. Click a color to select it or press the Shift key and click several colors to select more than one at a time. If you select more than one color at a time, the word MULT appears in the Library dialog box. Then, when you close all of the dialog boxes, the individual color names appear on the Colors palette. As a rule, you should accept the default names for the colors so that you know what you've selected when you consult swatch books and, when using spot colors, that the right name prints on the plates. However, you can edit the name of a color if you wish.

If you cannot locate a particular library in the Edit Color dialog box, the files may not be stored in the correct location on your hard drive. You need two files: the color-picker file, which is called Aldcolor.add, and the library file, which has an ACF or BCF extension. The color-picker file appears in the Plug-ins folder in the Adobe folder in your System folder. The color library file appears in the Color folder in the RSRC folder in the Adobe PageMaker 6.0 folder. You can always reinstall these files from the PageMaker installation disks.

Using Tints

To control your color printing costs, you may limit yourself to printing black and one spot color. You can expand your choices, however, by creating and using tints of that spot color. A tint, or *screen,* is a lightened version of a spot color that prints on the same spot-color overlay. PageMaker creates the tint by applying a halftone screen to the solid spot color and, thereby, changing the number and size of the dots of ink. You specify the size of the screen when you choose an exact percentage for the tint. Figure 10-21 and Plate 11 shows samples of tints.

PageMaker 6 allows you apply tints in five-degree increments from the Colors palette, discussed under the section, "The Colors Palette," later in this chapter. For 99.9 percent of all documents, you will never need tints with screen values between the five-degree increments. But PageMaker still allows you to create them. To create a tint, choose Define colors... from the Element menu. Click the New... button, then click the Tint option in Type. The dialog box changes, as shown in Figure 10-22, so that you can specify a tint. Choose the color on which you want to base the tint from the Base Color pop-up menu. Then, enter a value or use the scroll bars to specify the exact percentage of the tint. You can specify tints in increments as small as 1%. However, printing presses typically cannot hold a tint to that precise a level, so you may want to think in 5% or 10% increments.

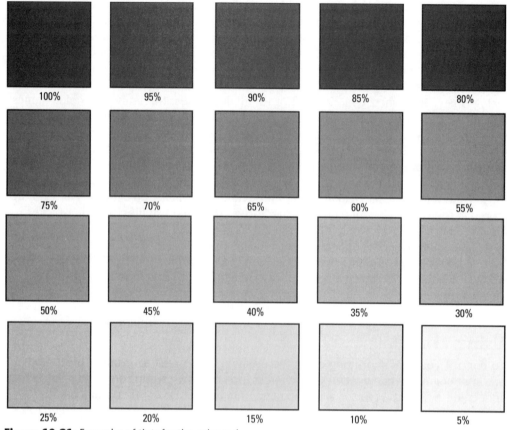

Figure 10-21: Examples of tints for the color red

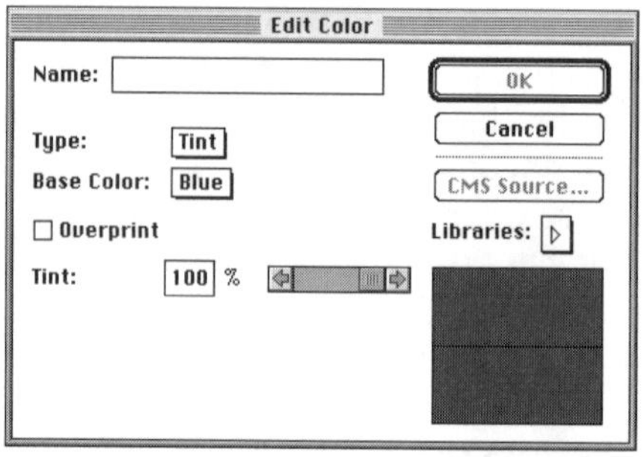

Figure 10-22:
The Edit Color dialog box
configured to work with tints

You should be wary of specifying tints below 20% — most presses cannot print that light a tint. You may want to consult your printer for advice about how fine a tint you can print. When you're done defining the tint, enter a name for it. As a rule, choose names that include the base color, so that you know what color you're applying when you use it in your document. Then click OK to close the dialog boxes.

 When to overprint tints: You can also specify that a tint overprints, so that any objects that have the tint applied will print on top of any objects behind them. This is a handy feature because there may be times when you want a color to knock out some objects and overprint others. To do that, you can create one color and then create a 100% tint of that color and set the tint to overprint (by checking the Overprint option). The color and the tint are identical, but one knocks out and the other overprints the objects it's applied to.

Note that when you apply tints from the Colors palette (discussed in "The Colors Palette" later in this chapter), objects use the overprinting value for the color selected. You cannot successfully overprint most screens without some show-through from the underlying color. So, if you want to knockout some instances of a color when you use a tint and overprint when you don't use a tint, you should use the above method to create new colors for the tints, rather than assign them from the Colors palette.

Here's one final suggestion on tints: Always consult your printer before applying tints — particularly light tints — to fine objects, such as hairline rules, small serif text, and so on. It's usually better to use a solid color to print fine objects because the objects hold their shapes better. However, your printer can best advise you on each particular object.

Editing Colors

After you create a color, you can always edit it. PageMaker will automatically update any objects to which the color is applied. It will also update any tints based on that color, so stand warned if that's not the result you're expecting. Note, as well, that you can edit the spot colors included in EPS graphics but not the process colors.

To edit a color, choose the Define Colors... command from the Element menu. (You can also press the Command key and click the color name on the Colors palette to quickly open the Edit Color dialog box and make changes.) In the Define Colors dialog box, click the color you want to edit, then click the Edit... button.

You can convert a process color into a spot color by holding down Command-Option-Shift and clicking the color name in the Colors palette.

When you edit colors, you should follow the same principles as when you create them. For example, don't rely on the color on screen to make your edits. Instead, work from printed swatch books of spot or process colors. Be particularly careful if you change a spot color into a process color because process-color inks can only simulate a spot-color ink. (Process colors are printed with translucent inks and spot colors with premixed, semi-opaque inks; the results look very different in print.) If you work from printed color charts, you'll get more predictable printed results. You should also note that Adobe doesn't recommend editing colors from the color matching systems. The companies that created the different color matching systems intended you to get very specific printed results by using their colors. If you don't want those results, then you should mix your own colors.

Editing Imported EPS Graphics

When you import EPS graphics into a PageMaker layout, spot colors contained in that image are added to the color list. PageMaker lets you edit imported spot colors the same as any other color — a feature that can save you time and money when you print. When you print color publications, you want to control the number of printed separations to save money. For example, in a five-color publication you'd pay for printed separations of the four process-color inks and one spot-color ink. You don't want to use a second spot color by accident, or you end up with an expensive extra separation when you print. Plus you incur the additional cost of having the printer strip together the two spot-color overlays so they both print on the same printing plate.

One of the easiest ways to end up with an unexpected extra separation is to import an EPS graphic that includes a different spot color than the one you're using in your publication. If that happens, you can always go back to the original application for the EPS, change the color, and then place it into PageMaker again. You may not have the original graphic file, though, or you may not want to spend the time to edit and reimport the graphic. That's where it's handy to edit the spot color in PageMaker.

Merging EPS spot colors with document colors: To merge spot colors in an imported EPS with spot colors in your publication, choose the Define Colors… command from the Element menu. In the color list, select the EPS color you want to edit. Click the Edit… button, then click the Tint button. For the Base color, select the color you want to merge with and then type 100% for the tint percentage. Then click OK to close the dialog boxes. Now, the spot-colored objects in the EPS graphic will print on the same overlay as the base color. You can also convert a spot color in an EPS graphic to a process color.

Replacing One Color with Another Color

Sometimes you may want to do more than edit a color. You may want to replace it with another color. You'll find having the ability to update objects automatically particularly useful if you work with long documents.

To replace one color with another color, choose Define Colors... from the Element menu. Click the color you want to replace, then click the Edit... button. Change the name of the color to the name of the color you want to replace it with. For example, if you want to get rid of a color named Purple and make all objects with Purple applied Mauve, you would change the name Purple to Mauve. If the color is a process color, you can change the CMYK values to the new specifications. Then click the OK button to close the Edit Color dialog box. An alert message will appear asking whether you really want to change all objects to the other color. Click the OK button to replace the colors, then click the OK button to close the Define Colors dialog box.

PageMaker removes the original color from the color list and replaces it with the new color. Any objects that had the original color applied now have the new color applied. Any tints that were based on the original color also change to the new color (which is why it pays to include the base color in your tint names — so you can predict what will change).

Importing Colors

You can define colors in one PageMaker publication and then quickly copy those colors into another publication. To copy a few colors from one publication to another, create one or more objects — such as rectangles, ellipses, or lines — in the publication that contains the colors you want. Apply the colors you want to the objects. Then, either cut and paste or copy and paste the objects into the other publication. The colors now appear on the color list in the other publication, so you can apply them to other objects.

To copy all of the colors from another publication, choose the Define Colors... command from Element menu. Click the Copy... button. When the Copy Colors dialog box (see Figure 10-23) opens, locate and double-click the PageMaker document that contains the colors you want. Click the OK button to close the Define Colors dialog box. All of the colors from the other publication now appear in the color list in your publication.

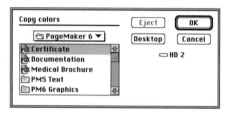

Figure 10-23:
The Copy colors dialog box

If a color you're copying has the same name and different specifications than a color in your publication, you should decide whether or not to replace the color. PageMaker displays an alert message that asks whether or not to replace the color. You can click the OK button to replace it or the Cancel button to retain the color in your publication. If two colors have the same name and specifications, PageMaker doesn't import the color.

Exporting Color Libraries

If you use a certain combination of colors over and over again, you may want to create them once and then turn them into a color library that you can access all the time. (You could also create a document template containing often used colors. However, when you create colors in a document template, all of the colors you create are present on the color list. (Templates are discussed in Chapter 4.) Creating a color library lets you have instant access to your standard colors but doesn't automatically clutter the list with colors that you won't necessarily use in every publication.

To create a custom color library, open a publication and specify all the colors you want to appear in that library. Be sure to give each color a meaningful name, so that you know what you're selecting from the library you create. Then, choose the Create Color Library... command from the PageMaker Plug-ins submenu on the Utilities menu. The dialog box shown in Figure 10-24 appears. For Library name, enter the name you want to appear in the Libraries list in the Edit Color dialog box. The File name, on the other hand, is the name of the actual color library file that's stored in the Color folder in the RSRC folder, in the Adobe PageMaker 6.0 folder. Obviously you'll want to choose unique names for each Library name and File name you create. For File name, either accept the default name or change it to a name you want. Be sure to include the BCF extension, however, or PageMaker won't recognize the library you create. Then, enter a number between 1 and 10 to specify the number of columns and rows of colors that appear at one time in your color library window. Click the Save button to save the library.

Figure 10-24:
The Create color library
dialog box

Create color library	Save
Library name:	Cancel
File name: Custom.bcf	Save as...
Preferences	
Colors per column: 5	
Colors per row: 3	
Notes:	

Deleting Colors

If you decide not to use a color in the document color list, you can easily remove it from your publication. You simply choose the Define Colors... command from the Element menu, click the name of the color you want to remove, and click Remove.

Delete unused colors: As a rule of thumb, you should delete colors from your publications if you decide not to use them — particularly spot colors and in long documents. It's just too easy to apply a color to some small object on page 52 of a 90-page publication and forget you've done it. Then, when you print separations of the publication, you end up with an extra, expensive separation. Deleting unnecessary colors ensures that you print only the correct number of separations.

The Colors Palette _____

The Colors palette is a key tool for applying colors in PageMaker. You use the palette to apply colors to the lines and fills of PageMaker objects, text, and imported graphics. To open the Colors palette, shown in Figure 10-25, you choose the Colors command (⌘-K) from the Window menu.

Figure 10-25:
The Colors palette

The Color List

The main thing you'll find on the Colors palette is a list of the colors you created or imported into your publication. A color swatch appears to the left of the color name, so you can get a quick idea of the color. Each color name reveals whether the color is a spot color, a process color, or a tint of one of those colors. Spot-color names appear in plain text, and while process color names appear in italic text. A percent (%) sign appears to the left of the tint names, which are either plain or italicized depending on whether they are spot- or process-color tints.

If you import an EPS graphic that contains spot colors, those colors appear on the palette list as well. You'll recognize those colors because an EPS symbol shows up between the color swatch and the color name. If you imported an EPS from Macromedia FreeHand that contains process colors, those colors also appear on the palette list. However, PageMaker does not display process colors that are imported in EPS graphics from other programs. (PageMaker prints those process colors — they just don't appear in the palette list. The reason they don't appear is that PostScript doesn't offer a standard way to describe process colors, so PageMaker doesn't have a way to capture information from other programs.) You can apply EPS colors to other objects in your PageMaker publication, just as you would any other color. You can also edit imported EPS spot colors. For more information, see "Editing Colors" earlier in this chapter.

Six colors are listed in the Colors palette by default — [Paper], [Black], [Registration], three spot colors (Red, Green, Blue), and the other three process colors, (Cyan, Magenta, Yellow). You can delete the Red, Green, and Blue colors at any time from any publication, or you can delete them when no publication is open to remove them from the default color list. (In fact, we recommend deleting them permanently as they serve no real purpose, unless you commonly use these three spot colors, which most people don't. To edit this default, choose the Define Colors... command when no publications are open, click one of the default spot colors, and click Remove. Repeat these steps two more times for the other two spot colors.) Another option is to edit these defaults or delete them and then replace them with other default colors that you use frequently.

You cannot remove the [Paper], [Black], and [Registration] options. These "colors" are used in all PageMaker publications, and are described below:

 ☞ **Paper:** The [Paper] option is a peculiar one. Basically, it's a non-color. When you apply it to an object, that object knocks out any colored items that appear behind it, so that the paper shows through. You can edit [Paper] to simulate on-screen the color of the paper you're printing on. That simulation doesn't print, however. It just gives you an on-screen sense of what your final design will look like.

⮑ **Black:** The [Black] option is a 100% process black ink, which you cannot edit. Any objects with this [Black] applied knock out objects placed behind them, with one critical exception — text. Black text automatically overprints anything placed behind it. In most instances, that's great — you want black text to overprint, particularly small, serif text that's difficult to trap. However, you may occasionally want black text to knock out (or other black items to overprint). You can accomplish this with PageMaker 6's new trapping option, discussed in the "Trapping in PageMaker" section later in this chapter.

 In PageMaker 4.2 and earlier versions, the default black color was a spot color. If you are used to using the default black as a spot color, you can convert the new process-color default into a spot color.

⮑ **Registration:** The [Registration] item is another non-color. Basically, you apply it to items that you want to print on every separation. If you create your own crop marks or registration marks, you can place them in your publications and apply [Registration] to them, so they'll print on every separation. Crop marks and registration marks are discussed in Chapter 13.

Applying Colors to Elements

Once the Colors palette is open, you use it by first selecting the element or elements to which you want to apply color and then selecting a color from the palette. You can apply colors to a variety of objects that you create in PageMaker, including text, lines, rectangles, and ellipses. You can also apply colors to some imported graphics, such as Encapsulated PostScript (EPS) files and monochrome or grayscale bitmapped images. Don't be fooled though — when you apply color to imported graphics, you're not changing the intrinsic color of these graphics. Instead, you're overriding the intrinsic color information. The color you apply in PageMaker dictates what separations the graphic prints on and, therefore, what spot or process inks are used to print the graphic. If you remove a color that you apply to an imported graphic, PageMaker uses the imported graphic's internal color information to print the graphic on the appropriate separations.

To apply colors to most objects, you select the object with the pointer tool and click the color name on the Colors palette list. There are a few exceptions to keep track of, though. You need to select text with the text tool to apply a color to it. Rectangles and ellipses require a few extra steps because you can apply different colors to the outlines and fills of these objects. After you select the rectangle or ellipse, you choose the Line, Fill, or Both icons on the Colors palette. They run left to right above the color list, as shown in Figure 10-26.

Figure 10-26: The Line, Fill, and Both buttons on the Colors palette

Using commands to assign colors: You can also choose the Line, Fill, or Fill and Line commands from the Element menu to apply separate fill and line colors. Choosing this command lets you specify a custom line weight between 0 and 800 points and lets you overprint the color you're applying to the line or fill, as discussed in Chapter 8. And you can apply color to text from the Type Specifications dialog box, as discussed in Chapter 6. For more information on overprinting, see the "Other Printing Issues" section earlier in this chapter.

Changing the colors of objects is as easy as applying colors to them. With lines and text, you simply apply a different color. So, for example, if you color a text block red and then decide that you want it to be black, you select the text again and click Black on the Colors palette. With rectangles and ellipses, select the object and then either choose None from the Line or Fill submenu on the Element menu or choose the Fill and Line... command on the Element menu and make changes in the dialog box that appears. With imported graphics, select the graphic and choose the Restore original color command from the Element menu.

Applying Tints

In addition to applying the tints you create using the method discussed earlier in this chapter under "Tints," you can also apply one of the 21 incremental tints (if you count both 100% and 0%) that PageMaker automatically creates for each color, as demonstrated in Figure 10-27. The method for applying tints is the same as applying other colors, except that it requires one more step. After you've selected the object and applied the desired color, simply select the tint percentage from the Tint pop-up menu in the Colors palette.

Figure 10-27:
The Colors palette Tints pop-up menu

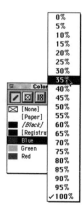

Trapping in PageMaker _____

 Earlier in this chapter we warned you about the need to trap abutting colored objects in PageMaker layouts. Remember that trapping compensates for inaccurate press registration, or slop. PageMaker 6 has a built-in trapping utility that works reasonably well, allowing the program to compensate printing press slop in most instances. This section looks at the new trapping feature. Before going into this discussion, though, we want to make a few of things perfectly clear about PageMaker's trapping — to keep you from getting into trouble:

⮑ **PageMaker cannot trap imported graphics:** Your Adobe Illustrator, Photoshop, and Macromedia FreeHand files are separate entities. PageMaker cannot perform its trapping magic on these files. You *must* trap abutting colors in the graphics application.

⮑ **PageMaker doesn't trap PageMaker objects that overlay imported objects:** If you need text or other objects placed over an imported graphical image in your layout, it's a good idea to apply them in the graphics application. PageMaker is great at trapping elements created in PageMaker, but it can't trap when mixing PageMaker elements with elements you place in your layout. Note, however, that this does not apply to imported text over PageMaker drawn boxes, lines, and ellipses. Imported text becomes a PageMaker object.

⮑ **PageMaker cannot trap text over text:** When you place a colored text object over another colored text object, PageMaker cannot create a trap. If you need effects like this, use your graphics application to create them and place the graphic in PageMaker.

⮑ **You don't have to do your own trapping:** If all this business about trapping seems daunting, relax. You don't have to do it yourself. Your service bureau has software, such as Adobe TrapWise, that can perform the trapping automatically. Many service bureaus also have technicians on staff who can create manual traps or apply PageMaker's trapping for you. Granted, the service bureau charges for these services, but not so much that it's worth pulling your hair out trying to figure out this darn trapping thing.

Using Trapping Options

You turn on and control PageMaker's trapping in the Trapping Options dialog box, shown in Figure 10-28. To get here, choose Trapping Options from the Utilities menu.

Figure 10-28:
The Trapping Options
dialog box

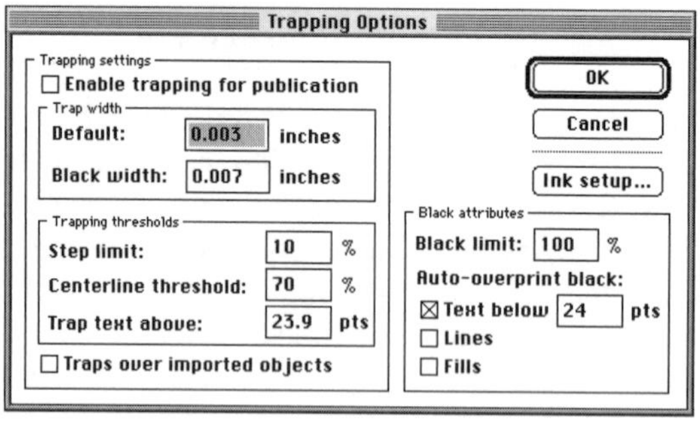

The following is a description of the Trapping Options dialog box:

- **Trapping settings:** Use these three options to turn on trapping for the current document (or make it the default with no document open), and to control the size of the trap. "Enable trapping for publication" turns on trapping. Trap width Default allows you to set the size of the trap. Before setting this option, you should consult the print shop, as you should with the third option, Black width, which tells PageMaker which size to create black traps.

- **Trapping thresholds:** These options tell PageMaker how to trap. Step limit tells PageMaker to begin trapping when one of the abutting colors is a certain percentage lighter than the other. For example, if this value is set to 10%, PageMaker begins trapping when one abutting color is 10% lighter than the other. A Centerline threshold percentage tells PageMaker when to use a centerline between colors with similar neutral densities. In these cases, PageMaker creates a centerline trap that straddles the area where the two colors meet. The Trap text above option tells PageMaker when to start trapping text. If this value is too low, you could wind up with misshapen characters. How low is too low depends on the font.

- **Traps over imported objects:** This option does not tell PageMaker to trap PageMaker elements to imported objects. Instead, it traps objects that overlay imported objects to PageMaker objects beneath the imported object. If you can believe that. Leave this one off.

- **Ink setup . . . :** This option lets you adjust the neutral density for each ink in the color list. The default neutral densities (relative lightness and darkness) are set by industry standard process inks in different parts of the world. The language version of PageMaker determines what values are used. Typically, you'd change these only if you're using a version of PageMaker that's targeted for a location different from the locale you'll be printing the publication in.

☞ **Black attributes:** These options control how PageMaker treats black objects. The Black limit setting tells PageMaker when to treat an object as if it's all black. For example, 100% tells PageMaker that all colors containing 100% black are black; therefore, they should be treated as black, affecting the Black width and Auto-overprint black options. Black limit also tells PageMaker when to determine whether a black is "solid" or "rich." Rich blacks contain percentages of one of the other CMYK colors. The Auto-overprint black option tells PageMaker at what size it should overprint black objects. Typically, you should always overprint black, but at small sizes in high-density colors it can get lost.

How PageMaker Traps

During printing, PageMaker looks at abutting colors and determines which is lighter and which is darker (neutral densities). It then decides whether to trap based on the settings in Trapping Options. When the program decides to trap an object, it spreads the lighter color into the abutting dark one, or darker ones when dealing with more than two colors. PageMaker then overprints the lighter colored trap over the edge of the darker color. The size of the trap depends on the Trap width setting in Trapping Options.

Which color PageMaker uses to trap also depends on the types of colors, process or spot:

☞ For abutting process colors that require trapping, PageMaker creates a trap color consisting of the CMYK values in the lighter color that are higher than the same values in the abutting color.

☞ For spot colors, PageMaker traps the darker color with the lighter color. This same process is used when a process color and spot color needs trapping.

■ ■

Summary

➠ Two kinds of color can be used in PageMaker: spot color and process color. Spot color uses colored opaque ink to reproduce the colors defined on-screen. Process color uses four translucent inks (cyan, magenta, yellow, and black) mixed to give the appearance of the defined color.

➠ Spot or process colors can be applied to elements within PageMaker, or colors can be applied in other applications before the elements are imported into PageMaker.

➠ When printing colored documents, there are many issues to consider, including registration, element knockouts and overprinting, and trapping. For this reason, you should work closely with your service bureau and commercial printer before producing color publications.

➠ The Define Colors. . . command and the Colors palette are the two main color tools in PageMaker. The Define Colors. . . command is used to create new spot or process colors, select colors from existing color libraries, and edit any existing colors. The Colors palette is used to apply colors to elements in your publication.

➠ PageMaker 6 allows you to edit spot colors from imported EPS graphics, which can save you time in production and avoid problems producing separations or reproducing your documents.

➠ There are several ways to move colors between publications. You can import colors from other PageMaker publications or existing color libraries, and export colors from your document to color libraries.

➠ PageMaker's built-in trapping lets you compensate for press misregistration when using abutting colors.

■ ■

Using PageMaker Plug-ins

CHAPTER 11

In This Chapter

- Introduction to PageMaker Plug-ins
- Review of in-the-box PageMaker Plug-ins
- Third-party Plug-ins

It's tough being popular. With over 1 million people all over the world using PageMaker for an incredibly diverse range of publications, it has become difficult (or impossible) for Adobe to add the "right" new features to each new PageMaker upgrade. Everyone has his or her own Top 10 list, depending on the type of publications he or she creates. Designers think Adobe should have more graphic design features. Book and technical documentation producers think PageMaker needs more long-document features. Office publishers would love to have more built-in text editing capabilities. And large publishing departments think more workgroup features would be the best area of improvement.

Of course, they're all right — it's just a matter of perspective. Realizing that it alone could not extend PageMaker far enough in every possible direction, Adobe has instead turned PageMaker into something of an open system with its PageMaker Plug-ins technology. This means that anyone can add features to PageMaker in order to satisfy some particular need or desire. The designers can add graphic design features, the technical publishers can add long-document features, and so on.

Did we say that anyone could add features to PageMaker? Well, that is theoretically true; although practically speaking, the programming skill required to create a new feature will probably stop most PageMaker users from doing so. Even if you don't want to do your own programming, you can still benefit by adding features that others have created to your copy of PageMaker. These might be features created by commercial software developers and then sold as PageMaker Plug-ins, or they might be features created by individuals and shared via user groups or on-line services. Adobe hopes that eventually there will be hundreds of different commercial, shareware, and public domain PageMaker Plug-ins for you to choose from. And to get the ball rolling, Adobe designers have written several Plug-ins that are included in the box along with PageMaker 6. Later in the chapter, we'll review each of these Plug-ins, plus a wide range of commercially available Plug-ins.

How Plug-ins Work

The core of PageMaker Plug-ins technology is the fact that instead of controlling PageMaker using only the existing menu commands, dialog boxes, tools, and keyboard equivalents, you can now control PageMaker by sending it commands. These commands can be sent by Plug-in modules that load into the PageMaker Plug-ins submenu or by other stand-alone applications. Let's take a closer look at each of these:

- **Loadable Plug-ins.** The Plug-ins formats you'll use most often are loadable Plug-ins like those provided with PageMaker 6. These Plug-ins must reside in the Plug-ins folder inside the RSRC folder in the Adobe PageMaker 6.0 folder. PageMaker checks for these Plug-ins during start-up and adds the name of each into the PageMaker Plug-ins submenu in the Utilities menu. Choosing a Plug-in from this menu executes that Plug-in, which can bring up a dialog box to present you further options or may immediately cause some action to occur. All of the bundled Plug-ins are introduced in the next section of this chapter, as are several commercially available loadable Plug-ins at the end of the chapter.

  Loadable Plug-ins must be written in the C programming language. These Plug-ins can both send commands to PageMaker and query PageMaker to get data about specific aspects of your publication. These capabilities make loadable Plug-ins more powerful than scripts.

- **Stand-alone applications.** Using Plug-ins technology, another application can also command PageMaker by sending Plug-ins commands via the System 7 Inter-Application Communication feature. Applications can send commands to PageMaker, query PageMaker, and receive query responses.

Plug-ins Technology

PageMaker Plug-ins provide a new way of controlling PageMaker (or more precisely, the software code that makes up PageMaker), but they do so indirectly. The Plug-ins themselves do not talk to the PageMaker code: Plug-ins send their commands or queries into a special "Plug-ins processor" module — called the Plug-ins Interface Manager — that exists within PageMaker. The Plug-ins Interface Manager interprets the Plug-ins' commands or queries, converts them into binary code that PageMaker itself can understand, and then calls the appropriate PageMaker code, technically known as either Action routines or Information routines.

This indirect method has both positive and negative implications. It is good in that it isolates Plug-in from changes in the PageMaker code, so Plug-ins will usually not require updating every time PageMaker itself is updated, and it limits the chance for a Plug-in to damage PageMaker files since they cannot directly modify PageMaker data. The downside is that this scheme limits a Plug-in's capabilities to only those things that PageMaker itself can already do. In other words, in a strict technical sense, you cannot add new capabilities to PageMaker with Plug-ins, but rather merely enhance the automation of the capabilities that could already be performed with some manual combination of existing PageMaker commands. This can be tremendously useful and time-saving, as the Plug-ins discussed later in this chapter will demonstrate, but this structure does impose technical limits as to what Plug-ins can accomplish.

The Plug-ins Bundled with PageMaker 6

The PageMaker Plug-ins are installed by the PageMaker Installer Utility, as explained in Appendix A. You can select among them, or just install all of them, as most people do. When installed, the Plug-ins are copied into the Plug-ins folder inside the RSRC folder within the Adobe PageMaker 6.0 folder.

 Getting rid of Plug-ins you don't need: If you ever need to save a little space on your hard drive, or if you want to speed up the loading of your copy of PageMaker by a few milliseconds, drag any Plug-ins you don't use out of the Plug-ins folder and into the trash. If you later discover that you need the deleted Plug-ins, just rerun the PageMaker Installer Utility.

If you've been using PageMaker version 5 before upgrading to PageMaker 6, you will notice that some of the Plug-ins aren't really new. Balance columns, Display Pub Info, Drop Cap, Build Booklet, and others are all holdovers, though a few have new names. Display Pub Info, for example, is now Pub Info.

Following is a short summary of every Plug-in that Adobe ships with PageMaker 6 except for HTML Author, which is discussed in Chapter 16. Also, some Plug-ins shipped with PageMaker install themselves into PageMaker menus, such as Sort Pages, Printer Styles, and a few others. This book treats them as commands and covers them in the appropriate chapters.

Add Cont'd Line

In any newspaper- or magazine-style layout where stories jump from column to column or page to page in irregular patterns, adding a continued-on or continued-from notice to the break points in your story is very helpful to your readers. This Plug-in is meant to automate the process of adding these notices, and it does a good job within its own limited scope.

To use the Plug-in, use the Pointer tool to select a text block to which you want a notice added and select the Add Cont'd Line Plug-in. (The Plug-in won't run if the text tool is selected.) The dialog box shown in Figure 11-1 appears, and you can choose to have the continuation notice added at the top or bottom of the text block. After you click OK, the Plug-in determines the correct page number reference and adds a new text block containing the "continued from" or "continued on" text just above or below the text block you selected.

Figure 11-1:
The Add Cont'd Line Plug-in
dialog box

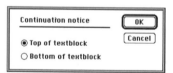

When "continued on" or "continued from" text is added, a new style sheet is automatically created for this new text block. The style sheet has the same type attributes as the adjacent text block, plus the bold type style and before and after paragraph rules. You can edit the definition of this style sheet, of course, or manually override the type style to apply any formatting you want.

Plate 1: Process-color printing combines percentages of four colors — cyan, magenta, yellow, and black (CMYK) — to create full color documents. The four colors are printed at varying angles and fit together like a puzzle to simulate a full-color effect.

Community CMC

StyleSystems Interational tower to open in May

Lorem ipsum dolor sit amet, consectetuer adipiscing elit, sed diam nonummy nibh euismod tincidunt ut laoreet dolore magna aliquam erat volutpat. Ut wisi enim ad minim veniam,

Lorem ipsum dolor sit amet, consectetuer adipiscing elit, sed diam nonummy nibh euismod tincidunt ut laoreet dolore magna aliquam erat volutpat. Ut wisi enim ad minim veniam, quis nostrud exerci tation. Duis autem vel eum iriure dolor in hendrerit in vulputate velit esse molestic consequat.

Lorem ipsum dolor sit amet, consectetuer adipiscing elit, sed diam nonummy nibh euismod tincidunt ut laoreet dolore magna.

Duis autem vel eum iriure dolor in hendrerit in vulputate velit esse molestic consequat, vel illum dolore eu feugiat nulla facilisis at vero eros et accumsan et iusto odio dignissim qui blandit praesent luptatum zzril delenit augue duis dolore te feugait nulla facilisi. Lorem ipsum dolor sit amet. Consectetuer adipiscing elit, sed diam nonummy nibh euismod tincidunt ut laoreet dolore magna aliquam erat volutpat. Ut wisi enim ad minim veniam, quis nostrud exerci tation ullamcorper suscipit lobortis nisl ut aliquip ex ea commodo consequat. Duis autem vel eum iriue dolor in hendrerit in vulputate velit esse molestie

consequat, vel illum.

Lorem ipsum dolor sit amet, consectetuer adipiscing elit, sed diam nonummy nibh euismod tincidunt ut laoreet dolore magna aliquam erat volutpat. Ut wisi enim ad minim veniam, quis nostrud exerci tation ullamcorper suscipit lobortis nisl ut aliquip ex ea commodo consequat. Duis autem vel eum iriure dolor in molestic consequat.

Vel illum dolore eu feugiat nulla

—Ambiguity Estivez
President, StyleSystems

Style Systems Tower

Spring/Summer 1994 StyleSystems Inc.

Plate 2: There are two types of color used to reproduce documents on a printing press: spot-color (top) and process-color (right). Spot-color is used to add intermittent color or to emphasize elements. Process-color is used to print more than three colors (for full-color photographs, book covers, magazines, and so forth).

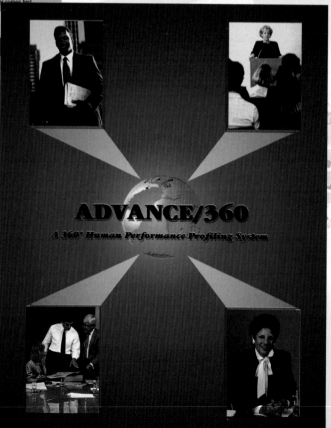

ADVANCE/360
A 360° Human Performance Profiling System

Final Spot Color document

Negative film for plates

Black-elements plate

Spot-colors plate

Plate 3: Color documents are reproduced on printing presses by creating plates for each color. In the top example, the spot-color document is printed from two plates, one for all black elements and one for all spot-color elements. Typically, you would print each plate as negative film on an imagesetter, which your print shop uses to burn the press plates. In the bottom example, each process-color has its own plate; these four plates are combined to create the final color document.

Process Color

Final color document   Negative film for plates

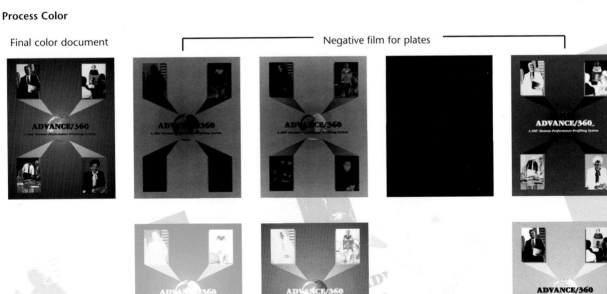

Cyan plate   Magenta plate   Yellow plate   Black plate

Misregistration

Misregistration

Plate 4: Due to paper stretching and printing press slop, abutting colors don't always line up as desired, as shown in these examples of poor press registration. These examples are exaggerated; real-world misregistration is more subtle but certainly noticeable. To avoid misregistration problems, you need to "trap" abutting colored objects, as shown in Plate 5.

Plate 5: To compensate for press misregistration, it is often necessary to "trap," or place an outline around one of the abutting colors, as shown here (the trap size is exaggerated for illustration purposes).

Plate 6: When printing a dark color under a lighter one, you should "knock out" the darker color beneath where the lighter color prints. Otherwise, the bottom color will show through and distort the top color. When printing darker colors over lighter ones, you can often "overprint" the darker objects, effectively avoiding the press misregistration problems shown in Plate 4.

Trap

Plate 7: When placing grayscale images over colored back-grounds or other colored objects, you should knock out the objects behind the image to keep the underlying color from showing through. Otherwise, your image will be discolored.

Knockout

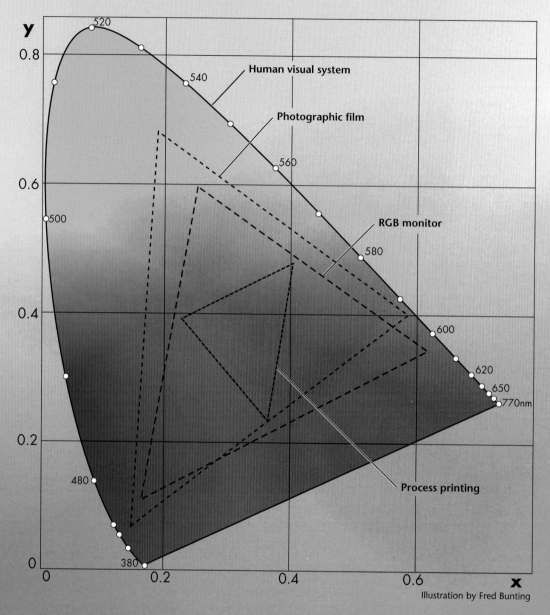

Plate 8: Each color device has its own color gamut, or range. Color monitors have the highest gamut, color printers have the next highest range, and printing presses have smaller gamuts than color printers. When designing documents, you should design toward the final output device's gamut, rather than your monitor or proof printer.

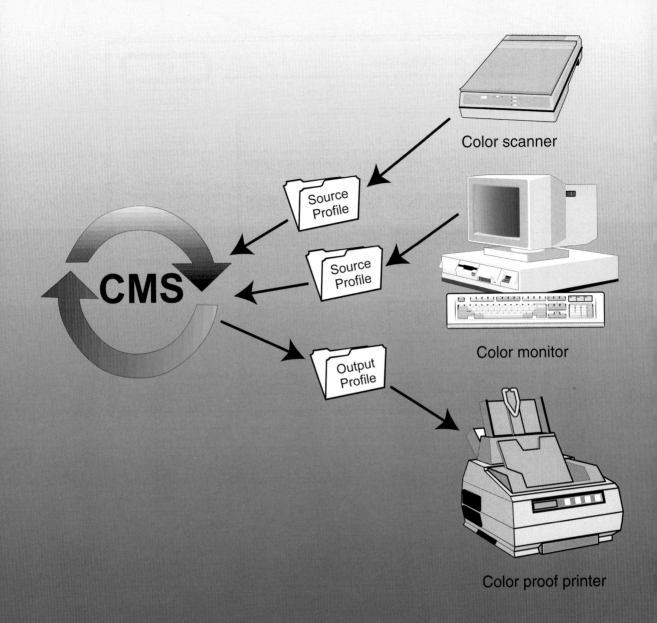

Color scanner

Source Profile

Source Profile

Color monitor

Output Profile

CMS

Color proof printer

Plate 9: A color management system (CMS) uses device profiles to define each color device's gamut, or color range. In this example, the CMS software reads the scanner's color gamut, then adjusts the image's color for the monitor. When you print, the CMS goes to work again, redefining the image's colors one more time for the color printer. When designing color images, use the CMS for the final target output device, such as a printing press, rather than your proof printer. Designating the CMS for the final output device will help avoid color shifts.

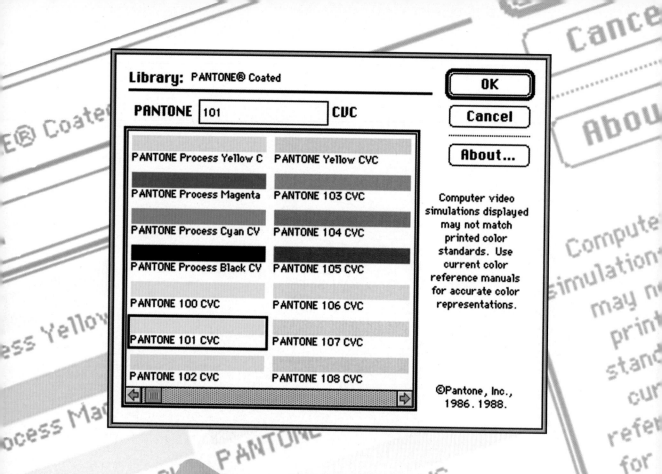

Plate 10: Several of PageMaker's color libraries correspond with ink matching systems used by print shops. In this example, PageMaker's PANTONE color library matches the colors in the PANTONE Matching System's swatch book. To pick colors, simply match the numbers in the swatch book with the numbers in the library dialog box. This system helps you control color output.

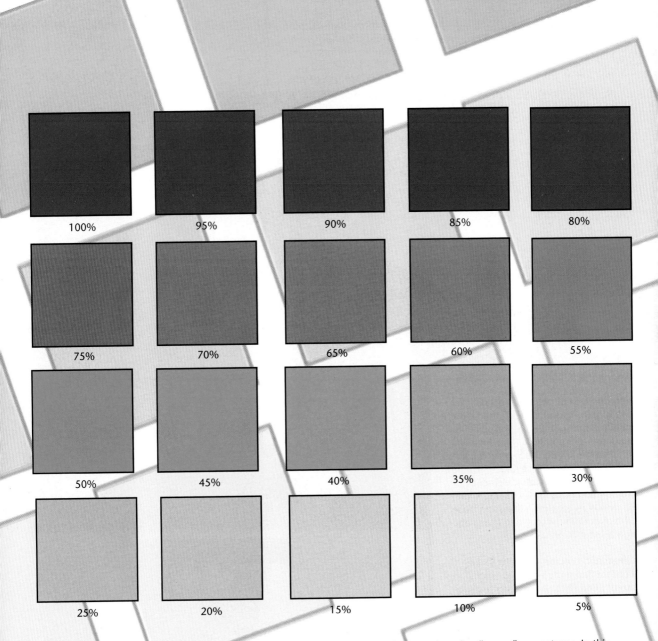

100% 95% 90% 85% 80%

75% 70% 65% 60% 55%

50% 45% 40% 35% 30%

25% 20% 15% 10% 5%

Plate 11: PageMaker's Tint option allows you to create new colors from existing ones by using "screen" percentages. In this example, the color red is screened in increments of 5 percent. This is a great way to save money on multiple-ink print runs.

Plate 12: You can use PageMaker's low-resolution and scanning capabilities to plan documents containing complex color graphics, as did Steven Brown, the designer of the brochure excerpted on this plate. In the text boxes of this excerpt, Brown explains how he integrated PageMaker, Illustrator, and Photoshop to complete the project. He did this job on a Power Mac 8100/80 with 48MB of RAM and a 1250MB disk drive.

Did you know?

How I Produced This Color Brochure

To produce the admissions brochure that this two-page spread comes from, I did preliminary planning in PageMaker using low-resolution scans and text. Once the client approved the layout, the file was exported as an EPS and placed into Adobe Illustrator where the layout of photos, elements, columns, and margins can be traced using the various vector tools. I like using these techniques for organizing and laying out large Photoshop files.

In Illustrator, I copied the paths to the Clipboard and pasted them as "paths" (not "pixels") into Photoshop. When copying paths, keep in mind that you can copy just what you need for particular tasks. When you transform photos, paths are very useful for alignment and placement. Paths can also be converted to selections and then saved as channels.

I did all shadows using channel operations. I prefer not having all four colors make up my shadow, so I added the opacity of the shadow to the black channel only. The photo channels were composited into one generic channel and duplicated out as a separate file and relinked into a PageMaker file for the varnish plate.

Byline: *Steven Brown*
Instructor
Graphic Design & Visual
Communication Program
UC Santa Barbara
805.893.3789
brown@id.ucsb.edu

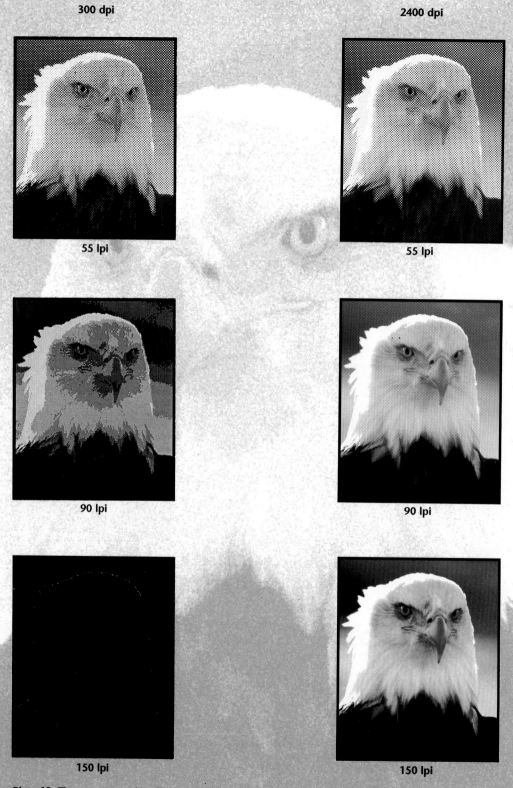

300 dpi

2400 dpi

55 lpi

55 lpi

90 lpi

90 lpi

150 lpi

150 lpi

Plate 13: These are examples of images printed at various line screens and resolutions. You'll often need to adjust line screens and resolutions to improve image quality on various paper types. Soft, uncoated paper, for example, requires loose screens. Coated paper holds screens better, so you can use higher line screens and achieve greater detail and more shades of gray.

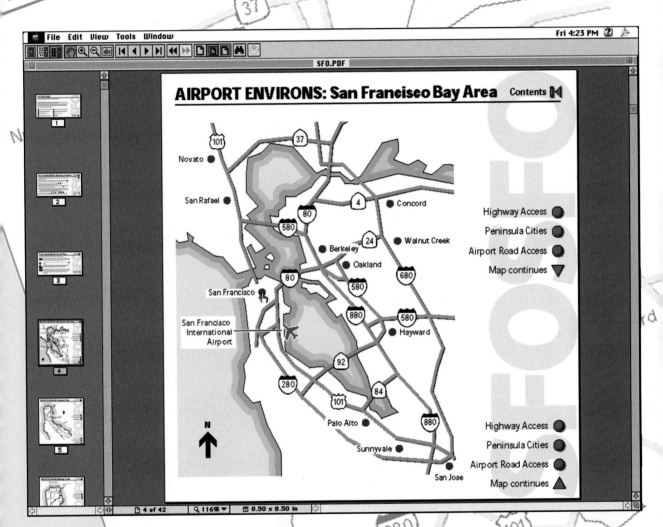

Plate 14: PageMaker's Create Adobe PDF command allows you to create portable document files from your PageMaker documents. PDF documents are hypertext documents meant to be viewed on-line. You can also use the PDF format for printing on demand.

Plate 15: PageMaker's HTML Author Plug-in allows you to create World Wide Web pages from PageMaker documents. This example shows Bill's home page, which you can see for yourself with a Web browser on the Internet at: http://www.west.net/~bharrel/. Web pages are hypertext documents that allow you to create links to any other document on the Web.

Continued line text blocks are not linked to their adjacent text blocks in any way, so if the text block moves, or if the text block they reference moves, the continued line is not automatically updated. You will have to change the reference page number manually or delete the continued line text block, if necessary.

Balance Columns

This simple Plug-in, shown in Figure 11-2, is meant to save you the trouble (if you find this sort of thing troubling) of figuring out how to get the tops or bottoms of side-by-side columns even. To use the Plug-in, select any number of side-by-side text blocks (with the Pointer tool), choose the Balance Columns Plug-in, and then select among the Alignment and Add leftover lines options. When you click OK, PageMaker will balance the columns.

Figure 11-2:
The Balance Columns Plug-in evens up columns in your layout.

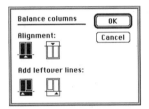

Build Booklet

Perhaps the most sophisticated of the Adobe-provided Plug-ins, Build Booklet is nothing less than a miniature version of the Adobe $2,000 PressWise page imposition program. Imposition, for those of you who didn't complete your printing apprenticeships, is the process of arranging the pages of a publication into signatures so that when printed, folded, and bound, the pages will wind up in the correct order. (An in-depth look at Adobe PressWise is included in Chapter 14.)

In order to use the Build Booklet Plug-in, which is shown in Figure 11-3, you need to know how your publication will be printed, folded, and bound. This can range anywhere from a relatively simple procedure where you fold all the pages in half and then put a staple through them, to a much more complex procedure (which would normally be done by your printer) where 4-, 8-, or 16-page spreads are created, folded, cut, and perfect bound. You can usually get this information from your print shop.

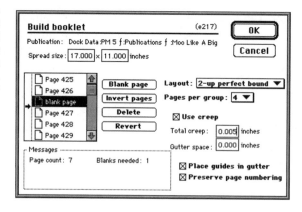

Figure 11-3:
Use the Build Booklet
Plug-in to impose the
pages in a publication
into signatures.

The benefit of electronic imposition, not surprisingly, is that it makes manual imposition unnecessary. Manual imposition is a difficult, slow, and expensive task — but one that is necessary in order to produce most multipage publications. You might have never heard of imposition before, even if you regularly create long documents, but that doesn't mean you haven't been paying for it. By imposing your own publications *before* they are imageset, you will probably be able to save considerable sums of money on your printing bill. Of course, to do this, you *must* talk to your printer and enter the correct imposition options or else you will make things worse instead of better and spend more money, not less.

Because the Build Booklet Plug-in cannot impose pages on more than one publication (it ignores any book list you may have created), you will not be able to use it to impose longer and more-complex publications. In that case, you should ask your service bureau or printer to use PageMaker PressWise to impose your electronic files before they are imageset.

Preparing to Use Build Booklet

The Build Booklet Plug-in automatically creates a copy of the current publication when it is run, and it then performs the imposition in this copy. This leaves your original file untouched, but it means that you must be completely finished with your publication before performing the imposition. You should finish all final text and page editing and create your index and table of contents, if necessary, before using the Build Booklet Plug-in. It is also a good idea to save your publication before choosing the Build Booklet Plug-in, and make sure that your hard drive has plenty of free space (usually an amount equal to twice the size of the publication is sufficient).

Build Booklet Options

The first option in the Build Booklet Plug-in is Spread size, which refers to the total size of your imposed pages. This will usually be two, three, or four times the size of each individual publication page. This Spread size option is automatically adjusted when the

Layout option is changed, but you may want to make further adjustments to provide room for crop marks or other items. Remember, the largest page size that PageMaker can support is 42 inches by 42 inches, and that is therefore the largest Spread size that it can support.

The scrolling page list provides a single page icon for every page in the current publication. You can rearrange the page order in this list by holding down the Option key and dragging a page to a new position. (Use the Shift key to select more than one page at a time for any manipulation.) You can also insert blank pages, leaving space for pages that will be manually pasted in later, or you can delete pages so that they will not be included in the imposed signatures.

The Layout option is the most important, defining the specific way that the Build Booklet Plug-in will rearrange your pages. The None option is used when you want to make a copy of the current publication without automatically imposing any pages (perhaps so that you can manually rearrange pages or change the spread size).

Three other binding styles are offered by the Layout option:

- **Saddle stitch.** A saddle stitch is the kind of binding you find in most magazines: The pages are folded over and stapled or sewn together at the spine. This is also the kind of binding most often used for office phone directories and other small business booklets.

   Saddle stitching is best used in smaller publications — perhaps fewer than 25 pages — because the thickness of the paper itself becomes an issue when folding a larger number of pages. The Use creep option, discussed below, can help in this situation, but in larger publications it will be necessary to use perfect binding.

- **Perfect binding.** This is the kind of binding you find most frequently in books: The pages are glued together into the spine.

- **Consecutive binding.** The consecutive binding puts two, three, or four pages together onto new, larger pages to save paper or film during imagesetting. In some cases, this repositioning can also be used to create multipanel brochure folds.

Another option in the Build Booklet dialog box lets you add and specify creep, which is compensation added to the space between two pages that makes up for the thickness of your paper and the effect this paper thickness has on the bound publication. You can see the need for creep yourself by taking 30 or 40 sheets of paper and folding them in half — the ends of the folded papers will be fanned, and not flush, because the outside sheets must travel further (around the thickness of the inside sheets) than the inside sheets. If this paper thickness is not accounted for when pages are positioned, the pages in a bound publication will gradually creep in and out as you move from the outside of the publication toward the center and then back to the outside. Creep values should be provided to you by your printer. The Gutter space option is more direct, adding space between pages in the signature. This directly affects the spread size and is applied equally to all pages in the publication.

Bullets and Numbering

This Plug-in inserts a bullet character or a number, and a tab, at the start of some specified number of paragraphs. To use the Plug-in, set the text cursor in the first paragraph you want to bullet or number and then choose the Bullets & Numbering Plug-in. Five different bullet character options appear by default, but you can select any character from any available font to use as a bullet by clicking the Edit... button. To add numbers instead of bullets, click the Numbers button and choose between the various numbering schemes.

The Range option lets you specify the paragraphs to which your bullets or numbers will be applied. Your alternatives are any number of sequential paragraphs, paragraphs formatted with a particular style sheet, every paragraph in the story, or selected paragraphs. When you click OK, the Plug-in moves through each specified paragraph, adding the appropriate bullet or number and then entering a tab character. The new bullets or numbers are automatically set at the same type size and leading as the paragraph into which they are placed. Figures 11-4 and 11-5 show the options you have in choosing bullets or numbers.

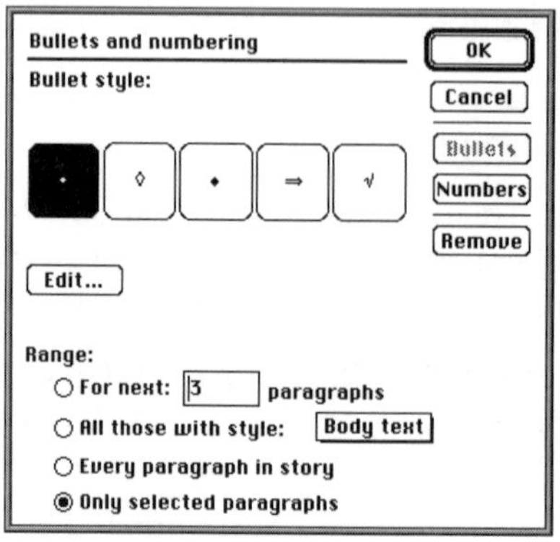

Figure 11-4:
The Bullets and Numbering Plug-in lets you select several types of bullets.

Figure 11-5:
The Bullets and Numbering
Plug-in lets you select among
several numbering styles.

Figure 11-5:
The Bullets and Numbering
Plug-in lets you select among
several numbering styles.

Bullets and numbering

OK

Numbering style:
- ● Arabic numeral 1,2,3...
- ○ Upper roman I,II,III...
- ○ Lower roman i,ii,iii...
- ○ Upper alphabetic A,B,C...
- ○ Lower alphabetic a,b,c...

Cancel

Bullets

Numbers

Separator: None

Remove

Start at: 1

Range:
- ● For next: 3 paragraphs
- ○ All those with style: Body text
- ○ Every paragraph in story
- ○ Only selected paragraphs

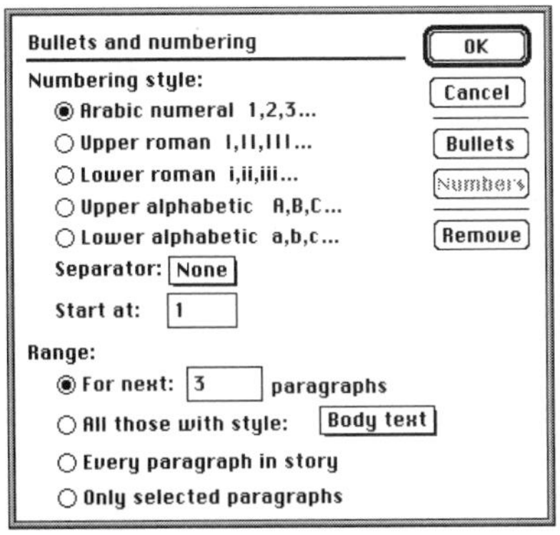

Create Color Library

This Plug-in helps you keep colors uniform between publications. This can be handy when you do lots of work for a specific client, project, or company and want to maintain color consistency. When run, the Plug-in skims through the open publication and creates a new color library that includes all of the colors in the publication. This color library can then be imported into other publications to ensure that the exact same colors are used. Figure 11-6 shows the Create Color Library dialog box.

Figure 11-6:
The Create Color Library
dialog box

Create Color Library

Library name: Medical Brochure

Save

File name: Custom.bcf

Cancel

Preferences

Colors per 5

Save as...

Colors per row: 3

Notes:

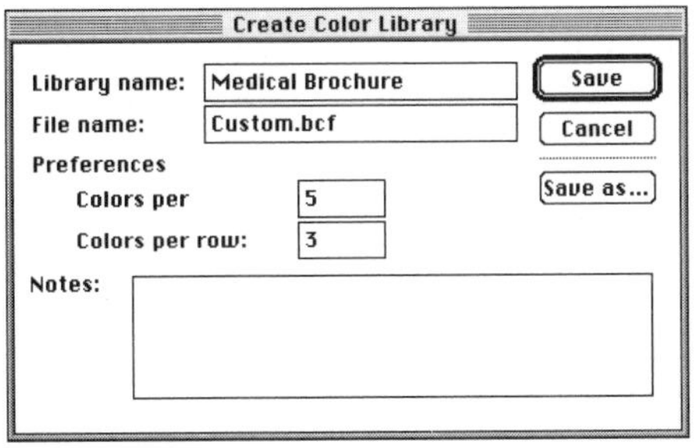

From here, you can name a color library, give it a filename, and define the number of columns and rows it should contain. Once the library is defined, you access it through the Libraries submenu in the Edit Color dialog box, as discussed in Chapter 10.

Drop Cap

This Plug-in creates a drop cap in the selected paragraph by enlarging the type size of the first letter in the paragraph and then lowering the baseline of that character so that it sits on the same baseline as the second or third line in the paragraph, depending on the option you select. Then, the Plug-in inserts tabs and line breaks to wrap the text in the second and third lines manually around the newly positioned drop cap. Not elegant in any way, but ultimately effective. Figure 11-7 shows a drop cap created with the Plug-in.

By 1991, VIA 1.618 employed more than 200 people includ ing 22 designers in its manufac- turing and design center just outside of Milan. We have also opened a wood products manufacturing facility in Karlskrona, Sweden, which employs the 27 craftsmen who fabricate our popular lines of pine, ash and juniper furniture.

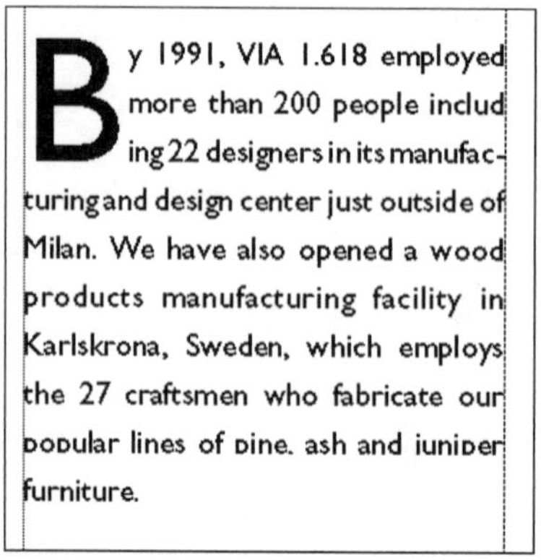

Figure 11-7: An example of a three-line drop cap created with the Drop Cap Plug-in

Beyond specifying the size of the drop cap you want to create, the Plug-in, shown in Figure 11-8, also allows you to jump to the previous or next paragraph in the story in order to apply drop caps there (although consecutive drop caps are rarely a wise decision), and it gives you a Remove button that will undo all of the smoke-and-mirrors formatting that makes the drop cap illusion work in the first place. This is important because if you have to edit the text in the first few lines of any paragraph where you have created a drop cap, you'll find that the text formatting becomes a terrible mess if you don't first remove the drop cap, then perform your editing, and then re-create the drop cap.

Drop cap
Drop cap
Size: 3 lines
Apply
Remove
Go to paragraph
Prev
Next
OK
Cancel

Figure 11-8: The Drop Cap Plug-in dialog box

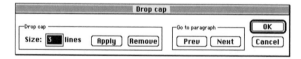

Old-Fashioned Drop Caps: An old PageMaker trick for creating drop caps can still be useful even now that the Drop Cap Plug-in is available. This trick calls for placing a graphic as your drop cap character and then using the Text Wrap feature, located on the Element menu, to make it look like a drop cap. See Figure 11-9 for an illustration.

There are three ways to get your drop cap character. Number one: Import a pre-made drop cap from a clip-art collection. A number of companies produce ornate alphabet clip-art just for this purpose. Number two: Produce your own drop cap art in your

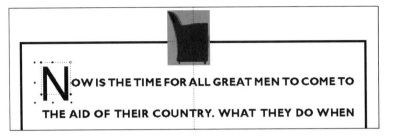

favorite graphics application. Number three: Turn a letter in your PageMaker file into a graphic and use that as a drop cap. To do this, you'll need nothing more than the Scrapbook desk accessory. (And you thought there was no real use for the Scrapbook, didn't you?)

STEPS:	**Creating a Drop Cap**
Step 1.	Cut the first letter of the paragraph to which you want to add a drop cap to the Clipboard.
Step 2.	Open the Scrapbook and paste the letter in as the first item in the Scrapbook.
Step 3.	Now, close the Scrapbook, choose the Pointer tool, and choose the Place command.
Step 4.	Select the Scrapbook file (it is usually found in your System Folder) and click OK in the Place dialog box.
Step 5.	The loaded placement cursor appears with the scrapbook icon. Position it roughly over the paragraph into which you want to insert the drop cap and click. You'll then have to choose the Pointer tool from the tool palette to get rid of the placement icon so that you don't place other graphics from your scrapbook.
Step 6.	Manually reposition and resize the drop cap graphic, as necessary.
Step 7.	Select the drop cap graphic and choose the Text Wrap command from the Element menu. Choose the center wrap option and click OK.
Step 8.	Customize the graphic boundary that controls the text wrap as necessary to get the look you want for your drop cap.

EPS Font Scanner

This nifty little utility scans the EPS graphics in your layout to make sure that there are no fonts used in them for which there are no screen font equivalents installed on your Mac. As you probably already know, the fonts may not print properly if there are no corresponding screen fonts available. You'll find this option partcularly useful if you use graphics originating on other computers in your layouts.

To use this Plug-in, follow this procedure: Select EPS Font Scanner from the PageMaker Plug-ins submenu. In the ensuing dialog box, click the On radio button, then click OK. Now print the document as you normally would. If the scanner finds fonts that are missing, a warning dialog box appears providing two options: Print Anyway or Do Not Print. If you want to stop and install the fonts before printing, click Do Not Print.

Guide Manager

Dragging multiple guides into a publication to set up a grid can be a time-consuming project, especially when you're working with multiple master pages. The Guide Manager Plug-in, shown in Figure 11-10, allows you to set guides and grids all at once. You can also save guide layouts for use in multiple documents.

Figure 11-10:
The Guide Manager
dialog box

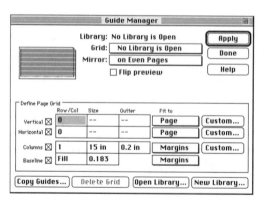

This powerful dialog box allows you to set up margin, column, and ruler guides by specifying values in the corresponding option boxes. You can also copy (by clicking the Copy Guides... button) and save the guides from an existing page, which means if you manually layout a grid you like, you can save it for later use in other publications. Guide layouts are kept in libraries that you save and name similarly to PageMaker's object libraries and color libraries. To start a new library, click New Library...; to open an existing library, click Open Library....

When you click on the Apply button, the Apply Guides to Page dialog box, shown in Figure 11-11, appears, allowing you to modify further the application of the new guides. From here, you can delete existing guides, determine which pages to apply the new guide layout and which, if any, master pages to assign the new guides. The Done button in Guide Manager saves the work you do in Guide Manager without applying the changes. Use this button to create and manage guide libraries.

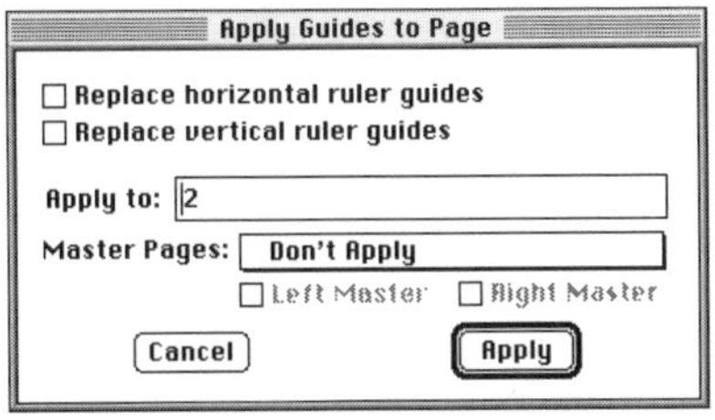

Figure 11-11:
The Apply Guides to Page
dialog box

Keyline

Called Create Keyline in Version 5, this Plug-in creates a box, or keyline, around text or graphic objects in your publication. This can be done as a design element or to trap the colors in adjacent objects. Using the Plug-in, which is shown in Figure 11-12, automates the manual process of creating boxes with the Rectangle tool and, of course, adds a level of precision that would be difficult for you to duplicate by hand. The Plug-in provides three primary options (Bring keyline to front of object, Send keyline behind object, and Knock out under keyline), plus the ability to set attributes for your keyline using the Fill and Line dialog box.

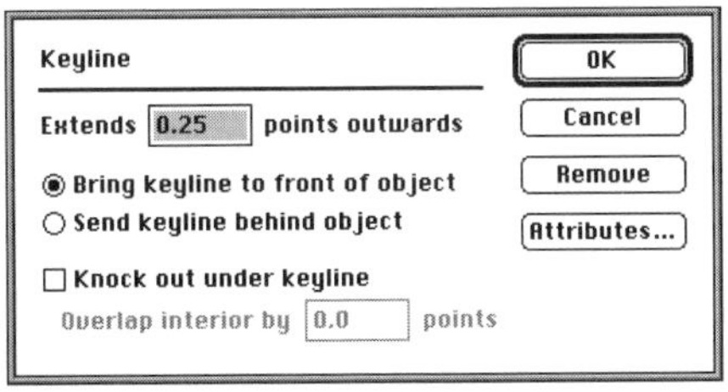

Figure 11-12:
The Keyline Plug-in

As shown in Figure 11-13, the options in the Keyline Plug-in dialog box let you define the positioning of the keyline relative to the outer boundary of the elements (this value can be positive in increments of $\frac{1}{100}$ point), whether the keyline object will be positioned in front of or behind the existing object, and the ability to knock out the keyline and define an overlap (trap) to that knockout. Clicking the Attributes button allows you to set line and fill options for your keyline box.

Figure 11-13:
The Keyline Plug-in allows you to stroke (trap) or knock out colored objects.

Keyline

Extends 0.25 points outwards

⦿ Bring keyline to front of object
○ Send keyline behind object

☒ Knock out under keyline
Overlap interior by 0.1 points

OK
Cancel
Remove
Attributes...

Open Template

This Plug-in, too, is more interesting for the capabilities it suggests than for those it actually delivers. The Open template dialog box, shown in Figure 11-14, enables you to create new publications (complete with custom page sizes, guidelines, and placeholder text, for 17 "popular" document types) by running scripts written in the PageMaker scripting language that describe the document to be created. The potential power in this is that by saving publications in the form of scripts instead of in the form of PageMaker publication files, you get publications that are much smaller, easier to transport, and easier to customize—if you know the PageMaker scripting language, that is.

Figure 11-14:
The Open Template Plug-in dialog box lists the scripted templates you can use to create publications.

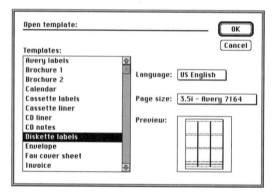

Open template:

OK
Cancel

Templates:
Avery labels
Brochure 1
Brochure 2
Calendar
Cassette labels
Cassette liner
CD liner
CD notes
Diskette labels
Envelope
Fax cover sheet
Invoice

Language: US English

Page size: 3.5i – Avery 7164

Preview:

Unfortunately, you cannot save your publications as this kind of template. The Template option offered by the Save As (File menu) command creates the same kind of template used in earlier versions of PageMaker, which is more like the Stationary Pad documents offered in System 7. In other words, you save a normal PageMaker document that, when opened, makes a copy of itself for you to modify.

Since you cannot create your own "scripted templates," you're left with the 17 that PageMaker has provided. These templates are stored in the Templates folder, inside the Plug-ins folder in the RSRC folder. These are mildly (very mildly) interesting, not particularly well implemented, and may save you a few minutes if you happen to need a publication exactly like one of the templates. In the future, someone will probably release a Plug-in that lets you save your publication in this "scripted template" format and maybe even a nice on-screen text editor that lets you modify these scripted templates before you open them. Until then, we're stuck with these.

Pub Info

Previously named Display Pub Info, this Plug-in, shown in Figure 11-15, is designed to prevent problems at your service bureau by providing you with a complete list of the fonts used in your publication, the availability of those fonts in your System Software, and any linked elements in the file. Also, it produces a list of the style sheets you've used. You can review the publication information on screen and save it to a text file to give to your service bureau along with your publication file. Or you can print the text file (using your word processor) and hand it to the service bureau when you place your output order.

Figure 11-15:
The Pub Info Plug-in dialog box displays useful information about your publication.

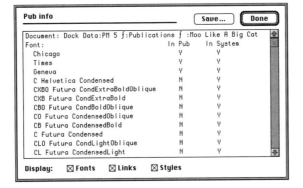

Running Headers and Footers

This Plug-in performs the fairly complex and useful task of creating unique running headers or footers for all of the pages in your publication based on some specific text on each page or text you create. It is a good example of automating an otherwise endlessly repetitive task, and it provides a range of options that allow you to create running headers and footers to suit even the most complex needs. Figure 11-16 shows the dialog box.

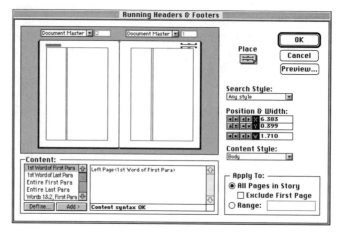

Figure 11-16:
The Running Headers
& Footers dialog box
automates creating
running headers and
footers from page
to page.

To use this Plug-in, you must first select, with the Pointer tool, a story that is threaded across all of the pages of your publication, or at least all of the pages where you want to apply headers and footers. Then, choose the Plug-in from the PageMaker Plug-ins submenu.

STEPS: Creating Running Headers and Footers

Step 1.   Above the pages in the preview area, select the page or Master page where you want the header and/or footer displayed.

Step 2.   Drag a set of window shade handles from the Place option to the point where you want the header or footer to appear in the preview window.

Step 3.   Use the options under Position and Width to place the placeholder window shade handles precisely. (The postions are relative to the zero intersection point, as you learned in Chapter 4.)

Step 4.   From the Content Style option, select the style sheet to apply to the header and/or footer. (It's a good idea to create header and footer style sheets in advance.)

Step 5.   Under the Apply To option, select a page range. You can use the same specifications for selecting page ranges available when printing a document, as discussed in Chapter 13.

Step 6.   Repeat steps 1 through 5 until all desired headers and footers are placed.

There are two ways to define the content of headers and footers: Type the content in the text field under Content or select one of the options in the scrolling list. You can use one or the other or a combination of both. The method you should use depends on the type of publication. Some directories and catalogs, for example, use the first and last entries in a text block to define header text. In these cases, you would use the options in the scrolling list, such as: *1st Word First Para* for the left header and *1st Word Last Para* in the right header.

You would use a combination of both options when you need both consistent and dynamic text to appear at the same time, such as *Section 5: Using the Print Command*. In this example, *Section 5* is the text entered manually, and *Using the Print Command* is the dynamic text gleaned from the first paragraph.

This is a complex Plug-in with a lot of power. You can get a preview of your work at any point by clicking the Preview button, which brings up the Preview dialog box shown in Figure 11-17. From here, you can zoom in and out on your page, select specific pages to preview, and jump between headers and footers by clicking the corresponding buttons.

Figure 11-17:
The Preview dialog box allows you to see the work as you define running headers and footers.

The running headers and footers this Plug-in creates are not linked to the text in your publication, and so they are not automatically updated to reflect any changes in the content or placement of your text. This means that you should not run this Plug-in until the body of your publication is complete, or if you do run it earlier, rerun it to collect the final correct data just before you save your finished publication before printing.

Update PPD

Basically, this Plug-in updates or creates a custom PostScript Printer Description (PPD) file for your printer. (PPDs are discussed in Chapter 13.) When you choose this Plug-in from the PageMaker Plug-ins submenu, the Plug-in first searches for the active printer connected to your Mac and gathers information about it from the Printers ROM. It then matches the printer to the appropriate PPD on your hard disk. Once this procedure is finished, the Update/customize PPD for: dialog box appears, as shown in Figure 11-18.

Figure 11-18:
The Update/customize PPD for: dialog box allows you to create custom PPDs or update existing ones.

Update/customize PPD for:	Update
	Cancel
Current printer: microLaser Pro	Options...
Printer model: microLaser Pro v2013.110	
Select PPD: TI microLaser Pro 600 L2 PS65	

If no PPD exists for your printer, PageMaker allows you to create a new one. Clicking the Options... button in the dialog box allows you to customize the information included in the PPD, as shown in Figure 11-19. As you can see from the Update PPD options... dialog box, you can include page sizes, font information, and the printer time-out interval from this Update PPD option dialog box. When you click Update from the Update/customize PPD for... dialog box, the PPD is updated or a new one is created.

Figure 11-19:
The Update PPD options... dialog box

Update PPD options...   OK

Cancel

☒ US page sizes
☐ European page sizes
☒ Max Page size
☒ Include fonts on the printer's hard disk
☐ Include fonts in printer's RAM

Give up waiting for printer to respond after :
○ 30 Seconds   ● 2 Minutes   ○ 5 Minutes

Third-Party Plug-ins

Using PageMaker 5 Plug-ins with PageMaker 6: At press time, the vendors listed in this section had not yet finished planning their PageMaker 6 Plug-ins. The list given here contains PageMaker 5 Plug-ins. The good news is that all of them should work with PageMaker 6. All you do after installation is drag them from the Aldus folder in the System Folder to the Plug-ins folder inside the RSRC folder in the Adobe PageMaker 6 folder.

In the long run, it will be third-party Plug-ins that make or break PageMaker Plug-ins technology. Remember, the idea behind Plug-ins is that they free PageMaker programmers to spend their time adding core features to the product and allow third parties to add specialized or vertical market features. So what have those third-party companies produced so far? The following is a look at a few of the best third-party Plug-ins products that were either shipping or in development when PageMaker 6 itself was released (August 1995).

Getting more Plug-in information: Undoubtedly, more Plug-ins will be available in the months and years ahead. To get a complete list of current PageMaker Plug-ins, call the Adobe Plug-ins Hotline (800-685-3547) or the Adobe Plug-in Source (206-489-3446). Both clearinghouses will be happy to send you a complete list of Plug-ins or catalogs at no charge.

PageTools

Extensis Corporation
(503) 274-2020

PageTools is a collection of Plug-ins that allow you to work faster and more efficiently in PageMaker. Adobe previously bundled this collection with PageMaker 5, but alas, now you'll have to buy them. One of the more interesting Plug-ins is PageBars, which adds a Word-like tool bar to the publication window. From the tool bar you can click to configure text and paragraphs, add tabs and indents, and easily open other Plug-ins.

Also interesting is PagePrinter, which allows you to see thumbnails of each page in your document to select specific ones for printing. This is handy when you don't want to print an entire document. This is a superb collection of utilities.

UPC-EAN BarCode, POSTNET Bar Code

Azalea Software
(206) 937-5919

If you need postal bar codes for your business or publishing work, these Plug-ins from Azalea will be a welcomed addition. (No pun intended.) They create EPS format bar codes for product labeling or postal sorting and place them into your publications. The Azalea UPC-EAN BarCode Plug-in creates version A, version E, EAN-8, EAN-13, and ISBN bar code symbols in an EPS format that can be put into the design. The POSTNET bar code Plug-in creates the kind of bar code that encodes ZIP codes on mail, saving you time and money, especially when creating business reply mail pieces. Finally, if these Plug-ins don't satisfy your bar code needs, you can also contact Azalea and buy a bar code font that lets you create bar codes in any Macintosh application.

Sundae Software

(800) 398-5050

Several separate Plug-ins are currently available from Sundae Software. Here's a quick rundown:

- ☞ **Baseline Grid** sets up a grid on a selected box on your page, which is an ideal way to keep track of the contents, orientation, and spacing of your text, much in the way ruled paper does. More importantly it also creates a baseline that keeps all columns perfectly lined up with each other. The dialog box provides a plethora of choices regarding the placement and spacing of the lines. Once I had completed placing all my text and graphics, I could remove the baselines altogether. PageMaker supposedly has a process for creating baselines, but it was so convoluted — a detailed process that involved traversing four dialog boxes repeatedly — that we could never get it to work as well as this $29 Plug-in.

- ☞ **Gridzoid** is best for creating forms or templates for items such as labels. It creates a rectangular grid on which you can place any number of evenly spaced horizontal and vertical lines. You enter the dimensions of the rectangle as well as the number of horizontal and vertical lines you want within the grid. You can't space out the lines unevenly in the dialog box, although lines can be deleted or added in the grid that this $39 Plug-in creates.

- ☞ **Safari** goes further down the path of grid complexity. It can create uneven grids or remove all gridlines from a publication at once. This Plug-in will create gridlines, horizontally and/or vertically around all objects or around selected objects in a publication. You can place or remove vertical and horizontal guides separately or work on both kinds of guides at once.

- ☞ **Marksmaker** is a must for anyone doing more than basic work with service bureaus. This $79 Plug-in places printer's marks, including crop and registration marks, guides, and color ramps on film for printing. Although PageMaker itself performs these functions also, it still doesn't recognize that film sheets rarely, if ever, correspond exactly to a publication's pages. Marksmaker lays out the pages of the publication onto the specified sheet of film, saving setup charges for users and time for service bureaus.

PMproKit

EDCO Services
(813) 962-7800, (800) 523-8973

This $149 collection offers seven well-implemented Plug-ins (a few of them were intended for PageMaker 4.2 and 5 and offer features now included in PageMaker 6, but the remaining capabilities are well worth the package cost):

- ☞ **Distort Type.** This Plug-in quickly expands or condenses selected type to the width of another type size. You can then, for example, set type that is 18 points high but only 15 points wide.

- ☞ **Kerning Pairs.** This kerning tool lets you add, delete, and modify automatic kern pairs while in PageMaker. The kern pairs take effect immediately and can be saved as part of the screen font.

- ☞ **Rotate & Merge Text.** You can select text and a horizontal or vertical line; the text will be condensed or stretched to fit the length of the rule and moved to the line. If you select a vertical rule, the text is rotated.

- ☞ **Pica Gauge.** Allows you to move any object, including text blocks, to any position within the page; or to reduce, enlarge, or distort the object to an exact size.

- ☞ **Set Up Columns.** Provides three options for setting up column guides: number of columns, relationship of columns to each other, and absolute column width.

- ☞ **Ruler.** Allows you to draw horizontal, vertical, or grid-pattern sets of rules.

- ☞ **Tab Text.** Establishes tab settings based on the width of the text lines, based on the longest text line in each column.

Figure 11-20 shows two of the features.

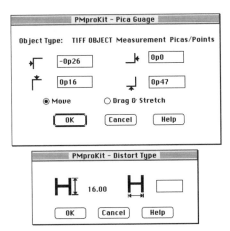

Figure 11-20:
Distort Type and Pica Gauge
Plug-ins from EDCO Services'
PMProKit Plug-ins

Framz Proportional Borders

ShadeTree Marketing
(602) 279-3713, (800) 678-8848

This $99 Plug-in provides a set of 101 stylized borders that you can place around any text block or graphic element in your publication. (See Figure 11-21 for a sample.) Many of the available frames are based on straight-line or box patterns, but there are also a few whimsical frames, such as running feet. If the default set of 100 borders is not enough for you, a second set of 100 frames is also available.

Figure 11-21:
The Framz Plug-in provides 100 fancy borders to include around layout options.

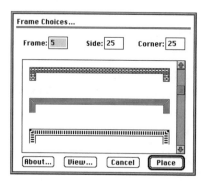

Summary

↝ PageMaker Plug-ins make PageMaker extensible, allowing third parties or end users to add new automation, features, and capabilities to suit their needs.

↝ There are three kinds of Plug-ins. Loadable Plug-ins are written in the C programming language, are placed in the Plug-ins folder inside the RSRC folder in the Adobe PageMaker 6.0 folder, and appear in the PageMaker Plug-ins submenu. Scripts are simple command sequences that work much like macros or HyperCard scripts to drive PageMaker commands and options. Stand-alone applications can also run as Plug-ins using inter-application communications to send commands and queries to PageMaker.

↝ More than 20 loadable Plug-ins are provided with PageMaker 6. Many of these are minor and unimportant, but several provide great capabilities, including Build Booklet, Running Headers and Footers, Edit Tracks, and Printer Styles.

↝ New Plug-ins from third-party companies should prove to be the real benefit of PageMaker Plug-ins technology. You can get a catalog of all currently available third-party Plug-ins by calling the Adobe Plug-ins Hotline at 800-685-3547.

Creating Long Documents

CHAPTER 12

In This Chapter

- ➤ Using the Book command to link multiple publications
- ➤ Creating a table of contents
- ➤ Indexing your publications
- ➤ Managing externally stored files

T he vast majority of PageMaker's capabilities work equally well on any kind of publication, from advertisements, to brochures, to newsletters, to magazines, to catalogs, to newspapers, to books. Longer documents frequently include textual components not encountered in shorter ones, such as tables of contents and indices. The real challenges longer documents present to the writer, however, concern the management of externally stored text and graphic files. We deal with both of these kinds of challenges in this chapter.

The Book Command

The core of PageMaker's long document capabilities is the Book. . . command (Utilities menu), which allows you to create logical connections among separate PageMaker files. Once you do this, you can index, create a table of contents, or print multiple PageMaker files as if they were one large document. This means that you don't have to create long documents as a single PageMaker file; instead you can break them down into a series of more natural and manageable documents while retaining the ability to perform operations across all parts of the final publication at once.

Specifically, you use the Book... command to create an ordered list, called the *book list*, of the PageMaker files associated with your final document. Then, when you use the Create Index..., Create TOC..., or Print... commands, you can apply them to all of the files in your book list at once. (From here on we'll use the word "book" to refer to the final document, but it could be any large document that spans more than one PageMaker file — including technical documentation, magazines, or anything else.)

How to Build a Book List

To build a book list, choose the Book... command from the Utilities menu. The Book publication list dialog box shown in Figure 12-1 then appears. On the left side of this dialog box is a list of the folders and files on your hard drive, and on the right side is the publication's book list. Files in the book list appear in the order in which they will be printed, indexed, and added to the table of contents. If you are using the auto renumbering option in Document Setup, the order of your book list also affects your page numbering.

Figure 12-1:
The Book publication list
dialog box

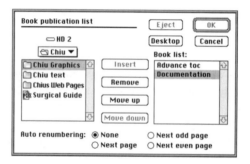

To add a PageMaker publication to the book list, locate it in the left window and select its filename (use the Desktop button and folder bar to navigate your drives, if necessary). Then click the Insert button or double-click the filename. The selected publication will then appear in the book list. Normally the last file in the book list is selected automatically, so new files are added to the end of the book list. If you want to add a new file to a specific location in the book list, select the file just above where you want the new publication to appear before you click the Insert button. Continue selecting files from your hard drive and adding them with the Insert button until you have completed your book list.

If any files accidentally get added in the wrong order, or if the order in which you plan to use the files changes, you can rearrange the list by selecting a filename in the Book list and then clicking the Move up or Move down button. You can also delete files from the book list using the Remove button. It is very common to have to remove files from the book list and then replace them with newer versions of those files that have slightly different filenames.

You control how your book's pages are numbered with Auto renumbering. If you choose None, the pages in each section of your book retain their original page numbers. Next page tells PageMaker to begin numbering the next section with the next number after the preceding section. In other words, the first section ends on page 30, the next section will begin on page 31. Next odd page tells PageMaker to begin numbering with the next available odd number, inserting blank pages where necessary to do so. Next even page works in the same manner.

When the book list presented on the right side of the dialog box is correct, click the OK button to close the Book publication list dialog box and save the book list. You can now use the Create Index..., Create TOC..., or Print entire book option, and all publications in your book list will be affected. Details on using each of these commands across multiple publications are provided later in this chapter.

When to Build a Book List

Since the Create Index..., Create TOC..., and Print... commands (when used on multiple publications) are all dependent on the book list, it is important to decide in which publication you will create your book list. Generally you'll need to create it in the publication in which you intend to lay out your index or table of contents, or in the publication from which you want to print all of the files in your book. Your index and table of contents are not likely to be in the same publication, although it is likely that you will print from the file containing the table of contents, so you'll have to create the book list at least twice if your publication has both an index and a table of contents (or use Cut and Paste). If you want to use the book-printing feature from a chapter other than the one containing the table of contents, then you may need to create the book list a third time as well.

Assigning the book list to all publications in the book list: Once you create your book list, you can send it to each of the other publications in the book list. To do this, hold down the Command key and choose the Book... command. A dialog box appears, documenting progress as the list is transferred into each publication. If any of these publications have existing book lists, they are overwritten by this process without warning. When the transfer is complete, the Book publication list dialog box appears, at which point the book lists are synchronized and you can close the dialog box by clicking OK or Cancel.

Exporting the book list to all of the publications in your list allows you to build a table of contents in any publication (although you'll usually only want to do this in one specific publication) and use the Print entire book option from any file in the book. Most importantly it is vital to the process of creating a complete index.

Since book lists are not automatically sent to every publication in the book list, there are a few book list tricks you can do. For example, you can use one file in many different book lists — let's say it's a one-page disclaimer that you include in all your publications. It doesn't matter if that same file is included in the book lists of 10 different publications, it will always be included in the table of contents, index, and book printing. You can also use the Book... command to chain-print a group of entirely unrelated publications. Do this by simply opening the first file you want to print and using the Book... command to build a book list of all the files you want to print. Then choose the Print... command and select the Print entire book option before clicking OK to begin printing.

Page Numbering in Long Documents

When printing the sequential publications in a book, you'll normally want PageMaker to renumber the pages of each publication automatically to reflect the count of pages in all preceding chapters. To do this, you must choose the Next page option in the Auto renumbering section in the Book publication list dialog box.

In some cases, however, you may not want to renumber every publication in your book automatically. You might want to number the opening pages sequentially using lower-case roman numerals, for example, and then begin pagination with page one in arabic numerals with the first page of the main text. To do this, set the page number style (using the Numbers... button in the Document Setup dialog box) to lowercase roman numerals in all of the files that contain pages placed prior to the main text (an introduction, preface, title page, etc.). Then in the first publication thereafter (the beginning of the main text), select the Restart page number option in the Document Setup dialog box, shown in Figure 12-2, and set the page number style option to standard numbering. You'll want to make sure that standard numbering is selected in all of the other files in the publication, too. Then choose the Auto renumbering option in the book list dialog box, and you're ready to print.

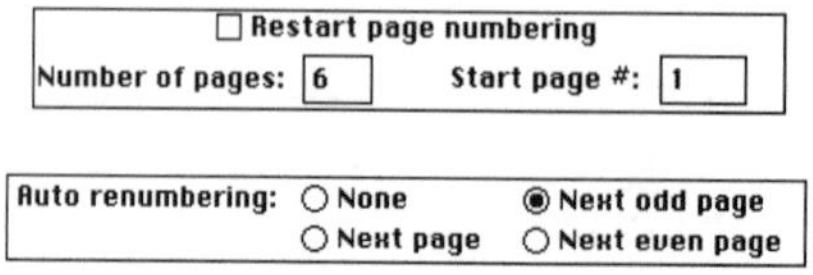

Figure 12-2:
The Restart page numbering option in the Document Setup dialog box and the Auto renumbering option in the Book publication list dialog box work together to let you create the proper page sequences for your publications.

☐ **Restart page numbering**

Number of pages: 6   Start page #: 1

Auto renumbering: ○ None   ● Next odd page
                    ○ Next page   ○ Next even page

Page Number Prefixes

If you want to include a prefix before the page numbers in the publications of your book — to indicate the book chapter or section — you can do so by typing the prefix in front of the page number placeholder on the master pages of each publication, as shown in Figure 12-3. This can be done in conjunction with the Restart page numbering option or independently. A book divided into chapters might have each page number in section one begin with the roman numeral I (as in I-1, I-2, etc.) and then have each page number in section two begin with the roman numeral II (as in II-17, II-18, etc.). Page numbering is discussed in Chapter 1.

Figure 12-3:
To add a prefix to a page number, simply type the desired text before the page number marker on master pages.

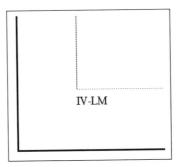

IV-LM

Alternatively, you might want the pages of your publications to be numbered without any prefix, but you find it useful to add a prefix to references to those pages when they appear in the index or table of contents. These prefixes may be chapter numbers, section numbers, issue numbers (in a compilation index of older publications), or any other identifying classification. To do this, open each publication, choose the Document Setup command, click the Numbers... button, and then in the Page Numbering dialog box enter the prefix you want to appear into the TOC and index prefix option, as shown in Figure 12-4. Save and close the publication.

Figure 12-4:
You can add index and table of contents prefixes through the Page Numbering dialog box nested in the Document Setup dialog box.

Page Numbering		OK
Style: ○ Arabic numeral	1, 2, 3, ...	Cancel
○ Upper Roman	I, II, III, ...	
◉ Lower Roman	i, ii, iii, ...	
○ Upper alphabetic	A, B, C, ... AA, BB, CC, ...	
○ Lower alphabetic	a, b, c, ... aa, bb, cc, ...	

TOC and index prefix: IV-

Table of Contents

In any document more than a few pages long, the table of contents is probably the most important page in the work. The table of contents provides your readers with a quick overview of your document, as well as help them to quickly locate sections of particular interest. You probably haven't seen too many magazines, newspapers, or nonfiction books that *didn't* include a table of contents. Even shorter documents such as newsletters and business reports can benefit from a table of contents: If you let your readers know "what's inside" and where specific information is located, they are far more likely to read the material than if they have to figure those things out for themselves. Yet many desktop publishers neglect to include this important feature, often because they assume constructing a table of contents would be too tedious.

In PageMaker, adding a table of contents is very easy. All you do is mark the text throughout your publication that you want included in the table of contents — usually paragraphs that are chapter names or major headlines — and then use the Create TOC... command to gather copies of these paragraphs together, along with the page numbers on which they are placed, into a new text story that you can position anywhere in your publication.

Marking TOC Paragraphs

To tell PageMaker that you want a specific paragraph included in your table of contents, position the text cursor in the paragraph, choose the Paragraph... command (⌘-M) from the Type menu, and select the Include in table of contents option in the Pagagraph Specifications dialog box, as shown in Figure 12-5. Click OK to close the dialog box. Then repeat this procedure to mark each paragraph in every publication in your book list that you want in the table of contents.

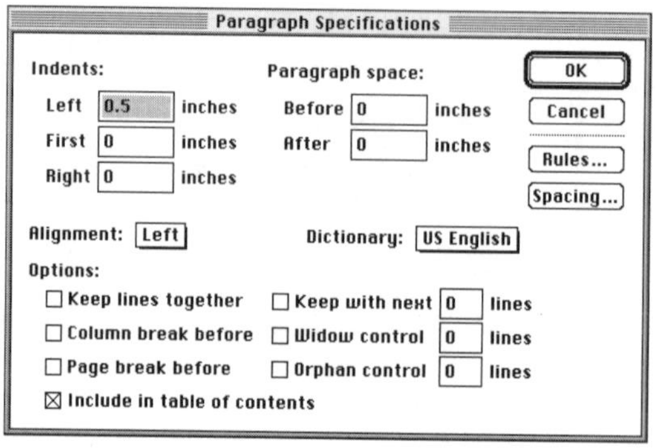

Figure 12-5:
You can use the Include in table of contents option in the Paragraph Specifications dialog box to mark paragraphs for inclusion in a table of contents.

Paragraph Specifications		
Indents:	Paragraph space:	OK
Left 0.5 inches	Before 0 inches	Cancel
First 0 inches	After 0 inches	
Right 0 inches		Rules...
		Spacing...
Alignment: Left	Dictionary: US English	

Options:
☐ Keep lines together   ☐ Keep with next 0 lines
☐ Column break before   ☐ Widow control 0 lines
☐ Page break before   ☐ Orphan control 0 lines
☒ Include in table of contents

If you use style sheets to format your documents (and after reading Chapter 7, who could resist?), you can build a good table of contents without manually setting this option in every paragraph: Just change the definitions of the style sheets used to format the paragraphs that should be in your table of contents (chapter titles and major headlines) so that the Include in table of contents option is selected in Paragraph Specifications.

To do this, choose the Define Styles command (⌘-3) and select the first style used to format paragraphs that should be in the table of contents. Click the Edit... button, then click the Para... button, then select the Include in table of contents option. Click OK twice to return to the Define Styles dialog box if you want to modify other style sheets, or hold down the Option key and click OK if you want to close all open dialog boxes and return to your publication window. Both dialog boxes are shown in Figure 12-6.

Figure 12-6:
The Define Styles and Edit Style
dialog box

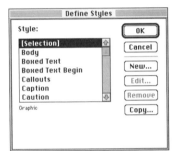

Of course, it is best to apply the Include in table of contents option in all appropriate paragraphs when the style sheets you use are first defined. This ensures that it will be applied correctly to all the different files that make up your book. If you have already formatted your entire book, however, and need to modify the style sheet definitions to add the Include in table of contents option, you only need to do this in one chapter and you can then move these updated style sheet definitions to all of the other chapters in your book. Do this by opening each publication, choosing the Define styles (⌘-3) command, and then using the Copy button to import the modified style sheets. Be sure to do this for each file in your book list or you will wind up missing the table of contents entries from the publications you forgot.

Generating a Table of Contents

After marking your table-of-contents entries, open the publication in which you want to lay out the table of contents. (Of course, if you are creating a table of contents for a document that is fully contained within a single PageMaker file, then use of the Book... command is unnecessary.) Select the Create TOC... command from the Utilities menu, and the dialog box shown in Figure 12-7 appears.

> **Create Table of Contents**
>
> Title: | Table of Contents |
>
>   (**OK**)
>
> ☐ Replace existing table of contents   (Cancel)
> ☒ Include book publications
>
> Format: ○ No page number
>   ○ Page number before entry
>   ● Page number after entry
>
> Between entry and page number: | ^t |

The options in this dialog box determine how PageMaker scans your publications to gather table of contents entries and how it formats the page numbers that it adds next to each entry.

These options include

- ❧ **Title.** The title you enter here will be placed at the top of the new story that is created to hold your table of contents. You can enter any title you want or leave the default title of "Contents." It doesn't really matter what you enter here, because you will be able to edit this title after the table of contents has been generated.

- ❧ **Replace existing table of contents.** If the file you are working in already contains a table of contents, the Replace existing table of contents option will be automatically selected. If you deselect this option, you will create a second table of contents. You'll generally want to leave it selected so that the new table of contents replaces the existing one. When you replace an existing table of contents in this way, any manual editing you have done to the existing table of contents will be lost. (As you will see later in this chapter, you will manually edit the table of contents for a variety of reasons.)

- ❧ **Include book publications.** If your document includes several different PageMaker publication files, and you have used the Book... command to build a book list, the Include book publications option is selected by default and table of contents entries will be collected from all PageMaker files in the book list. Deselect this option if you want to create a table of contents that contains only entries from the current file, ignoring other files in the book list.

- ❧ **Format.** This option determines where the page number is placed in each table of contents entry. The No page number option creates a table of contents that does not include any page number references; the Page number before entry option places the page number at the beginning of each entry in the table of contents; and the Page number after entry option places the page number at the end of each entry.

⊸ **Between entry and page number.** This option determines what is placed between the entry and page number on each line of the table of contents. The default setting is ^t, which inserts a single tab between the entry and the page number. Other possible settings are shown in Table 12-1.

Table 12-1		
Frequently Used Delimiter Characters and the Keys that Produce Them		
Character	*Keys*	
White space	^w or ^W	
Tab	^t or ^T	
Em space	^m or ^M	
En space	^>	
Thin space	^<	
En dash	^=	
Em dash	^_ (underscore)	

After setting the options in the Create Table of Contents dialog box, click the OK button to begin the actual compilation or click the Cancel button to return to the layout without generating a table of contents.

Placing the Table of Contents

After PageMaker gathers all of the table of contents entries, a loaded text placement icon appears just as if you had imported a new story with the Place command (unless you were in the Story Editor when the Create TOC… command was chosen, in which case the table of contents will appear as a new story window). Place the table of contents like any other story, positioning the text placement icon between existing column guides before clicking the mouse or drag-placing to create a custom-sized text block.

Once in position, the table of contents text may be edited freely, using either the text tool or the Story Editor. Frequently you'll have to edit some of the text because it is too long, or you may get a few paragraphs that don't belong in the table of contents and need to be deleted. You're also likely to want to modify some of the formatting for your table of contents, but don't do that until you read the next section of this chapter, which introduces TOC style sheets. Figure 12-8 shows a placed table of contents.

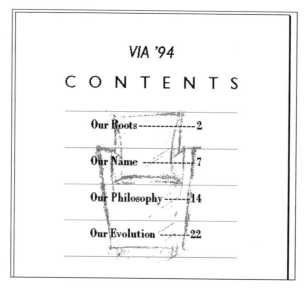

Another thing to keep in mind about editing the table of contents is that you'll usually have to rebuild the table of contents several times as you create your publication, unless you have far more will power than we do and actually wait until you are really finished laying out the document before constructing the TOC for the first time. PageMaker gathers table of contents entries as they exist when the Create TOC… command is chosen, but that table of contents remains accurate only until you edit your publication in such a way that any text in the publication reflows (moves to another page). The table of contents is not linked to the paragraphs they refer to as they exist on the pages of your publications, so when a table of contents entry flows from one page to another, the table of contents is not automatically updated. This means that, although you may create the table of contents one or more times before you finish your document, it is mandatory that you re-create the table of contents as the very last step in finishing your document, after all other changes have been made to all files in the document.

After creating the table of contents that last time, when you are sure nothing in any publications in the document will be changed (or at least not enough to move items between pages), then you can do any final editing to the table of contents text and verify the text formatting in the table of contents.

The Table of Contents Style Sheets

If your publications are formatted with style sheets, the Create TOC… command automatically creates new style sheets that are used to format your table of contents entries. It adds one new style sheet for each existing style sheet that has the Include in

TOC option selected. The new style sheets have the same names as the corresponding existing style sheets, with the letters TOC added to the front of their names, as shown in Figure 12-9.

Figure 12-9:
The new style sheets created for newly generated table of contents are automatically added to the Styles list.

These new style sheets are initially formatted using the same options and attributes as the style sheets on which they are based, but you are free to modify them as necessary to format the text in your table of contents properly. In most cases this will mean smaller type sizes, less space between paragraphs, and new tab settings. Any changes you make to the TOC style sheet definitions are not lost when the table of contents is re-created. This method allows you to format your table of contents — at least partially — even before the final edition is created.

Indexing

A good index is also vitally important to the success of any long document, but creating a good index is one of the most tedious jobs associated with publishing. As a result, before indexing features like those in PageMaker were available, it was necessary to endure the tedium or hire a professional indexing service to create a good index. Using PageMaker's indexing features, however, you can produce a very professional index with a fraction of the effort formerly required. PageMaker allows you to create an index across all of the publications in your book, with up to three levels of indexed items, cross-references, and a great flexibility in the type of page number citations used by each index entry.

PageMaker's indexing abilities are best described as semiautomatic: First you manually mark each index entry in each publication, and then PageMaker collects these entries and determines the correct page references. Specifically, a typical indexing project uses the following procedure:

    ☞ First, mark each text reference that you want included in the index. This can be done manually using the Index entry command, or the story editor's Change (Find & Change) command can be used to help automate this process.

꙰ Next, review your index with the Show Index command. This lets you review index entries alphabetically, making changes, adding or deleting entries.

꙰ Then choose the Create Index... command. This collects all of your index references, determines the page numbers on which the cited references appear, and compiles the index story.

꙰ The index then appears as a story you can place into your publication just like any story imported using the Place command.

꙰ Once the index is in position, you can edit the index text, correcting any problems or improving character or paragraph formatting.

꙰ Finally, if your publication is edited in any way that would affect your index — changes to the position of text or the text content — you'll have to re-create the index and redo any index edits.

The following sections describe each of these steps in detail.

Marking Index Topics

The first step in creating an index in PageMaker is marking each item in the text that you want to include in your index. PageMaker refers to each item you include in your index as a *topic reference*. A topic reference can be any text of up to 50 characters, including words, phrases, or proper names. To mark text as a topic reference, select it with the text tool and then choose the Index Entry... command (⌘-;) from the Utilities menu. The Index Entry dialog box, shown in Figure 12-10, then appears.

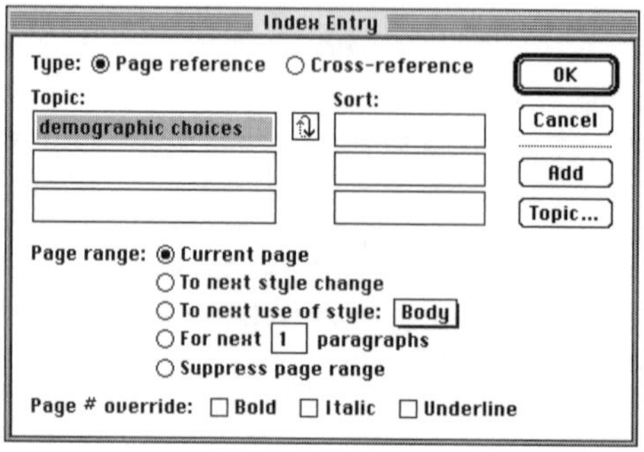

Figure 12-10:
Use the Index Entry dialog box to mark index entries.

If you want to create an index entry at a certain spot in your text but don't want to use any existing text as your topic reference, set the text insertion point and choose the Index Entry command (⌘-;). The same Index Entry dialog box appears, but no default text is included as the topic reference.

The Index Entry dialog box includes the following options:

↦ **Topic.** The upper-left section of the dialog box contains the topic option, which consists of three options boxes stacked below the word Topic. Any text that was selected when the Index Entry command was chosen is automatically placed in the top field, thus making this text the topic reference. You can modify this text as necessary to create the topic reference you desire.

The second and third fields below the Topic option are used for secondary or third-level references. Figure 12-11 shows a second-level reference. Second- and third-level references expand and clarify index references for complicated topics. In this book, for example, there are a number of references to the general topic of style sheets. Rather than producing an index with a single style sheets entry of 10 or more page references, secondary references are used to separate the style sheets entries into more-specific topics such as Creating, Importing, For table of contents entries, and so on. The second-level style sheet reference of Importing could also have third-level references to word processors and to other PageMaker publications.

Figure 12-11:
An example of a second-level topic reference

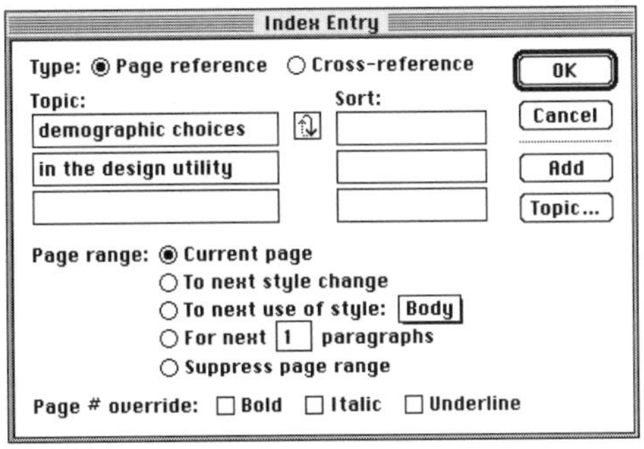

```
┌─────────────────── Index Entry ───────────────────┐
│ Type: ◉ Page reference  ○ Cross-reference    ┌──────┐ │
│                                              │  OK  │ │
│ Topic:                    Sort:              └──────┘ │
│ ┌─────────────────┐ ┌──┐ ┌─────────────────┐ ┌──────┐ │
│ │ demographic choices │ │↕ │ │                 │ │Cancel│ │
│ └─────────────────┘ └──┘ └─────────────────┘ └──────┘ │
│ ┌─────────────────┐      ┌─────────────────┐ ┌──────┐ │
│ │ in the design utility │  │                 │ │ Add  │ │
│ └─────────────────┘      └─────────────────┘ └──────┘ │
│ ┌─────────────────┐      ┌─────────────────┐ ┌──────┐ │
│ │                 │      │                 │ │Topic…│ │
│ └─────────────────┘      └─────────────────┘ └──────┘ │
│                                                      │
│ Page range: ◉ Current page                           │
│             ○ To next style change                   │
│             ○ To next use of style: ┌────┐           │
│                                     │Body│           │
│                                     └────┘           │
│             ○ For next ┌─┐ paragraphs                │
│                        │1│                           │
│                        └─┘                           │
│             ○ Suppress page range                    │
│ Page # override: ☐ Bold  ☐ Italic  ☐ Underline       │
└──────────────────────────────────────────────────────┘
```

To enter a second- or third-level reference, click the text tool in the appropriate field and enter the second- or third-level reference text. The reorder button, located next to the first index field, is used to exchange the text between the first-, second-, and third-level index fields. If you need to reorder an entry, click this button until the topic references are nested as you require them.

↦ **The Topic…** button. One problem with pulling topic references from your text, or entering them from the keyboard, is that any misspelling or terminology deviation will become a separate item in the index from that of the correct spelling or predominant terminology. For example, this book may contain references to both the LaserWriter and to the Apple LaserWriter. The best way to index these occurrences would be to have all index entries use one term of these terms (probably LaserWriter in this case) and have the other term cross-referenced (Apple LaserWriter. *See* LaserWriter).

To minimize this problem, PageMaker lets you check the current topic reference against a list of all existing topic references. This makes it easy to correct misspellings or select an alternate terminology so that all index entries will match. To check a topic reference, click the Topic... button. The Select Topic dialog box, as shown in Figure 12-12, then appears.

Figure 12-12:
The Select Topic dialog box

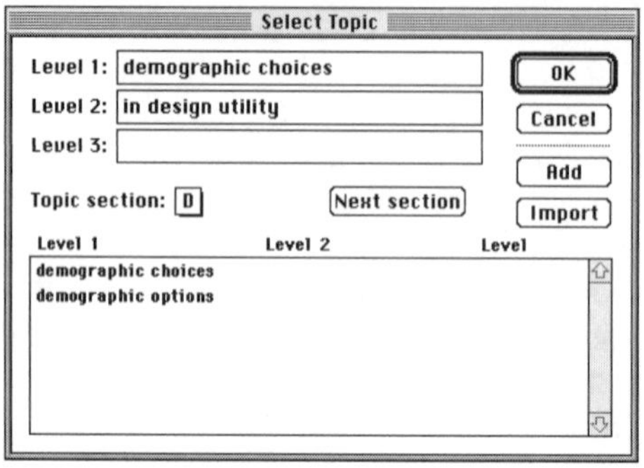

Your existing topic references (including first-, second-, and third-level references) appear in the top portion of the dialog box. Set the cursor in the box of the reference you wish to check. Then use the pop-up list next to the Index section option to select the first letter of the reference or of any alternate term you think might be used for that reference. A list of existing index entries for the letter you select appears in the lower portion of the dialog box. To check another set of existing index entries, choose another letter from the Index section option, or click the Next Section button, which moves you to the next alphabetical index section that contains at least one index entry.

If you find an existing entry you wish to use in place of the current topic reference, highlight it and click the OK button, or double-click the topic name. This will change the entry for the Topic option in the Index Entry dialog box. Click the Cancel button to return to the Index Entry dialog box without resetting the current topic.

The Import button. In order to get the topic references you've used in other publications in your book list to show up in the listing at the bottom of the dialog box, you have to use the Import button. This makes your search for alternate spellings and terms more complete and makes it easier to perform semiautomatic indexing as described later in this section. When the Import button is clicked, a list of all topics in the publications in the current book list appears.

The Import button will be dimmed if no book list has been created for the current publication or if all entries from the publications that are in the book list have already been imported.

↪ **Sort.** The Sort option in the Index Entry dialog box allows you to specify that a particular topic reference should be sorted as if it were spelled differently than it really is. For example, in most cases, topic references that begin with a number are sorted as if the number were spelled out (*2nd* is sorted as *second*). So if a topic reference were *2nd base*, you would write *second base* in the Sort option, and when PageMaker alphabetized the index, the *2nd base* item would be sorted in alphabetical order within the *S*'s.

↪ **Page range.** The Page range options, as shown in Figure 12-13, determine which pages are included in the citation of the current topic reference. These options appear after you select Page Reference in the Type: option at the top of the Index Entry dialog box. There are five options:

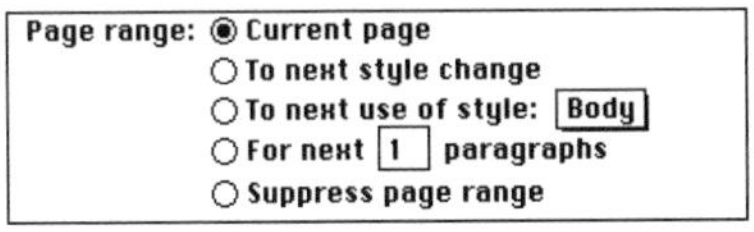

Figure 12-13:
The Index Entry Page range
options

Page range: ⦿ Current page
○ To next style change
○ To next use of style: [Body]
○ For next [1] paragraphs
○ Suppress page range

- **Current page.** When this option is selected, the index item lists only the specific page on which the topic reference is found.

- **To next style change.** When this option is selected, the index item lists a range of pages, starting with the page on which the topic reference is found and ending with the page containing the first paragraph that has a style different from that of the paragraph containing the topic reference.

- **To next use of style.** When this option is selected, the index item lists a range of pages, starting with the page containing the topic reference and ending with the page that contains the first paragraph using the style sheet specified in the pop-up menu following the option.

- **For next __ paragraphs.** When this option is selected, the index item lists the range of pages starting with the page containing the topic reference and ending on the page containing the nth paragraph after the one containing the topic reference, where you specify n in the field.

- **Suppress page range.** When this option is selected, the index item doesn't list a range of pages.

↪ **Cross-reference.** This option is used to create cross-references. Cross-references allow you to include alternate terminology or spellings in the index. Using our previous example, you would add an entry for LaserWriter and then select the Cross-reference option and use the Topic button to select the Apple LaserWriter entry as the cross-reference.

To create a cross-reference entry, click the Cross-reference (x-ref) option and then click the x-ref... button. This brings up the Select Topic dialog box, which you use to select the index item to which the current index entry will refer.

☞ **Page # Override/Reference Override.** In most cases, the text of each topic reference in your index and the page range for that entry will use the same type style. For some entries, however, you may want to use a bold, italic, or underline type style for the page reference to provide visual emphasis. The Reference override option makes it easy to do this: Just select the Bold, Italic, or Underline option in the Index Entry dialog box. If entries in your index are formatted using the selected type style already, the opposite style will be used. For example, if you select the Reference override: Bold option, but the text in your index is formatted as bold, then the page range will be formatted as not bold.

Note that when you change the Reference override option, that setting remains the default for all subsequent index entries until you change it again. So you won't have to select these options repeatedly unless you want to set the Reference override differently for different index entries. You usually don't want different index entries to use different reference overrides, because it will make your index unattractive and hard to read. You may, however, want to use one reference override for index entries and another for cross-references. In this case, be careful to set the Reference override option one way when creating index entries and the other way for when creating cross-references.

Even though the Reference override option will format your index automatically, you are still free to format the text manually.

Before clicking OK to close the Index Entry dialog box, double-check your option settings. The process of editing an entry already placed within an index is rather cumbersome (we describe this later), it is much easier to correct entries at this stage before placement. When you're sure everything is correct, click the OK button. This creates the index entry and closes the dialog box. Or click the Cancel button if you want to close the dialog box without creating the index entry.

In the layout view, there will be no visible result from your new index entry. In the Story Editor, however, a black diamond called an index marker will appear before each word or phrase that has been added to the index. If a word or phrase is indexed more than once, multiple index markers will appear. Multiple indexing is most frequently used for cross-referencing.. The first time you index the word Font, for example, you might add a standard page reference and a cross-reference from the word Typeface to the word Font.

Removing duplicate index markers: You may also find that two index markers appear before a word because it has been accidentally indexed twice. This can happen quite easily since there is no sign in the layout view that a word or phrase has been indexed. If you locate a doubly indexed word, you can remove one of the index entries by simply deleting one of the index markers.

Indexing Tips and Shortcuts

PageMaker includes a number of keyboard shortcuts and other commands you can use to complete indexing projects more quickly.

Quick Index with Defaults

To index a selected word or phrase without changing any of the default options in the Index Entry dialog box, use the ⌘-Shift-; (semicolon) keyboard shortcut. This indexes the selected text without opening the Index Entry dialog box, with the Range option set to Current page and no second- or third-level references included. You can modify the options for this entry later by selecting the text and choosing the Index Entry... command, or using the editing capabilities of the Show Index... command, as described in the next section.

Indexing Names and Titles

To index a proper name, select the name and press ⌘-Shift-Z. This indexes the name last name first. So if you index the name Robert Zimmerman, it will appear in the index as Zimmerman, Robert. To use this trick for names that have more than two words (like Hillary Rodham Clinton or J. R. Ewing), you must insert a non-breaking space (Shift-Spacebar) character by pressing Option-spacebar between each word except the last two then select the entire name and press ⌘-Shift-Z. In these examples, the non-breaking spaces would have to be inserted between *Hillary* and *Rodham* and between *J.* and *R.*, so the resulting index entries would be *Clinton, Hillary Rodham,* and *Ewing, J. R.*

Indexing with Search and Replace

When creating an index for a large publication, with many topic references and many occurrences of each topic reference, you can ensure that your index is complete by working in the Story Editor and using the Change... command. The Change... command allows you to search for all occurrences of a particular word or phrase in the current publication or in all open publications and add that word to your index. To do this, choose the Change command from the Utilities menu, enter the word or phrase you want to index into the Find what field, and enter ^; (caret + semicolon) into the Change to field. Click the Change All button, and every instance of your word or phrase is now in your index.

If you want to index only certain instances of the word or phrase or need to change the options in the Index Entry dialog box, use the Find button instead of the Change All button, and then use the Index Entry command and Change or Find next buttons as necessary.

Defining Index Topics in Advance

In most cases, you'll assign topic references as you go through your publications adding index entries. Alternatively, if you know in advance the topic references you want to use in your index, you can enter your list of topic references in advance. Doing this allows you to verify that, as you add index entries, each correctly corresponds to your predefined index specifications.

To enter your list of topic references, choose the Index Entry command (⌘-;) from the Utilities menu, and then click the Topic... button. The Select Topic dialog box will then appear. Enter each topic reference you want to add into the Level fields (you may enter a main reference or a secondary or third-level reference) and then click the Add button. Repeat this procedure until all of your topic references have been added. The lower portion of the dialog box displays a complete list of all existing reference topics, divided alphabetically, as illustrated in Figure 12-14.

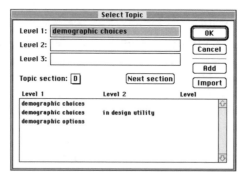

Figure 12-14:
An example of entering index topics in advance

After you have entered all topic references, click the OK command to close the Select Topic dialog box and then click Cancel to close the Index Entry dialog box. (Use the Cancel rather than the OK button so that you don't add a new index that isn't correctly attached to a topic in your publication.) You can then open other publications in your book and use the Import button in the Select Topic dialog box to copy your master topic reference list into each publication.

Editing Topic References

After you have indexed a number of topic references, you should review your index entries before creating the final index. This may reveal some missing index entries or alert you to index entries that need to be edited before they appear in the final index. Use the Show Index... command in the Utilities menu for a quick review of the current index entries for all publications in the current book list.

Using the Show Index Dialog Box

Choosing the Show Index… command causes PageMaker to read the index entries for the current publication and all other publications in the book list. If you want to limit the list to only entries from the current publication, hold down the ⌘ key when you choose the Show Index… command. A progress dialog box keeps you informed as entries are read, and then the Show Index dialog box appears as shown in Figure 12-15. This is similar to the dialog box that you saw when using the Topic… button in the Index Entry dialog box; it lists all of the existing topic references and the page references that are currently assigned to these topics. As you learned earlier, this dialog box displays topic references one alphabetical section at a time. Use the Index section pop-up or the Next section button to change to another alphabetical section of the entries.

Figure 12-15:
The Show Index
dialog box

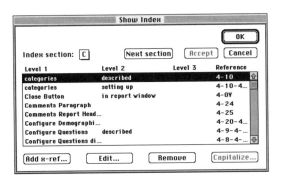

What you see in this dialog box is an alphabetical list of all topic references at level 1, level 2, and level 3, in addition to the current page reference. If any of your index entries are not found on a specific page, one of the following symbols in Table 12-2 may appear in the Reference column.

Table 12-2
Reference Column Symbols for Index Entries

Symbol	Meaning
PB	Pasteboard
LM	Left Master page
RM	Right Master page
OV	Overset Text (beyond end of a text block)
UN	Unplaced text (in a Story Editor window)
?	Location uncertain

Editing, Adding, and Deleting Topic References

From within the Show Index dialog box you can edit any topic reference, or the options associated with that topic reference, by selecting the topic reference in the list and then clicking the Edit... button. The Edit Index Entry dialog box then appears so that you can modify the topic reference or its options. The use of these options was discussed in the previous section of this chapter.

From the Show Index dialog box you can also add new topic references if they will be cross-references to other existing index entries. To do this, click the Add x-ref... button, and enter the name of the new topic reference in the Index Entry dialog box. The Cross-reference range option will be selected automatically. To assign a cross-reference, click the x-ref button and select one of the existing topic references from the Select Cross-Reference Topic dialog box. Then click the OK button. You can now enter new topic references that need corresponding page references from within the Show Index dialog.

You can also delete topic references from your index using the Show Index dialog box. Just select the entry you want to delete and then click the Remove button. The selected topic reference will be permanently deleted from your index. (If you delete any topic references and then wish you hadn't, click the Cancel button to close the Show Index dialog box and the deletion will be effectively undone.)

Capitalizing Topic References

The Capitalize... button lets you fix a common problem with index entries: incorrect capitalization. Unfortunately, this button is not available if your publication has a book list — it only works when indexing a single file. (Why does it only work on a single file? No good reason we can imagine. Although we're sure it was easier to program this way...) You can use the Capitalize... button to capitalize the first word of any selected entry, or all level 1 entries in your file, or of all index entries in the file. To capitalize a single entry, select that entry before clicking the Capitalize... button. In the Capitalize dialog box (shown in Figure 12-16), select one of the three options and then click OK to return to the Show Index dialog.

Figure 12-16:
The Capitalize dialog box

When you are finished checking or editing the index entries, click the OK button to save any changes you have made to the index and return to the layout, or the Cancel button to return to the layout without saving changes.

Show Index Dialog Box Shortcuts

There are a number of keyboard shortcuts to the Show Index dialog box that can help you do "index housekeeping" very easily, as shown in Table 12-3.

Table 12-3	
Keyboard Shortcuts for the Show Index Dialog Box	
Keyboard Shortcut	*Result*
Option + Add X-ref button	Deletes all index entries added since the Show Index dialog box was opened or since the Accept button was clicked.
Option + Remove... button	Undeletes all index entries deleted since the Show Index dialog box was opened or since the Accept button was clicked.
Command + Option + Remove... button	Deletes all index entries from the index.
Command + Shift + Remove... button	Deletes all cross-references from the index.
Command + Option + Shift + Remove... button	Deletes all index entries and cross-referneces from the index.

Generating an Index

When all of your topic references have been marked and your publication has stabilized to the point where text will no longer be flowing between pages, you are ready to create the actual index. You can create the index before all of your topic references are marked or when the layout is still in flux, but if you do, you will have to re-create the index later to get the final set of topic references and the final correct page references.

To create the index, open the PageMaker publication that will contain the index layout and use the Book... command (as described earlier in this chapter) to create or verify the book list. When the book list is correct, choose the Create Index... command from the Utilities menu, and the Create Index dialog box, shown in Figure 12-17, appears.

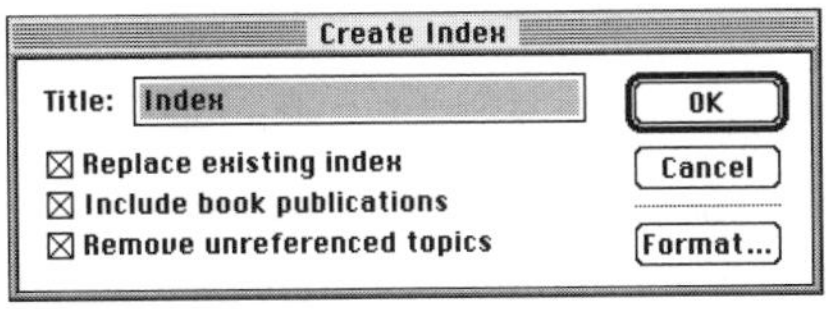

Figure 12-17:
The Create Index dialog box

This dialog box offers four options:

- ☞ **Title.** The Title option is used to enter the text that will appear as the header of the new index. You can edit this title after the index has been created, so the text entered here is not very important.

- ☞ **Replace existing index.** The Replace existing index option is automatically selected if the current file already contains an index, but you may want to deselect it. This option should be selected if you want the new index to replace the existing index in the current layout. Remember that if you have manually edited the existing index, replacing it will cause all your edits to be lost. If the current file contains more than one index, the most recently created index will be considered the existing index.

- ☞ **Include book publications.** The Include book publications option, which is selected by default, causes the index entries from all PageMaker files in the current book list to be included in the index that is generated. If you want to create an index that contains only entries from the current file, regardless of the number of files in the current book list, deselect this option.

- ☞ **Remove unreferenced topics.** This option, when selected, causes the new index to remove any topic references that do not occur at least once in the indexed text. If, for example, you had created an index entry for the name Bugs Bunny and later deleted the only paragraph containing the name Bugs Bunny, use of this option would cause the name to be removed from the index. If this option were not selected in this case, Bugs Bunny would be included in the index, without a page reference.

The Format... button in the Create Index dialog box provides access to a number of additional options that control the index compiled by the Create Index command.

The options in the Index format dialog box, shown in Figure 12-18, cover

- ☞ **Include index section headings.** When this option is selected, the name of each alphabetic section of the index will be included in the index. When this option is not selected, no section headings are included in the index, although space is placed between sections.

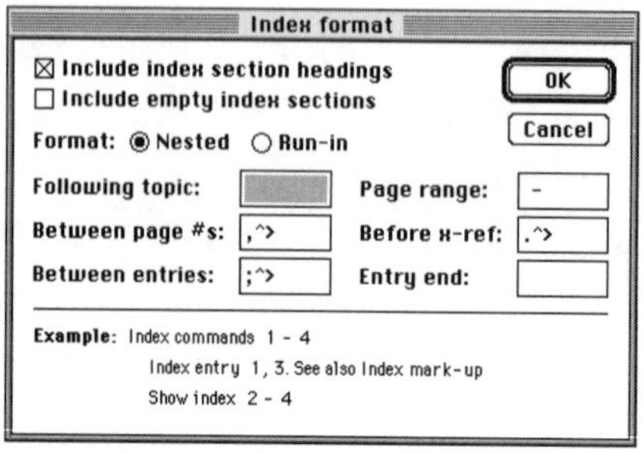

Figure 12-18:
The Index format dialog box

```
┌──────────── Index format ────────────┐
│ ☒ Include index section headings      ┌────────┐
│ ☐ Include empty index sections        │   OK   │
│                                       └────────┘
│ Format: ⦿ Nested  ○ Run-in            ┌────────┐
│                                       │ Cancel │
│ Following topic: [      ]   Page range: [ - ]
│ Between page #s: [,^>]   Before ×-ref: [,^>]
│ Between entries: [;^>]   Entry end: [    ]
│ ─────────────────────────────────────────
│ Example: Index commands  1 - 4
│          Index entry  1, 3. See also Index mark-up
│          Show index  2 - 4
└───────────────────────────────────────┘
```

⁂ **Include empty index sections.** When this option is selected, alphabetic sections of the index that do not contain any topic references are included in the index. When it is deselected, only sections of the index containing at least one topic reference are included.

⁂ **Format.** The index PageMaker creates can be in one of two formats — Nested or Run-in. In the Nested format, each first-level topic reference is placed on its own line, with second- and third-level topic references given their own lines, indented under the first-level item. In the Run-in format, each first-level topic reference begins a new line, but the second- and third-level topic references follow the preceding level, continuing on the same line. New lines are started only when the paragraph specifications of the index text force text to wrap to a new line. Figure 12-19 compares the Nested and Run-in formats.

In order to separate topic references, page references, entries, and cross-references, special characters called delimiters are inserted in the index. The remaining options in this dialog box control which types of delimiters are used in the various circumstances. Many of the characters used as delimiters, such as the en dash and en space, are produced with special key combinations, as listed here in Table 12-4.

C	C
categories	categories: described 4-10; setting up 4-10–4-14
described 4-10	Comments Paragraph 4-24
setting up 4-10–4-14	Comments Report Heading dialog box 4-25
Comments Paragraph 4-24	Configure Demographics dialog box 4-20–4-26
Comments Report Heading dialog box 4-25	Configure Questions: described 4-9–4-26
Configure Demographics dialog box 4-20–4-26	Configure Questions dialog box 4-8–4-26
Configure Questions	Current Page Field: in report window 4-26
described 4-9–4-26	
Configure Questions dialog box 4-8–4-26	**D**
Current Page Field	
in report window 4-26	demographic choices 4-20
	demographic titles 4-20

Figures 12-19: Examples of the Nested (left) and Run-in (right) index formats.

Table 12-4
Index Delimiter Characters

Character	Key Combination
White space	^w or ^W
Tab	^t or ^T
Em space	^m or ^M
En space	^>
Thin space	^<
En dash	^=
Em dash	^_ (underscore)

- ❧ **Following topic.** The entry made for this option determines the character that will be placed between each topic reference and the page numbers or cross-reference text. The default is two en spaces.

- ❧ **Page range.** The entry made for this option determines the character that will be placed between page numbers when a range of pages is listed. The default is an en dash.

- ❧ **Between page #s.** The entry made for this option determines the character that will be placed between multiple page references to a single topic reference. The default is a comma and an en space.

- ❧ **Before x-ref.** The entry made for this option determines the character that will be placed between a topic reference and its cross-reference text. The default is a period and an en space.

- ❧ **Between entries.** The entry made for this option determines the character that will be placed between secondary entries in the Run-in format. The default is a semicolon and an en space.

- ❧ **Entry end.** The entry made for this option determines the character that will be placed after the final topic reference when using the Nested format, or after each reference when using the Run-in format. There is no default character.

After completing all the options in the Index Format dialog box, click the OK button to return to the Create Index dialog box. If additional changes are not required in the Create Index dialog box, click the OK button to begin the index generation.

If the Include book publications option was selected, and any of the publications in the current book list are not in their original locations, a Find pub dialog box, as shown in Figure 12-20, will appear. Use the scrolling file list and the Drive button to locate any publications that have been moved, or use the Ignore or Ignore all buttons to create the index without the entries from any missing publications. If the name of any publication has changed, highlight the new file in the scrolling list and click the OK button to include the renamed publication in your index in place of the file that cannot be found.

Figure 12-20:
The Find pub dialog box

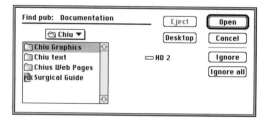

The process of creating your index may take several minutes, depending on the number of index entries that are included. The progress of the index generation will be shown in a progress dialog box. When the index is complete, one of three events will occur:

- ✏ If the Replace existing index option was selected, the new index will be placed in the text blocks that currently hold the previous version of the index.

- ✏ If you are in the layout view, and the Replace existing index option was not selected, a text placement icon will appear. You can then use the text placement icon to position and flow the index. See Chapter 5 for information on using the text placement icon to flow text.

- ✏ If the Story Editor is open, and the Replace existing index option was not selected, the index will appear in a new story window. You can edit the index text, if desired, as described in the next section. To place the index into your layout, choose the Place… command in the File menu. This will cause a text placement icon to appear; this icon can be used to flow the index text into the current publication.

Editing and Formatting the Index

Once placed, your index text can be edited and manipulated just like text imported from a word processor or created with the text tool. You can change any text or paragraph attributes in the index, modify the index style sheets, or apply new style sheets to the index text. Note that PageMaker automatically creates style sheets for your index entries and tags your entries with these style sheets, just as it did for your table of contents entries. These style sheets are

- ✏ **Index level 1.** This is the style sheet used to format first-level index entries.

- ✏ **Index level 2.** This is the style sheet used to format second-level index entries. It will be created only if your index includes second-level entries.

- ✏ **Index level 3.** This is the style sheet used to format third-level index entries. It will be created only if your index includes third-level entries.

- ✏ **Index section.** This is the style sheet used to format the section headings of the index.

- ✏ **Index title.** This style sheet is used to format the index title.

You can therefore reformat your entire index by modifying the formatting definitions of these style sheets. To do this, use the techniques explained in Chapter 7. You can also format the text directly, overriding the current style sheet applications, or tag your index entries with other style sheets.

You'll always want to take a very careful look at your index, searching for improper capitalization, topic references that are supposed to be identical but aren't, and ensuring the overall consistency of the entries. You can correct problems in your index in two ways: make corrections in your publication files and in the Show Index dialog box and then re-create the index, or edit the index story directly. If you will be using your publication files again in the future or aren't finished creating or editing the publication itself, you should definitely make corrections in the actual files and Show Index dialog box. If you choose to make corrections directly in the index story, remember that these corrections will be lost if you have to re-create the index later for any reason (if further editorial or layout changes make text flow across pages in any publication, for example). If you do not want to make corrections in the actual files and Show Index dialog box, you should nevertheless hold off performing the edits to the index story until you are sure that there will be no changes in the publication files.

Links and File Management

When you import a text or graphics file into a PageMaker publication, PageMaker automatically notes the location from which the imported file came (the drive and folder it came from) and the date and time the file was modified. This information is used later to determine if the original file has been modified since it was imported into PageMaker, and in some cases, to reduce the amount of disk space consumed by PageMaker files. The relationship between PageMaker and the external text and graphics file is called a *link*. Similar details are tracked for elements imported using the Subscribe to or Insert object commands, discussed in Chapter 5.

PageMaker has three commands that let you control the links between original files and your publication: the Links... command in the File menu, the Link Options... command in the Element menu, and the Link Info... command in the Element menu. With these commands, you can find out if the external versions of your text or graphic elements have been modified or the page number on which elements exist within your publication. You can also substitute one file for another by changing the link (or reconnect a file that has been moved to a new location on your hard drive), unlink files that you don't want to remain connected, and control the size of your publications by controlling which graphics files are fully stored within your publication.

The Links... Command

The Links... command (⌘-=) is the most powerful of the three link commands and the one you will use most often. Choosing the Links... command brings up the Links dialog box, which presents a list of all the text and graphics files that have been imported into the current publication. This list, as shown in Figure 12-21, gives the name of the file that was imported, the kind of file it is (Text, Image, EPS, PICT, OLE-linked, OLE-embedded, Subscriber), the page in the publication where the file is located, and a symbol indicating the status of the link.

Figure 12-21:
The Links
dialog box

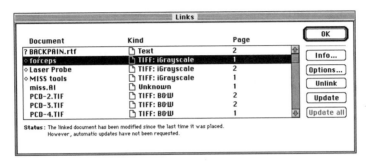

The symbols appear before each filename in the list. When a particular file is selected in this list, the meaning of that file's link status symbol appears just below the scrolling window (next to the word Status). The link symbols are as follows:

- **No Symbol.** If no symbol precedes the document name, the link is up-to-date, or no link information exists.

- **NA.** If the letters "NA" appear before a document name, there is no link information available, either because the document was pasted into your publication and no links exist, or because it is an OLE-embedded object.

- **Question Mark.** When a question mark appears, PageMaker is unable to locate the external file from which the file was imported. If the file has been moved or renamed and you would like to re-establish the link, or if you would like to link a different file, use the Info... button, as described later.

- **Solid black diamond.** When a solid black diamond appears before a filename, the external file has been modified since the text or graphic was imported into (or exported from) PageMaker, and this element is set (via the Link option defaults dialog box) for automatic updating. The newer version of this element will be brought into the publication the next time it is printed or opened. You can force the new element to be imported earlier by using the Update or Update all buttons.

- **Open diamond.** When an open diamond appears before a filename, the external file has been modified since the text or graphic was imported into (or exported from) PageMaker, but the element is not set for automatic updating in the Link option defaults dialog box. If you want to import the newer version of the external file, select the element name and then click the Update button.

↪ **Open triangle.** When an open triangle appears before a filename, both the external version of the element and the version of the element stored within your publication have been modified. If you select this element and click the Update button, the current external version will be imported and will overwrite the current version that exists in your publication, losing all of the changes that were made to that internal version.

The Page column lists the page number where the element was placed. If the imported element does not appear on one of the publication pages, one of the following symbols will appear:

↪ **Page#?.** The element is an inline graphic whose position has not yet been determined; the page number is currently unknown. When the story containing the graphic is placed, this symbol will be replaced with an actual page number.

↪ **LM.** The element is positioned on the left master page.

↪ **RM.** The element is positioned on the right master page.

↪ **PB.** The element is positioned on the pasteboard.

↪ **OV.** The element is hidden in a text block that has not yet been fully placed. When the text block containing the graphic is fully placed, this symbol will be replaced with an actual page number.

↪ **X.** The linked element is a story window that is open in the Story Editor and has not yet been placed. When the story containing the element is placed, this symbol will be replaced with an actual page number.

At the right of the Links dialog box, five buttons appear: Info…, Options…, Unlink, Update, and Update all.

↪ **Info…** is used to select a new file to link to the currently selected element. This button operates exactly like the Link Info… command, as described in the next section of this chapter.

↪ **Options…** opens the Link Options dialog box, which presents three options. When the Store copy in publication option is selected, a copy of the text or graphic element is kept in your PageMaker publication. This option is selected automatically for all text elements and cannot be deselected. When this option is not selected, only a screen image of the element is kept in the publication, and the external disk file is accessed when the actual element is needed for printing. In this case, changes made to the external file must be used by PageMaker in order to print the publication.

When the Update automatically option is selected, each time the publication is opened or printed, PageMaker determines if the linked file has been modified. If it has been modified, PageMaker imports the new version for use in your publication. When using this option, remember that any modifications you make to the copy of the element in your publication will be lost the next time the element is updated.

The Alert before updating option — which is available only when the Update automatically option is selected — determines whether PageMaker asks you to confirm the element update each time a new external disk version is found. When this option is selected, a dialog box will appear before the update takes place, thereby allowing you to cancel the update. If this option is not selected, automatic updates occur without warning each time your publication is opened or printed.

- ✑ **Unlink** breaks the link between the file and the PageMaker layout.

- ✑ **Update** replaces the current version of the selected element that is used in your publication with the newer version as found in the linked file.

- ✑ **Update all** replaces all linked elements in the publication, not just the one currently selected, with new versions as found in the linked files.

When you have finished modifying link information, click the OK button to close the Links dialog box. If you have modified any elements by updating links, these changes will now be reflected in your publication. You may want to examine your publication carefully to verify that all updated text is positioned properly and updated graphics are sized and positioned correctly.

The Link Info... Command

The Link Info... command, found in the Element menu, brings up the Link info dialog box (shown in Figure 12-22) just like the Info button in the Links dialog box. It is available as a separate command so that you can select one text or graphic element and check the link info of one specific element without having to go through the Links dialog box (and endure the associated wait while the Links dialog box checks every link in your publication).

Figure 12-22:
The Link info
dialog box

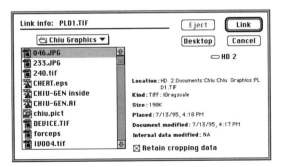

The scrolling window on the left side of this dialog box shows the contents of the folder where the linked file was originally found, with the linked file selected in some cases. The link information is presented on the right side. If PageMaker cannot locate the folder where the linked file was originally found, or if the linked file no longer exists, the correct folder or file will not be displayed in the scrolling file list.

If PageMaker has correctly located the linked file, and you do not wish to change this link, click the Cancel button to exit the Link info dialog box. Clicking the Link button causes PageMaker to replace the copy of the element as it currently exists within your publication with a copy of the element as it exists in the external file, regardless of whether the external file has been modified since it was imported into PageMaker.

You can determine if the external file has been modified since it was imported into PageMaker by comparing the dates and times listed for the Placed and Document modified lines on the right side of the dialog box. The Internal data modified line tells you when the copy of the element as it currently exists in your publication was last modified. If this date/time is later than the Placed date/time, some changes have been made to the element, and these will be lost if the link is updated. (You can also check the status of the link before updating it by closing this dialog box with the Cancel button and then using the Links... command from the File menu to check the current link status and update it, if necessary.)

You can also update the link manually, relinking a file that has been moved or renamed, or selecting a new file that you want to use as the source of text or graphic image for the current element. To do this, locate the file you want to link, select the filename, and click the Link button. This causes PageMaker to replace the current element with the information from the file you have selected.

If the Link button is clicked, and the result of the link update will be the loss of modifications made to the element inside PageMaker, a dialog box like the one shown in Figure 12-23 appears, warning you of the effect your link will have. Click the Yes button to complete the link and discard the current element or the No button to cancel the link and leave the element unchanged in your publication.

Figure 12-23:
The Link Update alert box

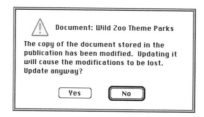

The Link Options... Command

The Link Options... command, found in the Element menu, works just like the Options button in the Links dialog box but lets you bypass the Links dialog box to verify or alter directly the link options for any selected text or graphic element. It also allows you to set the default link options, which cannot be done using the Link Options button in the Links dialog box.

To see the link options for any imported element, select the text or graphic with the arrow tool, and then choose the Link Options... command. The Link Options dialog box, as shown in Figure 12-24, will then appear. This dialog box presents three link options:

Figure 12-24:
The Link Options dialog box

- **Store copy in publication.** When the Store copy in publication option is selected, a copy of the text or graphic element is kept in your PageMaker publication. It is selected automatically for all text elements and OLE-linked objects and cannot be deselected. It cannot be used for OLE-embedded objects. (OLE is discussed in Chapter 5.)

  For graphic objects (except OLE objects), selecting this option causes a complete copy of the graphic file to be stored inside the PageMaker publication file. When it is not selected, only a screen image of the element is kept in the publication, and the external disk file is accessed when the actual element is needed for printing. In this case, PageMaker accesses the external file when printing the publication, so if you plan to print from another location, you have to be sure to take the externally linked graphic files along. You can do this by using the Copy linked files for remote printing option in the Save as dialog box, as discussed in Chapter 13.

- **Update automatically.** When the Update automatically option is selected, PageMaker determines whether the linked file has been modified each time your publication is opened or printed. If the element has been modified, PageMaker imports the new version for use in your publication. If PageMaker cannot find the external element when opening the file, you will be prompted to locate it. When using this option, remember that any modifications you make to the copy of the element in your publication will be lost the next time the element is updated.

- **Alert before updating.** The Alert before updating option, which is available only when the Update automatically option is selected, determines whether

PageMaker asks you to confirm the element update each time a new external disk version is found. When this option is selected, a dialog box will appear before the update takes place, allowing you to cancel the update. If this option is not selected, automatic updates occur without warning each time your publication is opened or printed.

To modify the default link options, select the Pointer tool from the toolbox, click the pasteboard or at some location on the current page where no element is located (so that nothing is selected), and then choose the Link Options... command from the Element menu. The Link Options: Defaults dialog box appears as shown in Figure 12-25. This dialog box presents the same options as the regular Link Options dialog box, but at this time their setting determines the default used by all text and graphics that have not yet been imported.

Figure 12-25:
The Link Options: Defaults
dialog box

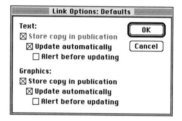

After setting the options for both text and graphic defaults, click the OK button to save the new defaults or the Cancel button to return to the publication without saving default modifications.

Working with Links

Each time you open a publication, or print from a publication, PageMaker checks the status of all linked elements and executes any scheduled automatic updates. If the linked file cannot be found for an element that is not stored in the publication and is scheduled for automatic updating, the Cannot find dialog box appears. Using this dialog box, you can locate an element that has moved to another folder or drive, or you can link a new file that has replaced the old version of the file.

When linked graphic elements are not stored in your publication file, it is easy to forget to include these files when backing up publications or copying publications to disk for transportation to another site. To avoid these mistakes, the Save publication as dialog box, shown in Figure 12-26, includes two options: the Copy Files for remote printing option and the Copy All linked files option.

Figure 12-26:
The Save
publication as
dialog box
allows you to
copy linked
files for
printing and
transporting.

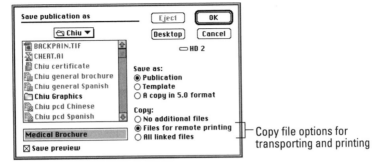

Copy file options for
transporting and printing

The Copy Files for remote printing option causes a copy of each file that is not stored in your publication to be placed in the same folder in which the publication is saved. The Copy All linked files option causes every linked file, whether stored in the publication or not, to be placed in the same folder in which the publication is saved. Of course, unless you are saving to some type of removable cartridge or tape, the total size of all files may exceed the available storage space on your disk, and unfortunately PageMaker's save operation will not prompt you for multiple disks during the save operation. Instead, it provides you with an error dialog box. In this case, save the publication and its linked files to a folder on your hard drive and manually copy them onto as many disks as are necessary.

■■

Summary

- ◆◆ The Book… command lets you create a list of PageMaker publication files to be treated or printed as a single document for purposes of creating a table of contents and index, with a single command.

- ◆◆ You don't have to build a book list in every publication in your book, but you do need one in the file that will contain the table of contents and index. You can export a book list from one publication to all others in that book list by holding down the ⌘ key while choosing the Book… command.

- ◆◆ To create a table of contents, you must first mark the paragraphs you want to include with the Include in TOC option in the Paragraph Specifications dialog box. You can also use this option in your style sheet definitions. Then open the publication in which you want to lay out the table of contents, verify that the book list is accurate, and choose the Create TOC… command.

- ◆◆ You can edit the table of contents text or change its formatting, but both will be lost if you later re-create the table of contents. The best way to format the text in the table of contents is by using the TOC style sheets that PageMaker automatically creates.

- ◆◆ To mark index entries, select the word or phrase you want to include and choose Index entry from the Utilities menu. For each index entry, you can specify up to three levels of topic references and select among five different methods of tracking page references. You can also create cross-references between topic references.

- ◆◆ To index a word or phrase quickly, select it and press ⌘-Shift-;.

- ◆◆ The Show Index… command lets you preview your index, checking all topic references and page references.

- ◆◆ Creating an index is much like creating a table of contents. Use the Create Index command, then place the new story. Style sheets are created automatically, and you can edit these or edit/format the text directly.

- ◆◆ Text files and embedded OLE files are automatically saved within your publication files. You can control whether graphic files are saved inside your publication or linked externally.

- ◆◆ The Links… command produces a list of all elements used in your publication and their link status. From the Links dialog box, you can modify, update, or remove links between elements in your publications and external text and graphic files.

■■

Printing Publications

13

In This Chapter

- ↠ Things to worry about before you print

- ↠ Resolution and screening

- ↠ A PostScript printing overview

- ↠ Printing to non-PostScript printers

- ↠ The Print command and dialog boxes

- ↠ Using printer styles

Printing your publication in PageMaker can be extremely easy or it can be somewhat complex, depending upon the colors used in the publication, the kind of printer you use, the way that you reproduce your publication, and the level of quality you're trying to achieve. To get the best printed output from PageMaker, there are a number of steps you have to follow. The first part of this chapter focuses on the commonly overlooked issues you have to worry about before you print your document. The last part of the chapter reviews the myriad options found in the cascading dialog boxes of the Print command.

Things to Worry About Before You Print

Most people don't think about printing until they're actually ready to choose the Print command. Unfortunately, most printing problems are caused by decisions you make while laying out the publication, adding text and graphic files, or specifying colors. The following list summarizes things you should keep in mind so that you can produce pages that have the best chance of printing without problems:

- **Page size versus paper size.** In order to print your publication at full size, the Page size you specify in the Page size pop-up menu in the Document Setup dialog box must be the same size or smaller than an available paper size supported by your printer. If your page size is larger than your paper size, each page of your document must be printed either at a reduced size or in sections (tiles). Both of these procedures are described in this chapter. Paper sizes available in your printer are listed in the Print Document dialog box, which is also described in the "Print Document Dialog Box" section of this chapter.

- **Imageable area.** Many printers cannot print to the edges of the paper due to an unprintable margin area. For laser printers, this area is usually ⅜ inch to ½ inch. Imagesetters can usually print edge-to-edge on any size paper. Once you select the appropriate PPD (PostScript Printer Description) file for your printer in the Print Document dialog box, the imageable area appears in the Print Paper dialog box, discussed later in this chapter under "Print Paper." (PPDs are discussed in "The Print Document Dialog Box," later this chapter.) Check these specifications before deciding on margins for your document or placing elements within the margin area. Items positioned in this unprintable margin will simply not appear on the printed page unless the publication is printed at a reduced size.

- **Scaled graphics.** Imported TIFF or bitmapped graphics will look best if you don't resize them, or if you resize them based on the resolution of your final output device. PageMaker makes it easy to do this by providing a "magic stretch" feature that calculates acceptable sizes of reduction and enlargement. To use this feature, first make sure that the correct printer type is chosen in the Chooser and that the correct PPD file is chosen in the Print Document dialog box, and then hold down the ⌘ key while resizing the graphic. Doing this limits the resizing to specific percentages that maintain maximum image quality on the target printer. For more details about this feature, see Chapter 8.

- **Fonts.** When preparing publications for final output on any PostScript laser printer or imagesetter, be sure to use only PostScript fonts or TrueType fonts. For other kinds of printers, you are best off using TrueType fonts or using PostScript fonts along with the Adobe Type Manager (ATM). You should also keep in mind that most desktop publishing service bureaus use only Adobe Type 1 PostScript fonts. You'll have the best success getting hassle-free imagesetter output if you use Type 1 fonts.

- **Text blocks.** When text blocks are not created properly, you'll often wind up with text that is not aligned as you expected or with missing text that is overset (not all text appears or prints at the end of the text block). Generally speaking, you should follow a few "rules" when working with text blocks: create your publication with as few text blocks as necessary; position most text blocks within column guides or ruler guides; and don't create text blocks that are too much wider than the actual width of the text they contain. You should also use tabs to align text in columns; don't use the spacebar. Proportionally spaced text (discussed in Chapter 6) does not line up properly when you use the spacebar to align it.

☞ **Delete unused elements.** Many printing problems are caused by elements that aren't even supposed to be printed. Before you print, use the Select All command from the Edit menu and look for text blocks that contain no text (they might have a font definition that will produce a Missing Font Error message), items that are totally covered up by other items, or elements that were dragged to the pasteboard but accidentally remain partially on the publication page.

An Overview of the Printing Process

Printing is an important step for your publication, whether you're going to print the final copy of your publication or just create a printed proof for review. Leaving aside the many options in the printing dialog boxes for a moment (these are examined in detail in the next section of this chapter), the printing process includes just three easy steps. The first is selecting the proper printer driver and printer with the Chooser. Next, you'll use the Print command (⌘-P) to access PageMaker's printing options. Finally, as your file prints, PageMaker will give you a progress report and detailed status messages.

Resolution and Screen Frequency

More than any other variable, resolution and screen frequency play essential roles in how well your graphics reproduce. The purpose of this section is to familiarize you with these terms and to present an overview of their importance.

Resolution

Most computer users are familiar with printer resolutions. For those who are not, let's review. Hard copy output devices—printers, imagesetters, slide recorders, plotters—print at various rates of dots per inch (dpi). Most laser printers, for example, print at

300 or 600 dpi. Imagesetters (photo-quality typesetters) print from 900 dpi up to 3,000 and beyond. The benefit of higher resolution is smaller dots. Smaller dots mean more detail and subtleties, sharper lines and curves, and, more important, cleaner halftone screens and photographs.

A combination of screen frequency and resolution affects image quality. Resolution is important because it determines the printer's ability to print higher screen frequencies.

Screen Frequency

Screens and *halftones* (these terms are used interchangeably) are percentages of solids. When you tell PageMaker to tint a box at 20 percent, you are creating a screen. Grayscale photographs, where shades of gray are made up of percentages of black, are also screens. So are the percentages of colors that make up a four-color drawing or photograph. Four-color images are created on a printing press by mixing percentages of cyan, magenta, yellow, and black (CMYK).

Conventionally, halftones are created with a camera. Fine-mesh screens (measured in lines per inch, or lpi) are laid over the object to be *screened*. The mesh separates the image into lines of tiny dots. The size and frequency of the dots determine where the printing press puts ink on paper, thus creating halftones.

Computers and scanners have all but eliminated the need for the fine-mesh screens, but printing presses still work primarily the same. It is important to consider screen fre-quency when preparing documents for the printing press, for a variety of reasons.

The most important consideration is how ink spreads on different paper types. For example, the difference in how soft newsprint and coated glossy paper accept ink is critical. On soft paper, ink soaks in and spreads, running together.

To compensate, halftones printed on newsprint require a *loose* screen, about 75 to 90 lpi, so that ink dots do not spread together, muddying the image. On coated paper, where ink spread is minimal, lpi works best at 133 or higher so that the coarseness of the screen is not noticeable. The trick is to match the lpi to the paper's absorbency so that as little as possible of the screen's coarseness shows, without degrading the halftone through ink spread.

Another aspect of halftone printing affected by lpi (and resolution) is gray scale. Manipulating screen frequency and gray scale can make a tremendous difference in the quality and clarity of *each* photograph. As you can see, this relationship between dpi and lpi is critical. Figure 13-1 and Plate 13 in the color section show grayscale images printed at four different resolutions and line screens. In addition to noticing the tightness and looseness of the various line screen settings, notice how differently the images print on the uncoated stock here from the coated stock in the color insert.

Figure 13-1:
Examples of images printed at various line screens and resolutions

Get help from the professionals: When preparing a document for the print shop, work closely with your service bureau and print shop. When creating graphics and laying out the document, decide the medium on which the work will be reproduced (paper type, copier, etc.). Then consult your service bureau and print shop regarding the best resolution and lpi settings for that medium. Don't worry about seeming like a beginner. All professional designers work very closely with their vendors to assure the best results.

The Macintosh Chooser

Using the Chooser to select the correct printer driver and printer not only determines where your document will print, but it also controls which printing options are presented when you choose the Print command. To access the Chooser, select it from your Apple menu. When the Chooser appears, an icon for each printer driver installed in your Extensions folder in the System Folder appears along the left edge of the dialog box, as shown in Figure 13-2.

Figure 13-2:
The Macintosh Chooser

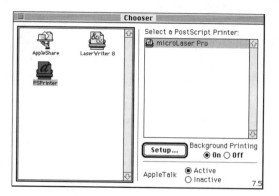

Printer drivers are really little conversion utilities that work at print time to translate your file from the native PageMaker format (in which they are stored on disk) into a format that the printer you select can use. As a result, you can print from PageMaker to any kind of printer for which you have a valid printer driver in the Chooser. Several kinds of printer drivers are common, including those for the LaserWriter, ImageWriter, StyleWriter, and various fax/modems. You can also purchase printer drivers that make it possible to print from your Macintosh to hundreds of different printers not originally designed for the Mac.

When you click the icon of a printer driver, a list of printers of that type currently connected to your Macintosh (either directly or via your network) appears on the right side of the dialog box. If you work on a large network, you'll also have to select a zone from a list that appears below the printer driver icons in order to see a list of available printers.

In order to print in PageMaker, you must select a printer driver in the Chooser even if you don't have any printers connected to your Macintosh, or if you have a printer but it is not the same type as the one on which your document will ultimately be printed. You have to select a specific printer only if you want to print on that printer directly. When printing a PostScript file to disk, you must select the PSPrinter (installed with PageMaker) or LaserWriter printer driver, but you do not need to select a specific printer. Printing to disk is discussed in "The Print Options Dialog Box," later in this chapter.

If you select the PSPrinter or LaserWriter driver, you are presented with a Setup… button, which you must use to select the PPD file for your printer. Click the Select PPD… button and choose the file that matches the printer you are using. If your printer is not listed, you may have not installed the correct PPD when you installed PageMaker, or Adobe may have not included a PPD file for your particular printer. You should contact Adobe or your printer manufacturer to obtain the correct PPD file, but in the meantime, you can click the Use Generic button to print your files.

Also available when the PSPrinter or LaserWriter driver is selected is the Background printing option, which appears just below the list of available printers. If you turn Background Printing on, when you print your file, your Mac spools the document to a file on your hard drive before actually sending it to the printer. The benefit of this is that it allows you to regain control of your Macintosh and continue working, in PageMaker or any other application, while your Mac prints in the background. If you use background printing, you'll need a good amount of free space on your start-up volume, sometimes several times the amount of space the file itself stores on disk (depending on the size of your linked graphic images).

The Print Command

After selecting a printer driver and printer, you are ready to print with either the Print or Printer Styles command. This chapter focuses on the Print command and the many options presented in its dialog boxes, but as described in the "Using Printer Styles" section of this chapter, you can also access them from the Printer Styles command.

When you choose the Print command (⌘-P), the Print Document dialog box appears. This looks like a normal dialog box, but in fact, it is a little different from most in that it is really five dialog boxes in one. This design was used because there are so many options related to printing that they couldn't possibly all fit into just one dialog box, and as demonstrated by the Paragraph Specifications dialog box, nested dialog boxes can get rather unwieldy. So in this dialog box, you can switch among different sets of options by clicking the buttons located just below the Print button. When printing to a PostScript printer, these buttons are Document, Paper, Options, Color, and Features, as shown in Figure 13-3.

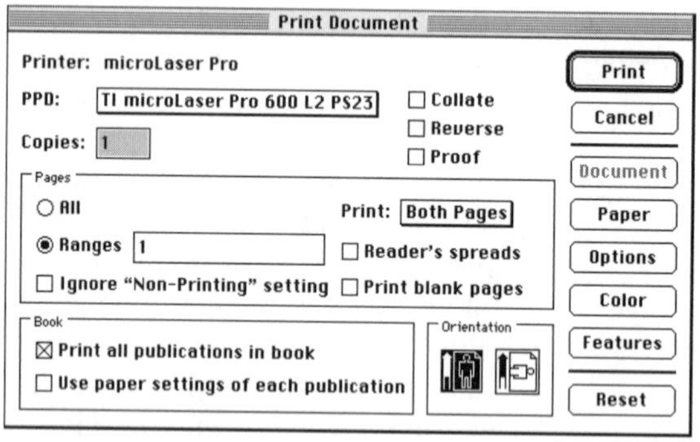

Figure 13-3:
The Print Document
dialog box.

Here's a quick look at the dialog boxes and options these buttons provide:

- **The Print Document dialog box.** This set of options controls the most basic printing issues, such as number of copies, orientation, range of pages to print, collation, proof printing, and whether or not all files in the book list will be printed. You also use this dialog box to select the PostScript Printer Description (PPD) file that corresponds to your output device.

- **The Print Paper dialog box.** This set of options defines the size of the paper onto which you are printing and the paper tray on your printer, and lets you specify reduction or enlargement of your pages. It also provides a tiling option that is used when a single page of the document cannot fit on a single sheet of paper.

- **The Print Options dialog box.** This set of options defines the quality at which graphics in your file print and what kind of printer marks are added to your pages. It also includes all the options for printing your file to disk, including control over the file, how downloaded fonts are handled, and the data format for included graphics.

- **The Print Color dialog box.** This set of options includes control over composite color or color separations, and mirror and invert options for printing film on

PostScript imagesetters. You can choose to print each spot- and process-color ink used in the document individually, and you can convert some or all spot colors to process colors. Other options include screen angles and screen rulings.

☞ **The Print Features dialog box.** This set of options allows you to configure your printer's memory, duplex printing options, and so on. The options that appear here depend on the specific printer and the PPD for that printer.

Each option in these four dialog boxes is described in detail in the following sections of this chapter. Once these options have been set, clicking the Print button begins printing. (When Write PostScript to File in the Print Options dialog box is checked, Print is replaced by Save.) If you're using the Background Printing option in your Chooser, the print file will be spooled into the background so that you can continue working while the file prints. Background printing is also discussed more fully later in this chapter.

Using printer styles to save time and maintain consistency: Most PageMaker users print to a variety of printers, such as desktop lasers for proofing and imagesetters for final output. Each printer requires different settings. You can save time and maintain consistency by using printer styles, as discussed in the "Using Printer Styles" section of this chapter.

Messages During Printing

After you click the Print button and printing begins, PageMaker does a very good job of informing you of what it is doing during the printing process. You are informed of the page number and (if applicable) color separation currently being printed and any fonts that are being downloaded. You also can see status messages that are sent back from your printer. Two different dialog boxes appear during printing, one of which provides the status messages and another that displays a progress thermometer and provides a Cancel button you can use to stop the printing. Another way to monitor printing progress is to watch the page number icons at the bottom of the publication window, which are highlighted as each page is printed.

If you are using the Background Printing option from the Chooser, the printing messages flash by quite quickly as your file is spooled to your hard disk. You can then, optionally, open the PrintMonitor window to watch the actual printing process. The PrintMonitor window, shown in Figure 13-4, provides much of the same feedback information, including page status, font downloading messages, and general printer feedback. You can also use PrintMonitor as a second chance to cancel printing or to reschedule printing for a later time.

Figure 13-4:
Use the PrintMonitor dialog box to control printing

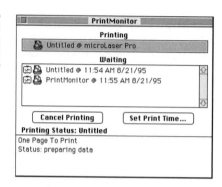

These are the messages that appear in the Print status dialog box and what they mean:

- **Looking for printer <printername>.** To begin the printing process, PageMaker looks over your network for the printer corresponding to the printer name last selected in the Chooser. If this printer is not available, an Alert box appears. In this case, select the Chooser, select the correct printer, and begin printing again.

- **Starting job.** Your computer is now beginning communications with the PostScript printer.

- **Busy.** PostScript printers can process only one job, or file, at a time. If you are not using background printing, and another user is printing to the same printer, you are placed in a queue until the printer is available. If you do not wish to wait, click the Cancel button and try again later or choose another available printer.

- **Preparing printer.** If the printer was just turned on and yours is the first document printed using the PSPrinter 8 or LaserWriter 8 driver, this message appears as the printer is prepared. Even though files such as Laser prep or Aldus Prep no longer exist, the PostScript printer still needs to have a prep file loaded. This job is done automatically by the PSPrinter 8 or LaserWriter 8 driver.

- **Preparing data.** This message appears when PageMaker is translating your publication into PostScript language and sending this information to the printer.

- **Processing job.** This message appears while the PostScript interpreter inside the printer executes the PostScript code.

- **Printing.** This message appears while a page is being printed by the printer.

- **Downloading <fontname>.** As PageMaker automatically downloads font information to the printer, this message displays the name of the font being downloaded.

- **<fontname> is not found.** This message appears in either of two cases: (1) Your document contains screen fonts that are no longer available (dimmed in the Font pop-up menu), or (2) you are using a screen font for which no printer font is available, either in the printer or for downloading.

As your document prints, the lights on your printer flash to indicate activity and, hopefully, progress. On some printers the flashing pattern of the lights actually has meaning: Consult your printer's user manual for specific details for your printer. On most Apple LaserWriters, for example, a double flash means that data is being received by the printer, and a single flash means that the printer is processing data.

The Print Command and Printing Dialog Boxes

When you choose the Print command in most Macintosh applications, you get a Print dialog box provided by the LaserWriter or PSPrinter driver and consequently the box shows very little variation from one application to another. In PageMaker however, choosing the Print command produces a very different dialog box than in other applications. This dialog box includes five selectable sections that offer literally dozens of new options to control the printing of your publication.

The Print Document Dialog Box

When you choose the Print command (⌘-P) from the File menu, the Print Document dialog box appears. This dialog box, shown in Figure 13-5, contains the most basic and frequently used options for controlling the printing process, plus the Paper, Options, Color, and Features buttons with which you select other sets of options for more specialized control over printing. The dialog boxes presented by each of these buttons are described in the subsequent sections of this chapter. Also available is the Reset button, which returns all options in the Print Document dialog box to their default settings.

Figure 13-5:
The Print Document dialog box

```
▒▒▒▒▒▒▒▒▒▒ Print Document ▒▒▒▒▒▒▒▒▒▒
Printer: microLaser Pro                              ┌──────────┐
                                                     │  Print   │
PPD:  [TI microLaser Pro 600 L2 PS23]  □ Collate     └──────────┘
                                       □ Reverse     ┌──────────┐
Copies: [1  ]                          □ Proof       │  Cancel  │
                                                     └──────────┘
┌─Pages────────────────────────────────────────┐    ┌──────────┐
│ ○ All                      Print: [Both Pages]│    │ Document │
│                                               │    ├──────────┤
│ ● Ranges [1        ]     □ Reader's spreads   │    │  Paper   │
│                                               │    ├──────────┤
│ □ Ignore "Non-Printing" setting □ Print blank │    │ Options  │
│   pages                                       │    ├──────────┤
└───────────────────────────────────────────────┘   │  Color   │
┌─Book──────────────────────┐ ┌─Orientation─┐       ├──────────┤
│ ☒ Print all publications  │ │  ▯  ▭       │       │ Features │
│   in book                 │ │             │       ├──────────┤
│ □ Use paper settings of   │ │             │       │  Reset   │
│   each publication        │ └─────────────┘       └──────────┘
└───────────────────────────┘
```

Using Non-LaserWriter Drivers

Even though PageMaker does not use the PSPrinter or LaserWriter Print dialog box, the dialog box presented in PageMaker is specific to the PSPrinter or LaserWriter drivers. If you have any other printer driver chosen when the Print command is selected (for printing to an ImageWriter, StyleWriter, or other QuickDraw printer), a similar but slightly different dialog box appears, as shown below. It does not offer the Type option, as non-PostScript printers do not use PPD files, and it does not offer the Page independence option since font downloading is also not an issue on non-PostScript printers. The Paper button and dialog box are replaced with the Setup... button and a dialog box specific to the chosen printer that allows you to set the paper size and other printer-specific options.

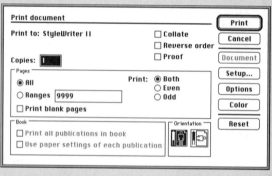

The Print Document dialog box options are

❧ **Printer.** The name of the printer currently selected via the Chooser is listed here. If this is not the printer on which you want to print your document, and you do not intend to print a PostScript file to disk, click the Cancel button to close the Print Document dialog box, and use the Chooser to select the correct printer. Using the Chooser to select your printer is discussed more fully earlier in this chapter.

❧ **PPD.** This pop-up menu lists all of the PPD files (PostScript Printer Description files) currently installed in the Printer Descriptions folder in your Extensions folder. PPD filenames are abbreviations for the name of the printer they represent and the version of the PostScript interpreter installed in them. Dozens of PPD files are provided and installed along with PageMaker 6, but you may also obtain

PPD files from printer manufacturers, Adobe Systems Inc., or your Macintosh dealer. Choose the one that corresponds to the PostScript printer on which you'll be printing your publication.

- **Copies.** Enter the number of copies that you want to print—any number from 1 to 32,000. In most cases, you should print only small quantities of your document directly from PageMaker, since it is usually faster and more economical to reproduce many copies of the publication by photocopying or offset printing.

  In fact, to discourage printing of large quantities directly from PageMaker, earlier versions supported a maximum quantity of only 100 copies. This limit has been removed to support new PostScript printers that are specifically made to handle large print runs, but it should not be used to overwork poor old laser printers.

- **Collate.** Checking this option forces PageMaker to print one complete copy of the requested page range (or selected book list) before starting on the next copy. This eliminates the need for manual collation but significantly increases printing time. Using the Collate option slows printing because it forces the printer to re-image each page for each copy of the publication. Without collation, the page is imaged only once, and then all copies of that page are printed at that time.

- **Reverse order.** Most printers normally print your pages in sequential order, although some naturally print in a last-to-first order. This option allows you to reverse your printer's natural page sequence, so that if you usually get the first page first, you'll instead get the last page first; and if you usually get the last page first, you'll instead get the first page first.

- **Proof.** Printing graphics, especially bitmapped images or TIFF files, is one of the slowest aspects of printing any page on a PostScript printer. This option removes all graphics from your publication and replaces them with rectangular placeholders. This allows you to proof the copy and basic page layout without wasting time printing the graphics. It may be the best kept secret in printing efficiency.

- **Pages/All.** This option causes every page of the publication to be printed. If the Print all publications in book option is also selected, every page in every document in the book list will be printed.

- **Pages/Ranges.** This option lets you specify individual pages for printing, a range of pages you want to print, or any beginning or ending portion of the publication that you want to print.

  To print individual pages, enter their page numbers separated by commas (3,7,19). To print a range of pages, enter the first and last page numbers in the range separated by a hyphen (6-9). To print a beginning section of the publication, enter a hyphen and then the last page number in the beginning section (-11). To print an ending section of the publication, enter the first page number in that section and then a hyphen (26-).

You can also combine these options. For example, to print pages 3, 5, 12, 14 through 26, and 39 through the end of the publication, you would enter: 3,5,12, 14-26,39-. To print page 77, 9 through 15, and all pages up to 6, you would enter: 77,9-15,-6.

- **Pages/Ignore "non-printing" settings.** This option coincides with PageMaker's Non-Printing command on the Element menu. When an object is defined as Non-Printing, PageMaker doesn't print it. Checking this option overrides Non-Printing, saving you from having to go back and redefine non-printing objects to printing objects when you want them printed.

- **Pages/Print.** Use the options on this pop-up to limit the pages printed to either even-numbered pages or odd-numbered pages. These options apply to both the All and the Ranges options; so even if you specified a range of pages that includes even page numbers but clicked the Odd Pages option, only the odd-numbered pages would print.

- **Pages/Reader's spreads.** This option tells PageMaker to print both pages of a spread on the same sheet of paper. This is primarily a proofing option that allows you to see both pages in a spread as they will print on a press. What this option does is reduce the size of each page, change the page orientation to landscape, and then print reduced pages.

- **Pages/Print blank pages.** Pages that have no elements (except Master-page elements) are normally suppressed from printing in order to avoid wasted paper or film. If you want to print the blank pages in your publication, click this option.

- **Book/Print all publications in book.** Checking this option causes the print job to include all publications in the current book list. (If there is no current book list, this option is dimmed.) When printing all publications in a book, the Pages/All, Pages/Ranges, Print Both Pages/Even Pages/Odd Pages, and Print Blank Pages options are honored for all publications printed. If the Pages/Ranges option is used, publication pages are not renumbered even if one of the Auto renumbering options is selected in the Book list dialog box. For more information about building a book list, see Chapter 12.

- **Book/Use paper settings of each publication.** When using the Print all publications in book option, checking this option causes each publication to use its own Size and Source settings from its Print Paper dialog box. This makes it possible to use a different size or type of paper and/or paper tray for each publication in the book list. (More details on these options are provided throughout this chapter.)

- **Orientation.** This option provides you with control over how the pages in your publication appear as they print. A page can be Tall (taller than wide) or Wide (wider than tall), as indicated by the two icon buttons. In most cases, this will match the orientation of the publication pages as set in the Document Setup dialog box, but when printing to imagesetters, you may want to rotate the page to use paper or film more efficiently.

After setting the options in the Print document dialog box, you can proceed in several ways:

ↈ **Click the Paper, Options, Color, or Features button.** Each of these brings up another set of options, as described in the rest of this section, that control your printing.

 Hold down Shift and click Print (or Save). This trick saves all the settings you've made in the Print Document, Print Paper, Print Options, Print Color, and Print Features dialog boxes as the current default settings but does not initiate a print job.

ↈ **Click the Print button.** This initiates the actual printing process.

ↈ **Click the Cancel button.** This cancels the printing process and returns you to the publication window.

The Print Paper Dialog Box

Clicking the Paper button in the Print Document dialog box, or any of the Print dialog boxes for that matter, causes the box to become the Print Paper dialog box. This dialog box, shown in Figure 13-6.

Figure 13-6:
The Print Paper
dialog box

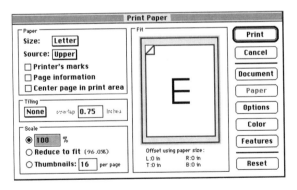

The Print Paper dialog box contains these options:

ↈ **Size.** This pop-up menu provides a list of the paper sizes available for the current printer based on the PPD file you've selected. Some PPD files also provide a Custom option that allows you to set any paper size you need. When you choose

Custom, the Custom Paper Size dialog box, shown in Figure 13-7, appears. From here you can set page width and height, paper margin, and a few other custom options, such as page orientation.

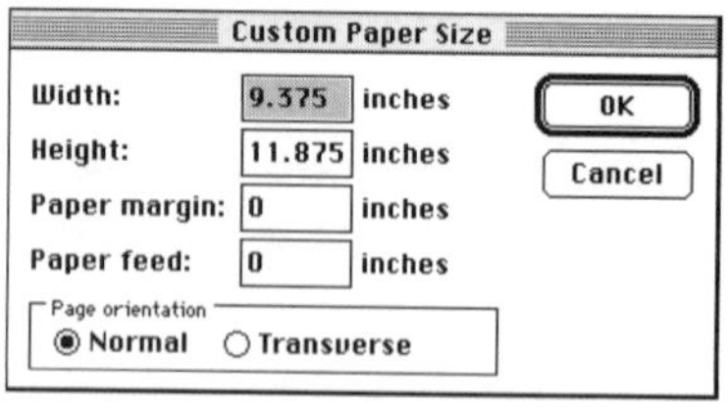

Figure 13-7:
The Custom Paper Size dialog box

Custom Paper Size		
Width:	9.375 inches	OK
Height:	11.875 inches	Cancel
Paper margin:	0 inches	
Paper feed:	0 inches	
Page orientation		
● Normal ○ Transverse		

Most laser printers can print only to within ¼ to ½ inch of their edges. For example, when you select a Letter paper size, the Size is listed as 8.5 by 11 inches for either the Apple LaserWriter NT or for the Linotronic 100; however, the Print area is only 8 by 10 inches for the LaserWriter NT, because the printer cannot actually print to the physical edges of the paper; but the Print area will be 8.5 by 11 inches for the Linotronic, because it is capable of printing to the physical edges of the paper. Any elements in your publication that are positioned outside the Print area for the selected paper size will not appear on the printed page. Most imagesetters can print edge to edge at most paper sizes.

In order for your document to print correctly, you must choose a paper size at least as large as the page size you selected in the Document Setup dialog box. Additional space must be provided for printer's marks and page information such as crop marks, registration marks, separation names, and so forth. If your paper size is not large enough for your pages, you can use the Scale options to reduce your publication, or print using the Tile option, as described in the next section.

Table 13-1 lists the amount of space required, in addition to the page size, to fit extra marks on printed pages.

Table 13-1
Space Requirements for Fitting Extra Marks on Printed Pages

Option	Vertical Space	Horizontal Space
Printer's marks	.75 inch	.75 inch
Page information	.5 inch	.5 inch
Both	.875 inch	.75 inch

Use the Fit option to determine the page-size to paper-size relationship: If you don't know how much space is available on the paper in your target printer, refer to the Fit section of the Print Paper dialog box for a visual representation of the page, print area, and paper size. Fit is discussed a little later in this section.

∞ **Source.** This pop-up menu presents the paper trays available for the current printer based on the PPD file you've selected.

∞ **Printer's marks.** Selecting this option adds crop marks, registration marks, density-control bars, and a color-control bar to your printed pages. (Color-control bars appear only when printing separations or to a color composite printer.)

Crop marks are used to trim your pages down to their final size after printing. Registration marks are used to align the various separations in a color printing job so that all colors and elements appear in their proper locations. Density-control bars print samples of each process or spot color used, in 10% increments, and help your service bureau or commercial printer check the calibration of the imagesetter on which your pages are printed. Color-control bars show 100% and 50% tints of the process colors and combinations of the process colors. These can be used to check color on a color printer, or they can be used by your service bureau or commercial printer to check the quality of your pages before and after printing. These marks will not appear if the selected paper size is not large enough. Figure 13-8 shows a page containing marks. Table 13-1, earlier in this chapter, detailed the space requirements for the marks.

∞ **Page information.** Selecting this option adds the filename, page number, current date, and color separation name (in 8-point Helvetica) to the lower-left corner of each page in your publication. These marks will not appear if the selected paper size is not large enough. This information is handy for identifying what file the page comes from, when it was printed, and so on. Also, the print shop can use it to identify separation plates.

∞ **Center page in print area.** Your pages are normally centered within the physical boundaries of the selected page size, but on some output devices, you may want to use this option to center the pages within the printable area instead.

∞ **Tiling.** The Tile option is used when your publication pages are larger than the paper on which you need to print your file (and you don't want to print the page at a reduction), or if you want to enlarge your pages so that they are larger than the largest available paper size. Tiling allows PageMaker to print each page in your publication in sections that can be pieced together after printing, as shown in Figure 13-9.

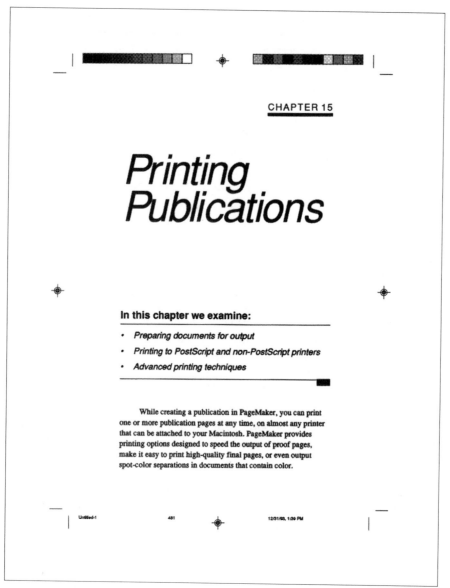

Figure 13-8: A page output with crop marks and color-separation marks

Figure 13-9:
The Tile option
allows you to
print oversize
pages and piece
them together.

You can control tiling manually or have PageMaker do it automatically. If you select the Manual tiling option, you print each section of your page individually, manually setting the exact portion of the page to be printed on each tile. To do this, position the ruler zero point in the publication window to designate the upper-left corner of each section you want to print. Then, with the Manual option selected, click the Print button (or press the Return or Enter key) to print the specified section. Continue this process, adjusting the zero point to specify another section of the page and then clicking Print in the Print Document dialog box until all necessary sections of the page have been printed. The main benefit of manual tiling is that it allows you to control how a page is broken into sections while avoiding page breaks that would make it difficult or impossible to reassemble the page accurately, such as in the middle of a photograph.

The Auto Overlap option, on the other hand, instructs PageMaker to create automatically all the tiles required to print each page. When this option is used, PageMaker starts at the upper-left corner of each page and continues to print sections of the page until the entire page has been output. Each section overlaps all other sections by the amount of space specified in the overlap field next to Tile. A larger overlap will result in easier reassembly (by avoiding awkward breaks) but will require more sections per page.

∞ **Scale.** To print your publication at any size other than 100% of normal size, use one of these three options. The Scale option itself allows you to enter any reduction or enlargement percentage between 5% and 1600% of the current size, in increments of .1%. Of course, enlargements may not fit on the selected paper size, so you may have to use the Tile option as well. When a page is printed at either a reduced size or an enlarged size, the printed page is drawn to the center of the paper.

∞ **Scale/Reduce to fit.** This option automatically calculates the amount of reduction necessary to fit the current page size on the currently selected paper size within the current printable area. If the Printer's marks and Page information options are chosen (described earlier), the reduction also makes sure these fit on the printed page. PageMaker shows the amount of reduction required next to this option.

Calculating reduction percentages: To calculate the reduction percentage needed to reduce a document to fit, divide the horizontal print area of the paper by the horizontal page size (such as 8/8.5 = 0.941) and the vertical print area by the vertical page size (such as 10.5/11 = 0.955). The smaller result corresponds to the largest possible percentage of the original size; in this case, 94.1%.

∞ **Scale/Thumbnails.** Thumbnails are small pictures of the pages in your document. They allow you to get an overview of the entire publication. Selecting the Thumbnails options allows you to print images of several pages of your publication on a single page, at a reduced size. As shown in Figure 13-10, thumbnails allow you to view several pages simultaneously for design, both individually and in relation to each other. The "per page" field to the right of the Thumbnails option specifies how many pages are to be printed on a single sheet of paper— the more thumbnails per page, the smaller the size of each one.

∞ **Fit.** The Fit section is the preview window in the middle of Print Paper. It provides a visual representation of the page in relation to the paper size selected and how the selection you make in several of the Print dialog boxes affects printing. When you choose Printer's marks, for example, the printer marks are displayed in Fit, as shown in Figure 13-11.

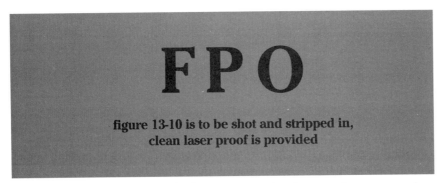

FPO

figure 13-10 is to be shot and stripped in,
clean laser proof is provided

Figure 13-10: Printing thumbnails allows you to preview the general appearance of your publication.

Figure 13-11:
The Fit preview showing printer
marks

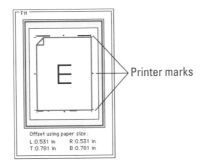

In Fit, the yellow area represents the paper size, and the white area inside the blue border represents the page. The "E" represents emulsion side up (mirrored) or emulsion side down. (Some printing presses require that the page be mirrored. When you select Mirror in Print Color, discussed later in this section under "Print Color," the "E" faces left.) When you select Negative in Print Color, the white page area turns black and the "E" is reversed.

The numbers below the preview show the page offset as L, R, T, and B. When the page is larger than the paper, these numbers are red.

Getting additional page information: You can get offset information about your page by double-clicking the page icon in the Fit preview, which brings up the Offset Calculation option shown in Figure 13-12. Double-clicking this area again returns you to the Fit view.

Figure 13-12:
The Offset Calculation option in Fit in the Print Paper dialog box

After setting the options in the Print Paper dialog box, you can proceed in several ways:

☞ **Click the Document, Options, Color, or Features button.** Each of these brings up another set of options that affect printing. (The Document options are described earlier; the Options options, Color options, and Features are described in the following parts of this section.)

☞ **Click the Print button.** This initiates the actual printing process. More information about this process is provided later in this chapter in the section "Messages During Printing."

☞ **Click the Cancel button.** This cancels the printing process and returns you to the publication window.

The Print Options Dialog Box

Clicking the Options button in the Print Document dialog box causes the box to become the Print Options dialog box. This dialog box is shown in Figure 13-13.

Figure 13-13:
The Print Options
dialog box

```
                          Print Options
  ┌ TIFFs/Images ───────────────────────────┐      ┌─────────┐
  │ Send image data:  Optimized             │      │  Print  │
  │ Data encoding:    Send binary image data│      └─────────┘
  └─────────────────────────────────────────┘      ┌─────────┐
  ┌ PostScript ─────────────────────────────┐      │ Cancel  │
  │ Download fonts:   PostScript and TrueType│      └─────────┘
  │ ☒ Use symbol font for special characters │      ┌─────────┐
  │ ☐ Include PostScript error handler       │      │Document │
  │ ☐ Write PostScript to file:  [    ] Save as...│  └─────────┘
  │ ◉ Normal        ☐ Page independence      │      ┌─────────┐
  │ ○ EPS           ☐ Extra image bleed      │      │  Paper  │
  │ ○ For prepress  ☐ Launch post-processor  │      └─────────┘
  └─────────────────────────────────────────┘      ┌─────────┐
  ┌ Printer communication ──────────────────┐      │ Options │
  │ ☐ Query printer for font and memory information│ └─────────┘
  └─────────────────────────────────────────┘      ┌─────────┐
                                                    │  Color  │
                                                    └─────────┘
                                                    ┌─────────┐
                                                    │Features │
                                                    └─────────┘
                                                    ┌─────────┐
                                                    │  Reset  │
                                                    └─────────┘
```

The following options are in the Print Options dialog box:

- **TIFFs/Images/Send image data.** This set of options determines how much data from your imported bitmapped and TIFF images gets sent to the printer. They do not affect EPS graphics. Using these options can reduce printing time by limiting the printed quality of your TIFF graphics. They present an alternative to the Proof option in the Print Document dialog box, which temporarily removes all imported graphics.

  The Normal option sends all the data so that the printer can produce the highest-quality representation of the image. The Optimized option resamples the data in your images, on the fly, to eliminate extra data in the graphics. Extra data means that the image was scanned or created at a resolution that is more than twice the current line screen of your output device. In this case, the printer cannot use all of the data the graphic includes, so PageMaker discards some data in order to speed printing. Unfortunately, this on-the-fly resampling may affect your image quality, so you are better off either resampling the graphic in Adobe Photoshop or Adobe PrePrint, rescanning it at the correct resolution, or printing using the Normal option, which may be slow but will not sacrifice quality.

  The Low resolution and Omit images options are the real time-savers and are not meant to be used for final output. Low resolution prints any TIFF or bitmapped graphics at 72 dpi, so you can see them but not at their maximum resolution. Omit images cuts the TIFF graphics out altogether.

- **TIFFs/Images/Data encoding.** These options affect the format in which data from your TIFF images and bitmapped graphics gets sent to your printer. They do not affect printing quality.

  The Send binary image data option cuts down on the time it takes graphics to be sent to your printer, but if you experience printing problems (such as time-out errors), you can use the Send ASCII image data option to improve the chances of successful printing.

- **PostScript/Download fonts.** Selecting one of these options tells PageMaker to include in the PostScript file the PostScript or TrueType printer fonts associated with any fonts used in the publication, unless these fonts are listed by the PPD file as being already resident in the target printer. PostScript files are discussed a little later in this section.

- **PostScript/Use Symbol font for special characters.** Many fonts do not have some important symbol characters (including ©, ®, ™, Σ, π, ∫, Ω, ¬, ≤, and ≥) in the "standard" Macintosh locations. Using this option causes the Symbol font, which is automatically installed in all versions of the Macintosh System Software, to be used instead of the selected font in order to ensure that these symbols are printed correctly.

Use the Symbol font option wisely: This feature provides a useful safety net when documents include symbols in text files that are first generated in a word processing program using some standard Macintosh font (such as Times, Helvetica, or even Geneva). When a document like this is transferred into PageMaker and formatted in a less standard font, especially in fonts not from Adobe Systems, there is a good chance that symbol characters will not translate correctly. Using this option can save you the trouble of manually locating every symbol and resetting it. The downside of this option, however, is that the resulting Symbol font characters, which are designed to match either the Times or Helvetica fonts, may stand out as a different type style than the fonts used in the rest of the publication.

⋙ **PostScript/Include PostScript error handler.** In the past, the only information you got when a document failed to print was a message that said "Document is OK but cannot be printed" — not very helpful. This option gives you the opportunity to have the PostScript error handler downloaded into your printer, which will cause a page to print whenever an error occurs, documenting the PostScript error type, the PostScript command that caused the error, and a possible solution to the problem. In order to benefit from this information, you'll usually need some understanding of the PostScript language, but you can also use this information when you call Adobe Technical Support to discuss a printing problem.

Get more help from an advanced PostScript error handler: A simple PostScript error handler is provided along with PageMaker, but service bureaus and other professionals may wish to purchase a third-party error handler that offers additional error information. You should not use this option when printing files to disk for output at a service bureau (discussed next), unless the service bureau requests that you do so, because printed error pages would waste their film and could result in additional charges on your output bill.

⋙ **PostScript/Write PostScript to file.** Rather than printing your publication directly to a PostScript printer, this option lets you capture the PostScript code created by the printing process in a disk file that can be easily transported for remote printing or used in some post-processing application such as Adobe TrapWise or Adobe PressWise.

Benefits of printing to disk: If your document is going to be printed at a remote location (such as a service bureau), there are three potential benefits of printing a PostScript file to disk instead of just sending the original PageMaker publication. First, it avoids the possibility of not having all the screen fonts that are used in the document available when the file is printed, causing faulty font printing (such as substituting Courier for the font you used in the document). You can also include any printer fonts that may not be available at the remote location. Second, it makes it impossible for anyone to accidentally change any aspect of the publication. Third, some service bureaus offer a discount for pre-PostScripted files.

By default, the name of the PostScript file you create is set as the existing publication name plus the extension .ps. If you choose the EPS or For prepress options (described next), other default names appear. You can change the name of the file by making any desired modifications to the name as it appears after this option. The PostScript file is saved to the same location as your publication file, by default, but you can click the Save As… button to select any other location where you want the PostScript file to be saved.

☞ **PostScript/Normal, EPS, For prepress.** These three radio buttons determine the format of your PostScript disk file. The Normal option creates a standard PostScript file, ready for downloading, containing all pages in your publication or book. The EPS option creates an EPS file for each page of your publication or book. Each page is automatically named with the existing publication filename, plus an underscore, the page number, and the .EPS extension. (So a publication named January News would create EPS files named January News_1.EPS, January News_2.EPS, and so on.) You can use this option to save a page from a PageMaker publication for use in other applications or even within another PageMaker publication, as shown in Figure 13-14.

The For Prepress option creates an OPI-compatible file that can be used in Adobe PrePrint, Adobe TrapWise 2.0, or other OPI-consuming post-processing applications. (OPI stands for Open Prepress Interface, which is a common interface among post-processing applications for creating separations.) OPI files are automatically named with the publication filename and the .SEP extension. For more on these prepress applications, see Chapter 14.

In order for PostScript printer fonts to be included in the file, they must reside in the Fonts folder inside the System Folder, or in the same folder as any screen fonts added using MasterJuggler or Suitcase II. If a PostScript screen font is used in the publication but its printer font is not available, it is not sent to the PostScript file, and the font will print incorrectly (Courier will be substituted) if it is not first downloaded to the output device before printing. Downloading fonts to a print file dramatically increases the size of PostScript files, and many service bureaus do not want you to embed fonts in your print files, anyway. Be sure to check with your service bureau to see if it has the fonts your document requires and, if not, whether it wants you to include them in your PostScript file.

↪ **PostScript/Page independence.** This option affects how font use is managed within the pages of your publication when it is downloaded to your printer or printed to a PostScript file on disk. Normally, all necessary fonts are downloaded at the beginning of a file, and then every page of the publication assumes that the fonts are available. When this option is selected, however, font calls (which cause downloading when the font is not already present) are made on a page-by-page basis. This can increase the size of print-to-disk files and may require more memory in the PostScript printer but provides additional flexibility in how print-to-disk files can be used.

You will not normally use this option when printing directly to a printer or if you are printing to disk and your publication will later be downloaded directly to a printer. You may need to use this option if your print-to-disk file will be manipulated with a separation, imposition, or trapping program that handles fonts differently than PageMaker. Your prepress service bureau should tell you if the use of this option is necessary for your files.

- **Extra image bleed.** When creating PostScript files, PageMaker normally includes only those elements, and parts of elements, that fit within the page margins. This option changes that default, including up to one inch of extra bleed in the file for cases when your PostScript files will be post-processed using applications like Adobe TrapWise that can take advantage of this extra data.

- **Launch post processor.** This is the "day late and dollar short" command. It exists because back when PrePrint was the only PageMaker alternative for creating color separations, Aldus (the previous publisher of PageMaker) got a lot of flack regarding the number of steps necessary to use two different programs to create separations. Using this option causes PrePrint (or another indicated post-processor) to be launched automatically and the PostScript file opened when the For prepress option is used. Now that PageMaker supports separations *and* trapping, you probably won't use this option.

After setting the options in the Print Options dialog box, you can proceed in several ways:

- **Click the Document, Paper, Color, or Features button.** Each of these brings up another set of options that affect printing. (The Document options and Paper options are described in the preceding part of this section; the Color and Features options are described in the following part of this section.)

- **Click the Print button.** This initiates the actual printing process. More information about this process is provided earlier in this chapter in the section "Messages During Printing."

- **Click the Cancel button.** This cancels the printing process and returns you to the publication window.

The Print Color Dialog Box

Clicking the Color button in the Print Document dialog box causes the box to become the Print Color dialog box. This dialog box is shown in Figure 13-15.

The options in the Print Color dialog box are

- **Composite/Grayscale (Color) /Print colors in black.** When a document contains colored elements, you use this option to print all elements in the document on a single piece of paper or film. In other words, this is how you print a color document without making color separations. If the current printer is a non-color (grayscale) printer, the option is titled Grayscale; if it is a color printer, the option is titled Color.

  When printing a composite version of a publication on a non-color printer, each color is represented by an appropriate level of gray when the default Composite option is selected. Alternatively, you can click the Print colors in black option, and all elements will be printed as 100% black regardless of their actual color.

  When printing on a color printer, each color in the document is printed as accurately as possible on the selected printer. If you want to defeat the colors from printing and print all colors as black (although we're not sure why you would do this), you can use the Print colors in black option.

- **Separations.** The alternative to making composite prints is to print separations, where each spot or process color on each page is printed on its own separate sheet. A document containing both process-color elements plus three spot colors would then produce seven plates for each publication page (one plate for each of the four process colors plus one page for each spot color.) Printing separations prepares the file for color reproduction via commercial printing. Before producing separations, you should review Chapter 10, read the *Print Publishing Guide* provided with your PageMaker documentation, and talk to your commercial printer.

  If you choose the Separations option, you can defeat the printing of any one color and convert all spot colors into process colors, using the Color list options described next.

If the Write PostScript to file option and the EPS option are selected in the Print Options dialog box, the Separations option is dimmed and unavailable.

∽ **Color list.** Below the Separations option is a scrolling list of every process and spot color used in your publication. The word Process precedes each of the four process colors (cyan, magenta, yellow, and black), and all other colors are spot colors. A check mark appears to the left of colors that are selected for printing. To toggle this check mark to include or remove a color, double-click the color name or select the color and click the Print this ink option. Use the Print all inks or Print no inks button to turn on or off all the colors.

If your document uses process colors, and you want to convert all the spot colors to process so that only four color separations will be produced for each page, click the All to process button. Note that this conversion occurs for printing purposes only—the spot colors remain defined and applied to the elements in your publication. If you want to convert a single spot color to process, you'll have to close the Print Color dialog box and return to the Edit Color dialog box for the color you want to convert and select Process from the Type menu. (To get to the Edit color dialog box, choose Define colors from the Element menu, select the color, and then click the Edit... button.)

∽ **Remove Unused.** This option removes the unused colors from the separation list. If the color isn't in use, you don't need it. You might as well remove it to keep from inadvertantly printing an unwanted plate.

∽ **Mirror.** When printing negatives on high-resolution imagesetters, the Mirror option is used to set emulsion up or down, depending on how film is loaded into the imagesetter. You'll have to ask your service bureau how this option should be set. It is normally selected to achieve right-reading emulsion down or wrong-reading emulsion up output, and deselected to achieve right-reading emulsion up or wrong-reading emulsion down output. The most common is Emulsion-down, meaning you should leave this option unchecked. But you should ask your print shop how they need the film produced.

∽ **Negative.** The Negative option prints a negative image of the publication, making all black items clear, all white items print black, and all screened items at 100% minus their value (80% screens will print at 20%, 20% screens at 80%). See Figure 13-16 for an example. Note that this setting should be used when preparing separations for the print shop.

∽ **Preserve EPS colors.** PageMaker lets you edit the colors used in any imported EPS graphics, as described in Chapter 10. Checking this option causes all EPS graphics to print with their original colors, as they were imported regardless of any changes you have made to those colors within PageMaker. If this option is not selected, EPS graphics will print using any color modifications you have made in PageMaker.

Figure 13-16:
An example of positive and negative output

☞ **Optimized screen.** When printing colors or halftones, the screen ruling and angles used in the halftoning process are critical to the quality of the resulting output. Screen rulings determine the number of halftone cells that print per linear inch and, along with the resolution of the output device, thereby determine the number of shades of gray (or the number of tints of a color) that can be produced. Angles (or *screen angles*, as they are more commonly called) determine the orientation of the lines in a halftone cell for each specific color. Each of the four process colors is normally set at a varying angle so that the colors appear to blend as smoothly as possible. When incorrect angles are used, unsightly moiré patterns become apparent in the final printed document.

The current PPD file provides PageMaker with information regarding the proper screen rulings and angles as defined by the printer manufacturer. Usually there are a variety of possible screen rulings and angles, and several resolutions at which the printer can be used. The Optimized screen option lets you choose among the available combinations of screen rulings and resolutions. Each of these combinations carries with it specific rules and angles for each process color.

To select a screen ruling and resolution, click the Optimized screen option pop-up menu and choose among the available combinations, as shown in Figure 13-17. Your choice for this option should be discussed with your service bureau and commercial printer, as limitations posed by the imagesetter that will be used to output your publication and the press on which your document will be reproduced usually determine the optimum screen ruling and resolution for your job. Screens and resolution are discussed at the beginning of this chapter.

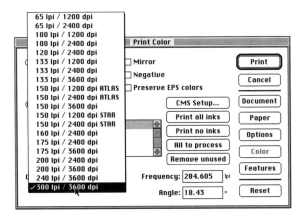

Figure 13-17:
The Optimized screen option pop-up menu presents screen rules and resolution options for the selected printer.

When you have selected a screen ruling/resolution combination, specific angles and rulings are applied to each process color and spot color in your publication. These values will apply to all elements in your publication, except those images for which the angle or rulings have been modified in the Image Control dialog box, discussed in Chapter 8. You can see the resulting angle and ruling for any specific color by selecting that color from the color list and looking at the values in the Frequency and Angle option boxes. You can modify any individual angle or ruling, but this is highly discouraged unless you have been directed to do so by, or have consulted with, your service bureau and commercial printer. If you modify any values for the Frequency and Angle options, the Optimized screen option will read Custom, indicating that a change has been made to the values provided by the PPD file.

⌐ **CMS Setup...** This button brings up the Color Management System Preferences dialog box, which allows you to set color management options, as discussed in Chapter 10. Color management is an involved subject; you should read the information covering it in Chapter 10 before making changes in Color Management System Preferences.

After setting the options in the Print Color dialog box, you can proceed in one of three ways:

⌐ **Click the Document, Paper, Options, or Features button.** Each of these brings up another set of options (as described in the preceding parts of this section) that affect printing.

⌐ **Click the Print button.** This initiates the actual printing process. More information about this process is provided earlier in this chapter in the section "Messages During Printing."

☞ **Click the Cancel button.** This cancels the printing process and returns you to the publication window.

The Print Features Dialog Box

The options that appear in the Print Features dialog box, shown in Figure 13-18, depend on your printer and specifications written into the PPD for that printer. Many PPDs don't have features defined in them. For Bill's MicroLaser 600, shown in the figure, he can switch between paper trays and tell PageMaker how much memory is available in the printer. Many of the options that show up in these highly varied dialog boxes are the same options you typically set from the printer's control panel. This dialog box saves you from having to mess with the printer for each print job, which is useful when the printer isn't nearby.

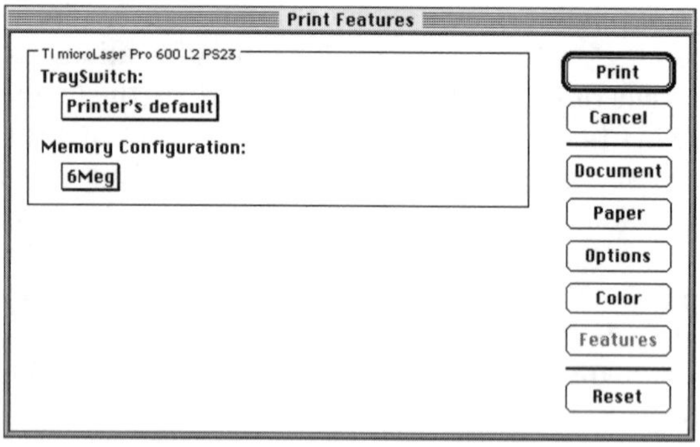

Figure 13-18:
The Print Features
dialog box

Using Printer Styles

Most desktop publishers print on several different types of devices, such as desktop lasers, color proof printers, and imagesetters. Each print job and device can require different settings in each of the five Print dialog boxes discussed in the previous section. To achieve desired results, you must remember to set them all correctly. Each time you change devices, you must remember to reset the options again, which can require too much time and costly print job errors. You can avoid all this setting and resetting up of devices by using PageMaker's Printer Styles command, which allows you to save settings for each type of print job. Then, when you get ready to print, all you do is select the appropriate style, and PageMaker does the rest.

To set up printer styles, select Define from the Printer Styles submenu on the File menu, which brings up Define Printer Styles dialog box shown in Figure 13-19. From here you can name the current printer setup as a printer style, create a new printer style, or edit an existing printer style.

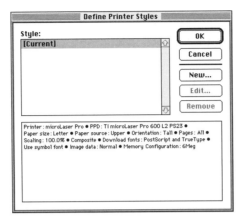

Figure 13-19:
The Define Printer Styles
dialog box

Notice in the figure that the Current printer setup is selected and described in the dialog box. You can name the current configuration simply by clicking the New... button. The Name Printer Style dialog box opens, allowing you to give the printer a name consisting of 1 to 31 characters. Once the printer style is named, you can edit it by clicking the Edit... button, which brings up the Print Document dialog box. From here you make changes to the selected printer style the same as you would set up a printer using the Print Document, Print Paper, Print Options, Print Color, and Print Features dialog boxes described in the previous sections of this chapter. The only difference in using this dialog box is that an OK button replaces the Print button, returning you to Define Printer Styles, rather than printing the document.

You should create printer styles for each printer you use in each configuration. For example, sometimes you print a 100 percent letter-sized sheet, and sometimes it's necessary to reduce a print job to make it fit on a letter-sized sheet. In the latter case, your printer would require different settings. Figure 13-20 shows several printer styles defined in the Define Printer Styles dialog box. When you finish setting up styles, they show up on the Printer Styles submenu, as shown in Figure 13-21. When you select a printer style from the list, the Print Document dialog box opens with the settings in the style, ready to print.

Setting up printer styles fast: You can easily set up several slightly different styles for the same printer by first defining the printer in Print Document and then using a combination of the Current option and New button in Define Printer Styles to make slight changes to the setup and giving each new printer style a descriptive name.

Figure 13-20:
A list of printer styles in the Define Printer Styles dialog box

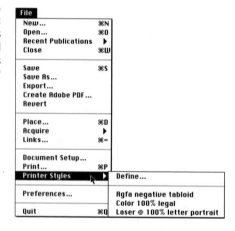

Figure 13-21:
Use the Printer Styles submenu to select predefined printer styles

Summary

●● Before you print your publication, you should check your document for common items that cause printing problems. These include incorrect page sizes, page elements placed beyond the printable margins of the printer, incorrectly scaled graphics, use of incompatible font formats, sloppy text blocks, and unnecessary page elements.

●● Two important considerations when printing graphics are resolution and screen frequency. They determine how well images reproduce on different types of paper.

●● Also before printing, you must use the Chooser to select at least a printer driver and, unless you are going to print a PostScript file to disk, the specific printer on which you want to print. Also, the Chooser is used to turn on background printing.

●● The Print dialog box is really five dialog boxes in one, which you control with five buttons along the box's right edge. When printing on PostScript printers, you can use the Print Document dialog box, the Print Paper options dialog box, the Print Options options dialog box, the Print Color options dialog box, and the Print Features dialog box.

●● The Printer Styles command lets you save printing settings in style sheets.

●● While your publication prints, PageMaker provides messages regarding printing status, font downloading, and printing errors.

●● You can set up output devices fast with printer styles.

Taking Advantage of Adobe's Prepress Tools

14

In This Chapter

- ➡ How PageMaker is used in the toolboxes of professional publishers
- ➡ Electronic imposition with Adobe PressWise
- ➡ Electronic trapping with Adobe TrapWise

The success that PageMaker has achieved over the past nine years has been due to the fact that beginners and experts alike can use the program to produce anything from office newsletters to newsstand magazines. But this is not to say that beginners and experts use PageMaker in exactly the same way: Professional publishers have much more exacting standards of precision, they use color more extensively in their documents, and they reproduce their publications in large quantities using offset printing. As a result, professional publishers must work more deliberately within PageMaker than casual publishers, but they must also supplement PageMaker with other desktop production tools, such as color separation utilities, trapping programs, and imposition software.

These tools are sometimes used by professional publishers themselves, but more often, color separation, trapping, and imposition are services provided to the desktop publisher by a service bureau or commercial printer. This marks a return to the kind of specialization that historically characterized the prepress and printing industry and is probably a positive change for desktop publishers. Each of these areas is technically complex and depends upon a detailed knowledge of prepress and printing that only these professionals can provide. Relying on service bureaus or printers to do the color separations, trapping, and imposition with electronic tools saves both time and money, not to mention the considerable burden of the technical expertise necessary for a professsional-quality job in these areas.

This chapter introduces two Adobe prepress products — Adobe PressWise and Adobe TrapWise — as well as Adobe Fetch, a nifty little image cataloging utility. These are largely used by service bureaus and commercial printers, but if you produce color publications or long documents, you should understand the features these programs provide and the capabilities they make available to you.

Adobe TrapWise

Before we discuss using Adobe TrapWise, let's take a look at trapping and some of the issues (and problems) involved in color printing.

What Is Trapping?

The term *trapping,* as used in desktop publishing parlance (or the larger domain of electronic prepress), describes the process of intentionally creating a small overlap of the colors in adjacent objects. This technique avoids problems caused by printing press misregistration: most significantly, small gaps between objects that allow the underlying paper color (usually white) to appear, and hue shifts caused by unintentional color overlaps. These gaps and hue shifts are easily noticeable and completely unacceptable in most color-printing situations.

Creating and controlling these intentional overlaps (*traps*) is not a trivial task. Accurate trapping depends on the colors, shapes, and relationships of the objects on the page and on the printing circumstances under which the document will be reproduced. For each trap, color, width, and placement must be defined. And for the best possible trapping, these attributes often must change as the color and relationship of the trapped objects change.

The process referred to here as trapping is also known by several other names, including *chokes and spreads, fatties and skinnies, lap register, making grips,* and *shrink and spread.* Complicating the definition further, the term *trapping* has also traditionally been used to describe issues relating to printing multiple layers of ink on top of each other and the way these overlapping inks react to each other. In this book (and in all Adobe documentation), *trapping* is defined as creating color overlaps.

Why Trapping?

In a perfect world, trapping would not be necessary because every color would print in the exact location intended. In reality, such perfection is improbable for a number of reasons.

The first procedure that makes trapping necessary is imagesetting, when the electronic file is printed and color separations are made. These separations should be aligned perfectly, or *in register*, but every imagesetter has some degree of inherent inaccuracy (sometimes called *slop*), and so misalignment is common.

The measure of imagesetter inaccuracy is known as repeatability, referring to the capacity to mark in the correct position page after page. This is a particular problem on older capstan-based imagesetters, many of which are still in use and which can be off by as much as .012 inch for every 18 inches of paper or film printed. This margin of error is too great for the generation of acceptable color separations. Capstan imagesetters manufactured in 1992 or later are far more consistent, potentially varying only .006 inch for every 48 inches of paper or film printed. Drum-based imagesetters perform even better, varying no more than .001 inch for every 24 inches of paper or film printed. Separations produced on drum-based imagesetters are well within the standards of the prepress and printing industries but still contribute to the need for trapping.

The next potential trouble spot that necessitates trapping occurs during film assembly, or *stripping,* where the stripper may inaccurately position a piece of film. This happens infrequently because most strippers are skilled professionals, and alignment marks make it easy to check their work, but it is possible — especially on more complicated jobs. Electronically created documents tend to require very little mechanical page assembly, however, so this problem is less common than it used to be. Errors can also be introduced during plate making, when vacuum pumps, exposure frames, and expo-sure systems are used to transfer film images onto plates. Nevertheless, misalignment, inaccurate exposure time, inconsistent light intensity, and operator error are all poten-tial trouble spots.

Once a job is on the printing press, the potential for register problems increases dra-matically. In fact, this is the most common place for significant misalignment to occur. As paper moves through the press at a high speed during printing, pressure from rollers and the pull of edge grippers propel the paper, and ink and water are applied as neces-sary. This can result in misregistration for a variety of reasons:

- ☞ The mechanical elements that move the paper can cause the paper to stretch, as can the heat resulting from this process.

- ↪ Ink and paper characteristics and humidity can also contribute to misregistration.

- ↪ Mechanical misalignment of one or more rollers or grippers can cause the paper to be out of position when ink is applied.

- ↪ As sheets of paper are accelerated through one part of the press and then stopped before being accelerated again by another set of rollers or grippers, "bounce" can occur, leaving the paper out of position.

Any one of these circumstances, or any combination of them, can result in preventing the colors involved from abutting as they should. Instead, these colors overlap in some areas and leave gaps where the paper remains visible in others. Proper trapping eliminates these problems.

Of course, trapping is not without its own problems and costs. Trapping is, by the given definition, the intentional addition of color overlaps, and when two colors overlap, a third color is almost always created, because process inks have a degree of transparency. The overlapping color allows some of the underlying color to show through, so the two colors appear as a mixed, or third, color.

Adding these overlaps (and the "third colors" they create) around the borders of many or most objects on a page is clearly not the preferred solution in terms of the aesthetic fidelity of the original image — it is the lesser of two evils: The small intentional overlaps and third colors caused by trapping are far preferable to the unintentional overlaps, third colors, and gaps that result when a document is not trapped.

Proper trapping minimizes the unpleasant effects of overlapping colors by using colors that produce the least noticeable overlaps possible and by positioning traps in such a way that most overlaps will be completely unnoticed by most viewers. It also minimizes these effects by applying traps in the correct widths, based on both the elements involved and the anticipated printing methods.

Trapping is not a subject in which most designers or production professionals are well versed. And with very limited exceptions, available desktop publishing software doesn't provide very good trapping tools, be they manual, automatic, or semiautomatic. Even PageMaker 6's trapping is only passable. As a result, even well-designed and otherwise well-constructed pages, when separated on PostScript imagesetters, can result in less-than-perfect results on press because of poor or nonexistent trapping in the electronic files.

Trapping electronic files has been a difficult problem for a variety of reasons. Good trapping requires extensive knowledge of color as well as the prepress and printing processes. And the inherent complexity of trapping requires commitment as well as patience. Until recently, good trapping was also waiting for technological breakthroughs because limits in existing software solutions were frustrating at best. There have been several different approaches to trapping implemented on the desktop, but each has provided only partial success and has imposed its own costs.

Adobe TrapWise largely solves the electronic trapping problem because it separates trapping from the design and production of electronic pages, it automates the complex and time-consuming aspects of accurate trapping, and it provides prepress professionals with a dedicated tool that they can use to produce precise trapping solutions that were never before available.

Color on the Desktop

To appreciate the importance of trapping, you have to think about how colors are defined in PageMaker (and your other software applications) and how color is applied to electronic objects, images, and pages. As you probably know, there are two broad color categories — spot color and process color — which correspond to the two different ways color is reproduced in the printing industry.

Spot colors are defined and used when documents will be printed with premixed semi- or fully opaque inks. Typically, spot colors are selected from a palette of existing colors, such as the PANTONE matching system, although you can create spot colors by mixing colors from any color model supported by your software application. For spot colors, the elements in an electronic file (and the subsequently output separations) designate only the location and tint of the colors used; the actual colors are based solely on the ink used by your printer. (Tints are lightened colors produced by limiting the number and size of the dots used to print the color.) With most desktop applications, you can define spot colors using any one of several color models, such as HSL (hue, saturation, lightness), HSB (hue, saturation, brightness), or RGB (red, green, blue), or by selecting from existing color-matching libraries, such as Dianippon, PANTONE matching system, or Toyo.

Process colors, in contrast, are defined as composite percentages of cyan, magenta, yellow, and black (CMYK) and are printed using overlapping dots (halftone screens) of these colors. By varying the number and size of the halftone dots printed for each CMYK color, you can produce about 50,000 different colors using only four ink colors. In PageMaker, you can define process colors in CMYK percentages, or you can select colors from CMYK matching libraries from PANTONE Inc., Focaltone, or TruMatch.

When you're ready to print the electronic file, you must create separations based on the number of inks that will be printed on the press. For documents that will be reproduced using spot-color inks containing only a few spot colors, a separation is produced for each page for each ink color; all the elements to which spot color #1 have been applied are on sheet 1, all the elements to which spot color #2 have been applied are on sheet 2, and so on.

When you print a document using process colors (also known as four-color printing), any elements in the document that are not already defined as CMYK colors must be converted into CMYK. This includes colors originally defined using the HSL, HSB, or RGB color models, colors selected from a spot-color matching library, and colors scanned and saved in an RGB format such as TIFF. This conversion, which is known as *color separation,* can be done either before or during printing on an imagesetter. (Usually, you can exclude any spot color from conversion, so that you can create a fifth color or varnish separation when needed.)

Trapping Basics

There are four basic trapping techniques — *overprinting, knocking out, spreading,* and *choking.* Each modifies the relationship between two color objects. *Overprinting* describes situations where one object is printed on top of another, thereby eliminating the primary problem that trapping is intended to avoid — gaps where paper can show through. This is not a panacea, however, because the transparent nature of process inks causes overprinting to yield an unacceptable third color in most situations. As a result, overprinting is the preferred solution only when the overprinting color is sufficiently darker than the underlying color to prevent a noticeable third color from being created or when opaque spot-color inks are being used.

Knocking out (or creating a knockout) describes the opposite situation, where the overlapped area of an object is removed so that the top object prints directly on the paper. It is this very situation that makes trapping necessary: When the top object isn't perfectly positioned within the knockout, portions will unintentionally overlap the underlying color (possibly creating third colors), and gaps will appear where the paper can show through. To compensate for these potential problems, spreads and chokes must be applied when objects are knocked out.

A *spread* is created by extending the edge of the top object so that it is larger than the area of the knockout where the object is supposed to print. This allows some margin for error, ensuring that even with a little misalignment, the knockout area will be fully covered. On the computer, it is relatively easy to spread most objects by adding or adjusting the stroke of their edges. A *choke* is the opposite of a spread — it shrinks the area of the knockout (as opposed to enlarging the size of the object that will fill the knockout) — but it has the same result, adding a margin for error to ensure that even with a little misalignment, the knockout area will be fully covered.

You can create overprints, knockouts, spreads, and chokes using traditional mechanical production techniques, using tools available within many desktop software applications, or using dedicated trapping software such as Adobe TrapWise. We describe each of these methods later in this chapter.

Defining Traps

Not every element needs to be trapped, only those that are physically adjacent to other objects *and* would be likely to cause noticeable color problems if shifted. These problems (paper showing through or distracting third-color overlap) are not likely to occur, for example, between two colors that have largely similar color components (because each contains similar percentages of cyan, magenta, yellow, and black inks) or when one color is substantially darker than the other color so that overprinting is a satisfactory trapping method.

When a trap is needed, the color, placement, and size of the trap must be defined. A basic rule of trapping suggests that the color of the lighter object should be used to create the trap, which should be positioned to overlap the darker object. This is generally true, but there is another important concern: The shape or edge between the colored objects must be maintained. Some objects — rectangular graphic elements, for example — can easily be spread or choked without dramatically changing their appearance, whereas other elements — small- to medium-sized text or delicate line art, for example — are easily disfigured by even subtle edge changes. As a rule, thin or delicate objects (including text) should be overprinted whenever possible, should be choked with lighter adjacent colors when overprinting is not possible, and should almost never be spread.

In many cases, rather than using one of the object colors as a trap color, you can get better results by using a tint of one of the object colors or a new, third color defined using the common color components of both object colors. To select a third color to use as a trap color between two process colors, you examine the component ink percentages of the two adjacent objects and then define a new color using the higher of the ink percentages for each color component. For example, if the color of one object is C25 M40 Y10 K15, and the color of the other object is C40 M10 Y70 K5, then the trap color that uses the higher of the common ink percentages should be C40 M40 Y70 K15.

Traps using tints or third colors are likely to be far less noticeable than traps using the color of the lighter object. Creating tint or third-color trap colors is difficult, if not impossible, using traditional methods, but is relatively easy with electronic publishing tools. As you will see, TrapWise creates these traps automatically and even varies the third color as the objects' colors change gradients and vignettes. (A *gradient* is a fade from one tint level of a color to another tint level of that same color. A *vignette* is a fade from one color to another, different color.)

Trapping gradients or vignettes has been nearly impossible with traditional techniques because of the need to vary the trap color and because these color changes require changing the location of the trap — shifting from a choke to a spread and perhaps back again — as the light-to-dark relationship of the objects changes. TrapWise positions these traps automatically as well.

The size of a trap, which is expressed most often in either inches or points, depends on the printing method used, the tolerances of the printing equipment, and the expertise of the operators. As a rule of thumb, most traps vary between .25 point and .5 point. Smaller traps are used for high-quality sheet-fed work, and larger traps for less demanding jobs like web-press newsprint. You should always obtain the size of the trap needed from your printer, who can base trap size on equipment and experience. Building traps too small will not overcome the undesirable effects of misregistration, and building traps that are too large will result in excess overlap, which creates third colors on your pages.

Traditional Trapping

With traditional prepress techniques, when overprinting cannot solve a potential trapping problem, traps are created by selectively overexposing film, thereby causing page elements to grow slightly and overlap adjacent elements. This is usually done by increasing the size of (*spreading*) the foreground object, so that it slightly overlaps the underlying background object. Alternatively, you can enlarge the background object (*choking*), so that it overlaps the foreground.

Film overexposures that create chokes or spreads are made by sandwiching an original film negative between the glass cover of a contact frame and clear spacer film over new contact film. A diffusion sheet is then placed on top of the contact frame's glass cover, and light is directed from above. Light rays passing through the diffusion sheet are set at various angles. As these angled rays pass through the original film, those near object edges travel an additional distance (due to the clear spacer film) before striking the new contact film. The result is a growth of the original object as it appears on the new film.

The amount of growth is controlled by the thickness of the clear spacer film used (normally .003 or .004 inch thick, although two or more sheets can be used for additional thickness, which makes additional growth possible) and the duration of the light exposure (longer exposures cause more growth).

Trapping with Desktop Applications

Some desktop applications provide features designed to help you perform basic trapping, such as options for defining knockouts or overprinting, and control over the stroke and fill of each individual object. These are especially prevalent in drawing applications, such as Adobe FreeHand, Adobe Illustrator, and Corel Draw!, and to a lesser extent in page layout packages such as PageMaker and QuarkXpress. Bitmap painting packages and image-editing software usually do not offer specific trapping capabilities because it generally isn't necessary to trap colors within one bitmapped graphic (although anti-aliasing to avoid sharp edges is sometimes helpful). More frequently, the bitmapped graphic needs to be trapped relative to other objects when it is imported into another graphic application or a page layout program.

To trap using knockout, overprint, stroke, and fill commands, you must determine the individual trapping needs of each element on your page and then set the options appropriately. This requires an understanding of trapping rules, certainty about how each color and each object will relate to other objects and colors when the piece is finished, and information from the printer about press requirements. Good results can be achieved in this way, and for simple pages containing simple color relationships or a small number of color interactions, it is often the best solution. For more complicated pages, however, achieving good results requires considerable time and diligence.

QuarkXpress offers several trapping options worth noting. Xpress's automatic trapping option applies a trap of a user-defined amount based on the program's calculation of the color relationship between adjacent objects. (The luminance of each color is checked, and then the lighter object is trapped to the darker.) You can define specific color relationships so that when an object of a certain color is adjacent to an object of another certain color an overprint, a knockout, a spread, or a choke is applied. This eliminates the need to make trapping decisions on an object-by-object basis, since the software will apply *color rule* trapping based on the selected colors. These rules are not optimal in all situations, however — small objects with delicate shapes often should not be treated like larger objects, regardless of similarities in the color relationships, for example. (There is a workaround for this deficiency: Two versions of the same color can be defined and named differently, with different trapping rules defined for each. Either version of the color can then be applied to an object, depending on the trapping needs.)

The limitation of Xpress's trapping capabilities is the same as that of other programs that allow you to create chokes and spreads on an object-by-object basis: When a single element is adjacent to more than one other element, or when the color of an element changes (as in gradients or vignettes), there is no way to apply the correct trapping color. In other words, if one part of an object needs one kind of trap, and another part of that object needs another kind of trap, your options are either to build a trap that will be right for part of the element and wrong for part of the element, build a trap that is the best compromise, or build no trap at all. Xpress provides control over this decision with its Indeterminate option, but there is no perfect decision in this frequently occurring situation; therefore, this method is not the optimal solution to such trapping problems.

PageMaker, on the other hand, looks at abutting colors and determines which is lighter and which is darker (neutral densities). It then decides whether to trap based on the settings in Trapping Options. When the program decides to trap an object, it spreads the lighter color into the abutting dark one, or darker ones when dealing with more than two colors. PageMaker then overprints the lighter colored trap over the edge of the darker color. The size of the trap depends on the Trap width setting in Trapping Options. This process is slightly superior to Quark's, but it is still not precise enough for sophisticated jobs.

Which color PageMaker uses to trap also depends on the types of colors, process or spot:

- For abutting process colors that require trapping, PageMaker creates a trap color consisting of the CMYK values in the lighter color that are higher than the same values in the abutting color.

- For spot colors, PageMaker traps the darker color with the lighter color. This same process is used when a process color and spot color need trapping.

Trapping with Adobe TrapWise

When files will be trapped with Adobe TrapWise, the designer and production professional are free to complete the pages without building any traps at all. In fact, while TrapWise can work with files in which manual traps have been built, it will generally work better if the files contain no traps at all. In order to use TrapWise, each page of the file that will be trapped must be saved as a separate single-page Encapsulated PostScript (EPS) file.

TrapWise 2.0 and later releases support multiple page PostScript files such as those created in PageMaker 6.

TrapWise builds traps automatically in a four-step process:

1. First, your file is passed through a software RIP (raster image processor), which converts the PostScript into a proprietary bitmapped format.

2. Then, TrapWise analyzes this bitmapped format to find the edges of every object on the page. This ability is based on patent-pending technology and is how TrapWise differs from all other electronic trapping solutions.

3. TrapWise then builds traps for all elements on the page, based on the size, color, and location of object edges and based on a set of trapping parameters that you have defined. TrapWise handles spot colors, process colors, and pages containing process colors and up to four spot colors. TrapWise is the only desktop solution that can vary the color, size, and positioning of traps as it moves along the edge of an object so that gradients or vignettes are trapped accurately.

4. Finally, TrapWise creates a new EPS file, containing the original, unmodified PostScript file with the traps appended to it. This EPS file is ready for imposition and/or imagesetting.

The only part of this process that takes any effort at all is the specification of the user-defined trapping parameters. These parameters, described next, make it possible to control the color relationships that TrapWise traps, the size of the traps TrapWise creates, and how TrapWise handles special situations like rich blacks, blends, spot colors, and more. To make TrapWise as efficient as possible, it can store all of these user-defined settings in trapping style sheets that it calls configuration (.CNF) files.

How TrapWise Builds Traps

TrapWise builds its traps by following a number of trapping rules and by considering the trapping parameters set in the Trapping Defaults dialog box. The first rule that TrapWise follows when building a trap is that it creates a trap that spreads lighter colors onto the darker colors. This tends to preserve the visual edge of darker objects and results in less noticeable traps. To do this, TrapWise must determine which color is "lighter" and which color is "darker" by measuring the *neutral density* of every color.

Neutral density is based on the amount of light reflected back from the paper to which the color is applied. It is calculated using a mathematical formula that converts the component ink percentage of each color to a precise neutral density value. This value is then displayed in TrapWise's Measured Color window when the densitometer tool is selected. Neutral density values reflect an inverse relationship between the amount of light and the neutral density value: Dark colors have high neutral density values based on the low amount of light they reflect, and light colors have low neutral density values based on the high amount of light they reflect.

Once TrapWise knows the neutral density of the adjacent objects, it then checks to see if a trap is necessary by comparing the difference between the values to the minimum step threshold option. This is important because it isn't necessary to create a trap every time one color abuts another, but only when the colors of the objects are likely to cause trapping problems in the event of press misregistration. The minimum step threshold specifies the amount of variation between the CMYK components of two adjacent colors before a trap *might* be needed. By default, the value of the minimum step threshold is 10%, so any color component (cyan, magenta, yellow, or black) in the first color that is within 10% of the corresponding component in the second color will not be trapped. If all color components are within 10% of each other, no traps will be added.

In addition to the presence of at least two component colors that vary by at least the minimum step threshold, at least one of these colors must be getting larger while at least one is getting smaller in order for a trap to be created. So if there are three colors that vary by an amount larger than the minimum step threshold, but they are all present in larger percentages in one object than in the other, no trap will be created. In that case, the result of a gap between the objects would be a color somewhere between the two colors, and, therefore, adding a trap would not improve the situation.

Once TrapWise knows that a trap must be created, it must decide on a trap color, trap width, and the placement of the trap. TrapWise can determine trap colors in two different ways. In its Overprint mode, the trap color includes only those component colors of the lighter object that are darker than those in the darker color. These colors are then overprinted on the darker color. Alternatively, in Conventional mode, traps are built as they were built traditionally, by using the higher component percentage of each component color.

In certain situations, an additional step is taken to achieve better results by slightly reducing the percentage of some or all component colors in the traps. This process is called trap color reduction and is supported by TrapWise in two ways. With manual trap reduction, you specify reductions for each process and spot color independently. This affects all common colors when you use conventional trapping (because all common colors are used in the trap), but only affects the darker components of the lighter color (because those are the only colors used in the trap) when overprint trapping is used. Automatic trap reduction is a built-in TrapWise feature that makes traps less noticeable without significantly changing their color. It does this by not selecting the higher of each available component ink percentage but instead using the smaller of the two values for each ink where the percentage difference does not exceed the minimum step threshold. This method is used only if two adjacent colors have three or more common color components.

Trap width is set as a trapping option and is set separately for Normal objects, traps set Under black, and traps set Over images. The normal trap width should be sufficient to compensate for any misalignment that might occur in prepress or on the printing press, and values between .002 and .005 inch are common. Trap widths for the Under black and Over images options are usually the same as the Normal option or smaller.

Determining the placement of a trap is easy when one element is clearly lighter than another. When adjacent elements have similar neutral densities or include graduated fills (fills in which the amount of color varies from one part of the object to another) or vignettes (blends in which the object changes from one color to another), determining trap placement is more complex. In these cases, the trap must be placed so that it partially overlaps the edge of each object. Fortunately, TrapWise manages trap placement automatically, sliding traps from one element to the other as neutral densities change.

Other TrapWise Features

Beyond this basic process of determining which elements on a page need to be trapped and building appropriate traps for those elements, TrapWise provides several other important features and capabilities:

- **Trapping black elements.** Because the color black is always as dark or darker than any adjacent elements, TrapWise handles black differently in a number of ways. First, since the edge of the black object always defines the relationship between a black object and another object, adjacent non-black colors always spread into blacks.

  If the black object is adjacent to a process color, the trap color is made up of the CMY components of that process color. If the black object is adjacent to a spot color, the spot color is used as the trap color. TrapWise does not create a trap when a black object abuts another black object. If the black object contains some percentage of cyan, magenta, and/or yellow ink, it is considered a *rich black*, and the non-black component colors are called *support screens*. Support screens are often used to ensure a deep, dark black that may not be possible with pure black ink alone. Support screens also add another trapping consideration: Misregistration can cause a support screen to become visible where it inadvertently extends beyond a black edge. To eliminate this possibility, support screens must be choked back from the edge of the black object in which they appear. TrapWise does this based on the value of the Under black option in the Trapping Defaults dialog box.

ᴔ **Trapping images.** When a file contains TIFF or MacPaint images (or OPI comments pointing to such files), TrapWise recognizes these images but does not create traps within these images: It traps the image only to any adjacent objects. In fact, each image is treated as a single object filled with a uniform color defined as 100% cyan, 100% magenta, 100% yellow, and 100% black. Because this is the darkest color possible, any adjacent element will always be lighter, and so TrapWise always traps by spreading the adjacent elements onto the image. The color of the trap, as in any other situation, is based on the component colors of the adjacent objects and on whether conventional or overprint trapping is being used. The width of the trap is defined by the Over images option in the Trapping Defaults dialog box. (TrapWise 2.0 adds the ability to trap continuous-tone images against other elements.)

ᴔ **Trapping resolution.** TrapWise allows you to specify the resolution at which the resulting file will be imageset, a value that determines the number of pixels TrapWise manipulates when it traps the file. Normally, this option is set at the actual imagesetting resolution, but in some cases, you can specify a value lower than the resolution at which the file will actually be imageset to get faster trapping and smaller resulting EPS files. Doing so, however, also produces somewhat lower-quality results because it affects the placement and shape of the traps, so this should only be done after some testing and consultation with your printer.

ᴔ **Ink control.** TrapWise can successfully trap EPS files containing up to four spot colors and the four process colors. (TrapWise 2.0 can trap files with up to 16 spot colors.) If your trapped file will be printed using a spot-color ink for each spot color present in the file, spot-color trapping is handled automatically. If any of the spot colors will be converted into process colors before (or during) separation, however, you must trap those colors as if they are process colors so that the correct trap colors will be applied.

ᴔ **Trap zones.** Although TrapWise is normally used to trap entire pages, on many pages only a small percentage of the page is actually at risk for trapping problems. In these cases, it is a waste of time to have TrapWise perform its complex conversion and analysis on the entire page. A page that is made up primarily of black text on a white background (which fills so much area on so many pages) but includes one complex EPS graphic is a good example. On a page like this, only the area of the EPS graphic really needs to be trapped. On other pages, different areas of the page might have very different kinds of graphics, and the trapping parameters that are right for one part of the page may be inappropriate for another.

To handle these situations, TrapWise supports *trap zones,* which allow you to define a set of trap parameters that apply only to specific areas of the page. By creating more than one trap zone on a page, you can trap different areas of your page using different trapping settings.

↪ **Trap previews.** To help you see the trapping decisions that TrapWise is making for your file, TrapWise can produce grayscale and full-color trap previews. Grayscale previews display traps in red so that trap locations are highly visible and it is easy to measure trap color with the densitometer tool. Full-color previews show the exact trap color, size, and placement (to the degree of accuracy possible on your monitor) and also allow you to analyze trap color with the densitometer tool.

↪ **RoboTrap.** This add-on program, provided with TrapWise at no extra cost, makes it possible to batch-process files through TrapWise or set up automatic trapping that takes all EPS files placed in a specific folder (or directory in Windows), traps them using a predefined configuration file, and places the resulting trapping file in another specified folder (or directory). With RoboTrap, the process of trapping files, which can be relatively time-consuming, can be set up and then run unattended (keeping the program busy all night, for example) until all trapping has been completed.

Imposition with Adobe PressWise _

When you create multiple page documents such as newsletters, magazines, or books, the publication pages that you finish in PageMaker are only the starting point of a complex process that ends when your finished publication is bound and ready to be distributed and read.

One of the vital steps in this process is combining the pages of your publication into *signatures*. Signatures are groups of 8, 16, or 32 pages that are arranged in such a way that once the signature is properly folded, trimmed, and bound, the final pages wind up in the proper order and orientation for reading. Determining which page goes where when building signatures is called *imposition*.

To get the general idea of imposition, fold a piece of paper into quarters, like a greeting card. Then number each panel, starting at the first page and continuing inside and out through the pages as you come across them, as if you were paginating a book. Now unfold the page, and you'll find that some of the numbers appear upside down and that page 1 is not on the same side of the same page as page 2. This is an imposition form. If you reprinted this page, front and back, on a new sheet of paper, you could fold the new paper like the original, trim away the top two folds, and staple the center folder. The result would be an eight-page, saddle stitch booklet.

To design an imposition form correctly, you must take into account the folding pattern, binding method, paper stock, and publication design that will be used. Each page must be positioned within the signature with great precision, to make sure that it is centered and correctly aligned after final trimming. This is a very complex task — there are literally hundreds of possible imposition forms, and only one or two will work for a specific printing job. And any mistakes in the imposition aren't likely to be found until after printing, when all pages are folded and it turns out that page 17 is upside down or page 32 follows page 6. Imposition must be done right the first time.

Traditionally, imposition was done by hand by a group of folks called *strippers*. (Very few of these strippers have any resemblance to Belle Star, although we do hear they get pretty wild at their annual convention — but that's another story.) Strippers manually build signatures by mechanically assembling page negatives. They follow imposition forms that they've learned over years of experience, and the entire process is relatively slow and accordingly quite expensive. Building signatures for a single 32-page four-color project can take even an experienced stripper as long as four hours.

When imposition is done electronically, the calculations that determine which page goes where are handled by the computer, and pages are positioned with perfect mathematical accuracy. Signatures that would literally takes hours and hours to produce manually are completed in just seconds, and pages come off the imagesetter ready to be burned into plates, or at least nearly ready. Electronic imposition has only recently become practical because of new wide-carriage imagesetters — between 40 and 60 inches in some cases — that are capable of printing 2-, 3-, or 4-page wide signatures as single sheets. If the width of the imagesetter is less than the size of the total signature, electronic imposition can still be done, but the signature is printed as tiles that are then stripped together. Even this saves $1/2$ to $1/3$ of the time and effort of manual stripping in most cases.

How PressWise Works

Adobe PressWise takes finished electronic pages from many different sources — Adobe PageMaker, QuarkXpress, Macromedia FreeHand, Adobe Illustrator, and others — and electronically imposes them so that they are ready for imagesetting. The program can save finished impositions to disk as PostScript files or can directly manage the printing of these files to imagesetters. The general workflow used with PressWise goes as follows:

1. **Finished files are saved in the PostScript file format.** To impose a publication electronically, you start by saving the finished PageMaker publication to disk as a PostScript file. If any pages of the publication you are creating were produced in other programs, such as QuarkXpress, Adobe FreeHand, Adobe Illustrator, or Adobe Photoshop, you must save these files as PostScript files.

2. **Launch PressWise.** Depending on your particular workflow, you can choose to impose your files before or after color separation and before or after electronic trapping. Usually, however, files are both separated and trapped before they're imposed.

3. **Load your PostScript files.** PressWise allows you to open the PostScript versions of all files (up to 32) that will be a part of your publication. As it opens each file, PressWise scans the PostScript code to learn about each page in the file and the fonts and colors used on those pages. The Page list, shown in Figure 14-1, includes an icon for each page in each file you have opened and the order in which those pages will appear in your final publication. You can reorder these pages freely — even rearranging pages between different publications. You can also delete pages or add blank pages that act as placeholders for pages that will be mechanically stripped in later.

Figure 14-1:
The Page list dialog box shows all open pages and publications.

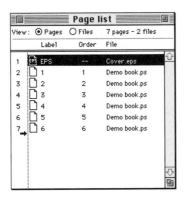

4. **Choose or create an imposition template.** PressWise uses templates much like PageMaker uses style sheets. A template file contains settings for every PressWise option regarding one specific imposition. Dozens of ready-to-use imposition templates are included with PressWise, and you can modify any of these, if necessary, or you can build your own templates from scratch. You can also get imposition templates from others and use them in your copy of PressWise. Figure 14-2 shows signature options, and Figure 14-3 shows template editing options.

Once an imposition template is selected, a preview of your imposed file appears on-screen, allowing you to check the page order and arrangement. You can then add, remove, or reorder pages and print a thumbnail signature.

5. **Print the imposed file to an imagesetter or to disk.** The resulting files are imposed signatures. Print these on a wide-format imagesetter and you're ready to go. Or tile them to a not-wide-enough format imagesetter.

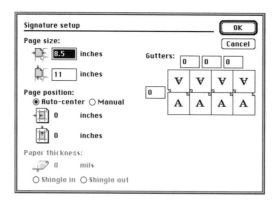

Figure 14-2:
The Signature setup
dialog box

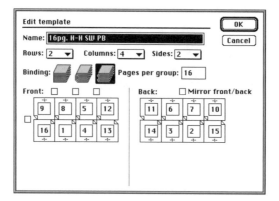

Figure 14-3:
The Edit template
dialog box

Imposition Templates and PressWise Features

PressWise imposition templates are essentially style sheets containing every option and parameter for one particular kind of imposition. Following is a quick overview of many of the options you can control for each PressWise imposition template, and some other key PressWise features:

- **Perfect bound, saddle stitch, or combination (Smyth) binding.** Selecting one of these three popular binding formats determines how PressWise arranges your pages and signatures.

- **Individual page rotation.** Any page in your form can be rotated to create head-to-head, tail-to-tail, or head-to-tail templates.

- **Form independent page numbering.** Page numbers are calculated, or manipulated, based on the total number of pages in a form (front and back), and PressWise automatically figures out the number of the back of the form when you change numbering on the front of the form, and applies numbering changes from the first form to all other forms in the template.

⬧ **Trim page size with shingled gutters.** You can define any fold in your template as a gutter, specifying the amount of space that should be added. In addition, you can specify shingled gutters where you define the paper thickness, and PressWise automatically adjusts pages to take into account the creep that occurs when folded pages move from the inside to the outside of a publication.

⬧ **Press Specifications.** PressWise lets you enter the press sheet size, specify gripper edges, and define side guides, center marks, and color bar positioning. Figure 14-4 shows the options.

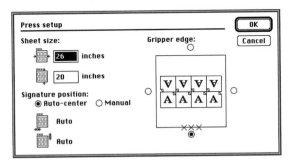

Figure 14-4:
The Press setup
dialog box

⬧ **Printing options.** PressWise offers a surprisingly powerful set of printing features. These include a wide range of printer's marks (crop marks, registration marks, collation marks, density bars, and color bars), tiling support for narrow carriage imagesetters, OPI support, and full support for PostScript Printer Description (PPD) files. The Print options dialog box is shown in Figure 14-5.

Figure-14-5:
The Print options
dialog box

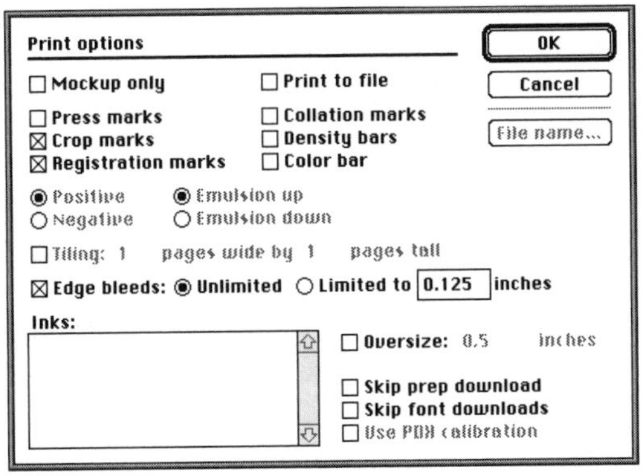

In addition, PressWise has its own built-in batch printing, which allows you to print multiple jobs in the background to multiple imagesetters simultaneously.

Image Cataloging with Adobe Fetch

Keeping track of graphic files has never been easy. Graphic files come in a great many file formats, usually don't have terribly evocative names, and often take up too much space and consequently wind up being moved around frequently. All of these problems occur even when your publishing output is quite modest, and they grow geometrically when you're working on lots of publications, doing graphic-intensive work, sharing files with others on a network, or using large amounts of clip art or stock photography.

 Note that Adobe Fetch has nothing to do with the FTP or gopher functions of the Internet or the Web. There are several search-programs for the Web with names like "Fetch" that have nothing to do with the operations of the Adobe Plug-in we are describing here.

Not too long ago, the idea of using a dedicated software package to keep track of your graphics would have been overkill. Today, the increasing size of hard drives, the introduction of Kodak's Photo CD technology, the vast amount of available high-quality clip art, the ease with which you can do your own color or grayscale scans, and the popularity of removable storage media like Syquest or Bernoulli drives or CD-ROM players make it nearly impossible to keep track of your graphic files *without* a software package dedicated to that task.

Adobe Fetch is designed to solve these problems by providing an image database with which desktop publishers can keep track of all their graphic files. When you use Fetch, you can create one big database to keep track of all of your graphics, or you can create any number of smaller databases, each of which tracks the graphics stored in one particular location or associated with one particular project. In each database, Fetch stores miniature versions of each cataloged graphic, as well as lots of information about each graphic, such as its size, file format, storage location, and any key words you associate with that graphic in order to help find it later.

Fetch lets you browse all of these items in a scrollable list or as graphic thumbnails, even if the actual files are stored on removable cartridges, network file servers, or CD-ROMs. Or instead of browsing, you can search for items by name, location, or keyword. Once you find an item you want to use, you can preview that item at full size from within Fetch, launch the application that created the file, or transfer the item into another application.

 There is a disabled sample of the Fetch application on the CD-ROM disc included with PageMaker.

Working with Fetch

To use Fetch, you create a database, called a *catalog*, in which you will store thumbnails of your graphics files, sounds, movies, and text files. You can create and maintain different catalogs for different purposes or keep just one Fetch catalog that contains all of your media assets. Figure 14-6 shows an example of images cataloged in a Fetch file.

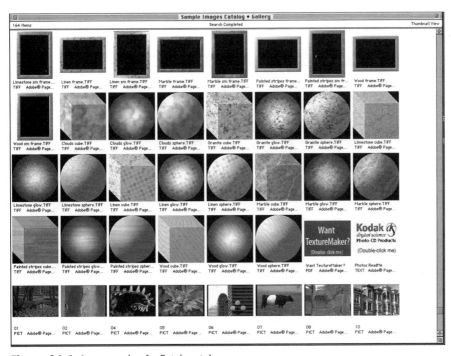

Figure 14-6: An example of a Fetch catalog

Once a catalog has been created, you add items to it by using Fetch to look at specific folders, hard drives, file servers, removable cartridges, or CD-ROMs and gather information on all available items. To do this, you use the Add/Update Items command (⌘-E) from Fetch's Admin menu. This opens the Add/Update Options dialog box, shown in Figure 14-7. Here you can specify what type of files you want to add to your catalog, the kind of thumbnails you want created (1-bit, 8-bit, 32-bit, or combinations), and what kind of compression you want applied to the thumbails. You also specify whether you want the item's name and location added as keywords, or if you want to be queried for additional keywords and item descriptions as each item is added. After setting all of the options, you then select the drive or folder that you want Fetch to scan.

Figure 14-7:
The Add/Update
Options dialog box

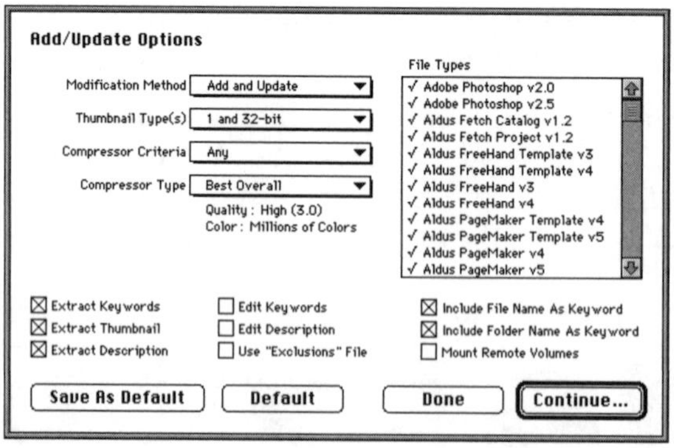

Fetch can read just about every popular graphics file format and many other kinds of files as well. Version 2.0 can read files in the following file formats: Adobe Photoshop 2.0, Adobe Fetch 2.5, and 3.0; Macromedia FreeHand 3.0, 4.0, and 5.0; PageMaker 4.0, 5.0, and 6.0; Adobe Persuasion 2.0 and 3.0; EPS; MacPaint; PICT; TIFF; Edition files; Finder Sounds; GIF; Jpeg; PhotoCD; Multi-ad Creator; SoundEdit; TEXT; RIFF; QuickTime; Storm JPEG; Targa; and more. And it ships with a copy of Apple's Macintosh Easy Open, which allows you to access even more file formats.

As Fetch reads the location you have selected, a progress dialog box shows you how many files have been added and displays the thumbnail of each item as it is added to your catalog. For most files, the thumbnail image is an actual miniature version of the file's content, but in some cases (such as sound files) the thumbnail is simply an icon that represents the file type. The process of adding items to the catalog takes some time, but you only have to do this once — if files are moved or renamed later, Fetch updates the catalog very quickly. When all files in the selected location have been added, the Find dialog box, shown in Figure 14-8, appears. Clicking the Find button will open a window that displays all items in the catalog, or you can use the dialog box to search for specific items by name, keyword, or description.

Figure 14-8:
The Find dialog box can
search for items by name,
keyword, location, file type,
or a combination of these
criteria.

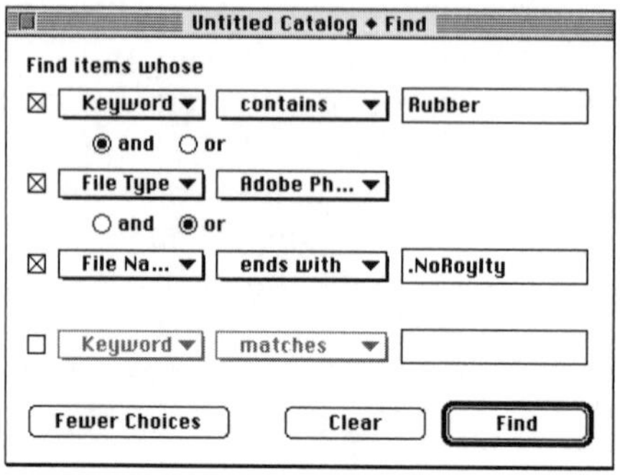

To continue building your catalog, you repeat the use of the Add/Update Items command until you have cataloged all desired items. This may mean scanning different hard drives, floppy disks, file servers, CD-ROMs, and removable drives. When you are done, you have a single Fetch catalog, small enough to keep on your hard drive, that includes thumbnails and information about all of the items stored in all of these locations.

To browse items in your catalog, you use the Fetch Gallery window, which you can display in text or thumbnails view. In the text view, you get a list of all items in the catalog (or the results of the last Find command search), and when you select any specific item, a thumbnail of that item and a list of keywords appear in the bottom of the window.

In the thumbnail view, you see a miniature image (about 1.5 inches by 1.5 inches) of every item along with the item name and file type. From the Gallery, you can get more information about any item by selecting it and choosing the Get Info command (⌘-I). The Info dialog box tells you the exact location of the original item, gives details about the file, and shows the current list of keywords and item description, as shown in Figure 14-9.

Figure 14-9:
The Info dialog box presents information about any item.

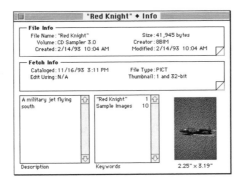

To preview any item from your catalog, double-click the item from the Gallery. At this point, Fetch reads the actual file, so if it is stored on a disk that is not mounted, you will be prompted to insert the disk, or if it is stored on a remote file server, that volume will be mounted. Then a new window will appear, showing the graphic at full size and full resolution or allowing you to preview the sound or QuickTime movie you selected. Graphic images can be magnified up to 3,200 percent.

Once you have located an item in the catalog that you want to use, Fetch provides several ways of transferring that item. Most directly, you can simply use the Copy command to transfer a copy of the original item to the Clipboard and then transfer to any other program and use the Paste command. If you locate items on remote servers, CD-ROMs, or removable cartridges and want to transfer a copy of the items to your hard drive (or some other location) where you can use it for a specific project, you can use the Copy Original command from the Item menu.

Fetch and PageMaker 6

You can move graphics from Fetch into a PageMaker 6 publication using the Copy command, or you can transfer any number of elements to the PageMaker 6 library palette. To do this, select the items you want to transfer in Fetch, choose the Copy References command from the Edit menu, and select the Include Thumbnails option. Switch to PageMaker 6, open or select the library palette, and choose the Import Fetch Items command from the Options menu. The copied items are added to the library. You can then transfer them into your publication just like any other item and save the library for use in other publications.

If you want to use Fetch to catalog all of your PageMaker publications themselves, make sure to select the Save Preview option in the Save As dialog box. This adds a thumbnail image to your saved publication, which Fetch uses when the file is added to a catalog. If you don't use this option, a PageMaker icon will be used in place of the thumbnail when the file is viewed in Fetch.

Summary

- For professional publishers, PageMaker alone is not enough. Your files and images require color separation, trapping, and imposition utilities. You probably won't have to acquire these programs yourself, because they are routinely used by prepress service bureaus and commercial printers.

- Adobe TrapWise provides complete electronic trapping for any PostScript page. The program analyzes each page to locate the edges of adjacent objects and to determine if these colors will require trapping. If trapping is required, a trap is automatically built, using the proper color, trap width, and trap placement. All trapping is done based on user-defined parameters that affect which objects are trapped, the color of each trap, and the placement of each trap.

- Adobe PressWise produces fully imposed signatures from pages in PageMaker, Xpress, FreeHand, or Illustrator files. You can freely rearrange the page order, even intermixing pages from different applications. Signatures are built by applying signature templates and defining options concerning the press and printing conditions you will be using. New templates can be defined to create signatures with up to 64 pages per side and in many bindery formats including sheet-fed, web-fed, perfect-bound, saddle-stitch, and combination binding.

Publishing Electronically— on the Web and Elsewhere

15

··

In This Chapter

- ➭ Understanding on-screen publishing

- ➭ Introduction to the World Wide Web

- ➭ Using the HTML Author Plug-in to publish World Wide Web pages

- ➭ Using Adobe's Portable Document Format (PDF)

- ➭ Using Create Adobe PDF to create on-screen documents

··

Frankly, when we started using PageMaker back when Aldus released version 1.0, neither of us thought we'd be dealing with this subject. PageMaker originated as a "page layout" program, meaning that you used it to create documents designed for printing on paper. We never thought we'd see PageMaker producing documents for the World Wide Web or other types of on-screen media. Here we are nearly 12 years later writing about how to use PageMaker to create documents for viewing on-screen, on the Internet, LANs, WANs, and other computer media. The times they are a changin'.

It's a long time coming, but the world's slowly on its way to a paperless office. This chapter shows you how to use PageMaker to help you participate in the electronic publishing revolution.

What Is On-Screen Publishing?

Now there's a loaded question. Nowadays, with computers becoming so pervasive in our lives, on-screen publishing means many things: from dynamic screen shows created with presentation programs, such as Microsoft PowerPoint, to multimedia extravaganzas created with high-powered multimedia authoring software, such as Macromedia Director. Even many of the movies you see at the theater and on TV are created on a computer, or at least partly.

Of course, this is not the level of sophistication you'll achieve with PageMaker's on-screen publishing tools. (Thank goodness. Do you know how long this book would be if we had to cover these topics, too?) Instead, on-screen publishing with PageMaker is much simpler. Basically, PageMaker's two on-screen publishing utilities, the HTML Author Plug-in and the Create Adobe PDF command, create relatively simple documents for viewing on-screen, either on the World Wide Web or with Adobe's Acrobat Exchange or Acrobat Reader.

Though publishing for each type of medium is somewhat similar, they do have some distinct differences. So, let's look at each type of publishing separately.

What Is the World Wide Web (WWW)?

Do you want the simplest answer? It's a service on the Internet. But then you knew that already, right? To be more specific, it's one of many services on the Internet. It is, many believe, one of the more interesting services on the Internet. Part of the reason for this is that it's one of the few places on the Internet that's graphical in nature; therefore, it's more fun and easier to navigate.

The WWW is also the fastest growing service on the Internet. Companies and individuals alike use it to advertise goods and services. Retailers and mail order services use it to provide electronic catalogs to debut their wares and sell products. It is a graphical world full of hot links that can, with a simple mouse click, jump the reader to any other page on the World Wide Web. It is the Information Age incarnate.

The Internet consists of individual segments of information called web pages. To access and display web pages on your computer, you must have access to the Internet through some type of information service, such as CompuServe, America Online, or a local Internet provider. You also must have a software interface known as a *web* browser, such as Netscape Navigator or Air Mosaic. Figure 15-1 shows an example of a web page displayed in a web browser; underlined texts and boxed graphics indicate hot links to other web pages. In Color Plate 15, the links are blue.

Figure 15-1:
An example of a web page in Netscape Navigator

Web pages are created with hypertext markup language (HTML). HTML is a simple page description language, which, when translated by a web browser (such as Netscape Navigator or Air Mosaic), is displayed as an on-screen document. Figure 15-2 shows an example of a web page and a corresponding HTML document in text format. Typically, HTML documents are created in text editors, such as SimpleText or Microsoft Word. PageMaker's HTML Author Plug-in makes the process of creating HTML documents a little easier: Instead of entering codes into the text file manually, this Plug-in allows you to design web pages in the same manner that you layout print documents in PageMaker.

Designing web pages opens an entirely new market for the desktop publisher graphics designer. The next section looks at creating web pages with PageMaker.

Browsing the World Wide Web

With all this talk about the World Wide Web, you may be wondering how you can get in on the action. First, you'll need access to the Internet, either from one of the popular information services — CompuServe, America Online, Prodigy — or through a local Internet provider in your area. Although the information services are easier to access and set up, we recommend that you choose a local provider.

Here's why: Money counts. The big information services, after giving you a few hours included in the base rate, charge by on-line time. The typical local Internet provider, on the other hand, charges a flat fee. Bill's service (west.net), for example, charges a flat fee of $22 per month, no matter how long he's on-line. When designing web pages, you could spend a lot of time making sure everything looks and works right, and uploading files.

Another drawback to using an information service as a gateway to the Internet is that most of them require you to use their web browser. Unfortunately, most browsers, including those used by CompuServe and America Online, do not read all of the HTML codes in a web page file. So, layouts don't look quite right, and some graphic elements, such as backgrounds, aren't displayed at all.

Also, at this writing, information services do not provide users with space on their servers to load and maintain personal web pages. If you're interested in designing web pages for yourself or your company, you'll need an individual SLIP or PPP account with a local provider.

A drawback to using local providers is that they don't always provide all the software you need to access all of the Internet services, or they don't provide the ones you want. To cruise the World Wide Web and create web pages, you'll need a good web browser. There are several out there, but we recommend Netscape Navigator, distributed by Netscape, Inc.

Netscape is quickly becoming the industry standard in web browsers. In addition to providing access to the most HTML options, it's easy to use. And the way it lets you view and reload HTML files off-line makes designing web pages easier.

 There are a number of ways to get Netscape Navigator. You can download it from the Netscape home page at http://www.netscape.com or from the company's file transfer protocol (FTP) site at ftp.netscape.com. If you aren't up and running on the Internet yet, simply call Netscape at 415-528-2800.

Using the HTML Author Plug-in to Create World Wide Web Pages ____

On its own, PageMaker is not capable of creating web pages. Instead, you must use the HTML Author Plug-in that Adobe ships with PageMaker. Before going any further, though, you should be warned that HTML Author is not a full-featured HTML authoring tool. It does not support several HTML codes, including some we consider highly important, such as: <FONT SIZE>, <TABLE>, <BODY BACKGROUND>, and several others. If you want to create truly sophisticated web pages, you'll need to edit your HTML files directly, which we'll look at under "Editing HTML Files," later in this chapter.

Here are a few more warnings that will save you some time:

- **Begin HTML pages from the ground up.** You may be tempted to try to convert existing PageMaker documents to web pages. Publishing for the screen is different from publishing on paper, for many of the reasons discussed in this list.

- **Use the right graphics formats.** Most web browsers support only GIF and JPEG graphics formats. Also, most monitors display at about 72 dpi. Creating graphics at higher resolutions serves no purpose, other than to slow down the display, which is a cardinal sin on the Internet. Remember this: *High-resolution graphics load slowly and take too long to display.* By the same token, you really shouldn't create any images for your web pages larger than about 40K, even backgrounds. There are too many slow modems out there. As more people move to high-speed modems, these files can be larger, but not yet.

- **Be case conscious.** Internet servers, usually UNIX systems, are case sensitive. When creating links to other files and naming files themselves, you must be mindful of how they're spelled, otherwise your links may not be recognized.

- **Use special characters sparingly.** Keep in mind that the Internet is a cross-platform medium. Different machines assign different addresses to extended characters (those not on your keyboard). You should avoid using characters not on your keyboard, such as fractions, em dashes, copyright symbols, and the like. If you need them, you should include them in your graphics. (A few symbols, such as the ampersand (&), are supported through special codes, most of which HTML Author knows and automatically inserts in your HTML files.) This is especially true when naming files. You should avoid spaces and special characters. Use only letters and characters to be safe.

↪ **Keep your web page elements in the same folder.** Web browsers look for supporting files in the same folder (unless you specify otherwise). In other words, if your main (home) page is in a folder named Web_Pages, you should also save all linked HTML files and graphics in the same folder. This becomes particularly important when placing the files on an Internet server (you should get instructions from the provider).

↪ **HTML Author does not support sound and animation links.** Many web browsers allow you to play sound and animation files on the World Wide Web through helper applications or small applets that launch automatically and play the file. PageMaker's HTML Author does not support the codes necessary to create this type of link. You'll have to add them manually by editing the HTML file.

Preparing to Create Web Pages in PageMaker

Before running the HTML Author Plug-in, you should first set up your pages. Remember, not too fancy, now. HTML is not a fancy medium. It's best to begin by creating a template for working with web pages, which includes choosing the correct paper size and a set of style sheets to match the HTML codes PageMaker supports.

Selecting a Page Size

OK. You're thinking, "What do you mean, *page size*? Aren't we designing for the monitor?" Yes, we are. But PageMaker thinks in pages. Version 6 contains several new page sizes for monitors. When beginning a web page, you should select a page size from the monitor list in the Document Setup dialog box, as shown in Figure 15-3.

Figure 15-3:
Selecting from one of PageMaker's six monitor sizes

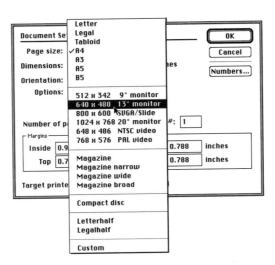

The most common monitor size is 13 inches (640 × 480 resolution). As more and more people upgrade their systems, this will change. But right now, that's the norm. We typically design for this size. If somebody logs on at a larger size, the web page formats a little differently from the original design, but it's usually still acceptable.

You should also deselect the Double-sided and Facing pages options, as your web pages cannot display side-by side on the Internet. In addition, all web pages start on page one. In fact, HTML Author will not run if you don't start the document on page one. The only other option in this dialog box relevant to the web page-creation process is the number of pages, but you can add pages as needed with Insert Pages on the Layout menu.

Setting Up Style Sheets

Let's get something straight from the beginning of this discussion of style sheets and HTML. Although HTML tags format text and graphics, they are not the same as PageMaker's tags. You cannot control typefaces and have only limited control over point sizes. Fonts are determined by the web browser reading the file, and type sizes are determined in large degree by the size of the display and the settings in the web browser reading the document. (This does not mean that you have absolutely no control over type size. We'll look at that in a minute.) You have no control over leading, kerning, tracking, rules, tabs, and the like. Don't bother applying these attributes to text targeted for HTML. They won't translate. In addition, HTML supports character-level tags, which PageMaker does not. You add HTML tags for boldface, italic, underline, and so on, to format words and letters, which you cannot do in PageMaker. (Of course, you can apply these same formats in PageMaker, but character-level styles are not sup-ported.) You add the HTML tags by editing the file in a text editor, which we'll show you how to do in "Editing HTML Files," later in this chapter.

 Create an HTML template: If you plan on doing more than one HTML docu-ment with PageMaker, you should create an HTML template. PageMaker supports only about 20 HTML codes. Once you create corresponding style sheets and save them in a template, you'll have them and won't have to do them again. (Templates are discussed in Chapter 7.)

HTML Author lets you link PageMaker style sheets to HTML tags. When you create style sheets for working with HTML Author, you can create style sheets for all of the HTML tags PageMaker supports or for just those you use in your document. Table 15-1 lists the HTML codes that HTML Author supports.

Table 15-1	
The HTML Codes Supported by HTML Author	
HTML code	**What it does in a web browser**
<TITLE></TITLE>	The text between these codes appears in the publication window title bar.
<H1></H1>	The text between these two codes formats as Heading 1 (H1), the largest heading style. There are six levels of headings: H1, H2, H3, H4, H5, and H6.
<ADDRESS></ADDRESS>	The text between these codes is set in short text blocks apart from the body text.
<BLOCKQUOTE></BLOCKQUOTE>	The text between these codes is set apart from the body text. It's typically used to set off larger blocks of text.
<BODY Text></BODY Text>	The text between these codes assumes normal formatting.
<MENU List></MENU List>	The text between these codes becomes a compact, numbered, or bulleted list.
<OL List></OL List>	The text between these codes becomes a numbered list. Most browsers insert numbers for each occurrence of the code.
<PREFORMATTED></PREFORMATTED>	The text between these codes retains its formatting, regardless of style settings made in the web browser reading it.
<UL List></UL List>	The text between these codes becomes a bulleted list, complete with bullets in most browsers.
<CITE></CITE>	The text between these codes is set off as a citation between quotes.*
<CODE></CODE>	The text between these codes usually depicts computer code, usually displayed in monospaced type.*
<DEFINITION></DEFINITION>	The text between these codes usually depicts a definition set off by quotes.*
<EMPHASIS></EMPHASIS>	The text between these is set off by italics.*
<SAMPLE></SAMPLE>	The text between these codes depicts computer status messages.*
<BOLD></BOLD>	The text between these codes is set off with bold.*

*Character-level formats in HTML; applied as paragraph styles in PageMaker.

Other useful codes: There are a bunch of other useful HTML codes the folks at Adobe neglected to include in HTML Author. We'll give you some of the more common ones in "Editing HTML Files," later in this chapter.

Again, the font and point size of your type on a web page is determined by the web browser and the size of the display system. You should name the style sheets as shown in Figure 15-4, which automatically matches the equivalents in HTML Author. You should also assign formatting to the styles similar to how they'll appear on the web page. The Code tag, for example, displays monospaced type, such as Courier. The heading tags (H1, H2, etc.) and body text are usually set in sans serif type, such as Arial, and the heading sizes start at about 30 points for H1 and work downward. Body text is about the equivalent to 12 points. But again, remember that *this all depends on browser settings and display size.*

Figure 15-4:
An example of a style palette set up to work with HTML Author

Figure 15-5 shows the same web page displayed at 640 × 480 and at 1024 × 780. Notice the difference in the display sizes and font sizes.

Figure 15-5:
An example of a web
page displayed at
different monitor
resolutions

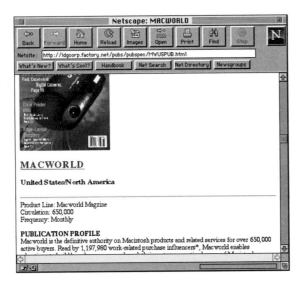

Laying Out Your Web Pages

After creating your style sheets, it's time to begin laying out your web pages. This is a simple process. You'll accomplish nothing by creating complicated layouts at this juncture. All that really matters is the tags that ultimately get assigned to the elements on your pages. The one thing to remember, though, is that all of your graphics should be in-line, which you learned how to do in Chapter 8. Oh yes, and don't forget that all images should be low-resolution GIF or JPEG. Keep in mind also that you can't resize HTML graphics in PageMaker. The web browser will read them at their saved size. So you should save them at the size at which you want them to be displayed by the graphics application. Figure 15-6 shows a typical web page beginning in PageMaker. Run this simple layout from page to page until all the information is used. Oh yeah, and don't forget to save all your graphics in the same file as the publication.

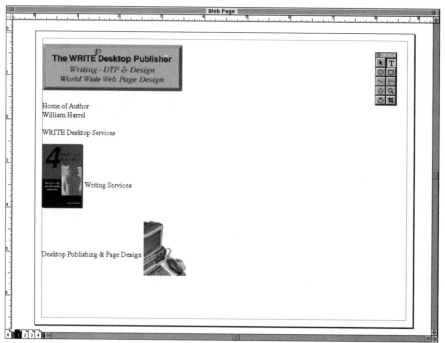

Figure 15-6: An example of a simple web page design beginning in PageMaker

Creating multiple pages from the same file: If you already know something about web pages, you know that most web locations consist of a home page (base) that branches off to several other linked pages. A strength of HTML Author is that it lets you create these auxiliary pages and links from the same file. So, go ahead and layout the entire web location in one PageMaker document.

After placing your text and graphics, go through and assign style sheets to each element in the layout, as shown in Figure 15-7. Don't worry about assigning justification or the placement of graphics. HTML Author won't recognize this type of formatting. We'll show you how to do this manually by editing the HTML file directly in "Editing HTML Files" in a bit.

You are now ready to open HTML Author.

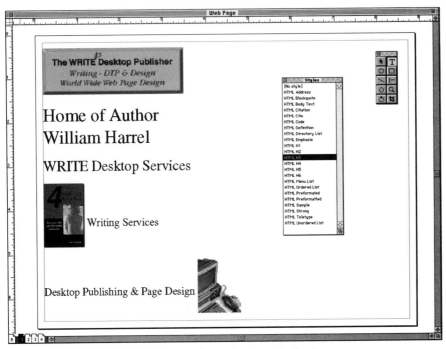

Figure 15-7: A sample of a web page after assigning style sheets

Setting Up Your Web Pages in HTML Author

Once you've laid out your pages and assigned style sheets to the elements in your layout, you're ready to create your HTML pages in HTML Author. Making sure that you have nothing selected, choose HTML Author from the PageMaker Plug-ins submenu. The dialog box in Figure 15-8 appears. You begin defining your HTML Pages here.

Note that there are four sections to this dialog box, including a Preferences section. If you create your style sheets as shown in the previous section, you really shouldn't need to edit preferences—unless you need to make new style-to-code associations. This is usually only necessary when you are creating a web page from an existing document. (OK. So we said you shouldn't try this, but some people will, undoubtedly.)

Figure 15-8:
PageMaker's HTML
Author Plug-in

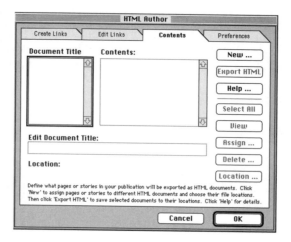

To begin a new HTML document, click the New... button in the Contents section of the Plug-in, which opens the New HTML Document dialog box (see Figure 15-9). Here you name the current web page. (This dialog box also allows you to select PageMaker stories rather than entire pages.) Each new HTML file is a separate web page. When you've finished naming the page, click Next.

Figure 15-9:
The New HTML Document
dialog box for naming a web
page

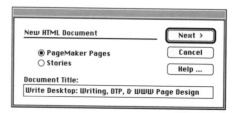

Figure 15-10 shows the Assign PageMaker Pages To dialog box. Web pages can be very long, allowing you to assign as many PageMaker pages to one web page as needed. In the example in Figure 15-10, two PageMaker pages are assigned to the current Web page. After assigning pages, you can click either Done or Next>. Done returns you to the HTML Author. Next> takes you to a dialog box that allows you to save the current HTML Document. You can export the document to HTML at any time. But if you want to link the pages in your site to one another, you should save them as you create them using the Next> option. That way you'll have filenames to link later in the process.

Repeat the process for each web page you want to create. When you finish, click OK to return to PageMaker.

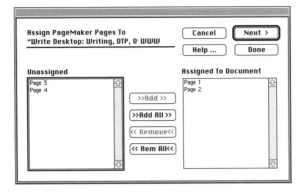

Figure 15-10:
The Assign PageMaker Pages To dialog box allows you to assign pages to a web page.

Assigning Hypertext Links

HTML Author allows you to create all kinds of links on the World Wide Web and the Internet in general, and it's far beyond the scope of this book to describe them all. You can, for example, create links to mail services, news services, file transfer sites, and so forth. You can also create links to any other page on the World Wide Web. For this discussion, though, we'll show you how to link the pages in your web site to each other.

To create a link, use the Text tool to select the graphic or text to which you want to assign a link. Then open HTML Author. The Plug-in opens ready to assign the link, as shown in Figure 15-11. All you do to create a link to another HTML document is type the document name in Enter URL. (A URL is an address on the Internet. Since your linked documents are kept in the same directory on your Internet provider's server, you don't need to designate a Link Type.) When you've typed in the name of the file (exactly as you named it), click Create and then OK to return to PageMaker.

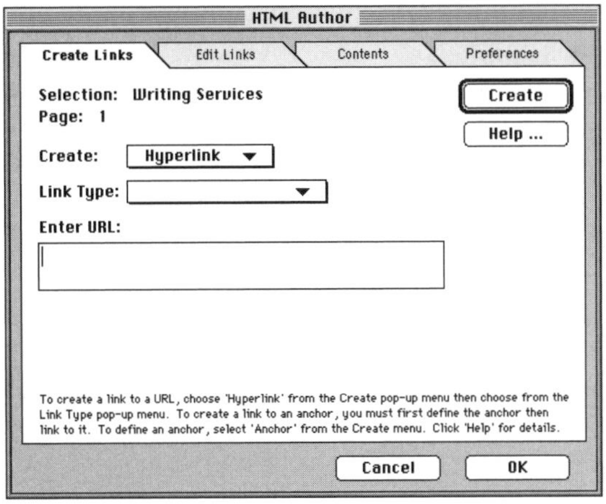

Figure 15-11:
The HTML Author ready to assign a hypertext link

Creating Internet links: Use the preceeding method to create all types of links all over the Internet. The typing of the URLs must be exact, including text case.

You'll have to complete this process for each link you want to create, selecting the text or graphic, then opening HTML Author and making the link. You can edit links, reassigning the link type and address, from the Edit Links section in HTML Author by clicking the Edit Links tab. This displays the dialog box shown in Figure 15-12. From here, you can reassign links, delete links, and so on. The Select Same button selects all links with the same destination, allowing you to edit them all at once.

Figure 15-12:
The HTML Author Edit
Links dialog box

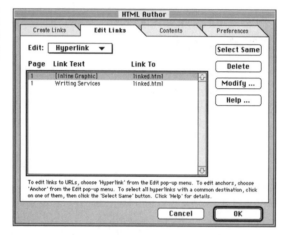

HTML Author Preferences

Clicking the Preferences tab in HTML Author brings up the Preferences portion of the dialog box, as shown in Figure 15-13. From here, you can change some aspects of how HTML Author works, such as assigning different codes to PageMaker style sheets. Again, we can't see any real reason to change any of the other items here. The only one that changes the way your web pages look is the Link Format option, which allows you to change the way links appear on the web page itself. But the standard on the World Wide Web is blue and underlined hypertext, which is HTML Author's default. You can get a description of the options in this dialog box by clicking the Help... button.

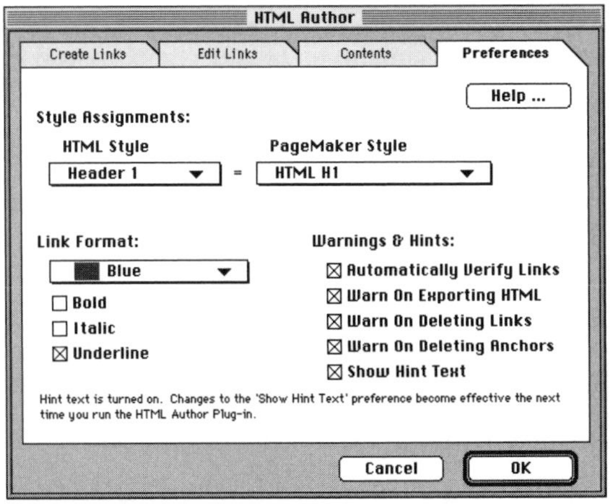

Figure 15-13:
The HTML Author
Preferences dialog box

Figure 15-13:
The HTML Author
Preferences dialog box

Exporting HTML Files

Once you've got all of your pages assigned to HTML files and all correspondence links assigned, you'll need to export to HTML. You should wait until you're as close to possible, because this is a one-way street. You can't edit the HTML files again in PageMaker. But you can edit the PageMaker files and export them again. HTML pages are exported from the Content section of HTML Author, as shown in Figure 15-14. From here you select the page you want to export, then select Export HTML. You can export all files at once by clicking Select All. To change the location of the HTML pages, click the Location... button, but keep in mind that all pages and supporting files should reside in the same directory.

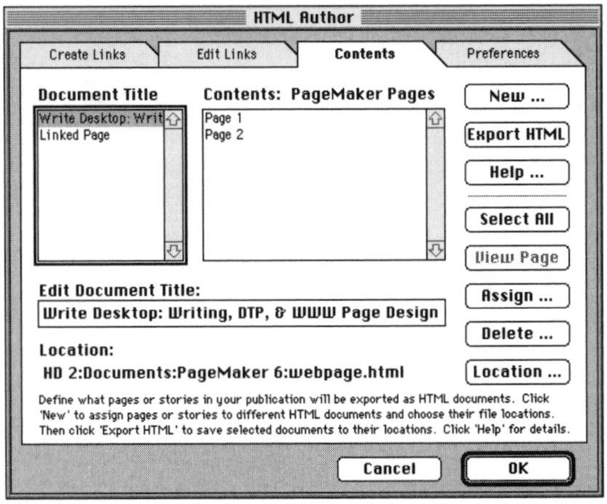

Figure 15-14:
The HTML Author
preparing to export
HTML files

Remember to give the HTML files names with no spaces and no special characters. Also remember that the Internet is case sensitive. We always use lower case letters when naming HTML files.

Figure 15-15 shows the finished web page document. Unfortunately, it's not too sophisticated. You can spruce up your web pages by editing the files directly, which is the topic of the next section.

Figure 15-15:
A web page created in
PageMaker.

Editing HTML Files

Unfortunately, HTML Author is not the ideal web page designing tool. It is, however, a great jumping-off point. It allows you to create your pages and links, which is a big part of the job. It also works well for assigning tags to large text files. It does not, however, support all the HTML options, especially the options provided with Netscape extensions. In this section, we'll look at sprucing up your web pages by editing the HTML file in your Mac's SimpleText utility.

Creating really cool web pages: It's way beyond the scope of this book to provide instruction on HTML programming. But if you're interested in this type of publishing, we can tell you where to go to get quick and easy help. We recommend *Macworld Creating Cool Web Pages with HTML* by Dave Taylor (IDG Books Worldwide). This small, helpfully organized book provides most of the HTML codes and gives great advice on how to use them.

Look again at Bill's home page in Figure 15-15. Pretty bleak, huh? Now look at Figure 15-16. What a transformation! Bill made these adjustments by inserting codes directly into the HTML file. (He also changed the top image.) Figure 15-17 shows the differences in the HTML files.

Figure 15-16:
A home page spruced up through direct HTML file editing

Figure 15-17:
Examples of
HTML files, one
created with
PageMaker (top)
and another
edited in
SimpleText
(bottom)

```
webpage.html

<!DOCTYPE HTML PUBLIC "-//W3O//DTD W3 HTML 2.0//EN">
<!-- This HTML document was generated by PageMaker -->
<!-- On Fri Sep 15 12:00:48 1995 from "HD 2:Documents:PageMaker 6:Web Page" -->
<HTML>
<HEAD>
<TITLE>Write Desktop: Writing, DTP, & WWW Page Design</TITLE>
</HEAD>
<BODY>

<!-- Generation of PM publication page 1 -->

<IMG SRC="../WebPage/Bharrel Web Pages/The_WRITE_Desktop.gif" ALIGN="BOTTOM">
<H1>
<P>Home of Author
<P>William Harrel
</H1>
<H2>
<P>WRITE Desktop Services
</H2>
<H3>
<A HREF="linked.html"><IMG SRC="../WebPage/Bharrel Web Pages/better_back.gif"
ALIGN="BOTTOM"></A>
 <A HREF="linked.html">Writing Services</A>
<P><A HREF="linked.html">Desktop Publishing &amp; Page Design <IMG
SRC="../WebPage/Bharrel Web Pages/dtp.gif" ALIGN="BOTTOM"></A>

<!-- Generation of PM publication page 2 -->
```

```
index.shtml

<BODY BACKGROUND="background.gif"><HTML>
<HEAD><TITLE>The WRITE Desktop: Writing, DTP & WWW Page Design</TITLE><HEAD>
<BODY>
<CENTER><IMG SRC="The_WRITE_Desktop.gif"><BR>
<P>
<H1><I>Home of Author<I></H1>
<P>
William Harrel<BR>
<FONT SIZE=3>
<A HREF="resume.html">Click here for resume.</A></BR>
</FONT>
</CENTER>
<P>
<FONT SIZE=8>
<CENTER>WRITE Desktop Services</CENTER>
</FONT>
<P>
<CENTER>
<A HREF="writing.html"><IMG SRC="coreldraw.gif" ALIGN=middle HSPACE=10><FONT
SIZE=6><I>Writing Services</FONT></I></A><BR>
<A HREF="dtp.html"><FONT SIZE=6><I>Desktop Publishing & Page Design</FONT></I><IMG
SRC="dtp.gif" ALIGN=middle HSPACE=10></A><BR>
<A HREF="wwwpage.html"><IMG SRC="globe.gif" ALIGN=middle HSPACE=10><FONT
SIZE=6><I>World Wide Web Page Design</FONT></I></A><BR>
<A HREF="consult.html"><FONT SIZE=6><I>Computer Consulting & Training</FONT></I><IMG
SRC="blocks.gif" ALIGN=middle HSPACE=10></A><BR></CENTER>
<HR>
<CENTER><H1><I>WORK IN PROGRESS<I></H1>
<A HREF="PM6B.HTML"><IMG SRC="PAGEMAKER.GIF"></A>
<HR>
```

To edit an HTML file, simply open it as text file in SimpleText or another text editor. Now you'll enter codes to adjust aspects of the page. Simply enter the codes where you want the effect to appear. When you're finished, save the file as straight text. Table 15-2 lists several useful codes, what they do, and how to use them.

Table 15-2
Some Useful HTML Codes

Code	What it does	How to use it
<BODY BACKGROUND>	Places an image behind the text and graphics on your page as a background.	Place at the beginning of the HTML document: <BODY BACKGROUND="imagename">.
<B> , <I>, <U>	Emboldens, italicizes, or underlines text at character level.	Place text between codes: <I>text</I>. You can also use combinations: <I><B>text</I></B>.
<CENTER>	Centers all text and graphics between codes.	Place at the beginning and end of the section of the web page you want centered: <CENTER>contents</CENTER> (this one is only recognized by Netscape).
<HR>	Creates a horizontal rule.	Place code where you want the rule. You can also adjust the size by pixels: <HR SIZE=5>.
<FONT SIZE>	Controls font size.	Place before and after text you want to resize: <FONT SIZE=5>text</FONT> (font sizes between -7 and 7 are supported).
<P>	Paragraph break.	Place where you want the break.
 	Line break.	Place where you want a line to break.
ALIGN=	Used in conjunction with image placement codes to align an image in relation to text on the same line.	Place inside image source brackets: <IMG SRC="image_file_name" ALIGN=middle> (top, middle, and bottom are supported).
VSPACE=, HSPACE=	Use to designate space between images and other objects, such as other images or text, on the page in pixels.	Place inside image source brackets: <IMG SRC="image_file_name" VSPACE=20>.

There are many other codes, and you can often use codes in conjunction with one another to get some pretty snazzy results. If you are serious about web page publishing, you really should get a book on HTML.

 Get help on-line: Ever look at something and wonder, "How did they do that?" Well, the beauty of the World Wide Web is that it's easy to see the source HTML file of any web page, depending on the browser you're using. In Netscape Navigator, for example, all you do is choose Source from the View menu. Also, there's plenty of information on web page creation at various web sites on the WWW. Yale University has a good one at: http://info.med.yale.edu/caim/StyleManual_Top.HTML.

On-Screen Publishing with Create Adobe PDF

Unlike HTML publishing, publishing documents in Adobe's Portable Document Format is much the same as creating any other document in PageMaker, except that it requires a few extra steps. Basically, any document you lay out in PageMaker for conventional printing can be converted to a PDF document for on-screen viewing.

To view (or print) PDF files, you'll need a copy of Acrobat Reader or Acrobat Exchange. Adobe includes Acrobat Reader on the PageMaker CD-ROM disc. Figure 15-18 and Color Plate 14 in the color insert show a PDF document in Acrobat Reader.

Here are some reasons for creating PDF files:

- **Documents for on-line viewing across a network.** You can use PDF documents for training and procedural documents on-line. Acrobat works across many platforms, including Mac, Windows, and UNIX.

- **Printing on demand.** When saved in PDF, documents are already PostScripted. You can print them from Adobe Acrobat Exchange without the host application (in this case, PageMaker).

- **World Wide Web publishing.** Although web browsers cannot read the PDF format directly, many of them, including Netscape Navigator, can use Acrobat Exchange or Acrobat Reader as a helper application. Once you have downloaded a PDF document to your computer, Netscape launches Acrobat and lets you read and navigate the document while still on-line.

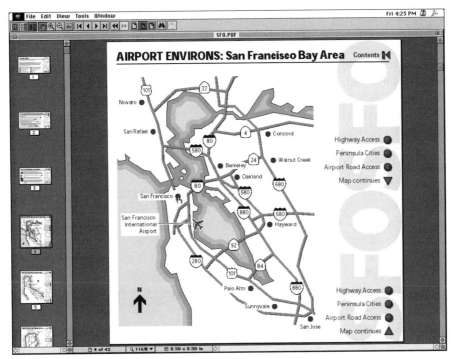

Figure 15-18: A PDF document in Acrobat Reader

Before continuing this discussion of PDF publishing, here a few things to consider:

- **All PDF files start at page one.** If you have a table of contents and other pages that are unnumbered pages, of if you start page numbering over again, you should renumber pages so that they start at page one and run sequentially.

- **Combine books and manuals.** PDF files are great for creating long on-line documents from multiple chapters and sections. Before running Create Adobe PDF, be sure that you have used the Book command on the Utilities menu to combine chapters and sections. This command is discussed in Chapter 12.

- **Keep tables of contents and indices current.** If you renumber your pages for PDF publishing, you should go back and regenerate your table of contents and indexes, because Create Adobe PDF allows you to create hot links between them and the pages they reference for easy navigating in long documents. Generating tables of contents and indexes is discussed in Chapter 12.

↪ **Decide beforehand whether the document is for on-screen viewing or printing on demand.** This is important. Determine which medium the document is designed for — screen or paper. This determines how Create Adobe PDF treats the graphics in the file. If you are going to print the document, you'll want to maintain image resolution and CMYK values. If you'll be using the document on-line, you'll want low-resolution RGB graphics. Create Adobe PDF can make these changes for you, but you have to tell it what to do.

Using Create Adobe PDF

After solving page numbering conflicts, updating the indexes and table of contents, and so on, you are ready to convert the PageMaker file to PDF with Create Adobe PDF (on the File menu), which, after offering you a chance to save your document, opens the Create Adobe PDF dialog box, as shown in Figure 15-19.

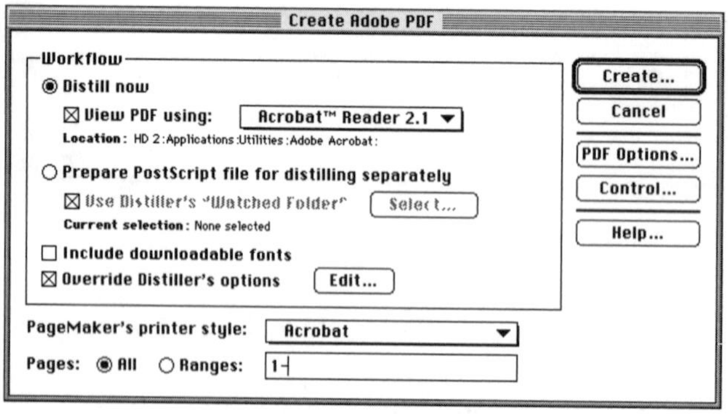

Figure 15-19:
The Create Adobe
PDF dialog box

The Create Adobe PDF dialog box offers the following options:

↪ **Distill now** tells PageMaker to create the PDF when you click the Create... button. In order for this option to work, you must have previously installed Acrobat Distiller from the PageMaker CD-ROM (or another Adobe application). The View PDF using suboption automatically launches the Acrobat application indicated in the pop-up menu. Unless you have purchased and installed Acrobat Exchange (the full-featured Adobe Acrobat program) only Acrobat Reader will be available, and this is only if you previously installed it from the PageMaker CD-ROM disc.

↪ **Prepare PostScript file for distilling separately** creates a file with all the markers Acrobat Distiller needs to convert it into a PDF file. You would typically choose this option if you don't have Distiller installed yet or wanted to distill the file on another computer — or if you don't want to wait for the distillation process at this time. The Use Distiller's "Watched Folder" allows you to save the PostScript file to the directory you have designated in Distiller as the directory to look in first for files to distill.

⊙ **Include downloadable fonts** embeds the fonts used in your document in either the PostScript file or the PDF file. Acrobat can simulate most common serif and sans serif fonts reasonably well, so there's really no reason to download them, unless you plan to use the file for printing on demand. However, the PDF font simulator cannot simulate decorative and symbol fonts. You should always download them.

⊙ **Override Distiller's options** allows you to modify Distiller's default parameters. Clicking the Edit... button displays the Distiller PDF Job Options dialog box, shown in Figure 15-20. Here you control several options, including whether to create thumbnails for each page in your PDF file, whether to download fonts, and so on. You also control image quality and resolution from here, which is important when you are creating images for printing on demand. Clicking the Help... button brings up a very good description of each option in this dialog box.

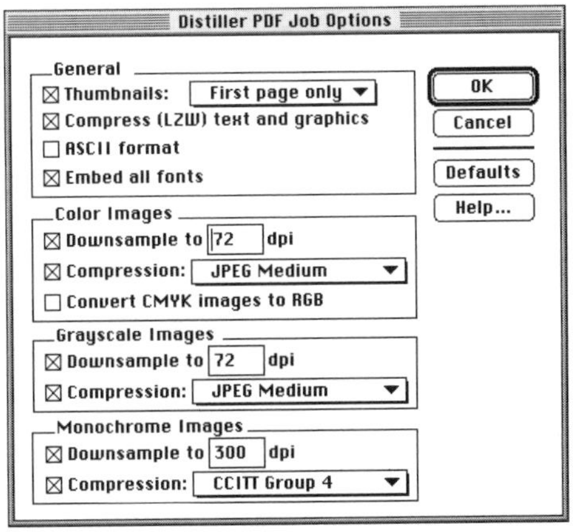

Figure 15-20:
Use the Distiller PDF Job Options dialog box to control different aspects of how the document is processed, including image resolution and quality.

⊙ **PageMaker's printer style** allows you to set the target printer from your printer style list. (Printer styles are discussed in Chapter 13.) Usually, unless you set the PDF file up as a print-on-demand document, you would set this option to Acrobat. When setting up a print-on-demand file, set this option to the printer style for the target printer.

⊙ **Pages**, of course, allows you to choose the page range to be processed by Create Adobe PDF.

⊙ **PDF Options...** opens the PDF Options dialog box, shown in Figure 15-21. Here you tell Create Adobe PDF whether to create hot links between tables of contents and index entries and the document. You can also determine whether to create bookmarks that jump the reader to specific places in the document. The Edit names... button in the TOC section of the dialog box opens the Edit Bookmark names dialog box, shown in Figure 15-22, which allows you to rename bookmarks. Clicking the Help... button in either of these dialog boxes displays a description of each option and tells you why you'd want to use it.

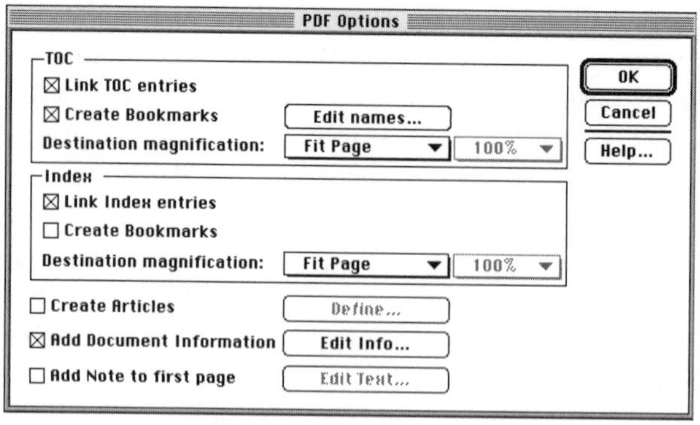

PDF Options

TOC
☒ Link TOC entries
☒ Create Bookmarks   Edit names...
Destination magnification: Fit Page ▼   100% ▼

Index
☒ Link Index entries
☐ Create Bookmarks
Destination magnification: Fit Page ▼   100% ▼

☐ Create Articles   Define...
☒ Add Document Information   Edit Info...
☐ Add Note to first page   Edit Text...

OK
Cancel
Help...

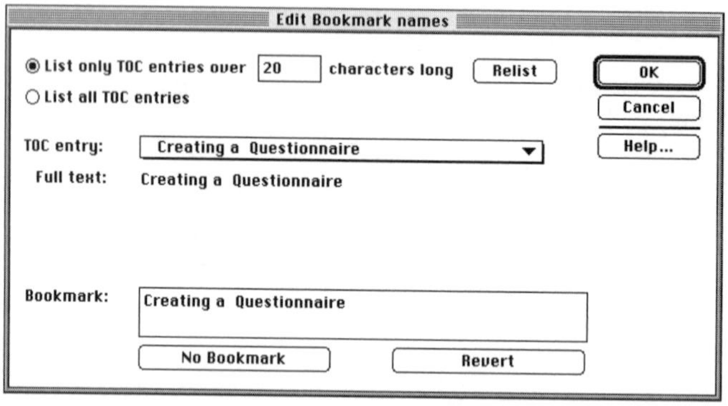

Edit Bookmark names

◉ List only TOC entries over 20 characters long   Relist
○ List all TOC entries

TOC entry: Creating a Questionnaire ▼

Full text: Creating a Questionnaire

Bookmark: Creating a Questionnaire

No Bookmark   Revert

OK
Cancel
Help...

☞ **Control...** displays the Control dialog box, shown in Figure 15-23. The options in this dialog box are preferences, such as always saving the current PageMaker file before opening Create Adobe PDF, and a few others. The Help... button provides a wealth of information about this dialog box's options.

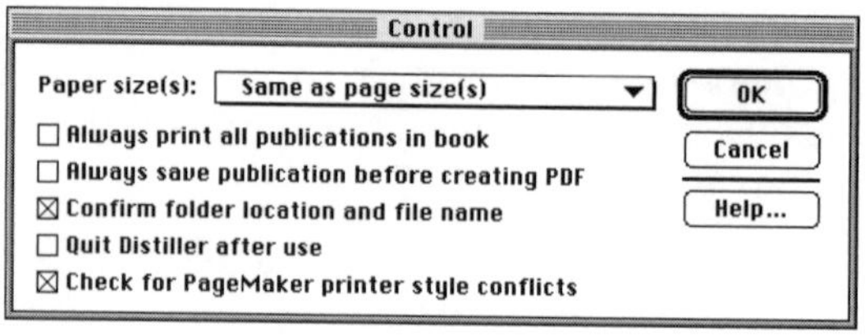

Control

Paper size(s):   Same as page size(s) ▼

☐ Always print all publications in book
☐ Always save publication before creating PDF
☒ Confirm folder location and file name
☐ Quit Distiller after use
☒ Check for PageMaker printer style conflicts

OK
Cancel
Help...

Learning more about PDF: Still a little confused about Acrobat and how it works? When you install Acrobat Reader and Acrobat Distiller from the PageMaker CD-ROM disc, several read-me and documentation files are also installed, including some extensive help files. There are also several PDF files on the CD explaining all types of PageMaker and electronic publishing issues. Take a minute to browse through the folders on the PageMaker Deluxe CD. Open and navigate some of the PDF files. You'll come away with a much better understanding of publishing for the computer screen.

Finally, the on-screen documents created by Create Adobe PDF do not take full advantage of the Acrobat medium. For example, each page in an Acrobat Exchange file can contain hot text and buttons for jumping to different pages throughout the document. To create these types of dynamic documents, you'll need to open your PDF files in Acrobat Exchange and edit them further. Acrobat Exchange is a separate product sold by Adobe.

Summary

↦ PageMaker allows you to publish for the World Wide Web with the HTML Author Plug-in.

↦ Setting up a PageMaker document for use with HTML Author requires that you use low-resolution GIF or JPEG graphics and simple layouts.

↦ Once you have generated your HTML files, you can make further changes to them in SimpleText or another text editor.

↦ If you're serious about web page publishing, you should get a book on HTML.

↦ You can create Adobe Acrobat PDF files with Create Adobe PDF on the File menu.

↦ With a few exceptions, PageMaker documents intended for PDF publishing are laid out the in the same way as other PageMaker publications.

Putting PageMaker to Work

The first three parts of this book cover a lot of ground. But we've found that nothing replaces hands-on experience. In this section, we guide you through three sample projects, a newsletter, a flyer, and a catalog. These projects reintroduce you to many PageMaker functions, and use most of PageMaker's typesetting and layout features. You can take advantage of the sample files included on the CD-ROM that accompanies this book. Have fun.

Creating a Newsletter

16

In This Chapter

- ❖ Preparing master pages
- ❖ Adding a masthead
- ❖ Importing a text file
- ❖ Making a drop cap
- ❖ Creating a sidebar

The project in this chapter reintroduces you to each of the features and methods discussed in the previous chapters while allowing you to work toward a real and tangible goal. This kind of experience will come in very handy when you start creating your own documents.

In this first project, you will use PageMaker to create a newsletter — the quintessential PageMaker document. During the creation of this document, you sample PageMaker's abilities and begin to see the ways in which these abilities can be used to create not only newsletters, but virtually any kind of document.

This newsletter project is the first of three sample projects presented in this book and therefore focuses on the elementary aspects of PageMaker's commands and features. For those who feel daunted by the prospect of creating a full-fledged document, you will find the newsletter to be surprisingly elementary. It consists of just two pages, including three short articles and a series of simple geometric elements created inside PageMaker. You are encouraged to follow the steps to create a newsletter, as I describe them — all you need to complete this project are the files in the Newsletters folder on the CD-ROM included with this book (see Figure 16-1) and Adobe PageMaker 6 itself.

You may either copy this folder to your hard drive or work directly off the CD-ROM. You will notice, however, that accessing a file from the CD-ROM is slower than from your hard disk.

Figure 16-1:
This folder includes all the elements necessary to create the newsletter in this chapter.

Newsletter files			
Name	Size	Kind	Label
Main Story 1	17K	Microsoft Word do...	—
Page 2 Sidebar	17K	Microsoft Word do...	—
Page 2 Story 1	17K	Microsoft Word do...	—

Although most of the PageMaker features used in this chapter have been introduced previously, a few may be new to you. The descriptions of each command here should be sufficient for your work in completing the sample project, even if you haven't read all the previous chapters. If you are having problems with any particular topic, feel free to locate the more complete discussions included in the reference chapters.

Creating Your Publication

To begin creating your publication, first launch PageMaker. There are two ways to do this:

- ☞ Double-click the PageMaker icon on your desktop.

- ☞ Use a launching application or utility such as Launcher, Now Utilities, QuicKeys, or On Cue. (Click your mouse button anywhere on your display to dispense with the copyright screen.)

Once you are in PageMaker choose the New command from the File menu or press ⌘-N to bring up the Document Setup dialog box, in which you delineate specifications for many global attributes of your document. Set the options as follows:

- • Page size: Letter

- • Double-sided: selected

- • Orientation: Tall

- • Facing pages: selected

- • Start page #: 1

- # of pages: 2

- Margin in inches: Inside: 0.5, Top: 1, Outside: 0.5, Bottom: 1

This project uses inches as the unit of measurement. To make this the current Measurement system, use the Preferences command in the File menu, as discussed in Chapter 1.

Figure 16-2 shows the completed Document Setup dialog box.

Figure 16-2:
The Document Setup
dialog box with the
specifications of your
newsletter

Document Setup	OK
Page size: Letter	Cancel
Dimensions: 8.5 by 11 inches	Numbers...
Orientation: ⦿ Tall ○ Wide	
Options: ☒ Double-sided	
☒ Facing pages	
☐ Restart page numbering	
Number of pages: 2 Start page #: 1	

Margins

| Inside 0.5 inches | Outside 0.5 inches |
| Top 1 inches | Bottom 1 inches |

Target printer resolution: 600 ▷ dpi

Tips for Working in Dialog Boxes

☞ When selecting or deselecting radio-button or checkbox options, you can click either inside the circle or square or on the option name next to the button or box.

☞ Press the Tab key to move to the next option box, selecting the current value there. Once selected, enter a new value to replace the selected value if necessary. Press Shift-Tab to move backward between option boxes.

☞ Double-clicking the value in an option box will also select it so that it can be overwritten (replaced).

☞ Setting the insertion point in an option box allows you to use the Backspace or Delete key to delete existing values.

When you have finished entering the specifications for the new publication, click the OK button or press Return or Enter to instruct PageMaker to create the document as you have specified. The new publication window displays the first page of your publication, as shown in Figure 16-3. The on-screen display includes page icons for the left and right master pages as well as pages 1 and 2, the toolbox, scroll bars, and the rulers. Your display may be different if the default settings have been changed. (If the rulers are not visible, press ⌘-R.)

Figure 16-3: The first page of your new newsletter

Preparing the Master Pages_____

Every PageMaker publication has at least one or two master pages (one if your document is single-sided; two if the double-sided option in the Document Setup dialog box is selected). You can add more as needed. These master pages are used to hold items that repeat from page to page, such as running heads or footers, page numbers, or graphics. By placing repeating elements on the master pages, you ensure that they will be positioned exactly on each page. This procedure saves you the effort of repeatedly positioning identical elements from page to page.

Master pages can also hold column guides and ruler guides, which can be used to create an alignment grid for elements that will be placed on the actual publication pages. For example, you may want the top of specific kinds of text blocks to begin some distance below what has been defined as the top margin of your pages. By placing a ruler guide at this position on the master page, you can easily and accurately execute your design without the effort and potential for error that can result from measuring the correct distance on every page.

The Right Master Page

To display a simple rule and company logo at the bottom of each page in your newsletter, use the following steps.

STEPS: Adding a Rule and Company Logo

Step 1.   Click on either of the master page icons, labeled L and R (for left and right) in the lower-right corner of the display. The master pages appear in the publication window.

Step 2.   ⌘-Option-click anywhere in the bottom half of the right page. This magnifies your screen display to the Actual size view. Then move the page with the hand icon — accessed by pressing the Option key and clicking with your mouse — until you can clearly view the bottom margin of the right page.

Step 3.   Drag downward from the horizontal ruler at the top of the display to create a ruler guide. This guide can be dragged up and down, very much as you would drag a block of text or other element. Drag the ruler guide until it is one-quarter inch below the bottom margin. This defines the location of the top of your simple line and logo.

Step 4.   Select the Constrained Line tool. Draw a line across the bottom margin of the right page, extending from the left margin to the right margin. While drawing your line, dragging into the edge of the window will scroll the display as needed.

Step 5.   Select the Pointer tool. Drag the line directly downward. Since you want to change only the vertical position of the line, press and hold the Shift key, and the movement of the line will be constrained in the first direction that you drag. For example, if you drag the line upward while pressing the Shift key, the line can move only up and down—not diagonally or horizontally.

This allows you to position your line precisely in one direction without disturbing its position in another direction. Using the Shift key to constrain movement works when moving any graphic or text element in PageMaker as well as in many other Macintosh applications. After pressing the Shift key, drag the line downward until the line snaps to the ruler guide.

Step 6. While the line remains selected, change its weight (thickness) by choosing the Line command from the Element menu. Hold down the mouse button as you choose this command, and a hierarchical pop-up menu of available line weights displays to the right of the Element menu. Keeping your mouse button pressed, move the arrow cursor horizontally in the direction of the hierarchical list until one of the line weights becomes highlighted. You can scroll up and down to choose different weights. After a little practice, working with these hierarchical pop-up menus will be almost as easy as any other mouse operation. Release the mouse when you are satisfied with your line weight selection. In this case, choose the 2 pt option.

Step 7. Drag another ruler guide, this time from the vertical ruler on the left of your display. Move this guideline until it lines up with your right margin. This will help you in locating the company logo.

Step 8. To represent the company logo, select the Rectangle tool and draw a rectangle one inch wide and one-quarter inch high. While the rectangle is still selected, choose the Hairline option from the hierarchical Line menu. Then choose the tight crosshatch pattern (third from the bottom) from the Fill pop-up, which is also under the Element menu. With the Pointer tool, position the makeshift logo one-eighth inch below the 2-point line that runs across the bottom of the page. The right side of the logo should be flush against the vertical ruler guide, as shown in Figure 16-4.

Figure 16-4: The right master page containing the line and logo elements you have created thus far

The Left Master Page

You now need to make a mirror image of the rule and logo for the left master page.

STEPS:	**Making a Mirror Image of the Rule and Logo**
Step 1.	Select both elements. You can do this by dragging with the Pointer tool, surrounding the line and logo with a rectangular marquee. Or you can click the line and then Shift-click the logo. After both elements are selected, choose the Copy command from the Edit menu or press ⌘-C. This puts a copy of both items into the Macintosh Clipboard, to be used later at your convenience.
Step 2.	Scroll over to the left master page, using the scroll bars or the grabber hand tool (accessed by pressing the Option key and clicking).
Step 3.	Notice that your horizontal ruler guide appears on this page, too. Horizontal guides always show up on both pages of a facing-page spread. However, you are missing the vertical ruler guide. So drag a guide from the vertical ruler, aligning it with the left margin of the left master page.
Step 4.	Choose the Paste command from the Edit menu or press ⌘-V. This produces a copy of your simple line and company logo in the center of your display. You want to position these elements slightly differently on the left master page than you did on the right master page.
Step 5.	When you paste one or more elements, they are selected immediately after they appear on your screen. This is so that they can be positioned easily. Taking care not to deselect the line and logo, drag at either element. If you begin your drag quickly, PageMaker represents the position of two elements as a thinly outlined rectangle. If you click and hold for a moment before moving your mouse, PageMaker correctly represents both elements as you drag. Move the elements so that the 2-point line snaps under the horizontal ruler guide and the left side of the line is flush with the vertical guide.
Step 6.	Deselect both elements by clicking a blank area of your display. Then scroll leftward, if necessary, and select the new copy of the company logo. For this exercise, you want the logo to be on the left side of the left master page, a mirror image of the right master page. While constraining your drag by pressing the Shift key, move the logo until its left side is flush with the vertical ruler guide.

Figure 16-5 shows how the completed master pages look.

Figure 16-5: The left and right master pages of your newsletter

Adding a Masthead to Page 1 _____

Now that you have your master page elements in place, you will want to add a masthead to the top of page 1. The masthead, also called a flag, is the title of your newsletter, represented in an eye-catching manner that visually states your purpose.

STEPS:	Creating the Masthead Text
Step 1.	Click the page 1 icon to turn to page 1. You could also use the Go to page... command from the Page menu (⌘-G), but it is usually faster to click the page icon or press ⌘-Tab.
Step 2.	Zoom in to the top area of page 1 by dragging a marquee with the Zoom tool. Select the Text tool from the toolbox and position the text entry cursor (also known as the I-beam) in the upper-left corner of the page, just inside the top

and left margins. Click the mouse button, and a flashing vertical cursor will appear against the left margin. The flashing I-beam cursor indicates that you can enter the text for your masthead.

Step 3. Type the characters **I-n-f-o-r-m-a-t-i-o-n-!**. Notice that they emerge from the left margin in 12-point Times Roman. This is the default type size and typeface specification used by PageMaker. (In the second sample project, you will learn how to alter the default settings used for type size, typeface, and many other PageMaker options.)

Step 4. To change the typeface and type size of your masthead, you must first select the text you want to alter. PageMaker uses the same principles of selection and modification employed by most Macintosh word processors: Text must be selected (highlighted) for any of its attributes to be changed. There are several ways to select text in PageMaker:

- Drag the I-beam cursor over the text to be selected.

- Double-click on a word in the text block to select the entire word. Select additional text one word at a time by holding the mouse button down after the second click and then dragging.

- Triple-click on a word to select the entire paragraph.

- After setting the text entry cursor within a text block, choose the Select all command (⌘-A) from the File menu to select the entire story, even if it spans many text blocks on many pages. In this case, you want to select the entire text block, which consists solely of the word Information!

Step 5. Once the text block is selected, choose the Font command from the Type menu. A hierarchical list of typefaces loaded into your System file or opened with Suitcase II or MasterJuggler will appear. Choose the Helvetica option from this list.

Step 6. Choose the Size command to display a pop-up list of commonly used type sizes. Choose the 48-point option. The result is a much-enlarged version of your masthead, which is more impressive and eye-catching than the original 12-point Times Roman type.

Step 7. Choose the Type style command from the Type menu to display a pop-up menu listing of styles, and choose the Bold option (or press Shift-⌘-B).

Step 8. To center your masthead, choose the Alignment command from the Type menu; then choose the Align center option from the corresponding pop-up listing (or press Shift-⌘-C). Your masthead text now appears in the font, type size, type style, and horizontal position, as shown in Figure 16-6.

I-n-f-o-r-m-a-t-i-o-n-!

Figure 16-6: The 48-point Helvetica-bold masthead on page 1.

Step 9.   Move the masthead text vertically, either by dragging the text block while pressing the Shift key or by dragging the tab on the upper windowshade, until the top of the text block snaps to the top margin as shown in Figure 16-7.

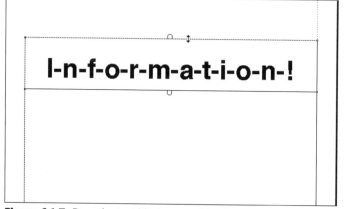

I-n-f-o-r-m-a-t-i-o-n-!

Figure 16-7: Drag the text block upward by dragging its upper window- shade until it snaps to the top margin.

A PageMaker text block is a discreet element that can be selected, moved, resized, and deleted. Text blocks are created automatically when you enter new text after clicking with the Text tool or when text is imported using the Place command from the File menu. When selected, text blocks are marked by windowshades that appear on the top and bottom of the text block. As you will see, windowshades can be moved in relation to each other by dragging at the small tab that extends upward or downward from the middle of the window-shade. To see the text block for your masthead text, select the Pointer tool from the toolbox and click the word Information!

With windowshades displayed, you can change the position of a text block by dragging it. Press and hold the mouse button down while pointing anywhere in the text block except on its handles or tabs. Since you want to alter only the vertical positioning of the text block, press the Shift key to constrain the drag movement. Another method of vertically positioning a text block without disturbing the block's horizontal positioning is to drag the tab on the upper window shade of the text block. By dragging upward on the windowshade and releasing, you cause the text block to rise. Dragging downward on the upper windowshade lowers the text. Note, however, that when you drag downward, the bottom windowshade will often remain motionless, so a line or more of text may remain hidden. If this happens, drag downward on the lower window-shade, which will contain a small down arrow. (The latter portion of this chapter includes more information on using the lower windowshade tab of a text block.)

Isolating the Masthead from the Newsletter

If you were to stop now, you would simply have a big word at the top of a page. There is nothing to distinguish the masthead from other large blocks of text, such as headlines. Although you won't be creating any 72-point headlines, the sheer immensity of a masthead is not necessarily enough to instruct a reader as to the purpose of this text block. But a simple graphic can go a long way to visually establishing a masthead for what it is. You will be using the simplest of all graphics — a straight line — to set your Information! masthead apart from the rest of your newsletter.

STEPS: Adding an 8-Point Rule Under the Masthead

Step 1.   With the Pointer tool, drag a guide down from the horizontal ruler to a point about one-quarter inch below the masthead text.

Step 2.   Select the Constrained Line tool from the toolbox and position the cursor at the intersection of the vertical ruler guide (from the right master page) and the new horizontal guide.

Step 3.   Draw a line to the right margin so that it stretches across the page. Make sure to drag slightly down from the horizontal guide so that the line sits just under the guide. If your view size does not display the entire width of the page, PageMaker will automatically scroll your display.

Step 4.   With the line selected, choose the 8 pt option from the Line pop-up listing under the Element menu. If you created your line under the guide as instructed in the previous step, the 8-point weight of the line will appear below the guide, as shown in Figure 16-8.

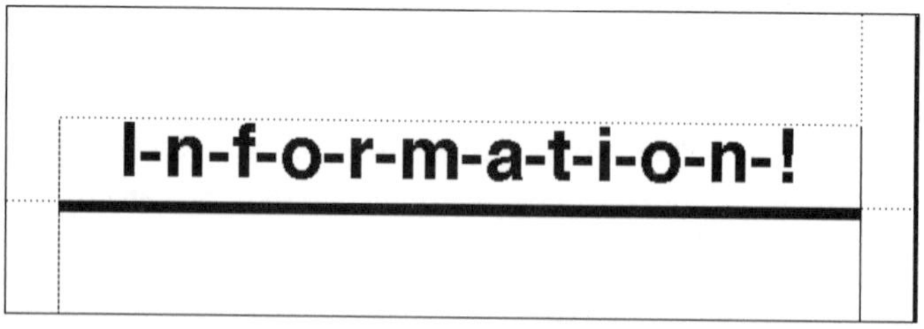

I-n-f-o-r-m-a-t-i-o-n-!

Figure 16-8: The completed masthead with text and an 8-point line

Arranging the Text

Now that you have completed the masthead, you are ready to add the first article to your newsletter. The format that you are going to use calls for the lead article to be set in two columns directly below the masthead. It is advisable to always define your columns prior to pouring text.

STEPS: Setting Column Guides

Step 1.   Choose the Column Guides command from the Layout menu. This command allows you to define up to 20 columns per page and to also specify the amount of space between columns. Choosing this command opens the Column Guides dialog box, which is shown in Figure 16-9. This dialog box defines the number and placement of equidistant column guides for the current page or pages. Setting the column guides while working on the master pages affects the guides on all corresponding publication pages.

Step 2.   Enter **2** for the Number of columns option.

Step 3.   Define the Space between columns as **0.5** (assuming you are still using inches as the units of measure).

Step 4.   Click the OK button to instruct PageMaker to close the dialog box and add the specified column guides to the page.

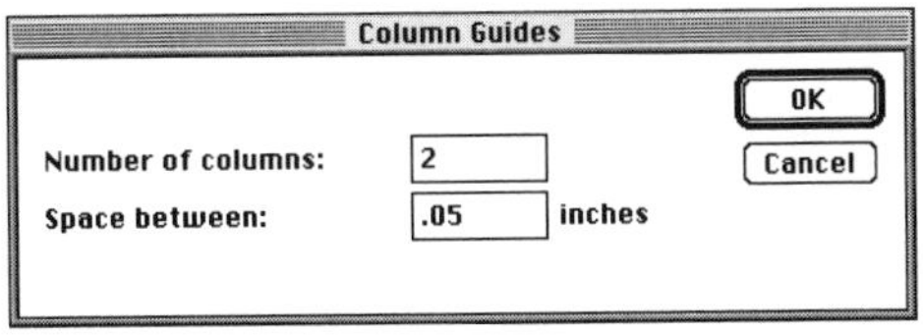

Figure 16-9: The Column Guides dialog box

To define the two columns, PageMaker has added three column guides to your page. One is in front of the left margin guide, one is in front of the right margin guide, and one is in the middle of the page with a one-half-inch gutter between its two sides (according to your specifications in the Column Guides dialog box). The amount of room between the left and center column guides and the center and right column guides is equal. PageMaker simply subtracts the combined gutters from the total width of a page and divides that amount by the number of columns. The result is the width of each column. In this case, each column is 3.5 inches wide. (In later chapters, you will learn how to move column guides to create individually wider or narrower columns.)

Placing Text

As discussed in the previous chapter, you can prepare your text in a word processor before using it in PageMaker. For the lead article in this newsletter, you will import a document previously created in a word processor.

STEPS: Importing an Article from a Word Processor

Step 1. Before you import the story text, drag down another ruler guide, which you will use to align the top of the text into the columns on your page. Drag the guide down from the horizontal ruler to a location about two inches below the 8-point line.

Step 2. Choose the Place command from the File menu (⌘-D). The Place document dialog box (shown in Figure 16-10) appears, allowing you to select the text file to be imported and to specify the way in which the text is used.

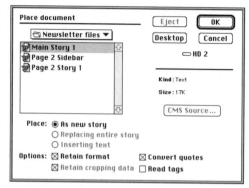

Figure 16-10: The Place document dialog box

Step 3. Locate and select the Main Story 1 file in the Project 1 folder on the disk accompanying this book. Click the OK button or press the Return or Enter key. The dialog box closes, and your cursor changes to the manual text flow icon, indicating that PageMaker is ready for you to put the selected article into position.

The scrolling file listing and the Eject and Desktop buttons in the Place document dialog box provide the standard means for locating files on any available disks or in any available folders. (Remember that you can use any text document that you have available for this exercise, provided it is at least one page long.) Once you have successfully located and selected a file to be used for the lead article, you may want to examine and perhaps manipulate some of the Place document dialog box options.

There are three Place radio buttons. The first option, As new story, is the only option that is not dimmed and is suitable for this purpose. (The remaining two options are useful when replacing existing text.)

There are also four Options check boxes. The Retain format option, which is selected by default, instructs PageMaker to utilize exactly the text and paragraph formatting of the incoming document. Deselecting this command would cause the placed document to be stripped of its character formatting (such as fonts, type sizes, and type styles) and paragraph formatting (margins, indents, and tabs). The Convert quotes option alerts PageMaker to substitute an opening or closing quote (" or ") in place of a leading or trailing standard quote ("). If this option is deselected, the quotation marks remain unchanged. The Read tags option is used when style sheet tags have been entered into a word processed document. The Retain cropping data option is used when there are crop marks in the document. We discuss style sheets, tags, and cropping in more detail in Chapter 7.

Besides importing texts from word processors, it is also possible to pour a story into your document manually.

STEPS: Manually Pouring a Story

Step 1. Position the manual text flow cursor at the intersection of the new ruler guide and the leftmost column guide; then click your mouse button. The text from your document will flow into the column, stopping when it reaches the bottom margin. (Now, if you like, you can reposition your ruler guide.) Since the entire document does not fit into a single column, there will be a down arrow in the tab of the lower windowshade of the new text block, indicating that more text remains to be placed.

Step 2. Click the down arrow, and the manual text flow cursor will reappear. Position your cursor in the right-hand column, vertically aligning it with the beginning of the text in the left column, and click the mouse button to begin the text flow in this column. If enough text remains in the document, the text will flow down to the bottom margin.

Step 3. Make sure that the tops of both columns are even with each other by selecting each text block and then dragging each upper window shade flush with the most recently created horizontal ruler guide.

Figure 16-11 shows how your document should appear now.

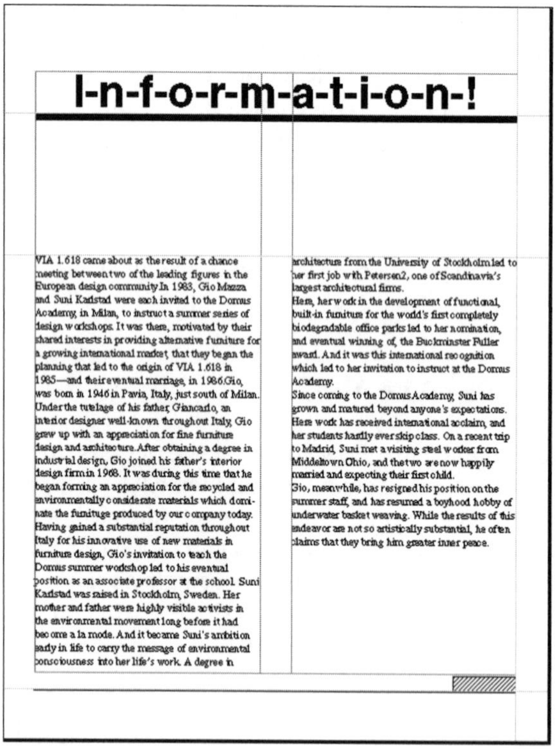

Figure 16-11:
The result of pouring
an article into two
columns with a one-
half-inch gutter

Formatting Text

Now that you have placed your first story in position, you can change the character and paragraph attributes of the text to fit both your design scheme and your personal preference. In the following steps, you will change the font for the entire article; set the type size, leading, and first-line indent; and create a headline as a separate text block.

STEPS: Changing Type Specifications

Step 1. Click anywhere inside the first or second column of the text and press ⌘-A or choose the Select all command from the Edit menu. This ensures that ensuing text changes will affect the entire article, even those portions you may not have poured yet. Choose Helvetica from the Font pop-up listing under the Type menu. Then choose the 10-point type size from the Size pop-up listing.

Step 2. Change the leading of your article. Like typeface, type size, and other text attributes, leading can be altered by way of a pop-up menu. The unique property of the Leading pop-up listing, however, is that the options offered vary depending on the current type size value. For example, if you select a 24-point type size, the Leading pop-up listing will contain 23-point through 26-point options in half-point increments, plus a few larger sizes. But if you select a 12-point type size, the half-point variations are offered in the 11-point to 14-point range.

Suppose that you want to change the leading to 12.5 points. Unfortunately, this value is not included in the Leading pop-up list when the type size is set to 10-point. To access other leadings, choose the Other option from the Leading pop-up menu; the Other Leading dialog box, shown in Figure 16-12, displays. Enter 12.5 into the option box and press Return. This gives you 10/12.5 type, or 10-point type size on 12.5-point leading, which is an extremely legible combination for most typefaces.

Figure 16-12:
The Other Leading dialog box allows you to enter a leading that does not appear in the pop-up menu.

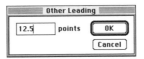

STEPS: **Changing Paragraph specifications**

Step 1. To increase the legibility of your text, you need to add a first-line indent to and some space below each paragraph. With your entire story still selected, choose the Paragraph command from the Type menu or press ⌘-M. This brings up the Paragraph Specifications dialog box, which controls a number of attributes that are applied to whole paragraphs. (For complete information about the Paragraph Specifications dialog box, refer to Chapter 6.) Here's a brief discussion of each of the options offered by this dialog box:

- The **Indents** options allow you to add specified amounts of horizontal space to selected paragraphs. The horizontal space indicated by the Left value is added between the left column guide and the selected text. The space indicated by the Right value is added between the right column guide and the selected text. The First option adds space between the left column guide and the first line of text in the paragraph. You will be using the First option to add a first-line indent to the newsletter text.

- The **Paragraph space** options allow you to add specified amounts of vertical space between selected paragraphs and their neighbors. The Before option inserts space between the first line of a selected paragraph and the preceding paragraph; the After option inserts space between the last line of a selected paragraph and the following paragraph.

- The **Alignment** pop-up menu allows you to select from five alignments: flush left, centered, flush right, justified, or force justified. These options perform identically to the options available from the Alignment pop-up under the Type menu, as explained in the following chapter.

- Finally, the **Options** check boxes allow you to determine the manner in which PageMaker breaks a paragraph at the end of a column. For example, you can prevent two paragraphs from becoming separated or specify that a paragraph never breaks between columns. Figure 16-13 shows how the Paragraph specifications dialog box appears.

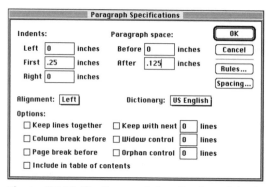

Figure 16-13: The Paragraph Specifications dialog box as it should appear before you click OK

Step 2. Of the Indents options, change the First value to 0.25, or one-quarter inch. Also change the After value in the Paragraph space column to 0.125, or one-eighth inch. Then click the OK button or press Return, directing PageMaker to implement your changes. You can now see that your indents call attention to the beginning of each paragraph. The space after each paragraph helps to set paragraphs apart slightly. The result is two very readable columns of text, as shown in Figure 16-14.

Incidentally, if your paragraphs already contain introductory tabs or multiple spaces, both of which are common typewriting devices for indicating the beginning of paragraphs, these should be deleted. First-line indents serve the same purpose and are much easier to implement and manipulate.

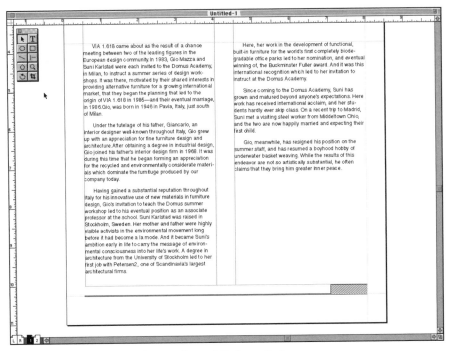

Figure 16-14: Your two columns of text, fully formatted

Creating a Drop Cap

You will now create a drop cap, a design device for introducing your article to a reader. You will set the first letter of your article in a larger type size so that it encompasses the first two lines of text. You will use one of the Adobe Plug-ins Additions that is included with PageMaker 5 to make the drop cap.

STEPS: **Creating a Drop Cap**

Step 1. Set the insertion point anywhere in the paragraph to which you want to add a drop cap.

Step 2. Go to the Utilities menu and hold down the mouse button while selecting the PageMaker Plug-ins command. A submenu of available Plug-ins appears. Scroll down the submenu and choose Drop Cap.

Step 3.   The Drop Cap Plug-in dialog box now appears. Enter **2** into the Number of lines option and click the OK button. The Plug-in will then manipulate the size of the initial character and insert tabs as necessary to have the other lines wrap around the drop cap character. Figure 16-15 shows the completed drop cap.

V IA 1.618 came about as the result of a chance
meeting between two of the leading figures in
the European design community.In 1983, Gio Mazza and
Suni Karlstad were each invited to the Domus Academy,
in Milan, to instruct a summer series of design workshops. It was there, motivated by their shared interests in
providing alternative furniture for a growing international
market, that they began the planning that led to the
origin of VIA 1.618 in 1985—and their eventual marriage,
in 1986.Gio, was born in 1946 in Pavia, Italy, just south
of Milan.

Figure 16-15: A two-line drop cap created with the Drop Cap Plug-in

Adding a Headline

The only element that this article still lacks is a headline. A headline is needed to introduce the article and summarize its purpose. You'll add this headline in the same manner as you created the masthead—by typing it directly into PageMaker. Generally, headlines are set as wide as the text they introduce. If an article is poured into a single column, the headline should be one column wide. If the article is poured into two columns, like yours, then the headline should stretch across both columns. Therefore, you need to create a headline that extends the entire width of the image area, from the left margin to the right margin.

The problem here is that you have set up two columns. If you were to click with the Text tool in one of these columns, your headline text block would only be one column wide. There are three ways to rectify this situation:

⤚ Choose the Column guides command from the Options menu and change the Number of columns option to 1. This would return your page to a one-column format and allow you to create a headline the width of the page. It will not alter the format of any two-column text already positioned.

☞ Click in one of the two columns and type your headline text. When you are finished, you can stretch the width of this existing text block to any width. (This method is demonstrated in the sample project in Chapter 17.)

☞ Override the column guides by drawing the width of your page with the Text tool. This is the quickest and easiest method, as demonstrated in Step 1 below.

STEPS: Adding a Headline

Step 1. You will be using the third method of overriding the column guides by dragging with the Text tool. First, use the Zoom tool to zoom in on the area above the text columns (the two-inch-high area between the masthead and the columns of type). Click the left column and, without releasing, drag the entire width of the page to the right edge of the right column. Figure 16-16 demonstrates how your drag should appear.

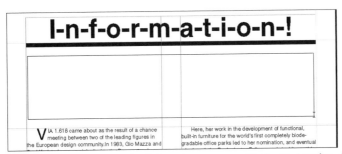

Figure 16-16: An example of dragging an area with the Text tool to define a text block

Step 2. Once you have defined the width of your text block, you can type in your headline. Type: **Two Faculty Members From Domus Academy Excel at Via**.

Step 3. Press ⌘-A to select all of the text in the headline. Change the typeface to Helvetica and the type size to 36-point, using the same methods described throughout this chapter. Also, make sure that the leading is set to Auto (Shift-⌘-A). Center the headline by pressing Shift-⌘-C or choose the Align Center option from the Alignment pop-up listing under the Type menu.

Step 4. Vertically position the headline text block evenly between the masthead and the two-column article by Shift-dragging with the Pointer tool. Figure 16-17 shows the final headline.

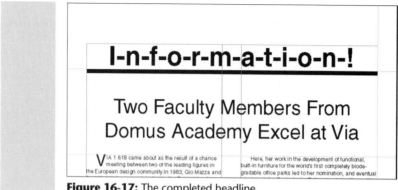

Figure 16-17: The completed headline

This ends the discussion of page 1. You have successfully created a masthead to announce your newsletter, a lead story to inform your readers, and a headline to introduce the lead story. Figure 16-18 shows the completed first page. On page 2, you will pour two more stories and give each article a headline. You will also draw a box around one of your stories to provide visual emphasis.

Creating the Second Page

You are now ready to create the second page of this two-page newsletter. You will be placing two more stories, both originally created using Microsoft Word.

Placing and Formatting a Three-Column Story

First, you need to change the page format to accommodate three columns of text. Then you can flow the text.

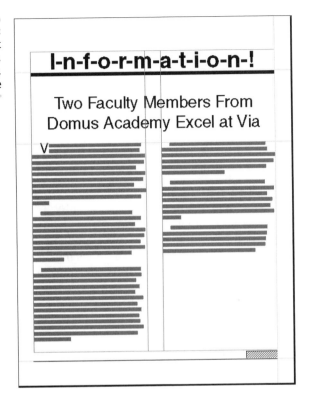

Figure 16-18:
The completed first page of your newsletter, complete with banner, body text, and headline

STEPS: **Changing the Number of Columns**

Step 1. Click the page 2 icon to turn to the second page. You can also reach page 2 by pressing ⌘-Tab.

Step 2. When your screen displays page 2, you will notice that it matches the left master page. The rule is at the bottom, the company logo rectangle is in the bottom-left corner, and there is only one column defined. On this page, you will be changing your format slightly to accommodate three columns of text. Therefore, choose the Column Guide command from the Utilities menu. After the Column Guides dialog box appears, enter **3** in the Number of columns option and **0.5** in the Space between columns option. Then click OK. Four column guides appear on the page, defining three equal columns.

Step 3. Drag a horizontal ruler guide down to a point two inches below the top margin. Assuming that you have not moved the zero point of your rulers, this point will correspond to the 3-inch tick mark on your vertical ruler. The area above this guide designates the area where you will create the first headline. Then drag another horizontal ruler guide down to a point corresponding to the 6-inch marking on the vertical ruler. Both guides will help you position the first article on this page.

Step 4.   Now that you have defined the boundaries for your article, you are ready to place the text. Choose the Place command from the File menu. Select the file "Page 2 Story 1" and double-click or press the OK button in the Place Document dialog box.

Step 5.   Position your manual text flow cursor up against the top ruler guide and inside the first column, and click. After PageMaker has poured the first column of your article, click the tab of the lower windowshade of the text block.

Step 6.   Next, click the manual text flow cursor at the intersection of the top ruler guide and the second column. The text will again flow to the bottom margin. For this purpose, however, you want this column of text to extend only down to the lower horizontal ruler guide. This means that you must drag the lower windowshade of the second text block up to the lower ruler guide and then click the lower tab, as shown in Figure 16-19.

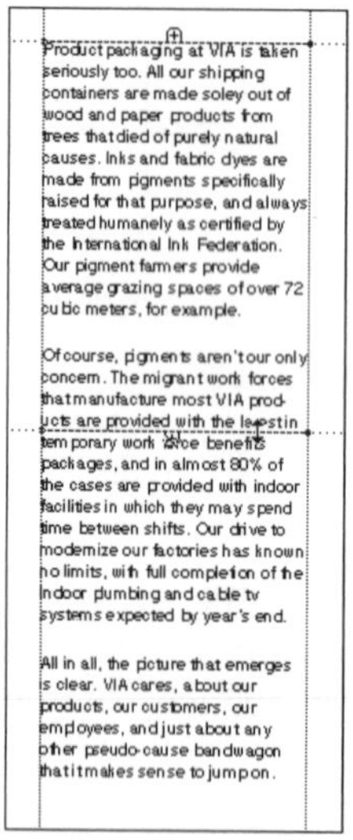

Figure 16-19: Shorten the second column by dragging up the lower windowshade of the text block.

Step 7.   Position your manual text flow cursor flush with the top ruler guide and click inside the third column. Like the second column, this column should extend only to the lower ruler guide. Since the text is not yet formatted properly, it will now flow somewhat beyond that boundary.

Now it is time to format the text.

STEPS: Formatting the Three-Column Story

Step 1. Select the Text tool, click inside any one of the columns of text, and press ⌘-A to select all of the text.

Step 2. Change the type specifications to 10/12.5 Helvetica, using the Font, Size, and Leading pop-up menus as described during the formatting of page 1.

Step 3. Add a first-line indent of 0.25 inch and an After spacing of 0.125 inch to your paragraph formatting. If your text is not already ragged right, select the Align left option from the Alignment pop-up menu. (If necessary, shorten column 1 by one line to get rid of the widow.) This article is now poured into three columns and fully formatted as shown in Figure 16-20.

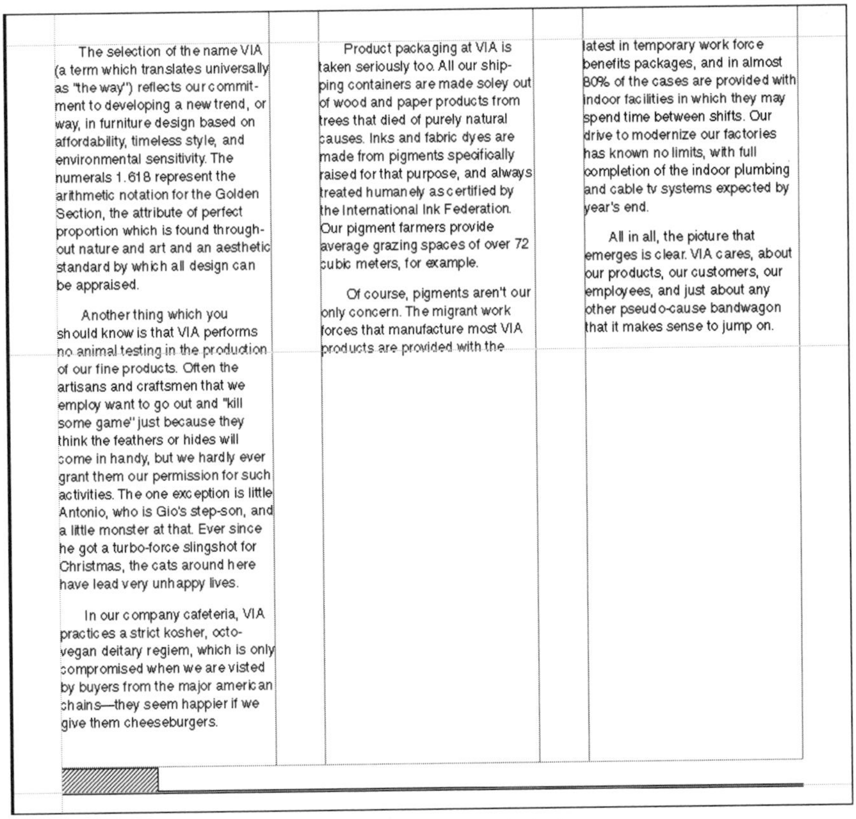

The selection of the name VIA (a term which translates universally as "the way") reflects our commitment to developing a new trend, or way, in furniture design based on affordability, timeless style, and environmental sensitivity. The numerals 1.618 represent the arithmetic notation for the Golden Section, the attribute of perfect proportion which is found throughout nature and art and an aesthetic standard by which all design can be appraised.

Another thing which you should know is that VIA performs no animal testing in the production of our fine products. Often the artisans and craftsmen that we employ want to go out and "kill some game" just because they think the feathers or hides will come in handy, but we hardly ever grant them our permission for such activities. The one exception is little Antonio, who is Gio's step-son, and a little monster at that. Ever since he got a turbo-force slingshot for Christmas, the cats around here have lead very unhappy lives.

In our company cafeteria, VIA practices a strict kosher, octo-vegan deitary regiem, which is only compromised when we are visted by buyers from the major american chains—they seem happier if we give them cheeseburgers.

Product packaging at VIA is taken seriously too. All our shipping containers are made soley out of wood and paper products from trees that died of purely natural causes. Inks and fabric dyes are made from pigments specifically raised for that purpose, and always treated humanely as certified by the International Ink Federation. Our pigment farmers provide average grazing spaces of over 72 cubic meters, for example.

Of course, pigments aren't our only concern. The migrant work forces that manufacture most VIA products are provided with the

latest in temporary work force benefits packages, and in almost 80% of the cases are provided with indoor facilities in which they may spend time between shifts. Our drive to modernize our factories has known no limits, with full completion of the indoor plumbing and cable tv systems expected by year's end.

All in all, the picture that emerges is clear. VIA cares, about our products, our customers, our employees, and just about any other pseudo-cause bandwagon that it makes sense to jump on.

Figure 16-20: This is how your three columns should look.

Notice that the format exactly matches the article on page 1. It is generally a good idea to keep your body text consistent throughout a newsletter or any document. This gives your pages a reliable design structure, which aids your readers by reducing potential confusion. The best type, after all, is type that goes unnoticed but not unread.

Creating a Headline and a Subhead

Your next step is to add both a headline and a subhead to this story. As mentioned earlier, a headline serves as an introduction to an article. A subhead further elucidates the story, often relating very closely to the headline both visually and conceptually. A headline might ask a question that is answered in the subhead. The headline might make a statement to which the subhead poses a logical question, which is answered in the text. In this case, you will create a direct, two-word headline designed simply to attract the reader. Your subhead will summarize the article and state its purpose.

STEPS: Adding a Headline and a Subhead

Step 1. First you will create a two-column headline. If you haven't already done so, magnify your screen display to Actual size view and position your display so that you can see the top of the page.

Step 2. Select the Text tool and position your cursor at the intersection of the top and left margins. Drag from this point to the right edge of the second column, as shown in Figure 16-21.

Figure 16-21: Drag a text box as shown here.

Step 3. Type **VIA Backgrounder**. Then select both words with the Text tool and format the entire text block to 36-point Helvetica Bold. Move the headline up until it is flush with the top margin.

Step 4.   To create a visual link between your two-column headline and your three-column text, you need to add a three-column subhead. Again using the Text tool, drag from a point between the headline and text on the left margin all the way across the page to the edge of the right column. Then type the subhead **Corporate responsibility a top priority in all aspects of the VIA operations**.

Step 5.   Select the whole text block and format the subhead to 24-point Helvetica. To distinguish the subhead from the headline even more clearly, select the Italic option from the Style pop-up menu under the Type menu (or press Shift-⌘-I), giving the subhead a visually interesting slant. Vertically position this text block between the headline and the article. The completed headline and subhead are shown in Figure 16-22.

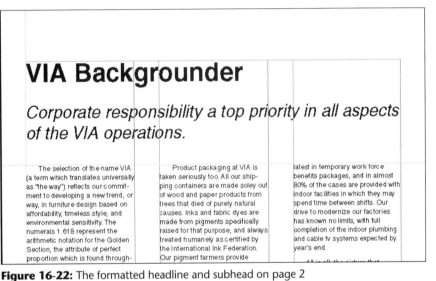

Figure 16-22: The formatted headline and subhead on page 2

Creating a Sidebar

The last article you will place into this newsletter will obviously have to fit in the empty area occupying the bottom-right third of the page. This area is purposefully much smaller than the area containing the three-column article, since the next story you pour will act visually as a supporting story, or sidebar, to the feature story. A sidebar includes additional information along the same lines as the feature story—information that is interesting, although not necessarily as important.

To distinguish it from the feature story, a sidebar is often set off by a box. To further highlight the article, its box might have a drop shadow. A drop shadow is a black or gray box, largely hidden in back of the first box, that gives your page a sense of dimension, as if the box surrounding the article is hovering above the page, casting a shadow onto the page. Before creating the sidebar, you should establish a border and a drop shadow. But first, you must set another ruler guide to help position your article and the graphic elements that surround it.

STEPS: Drawing a Box with a Drop Shadow

Step 1.   Drag a horizontal ruler guide down to one-quarter inch below the lower horizontal ruler guide. (This should be at the 6$\frac{1}{4}$-inch tick mark on the vertical ruler, provided that you have not moved your ruler's zero intersection point.)

Step 2.   The easiest way to create a drop shadow box is to create the shadow first. Select the rectangle tool and drag from the intersection of the new horizontal ruler guide and the left edge of the second column to the bottom right margin corner.

Step 3.   While the shape is still selected, choose the Line and Fill command under the Element menu, choose the None options from the Line pop-up, and set the fill to Solid and Tint to 40%. (If you don't know how to do this, refer to Chapter 8). The result is a rectangular, medium gray value screen with no outline. The box should look like Figure 16-23.

Figure 16-23: The gray box for your sidebar drop shadow

Step 4.   Create the box in front of the shadow. The box should be the same vertical and horizontal dimensions as the shadow to ensure a consistent and realistic relationship between them. The shadow is, after all, being cast by the box. Therefore, you can create the box by making a copy of the existing shadow. Assuming that the gray rectangle is still selected, choose the Copy command from the Edit menu or press ⌘-C. Then immediately bring a copy of the shadow from the Macintosh Clipboard to your page by choosing the Paste command from the Edit menu or pressing ⌘-V. The pasted rectangle will appear directly in front of the original rectangle.

Step 5. Drag the selected rectangle one-eighth inch above and to the left of the bottom right margin corner, as shown in Figure 16-24. In this way, it is just slightly offset from the original rectangle behind it. While the forward shape remains selected, choose the Paper option from the Fill pop-up listing and 1 pt from the Line pop-up listing.

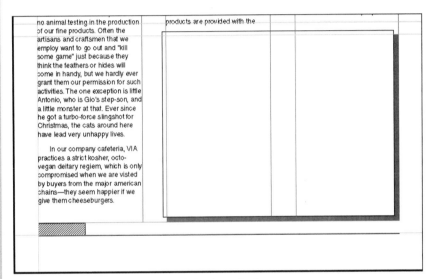

no animal testing in the production of our fine products. Often the artisans and craftsmen that we employ want to go out and "kill some game" just because they think the feathers or hides will come in handy, but we hardly ever grant them our permission for such activities. The one exception is little Antonio, who is Gio's step-son, and a little monster at that. Ever since he got a turbo-force slingshot for Christmas, the cats around here have lead very unhappy lives.

In our company cafeteria, VIA practices a strict kosher, octo-vegan deitary regiem, which is only compromised when we are visted by buyers from the major american chains—they seem happier if we give them cheeseburgers.

products are provided with the

Figure 16-24: The sidebar box and the drop shadow

Before pouring your text into the box, you should group the box and the drop shadow so that PageMaker treats them as one object and maintains their positional relationship to each other. After grouping the objects, you can then lock their positions on the page so that they cannot be moved with your mouse.

Step 6. With the front box still selected, Shift-click a visible portion of the gray box to select it, then choose Group from the Arrange menu. Now choose Lock Position from the Arrange menu. The items are now grouped and locked you can't move or change their positional relationship. Go ahead and try.

The box is now completed, appearing to be in front of the drop shadow. You are now ready to place the text into the box.

STEPS: Pouring and Formatting the Sidebar Text

Step 1.   Before you place your text, yet another ruler guide is required. This time, drag a vertical ruler guide to about one-quarter inch from the right margin (one-eighth inch in from the right edge of the box). This guide will define the right column guide of your sidebar text.

Step 2.   Choose the Place command or press ⌘-D, select the Page 2 Sidebar file, and press Return. When your manual text flow cursor appears, do not click. This time, you will draw the column width of your text with the Text tool, just as you did earlier when creating headlines and subheads. Drag with the manual text flow cursor from the intersection of the left edge of the second column and the lowest horizontal ruler guide (just inside the box) over to the newest vertical ruler guide.

Step 3.   After PageMaker pours your text, select all the sidebar text with the Text tool and change the type specifications, or specs, to 12-point Helvetica with Auto leading. Also make sure that the text is flush left and give each paragraph a 0.25-inch first-line indent and .125 Space after, as we did for the other text blocks in this exercise. Incidentally, this text is slightly larger than other text in the newsletter to highlight the sidebar more vividly. Because it is a small article with large text, it seems friendly, making a person more likely to read it. If it is well written, a sidebar may spark a reader's interest in the main article.

Step 4.   Click the text with the Pointer tool and, if necessary, adjust the lower windowshade of the text block to within one-eighth inch from the bottom edge of the box. The upper windowshade may need to be adjusted as well so that it touches the horizontal ruler guide.

Step 5.   Like any other article, a sidebar needs a headline. The headline will fit in the area between the feature article text and the sidebar box. Select the Text tool and drag in this area from the left edge of the second column to the vertical ruler guide on the far right of the page to define the headline column width. Then type **Guiding Principles** and change the specs to 24-point Helvetica Italic (known as Helvetica Oblique). If necessary, adjust the position of the headline vertically to match the position shown in Figure 16-25.

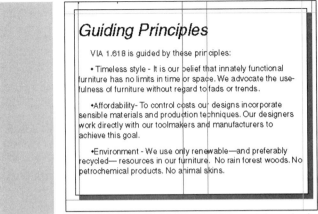

Figure 16-25: The finished sidebar and drop-shadow box

Your newsletter is now complete. If you wish, demagnify your display to Fit-in-window view size. It should closely match the page shown in Figure 16-26.

Figure 16-26:
Page 2 of the finished
newsletter.

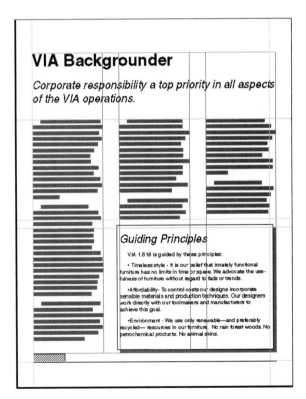

All that is left to do is save your newsletter to disk for future reference and print the file to an output device.

Saving the Newsletter to Disk

You always want to store files that you create to disk. Generally, you want to save a file before you are done creating it or soon after starting it. We've postponed the discussion of the Save command to this point in order to focus this sample project on the newsletter-creation process itself. When you create files of your own, however, we recommend that you execute the Save command frequently. This way, you won't lose very much information if you get a system error or if you are forced to restart your computer for some other reason.

When you save a file to disk, all your work is transcribed from your computer's memory to disk. The file that you save can be transferred to other floppy or hard disks and will thereby remain available should you want to use it again at a later date. You never know when you may want to access this file again, especially in the case of a periodical publication such as a newsletter. Once you have established a certain visual style, you will want to build on it again and again. For example, in future versions of this newsletter, you could open this same file to spare yourself the time and effort of re-creating your master page items and the masthead text. Considering that the creation of these items alone consumed the first third of this chapter, there is much to be gained by saving this file.

Choose the Save command from the File menu or press ⌘-S. Since you have never saved this file before, the Save publication as dialog box appears, as shown in Figure 16-27. The folder bar and Eject and Drive buttons allow you to determine to which disk or hard drive and to which folder you want to save your file. You must also enter a name for your file in the option box under the list of existing files. We suggest the name Two-page newsletter, but you can enter any name that you like.

Figure 16-27:
Saving the two-page newsletter to disk

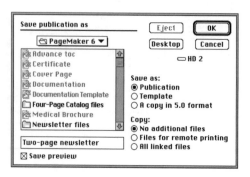

Determining a filename and location is a very important process. First-time users often make the mistake of giving their files very general or obscure names and saving them to arbitrary disks. In the short run, this can be fine. You may not have many files, only two or three folders' or disks' worth, and you can easily find them and tell them apart. But you would be surprised how little time it takes to amass a very large number of files. If you use PageMaker often, you can easily create enough files to fill many folders or disks every month, making random file storage an organizational nightmare. Here are a few tips for saving your files:

- Save similar files to the same folders. In other words, save newsletters to one folder or set of folders, flyers to another, business letters to another, and so on.

- When naming a file, ask yourself if you have provided enough information to recall the contents of the file a few months, or even years, later. Make your names specific and exact. Remember, you have 32 characters to name your file, so there is no need to be cryptic or overly brief.

- How will you be able to differentiate this version of your document from previous or future versions? You don't need to date your file, since the Macintosh System already provides this information, but adding a version or issue number to the end of a filename can be helpful in distinguishing similar files.

After determining a file destination and entering a filename, click the OK button or press the Return or Enter key. Your file is now saved so that you can reuse it in the future.

Printing a Two-Page Document ___

The last step in producing a document in PageMaker is to print it. PageMaker files can be printed to nearly any printer you have connected to your Macintosh or to a high-resolution imagesetter at a desktop publishing service bureau or commercial printer. There are many different printing options in PageMaker, but for now we'll just focus on the ones you need in order to print your newsletter.

STEPS: Printing a Two-Page Document

Step 1.   First, make sure that your printer is turned on. Then use the Chooser to select the printer driver that represents your printer (the LaserWriter or PostScript 8.x driver is used for all PostScript printers) and select your printer.

Step 2.   Choose the Print command from the File menu or press ⌘-P. This brings up the Print document dialog box, shown in Figure 16-28. Enter the number of copies of each page of your file you want to print in the Copies option. Usually, this number should be 1. If you want to print large quantities of copies, you generally can save money by outputting a single original and having photocopies or offset prints made from the original set. The Pages options control which pages in your file will print. Select the All radio button to print the entire file, or enter the page range in the Ranges option box. For example, if you wanted to print only page 1, you would enter **1** in this box.

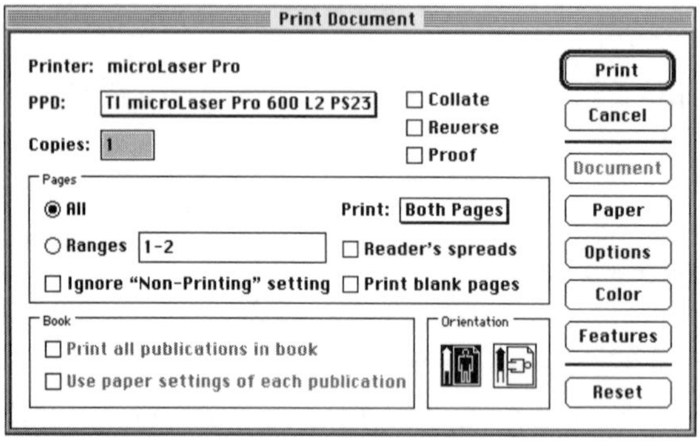

Figure 16-28: The Print Document dialog box

Step 3.   PageMaker lists the name of the printer that you have chosen at the top of the dialog box. If you are using a PostScript printer, just below the printer name is the PPD option, which you use to specify the specific make and model of printer you are using. This is done by selecting a PostScript Printer Description (PPD) file from the pop-up list. PPD files have somewhat cryptic names, but they generally include the name of the printer manufacturer, model, and version of PostScript. Select the one that represents your particular printer.

Step 4.   After all your specifications are complete, click the OK button to instruct PageMaker to print your file. The Print Document dialog box disappears and the Print status dialog box displays. The Print status dialog box lists various situations regarding your current print job, including fonts being down-loaded and error condition messages sent back by the printer. The Cancel button allows you to cancel the print job if you discover a problem.

After your pages print, examine them to make sure that they meet your expectations. If you see any problems, make the necessary changes to your document. You may even find it advantageous to make changes to your newsletter that are not outlined in this chapter. Try experimenting with the fonts and other type specifications. Try jazzing up the masthead.

 The newsletter outlined in this chapter is not designed to be used for your personal newsletter needs. But it can act as a structure upon which you can build a more complex, more personalized newsletter. Or, you may want to develop a newsletter in a completely different direction.

In either case, by successfully completing this project, you have demonstrated an understanding of the most-basic and essential commands and options offered by PageMaker.

Summary

➥ Every PageMaker publication has at least one or two master pages (one if your document is single-sided; two if the double-sided option in the Document Setup dialog box is selected). You can add more as needed.

➥ Master pages are used to hold items that repeat from page to page, such as running heads or footers, page numbers, or graphics. By placing repeating elements on the master pages, you ensure that they will be positioned exactly on each page. This procedure saves you the effort of repeatedly positioning identical elements from page to page.

➥ A PageMaker text block is a discreet element that can be selected, moved, resized, and deleted. Text blocks are created automatically when you enter new text after clicking with the Text tool or when text is imported using the Place command from the File menu.

➥ When selected, text blocks are marked by windowshades that appear on the top and bottom of the text block. As you will see, windowshades can be moved in relation to each other by dragging at the small tab that extends upward or downward from the middle of the windowshade.

➥ A headline serves as an introduction to an article. A subhead further elucidates the story, often relating very closely to the headline both visually and conceptually. A headline might ask a question that is answered in the subhead. The headline might make a statement to which the subhead poses a logical question, which is answered in the text.

➥ You should save a file before you are done creating it or soon after starting it. When you create files, we recommend that you execute the Save command frequently. This way, you won't lose very much information if you get a system error or if you are forced to restart your computer for some other reason.

Designing a Two-Sided Flyer

CHAPTER 17

In This Chapter

- ⟶ Changing PageMaker's default settings
- ⟶ Using symbols
- ⟶ Placing and cropping a graphic
- ⟶ Creating a border
- ⟶ Rotating text

In this chapter, you will use PageMaker to create a two-sided flyer like those commonly used for marketing and direct mail. The step-by-step explanation of this flyer represents the second of three sample projects presented in this book. This one helps you develop an intermediate-level understanding of Pagemaker commands and demonstrates how Pagemaker features can be used for a variety of publication production needs that the first project did not showcase.

Since your flyer will be two-sided, you will create it as a two-page document. You will also design the flyer to be folded into thirds for easy and inexpensive mailing. As an added customer incentive, you will include a discount clip-out coupon at the bottom of the flyer.

Flyers do not generally contain superfluous text, so for this project you will use only one fairly short text file. You will also import a graphic saved in the MacPaint format. Throughout the creation of this flyer, you will use the typefaces Palatino and Zapf Dingbats. If you do not already have the Palatino or Zapf Dingbats screen fonts loaded into your System file, copy them into the Fonts folder of your System Folder from your System Software floppy disks.

Step 1.   Launch PageMaker.

Step 2.   Click the mouse button to dispense with the copyright screen.

Changing PageMaker's Default Settings

Before you create a new file, you will alter some application default settings in PageMaker. Adobe has set PageMaker defaults to the most commonly used settings for each option. By changing these defaults according to your needs, you can save the time and energy it would take to change specific settings over and over again in each publication. Here are some examples of the default settings built into PageMaker:

- ☞ A new file is created for letter-size paper with Tall orientation.

- ☞ Inches is the default unit of measurement.

- ☞ Type specifications are set for 17-point type size, Times Roman typeface with automatic leading, and flush-left alignment.

- ☞ Two column guides are set to provide one column per page.

- ☞ The default line weight is 1 point and the default fill is None, providing transparent interiors for boxes drawn in PageMaker.

 Many of these defaults are useful, but as you continue to work in PageMaker, you will discover more and more defaults that are not pertinent to your way of working. PageMaker recognizes that your publication needs and page-creation working habits are as unique as you are, so the application allows you to specify your own defaults. If you create legal-size pages more often than letter-size, for example, you may want to change the default setting for the Page size option. Or if you prefer the typeface New Baskerville to Times Roman, you can change the Font option as well.

There are two ways to change default settings. The first method is to choose commands and select options at the PageMaker desktop while no publications are open. This resets the application defaults for every new file that you create from that point on, until you again reset the defaults. The second method is to choose commands and select options in an open file while no element is selected. These become publication defaults, which affect only the current file and do not affect files you create in the future.

STEPS: **Setting the Defaults for the Flyer**

Step 1. Choose the Preferences command from the File menu to display the Preferences dialog box. The Measurements in option in this dialog box determines the system of measurement used in the rulers and dialog boxes while you create documents. PageMaker offers five units of measurement:

- **Inch,** the most commonly used system of measurement in the United States.

- **Inch decimal,** which divides the standard inch into ten equal segments.

- **Millimeter,** a metric unit equal to $^1/_{1000}$ meter or $^1/_{10}$ centimeter. The metric system is used commonly throughout Europe.

- **Pica,** a unit of measure that is roughly $^1/_6$ inch. A pica is subdivided into 12 equally sized units called *points*. Picas and points are the traditional unit of measurement for American typesetting and page composition and are now the preferred system of measurement in desktop publishing applications.

- **Ciceros,** a unit of approximately $4^1/_2$ millimeters, the traditional unit of measurement for European typesetting. Like the pica, a cicero is subdivided into 12 points. (One cicero point is approximately equal to 1.06 pica points.)

 You can also select a unit of measure from the Vertical ruler column that affects the scale on your vertical ruler only. Generally, this option should be set to the same unit of measure selected from the Measurement system column.

Step 2. Choose the Picas option from the Measurement system pop-up menu. Also choose Picas from the Vertical ruler option.

Step 3. Click the OK button or press the Return or Enter key to confirm your changes. Figure 17-1 shows the new defaults.

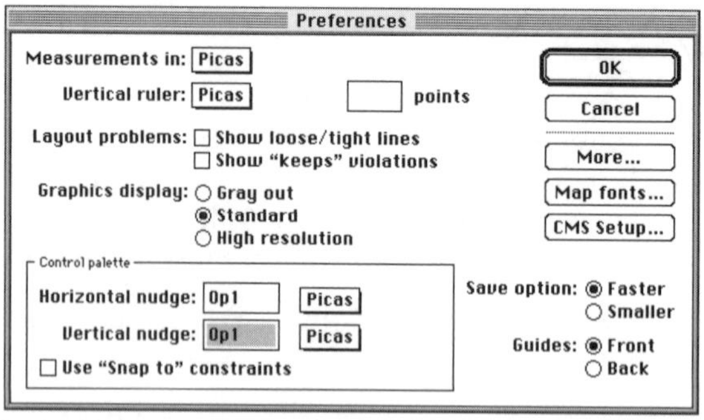

Figure 17-1:
The Preferences dialog
box showing the new
default settings

The Type Specifications Dialog Box

The first option in the Type Specifications dialog is the Font pop-up menu. The scrolling list of fonts available displayed by clicking the current typeface name contains the same options accessed by choosing the Font command from the Type menu. Clicking the arrows to the right of the Size and Leading pop-up menus offer the same choices available by choosing the Size and Leading commands. Alternatively, you can enter any value up to 650 for the Size option or 1300 for Leading. Values are accurate to $1/10$ point.

The Set width option allows you to condense or expand type. You can choose one of the preset options in the pop-up menu or enter a value between 5% and 250% in $1/10$ percent increments in the option box. Any value under 100% produces skinny type; any value over 100% creates wide type, relative to the normal width of the typeface characters.

Use the Color option to change the color of your type. All currently defined spot and process colors appear in the pop-up listing.

The Position pop-up menu allows you to create superscript or subscript text. This option is especially useful for fractions. The Case pop-up menu allows you to determine whether selected or default text is set as Normal (uppercase and lowercase characters), All caps (uppercase letters only), or Small caps (capitals the size of lowercase letters). The effects of these options are demonstrated later in this chapter.

The Track function in PageMaker alters the amount of space set between letters and between words. The amount of space varies depending on the current type size. See Chapter 9 for complete details on using the Tracking option.

The Type style options are identical to those displayed upon choosing the Type style command from the Type menu. They are merely presented in a different format for easier access.

This change in the default setting for Measurements in, from inches to picas, has now been saved to PageMaker's preferences file. Any new documents created in PageMaker will default to picas instead of inches, as long as Picas remains the default setting. Existing documents, however, will retain the same system of measurement that was chosen the last time each document was saved.

If you want to alter any other default settings, now is the time to do so. For this project, you will alter type specification defaults, line width and fill settings, and some settings in the Page setup dialog box.

STEPS: Altering the Type Specification Defaults

Step 1. Choose the Type specs... command from the Type menu or press ⌘-T. This opens the Type Specifications dialog box, in which you can change settings for font, style, size, and leading options in one location, rather than having to choose from several menu commands.

Step 2. For this project, the options in the Type Specifications dialog box, shown in Figure 17-2, should be set as follows:

- Font: Palatino

- Position: Normal

- Size: 36

- Case: Normal

- Leading: 37.5

- Track: No track

- Set width: Normal

- Color: Black

- Type style: select Bold and Italic options

- Line End: Break

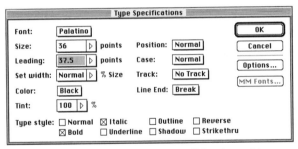

Figure 17-2: The Type Specifications dialog box with your new default settings.

Step 3.   Press the Return Key.

For the final default type specification, you will change the alignment of your text from flush left to centered.

STEPS: Changing the Alignment Default

Step 1.   Choose the Align center option from the Alignment pop-up menu under the Type menu or press Shift-⌘-C.

Step 2.   Click OK.

Now that you have altered the default settings for the font, style, size, leading, and alignment of your text, you are ready to set other defaults. The following settings can be changed without accessing dialog boxes.

STEPS: Creating a Border for the Coupon

Step 1.   Choose the Line command from the Element menu to display the list of line weights, and choose the second coupon border (the fifth option from the bottom).

Step 2.   Choose Paper from the Fill pop-up menu. (Any shape created with PageMaker's line or shape tools will have a coupon border outline and an opaque interior.)

Step 3.   Choose the Snap to rulers command from the Guides and Rulers submenu in the Layout menu or press ⌘-[. This activates PageMaker's Snap to Rulers feature, which constrains the creation and manipulation of elements to a grid determined by the current system of measurement. For example, since you'll be working in picas at the Actual view size, each tick mark on the horizontal and vertical ruler will indicate $1/4$ pica, or 3 points. When Snap to Rulers is turned on, you will be able to create or move elements only in increments of 3 points. This 3-point grid will help you to maintain consistency in the placement of text and graphics throughout your document.

The last group of default settings you will change affects the number of master and publication pages, as well as the margins you will use to create your flyer. Flyers generally require only one master page and two publication pages. For this flyer, your margins should be slightly smaller than PageMaker's present settings.

STEPS: **Changing the Master Pages Defaults**

Step 1. Choose the Document Setup command from the File menu.

Step 2. Set the options in the Document Setup dialog box, shown in Figure 17-3, as follows:

- Page size: Letter
- Double-sided: not selected
- Orientation: Tall
- Facing pages: dimmed
- Start page #: 1
- Margin in picas: Left: 3, Top: 3, Right: 3, and Bottom: 3
- Number of pages: 2

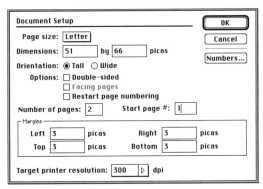

Figure 17-3: The Document Setup dialog box containing your new default settings

Step 3. Press Return.

Now that you have changed default settings for commands from every menu except the Pages and Windows menus, it is time to see how these altered defaults affect the creation of a new document.

STEPS: Checking the Altered Defaults

Step 1.   Choose the New command from the File menu or press ⌘-N. Notice that the resulting Document Setup dialog box contains all your new default settings. Press Return to confirm these settings and create a new file. A new publication window is displayed, showing the first page of your publication. Vertical and horizontal rulers should also be displayed, both measuring picas. (If necessary, press ⌘-R to display the rulers.) Notice that there is now only one master page icon, labeled R for right. Any element or guide that you put on this master page will be displayed on both pages of your flyer.

Step 2.   Click the master page icon in the bottom-left corner of your screen display. You will not create any elements on the master page because no text or graphic items will appear on both sides of the flyer. However, both sides will share the same basic layout, so you will use the master page to establish a consistent system of ruler guides.

Creating the Fold Lines _____

Creating a two-fold flyer is fairly tricky because you have to consider how each of three panels (on each side of the paper) will appear when viewed alone as well as when the flyer is fully opened. Therefore, each panel must be indicated by fold lines on your electronic pages. Two horizontal ruler guides will serve as these fold lines.

You must first determine the size of each panel. At first, this may seem easy. The page will be folded two times, with both folds in the same direction, to create three panels. Therefore, each panel should be one-third page in size. However, you will fold the two outer panels over the middle panel, so you must accommodate the thickness of the paper folding over on itself. The bottom panel must be the smallest. It will fold over the middle panel, which should be slightly longer to accommodate the thickness of the paper at the fold and to ensure that the edge of the bottom panel will not touch the second fold line. The third panel must be even longer because it will be folding over the thickness of two layers of paper. For a professional appearance, you want the edge of the outer panel to be flush with the edge created by the first fold.

To determine the exact size of each panel, you must first establish your overall page size 8 ½ inches wide by 11 inches tall, or 51 picas by 66 picas. You will fold the flyer lengthwise, so if each panel were exactly one-third page tall, it would measure $66 \div 3 = 22$ picas. The bottom panel should be the smallest, so you subtract one pica from it: $22 - 1 = 21$ picas. You add this 1 pica to the larger top panel: $22 + 1 = 23$ picas.

STEPS: Setting Up Ruler Guides

Step 1. The zero intersection point of your ruler is currently at the top-left corner of the master page. Drag down two ruler guides from the horizontal ruler at the top of your display to indicate the fold lines in your flyer.

Step 2. Drag the first horizontal ruler guide to the 23-pica mark of the vertical ruler (just at the center of the 24-pica label).

Step 3. Drag a second horizontal ruler guide down to the 23 + 22 = 45-pica mark of the vertical ruler (halfway between the 42- and 48-pica labels). This leaves a bottom panel that is appropriately 66 − 45 = 21 picas.

Throughout this project, you will create and use additional horizontal ruler guides. To avoid as much confusion as possible, we will refer to the two current horizontal ruler guides as the upper and lower *fold lines*.

Now you need a few more horizontal ruler guidelines to indicate the margins of each panel. Since the flyer as a whole has a 3-pica margin around all sides, each panel should have 3-pica margins of its own. You may notice that each panel already has left and right margins of 3 picas. However, the top panel is missing a bottom margin; the bottom panel is missing a top margin; and the middle panel is missing both a top and bottom margin.

STEPS: Setting Margins

Step 1. To establish the bottom margin of the top panel, drag a guide from the horizontal ruler to a position 3 picas above the upper fold line: 23 − 3 = the 20-pica mark on the vertical ruler.

Step 2. Drag another horizontal ruler guide to represent the top margin of the middle panel. This must be located at: 23 + 3 = the 26-pica mark on the vertical ruler.

Step 3. Represent the bottom margin of the middle panel by dragging a horizontal ruler guide to 3 picas above the lower fold line, at 45 − 3 = the 42-pica mark on the vertical ruler.

Step 4. Drag a guide to 45 + 3 = the 48-pica mark as the top margin of the bottom panel of the flyer.

From now on, we will refer to the four newest horizontal ruler guides as the first, second, third, and fourth *fold margins*, numbered from top to bottom of the page.

Having created all fold lines and fold margins required to guide you in the creation of your flyer, you are finished with the master page. Click the page 1 icon at the bottom of your display to return to publication page 1, which should appear as shown in Figure 17-4.

Figure 17-4:
Page 1 containing
the fold lines and
margin lines from
the master page

In the first sample project, we waited until you had finished creating the entire document before instructing you to save the file. In this way, we were able to isolate the description of the Save command. However, you will not normally want to wait until a document is completed before saving it to disk. Generally, it is advisable to save a document after your first major step in its creation. Considering your establishment of ruler guides on the master page as a major first step, you are now ready to save.

STEPS: **Saving the Document**

Step 1. Choose the Save command from the File menu or press ⌘-S.

Step 2. When the Save publication as dialog box appears, enter the name **Two-sided flyer,** or some other appropriate and sufficiently descriptive filename, into the option box under the list of filenames in the current folder.

Step 3. Using the Desktop and Eject buttons in combination with the folder bar to determine the destination to which your file will be saved, press the Return key or click OK. PageMaker will take a few moments to save your file to disk, after which the filename will appear at the top of your screen display in place of the word *Untitled* in the current title bar.

Now that your flyer is saved to disk, you should periodically update the file by choosing the Save command or pressing ⌘-S after each major step in creating your document. The Save command will no longer produce the Save publication as dialog box but will simply overwrite the existing file. If you want to produce the Save publication as dialog box, perhaps to save the file to a different folder or disk, choose the Save as command from the File menu.

Placing the Text and Graphics ___

You are now ready to create the text and graphic elements of your flyer. You begin by placing the body copy.

As mentioned at the beginning of this project, a flyer does not generally contain a large amount of text, because it is intended to be read quickly. Therefore, you will use a short text file, called Main Flyer Text, from the Two-sided flyer files folder on the CD-ROM included with this book. You can drag this folder from the CD onto your hard drive or use the files directly off the CD.

STEPS:	**Placing the Body Copy**
Step 1.	Choose the Place... command or press ⌘-D.
Step 2.	When the Place document dialog box appears, double-click the Main Flyer Text file from the Two-sided flyer files folder.
Step 3.	When the publication window reappears, click with your manual text flow cursor in the upper-left margin corner.

Changing Column Width

Since you did not set a new application default for the column width, and you did not adjust the column width on the master page, your story pours the entire width determined by the margins specified in the Page setup dialog box. However, this is most likely an unsuitable column width for flyer text, because body copy this wide (45 picas) is generally difficult to read. Reducing the width of an existing text block is a very simple task.

Surrounding your text block (assuming that it is selected) are four square handles, each located at an end of one of the two windowshades. These handles are useful for adjusting the column width of the text block.

You will also be making use of the small dotted tracking lines that appear on the vertical and horizontal rulers, monitoring the location of the cursor. As you move your cursor, these tracking lines also move to show the current cursor position. Tracking lines are very useful in positioning elements.

STEPS:	**Adjusting the Column Width of Existing Text**
Step 1.	If your text block is not selected, click it with the Pointer tool to display its windowshades and four square handles.
Step 2.	Click and hold the lower-left handle, and notice how a rectangle appears surrounding the text, demonstrating its horizontal and vertical dimensions. The tracking line on the horizontal ruler is at the 3-pica mark.

Step 3. Drag the lower-left handle to the right until the tracking line aligns with the 9-pica mark, then release.

Step 4. Drag the lower-right handle of the text block toward the left to the 42-point marker on the horizontal ruler. Once completed, you will have decreased the column width of your text block by 6 picas (or one inch) on each side, as demonstrated in Figure 17-5. Your new text block width is 33 picas, a more readable column width and thus more suitable to this project.

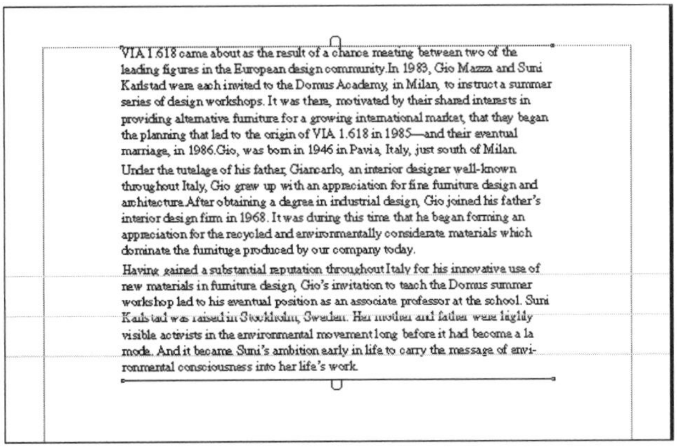

Figure 17-5: Your text block should now look like this.

Changing Type Specifications

The next step is to change or adjust the type specifications of your text. Notice that your current text is not in 36/37.5 Palatino Bold-Italic, the setting you specified when you altered the default type specifications. This is because this text was imported into — rather than created directly in — PageMaker. Regardless of the default type specs, a text file is generally imported from a word processor with its specifications intact. (An exception is a text file with style sheets, as we demonstrate in the sample project in Chapter 18.)

The easiest way to make changes to blocks of text is with the Control palette. To get you in the habit of using it, for the remainder of this chapter we will have you make changes in the text attributes with the Control palette wherever possible.

STEPS: Adjusting the Type Specifications of Text

Step 1.   Choose Control Palette from the Windows menu. (If necessary, position it out of the way at the bottom of the page.)

Step 2.   Select the Text tool. Click anywhere inside the imported text block and press ⌘-A (Select all).

Step 3.   On the Control palette, change the typeface, size, and leading to Palatino 12/Auto, as shown in Figure 17-6. (If you don't know how to use the Control palette, you should read Chapter 9.)

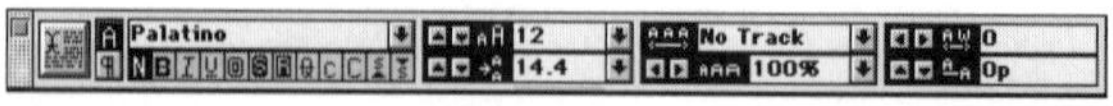

Figure 17-6: Your Control palette should look like this (selecting Auto for leading sets the leading option to 14.4).

Step 4.   This block of text will probably look better if you fully justify it so that the left and right edges of each line of text are flush with the edges of the text block itself. While the type is still selected, change the alignment from the Control palette (by clicking the Paragraph view button) or press Shift-⌘-J.

Step 5.   As usual, the final step in creating your text block is to adjust its position vertically by dragging at its upper and lower windowshades. Select the Pointer tool and drag the upper windowshade tab down to the 15-pica mark on the vertical ruler (as indicated by the tracking line). Then drag the lower windowshade to the bottom fold margin of the middle panel (the horizontal ruler guide 42 picas from the top of the page).

Step 6.   Press ⌘-S to update your file on disk.

The area from the top margin to the top of your body copy (15 picas) is allocated for a headline and a simple graphic. You will create the headline first.

STEPS: Creating a Headline with Default Type Specifications

Step 1.   Select the Text tool and ⌘-Option-Click at the top of the page to magnify your page to the Actual view size.

Step 2.   Click with the Text tool just below the top margin to establish a text entry cursor, and type: **What's a chance meeting got to(¶)do with great furniture?**

Step 3.   Select the Pointer tool and click on the text block.

Step 4.   Adjust the vertical placement of the headline by dragging its upper windowshade flush with the top margin of the page.

Step 5.   Once your headline appears as shown in Figure 17-7, press ⌘-S to save the file.

Figure 17-7:
Your headline
should look
like this
example.

What's a chance meeting got to do with great furniture?

VIA 1.618 came about as the result of a chance meeting between two of the leading figures in the European design community. In 1983, Gio Mazza and Suni Karlstad were each invited to the Domus Academy, in Milan, to instruct a summer series of design workshops. It was there, motivated by their shared interests in providing alternative furniture for a growing international market, that they began the planning that led to the origin of VIA

Once you have completed typing your headline text, notice how it looks. It is centered, 36/37.5 Palatino Bold-Italic, just as you specified in your default type specs! Because this is exactly what you want, no alterations are necessary. This is a good example of how you can save time and energy by establishing defaults before creating a new file.

Unfamiliar Symbols?

There are two symbols in Step 2 of the previous procedure that you may not recognize or know how to access. One is the paragraph sign (¶). In these sample projects, I use the paragraph sign to indicate a carriage return, marking the location at which you should press the Return key to set your cursor on the next line before typing the following words. You may not even recognize that the second symbol is not an ordinary character. It is the apostrophe ('), or right single quotation mark. You may have instead pressed the straight single quotation mark ('). In general, both the

(continued)

(continued)

straight single quote (') and the straight double quote (") should be avoided; the left and right single (' and ') and double ("and") quotes — which are more distinctive and attractive — are the correct symbols. Each quote is accessed by pressing the key combinations in Table 17-1.

Table 17-1
Types of Quote Symbols

Quote Symbol	Key Combination
Left double quote	Option-[
Right double quote	Shift-Option-[
Left single quote	Option-]
Right single quote (apostrophe)	Shift-Option-]

Placing a Graphic

The following steps outline the addition of a simple graphic between the headline text and the body copy on the first page of your flyer. PageMaker supports most popular graphic file formats — including MacPaint, PICT, EPS (Encapsulated PostScript), and TIFF (tagged image file format).

The graphic you'll use is in the two-sided flyer files folder on the CD-ROM.

STEPS: Adding a Simple Graphic

Step 1.   Choose the Place… command from the File menu or press ⌘-D. This opens the same Place document dialog box, shown in Figure 17-8, that you have used to import files.

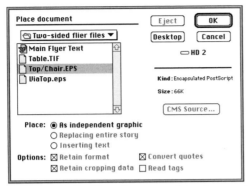

Figure 17-8: The Place document dialog box ready to import a graphic

Step 2. Select the Top/Chair.EPS file from the file listing. You will notice that as soon as you click an available graphic filename, some of the Place options change. Since no graphic is currently selected in your PageMaker file, the only option that is not dimmed is the As independent graphic option. This indicates that your graphic will be placed into your flyer normally rather than as a replacement for an existing graphic. If you had selected a graphic before choosing the Place command, a second option, reading Replacing entire story, would also become available for selection. This option would allow you to replace all of the copy with a placed graphic, including resizing and crop marks (both of which will be described shortly).

Step 3. After selecting a graphic filename to be placed, press Return.

Step 4. Your cursor will change to a small PS icon because you are using an EPS format graphic. When you place other file formats, you get other icon types: MacPaint files display a paintbrush, PICT files display a pencil, and the TIFF files display a small gray square. Position the PS cursor in the upper-left portion of your window and click to place the graphic.

Your graphic will now appear on page 1, surrounded by handles to demonstrate that it is selected. This graphic includes two elements, a top icon and a chair icon, as shown in Figure 17-9. In this case, you want to use only the top, so you'll have to crop out the chair. This is very common when importing clip-art files, for example. One page of clip-art often contains several drawings, which saves space and decreases the number of files on disk.

PageMaker provides a built-in cropping feature for removing extraneous images from an imported graphic file. To crop a graphic is to cut away some portion of the graphic so that it is no longer visible in your document. The cropped portion still exists, and you may re-expose it later if you want to, but it is hidden from view.

Figure 17-9:
An imported graphic with two
graphic elements

STEPS: Cropping a Graphic

Step 1. Select the crop tool (in the lower-right corner of the toolbox) and click your graphic to select it. Eight handles are displayed — one in each corner and one on each side.

Step 2. Click the right-most handle and drag left until only the top icon graphic is visible. (Be sure to click a handle! If you click inside the graphic with the crop tool, you will get a grabber hand icon, as discussed in the next few paragraphs.)

The crop tool works by cutting off horizontal or vertical strips of the image only, as shown in Figure 17-10. Therefore, you cannot effectively use the cropping tool to modify images that jut slightly into each other's perpendicular boundaries. Such fine-tuning operations must be performed in a graphics application prior to importation of the graphic.

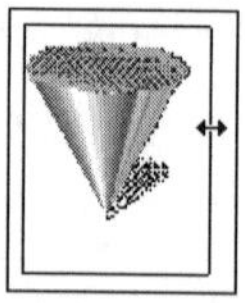

Figure 17-10: Cropping off a portion of a placed graphic

Step 3. After cropping out any extraneous portions of your graphic, select the Pointer tool and drag the graphic to center it between the headline and body copy.

Step 4. Once you have established the size of your graphic by cropping and have positioned it correctly, you may find that you have overcropped or under-cropped and need to make adjustments. Select the crop tool again and click the graphic to select it. This time, instead of clicking a handle, click inside the graphic and hold. Your cursor will change to a grabber hand icon, as shown in Figure 17-11. Now drag with the grabber hand. This moves your graphic independently of the cropping boundaries. This is especially useful if you have cropped the graphic to an exact size but aren't quite sure what details of the graphic you would like to see. Dragging with the grabber hand doesn't affect the size of the graphic, as does dragging at the handles; it affects only the portion of the graphic that is visible.

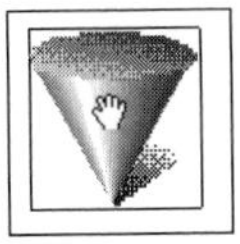

Figure 17-11: Using the Cropping tool to position a graphic within the cropping boundaries

Step 5. After you have cropped your graphic and until you are satisfied with its appearance, select the Pointer tool and click the graphic to select it. Then press ⌘-C to execute the Copy command. You will be using this copy of your image in a logo at the bottom of the page.

Step 6. Press ⌘-S to update your file on disk.

Creating a Clip-Out Coupon _____

In the next few steps, you will create a clip-out coupon on the bottom panel of the flyer. Inside this coupon, you will input some text directly into PageMaker, including a logo. This logo will also consist of a graphic element in the form of a reduced version of the image you will have just copied.

STEPS: Drawing the Border for the Coupon

Step 1. Scroll down to the bottom panel of page 1. Select the Rectangle tool and drag from the top left margin corner of the bottom panel to the bottom right margin corner. The resulting box should look like the one shown in Figure 17-12. Notice that the outline of this box is a medium-weight coupon border, the one you selected when setting defaults. The interior is white, also matching your new fill default, Paper.

Figure 17-12: A coupon border created with the Rectangle tool

Right now, your page has only one column, and the left and right column guides are flush with the left and right sides of your coupon border, respectively. This means that any text you create inside the coupon will be as wide as the coupon itself, which would make the edges of the text unreadable. Text inside a coupon border must have surrounding margins, just as text on a page must have margins. In order to establish these margins, you will move your column guides.

Step 2.   Select the Pointer tool and drag the left column guide to the right until you reach the 6-pica mark on the horizontal ruler. (If you cannot drag the column guide but instead find yourself dragging the coupon border, check that the Guides option is set to Front in the Preferences dialog box. Also make sure that the Lock guides command in the Options menu is deselected; that is, it does not have a check in front of it.)

Step 3.   Drag the right column guide to the left until you reach the 45-pica mark on the horizontal ruler.

Step 4.   Select the Text tool and click inside the coupon, anywhere between the column guides. Then type **All VIA tables, 20% off (¶) This month only**. (Remember that the symbol (¶) means that you should press the carriage return key.) Your text appears in the default type specs of centered 36/37.5 Palatino Bold-Italic. These type specs fit the requirements of the coupon to an extent, but some of the text will need to be changed. For example, the second line of text should be smaller to downplay its significance.

Step 5.   Triple-click the second line of text with the Text tool. This selects the entire paragraph, from carriage return to carriage return.

Step 6.   Use the Control palette to change the type size to 18 point, change the leading to Auto, and change the type style to Normal.

Step 7. With the second line of text still selected, press ⌘-M to access the Paragraph Specifications dialog box. Press the Tab key repeatedly until the After option is selected and change the value to 3 picas. Then press Return.

Step 8. Select the Text tool and drag at the text block to position it vertically, as shown in Figure 17-13. Then press ⌘-S to update your file on disk.

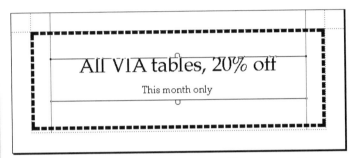

Figure 17-13: The text for your coupon positioned accurately

Adding a Graphic to the Coupon

In the next steps, you will add a graphic to the coupon. But first, you must make room for it. The graphic belongs between the words *VIA* and *tables* in the first line of text. To make room, you must insert spaces between these two words. Not ordinary spaces, but *fixed spaces*. When you press the spacebar, you create a *variable space* — a space that may be changed by PageMaker to accommodate the alignment of the text block. This occurs most commonly when you justify text, because PageMaker must stretch or shrink the amount of space between each word in a line of type to fill the column width. Fixed spaces are always the same width, regardless of whether the text block is justified, centered, or aligned left or right. Table 17-2 lists three kinds of fixed spaces, followed by the key commands used to access them.

Table 17-2 Types of Fixed Spaces		
Space	*Width*	*Key Combination*
Em space	a space as wide as the point size of the text	Shift-⌘-M
En space	a space half as wide as the point size	Shift-⌘-N
Thin space	one-quarter the width of the point size	Shift-⌘-T

A 17-point em space is 12 points wide, a 17-point en space is 6 points wide, and a 17-point thin space is 3 points wide.

STEPS: **Inserting a Graphic**

Step 1.   Click with the Text tool between the words *VIA* and *tables*.

Step 2.   Press Shift-⌘-M once and Shift-⌘-N once to create one em space and one en space. This amount of space will allow sufficient room for the logo graphic.

Step 3.   Choose the Place command, select the file Table.TIF, click the As independent graphic option, and click OK.

Step 4.   Place the graphic and use the Pointer tool to drag it into position. Figure 17-14 shows the coupon with the graphic in place.

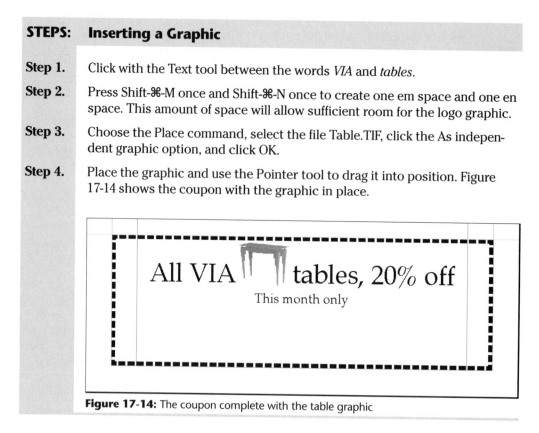

Figure 17-14: The coupon complete with the table graphic

The next two graphic elements you will add are two small pairs of scissors, which will indicate that the coupon is to be clipped from the flyer and brought into a local VIA retailer for friendly and courteous redemption. These scissors are accessed as characters of the typeface Zapf Dingbats, a standard PostScript font that contains graphic elements and symbols and is built into nearly all PostScript printers.

STEPS: **Adding Graphic Elements**

Step 1.   Select the Text tool. Without clicking, use the Control palette to change the type to 24/Auto Zapf Dingbats and select the Normal style option. Since no text is selected, you cannot immediately see the effect of your change.

This is also an indication that you have altered the default settings for this file from 36/37.5 Palatino Bold-Italic to 24/Auto Zapf Dingbats. This change does not affect any other files. Existing files will still use the same defaults they used when they had been previously saved, and new files will retain the standard default of 36/37.5 Palatino Bold-Italic.

Step 2.   With the Text tool, draw a box just above the coupon border from the left margin to the left column guide, a distance of 3 picas. (It does not matter how tall you draw the box.)

Step 3.   Press Shift-4. Although this key combination produces a dollar sign in most typefaces, in Zapf Dingbats it produces a pair of scissors.

Step 4.   Press Shift-⌘-L, the keyboard equivalent for flush-left text alignment.

Step 5.   Select the Pointer tool and position the text block vertically so that its lower windowshade rides just below the top coupon border.

Step 6.   Press ⌘-C to copy the symbol.

Step 7.   For the sake of symmetry, you might want to create a second pair of scissors, horizontally aligned with the first but positioned on the right side of the page. Press ⌘-Option-V to paste a copy of the scissors to your page exactly over the existing ones. Select the Pointer tool from the toolbox, select the top pair of scissors, hold down the Shift key, and drag the text block toward the right so that it is positioned between the right column guide and right margin, and its handles snap to the guides, as shown in Figure 17-15.

Figure 17-15: Your coupon should look like this, with both pairs of scissors placed in the margins of the coupon.

Step 8.   Press ⌘-S to update your file on disk. Then press ⌘-W to demagnify your display to the Fit in window view size. You have successfully completed the inner side of this two-sided flyer, as shown in Figure 17-16.

Figure 17-16: The finished first side of your flyer

Creating the Flyer's Exterior _____

You are now ready to create the second side of your two-sided flyer. The three panels on this side will include a mailer and two blocks of text imported from a graphics program. In building this next page, we will introduce you to rectangles with rounded corners; layering elements in front and in back of other elements; and reversing, rotating, and condensing text.

STEPS: Constructing the Flyer's Outer Sides

Step 1. Click the page 2 icon at the bottom of your display to go to page 2.

Step 2. ⌘-Option-click the middle of the page to magnify your view to Actual size. If necessary, scroll right so that the right margin of the page is visible.

Step 3. Select the Text tool and click and hold down your mouse button at the location where the horizontal ruler tracking line aligns with the 43-pica mark and the vertical ruler tracking line meets the 26-pica mark (flush with the top margin of the middle panel).

Step 4. Without releasing the mouse button, drag down and to the right about 5 picas (to the 48-pica mark) until the Text tool snaps to the right margin.

Step 5. Before typing, change the type specs to 9/10 Helvetica using the Control palette. This changes the type specs for this text block only, without altering your default settings.

Step 6. Type **Post office will not deliver without sufficient postage.**

Step 7. Press ⌘-A to select the entire block of text and press Shift-⌘-K to change the type to uppercase letters. The type should already be centered. (If you have changed the Alignment option, press Shift-⌘-C.)

Step 8. To position the vertical text block correctly, click it with the Pointer tool and Shift-drag it downward one-half pica, to the location shown in Figure 17-17. (Use the vertical ruler to measure.)

Figure 17-17: The new text block, selected to display the column width and vertical positioning

Step 9. Select the rectangle tool, which is the second tool on the bottom row of your toolbox. You will use this tool to create a small box around your text block, indicating the dimensions of a typical postage stamp.

Step 10. Position the rectangle tool cursor at the intersection of the top margin of the middle panel and the right margin of the page.

Step 11. Shift-drag down and to the left 5 picas to the 43-pica mark on the horizontal ruler and the 31-pica mark on the vertical ruler.

Step 12. Notice that your small square with rounded corners has a fat coupon border and a white interior (as specified by your defaults), thereby covering up your text. Perhaps this postage marker will attract more attention if it appears as a black box with the text in white. Therefore, while the shape is still selected, choose the Solid option from the Fill pop-up listing in the Element menu and select None from the Line pop-up listing.

Step 13. The rectangle shape could have a little more flair, which you can add by rounding its corners by choosing the Rounded corners command in the Element menu to bring up the Rounded Corners dialog box. This dialog box allows you to select from six corner options, ranging from perpendicular to very rounded. The fourth option is currently selected. Select the second option of the top row, as shown in Figure 17-18, and press Return. The rounded corners of the black shape are now greatly reduced. In fact, they appear to be almost perpendicular.

Figure 17-18: The Rounded Corners dialog box, with the second corner option selected

The text you typed into your document in Step 6 above is now hidden by a black square. Like most desktop publishing applications, PageMaker relies on a layering convention. Any on-screen element is considered to be in front of some elements and in back of others. Thus, when you create a document, you are really creating an electronic collage of lines, shapes, text blocks, and imported graphics. Every time you create a new element, you place it at the front of this electronic collage. Newest elements are always created in front of their predecessors, so the black square is currently in front of the text.

You can change the layering relationship among elements with the the Bring to Front/Bring Forward and Send to Back/Send Backward commands in the Element menu. These commands allow you to bring a selected element in front of one or all other elements on the page or send an element behind one or all other elements on the page. The next step demonstrates how you use these commands.

STEPS: Reversing the Color of Text

Step 1. Your black square should still be selected. Choose the Send Backward command from the Edit menu or press ⌘-9 to send the square to the back of the page, behind the text block.

Step 2. Your text is now in front of the black shape, but it remains invisible because the type is black, the same color as the shape behind it. To be sure that the text block is in front, select the Text tool and click in the middle of the black square. A text entry cursor will blink at your exact click point, indicating that there is indeed text there.

Step 3. To make this text visible, press ⌘-A to select the entire text block.

Step 4. Choose the Reverse option from the Control palette. This makes the text white.

Step 5. Click the Pointer tool to deselect the text, and you will see that it is now reversed against a black background, as shown in Figure 17-19. Press ⌘-S to update your file on disk.

Figure 17-19: The reversed text against a black background

No mailer would be complete without a return address. The next series of steps affixes the return address to the proper place on your flyer.

STEPS: **Affixing the Return Address**

Step 1. If necessary, scroll left until the left margin is clearly visible.

Step 2. Before typing any text, change the default type specs to 12/Auto Palatino Bold-Italic, using the Control palette.

Step 3. Select the Text tool and position your cursor at the intersection of the top margin of the middle panel and the left page margin.

Step 4. Click at this point and drag right 15 picas to the 18-pica mark on the horizontal ruler. Also drag down enough to accommodate a few lines of text.

Step 5. Press Shift-⌘-L to make the type in this text block align on the left.

Step 6. Type **VIA International (¶) 1205 University Ave.(¶) Northwestern, AU 34210**.

Step 7. VIA's company name looks nice in Palatino Bold-Italic type, but it is indistinguishable from the address. So triple-click the second line of the text block to select the entire first address line.

Step 8. Shift-click the third line, selecting it entirely as well.

Step 9. To make this text plain, press ⌘-Option-spacebar. (Or you could choose the Normal option from the Type style pop-up under the Type menu or click N in the Control palette.) The text is now set in Palatino Roman (plain style, without bold or italic), as shown in Figure 17-20. Press ⌘-S to update your file on disk.

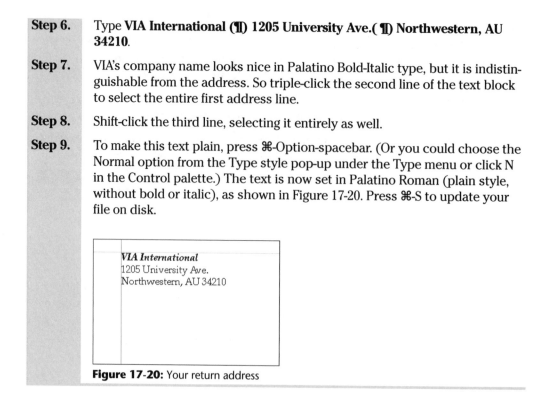

VIA International
1205 University Ave.
Northwestern, AU 34210

Figure 17-20: Your return address

Condensing and Rotating Text

The only portions of the flyer that remain incomplete are the top and bottom panels, which present a special challenge. Because of the way in which the folds of the flyer overlap each other, the text on both the top panel and the bottom panel must be upside down. This ensures that the customer, when unfolding the flyer, can continue to read each newly presented panel without having to turn the flyer upside down at any point. (To understand this concept visually, try folding your flyer after you have printed it.)

STEPS: Condensing the Text

Step 1. Scroll to the top panel of the current page.

Step 2. Select the Text tool and then, using the Control Palette, change the default type specs to 48/50 Palatino Bold-Italic, a larger type size than you have employed so far.

Step 3. Click somewhere near the top of the page. Type **Special Pricing (¶) On The Finest Italian Furniture**.

Step 4. You want to grab your reader's attention the moment he or she picks up your flyer. One way to do this is to alter the type slightly. In this case, you will condense the type, making it thinner than normal. While your text entry cursor remains in the text block, press ⌘-A to highlight both lines of type.

Step 5. Choose the Set Width command from the Type menu to access a pop-up list of possible compression or expansion percentages. Choose the 70 percent option. (You can also use the Set Width option on the Control palette.) Your text now appears approximately the same width as 36-point text, as shown in Figure 17-21.

Figure 17-21: Type compressed to 70 percent

Now to rotate your text. To do this, you'll use the Control palette.

STEPS: Rotating the Text

Step 1. Get the Pointer tool and select the text block.

Step 2. In the Control palette, click the middle of the *proxy*, which is the box that is the second element from the left edge. It looks like a small square with handles in each corner, on each edge, and in its center. Clicking in the middle should put a selection dot on the center handle. (If you accidentally click twice, the dot turns into an arrow. If this happens, click again to turn it back into a dot.) Selecting the dot in the middle of the proxy tells PageMaker that you want to rotate the selected text block from its center so that it stays in the same place on the page. If one of the corners or edges of the proxy was selected, the text block would move out of position when you rotate it.

Step 3. Since you want to flip the text block over, you can use the two reflecting options, which are the small buttons on the very right edge of the Control palette. Both show small "F" characters on them depicting the reflection they control. The top one is the Horizontal reflecting button, and the bottom one is the Vertical reflecting button. Click each of these buttons once. Figure 17-22 shows the rotated block.

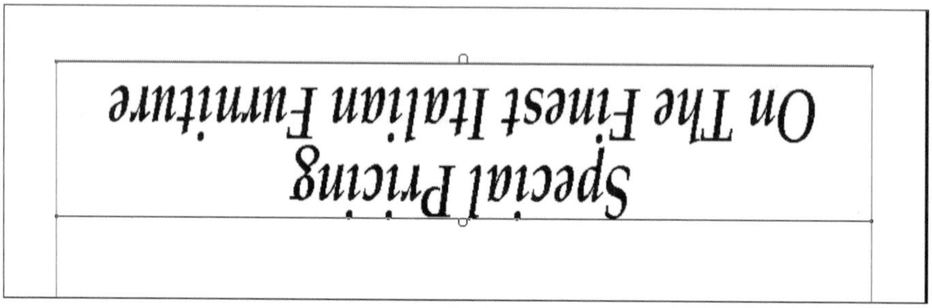

Figure 17-22: Your rotated text should look like this.

Step 4. To add text to the bottom panel, scroll down to the bottom of the page. Select the Text tool from the toolbox, click inside the bottom panel, and type **At prices like this, it just won't last. . .**

Step 5. Press ⌘-A to highlight all text and again choose the 70 percent option from the Set Width pop-up menu under the Type menu.

Step 6. Select the text block with the Text tool and reduce the text size to 36 points using the Control palette.

Step 7. Again you'll use the reflecting buttons on the Control palette to flip your text block over. Select the Pointer tool, select the text block, and then select the Control palette. Make sure that the center handle in the proxy is selected.

Step 8. Click the Horizontal reflection and then the Vertical reflection buttons.

Step 9. Press ⌘-W to demagnify your page to the Fit in window view size. Finally, press ⌘-S to update your file on disk. Figure 17-23 shows the completed second side.

Figure 17-23:
The finished flyer

Your flyer is now complete. The only step remaining is to print the finished document.

STEPS: Printing the Two-Sided Flyer

Step 1. Make sure that your printer is on and chosen, using the Macintosh Chooser desk accessory.

Step 2. Press⌘-P to access the Print Document dialog box. Indicate one copy, and print from page 1 to 2 as described at the end of the first sample project (see Chapter 16).

Step 3. When the two pages of your flyer are finished printing, put them back-to-back to simulate the document's look after it is photocopied or offset printed. Then try folding it. This will give you a sense of how two-fold flyers work.

Step 4. Examine your pages and make sure that they meet your expectations. If you see any problems, make the necessary changes to your file.

By successfully completing this sample project, you have gained an understanding of some intermediate functions and operations offered by PageMaker. This know-how will serve you well in understanding the remaining material in this book and will give you a greater appreciation of the material in the earlier chapters in their greater detail. You are now well on your way to a real proficiency with PageMaker.

Summary

- There are two ways to change default settings. The first method is to choose commands and select options at the PageMaker desktop while no publications are open. This resets the application defaults for every new file that you create from that point on, until you again reset the defaults. The second method is to choose commands and select options in an open file while no element is selected. These become publication defaults, which affect only the current file and do not affect files you create in the future.

- PageMaker relies on a layering convention. Any on-screen element is considered to be in front of some elements and in back of others. Thus, when you create a document, you are really creating an electronic collage of lines, shapes, text blocks, and imported graphics. Every time you create a new element, you place it at the front of this electronic collage. Newest elements are always created in front of their predecessors.

- You can change the layering relationship among elements with the the Bring to Front/Bring Forward and Send to Back/Send Backward commands in the Element menu. These commands allow you to bring a selected element in front of one or all other elements on the page or send an element behind one or all other elements on the page.

- Sometimes you may want to insert *fixed* spaces between words. When you press the spacebar, you create a *variable space* — a space that may be changed by PageMaker to accommodate the alignment of the text block. This occurs most commonly when you justify text, because PageMaker must stretch or shrink the amount of space between each word in a line of type to fill the column width. Fixed spaces are always the same width, regardless of whether the text block is justified, centered, or aligned left or right. The three most common fixed spaces are the em space, en space, and thin space.

- PageMaker provides a built-in cropping feature for removing extraneous images from an imported graphic file. To crop a graphic is to cut away some portion of the graphic so that it is no longer visible in your document. The cropped portion still exists, and you may re-expose it later if you want to, but it is hidden from view.

Laying Out a Four-Page Catalog

In This Chapter

- •◆ Toggling commands

- •◆ Creating banner text

- •◆ Creating a folio

- •◆ Wrapping text around objects

- •◆ Importing a graphic

- •◆ Overriding a style sheet

- •◆ Printing

I n this chapter, you use PageMaker to create a full-color, four-page catalog that includes a graphic, a photograph, a price list, and two spaces for advertisements. The completed catalog, shown in Figure 18-1, is the last of three sample projects presented in this book. This chapter focuses on the most-advanced commands and operations offered by PageMaker and, as always, demonstrates how these features can be used to satisfy a wide variety of your publication needs.

 The files you'll need for this project are found in the Four-page catalog files folder on the CD-ROM that accompanies this book. These files include the text and graphic images.

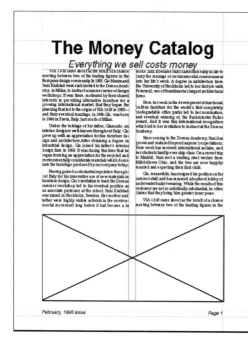

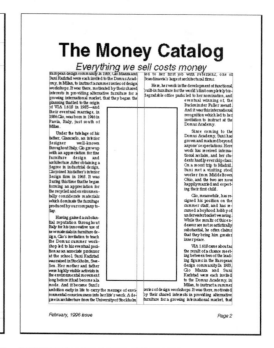

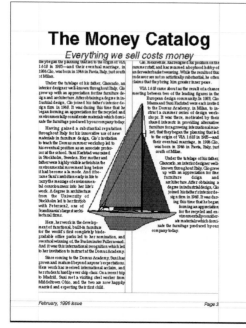

Figure 18-1: The four-page catalog you create in this chapter

STEPS:	**Launching PageMaker**
Step 1.	Launch PageMaker.
Step 2.	Click the mouse button to dispense with the copyright screen.

Changing Default Settings

Before creating a new file, you will first alter a few application default settings in PageMaker, just as you did in the second sample project. The defaults you will change include the system of measurement, the line weight and fill value, the column guides, and a variety of commands under the Utilities, Layout, and Windows menus.

The Toggling Commands

Throughout this book, I have described a number of commands that toggle various PageMaker attributes on and off. The following list contains the name of the toggling commands that you will use in this project and the effects of each:

- **Show Rulers:** displays horizontal and vertical rulers.

- **Snap to Rulers:** creates an invisible grid corresponding to each ruler tick mark.

- **Show Guides:** displays margins and column guides and allows you to create ruler guides.

- **Snap to Guides:** snaps cursor to margins, column guides, and ruler guides.

- **Autoflow:** automatically pours a placed text file into specified columns, adding pages to a document if necessary.

You will also use the following Windows menu commands:

- **Toolbox:** displays the toolbox.

- **Show Scroll Bars:** displays the scroll bars.

- **Control Palette:** displays the Control palette.

- **Styles:** displays the Styles palette beneath the toolbox, containing a scrolling list of all available style sheets.

- **Colors:** displays the Colors palette for assigning colors to objects.

STEPS: Changing the Measurements Defaults

Step 1. Choose the Preferences command from the File menu to display the Preferences dialog box.

Step 2. Select Inches decimal from the Measurement system and Vertical ruler pop-up menus and press Return. Unlike inches shown on a standard ruler, decimal inches are divided into tenths and twentieths. This means that you may be asked to position your cursor even with the 7.8-inch mark on the horizontal ruler and the 4.15-inch mark on the vertical ruler. All measurements will be annotated in decimals rather than fractions.

Step 3. Choose the Column Guides command from the Layout menu to open the Column Guides dialog box.

Step 4. Enter 2 for the Number of columns option. Then press the Tab key, enter 0.25 to replace the Space between columns value, and press Return.

Step 5. Choose the 2 pt weight from the Line pop-up listing and None from the Fill pop-up listing in the Element menu.

Step 6. If any of the toggle commands (see the sidebar on the previous page) under either the Layout or Windows menu is not checked, you should choose it at this time. When you are finished, your Layout and Windows menus will look like those shown in Figure 18-2.

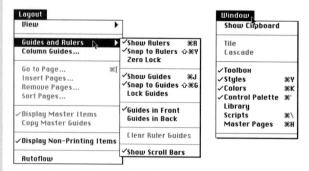

Figure 18-2: The default settings in the Layout (left) and Window (right) menus for this sample project

Preparing a Master Page_____

As always, your first step is to define and create items on the first master page for your document. In PageMaker 6 you can have multiple master pages, which you can create at the beginning of the layout process or as needed. We'll create the base master page now and another later in this exercise. In this case, your master page will contain not only a system of ruler guides but also a banner at the top of the page. The banner, which you will type directly into PageMaker, represents the name of the publication.

You will also learn how to create a master page *folio*. A folio contains general information and is positioned at the top or bottom of each page of a document. The text of the folio may include the name of a document or its issue date, along with the current page number.

STEPS:	Changing the Master Pages Defaults
Step 1.	Press ⌘-N to access the Document Setup dialog box.
Step 2.	The options in this dialog box should be set as follows:

       ☞ **Page size:** Letter

       ☞ **Double-sided:** not selected

       ☞ **Orientation:** Tall

       ☞ **Facing pages:** dimmed

       ☞ **Start page #:** 1

       ☞ **Margin in inches:** Left: 1, Top: 2, Right: 1, and Bottom: 1

       ☞ **Number of pages:** 4

Step 3.	When you have finished entering and selecting the specifications listed here, press the Return key to instruct PageMaker to create your new document, as shown in Figure 18-3.

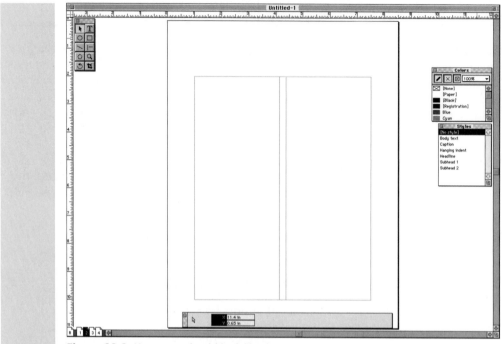

Figure 18-3: Your page should look like this.

STEPS: Creating the Master Pages

Step 1. Click the right master page icon, labeled R, at the bottom of your display.

Step 2. After the master page appears, drag two guides down from the horizontal ruler. One guide should be positioned at the 1.0-inch mark on the vertical ruler, and the other at the 1.8-inch mark.

Step 3. Drag two guides from the vertical ruler, positioning them exactly even with the two outermost column guides (flush with the left and right margins). These guides will provide a gridwork for text blocks created in the areas above and below the margins.

STEPS: **Creating the Banner Text**

Step 1. Use the Zoom tool to zoom in on the center of the two-inch area above the top margin ruler guide.

Step 2. Select the Text tool.

Step 3. Drag from the intersection of the upper ruler guide and the left margin to the intersection of the lower ruler guide and the right margin. This determines the column width of your banner text.

Step 4. Type **The Money Catalog**. This text will be displayed in the current default type and paragraph specifications. If you haven't created anything since the last sample project, your text will be in 48/50 Palatino Bold-Italic. But it really doesn't matter; you will be changing the type specs in the next step.

In previous sample projects, you altered the type specs of one or more selected words either by choosing options from the various pop-up commands in the Type menu, by accessing the Type Specifications dialog box, or from the Control palette. This time, however, you will specify the appearance of your text using style sheets. Style sheets contain specifications that you use to format entire paragraphs quickly, including font, type style, size, leading, horizontal scaling, tracking, alignment, indents, tabs, and more.

In PageMaker, style sheets are easy to create, edit, and apply. When used properly, they provide consistency for your publications and reduce formatting errors. If you want two paragraphs in a document to be identical in font, style, and so on, you merely choose the same style sheet for both. For example, all of your headlines can be set in one style, all your subheads in another, and all body text in still another. If you later decide to change the type specs of a group of paragraphs, you can edit the style sheet directly. All paragraphs to which that style has been applied will change, even if they are themselves separated by other paragraphs whose specifications you don't want to change. Style sheets save time and help to minimize errors and inconsistencies.

STEPS: **Changing the Type Specifications with Style Sheets**

Step 1. While your text entry cursor continues to blink in your text block, click the Headline option in the Styles palette. Immediately, your first line will change to 30-point Times-Bold, flush left, as shown in Figure 18-4.

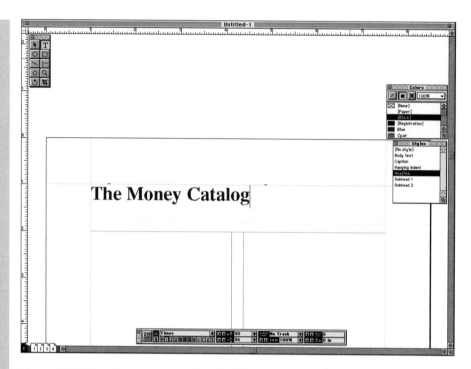

Figure 18-4: The effect of applying the Headline style sheet to the first line of banner text

Headline is one of PageMaker's default style sheets, available anytime PageMaker is launched. Unfortunately, 30-point Times-Bold is not well suited to this project. Times and Palatino do not generally complement each other, so Times is a poor choice for your banner. You will change these type specs by altering the Headline style sheet.

Step 2.   Select the Pointer tool to deselect your text. Although this is not an essential step, it will demonstrate that changing a style sheet also changes text tagged to that style, whether or not the text is currently selected.

Step 3.   To edit the Headline style, choose the Define Styles command from the Type menu or press ⌘-3. The Define Styles dialog box that appears provides full control over the manipulation of style sheets. Here, you can create a new style by clicking the New… button, alter an existing style by clicking the Edit… button, delete a style with the Remove button, and access any style contained in other PageMaker files by clicking the Copy… button. The scrolling Style list contains the same style sheet names that are available in the Styles palette.

Step 4. Click the Headline style to select it. Note that the specifications of the Headline style appear beneath the Style list. You can see that the Headline style sheet currently includes the typeface Times Bold, a 30-point type size, Auto leading, and so on, as shown in Figure 18-5. This display of type specs can be used to determine the attributes of any style sheet at a glance when you select its name from the scrolling style list.

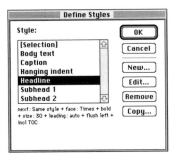

Figure 18-5: The Define Styles dialog box, with type specs for the Headline style displayed below the scrolling list

Step 5. Click the Edit... button, displaying the Edit Style dialog box, shown in Figure 18-6. This dialog box allows you to change the name of a style sheet or modify its attributes by using the dialog boxes associated with the Type..., Para..., Tabs..., and Hyph... buttons.

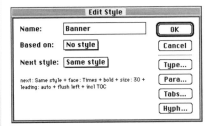

Figure 18-6: The Edit Style dialog box containing the new style name, Banner

Step 6. Enter the name *Banner* into the Name option, replacing the word Headline.

Step 7.   Click the Type... button to change the type specs of the current style sheet. The Type Specifications dialog box will appear (you may recognize it from previous sample projects). Using the methods outlined in Chapter 17, change the type specs to 46/40 Helvetica Bold. Then click the OK button to return to the Edit Style dialog box.

Step 8.   The only paragraph specification that you need to alter is the alignment. So click the Para... button to go to the familiar Paragraph Specifications dialog box, and then choose Center from the Alignment pop-up options. Now press the Return key three times. The first time returns you to the Edit Style dialog box, the second closes the Edit Style dialog box, and the third closes the Define Styles dialog box and returns you to the publication window, which appears as shown in Figure 18-7.

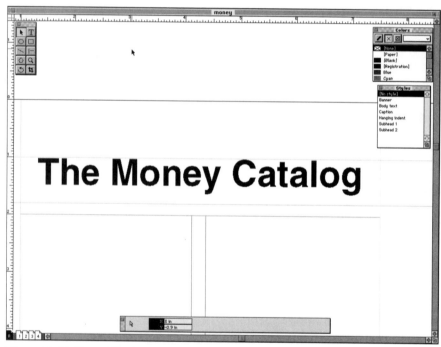

Figure 18-7: The publication window as it appears after completing alterations to the Banner style sheet

Although your banner text is no longer selected, it has been changed to your recent specifications. Once a paragraph has been tagged to a certain style sheet, it will continue to reflect any changes made to the style itself. The Styles palette no longer contains a Headline option. It has been replaced by a Banner option.

Your next operation is to create a new style that will be applied to a prospective second line of text in the banner. You can use either of two ways to create a new style sheet: Specify an entirely new style, determining type and paragraph specifications from scratch, or create a new style based on an existing style and build on prevailing specifications. In this case, you will use this second method.

STEPS:	Creating a New Style for the Banner Text

Step 1. Choose the Define Styles command from the Type menu or press ⌘-3.

Step 2. When the Define Styles dialog box appears, select the Banner style from the scrolling list and click the New... button. This opens the Edit Style dialog box. The Name option is empty, since this is a new style and so far has no name. However, the Based on pop-up option now contains the Banner style name.

Step 3. Click the Type... button, change the type specs to 24/Auto Helvetica-Italic, and press Return. Notice the specifications listing at the bottom of the Edit Style dialog box. The bold type style has been subtracted from the Banner style, and italic has been added. Your changes to the type size and leading are also noted, as shown in Figure 18-8. (The centered alignment from the Banner style sheet will be suitable for this style, so there is no need to alter the paragraph specifications for your new style.)

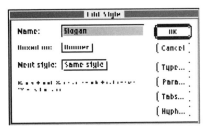

Figure 18-8: The Edit Style dialog box after creating a new style sheet based on the Banner style

Step 4. Enter **Slogan** into the Name option box, and press Return.

The new style has been designed especially to be applied to a slogan following the banner text. You can apply this style automatically by slightly altering the Banner style, as demonstrated in the following steps.

STEPS: **Applying the New Style to the Slogan**

Step 1. Inside the Define Styles dialog box, select the Banner style. Notice that the first item in the type spec readout is next: Same style. This indicates that any text you create directly following a paragraph set in the Banner style will also use the Banner style. If you prefer, however, you can instruct PageMaker to set succeeding paragraphs in a different style.

Step 2. Click the Edit... button.

Step 3. Click the Next style pop-up menu and choose the Slogan style from the list. Then press Return twice to execute your changes and go back to the publication window.

Step 4. Select the Text tool and click at the end of the word Catalog. Press Return to advance to the next line and type **Everything we sell costs money**. Because you changed the Next style option, your new paragraph changes to the 24-point Helvetica-Italic specs included in the Slogan style, as shown in Figure 18-9.

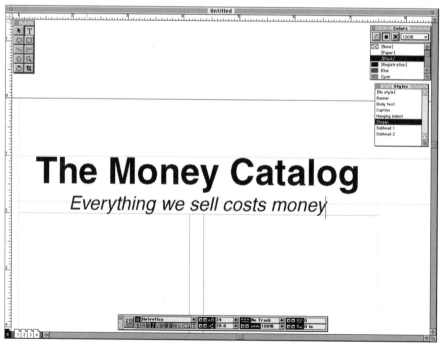

Figure 18-9: The Slogan style sheet has been applied to the second line of banner text.

Creating the Folio

Your banner and slogan are now complete. The next master page item to create is the folio, or page number text.

STEPS: Creating the Page Number Text for the Folio

Step 1.   Scroll down to the bottom of the page. Then drag two guides from the horizontal ruler to the 10.3-inch and 10.5-inch markers on the vertical rulers, respectively.

Step 2.   Select the Text tool and drag from the top-left ruler guide intersection to the bottom-right ruler guide intersection.

Step 3.   Type **February, 1996 issue** → **Page Ø**. (If PageMaker starts beeping at you or produces the alert dialog box shown in Figure 18-10, select the folio text with the Pointer tool and drag the lower windowshade down about an inch to display the second line of type. Then click in the text with the Text tool and continue typing.)

Cannot show the insertion point.

Turn the page, expand the text block, or place more of the story.   Note: Multiple paste may repeat this message.

Continue

Figure 18-10: If this alert appears, select your text with the Pointer tool and drag the lower windowshade down to display another line.

In Step 3, we used two more special character notations. The arrow symbol indicates that you should press the Tab key. This creates a gap between the date and the page number. The symbol Ø represents PageMaker's special page number character, produced by pressing ⌘-Option-P. On the master page, this character will appear as RM for right master, but on any other page, it will reflect the current page number, from 1 to 9999.

Your folio text probably looks strange right now. Since you edited the Banner style sheet while no text was selected, its type specifications have become your default settings. For this reason, your folio text is centered. Tabs don't work very well when inserted within centered text. The following steps demonstrate how to change the alignment and tab settings so that the date is positioned flush left and the page number is flush right.

STEPS: **Changing the Alignment and Tab Settings**

Step 1. With the Text tool, triple-click anywhere on your folio text to select the entire paragraph.

Step 2. Scroll up the Styles palette until you reach the top, and select the No style option. This untags your text so that it is no longer affected by any style sheet. No immediate change takes place, because your folio text retains the specifications of the Banner style sheet.

Step 3. Press ⌘-T to access the Type Specifications dialog box. Because you have accessed this dialog box directly without going through the Edit Style dialog box, your type spec changes will not affect any style sheet. Change the settings in this dialog box to 12/Auto Helvetica and press Return.

Step 4. Now choose the Indents/Tabs command from the Type menu or press ⌘-I to bring up the Indents/Tabs dialog box. This dialog box allows you to alter the location of tabbed and indented text in much the same way that you would move tabs on a typewriter. You can select from the following four styles of tabs:

ᠭ **Left**: the traditional tab, where the first letter of text after the tab character is flush left with the tab setting

ᠭ **Right**: where a section of text between one tab and another, or between the tab and a line return, is flush right with the tab setting

ᠭ **Center**: where a section of text between one tab and another, or between the tab and a line return, is centered at a specific point

ᠭ **Decimal**: where the decimal point in a tabbed number, such as $45.95, is aligned at the tab setting

Toward the bottom of the dialog box, a series of down-arrow icons are located on a ruler, indicating default tab positions. These will disappear when you set a tab of your own by selecting a tab button and clicking in the area just above the ruler. A tab appears instantly at the point where you click. The ruler allows you to measure the location of the tab from the left boundary of the selected text block. You relocate an existing tab by dragging it.

Step 5. Click and hold the scroll arrow to the right of the ruler until you can see the triangular column width indicator at the 6.5-inch ruler mark.

Step 6. Select the right tab button and click above the ruler at approximately the 5.5-inch marker. The right tab symbol will appear where you click, accompanied by a number in the Position option, displaying the exact location of the tab.

Step 7. Drag the right tab symbol right, all the way to the end of the column. (If you accidentally miss the existing tab and create a new one, drag the unwanted tab directly down, outside the dialog box, to remove it.) When you finish your drag, the number in the Position option should read 6.5, as shown in Figure 18-11. (You can also enter the value 6.5 directly into the Position option box if you prefer.) Then press the Return key or click the OK button.

Figure 18-11: The Indents/Tabs dialog box, showing your folio tab specifications

Don't worry if your page number is not flush right. As we mentioned earlier, tabs do not work correctly when a paragraph is centered. Generally, tabs work best when text is aligned flush left, so press Shift-⌘-L or choose the Align left option from the Alignment pop-up listing in the Type menu.

Now is a good time to save your document.

STEPS: Saving the Document

Step 1. Press ⌘-S or choose the Save command from the File menu.

Step 2. Enter the name **Four-page catalog** or some other appropriate name into the Save publication as dialog box.

Step 3. Press Return.

Figure 18-12 shows your progress so far.

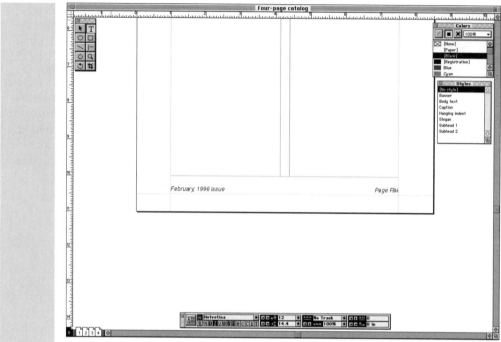

Figure 18-12: The master page folio, containing the flush-left date and flush-right page number character

Placing and Formatting Body Copy _

Now that you have finished creating master page items and ruler guides, you can move on to the actual pages. Your first operation is to place a long text file using PageMaker's autoflow feature.

STEPS: Placing a Text File with Autoflow

Step 1. Click the page 1 icon at the bottom of your screen display. Choose the Lock guides command from the Guides and rulers submenu in the Layout menu. This will prevent you from accidentally moving any master-page guides.

Step 2. Press ⌘-D or choose the Place command from the File menu, select Catalog Copy from the Four-page catalog files and press Return. When you placed text in previous sample projects, PageMaker displayed the manual text flow cursor. This time, however, you will be presented with the autoflow cursor because you set the Autoflow command from the Layout menu as an application default.

Step 3. Position your autoflow cursor at the top of the first column. Then click. On a fast computer, the text will pour very quickly. Once PageMaker finishes pouring the first column, it pours the second. Then it turns to the second page, pours those columns, turns to the third page and pours those columns, turns to the fourth page, and so on. If you don't stop it, PageMaker will continue to pour the entire article, creating pages as it goes. If you ever need to stop automatic text flow before it is completed, you can click the Cancel button in the text status dialog box.

As you can see in Figure 18-13, PageMaker created two additional pages. Later, you'll have to edit the text in your catalog copy if changing the type specifications does not make all of the text fit on the first four pages.

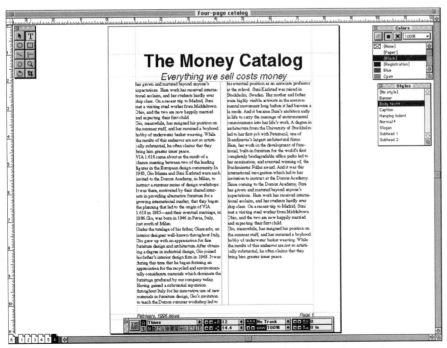

Figure 18-13: PageMaker continues to create pages until all the text is placed.

Editing the Body Copy Style Sheet

To format your new text file, you will use a style sheet just as you did on the master page.

STEPS: Formatting the New Text File

Step 1.   Click the page 1 icon to return to page 1. Select the Text tool and click anywhere in the text on page 1.

Step 2.   Press ⌘-A to select the entire file and click the Body text style in the Styles palette. Body text — another of PageMaker's preset style sheets — formats the text as 12/Auto Times Roman. Since you're using Palatino and Helvetica, however, the style will need to be edited.

Step 3.   Press ⌘ and click the Body text option in the Styles palette. ⌘-clicking a style sheet is a method of displaying the Edit Style dialog box without having to choose the Define Styles command.

Step 4.   Once the Edit Style dialog box appears, click the Type... button and change the type specs to 10/Auto Helvetica and press Return.

Step 5.   Click the Para... button to display the Paragraph Specifications dialog box. Select the Justify option, then enter 0.25 for the First option and 0.065 for the After option.

Step 6.   Press the Return key twice to return to the publication window.

Your text will automatically change to fully justified 12/Auto Helvetica. This completes your manipulation of the body copy. Now that the text fits onto the first four pages as it should, you need to delete pages 5 and 6, which were created by PageMaker when the text autoflowed.

STEPS: Deleting Pages

Step 1.   Choose the Remove Pages command from the Page menu. This opens the Remove Pages dialog box, as shown in Figure 18-14. The default values in this dialog box are the current page numbers.

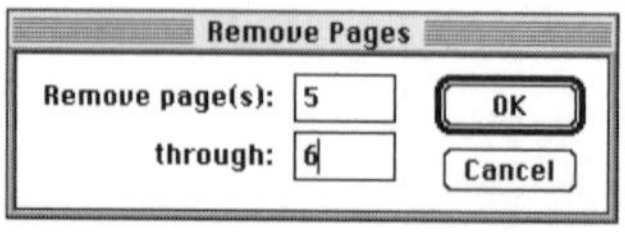

Figure 18-14: The Remove pages dialog box, containing your specifications

Step 2. Since you want to delete pages 5 and 6, enter the number 5 in the Remove page(s) field and 6 in the through field (deleting pages 5 through 6).

Step 3. Press Return. An alert dialog box displays, asking if you really want to delete the page and all items on it. If you are sure of your specifications, click the OK button or press Return.

Step 4. After you confirm the removal of pages 5 and 6, PageMaker deletes them. Since your next task will be to finish working on page 1, make sure that you are on page 1. Now press ⌘-S to update your file on disk.

This publication certainly has a large quantity of text for a catalog. Now it is time to clear spaces for advertisements, add graphic embellishments, and create a price listing. Sometimes when you create a document, you want to position your graphics first, then pour your text around them. But in PageMaker, it usually works best to pour your text first, as you have done, and then add the graphics.

Allocating Space for Graphic Elements

In the next few steps, you won't actually create ads, as it would be too time-consuming in the context of this sample project. Instead, you will place ads that have already been created, or in some cases simply create boxes that will act as markers, indicating where the ads can be later pasted into place after the file is printed or imported electronically into your PageMaker file.

Throughout the remainder of this chapter, you will be instructed to move your cursor using a coordinate system, in which H:0.0 = the 0-inch marker on the horizontal ruler and V:0.0 = the 0-inch marker on the vertical ruler. All other coordinates are measured from this point. For example, H:5.6 is equal to $5^6/_{10}$ inch.

STEPS: Creating Space for Ads and Graphics

Step 1. Press ⌘-Option and click near the bottom of page 1.

Step 2. Select the rectangle tool and drag from H:1.0, V:7.0 to H:7.5, V:10.0 to indicate the size of the ad space. Your rectangle should be the width of your margins, with a 2-point line weight and transparent interior, as shown in Figure 18-15.

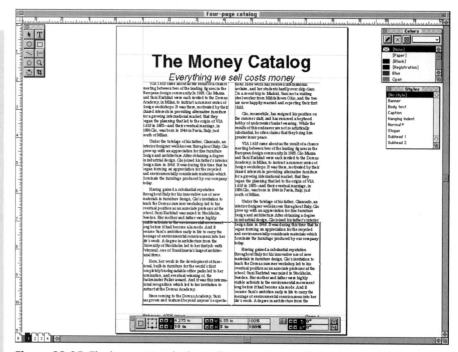

Figure 18-15: The large rectangle that will represent your ad space currently overlaps text.

Step 3. As you can see, your large rectangle overlaps about a third of the text on this page. This must be remedied by altering the length of each of the two text columns. Select the Pointer tool and click the first column.

Step 4. Drag the lower windowshade upward to approximately V:6.9, so that there is about $^1/_{10}$ inch between the end of the text and the rectangle. The text that is displaced by your shortening of this column will automatically wrap into the next column, and so on.

Step 5. Click the right column to select it and drag its lower windowshade upward to V:6.9 or thereabouts (see Figure 18-16).

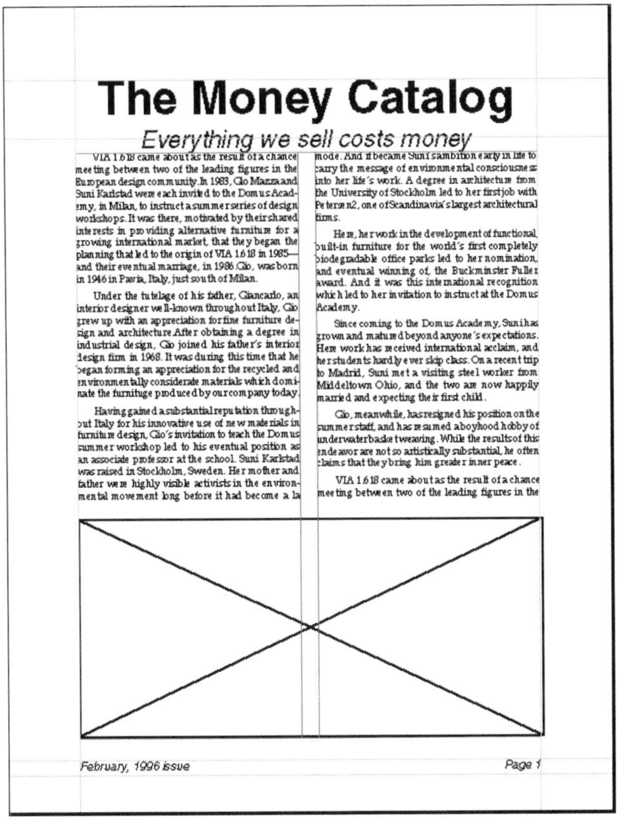

Figure 18-16: Lift the lower windowshades of each of your two columns of text so that they no longer overlap the rectangle.

Step 6. Now draw an X the size of your rectangle, indicating that it is not a real graphic but only a spaceholder.

Step 7. Select the diagonal line tool and drag from H:1.0, V:7.0 to H:7.5, V:10.0, the same coordinates you used to draw the rectangle. This creates a diagonal line from the upper-left corner to bottom-right corner of the rectangle, the first stroke of your five.

Step 8. Now, while the line remains selected, choose Hairline from the Line pop-up listing, reducing the weight of the line. For the second stroke of the five, draw from H:1.0, V:10.0 to H:7.5, V:7.0 with the diagonal line tool, joining the other two corners of the rectangle. Also change this line to a hairline.

Step 9. Press ⌘-W to zoom out to the Fit-in-window view size.

Step 10. Then press ⌘-S to update your file on disk. This completes page 1, as shown in Figure 18-17.

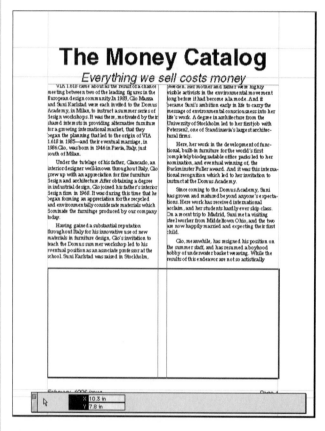

Figure 18-17: The completed page 1, with autoflowed text and an advertisement placeholder

Wrapping Text Around a Rectangular Object

Suppose that you want to create a space for an advertisement on page 2. Rather than positioning this ad at the bottom of the page, however, you want it to stand out more prominently to attract attention in a distinctive manner. To accomplish this, you will position a smaller vertical ad in the middle of the page, wrapping both columns of text around the rectangle. If you had to do this manually, it would be a difficult procedure; you would have to break your story into a number of additional columns, each with varying widths. PageMaker, however, provides an automatic text-wrapping feature, which you will use instead.

STEPS: Arranging Text with Automatic Text-Wrapping

Step 1. Hold down the Shift key and click the page 2 icon at the bottom of your screen display to go to the second page. Holding down the Shift key changes the view size to Fit-in-window and centers the page as you turn to a new page or set of pages.

Step 2. Drag a rectangle to the coordinates V:3.0, H:3.0 to V:9.0, H:5.5.

Step 3. Press ⌘-Option and click in the middle of the graphic, zooming in to Actual size. If necessary, press the Option key and drag to move your screen image until the rectangle is centered in your publication window.

Step 4. Your placeholder is now partially obscured by text. You can remedy this situation by taking advantage of PageMaker's text-wrapping feature. Select the graphic and choose the Text Wrap command from the Element menu. This opens the Text Wrap dialog box.

STEPS: Using the Text Wrap Dialog Box

Step 1. Select the second Wrap option icon. PageMaker will automatically select the second Text flow icon as well. However, since you will want text on the left and right sides of your rectangle, select the third Text flow icon instead.

Step 2. Enter .25 for the Left and Right options and .15 for the Top and Bottom options. Then press Return.

Step 3. A graphic boundary appears around your graphic to the specifications you entered. To get a better view of the graphic boundary and the manner in which your text has wrapped around the spaceholder, press ⌘-W to zoom out to Fit-in-window size, as shown in Figure 18-18. Then press ⌘-S to update your file on disk.

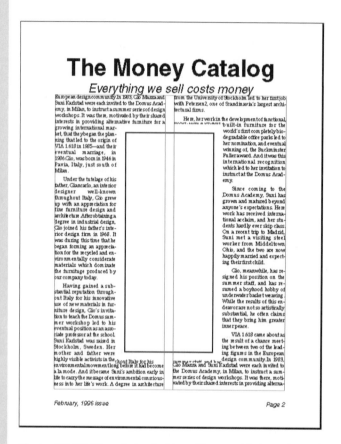

Figure 18-18: The ad placeholder with a graphic boundary, which causes text to flow around it in a rectangular manner

Don't worry when your graphic boundary disappears after saving your file. Text wrap boundaries appear only when a graphic is selected; the saving operation deselects all elements in your publication. If you want to see the boundary again, merely reselect the rectangle.

The Text Wrap Dialog Box

The Text Wrap dialog box, shown below, contains three Wrap option icons and three Text flow options. Each option is used to determine the visual manner in which overlapping text is forced to wrap around a selected graphic element. The first Wrap option icon, which is currently selected, indicates that text merely overlaps a graphic. The second icon specifies that text will wrap rectangularly around a graphic. The third icon, which is dimmed, is the custom wrap option; it allows you to wrap text around a complex graphic. You will get a chance to experiment with irregular text wrapping on page 3 of your catalog.

The Text flow icons determine where text is allowed to pour in reference to a graphic. The first option allows no text to pour below the selected graphic; the second allows for text above and below the graphic, but none to the left or right side; and the third allows text to wrap a graphic on all four sides.

The Standoff in inches options determine the dimensions of the graphic boundary. The Text Wrap... command creates a rectangular dotted line around the selected graphic. This graphic boundary forms a border of white space around an image, within which text will not appear. The Left, Right, Top, and Bottom values are measured outward from the selected graphic element.

Wrapping Text Around a Complex Graphic

For page 3, you'll import an existing graphic from the disk and then wrap text around it as you did on page 2. This time, however, the graphic isn't rectangular, so you'll customize the text wrap to follow the shape of the graphic.

STEPS: **Customizing the Text Wrap**

Step 1. Press ⌘-Tab to go to page 3 (or click the page 3 icon at the bottom of your screen display). Press ⌘-D, select Sailboat.eps from the Four-page catalog folder, and press Return. Click with your graphic placement icon in the upper-left area of your page.

Step 2. Display the Control palette (if it is not already displayed) by pressing ⌘-] or by choosing the Control Palette command from the Windows menu.

Step 3. Select the Pointer tool and click the graphic, and then click the Control palette to activate it.

Step 4. Select the Proportional scaling button so that it is on, as shown in Figure 18-19, and then enter 150 in the Horizontal scaling option and press Enter. The Vertical scaling option will change to 150 automatically, and the graphic will be enlarged to 150% of its original size.

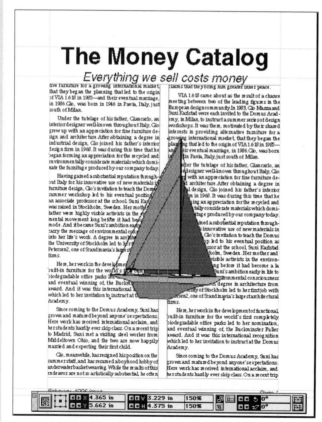

Figure 18-19: A graphic positioned in the middle of page 3

Step 5. Press ⌘-Option and click in the center of the graphic to zoom in. Center the graphic between the two columns using the Pointer tool.

Step 6. Since the text again overlaps your graphic, use the Text wrap command from the Element menu to bring up the Text Wrap dialog box.

As we mentioned earlier, you will wrap text irregularly around this image. So rather than creating a standard rectangular graphic boundary, you will want your boundary to imitate the outline of the graphic itself. It stands to reason that you should select the third Wrap option icon. Unfortunately, this option is dimmed. In PageMaker, you must always create a rectangular graphic boundary first and then manipulate that boundary in the publication window. The next few steps demonstrate how this works.

Step 7. Select the second Wrap option and the third Text flow option. Then enter 0.15 for each of the distance values, and press Return. A rectangular graphic boundary surrounds your image. Now you can alter the boundary around the graphic pictured in Figure 18-19. To wrap text irregularly around a graphic, you must manipulate the rectangular graphic boundary. Currently, the boundary has four handles, one at each corner. Each of these corners can be moved independently by dragging it.

Step 8. Pressing the Shift key while dragging constrains movement horizontally or vertically. You can also drag at the boundary *segments*, the dotted lines between handles, increasing or reducing the text wrap limitations from the value set for the rectangular boundary. This allows for limited irregular text wrapping. But the only way to imitate the outline of a graphic accurately is to add handles to the boundary by clicking a segment with the Pointer tool.

Step 9. Create new boundary handles by clicking the graphic boundary, and customize the fit of the graphic boundary by repositioning handles and moving boundary segments, as shown in Figure 18-20. As you change the graphic boundary, the surrounding text will reflow after each move in response to your progress. If you want to stop the text from reflowing temporarily, hold down the spacebar while adding handles or modifying the graphic boundary — this will stop the adjacent text from reflowing until you release the spacebar. The new graphic is shown in Figure 18-21.

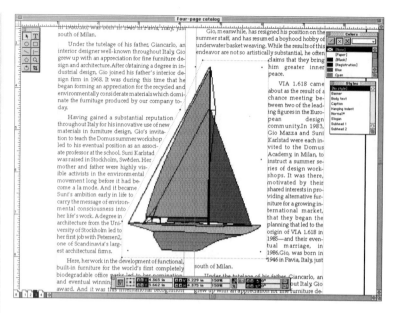

Figure 18-20: The graphic boundary is modified to more closely follow the edge of your graphic.

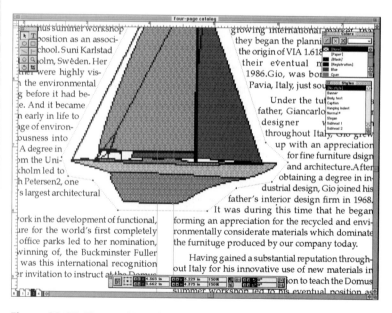

Figure 18-21: The graphic and its new graphic boundary, viewed at 200%

Creating a New Master Page _____

Page 3 now looks like Figure 18-22. (To get this view, press ⌘-0). After looking closely at your catalog, you've probably noticed that it has too much text. To remedy that, we're going to put a photograph and table on page 4, deleting all of the existing text on that page. We will then reformat the page with a new master page. Since we want to delete the text to the end of the document, we'll use Story Editor to select the desired text. Remember from Chapter 5 that Story Editor works similarly to a word processor, allowing you to select text as you would in Microsoft Word or another Mac text editor.

Figure 18-22:
Your page should look like this one.

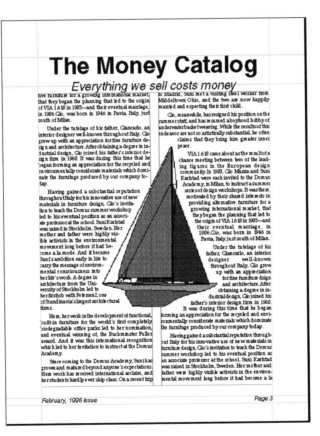

STEPS: **Deleting Excess Text**

Step 1. If you haven't already done so, press ⌘-0 to display page 3 in Fit-in-Window view. Then, using the Text tool, place the text cursor at the beginning of the last paragraph on the page.

Step 2. After placing the cursor, press ⌘-E to open the Story Editor. Notice that Story Editor opens with the cursor blinking at the position where you placed it in the previous step, as shown in Figure 18-23. You can now edit the text freely, in either direction. However, we want to delete the text to the end of the document.

	Four-page catalog:VIA 1.618 came abou:1
	interior design firm in 1968. It was during this time that he began forming an appreciation for the recycled and environmentally considerate materials which dominate the furnituge produced by our company today.
Body text	Having gained a substantial reputation throughout Italy for his innovative use of new materials in furniture design, Gio's invitation to teach the Domus summer workshop led to his eventual position as an associate professor at the school. Suni Karlstad was raised in Stockholm, Sweden. Her mother and father were highly visible activists in the environmental movement long before it had become a la mode. And it became Suni's ambition early in life to carry the message of environmental consciousness into her life's work. A degree in architecture from the University of Stockholm led to her first job with Petersen2, one of Scandinavia's largest architectural firms.
Body text	Here, her work in the development of functional, built-in furniture for the world's first completely biodegradable office parks led to her nomination, and eventual winning of, the Buckminster Fuller award. And it was this international recognition which led to her invitation to instruct at the Domus Academy.
Body text	Since coming to the Domus Academy, Suni has grown and matured beyond anyone's expectations. Here work has received international acclaim, and her students hardly ever skip class. On a recent trip to Madrid, Suni met a visiting steel worker from Middeltown Ohio, and the two are now happily married and expecting their first child.
Body text	Gio, meanwhile, has resigned his position on the summer staff, and has resumed a boyhood hobby of underwater basket weaving. While the results of this endeavor are not so artistically substantial, he often claims that they bring him greater inner peace.
Body text	VIA 1.618 came about as the result of a chance meeting between two of the leading figures in the European design community.In 1983, Gio Mazza and Suni Karlstad were each invited to the Domus Academy, in Milan, to instruct a summer series of design workshops. It was there, motivated by their shared interests in providing alternative furniture for a growing international market, that they began the planning that led to the origin of VIA 1.618 in 1985—and their eventual marriage, in 1986.Gio, was born in 1946 in Pavia, Italy, just south of Milan.
Body text	Under the tutelage of his father, Giancarlo, an interior designer well-known throughout Italy, Gio grew up with an appreciation for fine furniture design and architecture.After obtaining a degree in industrial design, Gio joined his father's interior design firm in 1968. It was during this time that he began forming an appreciation for the recycled and environmentally considerate materials which dominate the furnituge produced by our company today.

Figure 18-23: The Story Editor opens at the place where you inserted the cursor.

Step 3. Press Shift-End to select all the text from the current cursor position to the end of the document, then press Delete to delete the selected text. Now click the Story Editor close button to return to your layout.

You are now ready to create the new master page for page 4. Remember from Chapter 4 that you create new master pages with PageMaker 6's new Master Pages palette.

STEPS: **Using a Second Master Page to Reformat a Page**

Step 1. To create the new master page, select New Master from the Master Pages palette pop-up menu, as shown in Figure 18-24. This opens the Create New Master Page dialog box.

Figure 18-24: Create a new master page by choosing New Master . . . from the Master Pages palette.

Step 2. In the Create New Master Page dialog box, name the new master page Price List, and then change the number of columns to 1. Figure 18-25 shows the Create New Master Page dialog box with the settings for the new master page. After you finish making your changes, click Create.

```
┌───────── Create New Master Page ─────────┐
│                                          │
│  Name: │Price List        │  ⦿ One page  │
│                              ○ Two page   │
│  ┌─ Margins ───────────────────────────┐ │
│  │ Left:  │1│ inches  Right:  │1│ inches│ │
│  │ Top:   │2│ inches  Bottom: │1│ inches│ │
│  └─────────────────────────────────────┘ │
│  ┌─ Column Guides ─────────────────────┐ │
│  │ Columns:        │1│                 │ │
│  │ Space between:  │0.25│ inches        │ │
│  └─────────────────────────────────────┘ │
│              [ Cancel ]  [ Create ]       │
└──────────────────────────────────────────┘
```

Figure 18-25: The Create New Master Page dialog box with your new settings

After you click Create, PageMaker displays the new master page. PageMaker assumes that since you have just created a new master page, you'll want to format it. So, let's do so.

 Some of the master page items on the first master page we created earlier are also used on the new master page, though they are placed somewhat differently. We could have used the Duplicate command on the Master Palette menu to create the master page, which would have given us a new master with all the original elements intact. However, we wanted to make sure that you understood the process of creating a new master page from scratch.

STEPS: Formatting the New Master Page

Step 1.   Since we need both the banner and folio from the original document master, in the Master Pages palette, double-click the Document Master listing to go to that master page.

Step 2.   With the Pointer tool selected, choose Select All from the Edit menu, or press ⌘-A, to select both master page items. Then select Copy from the Edit menu to copy the items, or press ⌘-C. To return to the new master page, double-click Price List in the Master Pages palette.

Step 3.   Now that you're back on Price List master page, select Paste from the Edit menu, or press ⌘-V, to paste the master page elements onto Price List.

Step 4.   Click a blank space to deselect the objects.

Step 5.   Select and drag the banner down the page, so that the bottom windowshade lines up with the 6.5-inch mark on the vertical ruler.

Step 6.   Drag a horizontal ruler guide onto the page and place it at the 1-inch mark on the vertical rulers. Your page should look like Figure 18-26.

Step 7.   Applying a new master page is easy. Simply go to the page where you want to apply the new master page and then select the desired master page in the Master Pages palette.

Step 8.   Click the page 4 icon to go to page 4, and then click Price List to format the page with the new master page.

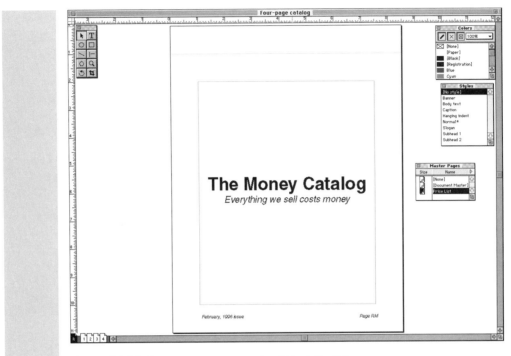

Figure 18-26: Your new master page should look like this one.

Importing and Modifying a TIFF Image

Now that you've formatted the new page, it's time to bring in the page elements. First you'll bring in a full-color photograph and then use a Photoshop Plug-in to modify it.

STEPS: Importing a TIFF image

Step 1.   Using the Place command, get and place the image money.tif from the Four-page catalog files folder, as shown in Figure 18-27. (You can use the Control palette to place the image precisely.)

Figure 18-27: Place the image as shown here.

Step 2.   Now that you've placed your image, we're going to apply a glass-effect special effects filter. PageMaker 6 allows you to apply Photoshop filters to TIFF images created in Adobe Photoshop. PageMaker ships with several Adobe Gallery Effects filters that are installed when you install PageMaker.

You can also access the filters you use with Photoshop by creating aliases of them and dragging the aliases to the Plug-ins folder in the RSRC folder inside the Adobe PageMaker 6 folder.

Step 3.   Making sure the image is still selected, choose Photoshop Effects from the Image submenu on the Element menu, which opens the Photoshop Effects dialog box. From here, you can select any of the installed filters.

Step 4.   Click on the Photoshop effect pop-up menu and select GE Glass, as shown in Figure 18-28, then click OK, which opens the Adobe Gallery Effects dialog box, shown in Figure 18-29.

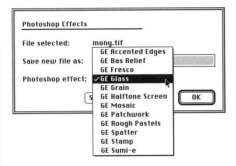

Figure 18-28: Choose GE Glass, as shown here.

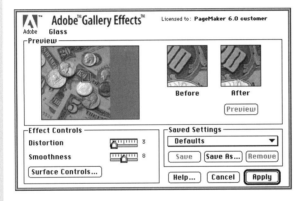

Figure 18-29: The Adobe Gallery Effects dialog box with your settings

The Photoshop Effects dialog box that comes up here depends on the Plug-in chosen. The one in this exercise is typical to Gallery Effects. The small square in the preview on the left allows you to adjust the area viewed in the Before and After previews on the right. The small sliders in the lower left allow you to adjust the degree of the special effect. In this example, you will create a slight glass distortion effect.

Step 5. Adjust the Distortion slider to 3 and then set the Smoothness slider to 8, as shown in Figure 18-29, then click Apply. Depending on your computer, it could take a few minutes to apply the effect.

Masking the Image

Now that we've applied a special effect, let's mask the image for an even more dramatic effect. Remember from Chapter 4 that masking places objects inside PageMaker-drawn shapes.

STEPS: Masking the Image

Step 1. Using the Ellipses tool, draw an oval like the one in Figure 18-30. You can match the settings in the Control palette to get the oval size exact.

Step 2. Using the Pointer tool, drag a marquee around the two objects (the picture and the oval) to select them both.

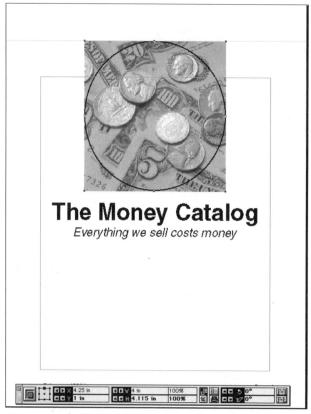

The Money Catalog
Everything we sell costs money

Figure 18-30: Draw an oval like this one.

Step 3. Select Mask from the Element menu to place the image inside the oval, as shown in Figure 18-31.

Step 4. Return to Fit-in-Window view by pressing ⌘-0.

Figure 18-31: An example of the masked image

Creating a Price List

Now that you have finished manipulating graphics, your next and near-final series of steps is devoted to the creation of a short price list, a fundamental part of any catalog.

STEPS: Creating a Price List

Step 1.   Click the Pointer tool icon to deselect all elements in the publication window.

Step 2.   Select the Body text style from the Styles palette. This style is now the default setting for this file.

Step 3.   Press ⌘ and click the No style option in the Styles palette. This opens the Edit Style dialog box, with an empty Name option and the Body text style listed for the Based on option. ⌘-clicking No style name allows you to create a new style based on the style that was previously selected.

Step 4.   Click the Tabs... button to open the Indents/tabs dialog box. You will insert two tabs. Select the Left option and click above the ruler at around the ^{3}/$_4$-inch mark. Alternatively, you can enter 0.75 into the Position option box. Create a second left tab at 2.5.

   Note: Look at the indent markers at the beginning of the ruler, as shown in Figure 18-32. The top half of the triangle is moved right slightly, indicating a first-line indent. Drag this top marker back to 0, eliminating the first-line indent, and press Return.

Figure 18-32: The Indents/tabs dialog box contains your specifications for the Price lists style sheet.

Step 6.   Enter **Price lists** for the style sheet name. Then press Return.

Step 7.   Before you create the price list, you need to create a ruler guide to help position the first line of text. So drag a guide down from the horizontal ruler to V:7.0. (If you incorrectly position the guide, you will not be able to move it because the Lock guides command is active. Choose the Lock guides command from the Options menu to deactivate it, move your ruler guide, and then reactivate the Lock guides command.)

Step 8.   Scroll down the Styles palette and select the Price lists option. This is now the default style sheet.

Step 9.   Then select the Text tool and click just below your ruler guide.

Step 10. Input the following text, using tabs for the → symbol and carriage returns for the ¶ symbol:

✧ 04024 → LCD clock radio → 139.95 ¶

✧ 04025 → Stereo clock radio → 229.95 ¶

✧ 07220 → Gold-plated watch → 79.95 ¶

✧ 07231 → w/ moon phases → 99.95 ¶

✧ 10188 → Knife sharpener → 69.95 ¶

✧ 43899 → 35-func calculator → 24.95 ¶

✧ 44899 → 2k data calculator → 34.95 ¶

✧ 57002 → 5-speed fan → 49.95 ¶

✧ 57305 → Portable heater → 179.95 ¶

✧ 57309 → Portable AC unit → 249.95 ¶

Step 11. Select the text with the Pointer tool, then shorten the windowshade handles and place the text, as shown in Figure 18-33.

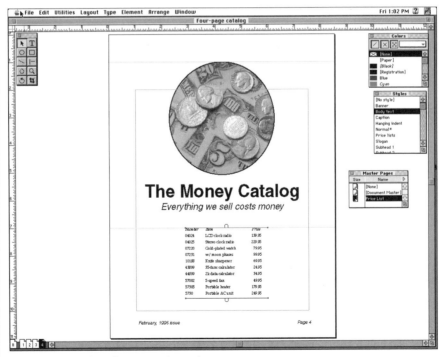

Figure 18-33: Place the text as shown here.

The numbers in your text are aligned rather strangely. The first numbers in each row are flush with each other, so that tens of dollars in one row line up with hundreds of dollars in another. To fix this, ⌘-click the Price lists style name in the Style palette.

Step 12. When the Edit Style dialog box appears, click the Tabs... button. The Indents/tabs dialog box displays the two left tabs above the ruler. Select the rightmost tab by clicking it and choose the Delete tab option from the Position pop-up menu. This dispenses with the inappropriate tab.

Step 13. Select the decimal tab icon and create a decimal tab at 2.75. Then press the Return key twice. Now the decimals in the price values line up, as is most commonly seen in a price list.

Overriding a Style Sheet

To complete the list, you need to distinguish the list headings visually — Number, Item, and Price — from the list itself. You will do this by directly assigning new type specs to the list headings, overriding their style sheet specifications.

STEPS: Overrriding Style Sheet Specifications

Step 1. Select the Text tool. Triple-click the top line of type in the first column.

Step 2. Press Shift-⌘-B to assign the bold style to the type. A bold style helps to differentiate the heading from the listed items, but it needs a little more. You may also want to rearrange the tabs so that the Price head is more centered above the dollar listings.

Step 3. Press ⌘-I to access the Indents/tabs dialog box, drag down on the decimal tab to dispense with it, select the left tab icon, and create a new tab at 2.5. Then press Return.

Notice the Styles palette. The Price lists option is followed by a plus sign, indicating that there are certain differences between the selected text and its style sheet. These differences will be retained unless you again click the Price lists style sheet while this line of type is selected.

Step 4. The headline might look even better with some additional paragraph spacing and a line between the headline and the list text. Press ⌘-M to open the Paragraph Specifications dialog box, and enter 0.15 for the After value.

Step 5. Click the Rules... button to display the Paragraph Rules dialog box. Here, you can create a rule above or below a line of text. This technique is preferable to underlining the headline with the line tool, since paragraph rules move with your text. Select the Rule below paragraph option and choose the 2 pt option from the Line style pop-up menu. Press Return twice to execute your paragraph specs.

Printing the Document

Your catalog is now complete. The only step remaining is to print the finished document.

STEPS: Printing

Step 1. Make sure that your printer is turned on and is chosen in the Chooser.

Step 2. Press ⌘-P to access the Print Document dialog box. Indicate one copy, and print from page 1 to 4, as described at the end of your first sample project (see Chapter 16).

Of course, if you were reproducing this catalog on a printing press, you'd be printing separations on an imagesetter.

Step 3. When your catalog is finished printing, examine the pages of your printed catalog, paying special attention to the results of your text wrapping and image control experiments. Make sure that they meet your expectations. If you see any problems, make the necessary changes to your file.

Successfully completing this chapter demonstrates an understanding of the most advanced functions and operations offered by PageMaker. We hope that this has helped you to better understand the topics covered throughout this book and provided you with a more developed working knowledge of PageMaker.

Summary

- Style sheets contain specifications that you use to format entire paragraphs quickly, including font, type style, size, leading, horizontal scaling, tracking, alignment, indents, tabs, and more. In PageMaker, style sheets are easy to create, edit, and apply. When used properly, they provide consistency for your publications and reduce formatting errors.

- A folio contains general information and is positioned at the top or bottom of each page of a document. The text of the folio may include the name of a document or its issue date, along with the current page number.

- The symbol **Ø** represents PageMaker's special page number character, produced by pressing ⌘-Option-P. On the master page, this character will appear as RM for right master, but on any other page, it will reflect the current page number, from 1 to 9999.

- The Text Wrap dialog box contains three Wrap option icons and three Text flow options. Each option is used to determine the visual manner in which overlapping text is forced to wrap around a selected graphic element. The first Wrap option icon, which is currently selected, indicates that text merely overlaps a graphic. The second icon specifies that text will wrap rectangularly around a graphic. The third icon is the custom wrap option; it allows you to wrap text around a complex graphic.

- The Text flow icons determine where text is allowed to pour in reference to a graphic. The first option allows no text to pour below the selected graphic; the second allows for text above and below the graphic, but none to the left or right side; and the third allows text to wrap a graphic on all four sides.

System Requirements and Installation

- -

In This Appendix

- ➡ System requirements and recommendations
- ➡ Adobe Type Manager

- -

In the Beginning

When Adobe released PageMaker 1.0 in June 1985, the system requirements and installation techniques for the application were fairly simple — PageMaker came on a single floppy disk and ran only on the Apple Macintosh 512K computer. And since Macintosh hard drives were virtually unheard of, installing PageMaker was as easy as inserting the disk.

Today, the system requirements and installation techniques for PageMaker version 6 are more complicated. PageMaker ships on half a dozen 1.44MB floppy disks or a CD-ROM disc, and the installation procedure is affected by the printers, scanners, word processors, and graphics applications you intend to use with the program.

This appendix explains the hardware and software requirements of PageMaker 6 and the procedures for installing the application. I'll begin by reviewing the basic system requirements prescribed by Adobe and then look at each aspect of a Macintosh publishing system in detail. Next, the actual software installation is reviewed. Finally, we'll cover some post-installation modifications to your system.

System Requirements and Recommendations

The minimum system requirement is not really the minimum hardware configuration on which PageMaker will run. It is the minimum hardware configuration on which Adobe believes you can use PageMaker without experiencing physical pain and calling the company to complain about how slow the thing is. It's a classic struggle between marketing and sales: On the one hand, the company wants to claim that almost anyone can run PageMaker on almost any Macintosh (which is actually true), but on the other hand, it wants to set a reasonable expectation so that people with under-powered Macs don't buy PageMaker and have an unpleasant experience. Like most other software companies, Adobe tends to err on the side of "A slow user is better than no user" or "Sell now — apologize later."

According to Adobe, the minimum system requirement for PageMaker 6 is:

- A 68030-equipped Mac with 10MB of RAM or a Power Macintosh with 12MB RAM
- 20MB to 40MB of free hard drive space
- System Software 7.1.x or later

A more realistic "recommended system" is:

- A 68040-based system, or, better yet, a Power Macintosh, with 24MB RAM
- 24-bit video capabilities
- A scanner
- A PostScript printer
- A CD-ROM drive

Living in the real world, we would call that configuration the "practical minimum" and recommend at least 70MHz Power Mac with 24MB of RAM, at least 100MB of free hard drive space, and System Software 7.5 or higher. The ideal system would include a Power Mac 9500 PCI with 32MB to 128MB RAM and a 1-gigabyte or larger hard drive.

The bottom line is that PageMaker appreciates horsepower as much or more than any other program you probably own, except for, perhaps, Photoshop. The measurable, real-world performance difference between PageMaker running on a 10MB Mac Centris 650 and PageMaker running on a 32MB 9500 PCI is several hundred percentage points. But we don't expect you to rush out and buy a new 9500 PCI system just because we recommend it. With that said, let's look at installing PageMaker.

Installing PageMaker

Before starting the actual installation of PageMaker 6, you need to decide what to do with your previous version of PageMaker. (If you do not have an older version of PageMaker on your hard drive, skip ahead to the next section; I'm not talking to you.)

You have two options: You can delete the old version of PageMaker (and all of its associated files) or you can move the old version (and all of its associated files) into one folder so that once you start using PageMaker 6, your Mac, you, or PageMaker 6 aren't confused by the older version's files.

 Maintaining Backward Compatibility: PageMaker 6 uses a new file format, so publications created in older versions must be converted to the new format before they can be edited or printed using PageMaker 6. This conversion automatically takes place when you open an older file in PageMaker 6, but it will change the files slightly, possibly altering the way words wrap or the exact position of graphic elements. In most cases, these changes are slight or unnoticeable, but they still require that you look over any converted publication before printing it.

As a result, many people choose to keep their older version of PageMaker around for a while so that minor changes to existing publications can be made quickly and easily without the time and effort of converting the files to the new format. There is no real reason not to keep your old copy of PageMaker around, except for the disk space it will continue to consume on your hard drive. If you want to keep PageMaker 5.0 around, you can do so without any special preparation. PageMaker 6.0 installs in a different manner from the previous version, keeping all supporting files and folders in the Adobe PageMaker 6.0 folder, rather than in the System Folder.

When you want to delete an old copy of PageMaker, drag the application and all of its associated files, including the Aldus (or Adobe, if you were using the Adobe version of PageMaker 5) folder, the PMx.x RSRC file, and Adobe Prep (these last two may be lying free in your System Folder), to the Trash. Then choose the Empty Trash command from the Special menu.

With your hardware in place and your old copy of PageMaker out of the way, you're ready to actually install PageMaker 6. Well, almost.

Before installing, it is a very good idea to restart your Macintosh with all extensions turned off. (Hold down the Shift key and choose Restart from the Special menu.) This turns off any virus-checking utilities, which is a good idea since Installer applications continually trip the alarms in virus checkers. PageMaker's Installer seems especially sensitive and has a better chance of success if all other extensions are temporarily out of the way.

Maintaining PageMaker 5 Custom Settings: If you made substantial customizations to PageMaker 5 defaults, you can transfer them to version 6 by copying the custom setting files in the Aldus folder in the System Folder to the RSRC folder in the Adobe PageMaker 6.0 folder. To simplify this task, use the PM5 Custom Settings utility that comes with PageMaker 6.

You might also want to defragment your hard drive before running the installer. This will improve the performance of your drive and prolong the drive's life. Defragmenting before a major installation will ensure that the program and all of its support files are written to your hard drive efficiently, thus getting you off to a good start with your new application. This is by no means mandatory, but worth the effort in most cases.

The last thing you should do before the actual installation is to verify that you have enough free space on the hard drive where you intend to install PageMaker and on the hard drive containing your System Folder. (If you have multiple hard drives, or hard drive partitions, these do not necessarily have to be the same drives.) PageMaker and its associated files will consume 15MB to 25MB at minimum and up to 40MB or over 50MB if you install all files and tutorials. In addition, the PostScript Printer 8.x driver and PPD files will need about another 1MB in your System Folder (they are placed inside the Extensions folder in System 7). The Installer will warn you of space deficiencies during the installation, but it is easier to make sure you have enough space before the process begins.

The PageMaker 6 Installation Program

PageMaker's installation is automated by the Adobe Installer/Utility program. This program copies the required files from the PageMaker disks or CD-ROM disc onto your hard drive, creating a new PageMaker folder. PageMaker must be installed from the floppy disks or CD-ROM using the installation program — it is impossible to copy the contents of the disks to your hard drive and then install the program.

Begin the installation by inserting Disk 1 into a disk drive or the Deluxe CD-ROM disc into your CD-ROM drive, and double-click the Adobe Installer/Utility application. Depending on the disc you use, you'll get one of two windows, as shown in Figure A-1. If you are using floppies, simply double-click the PageMaker 6 Installer/Utility icon. If you're using the CD-ROM, double-click the Adobe PageMaker 6.0 icon, then double-click the Install folder. Now you can double-click PageMaker 6 Installer/Utility. Whether you're using floppies or the CD-ROM disc, you are now in the PageMaker 6 Installer, shown in Figure A-2. From here, no matter what media you're using, installation is primarily the same. In addition to this installation information, you can get other valuable installation tips from the *Getting Started* booklet in the PageMaker package.

Figure A-1:
The folders that open when you
insert the PageMaker installation
disk 1 (top) and the CD-ROM
disc (bottom)

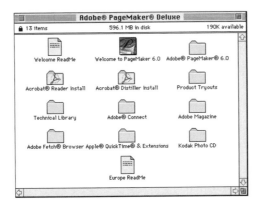

Figure A-2:
The PageMaker 6
Installer

From here you choose a language type. When you click the desired language, the
installer displays the Adobe Installer Main Window, which provides three installation
options, as shown in Figure A-3. Selecting either option displays a description of the
installation, what is installed, and how much hard disk space is required. The first two
options, Easy Install and Minimum Install, eliminate most of the choices from here on
out, installing the software automatically and stopping only occasionally to enable you
to choose a printer and filters. The third choice, Custom Install, changes the dialog box
to list all of the installation options, as shown in Figure A-4.

Installing PageMaker Components Later: During the installation process, you make several choices about what options to install. But don't worry, if you forget something or decide that you want to install something later, all you do is run the Installer again, making sure that you select only those options that you want to install.

Figure A-3:
The Adobe Installer Main
Window menu

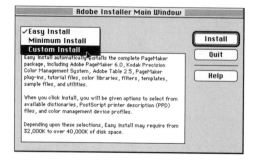

Figure A-4:
The Adobe Installer Main
Window menu in Custom
Install mode

From here, you pick and choose which options to install. The following is a description of each option:

- **Adobe PageMaker 6.0:** This option, of course, installs the PageMaker program. You'll need to install it to use PageMaker.

- **Adobe Table 2.5:** This is a utility that allows you to create tables for your PageMaker publications. It works okay, but if you use Excel or another spread-sheet, you'll get better tables.

- **Color Libraries:** These are the color libraries that are displayed in the Define Colors dialog box (discussed in Chapter 10), such as PANTONE, Focoltone, and so on. When you select this option, the installer will later give you a list of available color libraries from which you can choose.

- **Filters:** These are the import and export filters PageMaker uses to place and export your layouts, text and graphics. When you select this option, the installer will later give you a list of the available filters to choose from.

∞ **Kodak Precision CMS:** This is the color management system that ships with PageMaker (discussed in Chapter 10). When you select this option, the installer will later give you a list of available device profiles from which you can choose.

∞ **Plug-ins:** These are the PageMaker Plug-ins that ship with PageMaker (discussed in Chapter 11). When you select this option, the installer will later give you a list of available Plug-ins from which you can choose.

∞ **PostScript Printer Descriptions (PPDs):** PPDs are small files the Mac PostScript printer driver and PageMaker use to configure documents for your printer. When you select this option, the installer will later give you a list of available PPDs from which you can choose.

∞ **Templates & Scripts:** Templates are preformatted, professionally designed document shells into which you can import your own text and graphics to create publications. Scripts are automated tasks you can run to execute repetitive tasks in PageMaker. When you select this option, the installer will later give you a list of available templates and scripts from which you can choose.

∞ **Tutorial:** These are the files that correspond with the tutorial section of the PageMaker documentation. When you select this option, the installer will later give you a list of available files from which you can choose.

∞ **Utilities:** These are the many utilities that ship with PageMaker, such as KernEdit, Guides Maker, and several others.

After making your selections, click Install. The installer now displays a dialog box where you enter your name, company name, and serial number, as shown in Figure A-5. You must enter text in the Name field, and the Serial Number field must contain the serial number located on Disk 2 of the installation disks or on the bottom of the PageMaker box. Click OK and proceed to the next section.

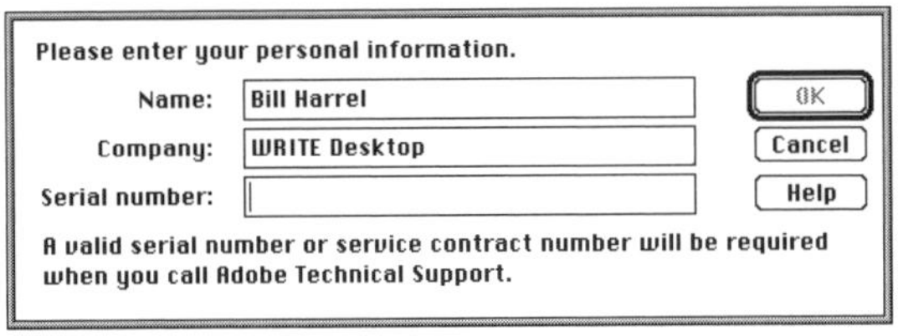

Figure A-5:
Enter your name, company, and serial number here.

Please enter your personal information.	
Name:	Bill Harrel
Company:	WRITE Desktop
Serial number:	

OK   Cancel   Help

A valid serial number or service contract number will be required when you call Adobe Technical Support.

Selecting Templates, PPDs, Plug-ins, and Filters

Depending on your installation options, you will now be asked to select the specific Plug-ins, templates, or PPD files that you want to install. Install only those files you think you will really need, since each will consume disk space and potentially slow down PageMaker's operation. On the other hand, each is relatively small and has only a small effect on performance, so don't hesitate to install any potentially useful files. If you are uncertain what you need, select and install all available files. To select more than one file, hold down Shift and click each filename you want in each dialog box before clicking the OK button to proceed.

Selecting a Location on Your Hard Drive

After personalizing your copy of PageMaker, the dialog box in which you designate the folder to install the program and files appears, as shown in Figure A-6. PageMaker uses this dialog to confirm that you have enough free space for the installation options you have selected. If adequate free space is not available, click the Cancel button to return to the Adobe Installer Main Window dialog box, and then select fewer installation options or quit and create more free space on your hard drive before trying the installation again.

Figure A-6:
Use this dialog box to choose a location for your PageMaker files.

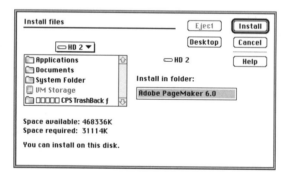

If enough free space is available, you may, if you wish, change the name of the folder into which PageMaker will be installed and the location on the drive where this folder will be placed. In most cases, you will probably not want to change the name of the Adobe PageMaker 6.0 folder, so there is no need to modify the "Install in folder" option. You should, however, use the scrolling window and drive button to select where you want the Adobe PageMaker 6.0 folder placed. When you have determined the location, click the Install button to continue.

The last thing the install program asks is where to put the PageMaker files. After you make this final selection, the installer prompts you for the floppies as needed to complete the installation (or installs the program directly from the one CD-ROM). When you restart the computer, PageMaker is ready to run.

Reinstalling PageMaker 6 _____

If the program is ever damaged or removed from your hard disk, you will need to reinstall it with the Adobe Installer/Utility, following the steps described previously for a first-time installation. Before reinstalling, delete the damaged program along with all of the other PageMaker 6 files, including those in the Adobe folder. Be careful not to delete any third-party Plug-ins or filters that were installed separately.

You can also use the Adobe Installer/Utility program to add or reinstall filters, PPDs, or Plug-ins without reinstalling PageMaker itself. To do this, either launch the Installer/Utility and then select the needed options (filters, PPDs, Plug-ins) or double-click any filter, PPD, or Addition from any original PageMaker disk. This will launch the install program and prompt you for a location for the selected file.

Adobe Type Manager (ATM)

This utility shouldn't be news to anyone working with PageMaker. ATM makes PostScript fonts look good on-screen by using the font outlines from printer-font files to clearly render screen fonts. ATM is vital in PageMaker because it allows you to use any font at any point size or in any type style and still have type that is clearly legible at any magnification. It also makes it easy to see fine detail of text placement and line endings and lets you see on-screen some (but clearly not all) of the effects of kerning and letter-spacing manipulations. Without ATM, a great many fonts are virtually illegible on-screen at many different view sizes.

In order to use ATM, you must load both the screen-font files and the printer-font files for all PostScript fonts. Keep the printer-font files in the same folder as the screen fonts — either in the Fonts folder in your System Folder or in the folder you use to store fonts accessed via Suitcase II or MasterJuggler.

ATM is located on the Type on Call CD-ROM disc that came with your PageMaker package.

What's on the CD?

Adobe ships a bunch of stuff with PageMaker, including about 150 fonts and some interesting backgrounds and clip art. So we thought long and hard about what to include on the CD-ROM. We didn't want to duplicate what Adobe provides, nor did we want to give you the same old stuff you got on the disc with another book. This appendix describes what we came up with — a lot of neat photos, Plug-ins, and graphics utilities to add productivity to your PageMaker sessions.

The Tutorial Chapter Files Folder __

In the last section of this book, there are three chapters that walk you through designing three PageMaker documents — a two-sided mailer (flyer), a newsletter, and four-page, process-color catalog. On the CD, there is a folder called "Tutorial Chapter Files." Inside this folder are three folders that correspond to the book chapters:

- The "Chapter 15" folder contains the two-sided flyer files.
- The "Chapter 16" folder contains the newsletter files.
- The "Chapter 17" folder contains the four-page catalog files.

Using the Tutorial Chapter Files

You can use the tutorial files directly from the CD or by copying them to your hard disk. When using files from the CD, simply access the folder as directed in the chapter text. To copy the folders to your hard disk, simply drag them from the CD to the desired folder in Finder. Finder will give you a message that the disc is locked and ask if you want to copy, rather than move, the files. Click Yes (or OK). Then use the files as directed in the chapter text.

The Plug-ins Folders

There are two types of Plug-ins on the CD: PageMaker Plug-ins and Photoshop Plug-ins. Both are located in separate folders, one for PageMaker and one for Photoshop. PageMaker Plug-ins can be used only with PageMaker. You can, however, use the Photoshop Plug-ins with either PageMaker (choose Element/Image/Photoshop Effects) or with Photoshop.

Installing the Plug-ins

To install either PageMaker Plug-ins or Photoshop Plug-ins for use with PageMaker, simply drag the icons from the CD to the Plug-ins folder inside the RSRC folder inside the Adobe PageMaker 6 folder. To use the Photoshop Plug-ins with both Photoshop and PageMaker, follow this procedure:

1. Drag the Photoshop Plug-in to the Plug-ins folder in your Photoshop folder.

2. Use Make Alias on the File menu to copy the Plug-in icon.

3. Drag the alias to the Plug-ins folder inside the RSRC folder inside the Adobe PageMaker 6 folder.

The Graphics Utilities Folder _____

This folder contains demos from various graphics software vendors. Each demo has its own Read-me file telling you how to run the demo and view the sample files.

The Stock Photography Folder _____

This folder contains samples of stock photography from various vendors. Inside this folder is a separate folder for each vendor. You can use these sample files in your layouts, and you can order other collections from the vendors. To use the photo samples, simply import them into your layout with PageMaker's Place command or, for faster access, drag them to your hard disk first.

Index

• **H** •

• **I** •

(continued)

The Fun & Easy Way™ to learn about computers and more!

Windows® 3.11 For Dummies,® 3rd Edition
by Andy Rathbone

ISBN: 1-56884-370-4
$16.95 USA/
$22.95 Canada

Mutual Funds For Dummies™
by Eric Tyson

ISBN: 1-56884-226-0
$16.99 USA/
$22.99 Canada

DOS For Dummies,® 2nd Edition
by Dan Gookin

ISBN: 1-878058-75-4
$16.95 USA/
$22.95 Canada

The Internet For Dummies,® 2nd Edition
by John Levine & Carol Baroudi

ISBN: 1-56884-222-8
$19.99 USA/
$26.99 Canada

Personal Finance For Dummies™
by Eric Tyson

ISBN: 1-56884-150-7
$16.95 USA/
$22.95 Canada

PCs For Dummies,® 3rd Edition
by Dan Gookin & Andy Rathbone

ISBN: 1-56884-904-4
$16.99 USA/
$22.99 Canada

Macs® For Dummies,® 3rd Edition
by David Pogue

ISBN: 1-56884-239-2
$19.99 USA/
$26.99 Canada

The SAT® I For Dummies™
by Suzee Vlk

ISBN: 1-56884-213-9
$14.99 USA/
$20.99 Canada

Here's a complete listing of IDG Books' ...For Dummies® titles

Title	Author	ISBN	Price
DATABASE			
Access 2 For Dummies®	by Scott Palmer	ISBN: 1-56884-090-X	$19.95 USA/$26.95 Canada
Access Programming For Dummies®	by Rob Krumm	ISBN: 1-56884-091-8	$19.95 USA/$26.95 Canada
Approach 3 For Windows® For Dummies®	by Doug Lowe	ISBN: 1-56884-233-3	$19.99 USA/$26.99 Canada
dBASE For DOS For Dummies®	by Scott Palmer & Michael Stabler	ISBN: 1-56884-188-4	$19.95 USA/$26.95 Canada
dBASE For Windows® For Dummies®	by Scott Palmer	ISBN: 1-56884-179-5	$19.95 USA/$26.95 Canada
dBASE 5 For Windows® Programming For Dummies®	by Ted Coombs & Jason Coombs	ISBN: 1-56884-215-5	$19.99 USA/$26.99 Canada
FoxPro 2.6 For Windows® For Dummies®	by John Kaufeld	ISBN: 1-56884-187-6	$19.95 USA/$26.95 Canada
Paradox 5 For Windows® For Dummies®	by John Kaufeld	ISBN: 1-56884-185-X	$19.95 USA/$26.95 Canada
DESKTOP PUBLISHING/ILLUSTRATION/GRAPHICS			
CorelDRAW! 5 For Dummies®	by Deke McClelland	ISBN: 1-56884-157-4	$19.95 USA/$26.95 Canada
CorelDRAW! For Dummies®	by Deke McClelland	ISBN: 1-56884-042-X	$19.95 USA/$26.95 Canada
Desktop Publishing & Design For Dummies®	by Roger C. Parker	ISBN: 1-56884-234-1	$19.99 USA/$26.99 Canada
Harvard Graphics 2 For Windows® For Dummies®	by Roger C. Parker	ISBN: 1-56884-092-6	$19.95 USA/$26.95 Canada
PageMaker 5 For Macs® For Dummies®	by Galen Gruman & Deke McClelland	ISBN: 1-56884-178-7	$19.95 USA/$26.95 Canada
PageMaker 5 For Windows® For Dummies®	by Deke McClelland & Galen Gruman	ISBN: 1-56884-160-4	$19.95 USA/$26.95 Canada
Photoshop 3 For Macs® For Dummies®	by Deke McClelland	ISBN: 1-56884-208-2	$19.99 USA/$26.99 Canada
QuarkXPress 3.3 For Dummies®	by Galen Gruman & Barbara Assadi	ISBN: 1-56884-217-1	$19.99 USA/$26.99 Canada
FINANCE/PERSONAL FINANCE/TEST TAKING REFERENCE			
Everyday Math For Dummies™	by Charles Seiter	ISBN: 1-56884-248-1	$14.99 USA/$22.99 Canada
Personal Finance For Dummies™ For Canadians	by Eric Tyson & Tony Martin	ISBN: 1-56884-378-X	$18.99 USA/$24.99 Canada
QuickBooks 3 For Dummies®	by Stephen L. Nelson	ISBN: 1-56884-227-9	$19.99 USA/$26.99 Canada
Quicken 8 For DOS For Dummies,® 2nd Edition	by Stephen L. Nelson	ISBN: 1-56884-210-4	$19.95 USA/$26.95 Canada
Quicken 5 For Macs® For Dummies®	by Stephen L. Nelson	ISBN: 1-56884-211-2	$19.95 USA/$26.95 Canada
Quicken 4 For Windows® For Dummies,® 2nd Edition	by Stephen L. Nelson	ISBN: 1-56884-209-0	$19.95 USA/$26.95 Canada
Taxes For Dummies,™ 1995 Edition	by Eric Tyson & David J. Silverman	ISBN: 1-56884-220-1	$14.99 USA/$20.99 Canada
The GMAT® For Dummies™	by Suzee Vlk, Series Editor	ISBN: 1-56884-376-3	$14.99 USA/$20.99 Canada
The GRE® For Dummies™	by Suzee Vlk, Series Editor	ISBN: 1-56884-375-5	$14.99 USA/$20.99 Canada
Time Management For Dummies™	by Jeffrey J. Mayer	ISBN: 1-56884-360-7	$16.99 USA/$22.99 Canada
TurboTax For Windows® For Dummies®	by Gail A. Helsel, CPA	ISBN: 1-56884-228-7	$19.99 USA/$26.99 Canada
GROUPWARE/INTEGRATED			
ClarisWorks For Macs® For Dummies®	by Frank Higgins	ISBN: 1-56884-363-1	$19.99 USA/$26.99 Canada
Lotus Notes For Dummies®	by Pat Freeland & Stephen Londergan	ISBN: 1-56884-212-0	$19.95 USA/$26.95 Canada
Microsoft® Office 4 For Windows® For Dummies®	by Roger C. Parker	ISBN: 1-56884-183-3	$19.95 USA/$26.95 Canada
Microsoft® Works 3 For Windows® For Dummies®	by David C. Kay	ISBN: 1-56884-214-7	$19.99 USA/$26.99 Canada
SmartSuite 3 For Dummies®	by Jan Weingarten & John Weingarten	ISBN: 1-56884-367-4	$19.99 USA/$26.99 Canada
INTERNET/COMMUNICATIONS/NETWORKING			
America Online® For Dummies,® 2nd Edition	by John Kaufeld	ISBN: 1-56884-933-8	$19.99 USA/$26.99 Canada
CompuServe For Dummies,® 2nd Edition	by Wallace Wang	ISBN: 1-56884-937-0	$19.99 USA/$26.99 Canada
Modems For Dummies,® 2nd Edition	by Tina Rathbone	ISBN: 1-56884-223-6	$19.99 USA/$26.99 Canada
MORE Internet For Dummies®	by John R. Levine & Margaret Levine Young	ISBN: 1-56884-164-7	$19.95 USA/$26.95 Canada
MORE Modems & On-line Services For Dummies®	by Tina Rathbone	ISBN: 1-56884-365-8	$19.99 USA/$26.99 Canada
Mosaic For Dummies,® Windows Edition	by David Angell & Brent Heslop	ISBN: 1-56884-242-2	$19.99 USA/$26.99 Canada
NetWare For Dummies,® 2nd Edition	by Ed Tittel, Deni Connor & Earl Follis	ISBN: 1-56884-369-0	$19.99 USA/$26.99 Canada
Networking For Dummies®	by Doug Lowe	ISBN: 1-56884-079-9	$19.95 USA/$26.95 Canada
PROCOMM PLUS 2 For Windows® For Dummies®	by Wallace Wang	ISBN: 1-56884-219-8	$19.99 USA/$26.99 Canada
TCP/IP For Dummies®	by Marshall Wilensky & Candace Leiden	ISBN: 1-56884-241-4	$19.99 USA/$26.99 Canada

For scholastic requests & educational orders please ll Educational Sales at 1. 800. 434. 2086

FOR MORE INFO OR TO ORDER, PLEASE CALL ▶ **800. 762. 2974**

For volume discounts & special orders please call Tony Real, Special Sales, at 415. 655. 3048

The Internet For Macs® For Dummies® 2nd Edition	by Charles Seiter	ISBN: 1-56884-371-2	$19.99 USA/$26.99 Canada
The Internet For Macs® For Dummies® Starter Kit	by Charles Seiter	ISBN: 1-56884-244-9	$29.99 USA/$39.99 Canada
The Internet For Macs® For Dummies® Starter Kit Bestseller Edition	by Charles Seiter	ISBN: 1-56884-245-7	$39.99 USA/$54.99 Canada
The Internet For Windows® For Dummies® Starter Kit	by John R. Levine & Margaret Levine Young	ISBN: 1-56884-237-6	$34.99 USA/$44.99 Canada
The Internet For Windows® For Dummies® Starter Kit, Bestseller Edition	by John R. Levine & Margaret Levine Young	ISBN: 1-56884-246-5	$39.99 USA/$54.99 Canada

MACINTOSH

Mac® Programming For Dummies®	by Dan Parks Sydow	ISBN: 1-56884-173-6	$19.95 USA/$26.95 Canada
Macintosh® System 7.5 For Dummies®	by Bob LeVitus	ISBN: 1-56884-197-3	$19.95 USA/$26.95 Canada
MORE Macs® For Dummies®	by David Pogue	ISBN: 1-56884-087-X	$19.95 USA/$26.95 Canada
PageMaker 5 For Macs® For Dummies®	by Galen Gruman & Deke McClelland	ISBN: 1-56884-178-7	$19.95 USA/$26.95 Canada
QuarkXPress 3.3 For Dummies®	by Galen Gruman & Barbara Assadi	ISBN: 1-56884-217-1	$19.99 USA/$26.99 Canada
Upgrading and Fixing Macs® For Dummies®	by Kearney Rietmann & Frank Higgins	ISBN: 1-56884-189-2	$19.95 USA/$26.95 Canada

MULTIMEDIA

Multimedia & CD-ROMs For Dummies® 2nd Edition	by Andy Rathbone	ISBN: 1-56884-907-9	$19.99 USA/$26.99 Canada
Multimedia & CD-ROMs For Dummies® Interactive Multimedia Value Pack, 2nd Edition	by Andy Rathbone	ISBN: 1-56884-909-5	$29.99 USA/$39.99 Canada

OPERATING SYSTEMS:

DOS

MORE DOS For Dummies®	by Dan Gookin	ISBN: 1-56884-046-2	$19.95 USA/$26.95 Canada
OS/2® Warp For Dummies® 2nd Edition	by Andy Rathbone	ISBN: 1-56884-205-8	$19.99 USA/$26.99 Canada

UNIX

MORE UNIX® For Dummies®	by John R. Levine & Margaret Levine Young	ISBN: 1-56884-361-5	$19.99 USA/$26.99 Canada
UNIX® For Dummies®	by John R. Levine & Margaret Levine Young	ISBN: 1-878058-58-4	$19.95 USA/$26.95 Canada

WINDOWS

MORE Windows® For Dummies® 2nd Edition	by Andy Rathbone	ISBN: 1-56884-048-9	$19.95 USA/$26.95 Canada
Windows® 95 For Dummies®	by Andy Rathbone	ISBN: 1-56884-240-6	$19.99 USA/$26.99 Canada

PCS/HARDWARE

Illustrated Computer Dictionary For Dummies® 2nd Edition	by Dan Gookin & Wallace Wang	ISBN: 1-56884-218-X	$12.95 USA/$16.95 Canada
Upgrading and Fixing PCs For Dummies® 2nd Edition	by Andy Rathbone	ISBN: 1-56884-903-6	$19.99 USA/$26.99 Canada

PRESENTATION/AUTOCAD

AutoCAD For Dummies®	by Bud Smith	ISBN: 1-56884-191-4	$19.95 USA/$26.95 Canada
PowerPoint 4 For Windows® For Dummies®	by Doug Lowe	ISBN: 1-56884-161-2	$16.99 USA/$22.99 Canada

PROGRAMMING

Borland C++ For Dummies®	by Michael Hyman	ISBN: 1-56884-162-0	$19.95 USA/$26.95 Canada
C For Dummies® Volume 1	by Dan Gookin	ISBN: 1-878058-78-9	$19.95 USA/$26.95 Canada
C++ For Dummies®	by Stephen R. Davis	ISBN: 1-56884-163-9	$19.95 USA/$26.95 Canada
Delphi Programming For Dummies®	by Neil Rubenking	ISBN: 1-56884-200-7	$19.99 USA/$26.99 Canada
Mac® Programming For Dummies®	by Dan Parks Sydow	ISBN: 1-56884-173-6	$19.95 USA/$26.95 Canada
PowerBuilder 4 Programming For Dummies®	by Ted Coombs & Jason Coombs	ISBN: 1-56884-325-9	$19.99 USA/$26.99 Canada
QBasic Programming For Dummies®	by Douglas Hergert	ISBN: 1-56884-093-4	$19.95 USA/$26.95 Canada
Visual Basic 3 For Dummies®	by Wallace Wang	ISBN: 1-56884-076-4	$19.95 USA/$26.95 Canada
Visual Basic "X" For Dummies®	by Wallace Wang	ISBN: 1-56884-230-9	$19.99 USA/$26.99 Canada
Visual C++ 2 For Dummies®	by Michael Hyman & Bob Arnson	ISBN: 1-56884-328-3	$19.99 USA/$26.99 Canada
Windows® 95 Programming For Dummies®	by S. Randy Davis	ISBN: 1-56884-327-5	$19.99 USA/$26.99 Canada

SPREADSHEET

1-2-3 For Dummies®	by Greg Harvey	ISBN: 1-878058-60-6	$16.95 USA/$22.95 Canada
1-2-3 For Windows® 5 For Dummies® 2nd Edition	by John Walkenbach	ISBN: 1-56884-216-3	$16.95 USA/$22.95 Canada
Excel 5 For Macs® For Dummies®	by Greg Harvey	ISBN: 1-56884-186-8	$19.95 USA/$26.95 Canada
Excel For Dummies® 2nd Edition	by Greg Harvey	ISBN: 1-56884-050-0	$16.95 USA/$22.95 Canada
MORE 1-2-3 For DOS For Dummies®	by John Weingarten	ISBN: 1-56884-224-4	$19.99 USA/$26.99 Canada
MORE Excel 5 For Windows® For Dummies®	by Greg Harvey	ISBN: 1-56884-207-4	$19.95 USA/$26.95 Canada
Quattro Pro 6 For Windows® For Dummies®	by John Walkenbach	ISBN: 1-56884-174-4	$19.95 USA/$26.95 Canada
Quattro Pro For DOS For Dummies®	by John Walkenbach	ISBN: 1-56884-023-3	$16.95 USA/$22.95 Canada

UTILITIES

Norton Utilities 8 For Dummies®	by Beth Slick	ISBN: 1-56884-166-3	$19.95 USA/$26.95 Canada

VCRS/CAMCORDERS

VCRs & Camcorders For Dummies™	by Gordon McComb & Andy Rathbone	ISBN: 1-56884-229-5	$14.99 USA/$20.99 Canada

WORD PROCESSING

Ami Pro For Dummies®	by Jim Meade	ISBN: 1-56884-049-7	$19.95 USA/$26.95 Canada
MORE Word For Windows® 6 For Dummies®	by Doug Lowe	ISBN: 1-56884-165-5	$19.95 USA/$26.95 Canada
MORE WordPerfect® 6 For Windows® For Dummies®	by Margaret Levine Young & David C. Kay	ISBN: 1-56884-206-6	$19.95 USA/$26.95 Canada
MORE WordPerfect® 6 For DOS For Dummies®	by Wallace Wang, edited by Dan Gookin	ISBN: 1-56884-047-0	$19.95 USA/$26.95 Canada
Word 6 For Macs® For Dummies®	by Dan Gookin	ISBN: 1-56884-190-6	$19.95 USA/$26.95 Canada
Word For Windows® 6 For Dummies®	by Dan Gookin	ISBN: 1-56884-075-6	$16.95 USA/$22.95 Canada
Word For Windows® For Dummies®	by Dan Gookin & Ray Werner	ISBN: 1-878058-86-X	$16.95 USA/$22.95 Canada
WordPerfect® 6 For DOS For Dummies®	by Dan Gookin	ISBN: 1-878058-77-0	$16.95 USA/$22.95 Canada
WordPerfect® 6.1 For Windows® For Dummies® 2nd Edition	by Margaret Levine Young & David Kay	ISBN: 1-56884-243-0	$16.95 USA/$22.95 Canada
WordPerfect® For Dummies®	by Dan Gookin	ISBN: 1-878058-52-5	$16.95 USA/$22.95 Canada

Fun, Fast, & Cheap!™

The Internet For Macs® For Dummies® Quick Reference
by Charles Seiter

ISBN:1-56884-967-2
$9.99 USA/$12.99 Canada

Windows® 95 For Dummies® Quick Reference
by Greg Harvey

ISBN: 1-56884-964-8
$9.99 USA/$12.99 Canada

Photoshop 3 For Macs® For Dummies® Quick Reference
by Deke McClelland

ISBN: 1-56884-968-0
$9.99 USA/$12.99 Canada

WordPerfect® For DOS For Dummies® Quick Reference
by Greg Harvey

ISBN: 1-56884-009-8
$8.95 USA/$12.95 Canada

Title	Author	ISBN	Price
DATABASE			
Access 2 For Dummies® Quick Reference	by Stuart J. Stuple	ISBN: 1-56884-167-1	$8.95 USA/$11.95 Canada
dBASE 5 For DOS For Dummies® Quick Reference	by Barrie Sosinsky	ISBN: 1-56884-954-0	$9.99 USA/$12.99 Canada
dBASE 5 For Windows® For Dummies® Quick Reference	by Stuart J. Stuple	ISBN: 1-56884-953-2	$9.99 USA/$12.99 Canada
Paradox 5 For Windows® For Dummies® Quick Reference	by Scott Palmer	ISBN: 1-56884-960-5	$9.99 USA/$12.99 Canada
DESKTOP PUBLISHING/ILLUSTRATION/GRAPHICS			
CorelDRAW! 5 For Dummies® Quick Reference	by Raymond E. Werner	ISBN: 1-56884-952-4	$9.99 USA/$12.99 Canada
Harvard Graphics For Windows® For Dummies® Quick Reference	by Raymond E. Werner	ISBN: 1-56884-962-1	$9.99 USA/$12.99 Canada
Photoshop 3 For Macs® For Dummies® Quick Reference	by Deke McClelland	ISBN: 1-56884-968-0	$9.99 USA/$12.99 Canada
FINANCE/PERSONAL FINANCE			
Quicken 4 For Windows® For Dummies® Quick Reference	by Stephen L. Nelson	ISBN: 1-56884-950-8	$9.95 USA/$12.95 Canada
GROUPWARE/INTEGRATED			
Microsoft® Office 4 For Windows® For Dummies® Quick Reference	by Doug Lowe	ISBN: 1-56884-958-3	$9.99 USA/$12.99 Canada
Microsoft® Works 3 For Windows® For Dummies® Quick Reference	by Michael Partington	ISBN: 1-56884-959-1	$9.99 USA/$12.99 Canada
INTERNET/COMMUNICATIONS/NETWORKING			
The Internet For Dummies® Quick Reference	by John R. Levine & Margaret Levine Young	ISBN: 1-56884-168-X	$8.95 USA/$11.95 Canada
MACINTOSH			
Macintosh® System 7.5 For Dummies® Quick Reference	by Stuart J. Stuple	ISBN: 1-56884-956-7	$9.99 USA/$12.99 Canada
OPERATING SYSTEMS:			
DOS			
DOS For Dummies® Quick Reference	by Greg Harvey	ISBN: 1-56884-007-1	$8.95 USA/$11.95 Canada
UNIX			
UNIX® For Dummies® Quick Reference	by John R. Levine & Margaret Levine Young	ISBN: 1-56884-094-2	$8.95 USA/$11.95 Canada
WINDOWS			
Windows® 3.1 For Dummies® Quick Reference, 2nd Edition	by Greg Harvey	ISBN: 1-56884-951-6	$8.95 USA/$11.95 Canada
PCs/HARDWARE			
Memory Management For Dummies® Quick Reference	by Doug Lowe	ISBN: 1-56884-362-3	$9.99 USA/$12.99 Canada
PRESENTATION/AUTOCAD			
AutoCAD For Dummies® Quick Reference	by Ellen Finkelstein	ISBN: 1-56884-198-1	$9.95 USA/$12.95 Canada
SPREADSHEET			
1-2-3 For Dummies® Quick Reference	by John Walkenbach	ISBN: 1-56884-027-6	$8.95 USA/$11.95 Canada
1-2-3 For Windows® 5 For Dummies® Quick Reference	by John Walkenbach	ISBN: 1-56884-957-5	$9.95 USA/$12.95 Canada
Excel For Windows® For Dummies® Quick Reference, 2nd Edition	by John Walkenbach	ISBN: 1-56884-096-9	$8.95 USA/$11.95 Canada
Quattro Pro 6 For Windows® For Dummies® Quick Reference	by Stuart J. Stuple	ISBN: 1-56884-172-8	$9.95 USA/$12.95 Canada
WORD PROCESSING			
Word For Windows® 6 For Dummies® Quick Reference	by George Lynch	ISBN: 1-56884-095-0	$8.95 USA/$11.95 Canada
Word For Windows® For Dummies® Quick Reference	by George Lynch	ISBN: 1-56884-029-2	$8.95 USA/$11.95 Canada
WordPerfect® 6.1 For Windows® For Dummies® Quick Reference, 2nd Edition	by Greg Harvey	ISBN: 1-56884-966-4	$9.99 USA/$12.99/Canada

"A lot easier to use than the book Excel gives you!"

Lisa Schmeckpeper, New Berlin, WI, on PC World Excel 5 For Windows Handbook

Official Hayes Modem Communications Companion
by Caroline M. Halliday
ISBN: 1-56884-072-1
$29.95 USA/$39.95 Canada
Includes software.

1,001 Komputer Answers from Kim Komando
by Kim Komando
ISBN: 1-56884-460-3
$29.99 USA/$39.99 Canada
Includes software.

PC World DOS 6 Handbook, 2nd Edition
by John Socha, Clint Hicks, & Devra Hall
ISBN: 1-878058-79-7
$34.95 USA/$44.95 Canada
Includes software.

PC World Word For Windows® 6 Handbook
by Brent Heslop & David Angell
ISBN: 1-56884-054-3
$34.95 USA/$44.95 Canada
Includes software.

PC World Microsoft® Access 2 Bible, 2nd Edition
by Cary N. Prague & Michael R. Irwin
ISBN: 1-56884-086-1
$39.95 USA/$52.95 Canada
Includes software.

PC World Excel 5 For Windows® Handbook, 2nd Edition
by John Walkenbach & Dave Maguiness
ISBN: 1-56884-056-X
$34.95 USA/$44.95 Canada
Includes software.

PC World WordPerfect® 6 Handbook
by Greg Harvey
ISBN: 1-878058-80-0
$34.95 USA/$44.95 Canada
Includes software.

QuarkXPress For Windows® Designer Handbook
by Barbara Assadi & Galen Gruman
ISBN: 1-878058-45-2
$29.95 USA/$39.95 Canada

Official XTree Companion, 3rd Edition
by Beth Slick
ISBN: 1-878058-57-6
$19.95 USA/$26.95 Canada

PC World DOS 6 Command Reference and Problem Solver
by John Socha & Devra Hall
ISBN: 1-56884-055-1
$24.95 USA/$32.95 Canada

Client/Server Strategies™: A Survival Guide for Corporate Reengineers
by David Vaskevitch
ISBN: 1-56884-064-0
$29.95 USA/$39.95 Canada

"*PC World Word For Windows 6 Handbook* is very easy to follow with lots of 'hands on' examples. The 'Task at a Glance' is very helpful!"

Jacqueline Martens, Tacoma, WA

"Thanks for publishing this book! It's the best money I've spent this year!"

Robert D. Templeton, Ft. Worth, TX, on MORE Windows 3.1 SECRETS

For scholastic requests & educational orders please call Educational Sales, at 1. 800. 434. 2086

FOR MORE INFO OR TO ORDER, PLEASE CALL ▶ 800 762 2974

For volume discounts & special orders please call Tony Real, Special Sales, at 415. 655. 3048

Unauthorized Windows® 95: A Developer's Guide to Exploring the Foundations of Windows "Chicago"
by Andrew Schulman

ISBN: 1-56884-169-8
$29.99 USA/$39.99 Canada

Unauthorized Windows® 95 Developer's Resource Kit
by Andrew Schulman

ISBN: 1-56884-305-4
$39.99 USA/$54.99 Canada

Best of the Net
by Seth Godin

ISBN: 1-56884-313-5
$22.99 USA/$32.99 Canada

Detour: The Truth About the Information Superhighway
by Michael Sullivan-Trainor

ISBN: 1-56884-307-0
$22.99 USA/$32.99 Canada

PowerPC Programming For Intel Programmers
by Kip McClanahan

ISBN: 1-56884-306-2
$49.99 USA/$64.99 Canada

Foundations™ of Visual C++ Programming For Windows® 95
by Paul Yao & Joseph Yao

ISBN: 1-56884-321-6
$39.99 USA/$54.99 Canada

Heavy Metal™ Visual C++ Programming
by Steve Holzner

ISBN: 1-56884-196-5
$39.95 USA/$54.95 Canada

Heavy Metal™ OLE 2.0 Programming
by Steve Holzner

ISBN: 1-56884-301-1
$39.95 USA/$54.95 Canada

Lotus Notes Application Development Handbook
by Erica Kerwien

ISBN: 1-56884-308-9
$39.99 USA/$54.99 Canada

The Internet Direct Connect Kit
by Peter John Harrison

ISBN: 1-56884-135-3
$29.95 USA/$39.95 Canada

Macworld® Ultimate Mac® Programming
by Dave Mark

ISBN: 1-56884-195-7
$39.95 USA/$54.95 Canada

The UNIX®-Haters Handbook
by Simson Garfinkel, Daniel Weise, & Steven Strassmann

ISBN: 1-56884-203-1
$16.95 USA/$22.95 Canada

Learn C++ Today!
by Martin Rinehart

ISBN: 1-56884-310-0
34.99 USA/$44.99 Canada

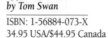

Type & Learn™ C
by Tom Swan

ISBN: 1-56884-073-X
34.95 USA/$44.95 Canada

Type & Learn™ Windows® Programming
by Tom Swan

ISBN: 1-56884-071-3
34.95 USA/$44.95 Canada

For scholastic requests & educational orders please call Educational Sales, at 1. 800. 434. 2086

FOR MORE INFO OR TO ORDER, PLEASE CALL ▶ 800. 762. 2974

For volume discounts & special orders please Tony Real, Special Sales, at 415. 655. 3048

COMPUTER
BOOK SERIES
FROM IDG

For Dummies
who want
to program...

Delphi Programming
For Dummies®
by Neil Rubenking

ISBN: 1-56884-200-7
$19.99 USA/$26.99 Canada

Access Programming
For Dummies®
by Rob Krumm

ISBN: 1-56884-091-8
$19.95 USA/$26.95 Canada

TCP/IP For Dummies®
by Marshall Wilensky &
Candace Leiden

ISBN: 1-56884-241-4
$19.99 USA/$26.99 Canada

HTML For Dummies®
by Ed Tittel & Carl de Cordova

ISBN: 1-56884-330-5
$29.99 USA/$39.99 Canada

Windows® 95 Programming
For Dummies®
by S. Randy Davis

ISBN: 1-56884-327-5
$19.99 USA/$26.99 Canada

Mac® Programming
For Dummies®
by Dan Parks Sydow

ISBN: 1-56884-173-6
$19.95 USA/$26.95 Canada

PowerBuilder 4 Programming
For Dummies®
by Ted Coombs & Jason Coombs

ISBN: 1-56884-325-9
$19.99 USA/$26.99 Canada

Visual Basic 3 For Dummies®
by Wallace Wang

ISBN: 1-56884-076-4
$19.95 USA/$26.95 Canada

Covers version 3.

ISDN For Dummies®
by David Angell

ISBN: 1-56884-331-3
$19.95 USA/$26.99 Canada

Visual C++ "2" For Dummies®
by Michael Hyman &
Bob Arnson

ISBN: 1-56884-328-3
$19.99 USA/$26.99 Canada

Borland C++ For Dummies®
by Michael Hyman

ISBN: 1-56884-162-0
$19.95 USA/$26.95 Canada

C For Dummies,® Volume I
by Dan Gookin

ISBN: 1-878058-78-9
$19.95 USA/$26.95 Canada

C++ For Dummies®
by Stephen R. Davis

ISBN: 1-56884-163-9
$19.95 USA/$26.95 Canada

QBasic Programming
For Dummies®
by Douglas Hergert

ISBN: 1-56884-093-4
$19.95 USA/$26.95 Canada

dBase 5 For Windows®
Programming For Dummies®
by Ted Coombs & Jason Coombs

ISBN: 1-56884-215-5
$19.99 USA/$26.99 Canada

For scholastic requests & educational orders please
call Educational Sales, at 1. 800. 434. 2086

FOR MORE INFO OR TO ORDER, PLEASE CALL ▶ 800. 762. 2974

For volume discounts & special orders please call
Tony Real, Special Sales, at 415. 655. 3048

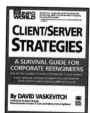

Order Center: **(800) 762-2974** *(8 a.m.–6 p.m., EST, weekdays)*

Quantity	ISBN	Title	Price	Total

Shipping & Handling Charges

	Description	First book	Each additional book	Total
Domestic	Normal	$4.50	$1.50	$
	Two Day Air	$8.50	$2.50	$
	Overnight	$18.00	$3.00	$
International	Surface	$8.00	$8.00	$
	Airmail	$16.00	$16.00	$
	DHL Air	$17.00	$17.00	$

*For large quantities call for shipping & handling charges.
**Prices are subject to change without notice.

Ship to:

Name _____

Company _____

Address _____

City/State/Zip _____

Daytime Phone _____

Payment: ☐ Check to IDG Books Worldwide (US Funds Only)

☐ VISA   ☐ MasterCard   ☐ American Express

Card # _____ Expires _____

Signature _____

Subtotal _____

CA residents add
applicable sales tax _____

IN, MA, and MD
residents add
5% sales tax _____

IL residents add
6.25% sales tax_____

RI residents add
7% sales tax_____

TX residents add
8.25% sales tax_____

Shipping_____

Total _____

Please send this order form to:

IDG Books Worldwide, Inc.
7260 Shadeland Station, Suite 100
Indianapolis, IN 46256

Allow up to 3 weeks for delivery.
Thank you!

IDG BOOKS WORLDWIDE LICENSE AGREEMENT

Important — read carefully before opening the software packet(s). This is a legal agreement between you (either an individual or an entity) and IDG Books Worldwide, Inc. (IDG). By opening the accompanying sealed packet containing the software disk(s), you acknowledge that you have read and accept the following IDG License Agreement. If you do not agree and do not want to be bound by the terms of this Agreement, promptly return the book and the unopened software packet(s) to the place you obtained them for a full refund.

1. License. This License Agreement (Agreement) permits you to use one copy of the enclosed Software program(s) on a single computer. The Software is in "use" on a computer when it is loaded into temporary memory (i.e., RAM) or installed into permanent memory (e.g., hard disk, CD-ROM, or other storage device) of that computer.

2. Copyright. The entire contents of the disk(s) and the compilation of the Software are copyrighted and protected by both United States copyright laws and international treaty provisions. You may only (a) make one copy of the Software for backup or archival purposes, or (b) transfer the Software to a single hard disk, provided that you keep the original for backup or archival purposes. The individual programs on the disk(s) are copyrighted by the authors of each program respectively. Each program has its own use permissions and limitations. To use each program, you must follow the individual requirements and restrictions detailed for each in Appendix B of this Book. Do not use a program if you do not want to follow its Licensing Agreement. None of the material on the disk(s) or listed in this Book may ever be distributed, in original or modified form, for commercial purposes.

3. Other Restrictions. You may not rent or lease the Software. You may transfer the Software and user documentation on a permanent basis provided you retain no copies and the recipient agrees to the terms of this Agreement. You may not reverse engineer, decompile, or disassemble the Software except to the extent that the foregoing restriction is expressly prohibited by applicable law. If the Software is an update or has been updated, any transfer must include the most recent update and all prior versions.

4. Limited Warranty. IDG warrants that the Software and disk(s) are free from defects in materials and workmanship for a period of sixty (60) days from the date of purchase of this Book. If IDG receives notification within the warranty period of defects in material or workmanship, IDG will replace the defective disk(s). IDG's entire liability and your exclusive remedy shall be limited to replacement of the Software, which is returned to IDG with a copy of your receipt. This Limited Warranty is void if failure of the Software has resulted from accident, abuse, or misapplication. Any replacement Software will be warranted for the remainder of the original warranty period or thirty (30) days, whichever is longer.

5. No Other Warranties. To the maximum extent permitted by applicable law, IDG and the author disclaim all other warranties, express or implied, including but not limited to implied warranties of merchantability and fitness for a particular purpose, with respect to the Software, the programs, the source code contained therein, and/or the techniques described in this Book. This limited warranty gives you specific legal rights. You may have others which vary from state/jurisdiction to state/jurisdiction.

6. No Liability for Consequential Damages. To the extent permitted by applicable law, in no event shall IDG or the author be liable for any damages whatsoever (including without limitation, damages for loss of business profits, business interruption, loss of business information, or any other pecuniary loss) arising out of the use of or inability to use the Book or the Software, even if IDG has been advised of the possibility of such damages. Because some states/jurisdictions do not allow the exclusion or limitation of liability for consequential or incidental damages, the above limitation may not apply to you.

7. U.S. Government Restricted Rights. Use, duplication, or disclosure of the Software by the U.S. Government is subject to restrictions stated in paragraph (c) (1) (ii) of the Rights in Technical Data and Computer Software clause of DFARS 252.227-7013, and in subparagraphs (a) through (d) of the Commercial Computer — Restricted Rights clause at FAR 52.227-19, and in similar clauses in the NASA FAR supplement, when applicable.

Replacement Disc. If a replacement CD-ROM is needed, please write to the following address: IDG Books Disc Fulfillment Center, Attn: *Macworld PageMaker 6 Bible*, IDG Books Worldwide, 7260 Shadeland Station, Indianapolis, IN 46256, or call 800-762-2974.

Disc Instructions

The CD-ROM contains tutorial files, and a lot of neat photos, clip art, Plug-ins, and graphics utilities to add productivity to your PageMaker sessions.

Using the Tutorial Chapter Files

To copy the tutorial chapter file folders to your hard disk, simply drag them from the CD to your hard disk. The Finder will give you a message that the disk is locked and ask if you want to copy, rather than move, the files. Click Yes (or OK).

Installing the Plug-ins

To install either PageMaker Plug-ins or Photoshop Plug-ins for use with PageMaker, simply drag the icons from the CD to the Plug-ins folder inside the RSRC folder inside the Adobe PageMaker 6 folder. To use the Photoshop Plug-ins with both Photoshop and PageMaker, drag the Photoshop Plug-in to the Plug-ins folder in your Photoshop folder. Use Make Alias on the File menu to copy the Plug-in icon. Drag the alias to the Plug-ins folder inside the RSRC folder inside the Adobe PageMaker 6 folder.

Running the Graphics Software Demos

There are several demos from various graphics software vendors. Each demo has its own README file telling you how to run the demo and view the sample files.

Importing the Stock Photographs

To use the stock photo samples, simply import them into your layout with PageMaker's Place command or, for faster access, drag them to your hard disk first.

IDG BOOKS WORLDWIDE REGISTRATION CARD

RETURN THIS REGISTRATION CARD FOR FREE CATALOG

Title of this book: Macworld PageMaker 6 Bible, 2E

My overall rating of this book: ❏ Very good [1] ❏ Good [2] ❏ Satisfactory [3] ❏ Fair [4] ❏ Poor [5]

How I first heard about this book:

❏ Found in bookstore; name: [6] _____ ❏ Book review: [7] _____

❏ Advertisement: [8] _____ ❏ Catalog: [9] _____

❏ Word of mouth; heard about book from friend, co-worker, etc.: [10] _____ ❏ Other: [11] _____

What I liked most about this book:

_____

_____

What I would change, add, delete, etc., in future editions of this book:

_____

_____

Other comments:

_____

Number of computer books I purchase in a year: ❏ 1 [12] ❏ 2-5 [13] ❏ 6-10 [14] ❏ More than 10 [15]

I would characterize my computer skills as: ❏ Beginner [16] ❏ Intermediate [17] ❏ Advanced [18] ❏ Professional [19]

I use ❏ DOS [20] ❏ Windows [21] ❏ OS/2 [22] ❏ Unix [23] ❏ Macintosh [24] ❏ Other: [25]_____
(please specify)

I would be interested in new books on the following subjects:
(please check all that apply, and use the spaces provided to identify specific software)

❏ Word processing: [26] _____ ❏ Spreadsheets: [27] _____

❏ Data bases: [28] _____ ❏ Desktop publishing: [29] _____

❏ File Utilities: [30] _____ ❏ Money management: [31] _____

❏ Networking: [32] _____ ❏ Programming languages: [33] _____

❏ Other: [34] _____

I use a PC at (please check all that apply): ❏ home [35] ❏ work [36] ❏ school [37] ❏ other: [38] _____

The disks I prefer to use are ❏ 5.25 [39] ❏ 3.5 [40] ❏ other: [41]_____

I have a CD ROM: ❏ yes [42] ❏ no [43]

I plan to buy or upgrade computer hardware this year: ❏ yes [44] ❏ no [45]

I plan to buy or upgrade computer software this year: ❏ yes [46] ❏ no [47]

Name: _____ Business title: [48] _____ Type of Business: [49] _____

Address (❏ home [50] ❏ work [51]/Company name: _____)

Street/Suite# _____

City [52]/State [53]/Zipcode [54]: _____ Country [55] _____

❏ **I liked this book!** You may quote me by name in future
IDG Books Worldwide promotional materials.

My daytime phone number is _____

IDG BOOKS

THE WORLD OF
COMPUTER
KNOWLEDGE

❑ **YES!**

Please keep me informed about IDG's World of Computer Knowledge.
Send me the latest IDG Books catalog.